DATE DUE

Demco. Inc. 38-293

The MMPI, MMPI-2, and MMPI-A in Court

The MMPI, MMPI-2, and MMPI-A in Court THIRD EDITION

A Practical Guide for
Expert Witnesses and Attorneys

Kenneth S. Pope
James N. Butcher
Joyce Seelen

AMERICAN PSYCHOLOGICAL ASSOCIATION
WASHINGTON, DC

Copyright © 2006 by the American Psychological Association. All rights reserved. Except as permitted under the United States Copyright Act of 1976, no part of this publication may be reproduced or distributed in any form or by any means, or stored in a database or retrieval system, without the prior written permission of the publisher.

Published by
American Psychological Association
750 First Street, NE
Washington, DC 20002
www.apa.org

To order
APA Order Department
P.O. Box 92984
Tel: (800) 374-2721, Direct: (202) 336-5510
Fax: (202) 336-5502, TDD/TTY: (202) 336-6123
Online: www.apa.org/books/
Email: order@apa.org

In the U.K., Europe, Africa, and the Middle East, copies may be ordered from
American Psychological Association
3 Henrietta Street
Covent Garden, London
WC2E 8LU England

Typeset in Berkeley by World Composition Services, Inc., Sterling, VA

Printer: United Book Press, Inc., Baltimore, MD
Cover Designer: Berg Design, Albany, NY
Project Manager: Debbie Hardin, Carlsbad, CA

The opinions and statements published are the responsibility of the authors, and such opinions and statements do not necessarily represent the policies of the American Psychological Association.

Library of Congress Cataloging-in-Publication Data
Pope, Kenneth S.
    The MMPI, MMPI-2 & MMPI-A in court : a practical guide for expert witnesses and attorneys / Kenneth S. Pope, James N. Butcher, and Joyce Seelen.—3rd ed.
        p. cm.
    Includes bibliographical references and index.
    ISBN 1-59147-397-7 (alk. paper)
    1. Forensic psychology—United States. 2. Evidence, Expert—United States. 3. Psychological tests—Law and legislation—United States.
    4. Minnesota Multiphasic Personality Inventory. I. Butcher, James Neal, 1933– II. Seelen, Joyce. III. Title.
    KF8965.P66   2006
    347.73'67—dc22   2005037695

British Library Cataloguing-in-Publication Data
A CIP record is available from the British Library.

Printed in the United States of America
Third Edition

Contents

Art on the Cover: *Vicksburg Courthouse*

Kate F. Hays

The noble and powerful majesty that courts and courthouses can represent is captured in the serene, calm, deliberate painting reproduced on the cover of this book. The artist's work, in case the reader has not yet noticed, is actively represented as well in the text, of which he is the second author.

James N. Butcher began developing his skills in watercolor painting in 2000, taking art classes during a sabbatical in England. Following up on a childhood skill, Butcher has found the process of painting, watercolors in particular, an exciting challenge in which the process is as satisfying as the product. He enjoys the increased sense of being able to convert a three-dimensional object to the two dimensions of a flat piece of paper. After a lifetime of working with people, he is especially drawn to portrayals of landscape and structures, entities that do not make demands or have expectations.

The painting is a representation of the Warren County Courthouse in Vicksburg, Mississippi. The courthouse was begun in 1858 and completed just before the Civil War. This Greek Revival structure was built by the Weldon brothers using skilled slave artisans. Jefferson Davis, a local planter, launched his political career from these grounds. Union troops raised the Stars and Stripes from the building's cupola during Vicksburg's surrender in 1863.

This building served as the official courthouse until 1939. It was selected in 1978 by the American Institute of Architects as one of the 20 most outstanding courthouses in America and has been designated a National Historic Landmark. Since 1948, it has been preserved as the Old Court House Museum and now houses artifacts ranging from prehistoric local Indian tribes to the current day. Dr. Butcher and his wife, Dr. Carolyn Williams, recently visited the Old Court House Museum during a tour of the Vicksburg battlefield and were struck with the beauty of this grand building. Butcher painted the watercolor from a photo taken by Williams.

Kate F. Hays, PhD, a clinical and sport psychologist, works with performing artists, athletes, and businesspeople through her consultation practice in Toronto, Ontario, Canada: The Performing Edge. She also serves as art coeditor for the *American Psychologist*.

List of Exhibits, Tables, and Figures

Preface to the Third Edition

Welcome to those who are new to this book, and welcome back to those who used the first or second editions.

Expert witnesses as well as attorneys work in a world of constant change. Surprising research continues to extend, deepen, and alter understanding of psychological assessment. New legislation and case law redefine the legal ground rules. Professional associations create new standards and guidelines. Innovative approaches catch the unprepared off guard.

We wrote this third edition to help expert witnesses and attorneys work effectively, ethically, and skillfully with the current versions of the Minnesota Multiphasic Personality Inventory (the MMPI–2 and MMPI–A, the adolescent version) within the context of constant change.

CONTINUING CHANGES

Significant changes to the MMPI prompted us to update the book. After the first edition, for example, the test publisher withdrew the original MMPI because it was determined to be scientifically, clinically, and forensically inappropriate. However, because the original MMPI will appear in court cases for years to come as part of previous medical or forensic records, this third edition provides information about the original MMPI, including its scales (Appendix W, this volume), its psychometric properties compared with current versions (Appendix X, this volume), and a procedure for converting original MMPI scores to MMPI–2 norms (Appendix Y, this volume).

After the first edition of the volume, the U.S. Supreme Court handed down its decision in *Daubert v. Merrell Dow Pharmaceuticals, Inc.* (509 U.S. 579 (1993)). *Daubert* created new standards for the courts in deciding what potential testimony qualifies as "expert" and admissible, and the appellate decisions—noted elsewhere in this third edition—following *Daubert*'s lead continue to redefine the courts' gate-keeping function in regard to admissible scientific evidence and expert testimony. "This gate-keeping function is important when one realizes that the expert testimony may be based on valid and reliable research, a combination of science and professional experience, professional experience alone, or personal values that become masked as professional opinion" (Sales & VandenBos, 1994, p. 4). Research is clarifying ways in which *Daubert* has (and has not) been applied in various kinds of cases (e.g., Dahir et al., 2005).

After the second edition of this book was published, the American Psychological Association (APA) issued new ethical standards (Appendix Q, this volume), and the requirements of the Health Insurance Portability and Accountability Act (HIPAA) for handling certain forms of health information began to take effect. HIPAA in turn prompted test publishers to create new rules for handling test booklets; individual test items; test manuals; test-user guides; scoring keys; templates; computer scoring programs; and certain test reports under copyright, trade secret, and similar laws (see Appendixes H, I, and J, this volume).

Finally, in the 6 years since the second edition of this book, research has continued to extend, refine, and sometimes redefine how we understand MMPI findings. The steady stream of research is not surprising in light of how many forensic specialists endorse the MMPI's forensic value. A survey of all psychologists holding a diplomate from the American Board of Forensic Psychology, for example, found that "a number of tests were fairly uniformly endorsed across the evaluation types. This includes the stalwarts of the MMPI–2 and the WAIS–III" (Lally, 2003, p. 496). In a key forensic area such as malingering, the survey found the MMPI–2 along with the Structured Interview of Reported Symptoms to be the only tests "recommended by the majority" (Lally, 2003, p. 495).

This book discusses the recent court decisions, research, and other factors that help both expert witnesses and attorneys understand what the three versions of the MMPI can and cannot do in forensic settings.

WHY WE WROTE—AND REVISED—THIS BOOK

The three of us come from diverse professional backgrounds. Yet all three have come to find the MMPI (both MMPI–2 and MMPI–A) and its use and abuse in court central to our professional concerns.

We joined together more than a decade ago to write the first edition of the book—and continued to update it—because we could not find anything like it anywhere else. Each of us wanted a single volume that we could use in preparing for trials and could take to court with us. We wanted an overview of the relevant issues, common practices, research, and laws. We wanted a single source in which we could find information on all three versions of the MMPI, validity and reliability data, the "Ethical Principles of Psychologists and Code of Conduct" (APA, 2002), the formal guidelines for forensic psychologists, and related documents and information. We also wanted a single volume that could serve as a checklist during preparation, something to help ensure that we did not overlook any crucial steps or resources while getting ready for deposition and trial. Finally, we wanted to gather the basic deposition and cross-examination questions that are central to expert testimony regarding psychological assessment.

This book focuses on the MMPI but also includes related material that can help expert witnesses and attorneys in their work (e.g., reaching formal agreements on fees and other working arrangements, obtaining informed consent for forensic evaluations, writing assessment reports). We gathered the kind of ideas, information, and resources that we and our colleagues find useful when preparing to go to court. We have tried to create a resource that would be helpful not only to seasoned experts but also to those who have never ventured near an MMPI or set foot in a courtroom. The appendix section in this third edition has grown to include resources that expert witnesses and attorneys can quickly lay their hands on in a trial's early stages, during deposition, or even in the courthouse.

ORGANIZATION OF THE BOOK

The pages ahead provide a detailed guide for expert witnesses and attorneys to the strengths and weaknesses of the MMPI, the MMPI–2, and the MMPI–A. Intended to be helpful not only to seasoned attorneys and expert witnesses but also to clinicians without legal–forensic experience and to attorneys who have never heard of the MMPI, this third edition includes general information in such areas as testing and assessment (e.g., understanding the validity and reliability of a test and recognizing responsibilities when test results indicate a risk of suicide or homicide), legal proceedings (e.g., subpoenas and depositions), witness–attorney interactions (e.g., handling initial contacts and setting fees), and discovery and cross-examination strategies (e.g., examination of an expert's understanding of basic psychometrics) that may not be inherently related to the MMPI but can play an important role in providing the proper foundation and context for MMPI-based assessment, testimony, and cross-examination.

Chapter 1 provides a brief introduction. Chapter 2 discusses the MMPI, the MMPI–2, and the MMPI–A in terms of their development; the validity, clinical, and content scales and their psychometric properties; and their applicability to forensic issues. Chapter 3 examines some common forensic settings in which MMPIs become a focus, such as criminal trials, personal injury suits, and so forth. Chapter 4 focuses on case law that defines the scope and limits of MMPI-based testimony. Chapter 5 provides a guide to preparation, procedures, and issues for the psychologist, expert witness, or other professional who offers MMPI-based testimony. As mentioned earlier, such professionals may appear in a variety of roles (e.g., a therapist who has administered an MMPI–2 or MMPI–A and is appearing as a percipient or fact witness, a professional retained by an attorney to offer expert testimony on the MMPI–2 or MMPI–A, or a court-appointed expert). Chapter 6 presents a guide to preparation, procedures, and issues for the attorney who retains an expert to testify on the MMPI or who encounters such testimony from an opposing witness. The next chapters of the book examine special topics relevant to forensic settings: assessing credibility (chap. 7) and the forensic assessment report (chap. 8). Chapter 9 presents a step-by-step guide to deposing and cross-examining the expert who is offering MMPI-based testimony. Reviewing these questions may help not only attorneys but also expert witnesses to prepare for deposition or cross-examination. Chapter 10 offers a few final thoughts on the MMPI and its applications. And as noted previously, this book also draws together under one cover a set of diverse resources in the form of 26 appendixes. We also include a glossary, list of references cited in the text, and a table of cases.

THE AUTHORS' BACKGROUNDS

Each of us came to the MMPI from diverse professional backgrounds and experience.[1] In 1965, James N. Butcher, a new faculty member of the University of Minnesota and just out of graduate school at the University of North Carolina, organized the Symposium on Recent Developments in the Use of the MMPI to provide a forum for researchers to discuss current and proposed research on the MMPI. Since then, over the 40 years of its existence, the annual symposium has served as a vehicle for many important new developments in the MMPI, has launched many research investigations, and has opened new areas for

---

[1] For additional information about each author, please see the section "About the Authors" on pp. 517–521, this volume.

research. A year after the inaugural MMPI symposium, the need for practical training in the use of the test became apparent because many psychologists were not receiving assessment training in their graduate programs. The MMPI symposium was expanded to include practical workshops on the clinical application of the MMPI. As a result, the MMPI Workshop Series has provided professional training on the MMPI, MMPI–2, and MMPI–A to thousands of psychologists.

Throughout his career in psychology, Butcher has been involved in studying the use of the MMPI in intercultural contexts. He has conducted research on psychopathology among different ethnic groups in the United States and has extensively explored the use of the MMPI in other cultures throughout the world. Over the years, he has conducted professional training programs in Belgium, Chile, China, Denmark, Egypt, Greece, Holland, Hong Kong, Iran, Israel, Italy, Japan, Korea, Mexico, Norway, and South Africa. In 1970, he founded the International Conference on Personality Assessment, which continues to be held every 2 years. The conference provides the opportunity for scholars from around the world to discuss their research and to exchange views on issues and techniques in personality assessment with professionals from other countries.

Butcher has conducted extensive research on the MMPI for more than 44 years in a broad range of contexts. His publications include basic research works in abnormal psychology, personality assessment, and the MMPI, including research methodology and computer applications of psychological tests.

Butcher was a central figure in the revision of the MMPI and the development of the MMPI–2 and MMPI–A. His contribution to the MMPI revision began in 1969, when he organized a national symposium to address the question of whether the MMPI needed to be revised and, if so, how. During the 1970s, he published articles and held additional meetings to keep alive the possibility of an MMPI revision. Finally, in 1982, the test publisher initiated a revision with a team comprising Butcher, Grant Dahlstrom, Jack R. Graham, and Auke Tellegen (who participated in the later stages of the project). The MMPI revision effort spanned 10 years and included scores of empirical studies with a broad range of normal and clinical populations. This revision effort culminated in the publication of the MMPI–2 in 1989 and the MMPI–A in 1992.

Butcher has authored a number of books on the MMPI and abnormal psychology. His published books include *A Practitioner's Guide to the MMPI–2* (2006), *A Beginner's Guide to the MMPI–2* (2nd ed., 2005a), *International Adaptations of the MMPI–2* (1996), *Use of the MMPI–2 in Treatment Planning* (1990b), *Computerized Psychological Assessment* (1987), *Essentials of MMPI–2 and MMPI–A Interpretation* (with Carolyn L. Williams, 1992a), *Abnormal Psychology and Modern Life* (12th ed., with Sue Mineka and Jill Hooley, 2004), and *Handbook of Research Methods in Clinical Psychology* (2nd ed., with Philip C. Kendall and Grayson Holmback, 1999).

Butcher's forensic testimony, the source of much material included in this book, has been extensive and covers many types of legal cases. As might be expected, his testimony almost always centers on the interpretation of MMPI–2 scores. Issues concerning technical aspects of the test or the likely meaning of a particular MMPI configuration are common themes in his court testimony. His forensic experience includes personal injury, criminal, family custody, and medical malpractice.

Joyce Seelen began working as an attorney in 1980 when she joined the Colorado state public defender's system. Learning how to examine and cross-examine psychological and psychiatric experts and how to understand psychological test results was a necessary part of representing poor people accused of committing crimes. Psychological assessment issues arose almost daily in connection with testimony about competency, sanity, and mental culpability.

In 1982, Seelen represented a patient who had been confined to the state psychiatric hospital for many years, after having been found not guilty of murder by reason of insanity. The patient maintained that he was sane. However, none of the doctors agreed. The heart of the subsequent trial was the cross-examination of the prosecution's doctors. A jury of six disregarded the stated opinions of the experts and decided that the patient was ready, with professional help, to begin life outside the hospital. (Colorado law has since been changed to limit a patient's opportunity to request release from a psychiatric hospitalization through a sanity trial.) That case provided a valuable lesson in the power of understanding and using psychological information.

When Seelen left the public defender's office in 1983, she began a private civil practice that emphasized representation of people exploited by those in positions of trust. In most exploitation and abuse litigations, the primary damages are psychological. The initial hurdle in emotional damages cases is finding a way to communicate the emotional injury to the jury as effectively as an X-ray or photograph can convey physical injury. Testimony on the basis of standardized psychological tests—particularly the MMPI—and other methods of psychological assessment provides that method of communication.

In 1990, Seelen championed the case of a young woman who had been harmed by both her minister and her church. In 1993, Colorado's highest court issued the opinion of *Moses v. The Diocese of Colorado* (863 P.2d 310 (Colo. 1993)), which resulted in Colorado becoming the leading state in the nation to hold religious organizations responsible for violating duties of trust to parishioners. In 1996, the Colorado court reiterated its opinion that the First Amendment to the U.S. Constitution does not protect religious organizations from their own breach of duty. The case, also brought by Seelen, was *Bear Valley Church of Christ v. DeBose* (928 P.2d 1315 (Colo. 1996)). Seelen defended against the church's petition to the U.S. Supreme Court, which asked the court to reverse the Colorado court on the basis of a number of First Amendment claims, including a claim that a biblical passage discussing "laying on of hands" protects ministers who placed their hands on the genitals of children. The U.S. Supreme Court refused to reverse the Colorado supreme court's decision. Seelen litigated psychological issues again in 2004 in a successful and precedent-setting action against Children's Hospital in Denver. The case is currently on appeal to the Colorado Court of Appeals (*Liggett v. Children's Hospital,* Colorado Court of Appeals #04CA 2262).

Ken has found the MMPI useful in his clinical and forensic practice; has encountered an amazing range of ways that tests can be used and misused; and finds issues regarding the administration, scoring, and interpretation of the MMPI arising in many cases in which he consults or testifies as an expert witness. Unlike his two coauthors, he lacks any of the interesting personal anecdotes about how he became involved with the MMPI and will resist the temptation to invent some fascinating accounts just so he will not look bad by comparison.

A NOTE ON TERMINOLOGY

Five general areas of terminology and format pose problems. First, for the sake of brevity and convenience, we do not want to refer constantly to "the MMPI, the MMPI–2, and the

MMPI–A." Therefore, we often shorten this cumbersome phrase to "the MMPI." Although this choice to use the MMPI in a generic sense to refer to all three versions of the test risks some confusion, we try to ensure that the context (and, in some cases, explicit qualifiers) will make it clear whether we are referring to the MMPI–2 alone or to the test as it appears in all three versions.

Second, it is easy to refer to attorneys. But what words should we use to refer to psychologists and other professionals who might be called to present testimony on the MMPI? Using the term *professional*, unless the context happened to make it clear, makes it ambiguous as to whether we are referring to attorneys as well, because they too are professionals. To refer always to *expert witnesses* unintentionally excludes some to whom this book is addressed. Clinical, counseling, and industrial–organizational psychologists as well as a variety of nonpsychology therapists, counselors, and other professionals might have administered the MMPI to clients, patients, job applicants, students, and others. In a subsequent legal action, they might be subpoenaed to testify as percipient witnesses (simply describing the results of the MMPI assessment and their sessions with the individual who was assessed without qualifying as an expert witness or offering professional opinions). Moreover, attorneys may retain an expert on the MMPI to help prepare a case (e.g., help the attorney to learn about the MMPI and help formulate deposition and cross-examination questions) while not designating the expert as a witness who would offer testimony. Coming up with no adequate, all-purpose term that did not seem bizarre, cumbersome, or confusing, we use such terms as *expert witness, expert, psychologist,* and so on, with the clear understanding that some of these terms may not fit all readers or even a particular reader in all cases.

Third, we had to decide what to term someone who takes the MMPI. The person might be a defendant, plaintiff, client, patient, research participant, job applicant, student, or a number of other possibilities. In creating case examples and discussing issues related to the MMPI, we use whatever designation seems to make or clarify the point at hand. We hope, however, that each reader will be able to generalize and adapt from our specific examples to those that will be most relevant and useful. Although the examples in almost any book will tend to reflect, at least to some degree, the experiences and concerns of its authors, we try to provide a variety of situations illustrating issues involving forensic uses of the MMPI. Finally, some forensic testimony focuses on people who have taken the MMPI in what might be called a mental health context. Some readers may have a preference for the term *patients* to refer to such individuals; others may prefer the term *clients*. However, in this book we use these terms interchangeably. Similarly, individual readers may prefer the term *therapy* or *counseling* in such contexts; again, we use these terms interchangeably.

Fourth, although we try to provide adequate explanations for each of the terms and concepts in the book, these explanations are not repeated throughout the volume. If the reader does not find the definition of a term in a particular chapter, the Glossary at the end of the book may provide a quick, convenient route to clarification rather than using the index. Readers unfamiliar with mathematical notation will come across symbols such as $\leq$ (less than or equal to) or $\geq$ (greater than or equal to).

Fifth, we do not adhere strictly to the citation and style format followed in most APA journals and books. For readers who are unfamiliar with the customary format, the authors' last names are listed in the text along with the dates of publication or presentation; the work may be looked up in the alphabetized reference section for a more complete citation. We also provide the legal citation for each case as we mention it in the text (rather than providing such information in the reference section). In addition, we provide a table of cases at the end of the book. We also often refer to people by using their first and last name, as well as other identifying information, in the text (rather than providing only the last name in the text and initials in the reference section). In addition, in a few places where there is a clump of citations that distract from the text, we use footnotes to list the citations.

Acknowledgments

We received an enormous amount of help in putting together all three editions of this book. We would particularly like to acknowledge the following individuals who offered useful comments, suggestions, or other help: Nancy Adel, JD, Adel & Pollack, Los Angeles, California; Cheri Adrian, PhD, UCLA Neuropsychiatric Institute and Hospital and independent practice, Los Angeles, California; Ray Arsenault, PhD, independent practice, Rocks Village, Massachusetts; Robert McKim Bell, JD, California Department of Justice, Los Angeles; Yossef Ben-Porath, PhD, Kent State University, Kent, Ohio; David Berry, PhD, University of Kentucky, Lexington; Bruce Bongar, PhD, Pacifica Graduate Institute, Palo Alto, California; Laura S. Brown, PhD, independent practice, Seattle, Washington; Kathleen Callanan, PhD, California Department of Consumer Affairs, Sacramento; Brandt Caudill, JD, Callahan, McCune & Willis, Tustin, California; Benjamin I. Collins, PhD, independent geologist, Denver, Colorado; Steven Edelstein, JD, independent practice, Miami, Florida; Philip Erdberg, PhD, independent practice, Corte Madera, California; James Eyman, PhD, independent practice, Topeka, Kansas; Jesse D. Geller, PhD, independent practice, New Haven, Connecticut; Joe George, PhD, JD, independent practice, Sacramento, California; William T. Gibson, PhD; Jack Graham, PhD, Kent State University, Kent, Ohio; Heather Hanneman, JD, independent practice, Denver, Colorado; Sheila Jensen, California Board of Behavioral Science Examiners, Sacramento; Alan Kaplan, JD, Herzfeld & Rubin, Los Angeles; Reneau Kennedy, PhD, independent forensic practice, Honolulu, Hawaii; Lawrence Majovski, PhD, independent practice, Los Angeles; the late Alan K. Malyon, PhD; J. Gary May, MD, Denver, Colorado; Helen L. McGonigle, JD, independent practice, Brookfield, Connecticut; Wendy J. Murphy, JD, New England School of Law, Boston, Massachusetts; Mark G. Ohnstad, JD, Thomsen & Nybeck, Minneapolis, Minnesota; Thomas S. O'Connor, formerly of the California Board of Psychology, Sacramento, California; Karen A. Olio, New England Mental Health Services, Norwalk, Connecticut; Robert Pelc, PhD, independent practice, Denver, Colorado; the late Allen Pinka; Carlos Raminez, JD, California Department of Justice, Los Angeles; Dan Recht, JD, independent practice, Denver, Colorado; Gary L. Sampley, JD, Bakersfield, California; David Shapiro, PhD, Nova Southeastern University, Fort Lauderdale, Florida; Jerome L. Singer, PhD, Yale University, New Haven, Connecticut; Susan K. Smith, JD, independent practice, Hartford, Connecticut; Janet L. Sonne, PhD, independent practice, Redlands, California; Melba J. T. Vasquez, PhD, independent practice, Austin, Texas; and Karen Zager, PhD, independent practice, New York City. We would also like to thank Jack

Graham for providing some case material presented in this book and Betty Kiminki for assistance on the references.

Finally, we owe a huge debt of gratitude to Susan Reynolds, Ron Teeter, Mary Lynn Skutley, Theodore J. Baroody, Julia Frank-McNeil, Valerie Montenegro, Margaret Schlegel, W. Ralph Eubanks, Susan Bedford, Catherine Hudson, Olin Nettles, Amy J. Clarke, Gary R. VandenBos, Jennifer Macomber, Emily Welsh, Anne Woodworth, and Debbie Hardin of the American Psychological Association for their exceptional generosity, skill, and support.

We would like to thank the following publishers for their kind permission to quote from the following copyrighted material:

THE AMERICAN PSYCHOLOGICAL ASSOCIATION for authorization to quote from *Casebook on Ethical Principles of Psychologists* (copyright 1987 by the American Psychological Association), "Ethical Principles of Psychologists and Code of Conduct" (copyright 2002 by the American Psychological Association), *General Guidelines for Providers of Psychological Services* (copyright 1987 by the American Psychological Association), *Guidelines for Computer-Based Tests and Interpretations* (copyright 1986 by the American Psychological Association), "Model Act for State Licensure of Psychologists" (copyright 1987 by the American Psychological Association), "Policy on Training for Psychologists Wishing to Change Their Specialty" (see Appendix R; copyright 1976 and 1982 by the American Psychological Association), and *Standards for Educational and Psychological Testing* (copyright 1985 by the American Psychological Association).

THE BOARD OF BAR COMMISSIONERS OF THE STATE BAR OF NEW MEXICO and WILLIAM E. FOOTE, PhD, OF THE NEW MEXICO PSYCHOLOGICAL ASSOCIATION for allowing us to reprint the *Statement of Principles Relating to the Responsibilities of Attorneys and Psychologists in Their Interprofessional Relations: An Interdisciplinary Agreement Between the New Mexico Bar Association and the New Mexico Psychological Association* (see Appendix T). Copyright 1986 by State Bar of New Mexico.

JOSSEY-BASS INC., PUBLISHERS, for permission to quote from K. S. Pope and M. J. T. Vasquez's *Ethics in Psychotherapy and Counseling: A Practical Guide, Second Edition.* Copyright 1998 by John Wiley & Sons, Inc.

LOUIS NIZER, ESQ., for permission to quote from L. Nizer's *My Life in Court* (Garden City, NY: Doubleday). Copyright 1961 by Louis Nizer.

PLENUM PUBLISHING COMPANY for permission to reprint the "Specialty Guidelines for Forensic Psychologists" (see Appendix S). These guidelines were published in Volume 15 (pp. 655–665) of the journal *Law and Human Behavior.* Copyright 1991 by Plenum Publishing Company.

UNIVERSITY OF MINNESOTA PRESS for permission to reprint materials on the MMPI, MMPI–2, and MMPI–A, and to incorporate profiles into the figures.

The MMPI, MMPI-2, and MMPI-A in Court

CHAPTER 1

A BRIEF OVERVIEW

A subpoena can suddenly land a clinician in court to testify under oath about the Minnesota Multiphasic Personality Inventory (MMPI). The MMPI may be the original (which appeared in 1940 and was discontinued in 1999), the MMPI–2 revision (which appeared in 1989), or the MMPI–A (adolescent version, which appeared in 1992). Imagine a clinician finding him- or herself in this situation who must testify as a fact witness—not an expert—about a client who terminated therapy years before. The former client could be suing for custody of children, for emotional damages from an accident, or for a surgeon's or former therapist's alleged malpractice. Even responding to a valid subpoena for test data in such situations can present complex challenges and pitfalls (Committee on Legal Issues for the American Psychological Association, 1996).

Courts can also appoint professionals to conduct independent psychological evaluations using the MMPI–2 (e.g., of a defendant's competence to stand trial or of a worker's compensation claim). Attorneys—and sometimes litigants themselves—retain professionals to administer standardized psychological tests as preparation for a court action. Expert witnesses testify about what the MMPI–2 has to say about individuals involved in violence, abuse, and discrimination (e.g., victims or perpetrators of rape, incest, battering, sexual harassment, racial discrimination in hiring, or hate crimes such as attacks on gays and lesbians). Whatever the path leading to the civil, criminal, or administrative courts, those who testify on such matters can profoundly affect the lives of others.

Likewise, attorneys encounter testimony about the MMPI in different guises. Testimony may describe the MMPI–2 or MMPI–A as an objective test that is far more scientific, accurate, and reliable than a so-called expert's subjective impressions, experience-based hunches, dogmatic assertions, and questionable opinions. Or the attorney may be stunned to hear testimony rhapsodizing about the instrument as a psychometric oracle whose Delphic powers provide the expert witness with a flawless roadmap to the human mind and infallible predictions about how test takers will behave (or will not behave, if they have been rehabilitated) tomorrow, next year, and for the rest of their lives. MMPI testimony may be decisive in some cases. Or it may strike judge and jury as nothing more than hokum for hire, the so-called findings clotted in strange bundles of professional jargon and multisyllabic words.

Why do expert witnesses and attorneys so often find expert testimony to be painfully frustrating or simply painful? Why does psychological testimony often confuse and distort matters for the jurors and judge rather than help them to understand the matters at hand?

Part of the problem, of course, is that some testimony is bogus and that some opposing attorneys and expert witnesses are unprepared to expose and counter fraud and hucksterism. Some experts are in the business of selling opinions-to-order, and some attorneys are looking to buy. In a national survey of the ethical dilemmas faced by psychologists, the participants' most contemptuous language (e.g., "whores") was used in describing these so-called experts, as in the following examples.

> There are psychologists who are "hired" guns who testify for whoever pays them. (Pope & Vetter, 1992, p. 402)

> A psychologist in my area is widely known to clients, psychologists, and the legal community to give whatever testimony is requested in court. He has a very commanding "presence" and it works. He will say anything, adamantly, for pay. Clients/lawyers continue to use him because if the other side uses him, that side will probably win the case (because he's so persuasive, though lying). (Pope & Vetter, 1992, p. 402)

Seemingly altruistic impulses—rather than greed and lack of integrity—can motivate false or distorted testimony. Judge David Bazelon, for example, observed that "psychiatrists have justified fudging their testimony on 'dangerousness'—a ground for involuntary confinement—when they were convinced that an individual was too sick to seek help voluntarily" (1974, p. 22).

Strong feelings about a topic can lead to slanted testimony. Kuehnle wrote, "Because of the strong emotions evoked by child sexual abuse and the polarization of views by some professionals involved in this area, litigated custody and visitation cases involving such accusations may lure the forensic evaluator from the role of a neutral scientist into the role of an advocate for the alleged victim or for the accused" (1998, p. 2).

Opposing attorneys (and other expert witnesses) may find themselves unprepared to challenge effectively an expert's subtly biased or downright bogus testimony. One goal of this book is to help expert witnesses prepare in ways that enable them to avoid giving biased or bogus testimony. The book gives both attorneys and expert witnesses the tools to counter misleading testimony effectively. Preparation is key. Trial attorney Louis Nizer wrote that "as any trial lawyer will admit, proper preparation

is the be all and end all of trial success" (1961, p. 8).

Too many expert witnesses struggle to provide a clear, compelling description of how an MMPI works, why it works, and what it means in the case at hand. Even if they make it through the sympathetic questioning of direct examination, many will cringe and wilt in the face of a skilled, carefully planned, fully informed cross-examination. Clinicians walking into the courtroom or facing informed, effective cross-examination for the first time may have no real idea of what to expect in this unfamiliar environment with its special customs and detailed rules. In his classic textbook *The Art of Cross-Examination*, Francis Wellman (1903/1936) quoted an apt statement about the plight of the witness.

> Of all unfortunate people in this world, none are more entitled to sympathy and commiseration than those whom circumstances oblige to appear upon the witness stand in court. . . . You are then arraigned before two legal gentlemen [sic], one of whom smiles at you blandly because you are on his side, the other eying you savagely for the opposite reason. The gentleman who smiles, proceeds to pump you of all you know; and having squeezed all he wants out of you, hands you over to the other, who proceeds to show you that you are entirely mistaken in all your supposition; that you never saw anything you have sworn to . . . in short, that you have committed direct perjury. He wants to know if you have ever been in state prison, and takes your denial with the air of a man who thinks you ought to have been there, asking all the questions over again in different ways; and tells you with an awe inspiring severity, to be very careful what you say. He wants to know if he understood you to say so and so, and also wants to know whether you meant something else. Having bullied

and scared you out of your wits, and convicted you in the eye of the jury of prevarication, he lets you go. (pp. 194–195)

Even experienced professionals may fall prey to the attorney who has taken the time to prepare properly, to master the MMPI's intricacies, to learn how to ask relevant questions about the normative sample, the psychometric structure, the validity and reliability statistics, the common interpretive errors, and so on. Properly prepared attorneys dismantle an expert so effectively that it stuns judge, jury, and expert. One trial attorney vividly described expert witness behaviors, indicating that it is time for "the cross-examiner to uncoil and strike."

> Have you ever seen a "treed" witness? Have you ever had the experience of watching a witness's posterior involuntarily twitch? Have you ever seen them wiggle in their chairs? Have you ever seen their mouths go dry? Have you seen the beads of perspiration form on their foreheads? Have you ever been close enough to watch their ancestral eyes dilating the pupil so that they would have adequate tunnel vision of the target that was attacking? (Burgess, 1984, p. 252)

Nizer (1961) wrote that the old process by which a person who testified was forced to "walk barefoot and blindfolded over red-hot plowshares laid lengthwise at unequal distances has been replaced by a stream of burning questions which a cross-examiner may hurl at the witness to drag from him the concealed truth" (p. 14).

The preface described the world of constant change in which expert witnesses and attorneys practice their professions. This constant evolution serves as another source of common problems with expert testimony. Expert witnesses and attorneys must keep up with advancing knowledge in areas such as forensic malingering (see, e.g., Pope, 2005a: Malingering Research Update, at http://kspope.com/assess/malinger.php), with new research on the uses and misuses of the MMPI, and with evolving legislation and case law governing the work of expert witnesses and attorneys.

This book's purpose is to give expert witnesses and attorneys information, ideas, and resources to practice effectively when the MMPI is at issue, and to identify, avoid, and address problems such as those described in this chapter. The first step in proper preparation for expert witnesses and attorneys is learning, updating, or reviewing information about the three versions of the MMPI, which is the topic of the next chapter.

Chapter 2

THE MMPI, MMPI–2, AND MMPI–A IN COURT TESTIMONY

The Minnesota Multiphasic Personality Inventory (MMPI), the most widely used personality test in clinical practice in the United States (e.g., Lubin, Larsen, & Matarazzo, 1984; Watkins, Campbell, Nieberding, & Hallmark, 1995), has become the preferred personality assessment instrument for evaluating individuals in forensic settings. Otto, for example, noted that "the MMPI–2 is the psychological testing instrument most frequently used in forensic treatment and evaluation contexts" (2002, p. 71; see also Boccaccini & Brodsky, 1999; Borum & Grisso, 1995; Lees-Haley, Smith, Williams, & Dunn, 1996). Lally surveyed forensic diplomates and reported that "a number of tests were fairly uniformly endorsed across the evaluation types. This includes the stalwarts of the MMPI–2 and the WAIS–III" (2003, p. 496).

This chapter summarizes the use of the MMPI, and its revised forms MMPI–2 and MMPI–A, in forensic settings and highlights the test characteristics (psychometric features) that support its use in forensic evaluations. It examines the similarities and differences among the MMPI, MMPI–2, and MMPI–A; their relative strengths and limitations in forensic assessment; and an expert witness's potential vulnerabilities when testifying with regard to the MMPI.

THE ORIGINAL MMPI

The original MMPI was a 566-item true–false personality questionnaire developed in the 1930s and early 1940s as a diagnostic aid for psychiatric and medical screening (Dahlstrom, Welsh, & Dahlstrom, 1972, 1975; Graham, 1977; R. Greene, 1980). The test's creators, Starke Hathaway and J. C. McKinley, developed the personality questionnaire using empirical-scale construction methods. The scales, which focus on abnormal behavior and symptoms of disorders such as depression and schizophrenia, were constructed by contrasting the response patterns of various patient groups with those of a sample of nonpsychiatric ("normal" or "normative") individuals.

The MMPI provided several sources of behavioral and symptomatic hypotheses about the person who takes the test. First, the validity scales yield information about how the person approached the test (e.g., test-taking attitudes) and whether the responses form a sufficient basis for additional inferences. If the pattern of validity scales indicated that the profile is invalid, no inferences may be drawn from the other scales or indexes. Chapter 7 focuses on the credibility of self-report in forensic settings.

The MMPI also contained objectively derived, scored, and interpreted scales that are associated with well-established symptoms or behaviors (see Appendix W, this volume). These scales and the patterns that they form provide hypotheses about personality and, if relevant and appropriate, about diagnosis and prognosis. They provide descriptive information that can help us understand personality traits and symptom patterns.

The MMPI in addition provided scales and indexes to identify or clarify specific problem areas (content themes). Focused scales, such as those designed to assess alcohol or drug abuse problems (MacAndrew [MAC] scale) or emotional control problems (Hostility scale [Ho]), focused on specific behavior problems.

Despite the original MMPI's broad use and recognized effectiveness in clinical and forensic assessment, a number of problems emerged that required that the test be revised and updated. For example, during the 1970s, serious questions were raised about the relevance and appropriateness of the items, the nature of the normative sample, and the datedness of the 1930s test norms (see, e.g., Butcher, 1972; Butcher & Owen, 1978). Some of these problems are outlined in more detail in Butcher (2000b).

In 1982, the MMPI copyright holder, the University of Minnesota Press, initiated an extensive revision of the MMPI item pool and launched an extensive study to collect new norms. The MMPI revision for use with adults (MMPI–2) was published in 1989. A number of articles and books have subsequently appeared detailing issues of reliability and validity.[1] *Basic Sources on the MMPI–2* (Butcher, 2000a) provides a compendium of articles on MMPI–2 scale development and validation along with several articles from the original MMPI clinical scale development. The revised version for adolescents (MMPI–A) appeared in 1992 (Butcher et al., 1992).

The original plan of the MMPI Restandardization Committee (James Butcher, Grant Dahlstrom, and John Graham) included the following.

- The revised versions of the inventory would have continuity with the original instrument in that the traditional validity and clinical scales would be maintained to ensure uninterrupted usage through continued reliance on the existing research base.
- To ensure that practitioners would have a smooth transition to the new versions of the MMPI, a phase-out period was implemented (originally planned to be 5 years, although it lasted until 1999) in which MMPI users could

become familiar with the new versions of the instrument—after which the original version would be withdrawn in favor of the revised forms.

By 1998, more than 95% of MMPI users had moved to the revised forms. The publisher withdrew the original MMPI—it is no longer recommended for clinical use—on September 1, 1999. As a consequence, the original version of the MMPI is no longer appropriate for forensic evaluations. This book includes some discussion and reference to the original MMPI because the original version still plays an occasional role in forensic cases—usually because it is contained in records from many years ago. This book focuses primarily on the MMPI–2 because this latest version is now the standard instrument for adults, and more than 20 years of accumulated research support its use.

THE MMPI–2

The MMPI–2 is the 1989 revised form of the MMPI designed for use with adults aged 18 or older. The MMPI revision project began in 1981 and included a number of clinical studies as well as the extensive normative data collection after the item pool revision was completed. Although the item pool was revised and expanded, continuity with the original instrument was ensured by keeping the original clinical and validity scales virtually intact (Butcher, Graham, Ben-Porath, Tellegen, Dahlstrom, & Kaemmer, 2001).

The norming of the MMPI–2 began with a large, contemporary normative sample (1,462 women and 1,138 men), generally representative of the national population (Butcher, Dahlstrom, Graham, Tellegen, & Kaemmer, 1989; Schinka & LaLone, 1997). This sample was randomly solicited from California, Minnesota, North Carolina, Ohio, Pennsylvania, Virginia, and Washington state.

This contemporary normative sample yielded new norms for the validity and clinical scales. The method of developing norms avoided the statistical problems plaguing the original *T* scores (i.e., the

---

[1] Archer, Griffin, and Aiduk (1995); Ben-Porath and Butcher (1989a, 1989b); Ben-Porath, Butcher, et al. (1991); Butcher and Graham (1991); Butcher, Graham, Dahlstrom, and Bowman (1990); Butcher, Jeffrey, et al. (1990); Butcher, Rouse, and Perry (2000); Egeland, Erickson, Butcher, and Ben-Porath (1991); Graham, Ben-Porath, and McNulty (1999); Hjemboe and Butcher (1991); L. Keller and Butcher (1991).

percentile values on the original were not consistent and uniform for given levels of *T* scores). *T* scores fall in a distribution in which the mean (or average) is 50 and the standard deviation (a statistical measure of the degree to which the individual scores are spread out from or are "bunched up" around the mean) is 10.

New personality and symptom scales assess content dimensions (clusters of symptoms) by using items in the expanded item pool (Butcher, Graham, Williams, & Ben-Porath, 1990). Several symptom-oriented scales, such as Bizarre Mentation scale (*BIZ*) and Depression scale (*DEP*), focus directly on symptom themes presented by individuals during the evaluation. Other scales assess clinical problems, such as Antisocial Practices scale (*ASP*) and Type A scale (*TPA*), and clinical problem areas, such as Work Interference scale (*WRK*) and Negative Treatment Indicators scale (*TRT*). Extensive research supports the validity and usefulness of these scales.[2]

The MMPI–2 retained some specific problem scales from the original MMPI—for example, Hostility scale (*Ho*), Anxiety scale (*ANX*), and Repression scale (*R*). The new item pool helped form other specific problem scales, such as the Addiction Potential scale (*APS*) and the Addiction Acknowledgement scale (*AAS*; Clements & Heintz, 2002; Weed, Butcher, Ben-Porath, & McKenna, 1992). Appendix W provides descriptions of the MMPI–2 content scales and supplemental scales. (For more detailed interpretive information, see Butcher [2006] or Butcher & Williams's [2000] textbook on the MMPI–2 and MMPI–A.)

THE MMPI–A

The MMPI Restandardization Committee recognized that the same instrument cannot adequately assess both adolescents and adults. As a consequence, in 1992 the committee developed the MMPI–A for people between the ages of 14 and 18.

This revised version of the MMPI for adolescents differs significantly from both the original MMPI and the MMPI–2.

First, although the MMPI–A retained the items necessary for scoring the traditional validity and clinical scales, a number of new items addressing specific adolescent problems and issues were added. Several items became more readable for adolescents through minor changes in wording.

Second, the MMPI–A used contemporary, nationally based norms for adolescents. The adolescent normative sample came from public and private schools in California, Minnesota, North Carolina, Ohio, Virginia, Pennsylvania, New York, and Washington state. The sample was balanced for age, gender, ethnicity, and other significant variables. The traditional clinical and validity scales used adolescent-specific norms.

Third, the MMPI–A contains new adolescent-specific scales based on both original MMPI items as well as newer items. A set of adolescent-specific content scales assessing important problem themes such as School Problems (*a–sch*), Low Aspirations (*a–las*), Conduct Problems (*a–con*), and Alienation (*a–aln*) are among the adolescent-specific content scales. Two additional scales—the Alcohol and Drug Problem Proneness (*PRO*) scale and the Alcohol and Drug Problem Acknowledgment (*ACK*) scale—assess the possibility of alcohol or drug problems. Appendix W in this volume describes the MMPI–A content and supplementary scales.

Fourth, an extensive clinical study incorporating adolescents in mental health settings, special school settings, and alcohol and drug treatment settings helped validate the traditional MMPI clinical and validity scales and the new MMPI–A scales.

The MMPI–A contains 478 items, is recommended for people between 14 and 18, and typically requires about an hour to an hour and a quarter to administer. For additional information about the MMPI–A scales and their uses, see Archer (1997b, 2005); Butcher, Cabiya, Lucio, Pena, Scott,

---

[2] For example, Bagby, Marshall, Basso, Nicholson, Bacchiochi, and Miller (2005); Barthlow, Graham, Ben-Porath, and McNulty (1999, 2004); Ben-Porath et al. (1991); Ben-Porath, McCully, and Almagor (1993); Bosquet and Egeland (2000); Brems and Lloyd (1995); Chisholm, Crowther, and Ben-Porath (1997); Clark (1994, 1996); Clements and Heintz (2002); Demarco (2002); Endler, Parker, and Butcher (1993); Englert, Weed, and Watson (2000); Graham, Ben-Porath, and McNulty (1999); Kopper, Osman, and Barrios (2001); Lilienfeld (1996); Lucio, Palacios, Duran, and Butcher (1999); Palav, Ortega, and McCaffrey (2001); Schill and Wang (1990); S. Smith, Hilsenroth, Castlebury, and Durham (1999); Strassberg and Russell (2000); Ward (1997).

and Ruben (1998); Butcher and Williams (1992a, 1992b); Butcher et al. (1992); Forbey (2002); McGrath, Pogge, and Stokes (2002); McLaughlin (1999); L. Pena, Megargee, and Brody (1996); C. L. Williams, Butcher, Ben-Porath, and Graham (1992). For a discussion using the MMPI–A in forensic settings beyond what this book provides, see Butcher and Pope (1992).

SIMILARITIES AND DIFFERENCES AMONG THE ORIGINAL MMPI, MMPI–2, AND MMPI–A

This section compares and contrasts the MMPI, MMPI–2, and MMPI–A. Appendix X provides a point-by-point comparative summary of the relevant features of the three instruments.

Relationship of the MMPI and MMPI–2

The MMPI–2 contains fewer objectionable items—that is, those items considered too personal or offensive—and more contemporary items than the original MMPI. The MMPI–2 addresses clinical problem areas and symptoms not covered by the original instrument. The clinical and traditional validity scales (Lie scale [L], Infrequency scale [F], and Defensiveness scale [K]) from the original MMPI and MMPI–2 are virtually identical in terms of item composition, reliability, and validity.

As previously noted, the MMPI Restandardization Committee used a research protocol that would maximize the continuity between the original MMPI and the revised version in terms of the traditional validity and clinical scales. With a few minor exceptions, the MMPI–2 item content is identical. A few items were deleted from a few scales: 4 on F (Infrequency), 1 on Hs (Hypochondriasis), 2 on D (Depression), 4 on Mf (Masculinity–Femininity), and 1 on Si (Social Introversion–Extraversion). The traditional scales did not use any new items. The MMPI–A dropped a few more items considered objectionable from the clinical scales.

Subsequent research confirmed that these minor modifications did not lower the reliability of the traditional validity and clinical scales (e.g., Ben-Porath & Butcher, 1989a). Therefore, most of the validity and clinical scales remain unchanged in

their measurement focus or have been shown to be psychometrically comparable. Ben-Porath and Butcher (1989a) conducted an empirical comparison of the MMPI and MMPI–2 using a test–retest research design. Half of the participants took the original version of the MMPI twice; the other half took the MMPI at one time and the MMPI–2 at another time. To correct for possible administration-order effects, the tests were administered in a counterbalanced order (i.e., some took the MMPI before taking the MMPI–2, and others took the MMPI–2 before taking the MMPI). Appendix X shows that the test–retest correlations between separate administrations of the original and revised versions are comparable to correlations between the different administrations of the original MMPI.

The congruence between the MMPI and MMPI–2 is evident in the comparability of the high point scores and profile codes (see, e.g., Graham, Timbrook, Ben-Porath, & Butcher, 1991). When the profile types are well-defined (i.e., the scales in the code are at least 5 points higher for the requiring scales in the code type), an individual's profile types tend to be similar when tested with either the MMPI or the MMPI–2 (Graham, Timbrook, et al., 1991).

Although the original MMPI and the MMPI–2 share many of the same items and scales, the norms of the MMPI–2 reflect a more contemporary, representative sample. The original MMPI's norms have been losing validity for contemporary evaluations. The original MMPI tended to overpathologize because the norms were out of date: When the norms for the original MMPI were used, test takers tend to show significantly more psychological problems than they actually have.

The three traditional validity scales of the MMPI–2 (Lie scale [L], Infrequency scale [F], and Defensiveness [K] scale) and clinical scales are essentially the same as the original MMPI versions in terms of the item composition (e.g., only five scales lost any items), scale reliabilities, and external correlates. The MMPI and MMPI–2 function in a similar manner psychometrically on these scales (Ben-Porath & Butcher, 1989a, 1989b; Chojenackie & Walsh, 1992; Graham, Watts, & Timbrook, 1991). Dahlstrom (1992) raised a question about the congruence of some MMPI and MMPI–2 codes, basing his concerns on a large sample of normal profiles available from the MMPI restandardization study. However, Tellegen and Ben-Porath (1993) pointed out that Dahlstrom's conclusions about congruence were based on a sample that included *only* normal-range profiles. These "normal" profiles have a significantly constricted range and would not be recommended for clinical interpretation because, in more than two thirds of the cases, *T* scores are below 60 and below 50 in many cases.

Gender Differences on the MMPI–2: Gender-Specific Versus Nongendered Norms

The authors of the original MMPI discovered some small differences between men and women that appeared to be unrelated to the pathological dimension (Hathaway & McKinley, 1940). They decided to plot MMPI scores for men and women using gender-based norms. Questions emerged in the 1990s, particularly in employment-related discrimination cases focusing on gender as a central issue—about why women's scores are compared only with the scores of other women, and men's scores only with those of other men. There were concerns that this represented differential treatment based on gender. To meet Equal Employment Opportunity guidelines, test developers began to eliminate the traditional practice of comparing people on specific gender-based norms and to provide nongendered norms for use in personnel selection.

When developing the MMPI–2 norms, the Revision Committee decided to follow the traditional practice of plotting scores on gender-specific norms to maintain continuity with the traditional MMPI. (Only a few MMPI–2 scales—e.g., the *Mf* scale and *ANX* scale—show any gender differences.) However, nongendered norms (Ben-Porath & Forbey, 2003; Tellegen, Butcher, & Hoeglund, 1993) are

available for situations in which they would be appropriate or required.

Relationship of the MMPI and MMPI–A

The 478 items of the MMPI–A contain the relevant items for scoring the traditional validity and clinical scales. As previously noted, additional adolescent-specific items were included to address more directly the problems and attitudes experienced by younger people. The Restandardization Committee ensured continuity between the two forms by keeping relatively intact the standard validity and clinical scales. The exception was the *F* scale, which was reconstructed to make it more appropriate for assessing adolescents.

The traditional MMPI clinical scales were cross-validated in adolescent clinical settings (Butcher et al., 1992; C. L. Williams & Butcher, 1989). As Appendix X shows, correlation coefficients between the MMPI–A and the original MMPI for the validity and clinical scales are quite high, indicating that the MMPI–A validity and clinical scales represent alternate measures of the original MMPI versions of those scales. Many traditional correlates established for the *Hs* (Hypochondriasis), *D* (Depression), *Hy* (Hysteria), *Pd* (Psychopathic Deviate), *Mf* (Masculinity–Femininity), *Pa* (Paranoia), *Pt* (Psychasthenia), *Sc* (Schizophrenia), *Ma* (Hypomania), and *Si* (Social Introversion–Extraversion) scales apply to adolescents in mental health, drug and alcohol, and special school settings (see Butcher et al., 1992). Extensive research on the MMPI–A has been published since it was introduced.[3]

VALUE OF USING THE MMPI–2 OR MMPI–A IN FORENSIC TESTIMONY

As noted earlier, the MMPI instruments have become the most widely used tests in the objective assessment of personality in forensic evaluations (Camara, Nathan, & Puente, 2000; Lally, 2003;

---

[3] Butcher and Pope (1992); Butcher, Ellertsen, et al. (2000); D. Carlson (2001); Cashel, Ovaert, and Holliman (2000); Conkey (2000); Contini de Gonzalez, Figueroa, Cohen, Imach, and Coronel de Pace (2001); Fontaine, Archer, Elkins, and Johansen (2001); Forbey and Ben-Porath (2001); Forbey, Handel, and Ben-Porath (2000); Forbey, Ben-Porath, and Davis (2000); Glaser, Calhoun, and Petrocelli (2002); Hammel (2001); Henry (1999); L. Hunter (2000); Krakauer, Archer, and Gordon (1993); Krishnamurthy and Archer (1999); Mcentee (1999); McGrath et al. (2000); McGrath, Pogge, and Stokes (2002); Micucci (2002); Moore, Thompson-Pope, and Whited (1996); Morton and Farris (2002); Morton, Farris, and Brenowitz (2002); Newsome, Archer, Trumbetta, and Gottesman (2003); Osberg and Poland (2002); Otto and Collins (1995); L. Pena (2001); Pogge, Stokes, McGrath, Bilginer, and DeLuca (2002); Powis (1999); Stein and Graham (2005); Weis, Crockett, and Vieth (2004).

EXHIBIT 2.1

Reasons for Using the MMPI/MMPI–2/MMPI–A in Court

- The MMPI is the most frequently used clinical test (Lally, 2003; Lubin et al., 1984). It is used in many court cases to provide personality information on defendants or litigants in which psychological adjustment factors are pertinent to resolution of the case.
- The inventory is relatively easy to administer, available in a printed booklet, on cassette tapes, and on computer. It usually takes between 1 and 1½ hours for adults to complete and 1 hour for adolescents.
- Individuals self-administer the test, under carefully monitored conditions, by simply responding "*T*" (*true*) or "*F*" (*false*) to each item on the basis of whether the statement applies to them. The items are written so that individuals with a sixth-grade reading level can understand them.
- The MMPI, MMPI–2, and MMPI–A are relatively easy to score. The item responses for each scale are tallied and recorded on a profile sheet. Scoring is simple and can be delegated to clerical staff to conserve more costly professional time. Computerized scoring programs are available and enhance the scoring process (i.e., reduce errors and score the numerous available scales quickly). The objective scoring ensures reliability in the processing of the test protocol, which is a critical determination in forensic cases.
- Forensic assessments involving people from different language or cultural backgrounds are often difficult to conduct because of the lack of appropriate, relevant assessment instruments. The MMPI and MMPI–2 have been extensively used in other countries, and there are many foreign-language versions of the MMPI and MMPI–2 available, including Spanish, Thai, Vietnamese, Chinese, Norwegian, Japanese, Dutch, Hebrew, and Italian. In cases in which the person being evaluated does not speak or read English, a foreign-language version of the instrument can be administered. In many cases, appropriate national norms can also be obtained.
- The MMPI–2 and MMPI–A possess a number of response-attitude measures, in addition to those that appear on the original MMPI, that appraise the test-taking attitudes of the test taker. Any self-report instrument is susceptible to manipulation, either conscious or unconscious; thus, it is imperative to have a means of assessing the person's test-taking attitudes at the time he or she completed the test (Bagby, Marshall, Bury, & Bacchiochi, 2006).
- The MMPI, MMPI–2, and MMPI–A are objectively interpreted instruments. Empirically validated scales possess clearly established meanings. A high score on a particular clinical scale is statistically associated with behavioral characteristics. These scale "meanings" are easily taught and are objectively applied to test takers. Clinical interpretation strategies are easily learned. The established correlates for the scales allow them to be interpreted objectively—even by computer.
- MMPI, MMPI–2, and MMPI–A scales possess high reliability (i.e., are quite stable over time). This well-established scale reliability is especially important in forensic application. MMPI–2 code types possess high stability when well-defined codes are used for interpretation (Munley, Germain, Tovar-Murray, & Borgman, 2004).
- The MMPI, MMPI–2, and MMPI–A provide clear, valid descriptions of people's problems, symptoms, and characteristics in a broadly accepted clinical language. Scale elevations and code-type descriptions provide a terminology that enables clinicians to describe test takers clearly. To say that a person possesses "high 4 characteristics" or exhibits features of a "2–7" communicates specific information to other psychologists. This clinical language can easily be translated into everyday language that makes sense to the lay public (Finn & Butcher, 1990).
- MMPI–2 and MMPI–A scores enable the practitioner to predict future behaviors and responses to different treatment or rehabilitation approaches, as was the case for the MMPI.
- MMPI, MMPI–2, and MMPI–A profiles are easy to explain in court. The variables and the means of score comparison are relatively easy for people to understand.

Lees-Haley, 1992; Lees-Haley et al., 1996; Otto, 2002). Several reasons, highlighted in Exhibit 2.1, account for the wide applicability of the MMPI–2 in forensic assessments.

First, each version of the MMPI assesses the credibility of the test-taker's responses. The MMPI–2 and MMPI–A added new measures of validity. Chapter 7 discusses these measures.

Second, the instrument can be interpreted in an objective manner based on external, empirically based correlates (Archer et al., 1995; Butcher,

Rouse, & Perry, 2000; Graham et al., 1999). The MMPI–2 provides an objective portrayal of mental health symptoms that is less dependent on subjective impressions than are many other widely used procedures. Use of the MMPI–2 helps to protect mental health professionals testifying in court from being vulnerable to the criticism that their interpretations are subjective (Ziskin, 1981b; see also chap. 4, this volume).

Third, the MMPI scales typically have high reliability (Dahlstrom et al., 1972; Leon, Gillum,

Gillum, & Gouze, 1979). Test–retest studies show that constructs measured by the scales tend to be consistent on retesting because many scales assess fairly stable traits or personality features. In a study of test–retest reliability, Jemelka, Wiegand, Walker, and Trupin (1992; see also Van Cleve, Jemelka, & Trupin, 1991) found that test scores of incoming state felony prisoners were stable, at least during the first month of incarceration. A test–retest study of 1,050 "normal" men who were administered the MMPI–2 on two occasions 5 years apart revealed that the clinical scale scores were quite stable over time. The stability coefficients ranged from .56 to .86, with a median stability index of .68 (Spiro, Butcher, Levenson, Aldwin, & Bossé, 2000), showing moderate to high reliability. This reliability is one key reason for the test's admissibility (see Appendixes A and B, this volume).

Fourth, MMPI–2 scale scores are statistically computed, setting it apart from some assessment instruments for which different—sometimes conflicting—methods are sometimes used to compute the scores. The standard interpretations for MMPI–2 patterns are based on empirical research. As a consequence, interpreters who possess adequate education, training, and experience with the instrument tend to show consistency in interpreting particular score patterns.

Fifth, the clinical scales have well-established correlates for describing aspects of personality. An extensive body of research published in peer-reviewed scientific and professional journals supports MMPI–2 in assessing personality characteristics (for reviews, see Butcher & Williams, 2000; Graham, 2006; R. Greene, 2000; Keller & Butcher, 1991).

Sixth, lay people find it relatively easy to grasp the nature, rationale, and workings of the test. Expert witnesses can explain the MMPI–2 and MMPI–A to judges, juries, and others without formal psychological training (see chap. 5, this volume).

POTENTIAL PROBLEMS TO ANTICIPATE IN TESTIMONY ABOUT THE MMPI OR MMPI–2

Expert witnesses often face two immediate challenges. First, they must convince the interpreter of the law, usually a judge, that the test is reliable.

Second, they must persuade the trier of fact, usually a jury, that the test has something meaningful to say about an issue that the jury must address.

Even though the original MMPI has been withdrawn from use, it is discussed in this chapter because it may yet be found in court cases for some time to come (e.g., because the individual involved might have been tested earlier when the original MMPI was in wide use). In this section, we discuss some of the possible questions or difficulties that psychologists might encounter (particularly in cross-examination) when presenting original MMPI-based testimony. This section examines some issues specific to using the different versions of the inventory, and explores questions that might apply regardless of which version is used.

Vulnerabilities in Testimony Regarding the Original MMPI

Trying to use the original MMPI at this time creates needless vulnerabilities for the expert witness. Cross-examination can focus on outmoded items, narrow normative sample, antiquated, inexact norms, and other problems discussed in this book.

Item-level problems

Possible question on direct or cross-examination: *Isn't it true that some of the items in the original MMPI are questionable because they are objectionable and antiquated?*

Criticism (e.g., Butcher & Tellegen, 1966) and litigation (e.g., *McKenna v. Fargo*, 451 F. Supp. 1355 (1978)) have shed light on the objectionable content of some of the items on the original MMPI. Lawsuits have focused on items containing religious- or gender-preference content. In these cases, the test was used to screen for high-stress positions (e.g., air traffic controllers) or positions involving a high degree of public responsibility and emotional stability (e.g., police officers or nuclear power plant operators).

The objectionable item content on the original MMPI can produce other negative effects for the person being evaluated. Awkward, antiquated, or objectionable items can lower motivation to answer the items appropriately. A woman taking the original MMPI before a custody hearing, for example, complained that "these items are stupid! I don't know what relevance my bowel movements being black or tarry could possibly have to keeping custody of my child." The MMPI–2 dropped these objectionable items.

Nonrepresentative standardization sample

Possible question on direct or cross-examination: *Is it true that the original MMPI normative data were collected in the 1930s? Is it true that these data are inappropriate for use with people today?*

The original normative sample comprised a relatively small number of mostly rural, middle-aged White visitors to the University of Minnesota Hospital (and a much smaller group of airline workers and Civilian Conservation Corps [CCC] workers) in the 1930s and 1940s who were selected for their notable lack of physical or mental health problems. The sample fails to meet the most basic expectation of representativeness. Various researchers noted this weakness when the original MMPI was used to evaluate individuals whose demographics (e.g., ethnicity) were missing from the "normative" sample (e.g., Butcher & Owen, 1978; Colligan, Osborne, Swenson, & Offord, 1983; Pancoast & Archer, 1989; Parkison & Fishburne, 1984). New norms were developed in the 1989 revision to address this issue.

Antiquated and inexact norms

Possible question on direct or cross-examination: *Isn't it true that the original MMPI norms are too inexact for use today? Isn't it true that the original MMPI tends to show more psychological problems than the individual really has?*

The original MMPI may make even those people without significant problems appear to be disturbed. The use of old norms in evaluating an individual in forensic assessments could lead an opposing attorney to make a motion to strike any MMPI-based testimony because it relied on an incorrect, outdated normative standard. As noted earlier, one of the reasons the MMPI revision was required was that the original MMPI norms tended to overpathologize contemporary individuals.

The scores of normal test-takers have risen significantly on the original MMPI over time because

psychologists started using different instructions than Hathaway and McKinley (1940) used in norming the original MMPI. Early test-takers, including those whose scores normed the test, were allowed to leave blank items they considered irrelevant. Contemporary test administrators instruct test takers to answer all items, if possible, and discourage item omissions. Interpreting the scores of people encouraged to complete all items using norms of those who were tacitly encouraged to omit irrelevant items violates the principles of standardization, is misleading, and tends to overpathologize test takers.

Conversion of MMPI scores to MMPI–2 norms: Procedures for modernizing. The original MMPI, although withdrawn from publication years ago, continues to appear in court cases when a litigant's mental health record includes an MMPI that was administered before the MMPI–2 was available. Forensic psychologists encountering the original MMPI in court cases should be able to translate scores on the original instrument into the MMPI–2 norms. The procedure takes little time and requires the original raw scores and the item response records (answer sheet). The procedure follows.

Step 1: Obtain the person's responses to the 13 MMPI items that were dropped from the original instrument (see Appendix Y).

Step 2: Note the direction (true or false) on which the individual responded to each of the 13 items.

Step 3: Modify the person's raw score for the scales on which these 13 items appear.

Step 4: Plot the revised raw score using an MMPI–2 profile form.

Note: Only the original validity scales (*L*, *F*, and *K*) and 10 standard or clinical scales can be processed in this manner. The MMPI–2 content scales and most of the special scales cannot be scored from the original MMPI.

Vulnerabilities in Testifying About the MMPI–2

Item changes

Possible questions on direct or cross-examination:

Is the MMPI–2 measuring the same things as the original validated MMPI scales? Because much of the established MMPI research was based on responses to the old item wordings, does the meaning of the items for the new inventory still apply?

The MMPI–2 has clear continuity with the original MMPI at the item and scale levels. Although a few of the original items were changed slightly to improve wording and clarity, most items are worded exactly the same in the MMPI–2 as in the original instrument. Research has provided evidence that item-wording changes have not altered an item's meaning or the psychological equivalence. Ben-Porath and Butcher (1989b), for example, found that people who took the original MMPI and a week later took the revised MMPI responded comparably to people who took the original MMPI and a week later took the original MMPI again.

Normative sample
Possible question on direct or cross-examination:
Does the MMPI–2 normative sample reflect the contemporary population of the United States?

The MMPI–2 normative sample comprised people randomly solicited from seven regions of the United States. The regions were chosen to ensure that the sample would reflect ethnic diversity. This large, general sample (Butcher, Graham, Williams, et al., 1990) serves as a more appropriate and diverse comparison group than was available for the original MMPI (Hathaway & McKinley, 1943). Schinka and Lalone (1997) found that "for clinical purposes, it would appear that deviations from estimated U.S. population demographic characteristics in the MMPI–2 restandardization sample do not have any more meaningful effects than those posed by the reliability limits of the MMPI–2 scales themselves" (pp. 310–311).

Importance of a Broad-Based Normative Population in the Interpretation of Personality Test Scores
Possible questions on direct or cross-examination:
What makes the MMPI–2 norms more appropriate than other personality tests? Another personality inventory was used instead of the MMPI–2. If you

chose to administer the "x" personality inventory rather than the most widely researched and used test, could you provide your rationale for selecting the "x" test instead of the MMPI–2? What research did you use to substantiate your decision?

As noted, the MMPI–2 norms are based on a broad sample of individuals drawn from across the United States and tested in a controlled setting according to standard test instructions. When an individual's score is plotted on MMPI–2 norms, his or her scale scores are compared with the most general and diverse reference group possible. This is not the case with many other personality scales. Butcher (1996) noted, for example, two exceptions to this traditional normative philosophy. These exceptions involve different approaches to understanding the scores than one finds with traditional normative scales.

The first example, a clear exception to the normative scale approach, involves the Basic Personality Inventory (BPI) published by Jackson (1989). This personality scale was developed to assess the clinical domains that are measured by the MMPI. Jackson used nonstandard and questionable normative data-collection procedures and analysis methods to develop norms that limit the test's generalizability. The BPI test norms were collected in an unusual manner—by mailing test booklets to potential participants inviting them to complete the items. This uncontrolled test administration procedure leaves potential test users with uncertainty as to who actually completed the items on which the "norms" are based. The normative sample is questionable because of inadequate procedures to ensure adequate ethnic representation and balance.

In the BPI normative data collection, some people who completed the testing responded only to one third of the inventory's items. Thus, few of the "normative" participants actually responded to the entire item pool in the normative sample—a procedure that limits any interpretations from data analyses requiring all of the items in the booklet, such as the alpha coefficient for the scales.

Finally, it is important for standardized instruments to be administered in a standardized manner. Aside from knowing that participants received the form in the mail, there can be no certainty—because the administration was not monitored—of the conditions under which each test booklet was filled out. Was the participant talking on the phone while filling it out, eating dinner and watching TV while responding, asking whoever was in the room their opinions about how to respond, or giving it to someone else to fill out?

A second personality questionnaire (Millon Clinical Multiaxial Inventory or MCMI; Millon, 1997) for which the authors used an extreme deviation from the use of standard normative practice involved the use of "base rate norms" against which to compare individual scores. The test developer used a sample of psychiatric patients as the reference group rather than individuals drawn from the general population. The scale scores, instead of reflecting a normative deviation, show the person's standing on the various scales as compared only with other psychiatric patients. This instrument does not allow for a client's scores to be interpreted according to a criterion of normality that might be an important factor to assess in a court case. The base rate norms do not allow for the description of normal behavior because there is no normal reference group. In effect, any score would be considered pathological. Most people who take the test would consequently obtain a fairly pathological picture because they are assumed to be a patient—the test does not detect differences from normality but only provides a perspective on what kind of patient a person might be. Therefore, the MCMI scales cannot be used for describing normal behavior as most other clinically oriented personality tests do. The meanings of MCMI–III (Millon, 1997) scale elevations are more narrowly defined than those of most personality measures that have a normative population. Otto and Butcher (1995) suggested that the MCMI–III should not be used in forensic assessment because it overpathologizes normals and cannot specifically address the question as to whether a client is experiencing psychological disorder. It should be noted that the test publisher includes language in the MCMI–III computer report outputs that warns users against using the test for applications (such as forensic or personnel applications) that differ from pretherapy planning for which the norms apply. Rogers, Salekin, and Sewell (1999)

concluded that "fundamental problems in the scientific validity and error rates for MCMI–III appear to preclude its admissibility under *Daubert* for the assessment of Axis II disorders" (p. 425).

A third instrument, the Personality Assessment Inventory (PAI; Morey, 1991; see also Boyle, 1996; A. Conger & Conger, 1996; Morey, 1996) poses problems in finding pertinent research for specific forensic use with specific populations. The absence of extensive validation studies for a specific forensic use leaves the expert witness, the litigants, the judge, and the jury in the dark about whether a standardized psychological test works. Rogers, Sewell, Cruise, Wang, and Ustad (1998) discussed concerns about the use of the PAI in forensic and correctional settings.

Comparability of *T* scores
Possible question on direct or cross-examination: ***Are the T scores in MMPI–2 comparable to the T scores in the original MMPI?***

The issue of comparability of *T* scores requires some explanation (see the Glossary, this volume, for a discussion of the standard score). Two factors account for the slight shift in *T* scores between the two versions of the MMPI. First, average raw score differences emerged between the normative samples for the original MMPI and MMPI–2 in large part because the original test allowed "*cannot say*" scores, which tended to lower scores. As noted earlier, many people in the original MMPI normative group left blank a significant number of items, which artificially lowered the raw scores and the *T*-score distribution for the scales. This later resulted in artificially inflating the *T* scores for contemporary individuals tested with the original MMPI (see Figure 2.1).

Second, the original *T* scores were not uniform with respect to the percentile rank across the clinical scales. This lack of uniformity meant that a *T* score of 70 on one scale might be at a percentile rank of 91 on another clinical scale and a percentile rank of 97 on still another. A new set of uniform *T* scores was developed to make the *T* scores comparable across percentile values of the clinical scales (Tellegen & Ben-Porath, 1992).

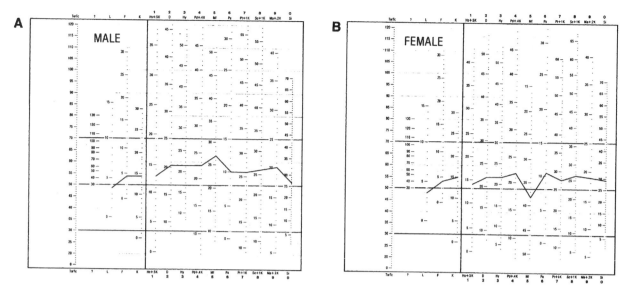

FIGURE 2.1. Group mean profiles of the MMPI–2 restandardization samples (*A*: N = 1,138; *B*: N = 1,462) plotted on the original MMPI norms to illustrate the inaccuracy of the original inventory to characterize "normal" individuals. From Appendix H of the *Manual for Administration and Scoring.* Copyright © 1942, 1943, 1951, 1967 (renewed 1970), 1989 The Regents of the University of Minnesota. All rights reserved. Used by permission of the University of Minnesota Press. "Minnesota Multiphasic Personality Inventory—2" and "MMPI–2" are trademarks owned by the University of Minnesota.

Although there are small differences between *T* scores, the relationship between the uniform *T*-score distribution and the original MMPI distribution is strong. Both are based on a linear *T*-score transformation for the raw scores. Correlations between linear *T* scores and uniform *T* scores are in the range of .99.

The MMPI–2 norms are more appropriate than the original MMPI norms for use with contemporary test takers. Take a look at the airline pilot applicant profiles in Figure 2.2 and Figure 2.3. These applicants are not clinical patients but are normal individuals applying for positions as airline pilots with a major air carrier. In general, typical airline pilot applicants tend to be well adjusted. They have usually been prescreened or preselected, and most have come through rigorous military screening programs. Finally, most are extremely defensive and take the MMPI with a response set to present a nonpathological pattern. Yet, when we plot their MMPI scores using the original MMPI norms, we find that most of their clinical scores are elevated at about one half to

nearly a full standard deviation above the mean. However, when their clinical scale scores are plotted using the MMPI–2 norms, their scores fall, as they should given their virtuous self-presentation, below the mean on all but one of the scales (Butcher, 1992c).

Validity considerations

Possible question on direct or cross-examination: *Has the MMPI–2 been validated to a reasonable degree of scientific certainty?*

Because the MMPI–2 and MMPI–A retained the validity and clinical scales of the original MMPI, there is continuity of validity. That is, the validity research on the original scales has been shown to apply equally well to the MMPI–2 (Graham, 1988) and the MMPI–A (Williams & Butcher, 1989). In addition, several studies have documented the validity of the traditional validity and clinical scales on the MMPI–2.[4] Several studies have also reported extensive validity with the MMPI–A (Butcher &

---

[4] Ben-Porath and Butcher (1989a, 1989b); Ben-Porath et al. (1991); Butcher et al. (1991); Butcher, Graham, et al. (1990); Butcher, Jeffrey, et al. (1990); Egeland et al. (1991); Hjemboe and Butcher (1991); Keller and Butcher (1991); Strassberg, Clutton, and Korboot (1991).

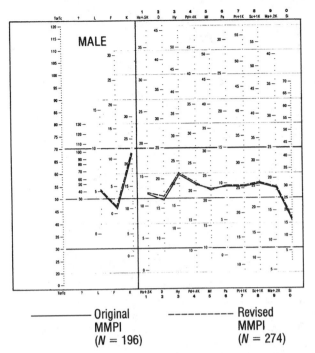

——————— Original
MMPI
(*N* = 196)

————— Revised
MMPI
(*N* = 274)

FIGURE 2.2. Basic profiles of two groups of airline pilot applicants who had been administered either the original MMPI or the MMPI–2, with both profiles plotted on the original MMPI norms. Used with permission of James N. Butcher.

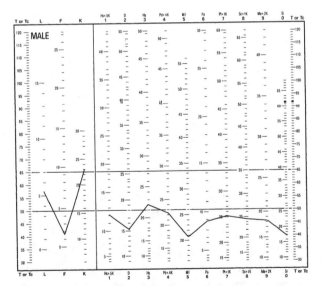

FIGURE 2.3. MMPI–2 basic profile of airline pilot applicants (*N* = 437), illustrating how well-adjusted individuals who present themselves in a positive light score on the MMPI–2 norms. Used with permission of James N. Butcher.

Williams, 1992a; Butcher et al., 1992; Williams et al., 1992).

Research supports the continuity of the original MMPI and MMPI–2 scores in samples of psychiatric patients. Blake et al. (1992), for example, conducted research showing "that all scales on the two forms were highly correlated. Discriminant function analyses show that there were essentially no differences between the two forms in the accurate classification of clinical and nonclinical groups" (p. 323).

Extensive research has studied MMPI and MMPI–2 in forensic settings (see, e.g., references provided in Appendixes C through G, this volume). Thus an appropriate experience base is available, for example, in personal injury assessments, child custody evaluations, and pretrial criminal assessment.

General Criticisms of the Empirical Approach to Personality Assessment

Several factors pertaining to response attitudes will be discussed in this section.

The Issue of Whether Response Sets Invalidate Empirical Scales

Possible question on direct or cross-examination: *Hasn't research shown that people do not answer each item in a completely truthful way but simply answer in a socially desirable way or acquiesce to the demands of the situation?*

Some researchers have claimed that personality questionnaires are susceptible to response sets and thus are not thought to present valid sources of personality information (Edwards, 1957; Jackson & Messick, 1962). However, Block (1965) showed that valid personality prediction could be obtained from MMPI items across a wide variety of samples regardless of the effects of response set. There is, however, a periodic reissue of the old response set criticism of the MMPI (see, e.g., Helmes & Reddon, 1993; Jackson, Fraboni, & Helmes, 1997).

Do differing motivations affect an individual's response to personality test items?

This is true with not only the MMPI but *any* personality questionnaire, including Jackson's Basic

Personality Inventory (Jackson, 1989). All such questionnaires are vulnerable to response motivational distortion. However, this is the reason why validity scales were developed—to detect the presence of invalidating motivational sets (see chap. 7 and Appendixes C and D, this volume).

Psychometric weakness: Low internal consistency of empirical scales

Possible question on direct or cross-examination: *Isn't it true that the MMPI–2 scales suffer from low internal consistencies and are therefore not reliable measures?*

Internal consistency is one way of estimating scale reliability. This statistic reflects the degree to which a scale measures a unitary construct as opposed to multiple characteristics. The higher the scale's internal consistency, the more likely it measures a single dimension or trait. The lower the scale's internal consistency the more likely it is focusing on multiple personality characteristics.

The internal consistencies of MMPI and MMPI–2 empirical scales differ widely. Some are relatively low (e.g., Scale 3); others are typically quite high (e.g., Scale 7). However, the internal consistencies of homogeneous content scales (such as the original MMPI's Wiggins [1966] content scales and the content scales of the MMPI–2) are typically quite high because internal consistency was incorporated in the scale construction approach.

The important thing to remember about internal consistency is that it is considered to be a less important scale statistic for scales that were derived by empirical means than for homogeneous or content scales. Test–retest reliability and eternal validity—the degree to which a scale actually measures behavior—are the empirical scale's ultimate criterion of worth. How the items of a scale relate to each other is relatively less important than that they, as a group, predict a particular criterion reliably. The MMPI clinical scales were developed to ensure that they measured or predicted behavior or characteristics.

Psychometric weakness: Overlapping items on the scales

Possible question on direct or cross-examination:

Isn't it true that the MMPI–2 is a weak measure of personality because its different scales contain overlapping items?

One important reason that item overlap occurs in omnibus-type personality scales is that psychological phenomena are not independent of each other. Clinical behaviors of interest to the practitioner are seldom isolated problems that are unrelated to other characteristics or traits. Depression as a symptomatic behavior is highly correlated with anxiety, social introversion, and low self-esteem. Any attempt to measure any one of these characteristics will result in an encounter with the others. It is difficult to measure depression in the absence of assessing (at least to some extent) these other qualities. In fact, an artificial elimination of item overlap may result in an incomplete assessment of psychological variables.

With regard to empirical scales, such as the MMPI–2 clinical scales, *external validity is the ultimate criterion* (see Archer et al., 1995; Butcher, Rouse, & Perry, 2000; Graham et al., 1999), and item overlap is of secondary importance. In the development of the MMPI–2 content scales, efforts were made to minimize item overlap to produce relatively pure content dimensions. Even in these instances, however, some item overlap was allowed because a particular item theoretically "belonged" on more than one scale. For example, an item might be empirically related to anxiety and appear on the MMPI–2 Anxiety (*ANX*) content scale. However, the same item may also be empirically related to work performance and appear on the Work Interference (*WRK*) content scale, in which it appears to assess an inability to work effectively. Such an item has content relevance and predictive validity for both scales.

Psychometric weakness: Test–retest reliability

Possible question on direct or cross-examination: *Isn't it true that you get different scale scores on the MMPI scales when you retest people at a later date?*

Most MMPI–2 scales have moderate to high test–retest reliabilities, depending on (a) the length of the scale (Scale 1 usually has a somewhat lower reliability coefficient than Scale 8, which is longer) or (b) the degree to which it measures stable "traits" in contrast to factors that are caused or evoked more by specific situations (see Appendix X, this volume).

Some MMPI–2 scales have exceptionally high test–retest stability. For example, the long-range test–retest stability for the *Si* scale was found to be .734 for a sample of normal men over a 30-year test–retest period (Leon et al., 1979). Spiro et al. (2000) found that the stability index for *Si* was .86 in a test–retest study of the MMPI–2 spanning 5 years. Matz, Altepeter, and Perlman (1992) found moderate to high stability coefficients (.60–.90) for the MMPI–2 validity scales in a sample of college students.

The meaning of individual items

Possible question on direct or cross-examination: ***Doesn't MMPI Item # "x" actually measure something different from the scale it appears on?***

It is generally not a good idea for expert witnesses who are testifying about the MMPI to introduce individual items—out of their scale context—in support of the interpretation. The MMPI is most valuable as an assessment instrument if the scale level rather than individual item level is the basis for interpretation. This is true for several reasons. First, items tend to be less reliable than groups of items or scales. Second, at least in the case of empirically derived measures, some items on the scale might have lower content relevance and validity than other items on the scale, and their inclusion as a focus in the testimony might detract from the overall value of the scale in assessing the personality features in question.

The late Jay Ziskin pointed out that

> there is a need to look at the subject's responses to individual items on the test. This statement may be objectionable to many psychologists who insist that evaluation should not be on the basis of the individual responses to items but rather on scale scores and configurations of scores. I am aware that is the way the test is used by most

psychologists. However, neither lawyers nor jurors are bound to that approach. (1981b, p. 8)

The following scenario illustrates possible problems psychologists might encounter when items are taken out of scale context.

Attorney: Tell me, Doctor, do you think most people inwardly dislike putting themselves out to help other people?

Psychologist: Er . . . no, I think most people would like to be helpful to others.

Attorney: That's interesting, Doctor. A "false" response to that question measures a point on the Paranoia scale, doesn't it, Doctor?

Psychologist: I don't remember the way particular items are scored.

Attorney: You don't know whether an item on a scale measures the characteristics of the scale, Doctor?

Psychologist: I only go by the total score of the scale.

Attorney: [Showing the items to the psychologist, having first asked the judge's permission to approach the witness] As you look at the items on the scale and the scoring key, is it your opinion that the item is scored on the Paranoia scale if it is answered "false"? Now, Doctor, doesn't it seem a bit strange to you that a "false" response to that item would measure paranoid thinking?

Psychologist: Could you repeat the question?

Attorney: Wouldn't you agree that a cynical, paranoid, mistrustful person would actually inwardly dislike putting themselves out to help other people, Doctor?

Psychologist: Er . . . yes, that would seem to be the case. But, you said that it was scored the other way.

Attorney: Wouldn't you agree then, Doctor, that the item is scored in the wrong direction on the Paranoia scale to actually measure paranoid thinking?

Psychologist: Intuitively, it would seem that more cynical people would answer the other way, but . . .

Attorney: Now, Doctor, are you aware of other items on the test that are incorrectly scored as this one is?

The attorney in this exchange was able to get the psychologist to question the accuracy of the test by reference to individual items. Chapter 6 discusses why attorneys cross-examining a witness often find it useful to ask about individual items and strategies they can use for that approach.

Cross-examination can cloud issues and make incorrect or misleading points by focusing on individual item responses. Expert witnesses can stay on much safer ground by referring to the full scale scores. They can do this by stating that items should not be considered individually. Interpreting at the scale level is more typical and psychometrically appropriate than taking items out of context.

A personal injury case highlighted the relative power of using scale-level interpretations rather than item descriptions. The litigant, a woman in her early 30s, was allegedly injured in an automobile accident while she was in a rental car (although she was not hospitalized nor did she seek treatment for the injury for a period of time following the accident). She claimed to have disabling physical and psychological symptoms (headaches, double vision, and troubling nightmares) and sued the car rental company for a considerable sum of money to compensate for her injury.

On the psychological evaluation, her MMPI–2 clinical profile showed some Scale 1 and Scale 2 elevation, indicating that she was presenting herself as having mood and somatic complaints. However, her validity configuration showed a clear pattern of response defensiveness often seen among personal injury claimants who are presenting unrealistic complaints (Butcher & Harlow, 1987). Her *L* (Lie) scale elevation (62 *T*) and *K* (Defensiveness) scale score (*T* = 70) showed a clear pattern of evasiveness. The expert witness testifying on behalf of the insurance carrier presented the MMPI–2 validity pattern as reflecting a conscious response attitude, with the litigant claiming excessive virtue and distorting self-presentation in an attempt to make her somatic complaints more believable. The presence of conscious defensive responding and lack of

frankness on the MMPI–2 profile called into question the truthfulness of her claims (for a discussion of credibility issues, see chap. 7, this volume).

During the cross-examination, the woman's attorney attempted to get the psychologist to establish the woman's disability by examining her responses to a few single items that stated her symptoms. For example, at one point the attorney attempted to get the psychologist to acknowledge that his client's response of *true* to the MMPI item related to trauma actually showed that she was having residual problems from the accident. Rather than acknowledging that the response to a single item showed any lingering disability, the psychologist called attention to the fact that her full-scale score on the Post-traumatic Stress Disorder Scale—Keane (*Pk*; Butcher et al., 1989; Fairbank, McCaffrey, & Keane, 1985; Keane, Malloy, & Fairbank, 1984; Keane, Wolfe, & Taylor, 1987; Lyons & Keane, 1992), which contained the item, was actually low. She did not appear to have problems of a posttraumatic nature because her scores on the MMPI–2 *Pk* scale were actually well within the normal range, despite her response to the one item.

At another point, the attorney attempted to get the psychologist to acknowledge his client's inability to work by her response to a single item.

Attorney: Doctor, I want to talk about individual questions. Wouldn't my client's response to the MMPI item that we've been focusing on indicate that she was disabled?

Psychologist: No. You are moving away from the reliability and validity of the scale when you interpret at the item level. . . . The way the MMPI–2 is actually used is by interpreting scales. Her low score on the Work Interference scale shows that she actually reports few problems in this area.

The psychologist testified that items like this actually appeared on the *WRK* scale, which addresses the general problem of low functioning in a work context. The woman's total score on that scale placed her in the normal range, indicating that she reported no more work adaptation difficulties than most people do.

In both of these instances in the testimony, the attorney's efforts to prove his case at the item level were frustrated by the fact that the client's total score on those scales actually showed her *not* to report many problems in those areas compared with most people. By focusing on individual items, the attorney was trying to force the psychologist to understate the cumulative effect of the individual items and the overall comparative nature of the instrument.

Can the MMPI–2 detect response to stress?

Possible questions on direct or cross-examination: *Can the MMPI–2 be used to determine if a person is experiencing a stress-related disorder? Is there a clear, definite pattern on the test that suggests posttraumatic stress disorder (PTSD)? Does a person who is presently living under stressful circumstances produce a single definable pattern? Is there a PTSD scale that can provide information about how much stress a person is undergoing?*

The answers to these questions are complex and have been studied extensively.

One of the earliest studies, for example, involved the classic research with the original MMPI during World War II by Ancel Keys and his colleagues (Brozek, Franklin, Guetzkow, & Keys, 1947; Keys, Brozek, Henschel, Michelson, & Taylor, 1950; Schiele & Brozek, 1948), who evaluated a group of conscientious objectors who volunteered to undergo systematic starvation in lieu of military service. The study was designed to provide information about the psychological and health effects of starvation. The most significant MMPI finding from the study was that the MMPI *F* scale increased substantially as the volunteers progressed through the stressful period of semistarvation, indicating an extensive amount of symptom development as their stress increased (see discussion in chap. 7, this volume).

In terms of prominent clinical scale changes over periods of stress, the *D* scale and *Pt* (Psychasthenia) scale are often found to be elevated. For a comprehensive review of the empirical research and clinical strategies to consider in assessing PTSD with the MMPI–2, see Penk, Rierdan, Losardo, and Robinowitz (2006). In addition, two review articles describing the interpretation of the MMPI–2 in medical and forensic evaluations have been published recently (see Arbisi, 2006; Arbisi & Seime, 2006).

There have been some specific scales developed to measure posttraumatic stress—for example, the most widely used and researched measure is the Post-traumatic Stress Disorder Scale—Keane (*Pk*) developed by Keane et al. (1984). This scale was developed using male Vietnam war combat veterans but has been used extensively with other populations as well (see Flamer & Buch, 1992; Forfar, 1993; Lyons & Keane, 1992; Lyons & Wheeler-Cox, 1999; Neighbours, 1991; Penk et al., 1989; see also the discussion on assessing PTSD with the MMPI–2 in chap. 3, this volume).

Psychologists interested in the wide range of studies that have addressed the assessment of PTSD with the MMPI/MMPI–2 can find a variety of articles listed in Appendix E.[5]

Reading Level

Possible question on direct or cross-examination: *What level of education is needed to understand MMPI–2 items?*

Forensic assessments may be complicated by the fact that the individual who is being assessed cannot adequately read or comprehend English. The MMPI–2 items were written in relatively simple English. It takes only about a sixth-grade reading level to understand the item content (Paolo, Ryan, &

---

[5] Many studies have provided information on using the test to assess people under stress; for example, to cite only a few: Albrecht and Talbert (Albrecht et al., 1994); Arbisi, Murdoch, Fortier, and McNulty (2004); Constans, Lenhoff, and McCarthy (1997); Elhai (2000); Elhai, Baugher, Quevillon, Sauvageot, and Frueh (2004); Elhai and Frueh (2001); Elhai, Flitter, Gold, and Sellers (2001); Elhai, Forbes, Creamer, McHugh, and Frueh (2003); Elhai, Frueh, Davis, Jacobs, and Hammer (2003); Elhai, Frueh, Gold, Hamner, and Gold (2000, 2001); Elhai, Gold, Mateus, and Astaphan (2001); Elhai, Gold, Sellers, and Dorfman (2001); Elhai et al. (2004); Elhai, Ruggiero, Frueh, Beckham, and Gold (2002); Forbes, Creamer, and McHugh (1999); Franklin, Repasky, Thompson, Shelton, and Uddo (2002, 2003); Gaston, Brunet, Koszycki, and Bradwejn (1996); Greenblatt and Davis (1999); Hiley-Young, Blake, Abueg, and Rozynko (1995); Keane, Weathers, and Kaloupek (1992); Litz et al. (1991); Lyons and Wheeler-Cox (1999); Neighbours (1991); Penk et al. (1989); Sloan, Arsenault, and Hilsenroth (1998).

Smith, 1991). However, some items are more difficult than a sixth-grade reading level. Dahlstrom, Archer, Hopkins, Jackson, and Dahlstrom (1994), in an extensive study of the reading level of MMPI–2 and MMPI–A items, found that more than 90% of the items required a reading level of fifth grade. These investigators suggested that when the reading level of a particular client is in doubt, then a reading test should be administered or the tester should administer a sample of the most difficult items to determine if the individual can comprehend the items.

Individuals with even lower reading skills can be tested by using a tape-recorded version of the instrument available through the test publisher. Research has established tape-recorded administration as comparable to written administration of the MMPI (Dahlstrom et al., 1972). Tape-recorded versions that are available from the test distributor include Spanish, English, and Hmong. Butcher (1996) presented several normative databases that might be used as a different reference sample for the client.

If the individual is able to read and understand the items at a fifth-grade level, he or she can likely respond to the items well enough to produce a valid, interpretable record. However, the validity scales *F, F(B), F(p)* (Infrequency Psychiatric), and *VRIN* (Variable Response Inconsistency scale) should be carefully evaluated to ensure that the person has responded appropriately to the content of the test items. People who cannot comprehend the items tend to produce high scores on *F, F(B), F(p),* and *VRIN* scales and may actually invalidate their test in a manner similar to a random response set.

Research also supports the use of MMPI items presented using American Sign Language to hearing-impaired individuals (Brauer, 1992). The interpreter should be aware, however, that this translation involved some item modification. For a discussion of practical and ethical issues in the assessment of hearing-impaired clients, see Brauer, Braden, Pollard, and Hardy-Braz (1998) and Pollard (2002).

Cultural Diversity and MMPI–2 Responses

Possible question on direct or cross-examination: *Can the MMPI–2 be used with people from minority backgrounds?*

The original MMPI was criticized because only White individuals were included in the normative sample, and the test seemed, at least in some instances, to produce misleading results for minorities.[6] In one MMPI study of a rural population, one MMPI item alone perfectly discriminated all Black test takers from all White test takers. A prominent computerized MMPI scoring and interpretation service, using data from this rural population, incorrectly classified 90% of the apparently normal Black test takers as showing profiles characteristic of psychiatric patients (Erdberg, 1970, 1988; Gynther, Fowler, & Erdberg, 1971; see also Hutton, Miner, Blades, & Langfeldt, 1992).[7]

Faschingbauer vividly underscored some of the difficulties facing the clinician attempting contemporary use of the original MMPI.

> The original Minnesota group . . . seems to be an inappropriate reference group for the 1980s. The median individual in that group had an eighth-grade education, was married, lived in a small town or on a farm, and was employed as a lower level clerk or skilled tradesman. None was under 16 or over 65 years of age, and all were white. As a clinician I find it difficult to justify comparing anyone to such a dated group. When the person is 14 years old, Chicano, and lives in Houston's poor fifth ward, use of the original norms seems sinful. (1979, p. 375)

---

[6] See *Standards for Educational and Psychological Testing* (APA, 1985), Standard 7.6, p. 47; and Pope and Vasquez's (1998) chapters "Assessment, Testing, and Diagnosis" (pp. 143–159) and "Cultural, Contextual, and Individual Differences" (pp. 210–222). See also Butcher (1985b, 2004); Butcher, Cheung, and Lim (2003); Butcher and Pancheri (1976); Cheung and Song (1989); Cheung, Zhao, and Wu (1992); Clark (1985); Hess (1992); H. Lee, Cheung, Man, and Hsu (1992); Manos (1985); Manos and Butcher (1982); Rissetti and Maltes (1985); Savasir and Erol (1990).

[7] For additional considerations regarding race, ethnicity, and assessment, see the chapters "Assessment, Testing, and Diagnosis" and "Cultural, Contextual, and Individual Differences" in Pope and Vasquez (1998).

TABLE 2.1

Means and Standard Deviations by Ethnic Origin for 1,138 Community Adult Males

Scale	White (N = 933)		Black (N = 126)		American Indian (N = 38)		Hispanic (N = 35)		Asian (N = 6)	
	M	SD	M	SD	M	SD	M	SD	M	SD
L	3.36	2.13	4.26	2.77	4.26	2.78	4.51	2.63	4.50	3.27
F	4.29	2.98	5.18	3.76	6.42	4.46	6.17	4.07	7.33	5.61
K	15.45	4.74	15.08	4.88	13.55	4.64	14.29	4.50	13.83	5.08
Hs	4.69	3.78	5.58	3.91	6.92	4.48	6.17	4.11	6.50	5.28
D	18.16	4.59	19.02	4.24	19.08	4.98	19.06	5.00	16.83	3.97
Hy	21.06	4.60	20.03	5.06	20.42	5.49	19.77	5.56	17.50	4.89
Pd	16.25	4.49	17.57	4.40	19.50	5.23	18.29	5.62	16.67	4.13
Mf	26.21	5.13	25.84	4.20	23.39	6.07	24.43	4.60	24.17	6.18
Pa	10.09	2.82	9.87	3.09	10.70	3.21	10.51	3.07	10.33	2.16
Pt	11.04	6.53	11.60	6.75	12.79	7.34	13.00	6.81	14.33	7.15
Sc	10.75	6.86	12.79	7.38	13.82	9.01	13.89	8.20	16.50	10.05
Ma	16.58	4.46	18.33	4.31	17.84	4.59	18.77	4.88	15.83	5.98
Si	25.80	8.70	25.56	7.43	28.32	8.63	24.77	8.26	32.17	9.45

Note. From Appendix H of the *Manual for Administration and Scoring.* Copyright © 1942, 1943, 1951, 1967 (renewed 1970), 1989 The Regents of the University of Minnesota. All rights reserved. Used by permission of the University of Minnesota Press. "Minnesota Multiphasic Personality Inventory—2" and "MMPI–2" are trademarks owned by the University of Minnesota.

In the MMPI–2 normative study, an effort was made to increase the relevance of the revised norms for minorities by including individuals from different regional and ethnic backgrounds in the normative sample. As a consequence, the instrument is based on a normative group that is more appropriate for testing a broad range of ethnically diverse people. The relative performance on MMPI–2 scores for different ethnic groups is presented in Tables 2.1 and 2.2.

Hall, Bansal, and Lopez (1999) conducted a meta analysis of all the available studies addressing the question of ethnic differences on the MMPI and MMPI–2. They concluded that the differences between MMPI profiles across these studies were trivial. For example, Timbrook and Graham (1994) showed that the empirical correlates for MMPI–2 scales apply equally for Black and White individuals.

Several other studies show that the MMPI–2 performances of ethnic minorities are similar to those of Caucasians in a nonclinical sample. McNulty, Graham, Ben-Porath, and Stein (1997) found similar results with mental health outpatients. A study of men undergoing court-ordered

evaluations provided an empirical evaluation of the relative unimportance of ethnic group differences on the MMPI–2, at least for certain groups under certain circumstances. Ben-Porath, Shondrick, and Stafford (1995) compared Black and White men who had been ordered by the court to take the MMPI as part of their pretrial evaluation. The group mean profiles of Black and White defendants are shown in Figures 2.4 and 2.5. The authors found relatively few scale-level differences between the two groups, indicating that the MMPI–2 normative sample is appropriate to use for Black as well as for majority individuals. Only Scale 9 on the clinical and validity profile and *CYN* (Cynicism scale) and *ASP* (Antisocial Practices scale) on the content scale profile were significantly different; these differences were slight, although statistically significant. Other research has supported the use of the MMPI–2 with Black clients (Reed, Walker, Williams, McCloud, & Jones, 1996).

The MMPI–2 has also been studied with other minority populations. Keefe, Sue, Enomoto, Durvasula, and Chao (1996), for example, found that acculturated Asian American college students scored in a similar manner on the MMPI–2 as White

TABLE 2.2

Means and Standard Deviations by Ethnic Origin for 1,462 Community Adult Females

	White (N = 1,184)		Black (N = 188)		American Indian (N = 39)		Hispanic (N = 38)		Asian (N = 13)	
Scale	M	SD	M	SD	M	SD	M	SD	M	SD
L	3.47	1.98	3.95	2.32	4.64	2.68	2.92	2.16	4.85	3.31
F	3.39	2.64	4.43	3.38	5.69	3.99	6.32	4.35	3.54	2.07
K	15.34	4.47	14.13	4.56	12.41	5.67	12.37	4.88	14.85	4.04
Hs	5.49	4.24	7.50	5.16	8.74	4.63	8.92	5.50	6.38	2.84
D	19.93	4.97	21.00	4.99	21.33	4.84	21.55	4.69	19.23	4.28
Hy	22.05	4.55	22.17	5.38	22.59	5.39	22.53	6.00	20.62	4.09
Pd	15.68	4.48	18.30	4.42	19.08	4.74	19.89	5.34	14.31	4.89
Mf	36.31	3.91	34.60	4.22	33.23	4.85	34.05	4.76	35.62	4.39
Pa	10.13	2.91	10.40	3.11	11.51	3.62	11.34	3.15	9.54	2.88
Pt	12.27	6.89	13.55	7.68	17.64	8.76	17.21	8.92	10.00	5.03
Sc	10.39	6.88	14.10	8.63	17.00	9.93	18.42	10.63	8.92	4.01
Ma	15.61	4.29	17.85	4.62	17.90	5.29	20.00	4.91	15.31	3.84
Si	27.78	9.36	28.37	8.54	32.26	7.25	27.45	7.79	28.77	7.67

Note. From Appendix H of the *Manual for Administration and Scoring.* Copyright © 1942, 1943, 1951, 1967 (renewed 1970), 1989 The Regents of the University of Minnesota. All rights reserved. Used by permission of the University of Minnesota Press. "Minnesota Multiphasic Personality Inventory—2" and "MMPI–2" are trademarks owned by the University of Minnesota.

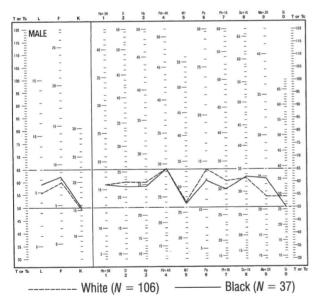

FIGURE 2.4. Group mean MMPI–2 clinical scale profile of White and Black men who had been court-ordered to take the MMPI–2. Data from D. D. Shondrick, Y. S. Ben-Porath, and K. Stafford. *Forensic Assessment With the MMPI–2: Characteristics of Individuals Undergoing Court-Ordered Evaluations.* Paper presented at the 27th Annual Symposium on Recent Developments in the Use of the MMPI (MMPI–2) Minneapolis, MN. Copyright by D. D. Shondrick, Y. S. Ben-Porath, and K. Stafford.

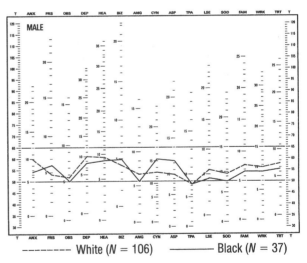

FIGURE 2.5. Group mean MMPI–2 content scale profile of White and Black men who had been court-ordered to take the MMPI–2. Data from D. D. Shondrick, Y. S. Ben-Porath, and K. Stafford. *Forensic Assessment With the MMPI–2: Characteristics of Individuals Undergoing Court-Ordered Evaluations.* Paper presented at the 27th Annual Symposium on Recent Developments in the Use of the MMPI (MMPI–2) Minneapolis, MN. Copyright by D. D. Shondrick, Y. S. Ben-Porath, and K. Stafford.

college students. And Velasquez et al. (1997) reported that the MMPI–2 can be effectively used in the assessment of Mexican American clients according to the American norms for the MMPI–2 (see a review of using the MMPI–2 with Caucasians by Garrido & Velasquez, 2006). Tinius and Ben-Porath (1993) reported that American Indian alcoholics produced similar MMPI–2 patterns as White alcoholics.

A recent study by Greene and his colleagues found some differences between American Indians and the MMPI–2 normative group on the five validity and clinical scales (*L, F,* Psychopathic Deviate [*Pd*], Schizophrenia [*Sc*], and Mania [*Ma*], six content scales (Depression scale [*DEP*], Health Concerns scale [*HEA*], Bizarre Mentation scale [*BIZ*], Cynicism scale [*CYN*], Antisocial Practices scale [*ASP*], and Negative Treatment Indicators scale [*TRT*]), and two supplementary scales (MacAndrew Scale—Revised [*MAC-R*] and Addiction Acknowledgment scale [*AAS*]). However, these differences were found to reflect actual substantive differences between the two groups rather than test bias. They concluded that "clinicians using the MMPI–2 with American Indians should not quickly dismiss elevations on these scales as reflecting test bias. Rather, these differences appear to accurately reflect the behaviors and symptoms that American Indian study participants were experiencing" (R. Greene, Robin, Albaugh, Caldwell, & Goldman, 2003, p. 368).

Non-English Language Versions of the MMPI–2

Possible question on direct or cross-examination:
Can the MMPI–2 be used with people from different cultures and languages?

It is not uncommon for forensic practitioners to be asked to evaluate people who are not native English speakers—for example, a parent from another country who is facing a child custody dispute. It is possible, if the person's English reading comprehension is sufficient, that a non-native English speaker can be administered the English language MMPI–2. In this case, the scale scores and interpretations of the test are considered to apply. For example, if the person has been in the United States

for several years, went to school in the United States, or works for an American firm and communicates in English, then the English language instrument and American norms would likely apply. If, however, the person is a recent immigrant and has problems comprehending the items, then an alternative means of assessment is required.

It may be possible to obtain an appropriate foreign language version of the MMPI–2 or MMPI–A and actually score the scales on an appropriate normative sample from the other country. Appendix K lists translations and translators. Butcher (1985b, 1996); Butcher, Cheung, et al. (2003); and Butcher, Derksen, Sloore, and Sirigatti (2003) discuss foreign language MMPI–2 translations.

Can a translated version of the MMPI–2 or MMPI–A produce equivalent measures? Yes, test translation procedures for the MMPI–2 have been well-developed and tested over many languages (see test translation information in Appendix K). Psychologists in other countries adapting the inventory in other languages and cultures follow strict translation procedures. If the translation is to be official, it needs to be cross-checked and approved by the test publisher, the University of Minnesota Press. There have been 32 translations of the MMPI–2 and 14 translations of the MMPI–A (for additional illustration of international assessment using the MMPI–2, see Butcher, Berah, et al., 1998; Butcher, Nezami, & Exner, 1998; Butcher, Tsai, Coelho, & Nezami, 2006).

Problems With Altered Instructions

Possible question on direct or cross-examination:
Can you change the instructions for the MMPI–2 to get at prior mental states?

Specifically, can an expert witness determine what test-takers were like *at the time* of a crime or *before* a traumatic event by asking them to fill out the MMPI–2 as if they were taking it at an earlier time? The answer is no. There are many problems with this approach—including the limitations of human memory in accurately remembering all the factors measured by the MMPI–2 as they were at a specific point in the past—but one of the most important is that the test was not standardized nor validated for this use. Research into altered instructions (Butcher, Morfitt, Rouse, & Holden, 1997; Cigrang & Staal, 2001; Fink & Butcher, 1972; Gucker & McNulty, 2004), for example, has demonstrated that the test instructions might be altered to reduce defensiveness at the time of the testing to produce more frank and open results, but no studies have provided scientific validation to support retrospectively administered tests.

Items Administered Out of Context

Possible question on direct or cross-examination: *Can specific MMPI–2 scales be excerpted from the test and administered separately?*

Some people have contended that the MMPI is too long and that one can simply extract specific scales out of context, for example, the MacAndrews Addiction Proneness Scale (*MAC–R*), and use that as the MMPI–2 based measure. Can an MMPI–2 scale, for example, the PTSD, the *MAC–R*, or the Hostility scale (*Ho*), be separately administered to clients without giving the entire MMPI–2? Some research has suggested that the test can be administered successfully in a modified form by taking the items out of the context of the other MMPI items (Scotti, Sturges, & Lyons, 1996). However, in forensic applications taking a scale of the MMPI–2 out of context by administering only a portion of the items can lead to problems of interpretation.

A central problem with administering a scale out of context is that it alters the response environment for the client in an unknown way. For example, administering only the items contained on a particular scale presents a number of similar items in sequence without the benefit of other nonconstruct-related items being interspersed. This piling up of a single item theme, such as depressed affect or antisocial problems (without a buffer of more neutral items), can affect the individual's response pattern in unknown ways.

Some research has shown that administering items out of context produces different scores; Megargee (1979) obtained a correlation of only .55 between Overcontrolled Hostility (*OH*) scores administered out of context and those administered in a full form administration. Another problem with ad-

ministering scales out of context is that the practitioner would not have available the all-important validity scales that guide forensic test interpretation so effectively. A third problem, to be discussed in the next section, involves the need to obtain permission of the copyright holder to modify a published instrument. Many publishers are unwilling to allow out-of-context use of scales from a published instrument.

Modified Administrative Formats: Abbreviated Versions of the MMPI–2

Possible question on direct or cross-examination: *Does one of the abbreviated or shortened versions of the MMPI–2 provide an adequate, valid assessment?*

Some have suggested using shortened versions of the MMPI to reduce the testing time. The use of an appropriate abbreviated version may be an acceptable alternative in some situations, for example, when time or physical limitations prevent the administration of the full form. The abbreviated form is created by reducing the number of items by presenting only the items contained on desired scales. For example, scores for the complete validity and clinical scales can be obtained by administering only the first 370 items of the MMPI–2 or the first 350 items of the MMPI–A. Reduced-item administration is relatively easy because all the items that make up the original clinical and validity scales are included in the first part of the test booklet. The actual number of items administered for each scale (e.g., the Depression scale) remains the same as when the full test is administered. An abbreviated form of the MMPI allows the psychologist to administer and score specific scales; the reliability and validity of these scales is not reduced by this procedure. However, the scales containing items in the back of the booklet, for example, the *MAC–R* scale or the MMPI–2 content scales, are not scorable.

MMPI–2 Short Forms

To shorten the time it takes to administer the test, a number of short forms of the MMPI–2 were published, such as the Mini-Mult (Kincannon, 1968), the MMPI 168 (Overall & Gomez-Mont, 1974), and the Faschingbauer scale (FAM; Faschingbauer, 1974). All of these short forms, however, were found to have a relatively poor performance at matching the clinical scale highpoints and configurations of the full-form MMPI (Butcher & Hostetler, 1990; Dahlstrom, 1980)—with only between 30% and 50% congruence rates between the short form scale estimates and the actual scale scores for the full form. As a consequence, these short forms do not provide an adequate basis for clinical or forensic decisions.

When the MMPI–2 was published, no short forms of the test surfaced during the first 10 years, in part because of the notably poor performance of the earlier short forms but also because, unlike with the original MMPI in which a large number of items were not used on the most widely used scales, *all* of the MMPI–2 items are used in working scales. The elimination of any items from an assessment would weaken the utility of the test because many standard MMPI–2 scales could not be scored.

However, in the past few years there has been a reemergence of MMPI–2 short forms that make similar promises of "saving time." And although they may have value in limited application for some situations (for example, in a research study where the findings will have no relevance to clinical or forensic decisions), until they have established adequate validity, reliability, sensitivity, and specificity for specific assessments, they lack a sufficient research base and track record for use in clinical or forensic assessments.

Three approaches to reducing item administration are described to illustrate their limitations for situations in which a thorough, reliable assessment is required.

Dahlstrom and Archer 180-item version of the MMPI–2. Dahlstrom and Archer (2000) recommended using the first 180 items of the MMPI–2 as a shortened version of the test. However, this short form was a poor predictor of the long-form scale score. In an evaluation of the Dahlstrom–Archer short form, Gass and Gonzalez (2003) conducted a study to examine its strengths and limitations and to determine the appropriate scope of its use in clinical applications. They used a psychiatric sample (N = 186) with normal neurological findings to examine short-form accuracy in predicting basic scale scores, profile code types, identifying high-point scales, and classifying scores as pathological ($T \geq 65$) or within normal limits. Gass and Gonzalez wrote, "The results suggest that the short form of the MMPI–2 is unreliable for predicting clinical code types, identifying the high-point scale, or predicting the scores on most of the basic scales" (Gass & Gonazalez, 2003, p. 521).

McGrath et al. short form. In another study, McGrath, Terranova, Pogge, and Kravic (2003) developed a short form for MMPI–2 that they thought would be more congruent in predicting full clinical scale scores than the Dahlstrom–Archer version but still shorter than the full length MMPI–2. These authors used a sample of 800 psychiatric inpatients and cross-validated with 658 inpatients and 266 outpatients. Although this short form does not offer full match with the full-form test, it reaches a higher degree of congruence but with the requirement of more items. Only the clinical scales are included.

Computer-adaptive administration: A tailor-made abbreviated form. Another type of abbreviated measure involves tailor-made or computer-adaptive MMPI–2 administration (CAT). A computer adaptive test is one that incorporates an individualized test administration format by having the client respond only to items that are needed to obtain a desired effect (such as the highest one or two clinical scale scores). A high point score or profile configuration can be obtained with minimal cost, in terms of items administered by the use of two established strategies: computer-adaptive testing using item response theory (IRT; Weiss, 1985) and the countdown method of administering items by computer (Butcher, Keller, & Bacon, 1985).

In CAT using IRT (developed primarily for ability testing), the first item that is administered is scored immediately to determine the difficulty and discrimination level of the next item. If the person responds to that item in a predetermined direction, the next item to be administered will be a more "difficult" item that has been determined to assess the hypothesized domain. The next item is administered and scored in the same manner, and additional items are administered as needed. The test administration is discontinued as soon as the "most probable" scores have been obtained. Only items that are appropriate for the examinee's level are presented, thereby abbreviating the administration. The advantage of CAT over conventional ability testing is its precision and capability of obtaining a reliable score with a minimum of items. Although the IRT strategy has been used to administer personality test items, it does not work as well with measures such as the MMPI–2 clinical scales that are heterogeneous in item content as it does with homogeneous keyed items (Waller & Reise, 1989).

Butcher et al. (1985) introduced an item-administration procedure referred to as the countdown method, as an alternative to IRT administration. Two different approaches to the countdown method have been suggested (Ben-Porath, Slutske, & Butcher, 1989; Butcher 1985). The first approach is referred to as classification procedure (CP); this strategy is most useful when the assessment question is simply to know whether the responses of the test takers fall below or beyond the cut off scores. In the second approach, full scores on elevated scales (FSES) strategy, the computer terminates the administration of a set of items when scale elevation is ruled out. That is, if the person is not able to obtain an elevated score, then administration of the items on that scale stop. However, if an individual reaches the clinical elevation level, all items in that scale are administered to obtain a full score on that scale. The countdown method provides perfect congruence with the highest MMPI–2 clinical scale or code type, and a number of studies have shown its effectiveness (Ben-Porath et al., 1989; Handel, Ben-Porath, & Watt, 1999; Roper, Ben-Porath, & Butcher, 1991). However, this is typically the only information obtained on the client—no other information is available about the client from special scales and the extensive validity scales.

The clearest reason for using a computer-adapted format for the MMPI–2 is that it allows for an abbreviated test administration—reducing the amount of time required to arrive at the most salient clinical scale scores. In some respects the computer-adaptive approach is similar to other short forms that have been published, and some of the criticisms made of short forms of the MMPI–2 can be applied (Butcher & Hostetler, 1990). The main problem with an abbreviated MMPI–2 administration is that a great deal of the information the interpreter is accustomed to using in a personality evaluation is not available—the extensive profile validity information, the content scales that represent "communications" between the client and the clinician, and the special problem scales such as the addiction measures or the Marital Distress scale are thus not available.

In most clinical and forensic applications in which the MMPI–2 is used, however, time considerations are tertiary. What is more important for the practitioner is to obtain a thorough psychological assessment—not a quick glimpse at the most apparent symptom or symptoms. In forensic settings, it is particularly important that the assessment be a reliable and valid description of symptoms and problems; saving of a half hour of assessment time is not typically important.

Dahlstrom (1980) pointed out that because using the objective inventories such as those of the MMPI for research or clinical purposes requires little professional time of the psychologist for administration or scoring, little is saved by using these abbreviated versions in direct cost to the practitioner or investigator, and a great deal may be lost to both the psychologist and client. Therefore, when time is not a primary factor but having a thorough and reliable assessment is, the use of a short form of the test such as those described becomes disadvantageous, and a full version of the instrument should be used.

RESPONSIBILITIES WHEN USING ALTERED FORMS AND SCORING SYSTEMS

The topic of altered forms of a test raises an important issue for forensic practitioners, although this may not apply to all altered forms. The publisher of the MMPI–2 seeks to ensure that no infringement of copyright occurs through the creation, marketing, and use of "new" tests that are based on improperly derived copyrighted items. It is important, whenever an expert witness encounters a new test that is based on a current, copyrighted instrument, that he or she make sure that the authors have obtained whatever relevant, necessary authorization may be legally required to use licensed or copyrighted items before the expert includes it in a forensic test battery.

Similarly, when the MMPI–2 or other psychological tests are scored by computer (see following sections), there may be important issues regarding licensing and copyright applicable to the scoring keys and resulting printout. Out-of-context or otherwise altered (e.g., translations into other languages; forms that are administered by computer) versions of valid, reliable, and standardized psychological tests may be both useful and legitimate. However, it is the expert witness's responsibility to ensure that a test is indeed both useful (e.g., is valid and reliable for the purposes to which it will be put; see chap. 5, this volume) and legitimate (e.g., that it does not violate copyright or other laws). If an expert witness is discovered to have used a modified test that violates copyright (and perhaps other) laws, it is obvious that a skilled cross-examination may call the integrity, carefulness, and credibility of the expert witness as well as the expert witness's testimony into serious question.

Forensic practitioners must also use exceptional care in regard to direct use of copyrighted test materials. Both stimulus materials (i.e., lists, figures, or other printed matter that are shown to the person taking a test either to explain the test or to form the basis for the person's response) and answer sheets (the printed forms on which either the person taking the test or the person administering the test records the test taker's responses) may be copyrighted. For example, the answer sheets for the Wechsler Adult Intelligence Scale—Revised (WAIS–III; Tulsky et al., 2003) are copyrighted. If the expert witness works in an institution (e.g., a large hospital or clinic offering extensive test services conducted by both senior staff and psychology interns) that conducts a high volume of assessments using such materials, it may be tempting (because it is less expensive), when the stock of response sheets is running low, to reproduce them through photocopying or offset printing rather than ordering them from the test publisher. Again, in ad-

dition to whatever ethical and related issues may be involved, forensic practitioners making use of materials that may violate copyright laws seem to invite, if the behavior is discovered, a cross-examination focusing on integrity, carefulness, and credibility of both the expert witness and his or her testimony.

Use of Non–K-Corrected Profiles in Forensic Evaluations

Possible question on direct or cross-examination: *Can psychometrically simplified, alternative strategies for displaying clinical scale scores (that is, can non–K-corrected scale scores) provide more refined assessments in forensic evaluations?*

In the original MMPI, Meehl and Hathaway (1946) devised a statistical procedure for assessing defensive responding—the K or subtle defensiveness scale. This measure was developed by examining the item responses of inpatients in a mental health facility who produced normal-range profiles that were then assumed to be defensive. In addition to evaluating test defensiveness the authors evaluated the extent to which various proportions of K would, if added to the patient's raw scale score, improve the assessment of their problems. The K scale became a standard means of correcting some clinical scales to improve the detection of psychopathology in patients who were overly defensive during the administration. Five MMPI scales (Hysteria [Hy], Psychopathic Deviate [Pd], Psychasthenia [Pt], Schizophrenia [Sc], Mania [Ma]) were considered to work more effectively by adding a portion of the K scale to the raw score. This test-scoring strategy has been the standard approach to profiling the MMPI–2 clinical scales in both research and practice since 1948. Some research has questioned the applicability of the interpretation literature in the absence of the K correction. For example, Wooten's (1984) research found that "the interpretive hypotheses available in the literature may not be applicable when K is not used. Overall, the data favor the use of the K correction" (p. 468).

Although most authorities have concluded that the K scale is effective at detecting defensive responses and problem denial (Butcher & Williams, 2000; Graham, 2000; R. Greene, 2000), and some recent research has applauded the *K* scale in identifying psychological contributions to understanding chronic pain complaints (McGrath, Sweeney, O'Malley, & Carlton, 1998) and to assess transplant cases (Putzke, Williams, Daniel, & Boll, 1999), the *K* weights have not been proven uniformly effective as a *correction* for defensiveness. Archer, Fontaine, and McCrae (1998), for example, found that "the *K*-correction procedure commonly used with the MMPI and MMPI–2 did not result in higher correlations with external criteria in comparison to non-*K*-corrected scores" (p. 87). See also Sines, Baucom, and Gruba (1979). Moreover, empirical efforts to modify the correction weights have not proven effective. For example, Weed (1993) attempted to increase the discriminative power of the *K* correction by using different weights that could be added to the scales that were deemed to be affected by defensiveness. However, Weed did not find other weight values that would substantially increase the discrimination.

Most research and clinical applications of the MMPI–2, since the *K* scale was introduced on the profile sheet in 1948, have been conducted using *K*-corrected *T* scores. Two methodological papers—Butcher and Tellegen (1978) and Butcher, Graham, and Ben-Porath (1995)—encouraged researchers to provide a more thorough examination of uncorrected scales by including non–*K*-corrected scores in MMPI validity research. However, most research has simply used *K*-corrected scores on a routine basis. As a consequence, it is difficult to find a sufficient non–*K*-corrected *T* score research database to support the interpretation of non-*K* scores for various forensic applications. Such issues of research are central to this book: For any measure, expert witnesses and attorneys must always ask whether there are sufficient independent research findings published in peer-reviewed journals, establishing adequate validity, reliability, sensitivity, and specificity for the relevant population *and* for the specific assessment question and context. Even though the *K* scale does not function successfully as a means of correcting for defensive responding as Meehl and Hathaway (1946) had thought, the practice of correcting for *K* in interpreting profiles continues. This situation occurs

(even with the revised version of the test) because the basic research on the clinical scales has involved *K*-corrected clinical scores. Interestingly, in most clinical settings, the use of *K*- and non–*K*-corrected profiles does not result in much profile difference. The differences in profile shapes and elevations between the *K*- and non–*K*-corrected profiles are typically minor. Some studies have shown that there are typically no differences between *K*-corrected and non–*K*-corrected scores. Barthlow, Graham, Ben-Porath, Tellegen, and McNulty (2002), for example, reported that "there were no significant differences between correlations of therapist ratings with *K*-corrected and uncorrected clinical scale scores" (p. 219). However, this conclusion has not always been obtained (Detrick, Chibnall, & Rosso, 2001).

In some circumstances the non–*K*-corrected profiles can appear somewhat different from the *K*-corrected profile, and require different interpretations, depending on which set of *T* scores is referenced. In some cases when the *K* scale is elevated and the *K* correction used, some of the clinical scale elevation can be accounted for by the elevation on *K*. When profile configurations or elevations differ between the *K*-corrected and non–*K*-corrected scores, the expert witness is faced with an interpretive dilemma—which of the two profiles should be used in the interpretation? Figures 2.6 and 2.7 provide an example of this discrepancy.

The expert witness must decide whether to use the *K* correction, and it is not an easy choice. Ben-Porath and Forbey (2004), for example, presented data suggesting that non–*K*-corrected scores were more closely associated than *K*-corrected scores with therapist-report and self-report measures.

One issue, as with any relatively new method—especially one that is not consistent with current practice—is whether non–*K*-corrected measures meet the *Daubert* or *Frye* criteria (*Daubert v. Merrell Dow Pharmaceuticals*, 509 U.S. 579 (1993); *Frye v. United States*, 293 F. 1013 (D.C. Cir. 1923)). Graham (2006) noted that "current practice is to use *K*-corrected scores routinely," although he stated that "this practice probably needs to be reexamined" (p. 224).

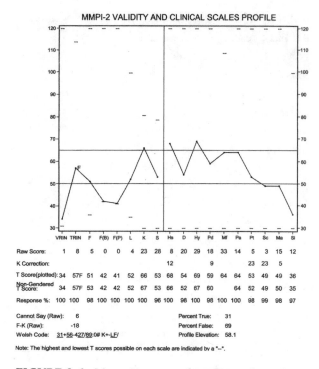

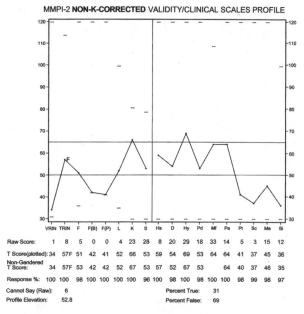

FIGURE 2.6. Mean *K*-corrected MMPI–2 clinical profile of a 55-year-old chronic pain patient seeking worker's compensation. Excerpted from the *MMPI–2 Extended Score Report*. Copyright © 1989, 1994, 2000, 2003 Regents of the University of Minnesota. Portions excerpted from the *MMPI–2 Manual for Administration, Scoring, and Interpretation, Revised Edition*, copyright © 2001 Regents of the University of Minnesota. All rights reserved. Used by permission of the University of Minnesota Press "Minnesota Multiphasic Personality Inventory—2" and "MMPI–2" are trademarks of the University of Minnesota.

FIGURE 2.7. Mean non–*K*-corrected MMPI–2 clinical profile of the same 55-year-old chronic pain patient seeking worker's compensation. Excerpted from the *MMPI–2 Extended Score Report*. Copyright © 1989, 1994, 2000, 2003 Regents of the University of Minnesota. Portions excerpted from the *MMPI–2 Manual for Administration, Scoring, and Interpretation, Revised Edition*, copyright © 2001 Regents of the University of Minnesota. All rights reserved. Used by permission of the University of Minnesota Press "Minnesota Multiphasic Personality Inventory—2" and "MMPI–2" are trademarks of the University of Minnesota.

The more fundamental question involves the research base. Graham (2006) described the choice facing those who revised the original MMPI: Should the *K* correction be maintained? He noted that

> the decision was made to maintain the *K*-correction for the MMPI–2. The argument for doing so was that decades of MMPI validity research was based on *K*-corrected scores, and to change to un-corrected scores could render that large research base inappropriate for guiding MMPI–2 interpretations. (p. 223)

As with any other measure, scoring method, or interpretive approach, the expert witness must determine whether there is adequate independent research, published in peer-reviewed journals, that establishes the validity, reliability, sensitivity, and specificity for the forensic question at issue, the relevant population, and the relevant context.[8]

---

[8] Published works addressing the issue of *K*-correction include Alperin, Archer, and Coates (1996); Archer, Fontaine, and McCrae (1998); Barthlow, Graham, Ben-Porath, Tellegen, and McNulty (2002); Butcher and Tellegen (1978); Clopton, Shanks, and Preng (1987); Colby (1989); Colligan and Offord (1991); Heilbrun (1963); Hsu (1986); Hunt, Cass, Carp, and Winder (1947); Ji, Gao, Li, Ji, Guo, and Fang (1999); Liu, Jiang, and Zhang (2002); McCrae et al. (1989); Putzke, Williams, Daniel, and Boll (1999); Ruch and Ruch (1967); Silver and Sines (1962); Sines et al. (1979); Williams et al. (2002); and Wooten (1984).

Interpretation of Newly Minted MMPI–2 Measures in Forensic Settings

Possible question on direct or cross-examination: *Can modified versions of the clinical scales provide acceptable interpretive descriptions for forensic assessment?*

The MMPI–2 provides an extensive domain for describing personality characteristics and the symptoms and problems people experience. The original MMPI clinical scales are not the only means of summarizing personality attributes. The large item pool, with its diverse and comprehensive content, makes it possible to characterize different human aspects in different ways. In fact, the first three decades of the MMPI saw many scales emerge. The vast literature on the original MMPI has discussed almost as many MMPI-based scales as there were items on the test.

One recently published and somewhat different approach to assessing clinical problems is the set of restructured clinical scales. The Restructured Clinical Scales (*RC*) by Tellegen, Ben-Porath, McNulty, Arbisi, Graham, and Kaemmer (2003) were developed to enhance interpretation of the traditional clinical scales by reducing item overlap of the scales, lowering the intercorrelation of the scales, and eliminating the so-called subtle items (i.e., items that are not content-related to the theme of the scale) in an effort to improve both the convergent and discriminant validity of the scales. In the test manual, the *RC* scales were recommended as supplemental measures and not considered to be replacements for the original clinical scales. (See also Ben-Porath, 2003.)

The resulting scales (*RCd* [Demoralization]; *RC1* [Somatic Complaints]; *RC2* [Low Positive Emotions]; *RC3* [Cynicism]; *RC4* [Antisocial Behavior]; *RC6* [Ideas of Persecution]; *RC7* [Dysfunctional Negative Emotions]; *RC8* [Aberrant Experiences]; and *RC9* [Hypomanic Activation]) were developed through a series of psychometric analyses using the responses of several groups of psychiatric patients. In the first stage in the development of the *RC* scales, the authors developed a Demoralization scale to assess the general maladjustment dimension that appeared to affect the existing clinical

scales by finding the items that overlap the clinical scales. The presence of the demoralization items on the traditional clinical scales was considered problematic; thus they were removed from the eight clinical scales to lessen their impact. The resulting seed scales for the eight *RC* scales consisted of the items remaining after the demoralization component was removed from the original scales.

The next stage of *RC* scale development broadened these residual measures through including items from the full MMPI–2 item pool by locating items that were correlated with the seed constructs. They then conducted both internal and external validity analyses to further understand the operation of the scales. The scale authors provided some analyses of the *RC* scales' internal validity and predictive validity using mental health patients from the Portage Path Outpatient Sample (Graham et al., 1999) and two inpatient samples (Arbisi, Ben-Porath, & McNulty, 2003). Their initial monograph reported that the *RC* scales have a comparable degree of association to external behavioral correlates to the traditional clinical scales.

This approach to the concept and implications of demoralization has not been free of controversy. Nichols (in press), for example, analyzed "several conceptual and methodological flaws in the construction of these scales . . . and the use of an atypical and depressively biased marker for unwanted ("first-factor") variances . . . [and] multiple important omissions."

As emphasized throughout this book, the expert witness bears the responsibility for reading the critiques of any new scale or measure, the responses to those critiques, and the relevant research findings published in peer-reviewed scientific and professional journals. Having considered the full range of evidence, the expert is then in a position to address a fundamental question: Do well-designed published research studies clearly establish the validity, reliability, sensitivity, and specificity of this scale or measure for the population, setting, and forensic use at issue? In addition to the works previously cited in this section, the following publications provide a good starting point for those seeking more detailed information about the

Restructured Clinical Scales: Butcher (2006); Butcher, Hamilton, Rouse, and Cumella (in press); Graham (2006); Sellbom and Ben-Porath (in press); Sellbom, Ben-Porath, Lilienfeld, Patrick, and Graham (in press); and Simms, Casillas, Clark, Watson, and Doebbeling (in press).

Computer-Based MMPI–2 Interpretation and Forensic Testimony

Possible question on direct or cross-examination: *Can the MMPI–2 be interpreted by computer?*

National survey research suggests that computer-based test scoring and interpretation services have been accepted and are widely used by psychologists: Already by the late 1980s, fewer than 40% of respondents reported that they had never used a computerized test interpretation service (Pope, Tabachnick, & Keith-Spiegel, 1987, 1988). In his review of computerized psychological assessment programs, B. L. Bloom (1992) concluded that "the very high level of professional vigilance over test administration and interpretation software undoubtedly accounts for the fact that computerized assessment programs have received such high marks" (p. 172; see also Zachary & Pope, 1984).

These automated services have also gained increased acceptance in forensic settings, even though there is discussion about how computer-based reports are to be incorporated in the clinical assessment (Atlis, Hahn, & Butcher, 2006; Fowler & Butcher, 1986; Garb, 1992; Matarazzo, 1986; Rogers, 2003; Rubenzer, 1991). Their broadened acceptance comes in large part as a result of their validity in describing and predicting behavior (Butcher, Perry, & Hahn, 2004; Shores & Carstairs, 1998). The late psychologist and attorney Jay Ziskin (1981b), for example, stated that he "would recommend for forensic purposes the utilization of one of the automated MMPI services" (p. 9). According to Ziskin, the advantages include the reduced possibility of scoring or transposition errors, the capacity of computers to store and use more quickly vast amounts of actuarial information, and the reduced likelihood that personal (i.e., examiner) biases will intrude on the process of gathering, scoring, and interpreting the test data.

As noted in Exhibit 2.1, one of the important reasons for the broad acceptance of the MMPI in forensic settings is that the profiles, being objectively and externally validated scales and indexes, can be interpreted with a great deal of objectivity. Any interpreter (or computer interpretation system developer) relying closely on the external empirical correlates of the scales and indexes would produce highly similar interpretations, eliminating or at least reducing the subjective sources of error (see chap. 5, this volume). The MMPI scale scores can be interpreted from an actuarial perspective (Butcher, 1987; Fowler, 1987; Gilberstadt, 1969; Graham et al., 1999) by referring to the established correlates for given scale elevations and profile types.

Although most computer-based psychological test interpretation programs are not full, actuarially derived systems—Fowler (1969, 1987) called them "automated clinicians"—they nevertheless can be viewed as objective interpretation systems when they provide hypotheses and personality descriptions in an automatic, consistent manner for the scores incorporated in the system.

It is important to emphasize again that the MMPI, even when scored and interpreted by a computer, produces *hypotheses* that must be considered in light of other sources of information. Almost anyone—including judges and juries—may tend to overlook this point when encountering an impressive computer printout of results from a scientifically based test (see, e.g., O'Dell, 1972).

ADVANTAGES OF USING COMPUTER-BASED PSYCHOLOGICAL TESTS IN FORENSIC TESTIMONY

The value of using a computer-based system for MMPI–2 interpretation can be summarized as follows: (a) Their use avoids or minimizes subjectivity in selecting and emphasizing interpretive material; (b) the reliability of the output can be ensured because the same interpretations will always be printed for particular scores or patterns; (c) the interpretations for a test provided by a computer are usually more thorough and better documented than those derived from a clinical or impressionistic assessment (depending, of course, on the knowledge, skill, and experience of the clinician); (d) biasing factors, such as halo effects (the tendency to see all aspects as "good" or "bad" without further differentiating), that can influence more subjective procedures such as clinical interviewing are usually avoided; and (e) computer-based reports can usually be explained and described clearly to a jury or judge, assuming that the expert witness is adequately familiar with database and inference rules on which the report is based. Appendix V provides an outline describing factors related to using computer-based MMPI–2 interpretations in court.

CAUTIONS OR QUESTIONS IN USING COMPUTERIZED REPORTS

A number of factors need to be taken into consideration in using computer-based personality test evaluations in forensic assessments. One key factor involves avoiding selective interpretation. Rogers (2003) pointed out that the term *objective tests* is a misnomer that may create a false impression among mental health professionals. Even though the scoring of a test is objective, the interpretation of them might not be. Clinicians need to be aware that one might select specific interpretations from a broad list of published possible interpretations (e.g., in an MMPI–2 handbook or a computerized report). He warns against selective picking of interpretations to provide a biased summary in a forensic practice.

When computer-processed test interpretation is included in a forensic case, it is important to establish the chain of custody involved in the processing of the test results (i.e., the record of the individual's responses). The expert witness must be able to document that the computer-based report is actually the report for the client in the case. For example, in cross-examination, an attorney might ask, "How do you know that the report actually matches the answer sheet filled in by the individual you assessed?" (see also chap. 9, this volume). The psychologist should be prepared to explain how the answer sheet was provided and to discuss how he or she knows that the computer-based results are actually those for the individual's answer sheet. There have

been cases in which the chain of custody was weakened by the fact that the psychologist was unable to ensure that the report provided for the person who was assessed was the correct one.

Similarly, the expert witness must establish that the particular interpretation in the computer-based report is an appropriate match between the person's scores on the test and the prototypal statements generated by the computer. An attorney in cross-examination might ask, "How do you know that the computer report actually fits the person?" (see chap. 9, this volume). Computer-based interpretation systems are essentially descriptors or correlates that are filed in a reference database analogous to a basic textbook or reference source except that the correlates or interpretive points are written in such a way as to flow in a narrative manner.

Computer-based psychological reports are usually prototypes and are generally actuarially based. Some—perhaps many—of the statements in a report may *not* be descriptive of a particular person. As emphasized in this book, the MMPI, whether scored and interpreted by an individual or a computer, produces *hypotheses*. A hypothesis is only a tentative supposition adapted to guide in additional investigation.

The psychologist should be prepared in direct or cross-examination to discuss computer-generated statements that do *not* fit the client. Typical questions to which the expert may be asked to respond include, "Do all of the computer-generated descriptions apply in this particular case? If not, how did you determine *which* ones would be used in this case?" and "What is there about the particular person in question that makes you conclude that the prototype does not fit?"

Direct and cross-examination questions may focus on the issue of whether the computer output can stand alone as a report. The issue of whether a psychologist needs to personally interview the client depends on the nature of testimony. As noted in chapter 1, some expert witnesses may be called to testify only about the nature of the MMPI; whether a particular profile, taken as a whole, is valid (i.e., whether the pattern of validity scores would preclude other inferences from being drawn on the basis of the test); and what hypotheses are produced, in light of the empirical research, by a particular profile. If, however, a psychologist is asked to testify about the psychological status or adjustment of a person, it is important to incorporate as much information as possible into the clinical evaluation (see, e.g., the explicit qualifications regarding validity in the forensic assessment report for Ms. Jones in chap. 8, this volume). The use of a computer-based report in isolation from other important information such as personal history, biographical data, interview observations, previous records, and so forth, may *not* be appropriate. However, as mentioned earlier, there are instances in which testimony that is based on the computer-generated MMPI report alone is appropriate and useful (e.g., if the issue of testimony involves a technical point concerning the use of the test itself or when the computer-generated report is used to cross-check an interpretation of a psychologist who perhaps also testified on the basis of the MMPI).

Another consideration in using computer-based test interpretations as part of a forensic evaluation and testimony centers on the possible lack of acceptance of high technology and fear of computers among some people in today's society. Some people mistrust automation and have a bias against mechanization of human affairs. There is always the possibility that a member of the jury or even the judge may have a bias against any mechanization when it comes to human personality. This possibility should be taken into consideration when explaining automated test results. Care should be taken to emphasize the strong reliability ("reproducibility") of results in computer interpretation and the general acceptance of automated reports by the profession.

Another point to consider in using a computer-based interpretation report in forensic assessment is that two different computer interpretation services might actually produce somewhat different interpretations for the same protocol (i.e., the record of test responses). In theory, all computer-based MMPI interpretations for a specific protocol should be quite similar because they are based on the same correlate research literature. The underlying assumption on which computer interpretation is based is that the actuarially based (objectively validated) correlates are automatically applied to test indexes. Computer systems that are based closely on research-validated indexes tend to have similar outputs. However, in practice, commercially available systems differ with respect to the information presented and the accuracy of the interpretations (Eyde, Kowal, & Fishburne, 1991). For example, one system might place more interpretive emphasis on the standard scores and another might allow more incorporation of supplemental scales or even non-MMPI–2 measures.

The psychologist using an automated interpretation system in court should be familiar with the issues of computerized test interpretation generally and the validity research on the particular system used (see Atlis et al., 2006; Butcher, Perry, & Atlis, 2000; Eyde et al., 1991; Moreland, 1987).

Once expert witnesses and attorneys have become fluent in these basic aspects of the MMPI in court, they are prepared to examine the constantly evolving research base for MMPI–2 and MMPI–A use in specific forensic contexts, which is the focus of the next chapter.

CHAPTER 3

FORENSIC ASSESSMENT SETTINGS

Although personality evaluations in different forensic settings vary widely, the Minnesota Multiphasic Personality Inventory (MMPI–2) is typically the central player in the test battery and provides an objective framework for evaluating the clients involved. This chapter examines three of the most typical settings for MMPI–2-based forensic assessments: personal injury, custody, and criminal or correctional cases. Forensic assessments using the MMPI–2 and similar standardized tests describe psychological characteristics, traits, states, symptoms, or adjustment and does not per se validate a particular legal proposition. Expert witnesses should avoid trying to infer legal concepts from psychological test data. For example, the results of a psychological test alone cannot tell us if a person is competent to stand trial or is not guilty by reason of insanity. MMPI–2-based forensic assessment can shed light on the individual's psychological adjustment as he or she sees it and is willing to share self-observations with others.

ASSESSING PERSONAL INJURY CASES

One of the most frequent forensic applications of the MMPI–2 involves its use in personal injury litigation. The test is widely used to assess the psychological status of litigants who claim damage or disability and seek compensation for the injuries or consequences of the event. The MMPI–2 is typically used in this context to evaluate the mental status of people who are alleging that they have been psychologically damaged. These claims of psycho-

logical injury may occur, for example, in lawsuits involving accidental injury, medical malpractice, sexual harassment, hate crimes (which may be the basis for later civil actions focusing on personal injury), or occupational stress. The injury might be one of a physical nature, for example, as a result of an automobile accident or slip-and-fall accident in which the individual claims to be disabled by chronic pain as a result of injuries. Or the claim might center on the litigant's reported psychological disability following a psychological trauma such as work-place harassment.

Several resources focus on personal injury or workers' compensation cases (Arbisi, 2006; Butcher & Miller, 2006). In addition, there have been a number of articles published on the MMPI in personal injury litigation. Moyer, Burkhardt, and Gordon (2002), for example, addressed the concern that clients can be coached to fake posttraumatic stress disorder (PTSD) Moyer and colleagues found that those who were coached (i.e., "given *Diagnostic and Statistical Manual of Mental Disorders, Fourth Edition* [*DSM–IV*] diagnostic criteria for PTSD prior to testing") were not able to fool the test. The findings showed "that knowledge about the specific symptoms of PTSD did not create a more accurate profile, but rather was likely to produce more invalid ($F > T89$) profiles, detecting them as malingerers" (p. 81). Alexy and Webb (1999); Butcher (1985a); and Dush, Simons, Platt, and Nation (1994) have provided articles addressing the MMPI in diverse aspects of personal injury suits. There also have been a number of articles addressing the outcome of litigation and personality assessment (R. Evans, 1994; Oleske, Andersson, Lavender, & Hahn, 2000; Patrick, 1988). Other studies have addressed the personality characteristics of litigators (Lanyon & Almer, 2002; Long, Rouse, Nelson, & Butcher, 2004) or personality and compensation-seeking status (Frueh, Smith, & Barker, 1996; Gandolfo, 1995; Gatchel & Gardea, 1999; Gold & Frueh, 1999). Moreover, a number of studies such as those by Bury and Bagby (2002) or Moyer et al. (2002), have focused on the credibility of the litigant's MMPI–2 profile. Appendix E of this book lists references involving the MMPI and MMPI–2 and personal injury litigation in areas of head injury, chronic pain, and PTSD.

The study of psychological factors in medical applications was an original focus of the MMPI (Hathaway & McKinley, 1940). Decades of MMPI and MMPI–2 research support the use of the test in medical settings (see recent reviews by Arbisi & Butcher, 2004a, 2004b, 2004c; Arbisi & Seime, 2006). As a result of the extensive accumulated database on the MMPI in medical settings, the test can be used as an aid in evaluating the presence of psychological distress or dysfunction (often relevant to legal claims for "pain and suffering") in litigants because the scales show the existence of symptoms in a reliable, valid manner in an objective framework. A higher degree of credence is usually placed on objectively interpreted procedures than on other types of information available to the psychologist (Arbisi, 2006; Butcher, 1995; Butcher & Miller, 2006).

Personal injury cases often ask the court or jury to decide to what extent, if at all, the litigant has been psychologically injured or disabled and what amount of compensation should be awarded for the claim. Faced with such questions, expert witnesses testifying in the case may be asked to assess whether a plaintiff's complaints of psychological damage are a result of one or more of the following: the alleged tort itself; one or more preexisting (i.e., before the alleged tort) conditions; harmful events or conditions that occurred after the alleged tort and for which the defendant is not alleged (by the plaintiff) to be responsible; stress; factitious disorder; malingering; paranoid delusion; or other fac-

tors. If the expert concludes that more than one factor is involved, he or she may be asked to make the much more difficult determination regarding the relative importance and possible interaction of each factor.

The MMPI–2 is widely used in personal injury evaluations (Boccaccini & Brodsky, 1999; Lally, 2003; Lees-Haley, Smith, Williams, & Dunn, 1996) and for the assessment of chronic pain (Piotrowski, 1998). Forensic evaluations in personal injury cases may involve several elements: (a) the credibility of the litigant's self-report (see chap. 7, this volume); (b) the symptoms that the individual is reportedly experiencing; (c) the likely causes of actual symptoms; and (d) the intensity and extent of actual distress or dysfunction and likely (or possible) course of recovery.

Psychological evaluations in disability determinations face inherent limitations. Sometimes it is impossible to determine whether a claimant's injuries are *actually* the result of organic posttraumatic changes or are based on preexisting personality factors (Marcus, 1983). No completely foolproof method of determining such distinctions is available at this time, although carefully conducted comprehensive psychological and neuropsychological assessments can help address the question. By selecting tests appropriate to the complaints, conducting careful interviews when possible, using the most valid and reliable test instruments, recording case notes and test reports, and reviewing relevant documents (such as previous records of assessment and treatment, school records, and records of previous civil or criminal legal cases), clinicians can be helpful in clarifying psychological factors in personal injury cases. If, for example, the individual responds to the MMPI–2 in a cooperative manner and the validity scales do not show evidence of malingering or other distortions, the test profiles are likely to provide valuable information.

A number of MMPI–2 measures can aid in determining whether an individual has attempted to present him- or herself in a slanted way. See chapter 7 for a discussion of the use of the MMPI–2 validity scales to assess malingering and other distortions. (See also the bibliography on the validity scales of the MMPI and MMPI–2 in Appendixes C and D, this volume, and Malingering Update at http://kspope.com/assess/malinger.php.)

Psychological testing can be of value in disability determinations in several ways. If the individual's approach to the test is valid, the test results can provide a useful evaluation of the client's symptomatic status. Psychological testing can also provide an indication of the severity of an individual's problems and the possible long-term course of the disorder.

In determining whether an individual who claims to have difficulties as a result of an injury, stressful experience, or exposure to toxic substances is manifesting symptoms consistent with such occurrences, several factors should be considered. As a baseline from which to judge personality test performances of disability claimants with cases pending, it is important to know how truly disabled people have responded on the relevant psychological measures. Research on personality characteristics of individuals who were actually disabled and were not awaiting a disability determination decision has been published. For example, Wiener (1948a) and Warren and Weiss (1969) reported that groups of individuals who were actually disabled tended to produce MMPI profiles with scale scores in the nonpathological range, below a T of 70. Moreover, there were no characteristic MMPI profiles found for the various disability groups when disabled patients were classified according to type of disability.

Symptomatic claims of personal injury litigants pending disability determination, on the other hand, appear to be more exaggerated and generally more pathological (Binder & Rohling, 1996; Pollack & Grainey, 1984; Rohling, Binder, & Langhinrichsen-Rohling, 1995; Sternbach, Wolf, Murphy, & Akeson, 1973). Expert witnesses must be familiar with the strengths and limitations of the research studies relevant to the assessment at issue. It is possible, for example, that the differences emerging from the studies cited may be due to an element of acuteness in the disorder or a trend toward excessive symptom claiming to emphasize perceived disability, or they may indicate other factors (Butcher, 1995).

Most MMPI research involving compensation cases reflects this increased level of psychological symptoms. In cases in which physical injury is claimed, the MMPI profile of compensation cases usually involves extreme scale elevations on Hypochondria (*Hs*), Depression (*D*), and Hysteria (*Hy;* Repko & Cooper, 1983; Shaffer, Nussbaum, & Little, 1972). Snibbe, Peterson, and Sosner (1980) found that workers' compensation applicants had generally rather disturbed MMPI profiles (with high elevations on Infrequency [*F*], Schizophrenia [*Sc*], *D, Hs, Hy,* and Psychopathic Deviate [*Pd*] scales), even though the 47 individuals in the research group had been drawn from four diagnostic groups according to type of claim (e.g., head injury, psychological stress and strain, low back pain, and miscellaneous). In a study of workers' compensation claims involving harassment, the *Pa* scale was the most prominent difference when compared with nonharassment cases (Gandolfo, 1995).

In a study to determine possible motivational differences among disability applicants, Pollack and Grainey (1984) reported that claimants may respond to the test in an exaggerated manner to receive financial benefits. The idea that claimants present a more exaggerated picture of their adjustment than others was also supported by Parker, Doerfler, Tatten, and Hewett (1983), who found that individuals with prominent MMPI Psychasthenia (*Pt*) scale scores in their profile code tended to report much more intense pain. Therefore, even when the test profiles are valid and interpretable, there may be some excessive responding in actually disabled clients.

As discussed in chapter 8, people may be motivated to respond in forensic evaluations in different ways—either to look virtuous or severely disturbed, depending on the specifics of the case. Some people who are attempting to appear psychologically disturbed in psychological disability claims may exaggerate complaints whereas others present purely physical complaints in the context of a defensive protocol (see Long et al., 2004).

In a study assessing the possible psychological effects of exposure to Agent Orange during the Vietnam War, Korgeski and Leon (1983) contrasted veterans on the basis of whether there was objective evidence of exposure to the chemical during the war and whether the veteran believed that he or she had been exposed to the chemical. In the first comparison, there were no neurological or personality differences between the veterans with an objectively determined probability of being exposed and those who were clearly not exposed to Agent Orange. However, veterans who *believed* themselves to have been exposed to Agent Orange (whether there was evidence or not) reported more significant psychological disturbance than those who did not believe they had been exposed. Frueh et al. (1996) found significantly more symptoms among compensation-seeking than noncompensation-seeking veterans. Expert witnesses must evaluate the possibility of secondary gain in symptom presentation (see, e.g., Binder & Rohling, 1996; Rohling et al., 1995). These evaluations are complex, involving a tangle of factors and possible interpretations. Are those who seek compensation, for example, showing more extreme symptoms because they wish to invent ways to get money, or are they seeking compensation because they suffer greater subjective pain and objective disturbance?

The claimant's overresponding often takes the form of exaggerating psychological symptoms, resulting in an elevated *F* scale score (Dearth et al., 2005). Schneider (1979) found that the *F* scale of the MMPI identified the individuals who were presenting a great deal of psychopathology in connection with their disability determinations for a pension on grounds of having service-connected psychopathology. These findings are consistent with the research of Keller, Wigdor, and Lundell (1973), who studied individuals seeking compensation on the basis of psychologically disabling symptoms, specifically on grounds that they were not employable but had no physical disability. These individuals were found to be identifiable with respect to MMPI-measured personality factors and lifestyle. Primarily, they produced elevated *F*-scale scores, indicating an exaggeration of symptoms. Schneider (1979) reported that individuals

applying for disability benefits as a result of psychopathology had elevated Paranoia (*Pa*) and *Sc* scores, reflecting an expression of severe and chronic disorder involving thought disturbance and personal deterioration. Similarly, in the study by Keller et al. (1973), these individuals presented significantly more psychopathology than controls on the MMPI, with scale elevations on *Hs, D, Hy, Pt,* and *Sc.* In addition, they were found to be low in self-esteem, dependent, depressed, and socially isolated.

Research suggests that individuals seeking compensation for different problems may produce somewhat different MMPI profile patterns. Bowler, Rauch, Becker, Hawes, and Cone (1989), for example, reported that individuals manifesting somatoform disorder produced different profiles than those for whom depression or anxiety was the prominent complaint.

Long-range consequences of disability are often at issue in personal injury cases. Psychologists may be asked to evaluate the extent of injury or damage to the individual and the possible length of time involved in the disability for purposes of establishing the amount of award in the suit. Personality assessment might be valuable in estimating how individuals will respond to rehabilitative efforts. Some research on the long-term consequences of physical and psychological disability in compensation claims has been reported with the MMPI, and it is important for the expert witness to be familiar with this material when addressing the course of disability or response to treatment.[1]

When considering the research that bears on MMPI-based assessments in personal injury cases (as in other types of forensic assessments), it is essential to evaluate the degree to which the participants in the research are truly comparable to the individual who is alleging personal injury, the degree to which the circumstances under which the research was conducted support or limit its applicability to the individual's situation, and the appro-

---

[1] Cairns, Mooney, and Crane (1984); Carragee (2001); Colotla, Bowman, and Shercliffe (2001); Drasgow and Dreher (1965); Dzioba and Doxey (1984); Flynn and Salomone (1977); Gilbert and Lester (1970); Heaton, Chelune, and Lehman (1978); Kubiszyn (1984); Kuperman and Golden (1979); Kurman, Hursey, and Mathew (1992); Levenson, Hirschfeld, and Hirschfeld (1985); Newnan, Heaton, and Lehman (1978); Oleske et al. (2000); Reitan and Wolfson (1997); Roberts (1984); Roberts and Reinhardt (1980); Salomone (1972); Wiltse and Rocchio (1975); Youngjohn, Davis, and Wolf (1997); Zwart, Ellertsen, and Bovim (1996).

priate weight to accord a particular research finding in light of the general array of relevant research findings (or absence of other applicable research findings).

The assessment report must explicitly address qualifications or reservations about validity (see chap. 8, this volume). Arbisi (2006) pointed out that given the clear involvement of nonanatomic factors in the recovery from injury, it is essential that a broadband measure such as the MMPI–2 be used in the assessment of disability related to work injury to determine the relative contribution of psychological factors in the continuing disability.

As emphasized throughout this book, the expert witness must determine the degree to which well-designed research demonstrates the validity, reliability, sensitivity, and specificity of the MMPI and other tests or assessment approaches for the specific question at hand, for the specific context, and for the specific population.

ASSESSING POSTTRAUMATIC STRESS DISORDER IN INJURED WORKERS

Penk and his colleagues (Penk, Drebing, & Schutt, 2002; Penk, Rierdan, Losardo, & Robinowitz, 2006; see also Arbisi, 2006) addressed questions of PTSD as they arise in personal injury cases. These reviews provide a comprehensive look at the use of the MMPI–2 in work-related and other posttraumatic stress disorder litigation. This section addresses some specific MMPI–2-based research relevant to assessing PTSD in personal injury litigation. (See also references in Appendix E, this volume.)

The Post-traumatic Stress Disorder Scale— Keane (*Pk*) in the MMPI–2 appears to measure negative response to stressful situations, as did the Keane scale in the original MMPI (Litz et al., 1991). A study by Lyons and Keane (1992) provided additional support for the MMPI–2 version of the *Pk* scale, as have several additional studies (Knisely, Barker, Ingersoll, & Dawson, 2000; Korestzky & Peck, 1990; Morrell & Rubin, 2001; Perrin, Van Hasselt, & Hersen, 1997). Other studies, however, have not provided support for use of the scale (Miller, Goldberg, & Streiner, 1995; Scheibe, Bagby, Miller, & Dorian, 2001).

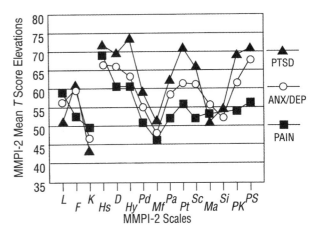

FIGURE 3.1. Mean MMPI–2 clinical profiles for PTSD, anxiety/depression, and chronic pain samples. From "Mean MMPI–2 Profiles for PTSD, Anxiety–Depression, and Chronic Pain Patients," by S. Flamer and W. Buch (1992, May). Paper presented at the 27th Annual Symposium on Recent Developments in the Use of the MMPI (MMPI–2), Minneapolis, MN. Copyright 1992 by S. Flamer. Adapted with permission.

Flamer and Buch (1992) conducted an investigation to determine if workers who were injured in industrial accidents showed more measurable psychopathology, particularly PTSD, than individuals who were reportedly experiencing chronic pain. Using workers' compensation claims, they grouped cases into three categories on the basis of the documented source of disability: workers with posttraumatic stress disorders (most of whom were also physically injured), chronic pain patients, and emotionally disturbed mental health patients. They examined their MMPI–2 clinical profiles and their scores on the *Pk* and Schlenger PTSD scales (Butcher, Graham, et al., 1990; Jordan et al., 1991; Schlenger & Kukla, 1987; Schlenger et al., 1989). Their MMPI–2 profiles are shown in Figure 3.1.

Consistent with the correlates for MMPI–2 scales, those workers with clearly defined posttraumatic symptoms showed more marked profile elevation on Scales 1, 2, 3, and 7 than did the other groups. In addition, the PTSD group showed more significant scale elevation on the PTSD scales than did the other groups. These findings are consistent with the observation that many individuals who are experiencing a reaction (either an immediate-onset or a delayed reaction) to a traumatic event show increased scale elevation on Scales 2 (Depression) and 7 (Psychasthenia).

In addition to evaluating these published MMPI–2 scales, Flamer and Buch (1992) have conducted research on a PTSD scale for assessing posttraumatic symptomatology related to work injury. They developed a 35-item scale that significantly differentiated the posttraumatic injury cases from cases involving other claimants. This scale, provisionally titled the Work Place Trauma Scale for the MMPI–2, significantly differentiated the developmental group from other workers and showed sufficient specificity and sensitivity, detecting PTSD in 20 out of 24 cases.

Flamer and Buch (1992) cross-validated the scale with an additional 20 workers' compensation claimants and found that it differentiated well on cross-validation, detecting PTSD in 18 of 20 new cases. Although additional work needs to replicate these findings in other settings, this promising research supports the effectiveness of the MMPI–2 in identifying and differentiating individuals who are experiencing work-related stress.

Of course, PTSD also occurs among other populations and in other contexts (e.g., among military combatants, torture victims, and asylum seekers). The extensive research literature on the MMPI and MMPI–2 provides resources specifically relevant to these special populations and contexts.[2] Appendix E lists published works on the MMPI and MMPI–2 and personal injury (including PTSD) assessments.

FORENSIC EXAMINATIONS RELEVANT TO EXPERIENCED POSTTRAUMATIC STRESS DISORDER IN ASYLUM SEEKERS, TORTURE VICTIMS, AND REFUGEE POPULATIONS

Recent years have seen thousands of refugees from other countries such as Rwanda, Ethiopia, Cambodia, and Bosnia, to mention only a few, enter the United States. Many of these individuals have experienced great trauma in being uprooted from their homes, and many have been subjected to inhumane acts such as rape, torture, and witnessing family members murdered (Jaranson & Popkin, 1998). Many of these individuals seek asylum in the United States and are required to undergo great scrutiny as a part of their immigration process. Legal proceedings relevant to the rights, personal history, and current condition of asylum seekers, torture victims, and refugee populations may focus on the individual's credibility.

A critical aspect of asylum cases is the applicant's ability to convince the judge that he or she has a well-founded fear of persecution. In some cases, the applicant's own testimony may be the only evidence available.

Credibility is undercut by generalities, avoidance of eye contact, evasiveness and apparent uncooperativeness in answering questions. Some of these behaviors are culturally dependent, while others may be the consequences of the experiences that caused the applicant to seek asylum.

Victims of torture or other severe trauma may be poor witnesses for themselves. Their shame and humiliation, anxiety, memory impairments and lack of trust often lead to confusing and apparently contradictory statements; an inability to recall times, dates and events; and a lack of emotional affect which may make their testimony unconvincing. . . . .

The very trauma or other form of persecution on which the asylum claim is based may contribute to a numbed responsiveness, the appearance of which ironically harms the applicant's credibility as a witness. The applicant, for example, may not cry when relating how his or her child was abducted by

[2] For example, Eberly, Harkness, and Engdahl (1991); Fairbank, Keane, and Malloy (1983); Frueh et al. (1996); Hyer, Leach, Boudewyns, and Davis (1991); Keane, Weathers, and Kaloupek (1992); Kenderdine, Phillips, and Scurfield (1992); Lyons and Keane (1992); McCormick, Taber, and Kruedelbach (1989); Munley, Bains, Bloem, and Busby (1995); Nichols and Czirr (1986); Penk et al. (1989); Pope and Garcia-Peltoniemi (1991); Powell, Illovsky, O'Leary, and Gazda (1988); Sloan, Arsenault, McCormick, Dunn, and Scalf (1992); Sutker, Bugg, and Allain (1991); Wilson and Walker (1990); Wise (1996); see also chapter 6, this volume.

the police and never seen again. (Physicians for Human Rights, 1991, pp. 12, 20)[3]

The MMPI–2 has been adapted in several languages spoken by refugees to the United States (e.g., Spanish, Hmong, Vietnamese, Ethiopian, etc.) who resettled from countries in which torture or severe war trauma was common (see Appendix K, this volume). When the test is used with people from these groups, the MMPI validity scales can be exceptionally helpful in providing evidence of the individual's credibility.

The two more typical forensic uses of the MMPI–2 validity scales can make it easy to overlook the usefulness of the MMPI–2 with these populations. The first more typical forensic use of the MMPI–2 validity scales is to help differentiate those who are *trying* to appear dysfunctional but are *feigning* (e.g., to escape responsibility for criminal acts or to obtain undeserved disability benefits) from those who not only *appear* but actually *are* dysfunctional. The second more typical use of the validity scales is to help differentiate those who are trying to falsely appear as if they lacked significant distress and dysfunction (e.g., to obtain a job or to be granted custody rights) from those who not only appear to but also *actually* do lack significant distress and dysfunction. Chapter 7 discusses these and other common uses of the validity scales.

Although these other more frequent forensic uses of the validity scales are important, it is also crucial to remember that some people may seem (e.g., during a clinical or job interview, during a deportation hearing, or during a custody or criminal trial) as if they are feigning, exaggerating, or otherwise distorting the truth when in fact they are not. They may appear guilty when in fact they are innocent. They may appear unharmed when in fact they are deeply damaged. They may appear to be concocting the wildest, most improbable lies when in fact they are telling the truth. In such situations, the validity scales can help establish or support the

individual's credibility. As the passage quoted earlier (as well as the secondary references that were cited) emphasize, this use of the validity scales may be particularly helpful when conducting forensic examinations of asylum seekers, torture victims, and refugee populations.

Refugees, many of whom are likely to have been mistreated or tortured before fleeing to another country, often show significant psychopathology (Jaranson et al., 2004), particularly on measures such as the MMPI–2 (see studies by Keefe et al., 1996; Tran, 1996, for a discussion of the impact of acculturation on MMPI–2 scores). Additional resources for those who are assessing torture victims, refugees, and asylum seekers are available at http://kspope.com/torvic/torture.php; http://kspope.com/torvic/torture1.php; http://kspope.com/torvic/torture-abst.php; see also Pope (2005b).

PHYSICAL DISABILITY: CHRONIC PAIN AND HEAD INJURY

A review of the literature on the use of the MMPI and MMPI–2 in the assessment of chronic pain would uncover over 300 relevant papers (Arbisi & Butcher, 2004b). It is beyond the scope of this volume to provide a complete survey of this literature; however, Appendix E lists many studies particularly pertinent to personal injury litigation.

Assessment of Behavioral and Emotional Consequences of Head Injury

Neuropsychological evaluation batteries typically incorporate the MMPI–2 (Adams & Putnam, 1992; Berry, 1995; Berry & Butcher, 1997; Gass, 1991, 1992, 2000; Nelson, 1995; Ogloff, 1995). As one example, Boccaccini and Brodsky (1999) conducted a survey of diagnostic test usage by forensic psychologists in emotional injury cases. They found that "the MMPI was by far the most frequently utilized instrument, with Version 1 or 2 being used by 94% of emotional injury

---

[3] See also Butcher, Egli, Shiota, and Ben-Porath (1988); Deinard, Butcher, Thao, Moua Vang, and Hang (1996); Herman (1992); Keefe et al. (1996); Pope and Garcia-Peltoniemi (1991); Thomsen, Helwig-Larsen, and Rasmussen (1984); Tran (1996); Westermeyer, Williams, and Nguyen (1992).

practitioners and in 89% of all emotional injury evaluations" (p. 255).

In a 1992 study, Beniak, Heck, and Erdahl administered both the MMPI and the MMPI–2 to a sample of people suffering from epilepsy and reported that the two versions of the MMPI produced comparable profiles. Those suffering from epilepsy tended to score high on the clinical Scales 2 and 8 on both forms. Scale 8 tends to be elevated in those who have epilepsy because of the neurological symptoms reflected in the subgroup of items on the scale (i.e., items pertaining to sensory and perceptual–motor problems). Thus, elevations on Scale 8 are often problematic because they do not allow for the important differential diagnosis between epilepsy and schizophrenia. However, Beniak et al. (1992) found that the MMPI–2 content scale Bizarre Mentation (*BIZ*), which is elevated for those suffering from schizophrenia, was *not* elevated for those suffering from epilepsy. This finding may provide important differential information for assessing those suffering from temporal lobe epilepsy. Although most of the validity research in brain-injured clients involved the clinical scales, one study (Palav, Ortega, & McCaffrey, 2001) found the MMPI–2 content scales provided information about symptoms beyond what was obtained through the clinical scales, about 4% to 36%.

Importance of Referencing Population Base Rates

When psychologists encounter a puzzling or unusual MMPI–2 profile pattern, it is important to examine the available clinical scale codebook resources for the scales obtained to determine if there are established correlates for the scale scores or code involved. It may turn out, of course, that the particular scale combination has not been prominent in similar cases and that little information exists in the published resources.

What, then, can the psychologist use from the empirical literature to guide interpretation of this particular profile code? The interpreter can, of course, resort to generic scale descriptions in developing conclusions. However, it might be more useful to first examine the relative frequency of the clinical profile in the particular setting—that is, it might be important to refer to the base-rate information that is available on the setting involved to place the profile into proper empirical perspective.

The base rate of the population refers to the probability (usually expressed in a percentage) of particular events occurring. For example, what are your chances of living to 110? Of winning a lottery? Of developing schizophrenia? Base rates are often calculated for clinical settings to determine the relative frequency of particular diagnoses being admitted to a hospital. For example, if 2 out of every 100 of your clients try to commit suicide, the base rate of suicide attempts in your practice is 2% (see discussion by Kamphuis & Finn, 2002; see also chaps. 5 and 9, this volume).

Lees-Haley (1997b) reported on the frequencies of various MMPI–2 scales from a clinical-forensic practice in California. The data were obtained largely from trauma cases and can prove valuable for giving a perspective on MMPI–2 profiles in personal injury litigation cases. The data were not analyzed separately for differing motivations to present in either a favorable or "symptom checking" manner, as noted earlier.

Butcher (1997, 1998a) provided additional information on base rates in a personal injury context with the differing motivational sets taken into consideration. In this study a total of 157 cases that were being assessed in various personal injury cases were obtained from nine forensic mental health practitioners who see a variety of cases. The cases involved people assessed from the perspective of the plaintiff's side as well as from the defense. The cases provided in the research sample centered on a variety of complaints, including age discrimination, workplace harassment, sexual harassment, slip-and-fall injury complaints, and posttraumatic injury from incidents such as accidents, rape, and workplace trauma.

THE GASS CORRECTION FACTOR FOR CLOSED HEAD INJURY

Some items contained on the MMPI–2 are commonly responded to in the same direction by individuals who have experienced a head injury. Individuals who have experienced a head injury tend to produce scale elevation on certain MMPI–2 scales because they are experiencing head injury symptoms. Some researchers have recommended that the MMPI (MMPI–2) scales be adjusted to take into consideration the impact of these common head injury symptoms. Kendall, Edinger, and Eberly (1978) suggested a rigorous empirical approach to correcting personality profiles for individuals who have experienced a spinal cord injury. Alfano, Paniak, and Finlayson (1993) developed a set of 13 items to correct for closed head injury in the original MMPI. Similarly, Gass (1991, 1992) developed an approach to the assessment of closed head injury patients for the MMPI–2.

The Gass correction for closed head injury comprises 14 items that were found to be associated with closed head injury (Gass, 2006). The items were obtained through a series of successive hurdles. First the items initially distinguished between a sample of 75 closed head injury cases and the MMPI–2 normative sample. Next, every item on the provisional scale was endorsed by at least 25% of the head-injury sample. Then the items were found to have high scale homogeneity through factor analysis; they showed high internal consistency with an alpha coefficient of .80. In this study, the items were found to have content validity in that each item appeared to reflect a common symptom of head injury. Several studies support using the Gass correction (e.g., Gass, 2000; Gass, Luis, Rayls, & Mittenberg, 1999; Rayls, Mittenberg, Burns, & Theroux, 2000). They examined the records of clients with traumatic brain injury and found that injury victims in their study (and the clients' relatives) independently reported that the correction items were endorsed by the patient specifically because of problems resulting from the injury and were not pertinent before the injury.

How does the practitioner use the Gass correction? The correction factor simply provides the expert witness with a way of taking into consideration the possible impact that the head injury could have on the clinical elevation. The items on the Gass correction are checked for scored direction and then subtracted from the raw score of the scales on which they appear if they are in the head-injury direction. A second profile is plotted (along with the client's complete profile) to obtain a picture of the influence of the neurological symptoms the client endorsed.

Some neuropsychologists have opposed the use of neuropsychological corrections as being too risky in that important psychopathology might be missed by dropping out the items on the correction (Cripe, Maxwell, & Hill, 1995). Others have criticized this approach for assuming too much homogeneity among neurological cases (R. Greene, Gwin, & Staal, 1997). However, cautious use of this correction factor might provide the clinician with important information that he or she would not have otherwise had—for example, the individual's likelihood of having symptoms of a psychotic disorder.

It is important to keep in mind that the Gass head-injury correction is never used to detect the possibility of head-injury symptoms. It is for use only in cases in which there has been a documented head injury. The head-injury correction is used to give the practitioner a view of the individual's scale score elevation without the head-injury symptoms contributing to the total score of the items that contain head-injury symptoms. The 14 items on the correction are noted and subtracted from the total raw score of the scales involved.

IMPORTANCE OF ASSESSING VALIDITY PATTERNS IN PERSONAL-INJURY LITIGATION CASES

Chapter 8 discusses assessing protocol validity more fully; however, because the MMPI–2 performance of clients in personal injury cases is often key information, its importance is noted in this chapter as well. Interpretation of profiles in personal injury cases is often complicated by individual motivation to present in a particular manner, depending on the type of personal injury complaint. Some litigants are motivated to present themselves in a defensive manner whereas others are motivated to present themselves as much more disturbed psychologically than they actually are. Butcher (1997) reported the following.

> When the total sample is considered without regard to response attitudes[,] three scales receive high prominence.

The *Hy* scale is the highest peak score with 17.2 percent of the cases producing elevated and well-defined peak scores; the *D* scale is the second most frequent peak with 7.6% frequency as an elevated and well-defined peak; and the *Pa* score is the third highest spike score occurring with 6.4% frequency as an elevated and well-defined score. However, when the response attitudes are taken into consideration (that is when the profiles are grouped according to defensive (likely feigned) versus exaggerated (likely malingered psychological symptoms), [D] then the picture changes markedly: The frequency of well-defined *Hy* scores increases to 22.2 percent in the defensive (possibly feigned symptom group); however, when the exaggerated (possibly exaggerated–malingered) profiles are grouped together the profile peak becomes one of high *Pa* (14.6% have well-defined scores at or above a *T* of 65D). (p. 3)

The data from this base-rate study suggest that it is important to keep the litigant's motivation in perspective when interpreting MMPI–2 profiles in personal injury cases.

PSYCHOLOGICAL ASSESSMENT IN FAMILY CUSTODY CASES

Psychologists and other mental health professionals are increasingly being called on to provide consultation on the personality and mental health adjustment of individuals who are involved in family custody dispute cases. Deed (1991) reviewed the pitfalls and challenges for psychologists conducting domestic court evaluations.

In providing expertise in forensic evaluations, psychologists are often asked to provide expert opinions about the emotional health of the parents and to assess possible adjustment problems and developmental issues for the child. Evaluations of parents and children tend to focus on family ad-

justment factors as well as potential problems in the family that might bear on the welfare of the minor. The use of psychological tests in family custody evaluations has been widely explored (e.g., Ackerman & Ackerman, 1997; Barnard & Jenson, 1984; Kelin & Bloom, 1986; Landberg, 1982; McDermott, Tseng, Char, & Fukunaga, 1978). Postuma and Harper (1998) provided strong support for using the MMPI–2 in child custody evaluations. In particular, the investigation provided strong support for using both the standard and supplemental validity scales and indexes to assess any possible response bias in the person's approach to the MMPI–2 in the evaluation. (See also discussion on the MMPI–A: Archer, 1997a.)

Research suggests that the MMPI/MMPI–2 is the most frequently administered personality test in custody cases (Ackerman & Ackerman, 1997; Kelin & Bloom, 1986). Ackerman and Ackerman's 1997 study, for example, found that "although the Minnesota Multiphasic Personality Inventory (MMPI) has remained the most frequently used test, it is used by 20% more respondents now than it was 10 years ago" (p. 139).

Personality assessments of parents who are enmeshed in family custody disputes are among the most difficult that psychologists face. Two major difficulties are often encountered. First, the quality of information that psychologists have available is often suspect. Second, there is a general lack of appropriate measures for the setting.

With regard to the first problem, men and women in custody disputes tend to be self-protective and assert their lack of problems, while at the same time tend to provide extremely negative and acrimonious information about their spouse. It is crucial that the professional conducting or reviewing the evaluation avoid reflexively accepting or rejecting these self-protective responses and claims about others; such aspects of the person's responses must be carefully explored and evaluated. Chapter 8 presents information on self-protective response sets that may be useful in such evaluations.

Second, available personality measures are often not developed with family custody considerations in mind and consequently need to be adapted for that purpose. Psychological test results in family court settings need to be interpreted from a somewhat different perspective than results in other settings. Appendix F provides an extensive array of MMPI research on parental behavior, personality, and custody.

Base Rate Information on MMPI–2 Profiles in Family Custody Cases

Parents who take the MMPI–2 in the context of a family custody evaluation tend to endorse the symptoms and behaviors in a manner that is different from people who take the test in personal injury cases. As discussed in chapter 8, these differing motivations can affect the validity and must be carefully considered. Several recent studies have addressed the question of how different MMPI–2 profiles are in family custody evaluations by seeking to obtain empirical data on the relative frequency of different MMPI–2 scale scores and profiles that are obtained in family custody cases (Postuma & Harper, 1998). Two studies provide valuable information on the relative frequency of MMPI–2 patterns in family custody cases.

Bathurst, Gottfried, and Gottfried (1997) conducted an extensive study of 258 men and 250 women who were involved in child custody evaluations to provide information on parents undergoing evaluations. The data from this study were also incorporated in a larger sample of child custody cases reported by Butcher (1997). The reader is referred to the article by Bathurst et al. (1997) for a discussion of their methods and procedures. We summarize the larger study by Butcher (1997). Butcher (1997) collected data on parents involved in the family custody cases by asking 19 clinicians who evaluated men and women in family custody disputes from varying practices across the United States and from Australia to provide cases for development of custody case base rates. A total of 1,799 cases (881 men and 918 women) involving a broad range of family custody assessment issues were included in the analysis. The data from this diverse range of cases have provided a rich picture of custody-based MMPI–2 profiles that enables practitioners to appraise the profile context more clearly (Butcher, 1998b).

Parents in custody cases are often concerned over their social image, so they tend to produce extremely defensive profiles. Parents who take the MMPI–2 in a child custody evaluation tend to present an overly positive self-appraisal, with high scores on the Lie scale (*L*) or Defensiveness scale (*K*). However, the majority of parents do produce valid interpretable profiles. For example, the mean score on the *L* scale for the custody sample as a whole was 56.5, or less than 1 standard deviation above the mean of the normal sample. The mean value of the *K* score for the custody sample was 56.5. The mean value for the *S* scale, the most sensitive measure of test defensiveness in this group, was 58.8 for the combined custody sample.

What is the range of clinical scale elevation in custody cases? The majority of people undergoing custody evaluations do not score in the pathological range. However, almost 20% of the men and 23.5% of the women produced well-defined clinical scale scores above a *T* score of 65—that is, within the interpretable, clinical range. In addition, well-defined 2-point MMPI–2 codes were found for 10.5% of men and 11.9% of women. There are clear trends in the scales that are elevated, with the *Pa* scale occurring as the most prominent spike in men (8.5%) and in women (7.6%). The second most prominent spike score for men is Mania (*Ma*; 3.2%) and for women is *Pd* (6.0%).

This study shows the majority of individuals undergoing custody evaluations do *not* report extensive mental health problems characteristic of a mental health center population. However, a substantial number of these people do show psychopathology on the MMPI–2. Some studies suggest that particular MMPI patterns may be differentially associated with patients who do and who do not receive custody (e.g., Ollendick, 1984; Ollendick & Otto, 1983). Several other lines of empirical investigation bear on family custody evaluations, as described in the next section.

MMPI Profiles of Parents of Disturbed Children

Several extensive reviews of research on parent personality in relation to child and adolescent psychopathology have been published (Hafner, Butcher,

Hall, & Quast, 1969; Lachar & Sharp, 1979). Lahey, Russo, Walker, and Piacentini (1989), for example, found that mothers of children exhibiting conduct disorders had more deviant MMPI profiles when compared with mothers of children who suffered from other types of problems.

> These results support the prediction that disturbances of maternal personality, as measured by the MMPI, would be associated with CD [conduct disorder], but not ADD/H [attention-deficit disorder/hyperactivity], in their children. The pattern of MMPI elevations is consistent, furthermore, with previous findings showing a weak but consistent link between CD in children and both antisocial behavior and hysteria/histrionic personality in their mothers (Stewart & Leone, 1978) and with studies that found that the mothers of clinic-referred children who apparently had primarily disruptive behavior disorders showed elevations on MMPI scales indicative of both antisocial behavior and hysteria/histrionic personality.
>
> The present findings suggest further that objective personality tests provide a sensitive tool for the study of disturbances in the psychological functioning of the mothers of children with psychological disorders (Butcher & Pope, 1992a). These findings suggest that subtle disturbances of personality in the mothers of children with CD are far more common than previous studies using only categorical diagnoses have indicated. (p. 514)

Any inferences drawn from such research must take into account the difficulties of attempting to interpret statistical associations (e.g., caring for a child who suffers from a serious conduct disorder—as distinct from another disorder—may be so stressful for a parent that MMPI-elevated scales may be a natural and understandable consequence).

Research on personality factors in marital distress. The MMPI has been used to help understand the personality characteristics of individuals who are experiencing marital distress. Some personality problems that are relevant to custody evaluations are reflected in MMPI responses.[4]

The Marital Distress scale for the MMPI–2 (Hjemboe, Almagor, & Butcher, 1992) can be of value in assessing couples participating in custody litigation. For example, some parties involved in family custody disputes may be remarried and are presently seeking custody of their children from a previous marriage now that they have become more maritally stable. Seeking a new custodial relationship with their children from their previous marriage, they may put the quality of their current marriage at issue before the family law court (if the state provides special courts that focus on family law).

Research on personality and adjustment factors in child physical and sexual abuse. A number of studies have attempted to identify responses that might characterize parents who abuse their children (Bosquet & Egeland, 2000). The research suggests that some MMPI scale scores are statistically associated with higher risk for child abuse.[5] Other studies have focused on how abuse (e.g., incest) affects the personality and development of the victim/survivor (e.g., Holifield, Nelson, & Hart, 2002). The empirical literature indicates that there may be special issues in interpreting MMPI profiles when abuse is at issue. Findings from a study by Flitter, Elhai, and Gold (2003), for example, "suggest that high F elevations may reflect genuine problem areas often found among CSA [childhood sex abuse] victims, rather than symptom overreporting" (p. 269). Psychological assessments of

---

[4] See, for example, Arnold (1970); Barrett (1973); Barry, Anderson, and Thomas (1967); Bloomquist and Harris (1984); Cookerly (1974); Hjemboe and Butcher (1991); McAdoo and Connolly (1975); Murstein and Glaudin (1968); Ollendick, Otto, and Heider (1983); Osborne (1971); Snyder and Regts (1990); Swan (1957).

[5] Egeland, Erickson, Butcher, and Ben-Porath (1991); Khan, Welch, and Zilmer (1993); Land (1968); Lund (1975); Paulson, Afifi, Chaleff, Thomason, and Lui (1975); Paulson, Afifi, Thomason, and Chaleff (1974); Paulson, Schwemer, and Bendel (1976); L. Wright (1970, 1976).

abuse victims–survivors need to consider the possibility of long-term consequences (Follette, Naugle, & Follette, 1997; Scott & Stone, 1986a, 1986b). When custody is at issue, the MMPI can be used to help assess the credibility of a parent's (or potential foster parent's) self-report, possible psychopathology, problems with alcohol or drugs, and characteristics that seem to be associated with safe, appropriate, and effective parenting.

It is essential to note that *no* MMPI scale, profile, or pattern to date can reliably differentiate people who abuse children from people who do not abuse children or people who have been abused from people who have not been abused. When expert witnesses or attorneys encounter claims that a particular MMPI scale, profile, or pattern definitely shows that a person has or has not abused someone or that a person has or has not been abused, it is important to ask for the published studies demonstrating the validity, reliability, sensitivity, and specificity of the instrument for this particular determination in this setting with this population.

ASSESSING CLIENTS IN CRIMINAL CASES

The original version of the MMPI has been used in criminal justice and correctional settings since the early 1940s (Megargee, 2006). For example, early studies by Capwell (1945), Fry (1949), Hathaway and Monachesi (1963), and Panton (1970, 1973), among others, established the test as an effective instrument for assessing criminal offenders. Borum and Grisso's (1995) survey found that

> when psychological testing was used, certain tests (e.g., WAIS–R, MMPI) were cited with exceptionally high frequency. This result suggests the possibility that even if testing is not seen as essential across cases, certain tests may represent standard practice for experienced forensic psychologists in those cases in which testing is used. (p. 471)

Evaluating Criminal Responsibility and Competence to Stand Trial

Using the MMPI to help determine whether an individual is psychologically able to stand trial is con-

sistent with one of the main purposes of the original instrument. Starke Hathaway (1965) pointed out that "the MMPI was intended as an objective aid in the routine psychiatric case work-up of adult patients and as a method for determining the severity of the conditions" (p. 463). As a consequence, much of the traditional MMPI research literature on clinical scale meanings and profile type correlates bears directly on the question as to the presence and extent of current, severe psychological problems.

More than 30 years ago, Dahlstrom and his colleagues (1975), in reviewing the literature on the use of the MMPI in the assessment of criminal behavior, observed that the instrument is frequently used in cases involving the question of whether defendants are competent to stand trial. In the same vein, Jay Ziskin (1981b) focused on the ways in which "assessment of psychopathology by means of the MMPI can be related to a number of legal issues" (p. 4). Although emphasizing that *insanity* is a legal term that is not equivalent to a psychotic state, Ziskin noted that a psychotic state seemed to be an essential prerequisite for a professional opinion regarding issues of insanity.

> If psychosis is present, then a description of the characteristics of the psychosis may support inferences concerning possession or lack of the requisite capacities for criminal responsibility. Conversely, in actual practice, failure to establish a psychosis will frequently negate lack of the requisite capacity. Also, in the criminal area, findings relative to prognosis or treatability may be relevant to disposition where a guilty verdict has been rendered. Availability of treatment and prospects for its success are factors the judge will take into consideration in the sentencing phase of the matter. (1981b, pp. 4–5)

A number of studies have attempted to assess the effectiveness of the MMPI in forensic insanity determinations or in determinations of possible differences between potentially insane individuals and those who have committed criminal offenses but are not legally insane.[6] It is important to keep in mind that when the MMPI is administered at some point after the crime, the results, if valid, reflect the individual's current (i.e., at the time of test administration) mental status, which may or may not be similar to the individual's mental status at the time that the crime was committed.

As with other forensic evaluations using the MMPI, evaluation of the defendant's test validity is especially important. Many individuals undergoing psychological evaluation in a correctional setting may attempt to dissemble to secure the most desirable verdict or sentence (see, e.g., Grossman & Wasyliw, 1988; McNulty, Harkness, & de Raad, 2002; Parwatikar, Holcomb, & Menninger, 1985; Rogers, Gillis, McMain, & Dickens, 1988; Wasyliw, Grossman, Haywood, & Cavanaugh, 1988).

Assessment of Sex Offenders

A great deal of research on MMPI–2 characteristics among sex offenders has been published. As one might expect, a number of studies have been devoted to an examination of the difficulties that can limit or lower the accuracy of a psychological assessment because of the lack of cooperation in the self-report that is found among some offenders. Several studies have addressed problem denial or inaccurate reporting by sex offenders (Baldwin & Roys, 1998; M. W. Clark, 1997; Karle-Brueck, 2003; Koss, Leonard, Beezley, & Oros, 1985; Lanyon, 1993; Lanyon & Lutz, 1984; Schattner, 2003; Wasyliw, Grossman, & Haywood, 1994; Whitacre, 1995).

The personality characteristics of sex offenders have also been studied extensively. A number of the published studies have attempted to provide a classification of offenders based on their assessed personality characteristics (Anderson, Kunce, & Rich, 1979; Armentrout & Hauer, 1978; Kieliszewski, 1999; Langevin, Wright, & Handy, 1990a, 1990b; Levin & Stava, 1987; Losada-Paisey, 1998; Melonas, 1998; Pirrello, 1999; Schlank,

1995; Shealy, Kalichman, Henderson, & Szymanowski, 1991; Siegel, 2002; Simkins, 1993).

Several works have addressed other medical or psychological factors in samples of sex offenders, for example, neuropsychological functioning (Knox-Jones, 1995; Veneziano, Veneziano, Le-Grand, & Richards, 2004); intellectual disability (Boer, Tough, & Haaven, 2004; Harris & Tough, 2004), diabetes (Langevin & Bain, 1992); and posttraumatic stress disorder (Weiner, 1997). In addition, a number of status variables among sex offenders have been researched—for example, previous sexual abuse (Langevin, Wright, & Handy, 1989), ethnicity (Maness, Silkowski, Velasquez, Savino, & Frank, 2001; Velasquez, Callahan, & Carrillo, 1989), military service (Walters, 1987), female sex offenders (Hudson, 1996), and priests (Plante, Manuel, & Bryant, 1996). Finally, a number of studies have addressed the treatment of sex offenders or predicting recidivism in sex offender populations (Aldridge, 1999; Lessin, 1997; Miner & Dwyer, 1995; Miner, Marques, Day, & Nelson, 1990; Valliant & Blasutti, 1992). For a review of the complex issues in assessing sex offenders, see Salter (1988, 2003).

Base Rate Information From Correctional Settings

Butcher (1997) reported base rate information provided by 13 clinicians who evaluated men in correctional facilities in the United States and Canada. A total of 322 men who were being assessed in a broad range of cases were included in the archival sample.

Validity patterns in correctional cases. The base rates of correctional cases provide information about the types of response sets used by convicted felons assessed in prison. First, a total of 61 men produced technically invalid profiles in this setting and were excluded from further analyses. These cases were eliminated because of high F, Infrequency-Back scale ($F[B]$), Variable Response

---

[6] Arce, del Carmen Pampillon, and Farina (2002); Blackburn (1968); Boardman (1996); Boehnert (1987a, 1987b); Claghorn, Hays, Webb, and Lewis (1991); Craddick (1962); Hays (1999); Moskowitz, Lewis, Ito, and Ehrmentraut (1999); Rogers, Salekin, Sewell, Goldstein, and Leonard (1998); Roman and Gerbing (1989); Schmalz, Fehr, and Dalby (1989); Schretlen and Arkowitz (1990); Schretlen, Wilkins, Van Gorp, and Bobholz (1992); Villanueva, Roman, and Tuley (1988); Wilcock (1964).

Inconsistency scale (*VRIN*), or True Response Inconsistency scale (*TRIN*). The remaining profiles were examined as to validity pattern. The mean validity scale performance for the group was as follows: $L = 55.9$, $F = 63.8$, $K = 46.5$, and $S = 45.8$.

Consistent with the correctional literature, a preponderance of *Pd* scale elevations was found among incarcerated felons. The *Pd* scale was the most prominent score of people undergoing psychological evaluations in correctional contexts, with 30.3% of the cases producing this profile high point score, and 16.9% of these cases were well-defined peaks at or greater than a *T* score of 65. The mean *Pd* score for the correctional sample was 67.4, with the *Pa* scale (Scale 6) close behind at 64.1. The majority of individuals undergoing evaluations in this sample would be considered as having some type of personality disorder.

Hispanic inmates. Butcher (1997) also reported data provided by Dr. Jose Cabiya from San Juan, Puerto Rico, on the basis of a large sample of inmates from the Puerto Rican prison system who took the MMPI–2 in Spanish. These evaluations were part of an extensive evaluation of 321 inmates in San Juan using the Spanish-language version of the MMPI–2. A somewhat different pattern of scores was reported for the inmates in the Puerto Rican prison system than those reported for prisoners on the United States mainland because these inmates were largely drug abusers. The highest prevalence of well-defined code types at or above a *T* score of 65 in this sample was 6-8/8-6 (10.3%) and 8-9/9-8 (5.0%). Cabiya found for this population that well-defined single-point scores that were at or above a *T* score of 65 were *Sc* (14.3%), *Pa* (9.3%), *Ma* (8.1%), and *Pd* (5.3%).

Personality Adjustment of Criminal Offenders

To develop a comprehensive system for classifying convicted felons, Megargee and Bohn (1977, 1979); Megargee and Carbonell (1995); Megargee, Carbonell, Bohn, and Sliger (2001); and Megargee (1994, 1995, 1997, 2006) identified 10 types of criminal offenders by using their response to the MMPI.

1. Able: This profile type has moderate clinical scale elevations, usually on Scales 4 and 9. These individuals are considered to be charming, impulsive, and usually quite manipulative.
2. Baker: This profile cluster has moderate elevations with peak scores usually on Scales 2 and 4. These individuals tend to be considered inadequate, anxious, and constricted. Alcohol abuse is frequent.
3. Charlie: This profile tends to be indicative of extremely poor adjustment. Profile elevations are usually high, with several scale scores elevated above 70. The individuals are usually described as hostile, misanthropic, alienated, aggressive, and antisocial. A history of deviant behavior, criminal convictions, and substance abuse is common.
4. Delta: This profile configuration has a moderate to high elevation on Scale 4. These individuals are usually considered amoral, hedonistic, manipulative, and self-centered. They are viewed as impulsive stimulation seekers.
5. Easy: This profile type typically has low elevations, often below 70, with peak scores on Scales 4 and 3. These individuals tend to be bright and stable with good adjustment. Many show good personal relationships.
6. Foxtrot: Very high scale elevations (above 80) are characteristic. Scales 8, 9, and 4 tend to be elevated. These individuals are usually described as streetwise, tough, cynical, and antisocial. Long criminal histories and poor prison adjustment are common.
7. George: Moderate elevations are typical, particularly on Scales 1, 2, and 3. These individuals are usually described as hard working, submissive, and anxious. They are often able to make use of educational and other resources, if available.
8. How: Very high elevations are found with scores on at least three scales above 70. These individuals are described as unstable, agitated, and psychologically disturbed.
9. Item: This profile type contains low scale scores (usually below 70). This group is considered to be generally stable with minimal psychological problems.

10. Jupiter: This configuration has moderate to high elevations, typically on Scales 9, 7, and 8. Individuals in this category tend to be described as overcoming deprived backgrounds. They often do better than expected when released from prison.

The Megargee and Bohn typology (1977), hereinafter known as Megargee types, has been widely studied, and a number of demographic variables and prison behaviors have been associated with these profile types. The typology has been supported in international studies; in Italy (Sirigatti, Giannini, Laura-Grotto, & Giangrasso, 2002) and Belgium (Sneyers, Sloore, Rossi, & Derksen, 2005). Megargee (2004) has also developed a validity scale (*Fc*; Infrequency Correctional) for use with criminal offenders to ensure that profile classification in correctional settings are conducted on valid profiles. In addition, the system's validity and reliability in the classification of felons has been widely explored. T. D. Kennedy (1986; see also Zager, 1988) provided a useful review of the research on the Megargee classification system, noting several studies that provided empirical tests of the system.[7]

A number of studies have supported the replicability of the 10 Megargee types across different inmate samples; the same types are found in fairly similar proportions across maximum- and medium-security facilities as well as minimum-security programs and halfway houses.[8] However, the proportions of inmates in each classification vary somewhat according to the setting. Specific sample characteristics appear not to be associated with proportions of the different types across settings. There is now empirical support for applying this classification scheme to women inmates. Although the Megargee types can be found in many settings, correlates of the types have not been consistently found to generalize across settings. Some studies found *no* personal history, psychiatric, demographic, prison adjustment, or outcome variables to be differentially associated with any of the types. One type, 3, or Charlie, seems to be one that has most consistently been found to be predictive of psychiatric and behavioral maladjustment, including poor prison adjustment. Another type, 8, or How, also seems to be fairly consistently correlated with psychological and adjustment problems.

There is not enough information available at this time to address the question of which types are more stable. Some studies have questioned the stability of *any* of the Megargee types, finding a 60% to 90% change in type after only 4 months (Dahlstrom et al., 1986; Johnson et al., 1983; Simmons et al., 1981). However, the issue of whether these changes reflect invalidating instability or actual personality changes in inmates remains open (Zager, 1983). For example, in one study of death row inmates who had their sentences commuted, the shifts away from pathological types Charlie and How into less pathological types Item, Easy, or George might be a valid reflection of changes in their mental state (Dahlstrom et al., 1986).

In criminal cases, it may be helpful to appraise people according to the Megargee felon classification typology in light of the research-based wealth of descriptive information (Wrobel et al., 1991). The resulting type can best be viewed, as with other aspects of MMPI profiles, as a source of potentially useful hypotheses. These hypotheses can then be evaluated in the context of the full range of other information available.

The typology can be scored and processed manually, although it can be a somewhat onerous task. Many users of the classification system find computer-based processing faster and more cost effective. Megargee (1992) found that a revised version of the Megargee rules for MMPI–2 classified 84% of the cases identically to the rules prepared for the original MMPI. The system has now been made available on computer from Pearson Assessments (Megargee, 2006).

---

[7] Bohn (1979); Booth and Howell (1980); Dahlstrom, Panton, Bain, and Dahlstrom (1986); Edinger (1979); Edinger, Reuterfors, and Logue (1982); Hanson, Moss, Hosford, and Johnson (1983); Johnson, Simmons, and Gordon (1983); Louscher, Hosford, and Moss (1983); Megargee (1984); Moss, Johnson, and Hosford (1984); Motiuk, Bonta, and Andrews (1986); Mrad, Kabacoff, and Duckro (1983); Simmons, Johnson, Gouvier, and Muzyczka (1981); Walters (1986); Wrobel, Calovini, and Martin (1991); Zager (1983).

[8] Dahlstrom et al. (1986); Edinger (1979); Edinger et al. (1982); Johnson et al. (1983); Mrad et al. (1983); Walters (1986).

In the numerous published MMPI and MMPI–2 studies, there are, of course, sources presenting the relationship of MMPI profiles to other classification systems and to special types of criminal offenders.[9] Most of the original MMPI research in forensic populations involved use of the clinical scales; however, other measures have received attention as well. Osberg (1999), for example, reported that the Harris–Lingoes subscales were effective at describing problems of prisoners.

In light of the background in this chapter and the preceding one about the development of the MMPI, MMPI–2, and MMPI–A in their forensic capacities, it is now time to look at the ways in which the courts have recognized, used, and restricted MMPI–based testimony.

---

[9] See, for example, T. Adams (1976); Anderson and Holcomb (1983); Duthie and McIvor (1990); W. Erickson, Luxenberg, Walbeck, and Seely (1987); Forgac and Michaels (1982); Grossman and Cavanaugh (1989); Hall, Graham, and Shepherd (1991); Hall, Maiuro, Vitaliano, and Proctor (1986); Hall, Shepherd, and Mudrak (1992); Holcomb, Adams, and Ponder (1985); Hunter, Childers, and Esmaili (1990); Kalichman (1990, 1991); Kalichman et al. (1989); Kalichman and Henderson (1991); Kalichman, Shealy, and Craig (1990); Kalichman, Szymanowski, McKee, Taylor, and Craig (1989); C. Pena, Cabiya, and Echevarria (1998); Rader (1977); Shealy, Kalichman, Henderson, Szymanowski, and McKee (1991); Sutker, Allain, and Geyer (1978).

CHAPTER 4

THE COURTS' RECOGNITION, USE, AND RESTRICTION OF MMPI-BASED TESTIMONY

Federal and state courts have ruled extensively (see Appendixes A and B, this volume) on the admissibility of various forensic uses of the Minnesota Multiphasic Personality Inventory (MMPI–2). This is not surprising because "the MMPI–2 is the psychological testing instrument most frequently used in forensic treatment and evaluation contexts" (Otto, 2002, p. 71). This chapter examines the courts' wide acceptance of the MMPI-based testimony in civil and criminal litigation, as well as the limits imposed in certain situations.

GENERAL EVIDENTIARY CONSIDERATIONS

The evidentiary admissibility of testing and interpretation based on one of the forms of the MMPI is controlled by the *Federal Rules of Evidence* (FED. R. EVID.) in federal courts and by the specific evidentiary rules of the state in which a state court evaluating its admissibility sits. All but six states have adopted the *Federal Rules of Evidence* in whole or in part, and evidentiary considerations tend to be similar from state to state.[1] In the decades after the *Federal Rules* were enacted in 1974, courts throughout the United States have decided exactly what the rules mean, often with conflicting conclusions.

The fundamental admissibility of MMPI results is governed by FED. R. EVID. 401, 402, and 404, or the state rules controlling relevancy and its limits.

"Relevant evidence" is, according to FED. R. EVID. 401, "evidence having any tendency to make the existence of any fact that is of consequence to the determination of the action more probable or less probable than it would be without the evidence." The remainder of art. IV of FED. R. EVID. limits the all-encompassing inquiry that R. 401 seems to allow. For example, R. 403 provides for the exclusion of relevant evidence on the grounds of prejudice, confusion, or waste of time; 404 excludes evidence of a person's character, with listed exceptions. The considerations discussed in R. 403 and 404 provide a basis on which MMPI results can be excluded from evidence.

Once the fundamental relevance questions are answered, the MMPI results are generally introduced into evidence as a basis of opinion testimony by expert witnesses. FED. R. EVID. 703 specifically authorizes use of information "reasonably relied upon by experts."

Within the parameters of the rules described, expert witnesses are allowed to testify about specialized knowledge that will assist the judge or jury to understand the evidence or to decide a fact in issue. The threshold question in determining admissibility of MMPI results in individual cases focuses on whether those results are sufficiently trustworthy to warrant their acceptance.

A federal court explored the origins and scientific bases of the test itself in copyright disputes

---

[1] California, Connecticut, Georgia, Illinois, Maryland, and New York have not adopted a state version of FED. R. EVID. 702 or 703.

regarding the original MMPI. As background, the federal eighth circuit court of appeals gave this description in its 1989 opinion in *Applied Innovations, Inc. v. Regents of the University of Minnesota* (876 F.2d 626 (8th Cir. 1989)).

> Their basic hypothesis was that individuals who share a particular psychological symptom or personality trait or characteristic were likely to respond to certain groups of test statements in the same way and that each response to a particular test statement was indicative of a particular psychological symptom or personality trait or characteristic. (876 F.2d at 629)

> The MMPI schedule was a comprehensive work and contained the 550 test statements, scale membership, scoring direction and *T*-score conversion data for the hypochondriasis, depression, hysteria, psychopathic deviate, sexual interest, question, truthfulness, and validity scales. (876 F.2d at 629)

The process of identifying the personality traits in individuals and groups of people, known as "building scales," was described in the trial court's factual findings and set forth in an earlier court's decision in *Regents of the University of Minnesota v. Applied Innovations, Inc.* (685 F. Supp. 698 (D.C. Minn. 1987)).

> The authors then commenced on the long and tedious process of determining which of their 1,000 plus test items assisted in identification of particular personality traits, a process appropriately called building scales. Although there were some minor variations in the building of the individual scales, a crude, general description of the process is as follows. The authors selected individuals that had been diagnosed as manifesting the personality trait they were attempting to identify. Then Hathaway and McKinley would compare their responses to the test items to the responses of a group of Minnesota adults (typically friends and relatives of patients at the University of Minnesota Hospital) and a control group of University of Minnesota students. Based on this comparison, a particular test item was initially selected as a discriminating test item if the percentage frequency difference between the criterion group (individuals manifesting the clinical trait) and the group of Minnesota adults ("normals") was a statistically significant amount, which varied from one scale to another. (685 F. Supp. at 701)

For years, the MMPI has been recognized by appellate courts across the country as a standard, reliable test when used correctly and appropriately, although the analysis has taken different directions in recent years. In general, the longstanding recognition allows proponents of MMPI testing to avoid evidence restrictions placed on more experimental testing.

The most recent dialogue in the legal and psychological communities concerning admissibility of psychological testing began with a 1993 case decided by the U.S. Supreme Court. *Daubert v. Merrell Dow Pharmaceuticals, Inc.* (509 U.S. 579 (1993)) changed the way federal courts and most state courts evaluated the admissibility of scientific expert testimony. Before that time, scientific testing that was new or novel was generally severely restricted in courtroom use. Restrictions governing admission of experimental techniques had been implemented in the 1923 case *Frye v. United States* (293 F. 1013 (D.C. Cir. 1923)). The *Frye* court held that general acceptance in the scientific community was a prerequisite to admissibility of scientific testimony. For decades, the restrictions discussed in the *Frye* case controlled admission of much of the expert testimony in courts across the country. After the FED. R. EVID. were implemented in 1974, questions were asked about whether the *Frye* guidelines still applied to expert testimony. Nothing in R. 702 established general acceptance as a prerequisite to admissibility. Nonetheless, even after passage of the FED. R. EVID., most courts continued to follow *Frye*. For example, the California supreme court looked to *Frye* when it decided in 1989 that the MMPI was a standardized test that could no longer be considered novel or experimental. In deciding that no special showing was required for expert opinion that relied on the MMPI, the court in *People v. Stoll* (49 Cal. 3d 1136, 265 Cal. Rptr. 111, 783 P.2d 698 (1989)), declared that

> No precise legal rules dictate the proper basis for an expert's journey into a patient's mind to make judgments about his behavior. In effect, however, California courts have deferred to a qualified expert's decision to rely on "standardized" psychological tests such as the MMPI to reach an opinion on mental state at the time acts were committed. . . . Such deference is no less appropriate here. Indeed, voir dire testimony indicated that qualified professionals routinely use raw material from the MMPI . . . as a basis for assessing personality, and drawing behavioral conclusions therefrom. (49 Cal. 3d at 1154, 265 Cal. Rptr. at 122, 783 P.2d at 709)

> The psychological testimony proffered here raises none of the concerns addressed by Kelly/Frye. The methods employed are not new to psychology or the law, and they carry no misleading aura of scientific infallibility (49 Cal. 3d at 1157, 265 Cal. Rptr. at 124, 783 P.2d at 711). Moreover, as Dr. Mitchell testified, diagnostic use of written personality inventories such as the MMPI . . . has been established for

decades. Modern courts have not resisted reference to these tests. (*Id.*)

> Contrary to the dissent's claim, expert reliance on the MMPI . . . for this particular purpose is not a "revolutionary" development. (49 Cal. 3d at 1158, 265 Cal. Rptr. at 125, 783 P.2d at 712)

> It would be anomalous to view the MMPI and similar tests as a "new" technique at this late date. (*Id.*)

In the decades before *Daubert* was decided, however, states had become increasingly critical of the *Frye* test for determining admissibility of scientific evidence. Twenty states had either directly rejected or severely limited their use of the *Frye* test. See Meaney (1995) for a state-by-state analysis.

In *Daubert,* the U.S. Supreme Court said clearly that the *Frye* standard for governing the admissibility of expert testimony had been displaced in 1974 by the Federal Rules of Evidence.[2] Therefore, in those states that have adopted the federal rules, the *Frye* test is gone.[3] Under *Daubert*, the trial judge is assigned to function as a gatekeeper, making sure that the expert evidence provided is both reliable and relevant. *Daubert* lists factors to be considered by the judge in deciding whether or not scientific evidence is reliable. Those factors include whether the scientific theory at issue has been or can be tested; whether the theory has been subjected to a peer-review process that included recognized publication and discussion; whether there is a statistical error rate that shows that the theory is statistically reliable; and whether the theory has been generally accepted in the relevant field.

Daubert sparked legal discussion around the country. Whether the case created a more stringent or lenient standard for admissibility than existed

---

[2] The court described the *Frye* analysis as an "austere standard, absent from and incompatible with the Federal Rules of Evidence (and) should not be applied in federal trials" (*Daubert*, 509 U.S. at 588).

[3] Of the six states that have no state version of FED. R. EVID. 702, all have addressed the *Daubert* issue. Georgia and Connecticut have either adopted *Daubert* or a *Daubert*-like standard (*Lattarulo v. State*, 401 S.E.2d 516 (Ga. 1991) requires "a scientific stage of verifiable certainty"; *State v. Porter*, 698 A.2d 739 (Conn. 1997) specifically rejected *Frye* and adopted *Daubert*, as did *Alexandru v. Dowd*, 830 A.2d 352 (Conn. App. 2003)). Four states without a rule 702 analogue—California, Illinois, Maryland, and New York—have expressly rejected *Daubert* and retained *Frye* (*People v. Leahy*, 882 P.2d 321 (Cal. 1994); *Roberti v. Andy's Termite & Pest Control, Inc.*, 113 Cal. App. 4th 893 (2000); *First Midwest Trust Co. v. Rogers*, 196 Ill. App. 3d 416 (1998); *People v. Wesley*, 633 N.E.2d 451 (N.Y. 1994)). Maryland decided that "persuasive reliance" on *Daubert* is "misplaced" and viewed *Kumho Tire* as a "tediously fact-specific 'tempest in a teapot'" (*CSX v. Miller*, 859 A.2d 1025 (Md. App. 2004). *See also State v. Smullen*, 844 A.2d 429 (Md. 2004)).

under the *Frye* case was the subject of debate (e.g., *United States v. Jones*, 107 F.3d 1147 (6th Cir.), *cert. denied*, 117 S. Ct. 2527 (1997); *Peitzmeier v. Hennessy Indus.*, 97 F.3d 293 (8th Cir. 1996), *cert. denied*, 117 S. Ct. 1552 (1997)). Legal scholars then asked a second question concerning whether or not *Daubert*, which involved scientific testimony concerning epidemiological studies, could be applied to nonscientific expert testimony that is based solely on experience or training, such as psychological testimony, at all (e.g., Imwinkelrind, 1994). The courts were divided again (e.g., *Vadala v. Teledyne Industry*, 44 F.3d 36 (1st Cir. 1995); *Pestel v. Vermeer Mfg. Co.*, 64 F.3d 382 (8th Cir. 1995)). The U.S. Supreme Court answered the first question in December of 1997 and the second in March of 1999.

In December of 1997, in response to the courts that were applying *Daubert* differently, often times exactly the opposite from each other, the U.S. Supreme Court elaborated on how courts should conduct a *Daubert* analysis in *General Electric Co. v. Joiner*, 118 S. Ct. 512 (1997), 522 U.S. 136 (1997). *Joiner* said that the *Federal Rules of Evidence* admitted a somewhat broader range of scientific testimony than would have been admissible under *Frye*. Clearly, the U.S. Supreme Court in *Daubert* had intended to give the trial courts more—not less—flexibility in admitting scientific expert testimony. The court also said that under the gate-keeper role, the trial judge was responsible for screening the reliability of the scientific evidence and that the trial judge's decision would not be reversed absent an abuse of discretion. The court did not, however, address the issue of whether experts testifying as psychologists should be subjected to a *Daubert* analysis at all.

In March of 1999, the U.S. Supreme Court addressed the second question that had gone unanswered in *Daubert*. In *Kumho Tire Co., Ltd. v. Carmichael*, 526 S. Ct. 137, 1999 WL 152455 (U.S. Mar. 1999), the U.S. Supreme Court answered clearly that the *Daubert* analysis applies to the testimony of all experts. The Court held that *Daubert*, which had required that a trial court judge serve a gate-keeping obligation in admissibility of expert testimony, "applies not only to testimony based on

'scientific' knowledge, but also to testimony based on 'technical' and 'other specialized knowledge'" (526 U.S. at 144). The other specialized knowledge category generally forms the basis of a psychologist's expert testimony. The *Kumho* Court also said that the list of specific factors that it had set out in *Daubert* to help a trial court determine the reliability of expert testimony were not exclusive and that a trial court had broad latitude in deciding how to determine that reliability. It is under the *Kumho* case that psychological testimony is most often analyzed.

Although the general state of the law of admissibility of expert testimony remains in flux, the MMPI and MMPI–2 results have such wide acceptance that they sail past the first part of a *Daubert* test. The test itself has been subjected to peer review and publication and is generally accepted. Likely because of the widespread acceptance of MMPI testing, much of the provocative discussion in recent years concerning the admissibility of psychological testing has revolved around other types of testing. Penile plethysmographs have been held to be unreliable under *Daubert* (e.g., *Doe v. Glazner*, 232 F.3d 1258 (9th Cir. 2000)); use of the Psychopathy Checklist Revised was allowed during the death penalty phase of a capital trial despite an argument that the test had not been standardized as to the Black or post-middle-age populations (*United States v. Barnette*, 211 F.3d 803 (4th Cir. 2000)); but the Able Assessment of Sexual Interest, which involves having the subject respond to a questionnaire and review pictures of clothed and unclothed people was excluded because there was no evidence the assessment had been standardized with a statistically significant sample of Native Americans (*United States v. White Horse*, 316 F.3d 769 (8th Cir.), *cert. denied*, 124 S. Ct. 116 (2003)).

Thus the first step in resisting any *Daubert* challenge to admissibility of MMPI results—establishing reliability—is fairly simple. The second step in resisting a *Daubert* challenge focuses on establishing the relevance necessary to ensure the test's admissibility. The lawyer must convince the court that the testimony concerning the results of a particular test will assist the trier of fact to understand or determine a fact at issue. Indeed, subsequent to

Daubert, some authors have recommended severely limiting the testimony of psychologists, claiming that "if there is a category of expert testimony that richly deserves the characterization of 'junk science,' it is the clinical opinion testimony of psychiatrists and psychologists. . . . psychologists and psychiatrists are loose cannons on the decks of courtrooms" (Mantell, 1994, p. 57). However, even the Mantell article differentiates between psychometric testing, which the article agrees is statistically valid and inherently reliable, and "clinical judgment," which the author argues is inadmissible under *Daubert*. Case law, nonetheless, generally supports the admissibility of clinical psychological testimony. However, given the clear statement in *Joiner* and in *Kumho* that the trial judge's decision will not be reversed absent an abuse of discretion, a prudent attorney should anticipate the possibility that he or she is facing a judge who believes that psychological testimony is junk science and be prepared to refute that impression with strong evidence. The lawyer should be familiar with the admissibility requirements under the rules of his or her state and under *Daubert*, *Joiner*, and *Kumho*, and should prepare to meet the most stringent standards. MMPI results should be admissible under virtually any interpretation of *Daubert*, *Joiner*, or *Kumho* discussed in lower courts as long as the results help the trier of fact decide something that is relevant. At its core, every test announced to deal with the admissibility of expert testimony, whether analyzed under rules or through appellate court decisions, attempts to ensure that only reliable and relevant expert testimony makes its way to the jury. Chapter 2 discusses the relationship among the MMPI, MMPI–2, and MMPI–A and provides various indicia of reliability. In summary of the details provided in chapter 2, testimony concerning the MMPI as long as it is relevant, would seem likely to be admitted under any of the reliability questions being asked by the courts because the revised versions of the MMPI have maintained the traditional validity and clinical scales and because the psychometric properties are nearly identical between the MMPI and each of the revised versions.

Courts generally treat the MMPI test results with deference because of their objective status. However,

sometimes that deference leads courts to conclude that the test results are able to impart more information than they were designed to give. For example, in *Ryan v. Clarke* (387 F.3d 785 (8th Cir. Neb. 2004)), the trial judge found—and the appellate court affirmed—that the MMPI results were credible because the test was "a respected objective psychological test (which) showed that while Ryan had an odd personality, he had no mental illness that would cause him to be incompetent" (*Id.*, at 795).

Most often, however, appellate courts use their watchdog status to ensure that test results are not misused. In *Carradine v. Barnhart* (360 F.3d 751 (7th Cir. Ind. 2004)), an appellate court reversed the decision of an administrative law judge (ALJ) based on its finding that the ALJ had made two serious errors in his reasoning process. The first, and most central to the decision of the appellate court, involved the MMPI. The ALJ had noted that the results of the MMPI "did not indicate invalid responses or exaggeration of psychological symptoms" but did suggest "somatization." From those valid MMPI results the ALJ found that the MMPI performance "implies she [the claimant] exaggerates the severity of symptoms she reports." The appellate court properly rejected the ALJ's reasoning, saying, "It implies no such thing. It implies merely that the source of Carradine's pain is psychological rather than physical. If pain is disabling, the fact that the source is purely psychological does not disentitle the applicant to benefits" (p. 754). The appellate court, in its gatekeeper function, refused to allow the somatization suggested by the test results to be misused to support a malingering defense.

In summary, an expert who testifies to the indicia of reliability should provide sufficient support for the admissibility of the test. However, both the expert and the attorney should be vigilant to focus attention beyond the reliability issue to include the more debatable issues surrounding relevance. Regarding the specific *Daubert* analysis, the U.S. Supreme Court, in *Kumho*, expanded the role that trial courts will likely play in determining admissibility of psychological testimony and directed the trial court to look at any information it decides is relevant.

Even though courts accept the reliability of MMPI testing, individual courts acknowledge the fallibility of this testing in particular circumstances. Courts deny evidentiary admission when the results of psychological testing may be misleading or inappropriate or when other testimony from experts suggests that the results should not be relied on as a source of the expert's opinion.

USE IN CRIMINAL CASES

Many appellate decisions that discuss the courtroom use of MMPI results involve criminal cases. In criminal cases, the use of the MMPI often focuses on whether test results indicate that the defendant's mental ability or functioning is sufficiently impaired to provide a defense to the crime charged.

Defenses of diminished capacity, impaired mental condition, and insanity are technical defenses that differ from state to state and are controlled by individual statutes. Use of the MMPI in criminal contexts may involve defensive use by the criminal defendant or rebuttal use by the prosecution faced with a defense of impaired mental functioning (see, e.g., *United States v. Mason*, 935 F. Supp. 745 (W.D. N.C. 1996); *Brown v. State*, 686 So.2d 385 (Ala. Crim. App. 1995)). In addition, defendants have used the MMPI–2 to challenge the admissibility of their confessions. For example, in 1996 an appellate court held that MMPI–2 results that showed that the defendant had difficulty controlling or checking anger were insufficient to render his confession involuntary (*State v. Lapointe*, 678 A.2d 942 (Conn. 1996)).

The MMPI has been held to provide a reliable basis for a variety of expert opinions in criminal litigation. The *Stoll* court said that expert opinions that rely in part on the MMPI or on other standardized tests have been admitted "as circumstantial evidence that the defendant did not harbor the requisite criminal intent or mental state at the time he committed the charged act" or that the "defendant was not likely to commit certain acts in the future" (783 P.2d at 711).

Another area of criminal law in which the MMPI has been increasingly used and criticized in the past several years involves its use in establishing a composite picture or profile (not to be confused with an MMPI–2 profile). The appellate court cases focus on whether testing may be used by a defendant to show that it is unlikely that he or she committed the crime charged because commission of the crime is inconsistent with the characterological (e.g. "sexual offender") profile.

The appellate decisions reflect a dilemma with which criminal courts are increasingly faced: Psychological testimony may provide relevant testimony to assist the judge or jury in deciding whether the defendant had a culpable mental state, but psychological testimony should not be used to usurp the jury's role in deciding guilt or innocence. The decisions of courts across the country reflect both conflicting sides of this dilemma. Various decisions have both affirmed and rejected the use of MMPI–2 profile evidence. The profile discussion often revolves around whether or not the MMPI–2 results are being improperly used to prove guilt or to attack or bolster character.

For example, in *R.D. v. State* (706 So.2d 770 (Ala. Crim. App. 1997)), the appellate court agreed that the MMPI–2 is considered valid and reliable. However, because neither the MMPI–2 nor any other test can determine whether or not a person is a sex offender, any professional opinion that the defendant "showed none of the characteristics that would indicate . . . sexual acting out" (706 So.2d at 773) amounted to improper and inadmissible character evidence. Contrast that with *State v. Blubaugh* (904 P.2d 688 (Utah Ct. App. 1995)), which allowed testimony of propensity for violence in part on the basis of the results of the MMPI–2.

Appellate courts within the same state often disagree about the use of MMPI profile evidence. Two Indiana appellate court decisions reflect the ongoing controversy. The opinion of an Indiana appellate court in *Byrd v. State* (579 N.E.2d 457 (Ind. App. 1st Dist. 1991)) was reversed after the appellate court had approved the introduction of MMPI results to show that the criminal defendant's psychological profile was inconsistent with the mental requirement of committing the act "knowingly," an element of the crime of murder. The court of appeals had said,

Byrd offered Dr. Davis's testimony only to show that Byrd's psychological profile and the MMPI test results were inconsistent with the knowing element of the crime of murder. Record at 1156, 1176–77; the results were not offered to show that Dr. Davis himself opined that Byrd did not knowingly kill Chafin. The MMPI results were admitted into evidence, so Dr. Davis's proffered testimony was based on facts in evidence; therefore, Dr. Davis's testimony met the proper foundational requirements for admissibility. (579 N.E.2d at 461)

That portion of the decision was vacated by the Indiana state supreme court in *Byrd v. State* (593 N.E.2d 1183 (Ind. 1992)).

The question is whether the results of a Minnesota Multiphasic Personality Inventory (MMPI) may be admitted to prove that a defendant's character is inconsistent with committing intentional murder. We hold that they may not. (593 N.E.2d at 1184)

The Indiana supreme court then maintained that the MMPI is properly an assessment device intended to assist a psychologist in treating a patient, "not for determining whether the particular conduct has occurred in the criminal context" (593 N.E.2d at 1186).

The most often reported use of profile testimony involves criminal allegations of sexual abuse, including pedophilia. In 1990, a California appellate court decided in the case of *People v. Ruiz* (222 Cal. App. 3d 1241, 272 Cal. Rptr. 368 (Cal. App. 1st Dist. 1990)) that the MMPI profile-type evidence that formed a basis for expert opinion would be admissible under the previous *Stoll* decision if the proper foundation for its use could be laid by the lawyers.

It follows that in the present situation, Ruiz was entitled to have Dr. Berg state his opinion that Ruiz was not a sexual deviant, or was not a pedophile, or was not likely to have committed the charged acts.

Dr. Berg apparently had no intention of stating an opinion on any of these matters. Rather, he planned to testify that Ruiz did not have the psychological characteristics of a person suffering from pedophilia; i.e., that he did not match the profile of a pedophile. (222 Cal. App. 3d at 1245, 272 Cal. Rptr. at 371)

Nonetheless, we see little reason to distinguish between the material underlying the expert's opinion in Stoll and the type of "profile" evidence underlying Dr. Berg's opinion in the present case. (*Id.*)

Courts require that the use of the MMPI–2 be based on the purposes for which the test was designed and that expert testimony accompany its use. In 1986, a California appellate court in *People v. John W.* (185 Cal. App. 3d 801, 229 Cal. Rptr. 783 (Cal. App. 1st Dist. 1986)) said that the test was not designed to inquire into certain topics. The expert witness had testified that the MMPI was "not particularly useful as applied to the topic of deviant sexuality" (185 Cal. App. 3d at 805, 229 Cal Rptr. at 785) and thus could not have been, according to the reviewing court, the basis of the expert witness's final opinion that the defendant was not a sexual deviant.

While Dr. Walker stated his belief that the MMPI was a reliable test, he conceded that it had never been "standardized in a sexual deviant population." Specifically, he stated that the publishers of the MMPI had not produced any profiles that one would expect from a person who is suffering from any sexual deviancy, so that the test is not particularly useful as applied to the topic of deviant sexuality. In that regard he admitted that "the main usefulness [of the MMPI] is whether they were honest or not on the test." (185 Cal. App. 3d at 804–805, 229 Cal. Rptr. at 784)

This decision incorporates inexact and misleading wording that psychological tests need to be *standardized* on various clinical groups. A more appropriate wording would involve the concept of having been *validated* for the specific group in question.

The courts also carefully acknowledged that MMPI–2 results are fallible. The MMPI–2 results and the expert opinion that accompanies these results are evidence to be weighed as any other scientific evidence presented to the trier of fact.

> We also are persuaded that no reasonable juror would mistake an expert's reliance on standardized tests as a source of infallible "truth" on issues of personality, predisposition, or criminal guilt. Here, for example, Dr. Mitchell stated that the MMPI was essentially 70 percent accurate in diagnosing some patients, but "completely invalid" as to others. Although the witness expressed faith in his own methods, he recounted one instance in which an "admitted" child sex offender had tested "normal" on the MMPI. Thus, despite testimony regarding "validity scales," the test results—which were never actually described below—were not made to appear "fool proof." (*Stoll*, 49 Cal. 3d at 1159, 265 Cal. Rptr. at 125, 783 P.2d at 712)

Underscoring the difficulty in evidentiary ruling regarding such issues as sexual deviance, *People v. John W.* was disapproved by the California supreme court in *People v. Stoll* as follows.

> In *People v. John W.* (1986) [185 Cal. App. 3d 801, 806–808, 229 Cal. Rptr. 783], the court suggested that repeal of the sexual psychopathy and MDSO [mentally disordered sex offenders] schemes undercut *People v. Jones*, 42 Cal. 2d 219, 266 P.2d 38 [1954] insofar as Jones authorizes admission of defense expert opinion on lack of deviance. However, the *John W.* court

overlooked codification of the Jones character evidence rule in section 1102 [of the California Evidence Code]. To the extent *John W.* is inconsistent with our opinion on this point, it is disapproved. (49 Cal. 3d at 1153, n. 18, 265 Cal. Rptr. at 121, 783 P.2d at 708)

The California court in *Stoll* and other courts around the country continue to be unwilling to permit an expert witness to opine on the truth or falsity of the criminal charges. That decision remains the sole determination of the jury. A psychologist, called to testify as an expert on the existence of certain personality traits and likelihood of certain behavior, is generally not competent to testify about the truth or falsity of criminal charges. Although opinion testimony is not made inadmissible solely because it embraces the ultimate issue to be decided by the trier of fact, an expert giving such an opinion must be otherwise qualified to do so. As the *Stoll* court reasoned,

> here, of course, nothing in the voir dire testimony suggested that Dr. Mitchell was qualified to render a legal opinion as to whether all elements of the charged crimes could be proven beyond a reasonable doubt against Grafton and Palomo. However, since Dr. Mitchell immediately retracted his assessment of the charges, we need not explore this issue further. (49 Cal. 3d at 1149, n. 13, 265 Cal. Rptr. at 118, 783 P.2d at 705)

Other uses of psychological testing in criminal litigation settings include its offensive and defensive use in the sentencing phase of death penalty cases. In the states that use death as a sentence alternative to life imprisonment in designated cases (37 state and federal jurisdictions use death as a sentence for designated criminal activities), a sentencing inquisition into aggravating and mitigating circumstances follows conviction and precedes sentencing. The aggravation or mitigation evidence may include a variety of MMPI–2 uses. Testing may show personality features that suggest reduced culpability. The treatment alternatives for a previously undiagnosed and untreated mental illness may argue against the likelihood of recidivism.

Because the stakes are so high, appellate courts allow the criminal defendant every opportunity to convince the judge or jury that life is a more appropriate sentence than death. Testing becomes an issue in reversal of death sentences most often when an attorney fails to raise or investigate relevant psychological testing. Such failure when a life is at issue often supports an ineffective assistance of counsel attack on the death sentence. The third circuit reversed and remanded a death sentence based on ineffective assistance of counsel in a case in which the attorney had not investigated mitigating information, including psychological testing in *Rompilla v. Horn* (355 F.3d 233 (3d Cir. Pa. 2004)). However, the U.S. Supreme Court reversed *Thompson v. Bell* (373 F.3d 688 (6th Cir. Tenn. 2004)), in which the appellate court stayed an inmate's execution and remanded for further proceedings when information learned after the trial suggested that the MMPI testimony had given the jury an inaccurate impression (*Bell v. Thompson*, No. 04-514 (U.S. 2005)).

USE IN CIVIL LITIGATION CASES

Versions of the MMPI have also been used extensively in a variety of civil litigation contexts. The issue of admissibility is generally raised through the expert's report, which is disclosed under FED. R. CIV. P. Rule 26. MMPI–2 test results have been used routinely in evaluating psychological injury in civil litigation cases. Plaintiffs, of course, tend to stress those MMPI–2 results that are consistent with trauma; defendants tend to stress those MMPI–2 results that are consistent with problematic personality traits that preceded the accident or incident in question. For example, in *Davis v. Medical Arts Laboratory* (952 P.2d 52 (Okla. Civ. App. 1997)), an MMPI–2 administered to a claimant alleging injury from the bombing of the Alfred P. Murrah Federal Building in Oklahoma City in 1995 showed that the claimant's psychological condition preexisted the bombing. In another example, in *Doe v. Lutz* (668 N.E.2d 564 (Ill. App. 1st Dist. 1996)), an ex-

pert testified that, on the basis of the MMPI–2 results, a child claiming to have been abused by a priest was not suffering from posttraumatic stress disorder, depression, or a generalized anxiety disorder. In *Carradine v. Barnhart* (360 F.3d 751 (7th Cir. Ind. 2004)), the court said that pain resulting from a psychological source is real pain and can be as disabling as pain from a physical source. The psychological source was documented through "somatization" findings of the MMPI testing . Lawsuits involving psychological damages have dramatically increased over the past few decades. With awards reaching as high as millions of dollars for damages that cannot be physically identified with the precision that an X-ray provides in defining a fracture, psychological testing has gained increased importance in civil litigation. Except for physical injuries resulting from self-mutilation and suicide attempts associated with psychological trauma, the damages claimed in cases are almost always physically unobservable psychological reactions to the exploitation. Predictably, attorneys for the plaintiff attempt to make the damages "real" for the jury (personal injury attorney William A. Barton addressed this problem in his 1990 book, *Recovering for Psychological Injuries*), whereas attorneys for the defendant attempt to emphasize the difficulties in assessing injury inherent in relying on the self-report of the plaintiff.

Defensive use of the MMPI–2 to show that a personal injury plaintiff is fabricating or distorting unobservable illnesses such as chronic pain or psychological impairment has become more frequent. Questions regarding use of the MMPI–2 to identify possible malingering in litigation contexts has been the source of numerous psychological journal articles (see chap. 7, this volume; see also *Malingering Research Update* at http://kspope.com/assess/malinger.php).

USE IN DOMESTIC RELATIONS CASES

The MMPI–2 has been cited extensively in appellate cases involving custody evaluations and attempts to limit parental rights for the sake of the children's welfare. The general goal in custody evaluations is to establish custody and visitation arrangements that are in the best interests of the children involved. Courts are often faced with acrimonious dissolution proceedings in which allegations including neglect and abuse are leveled against one or both parents. MMPI-based assessment of parents can provide valuable information in identifying not only psychological and behavioral (e.g., substance abuse) problems that might argue against a grant of custody but also characteristics that may suggest mature parenting abilities (see chap. 2, this volume).

In *Fisher v. Fisher* (691 A.2d 619 (Del. Super. Ct. 1997)), custody was awarded to a father after psychological tests, including the MMPI-2, showed the mother to be erratic. In *D.J. v. State Department of Human Resources* (578 So.2d 1351 (Ala. Civ. App. 1991)), the MMPI was accepted as evidence of a mother's mental state; the MMPI was accepted in a father's evaluation in *In re Rodrigo S., San Francisco Department of Social Services v. Joan R.* (225 Cal. App. 3d 1179, 276 Cal. Rptr. 183 (Cal. App. 1st Dist. 1990)); MMPI-based testing was appropriately used to evaluate the family in the custody dispute discussed in *Gootee v. Lightner* (224 Cal. App. 3d 587, 274 Cal. Rptr. 697 (Cal. App. 4th Dist. 1990)); and in *Utz v. Keinzle* (574 So.2d 1288 (La. App. 3d Cir. 1991)), the MMPI was used in a custody dispute to evaluate two sets of parents.

MMPI-2 testing has also been used to determine whether parental rights should be terminated (*State ex rel. LEAS in Interest of O'Neal*, 303 N.W.2d 414 (Iowa 1981)) and to decide when parental rights should be given to potential adoptive parents (*Commonwealth v. Jarboe*, 464 S.W.2d 287 (Ky. 1971)).

POSTTRAUMATIC STRESS DISORDER CONSIDERATIONS

The diagnosis of posttraumatic stress disorder (PTSD), and the use of the MMPI to identify or detect the disorder, have played an increasing role in criminal and civil litigation since the conclusion of the war in Vietnam. For example, in *Johnson v. May* (585 N.E.2d 224 (Ill. App. 5th Dist. 1992)), a jury's award of no dollars for disability was reversed when psychological testing, including the

MMPI, supported a diagnosis of severe PTSD. The presence of posttraumatic symptoms has been used as a defense in criminal prosecutions in cases in which veterans have had flashbacks to war experiences. In *State v. Felde* (422 So.2d 370 (La. 1982), *cert. denied,* 461 U.S. 918 (1983)), the test was used in the evaluation of a defendant diagnosed as suffering from PTSD. The test has also been used in civil litigations when psychological difficulties have followed, and may have been caused by, a traumatic event (see Lees-Haley, 1989; see also chap. 7, this volume).

CONSTITUTIONAL AND STATUTORY CONSIDERATIONS

Mandatory MMPI-2 testing as a prerequisite for entry into colleges or jobs has been challenged in recent years. These challenges have generally questioned whether mandatory testing violates any constitutionally protected rights, such as rights to privacy. Although there is some conflict, most courts have found that the testing does not violate state or federal constitutions.

Psychological testing is increasingly used in connection with employment applications. In *Lambley v. Kameny* (682 N.E.2d 907 (Mass. App. Ct. (1997)), a job applicant sued the doctor who examined the applicant at the request of the prospective employer. The MMPI-2 was a part of the evaluation process. *McKenna v. Fargo* (451 F. Supp. 1355 (D.N.J. 1978), *aff'd,* 601 F.2d 575 (3d Cir. 1979)) examined possible violations of the U.S. Constitution. Firefighters had sued the personnel manager and city of Jersey City, New Jersey, alleging that use of the MMPI in the selection process violated the First and Fourteenth Amendments of the U.S. Constitution. The court ruled against the plaintiffs. As Judge Coolahan's decision stated,

> Rarely does a case involve conflicting interests as important and as difficult to reconcile as those in this litigation. The psychological testing which Jersey City uses to screen applicants for its fire department has been challenged by plaintiffs as an invasion of the appli-

cants' constitutional rights. In plaintiff's view, conditioning employment on psychological testing of questionable validity puts the applicants to a prohibited choice of sacrificing constitutional freedoms to secure prized employment or of looking for work elsewhere. Defendants contend that the condition is a reasonable and necessary one because the task of fighting fires is no ordinary job in difficulty or importance and because success depends critically on the psychological capabilities of firemen.

There is good reason to scrutinize a government requirement which joins the words psychology and testing. Psychology is not yet the science that medicine is and tests are too frequently used like talismanic formulas. The Court has, therefore, carefully reviewed the extensive evidence generated by a long trial and has not arrived lightly at the conclusion that the defendant's psychological testing is constitutional. (451 F. Supp. at 1357)

In Pennsylvania, a federal court emphasized the reliability of the MMPI testing. Although one expert had testified in *Pennsylvania v. Flaherty* (760 F. Supp. 472 (W. Dist. Pa. 1991)) that "some studies have found the MMPI . . . 'inadequate' in predicting police and fire fighter performance" (760 F. Supp. at 486), the Pennsylvania court also found that "no one disputes that properly used psychological examinations help to screen out candidates whose temperament or personality may be incompatible with the critical demanding work of a police officer" (*Id.*). The expert who testified that the MMPI was "inadequate" conceded that the MMPI–2, a revision of the MMPI, was intended to reduce cultural and racial bias, although it was "too early to determine" its effectiveness (*Id.*).

In an earlier case, *Valle-Axelberd and Associates, Inc. v. Metropolitan Dade County* (440 So.2d 606 (Fla. 3d Dist. Ct. App.1983)), a Florida appellate court had upheld a county's choice of the second lowest bidder on contractual services because the lowest bidder used the MMPI, which the community, witnesses said, perceived to be a "racially skewed" test.

In a similar inquiry, an Illinois court also emphasized the longstanding acceptance of the MMPI in deciding that the testing could be used as a college admission criterion. The use of the results of the MMPI and related psychological consultations was found not to be an arbitrary or capricious basis for denying admission of a student to a private college.

Use of the MMPI–2 has also been attacked under the Americans With Disabilities Act (ADA; 42 U.S.C. § 12112), generally without success. In *Miller v. City of Springfield* (146 F.3d 612 (8th Cir. 1998)), a woman was denied employment as a police recruit because results of an MMPI–2 suggested above-normal depression. The court concluded that the level of depression did not rise to a substantial limitation as required under the ADA and "(i)n any event, we easily conclude that appropriate psychological screening is job-related and consistent with business necessity where the selection of individuals to train for the position of police officer is concerned" (146 F.3d at 614–615).

SPECIAL LIMITATIONS

Raw data from the MMPI–2, without accompanying expert opinion and other data, such as personal interviews of the individual, may be inadmissible. MMPI–2 data are often viewed as a springboard for the expert opinion. For example, in *Wesley v. State* (575 So.2d 108 (Ala. Crim. App. 1989)), the court held that testimony regarding MMPI results should be limited to the administering doctor. The conviction in *Wesley* was reversed at a higher state level because the lower court had allowed a doctor's testimony of opinion on the basis of evidence that was not admitted (*Wesley v. State*). However, in another Alabama case, *Bailey v. Gold Kist, Inc.* (482 So.2d 1224 (Ala. Civ. App. 1985)), a doctor was allowed to use the results of the MMPI evaluated by another psychologist to testify about the plaintiff's behavior patterns.

The *Byrd* court of appeals decision had acknowledged the limitations of MMPI results and held that its use is "not as a primary source of information, but instead as a means of confirming or challenging clinical impressions previously gained through direct contact with the patient" (579 N.E.2d at 460). The *Byrd* state supreme court decision went further, holding that "(u)nlike other more objective scientific tests (such as DNA testing), there is no suggestion that the MMPI is an accurate or objective indicator of whether a particular defendant committed the crime charged" (593 N.E.2d at 1186). The *Carradine* court refused to allow an ALJ to misuse the test to equate "somatization" with malingering.

Computer-generated MMPI–2 profiles have raised special concerns for the courts. The computer analysis, rather than forming a part of the basis of an expert's opinion, may actually appear to give an opinion. That analysis was excluded from evidence in the Indiana case of *Sullivan v. Fairmont Homes, Inc.* (543 N.E.2d 1130 (Ind. App. 1st Dist. 1989)), when the expert's opinion was based on MMPI interpretations in which the testifying expert did not participate.

> Dr. Bartleson does not consider himself to be an expert in the interpretation of the MMPI. The record does not show who programmed the computer, how the information provided by Sullivan was recorded and fed into the computer, or the scientific acceptability or reliability of the computerized result. (543 N.E.2d at 1133)

Courts have also addressed the difficulty of using the original MMPI in the evaluation of adolescents. In his article "Use of the MMPI With Adolescents in Forensic Settings," Robert Archer (1989) examined the problems inherent in using the MMPI to evaluate adolescents in litigation contexts because little cross-validation work has been done to determine how reliable the results are with adolescents. For a variety of reasons, including such criticisms, MMPI–A (Butcher et al., 1992)—rather than the original MMPI—should be used with adolescents.

In summary, courts allow psychological evidence that is both authoritative and relevant. MMPI results generally pass the authoritative admission requirement. The final admission requirement—determination of relevancy—rests on whether the test results will assist the trier of fact to resolve a question at issue.

The expert witness planning assessment and testimony confronts an array of challenges in the evolving contexts of research, legislation, and case law relevant to the MMPI. A practical approach to these challenges is the focus of chapter 5.

Chapter 5

THE EXPERT WITNESS PREPARES AND PRESENTS

Readers wanting to become—or improve as—expert witnesses may be thinking, "OK, I've learned about the MMPI–2 and about the law, but what do I *do*?" This chapter provides a guide to the steps an expert witness can take in preparing for, conducting, and testifying about a forensic assessment.

The first section discusses some crucial topics to address during the initial contact with the attorney The second section examines essential steps to take when planning, conducting, and writing up the assessment. The third section examines factors that can undermine the expert's deposition and courtroom testimony.

THE INITIAL CONTACT WITH THE ATTORNEY

Psychologists and other professionals who testify about the Minnesota Multiphasic Personality Inventory (MMPI–2) in court may wind up there in a variety of ways. Some may specialize in forensic assessments and market their services to encourage attorneys. Some may focus on providing services to populations who frequently appear before the courts (e.g., battered women seeking restraining orders; parents who are divorcing and seeking custody of their children; chronic pain patients who suffer from a work-related injury). Some psychologists with recognized expertise on the MMPI–2 testify on technical aspects of MMPI–2 administration,

scoring, results, and interpretations. And some, never having been to court before, may be surprised by a subpoena for the testing records of a patient they have not seen for several years.

Whatever the path to the court, the initial contact with the attorney is crucial. All too often, however, both attorney and potential expert witness may be rushed. A hurried phone conversation in which each individual finds no explicit disconfirmation of what he or she hopes or expects about possible arrangements can provide a misleading and dangerous substitute for carefully exploring a potential working relationship.

No set of factors can cover all situations, but addressing the following issues can help prevent mishaps and catastrophes.

The Task and the Client

What does the attorney want? Many may reply that what they want is "consultation" or for the clinician to "look at the case." This is a good start, but what *exactly* does the attorney have in mind?

Does the attorney need someone to conduct a forensic assessment? Does the attorney need an expert to review someone else's assessment and testify about it? Does the attorney just need help—but *not* an expert witness—in understanding the psychological aspects of a case?

Some attorneys can tell you exactly what they are looking for (e.g., "I need someone to conduct a

This chapter contains quotes from *Ethics in Psychotherapy and Counseling: A Practical Guide, Second Edition,* by K. S. Pope and M. J. T Vasquez, © 1998 by Jossey-Bass. Reprinted with permission from John Wiley & Sons, Inc.

psychological evaluation of my client to determine whether she is competent to execute a will"). Some will use a step-by-step "survivor" model: The potential expert advances to the next step only by successfully completing the previous step. For example, imagine the attorney has a new client who claims that an accident at work has caused severe psychological disability. The attorney starts to search for the "right" expert witness.

The attorney begins by giving a potential expert a brief description of the "facts" of the case. The potential expert responds that the symptoms as described do not seem to constitute a severe psychological disability. The no-longer-potential expert hears a quick "thanks for your time" and the dial tone. Unless potential experts arrange to be paid for this consultation, this "thanks" may be all that they receive for phone discussions that may have run on for an hour or two (and for which the attorney bills the client).

The attorney continues to call potential experts until someone says that it is likely or at least possible that the job incidents caused a severe disability. The attorney may then ask the candidate to review the records.

Potential experts who continue to express an opinion favorable to the attorney's case may advance to the next step: conducting a psychological assessment of the client. The attorney may ask for an oral summary of the potential expert's test findings and opinion. If these do not suit the needs of the attorney's case, the process can end right there. If the findings and opinion support the attorney's case, the attorney may hire the potential expert for the next steps: preparing a written assessment report (see chap. 8, this volume) and testifying at a deposition and trial.

That the potential expert's responses at each step allow the process to keep going (i.e., the clinician receives more business and more pay) or stop (perhaps making it unlikely that this particular attorney will contact the potential expert for future cases) can create subtle and not-so-subtle pressures on expert witnesses, a topic discussed later in this book.

There is another reason an attorney may call. In a particular topic area (e.g., using the MMPI–2 to screen applicants for police force or airline pilot positions; using the MMPI–2 to assess psychological harm suffered by rape victims/survivors) or geographic locale, there may be only a few widely known experts whose experience seems to qualify them almost uniquely for a particular case. Sometimes the attorney contacts such experts with no intention of hiring them. The attorney may believe (whether or not accurately) that the expert's testimony would be inherently damaging to his or her case. The attorney may, however, consult these experts so that they are no longer available to the opposing parties in the case. For example, a defense attorney may claim that information that was both confidential and privileged was discussed during the initial consultation, and that a prosecution expert witness should not have this information.

Attorneys have several strategies to block an expert from testifying for the opposing attorney. The attorney may telephone the potential expert and, without offering to retain the expert, simply ask if he or she could spare perhaps 5 minutes to discuss an urgent matter. The attorney may imply that the clinician is being considered as a potential expert.

Or the attorney may prevail on the clinician's (presumed) good nature, generosity, or collegiality, asking for some supposedly minor professional-to-professional consultation for which it would be greedy for the clinician to even think of charging. (After all, the whole conversation will take less than 5 minutes, and the attorney only wants to ask one very brief, very minor question.) The attorney may then give a two- or three-sentence summary of the case and ask a simple question (e.g., "Would the MMPI–2 be a good test to use in evaluating this plaintiff?" or "Is there a professional code of ethics that might be relevant?"). Having kept careful records of this professional consultation in which "crucial" information was shared with the clinician, the attorney is then in a position to move to exclude the expert from testifying for opposing counsel.

The clinician's own personal attorney may help in such situations. The other attorney's conduct could be considered unethical in some jurisdictions. If a pattern of such conduct can be shown, the court may grant other relief, such as allowing the expert witness to be retained by the other side despite the nominal consultation by the previous attorney.

Yet another variation involves the attorney asking his or her client to call the clinician to ask for some information or advice (again involving a brief disclosure of information about the case). Awareness of such strategies to tie up experts can enable potential experts to develop better procedures for handling consultations.

Some attorneys may contact a clinician for the first time through a subpoena for a current or former client's record. The clinician, seeing what appears to be a valid, court-authorized (i.e., perhaps signed by a judge, although some are simply signed by an attorney) demand, may blunder by immediately turning over the requested records to the attorney. This may be a terrible misstep because, depending on the circumstances, the clinician may have been legally required to claim privilege (therapist–patient) on behalf of his or her client. We recommend that a clinician receiving a subpoena consult with his or her own attorney before taking further action. Responding to the subpoena may become a more complex situation if the subpoena demands test items, scoring manuals, and similar materials (see, e.g., Appendixes H, I, and J, this volume).

Finally, in clarifying the task, the expert must figure out who the client is and where the responsibilities lie. Is the expert working for (e.g., is employed and paid by) the attorney? What problems may arise because the attorney's legal client becomes, in effect, the clinician's assessment client? Any potential conflicts need to be addressed during the initial contacts with the attorney. Clarification can become much more difficult in the criminal justice system, such as in cases involving court-ordered assessments. Even if they are working under severe time pressures, clinicians must make sure that they clearly understand the tasks and that they do not violate the accused's rights (e.g., R. D. Miller, 1990). In situations in which the clinician is called on to provide assessment (or treatment) services that are unwanted by the defendant or prisoner, Fersch (1980) has argued that

> it is easier to say that the psychologists' responsibility is to the judges or proba-

tion officers or whoever directs their work in the court. If these court personnel share a similar philosophy, then psychologists have at least two clients, the defendants (the traditional clients) and the court personnel, and psychologists' responsibilities to the two are bound to conflict at times. The ethical problems become more complex, however, when the various personnel within the court have differing philosophies, for this then multiplies the psychologists' clients. (p. 55)

Experts must clarify whether the task is solely assessment or may include treatment or other interventions. Elwork (1992) presented a useful discussion of "psycholegal interventions that integrate traditional psychotherapeutic approaches with the contingencies of the legal context" (p. 181; see also Appendix S, this volume).

Readers interested in a more extensive discussion of issues related to conflicting responsibilities in the forensic arena are referred to *Who Is the Client? The Ethics of Psychological Intervention in the Criminal Justice System* (Monahan, 1980). Other potential conflicts of interest are discussed in some of the following sections in this book.

Distinguishing Therapeutic and Forensic Roles

The attorney may be asking the client's current or previous therapist to conduct an assessment and serve as an expert witness. Potential expert witnesses must clearly distinguish between therapeutic and forensic roles and identify any potential problems in trying to combine the roles. Especially for those new to forensic practice, reading the relevant literature in this controversial area is crucial. Greenberg and Shuman (1997), for example, wrote,

> Expert persons may testify as fact witnesses as well as either of two types of expert witnesses: treating experts and forensic experts. . . . However, a role conflict arises when a treating therapist also attempts to testify as a forensic

expert addressing the psycholegal issues in the case (e.g., testamentary capacity, proximate cause of injury, parental capacity). Although in the preceding description the therapeutic relationship occurs first and the forensic role second, there are parallel concerns with the reverse sequence (i.e., the subsequent provision of therapy by a psychologist or psychiatrist who previously provided a forensic assessment of that litigant). There are also similar concerns about the treating therapist's role in criminal litigation. (p. 50)

The authors discuss "10 principles that underlie why combining these roles is conflicting and problematical" (p. 50). Expert witnesses must be able to provide clear, thoughtful, informed rationales for the roles they assume and anticipate and disclose any potential tensions between their roles.

Two Often Overlooked Restrictions

Health care professionals and others who serve as expert witnesses often overlook two restrictions that can cause problems.

First, professionals considering serving as expert witnesses must find out what restrictions, if any, determine who can testify as an expert witness in the relevant jurisdiction. For example, legislation, case law, or other regulations may specify that only a person with a particular license (e.g., only a licensed physician can testify in a trial in which a physician is accused of malpractice), a particular specialty (e.g., only a cardiac specialist can testify about the standard of care in diagnosing and treating cardiac conditions), or geographic area (e.g., only a person from the relevant state or one of the surrounding states can testify about the standard of care) can testify as an expert witness.

Second, if expert witnesses will be traveling to another state, they must determine whether the work they will be doing (e.g., conducting a psychological and neuropsychological assessment of a litigant) requires a license and, if so, what provisions, if any, the relevant jurisdiction makes for someone who is licensed in another state. Is someone licensed as a psychologist in another state allowed to practice as a psychologist in the relevant state for 30 or 60 days per year, or must the psychologist be licensed in the relevant state to practice in that state? If it is unclear whether the work that the expert witness will be doing in the relevant state requires a license, that should be clarified before the expert witness agrees to do the work.

Competence

The attorney may be looking to the clinician for help in understanding the psychological issues relevant to the case. It is the clinician who bears the responsibility to clarify what the issues are and to ensure that he or she possesses adequate competence or expertise to address those issues. To a psychologist who has never had any training or experience in assessing children and who is about $500 short on office expenses in a given month, a call from an attorney looking for an expert to conduct a psychological evaluation of two children who may have experienced psychological trauma as the result of an auto accident can be difficult to turn away. To a psychologist who has been in practice many years, it is easy to assume that sheer length of experience translates into the ability to hold forth competently on virtually any issue. But not only is the lack of education, training, and supervised experience in a particular area of practice relevant, research suggests that years of experience is no guarantee of expertise and may sometimes be negatively associated with quality of care (see, e.g., Choudhry, Fletcher, & Soumerai, 2005).

Clinicians have an ethical responsibility to be frank with the attorney about whether they have the proper background and credentials to serve as an expert in this particular case. In some instances, the clinician, even though thoroughly qualified to serve as an expert, may refer the attorney to someone whose particular history, skills, and characteristics seem better matched to a given case. For example, a psychologist may have conducted literally thousands of personality assessments using the MMPI–2 and be thoroughly qualified to conduct an assessment of a young woman who is experiencing job stress because of alleged sexual harassment. However, the psychologist may want to suggest that the attorney consider hiring another assessment specialist who focuses on cases of sexual harassment in the workplace, has conducted research in that area, and has served as an expert witness in previous cases of this type.

The Golden Rule may be useful here: Imagine that the potential expert witness must face a malpractice suit sometime in the future and contacts a defense attorney. Would the potential expert want the attorney to grab the case no matter what or refer the expert to another attorney with expertise in the areas of the particular case?

American Psychological Association (APA) policy documents emphasize the necessity of practicing only within the bounds of demonstrable competence and of accurately representing this competence (e.g., APA, 1981, 2002). State licensing laws and administrative regulations may also explicitly require that psychologists limit their practice to areas of demonstrable competence. For example, art. 8 ("Rules of Professional Conduct"), sec. 1396 of California Title 16 states, "The psychologist shall not function outside his or her particular field or fields of competence as established by his or her education, training and experience."

Consider the following scenario: An attorney asks a psychologist with a doctorate in experimental psychology to clinically assess a litigant and prepare a report. One step a psychologist might take in considering whether he or she possessed adequate general education and training in the clinical area would be to review the "American Psychological Association Policy on Training for Psychologists Wishing to Change Their Specialty" (see Appendix R, this volume). The individual must possesses adequate education, training, and experience in the general area (e.g., clinical psychology) of relevant practice as well the specific skills (e.g., administering and interpreting the MMPI–2 or evaluating whether an individual is competent to stand trial).

Conflicts of Interest

The potential expert witness must find out whether there are people, issues, or factors that would create an unacceptable actual or apparent conflict of interest. For example, an attorney may ask a clinician to assess a woman who is suing for custody of her children. The clinician, however, may once have been intimately involved with the woman and be in no position to provide an objective assessment.

As another example, an attorney may ask a psychologist to assess a plaintiff who is filing a malpractice suit against a local hospital. The psychologist may have applied to the hospital repeatedly but unsuccessfully for a staff position. The psychologist's objectivity would be open to serious question. If the psychologist were to conclude that the plaintiff had been severely harmed by the hospital's wrongful acts, it might seem to some that the psychologist's anger and resentment biased the assessment. On the other hand, if the psychologist were to conclude that the plaintiff had suffered no harm whatsoever, it might appear to some that he or she were trying to curry favor with the hospital, hoping to be hired.

In some instances, the potential expert witness must unilaterally decline (despite any urgings by the attorney) a case because of actual or apparent conflicts of interest. If there are relationships that involve confidentiality (e.g., the potential expert, as therapist, provided psychotherapy to the opposing attorney in this case), the potential expert may not be able to provide any specific information but may simply answer any of the attorney's requests for additional information with a statement such as, "I'm sorry, but participating in this case would constitute a potential or actual conflict of interest that I'm not at liberty to discuss."

In other instances, the potential expert bears a responsibility to disclose to the attorney factors that may be relevant to the case and that the attorney needs to be aware of in considering whether to retain the expert. In these instances, the potential expert has decided that the factors do not represent a legal, ethical, clinical, or professional barrier to participation in the case but that the attorney, apprised of these factors, may decide that another professional may be better suited to this case (e.g., that the attorney would be more comfortable working with another professional or that using this particular professional would needlessly complicate the case). For example, the potential expert may be best friends with—or, on the other hand, may have filed formal complaints against—the opposing attorney.

Additional Aspects of Adequate Disclosure

Potential experts owe it to the attorney to provide an accurate picture of their strengths and weaknesses relevant to the case at hand. Obviously, a conflict of interest or a lack of competence in the relevant issues are two of the primary aspects, but there are others. For example, is the potential expert currently under investigation by a hospital peer review committee, a professional ethics committee, or a state licensing agency? Has any agency sustained a complaint against the potential expert? Is there any record of significant violation of the law (something more than, say, a few parking tickets)? Has the expert ever been dismissed for cause from a paid or unpaid position?

Especially if attorneys are handling a mental health case for the first time, they may not understand professional terminology. For example, an attorney who addresses a potential expert witness as "Doctor" may need to be told whether the witness actually does possess a degree at the doctoral level and whether that doctorate is a PhD, a PsyD, an EdD, an MD, a DSW, and so on, and what these various degrees mean. This matter can become exceptionally troublesome if the potential expert has become accustomed to misstating his or her credentials or allowing others to make incorrect assumptions about his or her titles by not offering prompt correction and clarification. Consider the following example.

> Many hospitals function as training institutions. Unfortunately, both the institution and the trainee may engage in extensive rationalization to attempt to justify fraudulently presenting therapists as having qualifications or credentials that they do not possess. Upper level graduate students may be introduced to patients and the public as "Dr. _____." Similarly, interns who are prohibited by the laws of their states and by formal ethical principles

> from presenting themselves as psychologists because they have not yet been licensed may be presented to patients and the public in a flagrantly deceptive manner. (Pope, 1990, p. 1069)

The potential expert must disclose at least three facts about credentialing—(a) degree level, (b) area of degree, and (c) licensing status—and know the relevant professional association policies regarding these issues. For psychologists, the relevant documents include the "Ethical Principles of Psychologists and Code of Conduct" (APA, 2002; these principles and code are presented in Appendix Q, this volume), the *General Guidelines for Providers of Psychological Services* (APA, 1987b), the "Specialty Guidelines for the Delivery of Services" (APA, 1981), "Specialty Guidelines for Forensic Psychologists" (Committee on Ethical Guidelines for Forensic Psychologists, 1991; these guidelines are presented as Appendix S, this volume), the "American Psychological Association Policy on Training for Psychologists Wishing to Change Their Specialty" (Abeles, 1982; J. Conger, 1976; this policy on training is presented as Appendix R, this volume), and the lists of APA-accredited doctoral programs and APA-accredited predoctoral internship programs that generally appear in the December issue of *American Psychologist* (with supplementary lists sometimes appearing in the July issue). The Web page *Ethics Codes & Practice Guidelines for Assessment, Therapy, Counseling, & Forensic Practice* (2005) at http://kspope.com/ethcodes/index.php provides online copies of more than 80 therapy, counseling, forensic, and related ethics and practice codes developed by professional organizations (e.g., of psychologists, psychiatrists, social workers, marriage and family counselors). The section in chapter 9 (this volume) on education and training gives examples of ways in which opposing attorneys can explore these issues during deposition and cross-examination.

No witness or attorney should be blindsided by information that should have been disclosed at an earlier point. Pope and Vetter (1991) provided one example in which a woman brought suit against a previous therapist for engaging in sexual intimacies with her. Her subsequent treating therapist was scheduled to testify on her behalf concerning the standard of care and the way in which the intimacies with the previous therapist had affected the woman. Only at a point immediately before he was to be deposed did the subsequent treating therapist tell the woman's attorney that he himself had been a perpetrator of therapist–patient sex. As emphasized earlier, the Golden Rule exemplifies an important aspect of professional responsibility: The professional must tell the attorney all relevant information, just as the professional expects and wants the attorney to disclose all relevant information.

The Expert as Human

Each expert is a unique, vulnerable human being, and no one has grown up in a vacuum. Everyone has specific historical, cultural, and personal experiences, influences, and viewpoints. These may shape the way one goes about planning, conducting, and interpreting a forensic assessment. A client's condition, words, or behavior can evoke strong reactions from a professional (see, e.g., Epstein & Feiner, 1979; Fromm & Pope, 1990; Heimann, 1950; Pope, 1994; Pope, Sonne, & Greene, 2006; Pope, Sonne, & Holroyd, 1993; Pope & Tabachnick, 1993, 1994; Pope & Vasquez, 2005, in press; Shafer, 1954; Singer, Sincoff, & Kolligian, 1989; see also the section of research articles on "The Therapist As a Person" at http://kspope.com (2006). In some instances, for example, when a psychologist who was sexually abused as a child or was raped or battered as an adult conducts an assessment to determine how deeply sexual or physical abuse may have harmed another individual it is possible that the personal history of the psychologist may influence how he or she conducts the assessment (see Pope & Feldman-Summers, 1992, for a discussion of this issue). Table 5.1 presents data suggesting that two thirds of female and one third of male clinical and counseling psychologists have experienced some form of sexual or physical abuse.

To the degree that expert witnesses are "open and alert to these reactions, and can acknowledge . . . them nondefensively," it is possible that they

TABLE 5.1

Percentage of Male and Female Participants Reporting Abuse

Type of abuse	Men	Women
Abuse during childhood or adolescence		
Sexual abuse by relative	5.84	21.05
Sexual abuse by teacher	0.73	1.96
Sexual abuse by physician	0.0	1.96
Sexual abuse by therapist	0.0	0.0
Sexual abuse by nonrelative (other than those previously listed)	9.49	16.34
Nonsexual physical abuse	13.14	9.15
At least one of the above	26.28	39.22
Abuse during adulthood		
Sexual harassment	1.46	37.91
Attempted rape	0.73	13.07
Acquaintance rape	0.0	6.54
Stranger rape	0.73	1.31
Nonsexual physical abuse by a spouse or partner	6.57	12.42
Nonsexual physical abuse by an acquaintance	0.0	2.61
Nonsexual physical abuse by a stranger	4.38	7.19
Sexual involvement with a therapist	2.19	4.58
Sexual involvement with a physician	0.0	1.96
At least one of the above	13.87	56.86
Abuse during childhood, adolescence, or adulthood	32.85	69.93

Note. From "National Survey of Psychologists' Sexual and Physical Abuse History and Their Evaluation of Training and Competence in these areas," by K. S. Pope and S. Feldman-Summers, 1992, *Professional Psychology: Research and Practice, 23,* p. 355. Copyright 1992 by the American Psychological Association.

may even "constitute valuable sources of information" (Sonne & Pope, 1991, p. 176) that help the professional make sure that the assessment is conducted sensitively, respectfully, and fairly. To be aware of one's limitations or potential biases—as well as one's strengths and potential to recognize and avoid, transcend, or at least take into account bias—is a significant responsibility.

Psychologists and other expert witnesses are not invulnerable to intense emotional distress. A national survey of psychologists who worked as therapists found that more than one half (61%) reported experiencing clinical depression, more than one fourth (29%) reported having felt suicidal, and approximately 1/25 (4%) reported having been hospitalized as part of their mental health treatment (Pope

& Tabachnick, 1994). Expert witnesses must maintain *emotional competence* (see Pope & Brown, 1996; Pope & Vasquez, 1998, 2005).

Sometimes cases challenge mental health professionals because of personal beliefs, opinions, or values. Loftus, for example, described her agonizing decision about whether to testify about the problems with eyewitness identification and the fallibility of memory in the defense of a man accused of committing almost unimaginably heinous acts (Loftus & Ketcham, 1991). In this case, the accused—John Demjanjuk, whom people had identified as "Ivan the Terrible" from the Nazi death camps during World War II—maintained that he was the victim of mistaken identity. Loftus believed that the identification process was flawed.

> A case that relied on thirty-five-year-old memories should have been enough by itself. Add to those decaying memories the fact that the witnesses knew before they looked at the photographs that the police had a suspect, and they were even given the suspect's first and last name—Ivan Demjanjuk. Add to that scenario the fact that the Israeli investigators asked the witnesses if they could identify John Demjanjuk, a clearly prejudicial and leading question. Add to that the fact that the witnesses almost certainly talked about their identification afterward, possibly contaminating subsequent identifications. Add to that the repeated showing of John Demjanjuk's photograph so that with each exposure, his face became more and more familiar and the witnesses became more and more confident and convincing. (Loftus & Ketcham, 1991, p. 224)

Should the accused have access to her impartial scientific testimony on such issues as previous defendants have had, or did the special nature of the accusations and the special group of survivors pose an insurmountable barrier? On the one hand, "To be true to my work, I must judge this case as I have judged every case before it. If there are problems

with the eyewitness identification, I must testify. It's the consistent thing to do" (p. 232). But in the end, Loftus decided not to testify because of the special value she places on the memories of this particular group of survivors and the fact that her impartial scientific testimony about the fallibility of memory would have come across as an indictment of or attack on the memories of these survivors. "I could only think how precious the survivors' memories were. . . . I could not have taken the stand and talked about the fallibility of memory without every person in that audience believing that I was indicting the specific memories of the survivors. I would have been perceived as attacking their memories. I couldn't do it" (p. 237).

Each expert witness has an inescapable responsibility to conduct this kind of searching inventory of personal beliefs, opinions, and values and to determine their potential influences. To use the categories that Loftus set forth, are there defendants for whom we could not testify, regardless of serious questions about guilt or innocence, because of the nature of the charges they are facing? Are there other categories of defendants for whom we might be eager to testify? Are there certain groups of survivors whose memories seem so precious that we would feel it impossible to testify about the fallibility of memory because it might, however invalidly, be perceived as an attack on their memories? Are there other groups of survivors about whom we would have no qualms testifying, or whose memories we might be eager to attack?

Sometimes the potential influence of our own beliefs, personal (rather than expert) opinions, and values are reasonably clear to us, but many times these influences are elusive, subtle, complex, and easy to escape notice. The expert must make sure that these factors do not bias expert testimony.

Scheduling

Consider the following hypothetical scenario.

Attorney: Hello, Dr. Smith. I'm an attorney representing a plaintiff in a personal injury suit. My client was badly injured in an automobile accident. I believe it is clear that this trauma has affected her personality, her ability to work, her relationship with her family, and virtually all aspects of her life. I need someone to take a look at her medical records, talk with her husband and her work supervisor, talk with her, and—I wouldn't presume to tell you how to do your job, but—give her some general personality tests to find any evidence of neuropsychological impairment. I need someone who can tell the jury how tragically this accident has affected her and her life. You come highly recommended by [the attorney gives the name of someone you've never heard of]. Would you be interested?

Potential Expert: Well, I've done that kind of work before; it's a field I've specialized in. Part of my decision would depend on the time frame. Can you tell me what sort of schedule you have in mind?

Attorney: We're moving right along on this case. If you could review the records and complete the examination this evening and tomorrow morning—I can make my client available to you at your convenience any time this evening or before lunch tomorrow—I'd like to put you on the stand tomorrow afternoon.

This scenario may strike some readers as a wild exaggeration. Others will find it hauntingly familiar. In any event, it is crucial that the potential experts make sure they have time to do their work.

A basic question is how much work will this take? A comprehensive psychological and neuropsychological assessment—maybe including family, employer, and coworker interviews—can take much more time than an attorney had in mind. Some psychological examinations take several sessions, which may need to be spaced out over several days or weeks.

Scheduling must also take account of the availability of documents for review. It can take a long while and much work to track down school, court, or employment records—some of them quite dated—necessary to understand the client's current condition and how distant or more recent events (such as surviving an airplane crash, being battered by a partner, or losing a child because of medical malpractice) may have affected that condition.

It is easy to underestimate the potential expert's current work load and the sometimes unpredictable nature of forensic work. New cases tempt even professionals who are already overworked and overbooked. Taking on a forensic case can mean canceling a day of patient appointments because of a deposition, only to find the scheduled deposition cancelled several times at the last moment. Forensic cases can also lead professionals to clear a week of patient appointments so that they may travel to another city to testify, only to find the trial continued a number of times. It can be hard—sometimes impossible—to meet patients' clinical needs while juggling court cases calling for us to leave town. Each professional's approach to treatment, clientele, personal resources, resilience, and ability to maintain a solid clinical practice despite sometimes unpredictable calls to testify are unique. Professionals must carefully monitor their current work load, potential for burnout, and chances of being stretched too thin (see the chapter on "Creating Strategies for Self-Care" in Pope & Vasquez, 2005).

Financial Arrangements

Discussing fee issues makes some health service providers uncomfortable, but expert witnesses must discuss money with attorneys during initial contacts. The professional must make clear the charges, the methods and schedules of payment, reimbursement for expenses, payment for travel and lodging, and anything else that is relevant.

Does the attorney want the professional to testify as an expert witness, a fact witness, or both? Local laws can create different payments for an expert witness (i.e., one who has special knowledge and opinions that might help the trier-of-fact to understand the facts and issues) and as a percipient witness (also termed a lay or fact witness; i.e., one who was involved in some way, perhaps as an eyewitness or the subsequent treating therapist, and can help establish the facts of the case). Expert witnesses can usually command their customary fees, as long as they are reasonable. Local laws may set specific fees for percipient witnesses, generally at a much lower level than what expert witnesses can charge. Attorneys who hire experts tend to pay most of the fees, but opposing counsels will often, depending on the jurisdiction, pay the deposition fees for any witnesses they depose.

Expert witnesses use different methods to charge for their time. The hourly charge is probably most common. Some charge different amounts per hour depending on the work. They may, for example, charge more for court appearances. Experts must make clear the charges for the different kinds of work they do—for example, phone consultations with the attorneys, interviews, psychological testing, scoring and interpreting tests, reviewing records, providing feedback about findings in oral or written form, traveling to and from depositions and courtroom testimony, time spent waiting to testify, time scheduled for testing sessions or depositions that are cancelled without enough notice, time spent in depositions or courtroom testimony. It is a good idea to tell the attorney the estimated time and expense if things go relatively smoothly and the time and expense if Murphy's Law takes over.

Some professionals find it easier to charge a set fee for each task. The professional bases the charges on the average time the work tends to take. Obviously, if the tasks take a shorter time, the professional comes out ahead. But one case in which nothing goes right can erase those windfalls.

One benefit of the set fee for each task is that it clarifies completely for the attorney (and the attorney's client) exactly how much retaining this expert will cost. By contrast, when the expert charges by the hour, both the expert and the attorney may have no idea how many hours will be needed to review the hundreds or thousands of pages of relevant documents that accumulate during legal proceedings (e.g., previous medical, psychological, educational, and legal records and depositions by other experts and by percipient witnesses).

An expert may also carefully research the professional literature. Even though the expert *is* an authentic expert, preparation may require carefully examining—or reexamining—many books, articles, and other documents. If the expert does not tell the attorney about this process before the initial agreement is signed, the charges may seem like outrageous padding.

Expert and attorney should discuss the ways opposing attorneys can challenge the fee arrangement.

For example, assume the expert charges $300 for every hour spent on the case. The expert travels to another city for the trial and charges for every hour he or she is out of town. The expert explains that travel is case-related and each hour out of town is an hour away from the therapy practice or other income-producing work. The expert boards a plane at night, flies to the city in which the trial is held, spends the night at a hotel near the courthouse, testifies one day, then flies home exactly 24 hours after leaving. The expert earns $7,200 for this trip (i.e., 24 hours × $300 per hour). The cross-examination might go as follows.

Attorney: Let's see, you arrived in our fair city about 10 p.m. and checked into a hotel last night—is that your testimony?

Expert: Yes.

Attorney: And what time did you go to sleep?

Expert: Around 11 p.m.

Attorney: And what time did you get up this morning?

Expert: At 6 a.m.

Attorney: You slept from 11 p.m. last night until 6 a.m. this morning?

Expert: Yes.

Attorney: While you were asleep last night from 11 p.m. until midnight, you earned $300?

Expert: Well, actually I wouldn't put it quite that way. You have to understand that I calculate my fees so that . . .

Attorney: Would you please answer the question with a "yes" or "no": Did you earn $300 while you were asleep last night from 11 p.m. to midnight?

Expert: [after looking to his or her attorney who remains unhelpfully silent] If you put it that way, yes.

Attorney: [looking at the jury who may be comparing and contrasting the way they earn wages to the way the expert earns wages] And you slept from midnight to 1 a.m.?

Expert: Yes.

Attorney: And during that hour of sleep you also earned $300?

Expert: Yes.

Attorney: So by 1 a.m.—just to make sure I have it right—you've earned [the attorney may have developed interesting ways of pronouncing, inflecting, and emphasizing the word *earned*] a total of $600 in regard to your participation as an expert witness in this case by sleeping two hours at the hotel. Is that correct?

Expert: Yes.

Attorney: Now from 1 a.m. to 2 a.m. you were also asleep, is that your testimony?

Perhaps the greatest blunder that a potential expert witness can make in creating fee arrangements is to make the fee dependent in any way on the outcome of the case. In some states, it is unethical for an attorney to pay such a fee to an expert witness.

On the face of it, these fee arrangements create a clear conflict of interest. Judges and juries can reason that the expert witness faces a constant choice while gathering data, examining it, and testifying: certain testimony will maximize the chances that the expert will get paid *and* will receive the highest possible amount.

Opposing attorneys can use several methods to discredit an expert using contingency fees. For example, attorneys may ask experts to read from standard forensic psychology texts and comment on the prohibitions against contingency fees. David Shapiro, for example, served as president of the American Academy of Forensic Psychology and as chair of the ethics committee of the American Board of Professional Psychology. In his book *Forensic Psychological Assessment*, he emphasized, "the expert witness should never, under any circumstances, accept a referral on a contingent fee basis" (1991, p. 230). Another forensic specialist, the late Theodore Blau, who served as president of the APA, also stressed in his text *The Psychologist as Expert Witness* that "the psychologist should never accept a fee contingent upon the outcome of a case" (1984b, p. 336).

This is crucial: The expert is never paid to produce a particular opinion. Clever cross-examination can trip up the unprepared expert and make it appear that the expert has agreed to mouth an opinion-for-hire. Experts must always make clear that they are paid for performing a professional task or for their time and *not* for producing specific testimony. Pope and Bouhoutsos (1986) described an instance in which an attorney was cross-examining an expert witness about her fee. The attorney asked the expert how much she was being paid to recite the opinion. The expert responded that the fee she charged was not for her opinion but for her time. "And just how much will you be paid for that?" sneered the attorney. The witness replied, "That depends on how long you keep me up here" (p. 140).

Each legitimate form of charging has strengths and weaknesses. What is essential is that both expert and attorney clarify the nature of charges by the expert, how the fee is to be determined, and the schedule for payment (see Appendixes L, M, N, and O, this volume). Some experts, for example, may require all fees be paid in advance. Others specify that fees are to be paid within 30 days of submission of a written bill. Whatever the payment arrangements, the formal agreement must answer the question, "What, if anything, happens if the expert is not paid at the time specified for payment?"

Once an agreement on the nature, method, schedule, and other factors related to payments has been reached, a written agreement should be prepared to prevent future disagreements stemming from divergent memories of the original financial arrangements (see Appendix L, this volume).

Recordings and Third-Party Observers

Sometimes attorneys attempt to arrange for a third party to be present during the assessment or for a recording (videotape, audiotape, transcription, etc.) to be made (see chap. 6, this volume). If there is an objection and the attorneys cannot settle the issue between themselves, the judge may have to rule on what kind of observer or recording, if any, is to be a part of the assessment process.

Experts must be familiar with the relevant policy statements, research, and other articles. For example, if the assessment involves neuropsychological issues, the expert witness should know such articles as the American Academy of Clinical Neuropsychology's (2001) Policy Statement on the Presence of Third Party Observers in Neuropsychological Assessment, Axelrod et al.'s (2000) Presence of Third Party Observers During Neuropsychological Testing: Official Statement of the National Academy of Neuropsychology, and McSweeny et al.'s (1998) Ethical Issues Related to the Presence of Third Party Observers in Clinical Neuropsychological Evaluations. The expert should also be familiar with Constantinou, Ashendorf, and McCaffrey's (2002) finding that "in the presence of an audio-recorder the performance of the participants on memory tests declined. Performance on motor tests, on the other hand, was not affected by the presence of an audio-recorder" (p. 407).

Communication, Privilege, Secrets, and Surprises

Lines of communication among participants in a legal case can become tangled unless the expert and the attorney discuss mandatory, discretionary, and prohibited communications during their initial contacts. Depending on the circumstances and the jurisdiction, a professional hired as a consultant to an attorney may be both able and required to keep confidential—from the court and from the opposing attorneys—all aspects of the consultant work. Such work may be privileged and shielded—at least under normal circumstances—from all who are not directly involved in preparing the attorney's case.

Again, depending on the circumstances and the jurisdiction, an expert witness may be obligated to disclose virtually all relevant information and opinions to the opposing attorney during deposition. In some situations, there may be exceptions; some communications between expert witnesses and attorneys may be privileged, and some of the professional's work for the attorney may be shielded as "work product."

If the professional plans to administer, score, and interpret an MMPI–2 as part of an assessment of the lawyer's client, to whom is the professional expected to provide the final report, the raw test data, and the MMPI–2 form itself? How, for example, will the client receive feedback concerning the

test (see, e.g., Butcher, 1990b; Finn & Tonsager, 1992; Fischer, 1985; Gass & Brown, 1992; Pope, 1992; Pope & Vasquez, 1998)? Is the professional expected to meet with the client to review and discuss the results? Is it possible the client will hear the results (and their implications) for the first time while the professional testifies as an expert witness in court? Is the professional obligated to provide the test report, raw test data, and the MMPI–2 form to opposing counsel? Will the professional be able to request that such documents be delivered to a qualified psychologist who works for opposing counsel? If such a request is made, is there legal support for it in the jurisdiction? Discussion and clarification of such issues are crucial during initial contacts. (Some of these issues are addressed in Appendixes L and N, this volume.)

Communication can become tangled if an attorney's initial contact with a professional is through a subpoena to provide information about a psychological evaluation that was conducted some time in the past. Because *any* evaluation may become the focus of a lawsuit or other demand for information, those who conduct evaluations must clarify the ethical and legal ground rules for providing or withholding information about an evaluation. Clarification should become a routine part of any assessment.

Pope and Vasquez (1998) presented a fictional vignette highlighting the sometimes bewildering aspects of unexpected demands for information.

> A seventeen-year-old boy comes to your office and asks for a comprehensive psychological evaluation. He has been experiencing some headaches, anxiety, and depression. A high school dropout, he has been married for a year and has a one-year-old baby, but has left his wife and child and returned to live with his parents. He works full time as an auto mechanic and has insurance that covers the testing procedures.
>
> You complete the testing. During the following year you receive requests for information about the testing from:

- the boy's physician, an internist
- the boy's parents, who are concerned about his depression
- the boy's employer, in connection with a worker's compensation claim filed by the boy
- the attorney for the insurance company that is contesting the worker's compensation claim
- the attorney for the boy's wife, who is suing for divorce and for custody of the baby
- the boy's attorney, who is considering suing you because he does not like the results of the tests

Each of the requests asks for: the full formal report, the original test data, and copies of each of the tests you administered (for example, instructions and all items for the MMPI).

To which of these people are you ethically or legally obligated to supply all information requested, partial information, a summary of the report, or no information at all? For which requests is having the boy's written informed consent for release of information relevant? (pp. 147–148)

Some attorneys do not know all the requirements that may affect a psychologist or other professional conducting an assessment. For example, the attorney may be handling a wrongful discharge suit on behalf of a company's former employee. The attorney specializes in employment law but is new to mental health law. The attorney hires a psychologist to conduct a comprehensive psychological evaluation of the woman who was fired and asks that information from her family also be gathered so that the psychologist can testify not only about the harm that the firing caused the former employee but also about the collateral stresses and disruptions the firing caused the woman's family.

The psychologist schedules a meeting with the woman, her husband, and their 10-year-old daughter. He asks them as a group to discuss their history as a family, what life was like while the mother was

employed by the company, and what happened after she was fired. The daughter suddenly discloses a secret: that she had been sexually molested by her uncle. The father rushes from the room, shouting that he is going to kill the man who molested his daughter as soon as he can find him. At this point, the psychologist may face two responsibilities (again, depending on applicable law in that jurisdiction and the specific circumstances). The law may require the psychologist to make an oral and subsequent written report to child protective services within a specified period of time regarding suspicions of child abuse. The law may also require the psychologist to take reasonable steps to protect an identified third party (i.e., the uncle), whom the father has threatened to kill. These protective steps may involve disclosing information that would otherwise remain confidential. The expert and attorney need to discuss such possibilities, however unlikely they may seem.

Other Needs and Expectations

Experts and attorneys must discuss other services, materials, and so on, that each may need and expect from the other. Experts, for example, may need a variety of previous records to form an adequate professional opinion. They may need records of previous assessments (particularly any previous administrations of the MMPI–2), school records, employment records, and medical records. If these are not already available, it may be much more efficient and effective for the attorney to secure them. A clinician in independent practice may make many calls and send repeated written requests (accompanied by a written release of information form signed by the client) to an employer, the client's previous therapist, a school system, or an attorney who handled previous cases for the client. These calls and requests may bring no response. A phone call from an attorney or a written request on stationery with a law firm's letterhead may attract much greater attention from the recipient. Putting the written request in the form of a subpoena also tends to catch attention.

The expert can make clear during initial contacts why and how such previous records are a necessary part of the forensic assessment process and can reach agreement with the attorney—in writing—about how the records are to be obtained.

As another example, the expert may also require time and services from the attorney in preparing for the deposition or for courtroom testimony. The expert may want to meet with the attorney several days before the deposition (and again immediately before the trial) to discuss findings, to cover questions to be asked during direct examination, and to anticipate the opposing attorney's possible approaches to cross-examination. Some experts find these sessions essential and invaluable. Some attorneys resist preparatory sessions as a waste of time and money, but many recognize the benefits.

CONDUCTING AN ASSESSMENT

This part of the expert's work can *seem* so simple—what could be so hard about administering a few tests?—that it can cause major problems that do not show up until deposition and cross-examination. The following section provides a step-by-step guide to major issues and pitfalls in conducting an assessment.

Reviewing the Issues and the Literature

The expert witness must be competent and current on all relevant aspects of the evaluation. Assume, for example, that an attorney hires an expert to conduct a custody evaluation. The professional has vast experience in this area. In this particular case, however, while making an initial review of the case documents, the professional discovers that one of the parents has a chronic disease with which the professional has little familiarity. The rare disease tends to be associated with a somewhat shortened life span and may, in some instances, become debilitating. Part of the preparation for the assessment may involve consulting medical specialists, reviewing the professional literature to see if there is any discussion of a potential relation between the disease and the ability to provide adequate parenting, and checking the assessment literature to determine the degree to which disease has been included or studied as a variable.

Virtually any case will have aspects for which the expert will need to brush up on recent research.

Sometimes these aspects may not be discovered until the middle of the assessment process. The professional may need to tell an attorney that an assessment-in-progress should be supplemented—or replaced—by an assessment conducted by a specialist. For example, a clinician who specializes in assessing women who have been raped may come to suspect, during the assessment process, that the woman shows signs of neuropsychological problems. These problems may be caused by the rape (e.g., the rapist struck her head) or unrelated to the rape (perhaps involving a tumor, a blood clot, or a vessel rupture in the brain). The clinician who lacks expertise in neuropsychological assessment needs to note the signs of possible neuropsychological impairment and recommend that a qualified neuropsychologist or similar specialist conduct an assessment (or at least review the data from the current assessment to see if evaluation is warranted).

Choosing the Tests to Fit the Tasks

Imagine that an attorney pitches the following proposition.

I handle only cases in which large companies have reason to believe that an employee has engaged in theft from the company's store. I represent the company. What I want you to do is to administer an MMPI–2 to each employee that one of my client companies suspects is stealing and let me know if they're guilty or not. I'll pay you $2,000 per employee, and I can guarantee that you'll be testing at least 10 employees a month. I don't need you to swear that you're absolutely certain that the person committed the theft or not. All I want is for you to write a test report giving your best professional opinion based solely on the MMPI–2 as to whether you believe that the employee likely engaged in theft or not. All I want is some general indication so that we'll know whether to follow-up on the employee or not. Plus, we want something to put in the employee's personnel file to document that we had some reason to investigate fully and, where warranted, to fire them. You won't need to worry about getting sued: The companies will indemnify you, and I'll take out a $25 million professional liability policy on you. But I need an answer right now because I want to start the testing program this week. Will you take the job?

Maybe there are a few psychologists somewhere who would not be painfully tempted. The attorney is offering a minimum payment of $20,000 per month for administering and interpreting a few MMPI–2s, along with a policy to protect against losses from malpractice suits.

Here is the cold water: The psychologist *must* ask, "Has the MMPI–2 been adequately validated for this purpose? Do methodologically sound studies published in peer-reviewed journals provide evidence that the MMPI–2 can effectively distinguish between employees who have been stealing from their companies and employees who have not engaged in such theft?" Sections 9.02(a) and 9.02(b) of the American Psychological Association's (2002) "Ethical Principles of Psychologists and Code of Conduct" speak clearly to this issue.

9.02 Use of Assessments

(a) Psychologists administer, adapt, score, interpret, or use assessment techniques, interviews, tests, or instruments in a manner and for purposes that are appropriate in light of the research on or evidence of the usefulness and proper application of the techniques.

(b) Psychologists use assessment instruments whose validity and reliability have been established for use with members of the population tested. When such validity or reliability has not been established, psychologists describe the strengths and limitations of test results and interpretation.

As another example, there is no adequate evidence that MMPI–2 scores, in and of themselves, provide comprehensive and adequate screening for neuropsychological damage. The MMPI–2, of course, may be used as *one* of the tests in a comprehensive psychological and neuropsychological assessment. Reitan and Wolfson (1985), for example, wrote that "the Minnesota Multiphasic Personality Inventory is also frequently administered with the HRNB (Halstead–Reitan Neuropsychological Test Battery), not as a neuropsychological procedure for evaluation of brain functions, but to provide information regarding any emotional distress or personality disturbance the patient may be experiencing" (p. 39). Similarly, Lezak (1983) noted that

the sheer variety of brain injuries and of problems attendant upon organicity probably helps explain the unsatisfactory results of MMPI–2 scale and sign approaches. Moreover, the MMPI–2 was not constructed for neuropsychological assessment and may be inherently inappropriate for this purpose.

. . .

Thus, for brain damaged patients, acknowledgment of specific symptoms accounts for some of the elevation of specific scales. Premorbid tendencies and the patient's reactions to his disabilities also contribute to the MMPI–2 profile. The combination of symptom description, the anxiety and distress occasioned by central nervous system defects, and the need for heroic adaptive measures probably account for the frequency with which brain damaged patients produce neurotic profiles. (pp. 611–613)

Psychologist Kirk Heilbrun (1992) of the Medical College of Virginia outlined several considerations for psychologists who are planning forensic assessments. He wrote that adequate availability and documentation are two important criteria for test selection.

The test is commercially available and adequately documented in two

81

sources. First, it is accompanied by a manual describing its development, psychometric properties, and procedure for administration. Second, it is listed and reviewed in *Mental Measurements Yearbook* or some other readily available source. (p. 264)

Tests should also meet the more general criteria (i.e., for use in nonforensic as well as forensic settings) regarding validity, reliability, administration, scoring, and interpretation as set forth in *Standards for Educational and Psychological Testing* (APA, 1999) and similar policy documents. Chapter 9 provides examples of detailed deposition and cross-examination questions to explore issues relating tests to assessment tasks in forensic settings.

United States. v. Huberty (50 M.J. 704 (A.F. Ct. Crim. App. 2000)), in which an appellate court upheld a decision to preclude a psychologist's MMPI–2-based testimony, provides an example of the reasoning courts may use in deciding whether a psychological test fits the task at hand and is used in a way that is supported by research and has gained widespread acceptance in the scientific community.

The military judge did not allow Dr. Campbell to testify that: only an exhibitionist would have conducted himself in the manner that BV testified; that exhibitionists will consistently produce certain test results on the MMPI–2; that appellant did not produce those results; and, therefore, that appellant is not an exhibitionist.

Appellant was unable to establish that the challenged testimony has gained widespread acceptability in the scientific community. In fact, Dr. Campbell testified that he was only aware of one psychologist who attempted to offer a similar theory in another jurisdiction. Dr. Campbell also admitted that there are no published studies supporting the theory that psychological testing can exclude a person from a psychological diagnosis of exhibitionism. Because this theory was unpublished (and thereby not subjected to peer review), Dr. Campbell also acknowledged it had yet to be subjected to testing. We hold, therefore, that the military judge did not err in excluding this testimony because it was unreliable. (See *United States v. Latorre,* 53 M.J. 179 (2000))

Even if the military judge had admitted the testimony that Dr. Campbell was unable to characterize appellant as an exhibitionist, the remainder of the proposed testimony at issue was not legally relevant. See Houser, supra. As the military judge noted, "The issue before the court was not whether or not the accused was an exhibitionist, but whether, on one particular occasion, he exposed himself in a public place." At a minimum, Dr. Campbell's proferred extrapolation—that, because he could not characterize appellant as an exhibitionist, he could absolutely eliminate appellant as someone who would commit the charged conduct at the pool—would have constituted improper use of profile evidence. (See *United States v. Banks,* 36 M.J. 150, 160–163 (C.M.A. 1992))

Choosing the Tests to Fit the Individual

Tests must demonstrate adequate validity and reliability not only for the task at hand but also for the test taker. Does research validate the scoring and interpretation hypotheses using a specific test with individuals who match the client's age, sex, race, and culture if these are salient variables? To take an extreme example of tests not fitting the individual, imagine giving the English-language MMPI–2 to someone who did not read English or giving the MMPI–2 (instead of the MMPI–A) to a 14-year-old.

Some individuals with disabilities may require reasonable accommodations that include departing from the usual methods of test administration. D. Lee, Reynolds, and Willson (2003) noted that

> 1999 Standards for Educational and Psychological Testing adopted by AERA [American Educational Research Association], APA, and NCME [National Council on Measurement in Education] requires examiners to make reasonable accommodations for individuals with disabilities when administering psychological tests to such persons. Changes in test administration may be required, but the Standards also require the examiner to provide evidence associated with the validity of test score interpretation in the face of such changes in administration. (p. 55)

Informing the Client

Professionals must make sure that clients understand why they are in a professional's office and what is going to happen to them. Some clients may have no idea why they have been sent to see a mental health professional. Some may not understand that the professional *is* a professional (e.g., a psychologist), what that sort of professional does, and so on.

The professional often has legal responsibility to ensure that the client understands the process and freely consents to it. A written form may be useful in documenting such consent and making sure that all relevant items are covered (see Appendix M, this volume). For example, does the client understand that you have been retained by the client's attorney (if that is the case) to conduct a psychological assessment? Does the client understand that you will be preparing a written report (if that is the case) and to whom you will be submitting the report (e.g., to the client's attorney)? Does the client understand that confidentiality may *not* apply, that you may testify about the assessment? Does the client understand this arrangement and consent to it?

Does the client have any questions, even if they concern topics that you have not covered?

The issues become more complicated if the professional has not been retained by the client's attorney but by the opposing attorney or if the court has ordered the testing.

Taking Adequate Notes

Professionals must make sure that they preserve adequate accurate information. Opposing attorneys can take advantage of the ways in which the passage of time may obliterate or significantly distort the professional's memory of an assessment, the client, and the conditions of the assessment. For example, the professional who conducts 100 assessments each year may have a hard time remembering each client.

In one case, an attorney deposed a psychologist several years after the psychologist's last assessment session with the client. The attorney asked the psychologist to describe the client. The psychologist had complete records of the test data, scoring, and interpretation but had not written down anything about the client's appearance, Unable to remember what the client looked like, the psychologist had to admit—under oath and with a court reporter taking down every word—that he had no idea whether the client was 4'10" or 6'2"; whether the client weighed around 120 or 250 lbs; whether the client did not need glasses or contact lenses, customarily wore glasses or contacts, wore them only for reading, or wore them while taking the psychological tests; whether the man had black hair, white hair, or was bald; and that he did not know whether the man had any facial scars or distinguishing characteristics. He did not even know the client's race or ethnic group.

Experts must keep in mind that their notes are not private in legal cases. They are likely to be scrutinized—*carefully*—by opposing attorneys. Even the shortest, seemingly most trivial phrase in the notes can wind up as the focus of extensive deposition questioning and cross examination. Attorneys may make excerpts from the notes into large displays and use them effectively during cross-examination. Avoid notes that are ambiguous, easily misconstrued, or without adequate context (so that the expert can point out if a misleading fragment has clearly been taken out of context).

Addressing Special Needs and Circumstances

Special needs and circumstances can—if not identified and adequately addressed—undermine the validity of a forensic assessment.

Vision. If the testing depends on the ability to see (e.g., a test involving copying geometric shapes, reading, or recognizing visual patterns), the professional must find out if the individual has any visual difficulties. For example, does the client normally wear glasses or contact lenses for reading or for the types of tasks involved in the assessment? If so, is the client wearing those glasses or contacts during assessment? Unless asked, some clients may be reluctant to disclose that they forgot to bring their reading glasses; they may attempt to take the tests with a visual problem that will affect their responses. Some professionals who administer psychological tests find it useful to keep some inexpensive reading glasses of different strengths in their office. If an examinee has forgotten to bring reading glasses, the professional might have some of the same strength and the assessment will not have to be rescheduled.

Is the light in the room adequate, or does it cause any problems? Does the light produce an annoying glare, or is it shining directly in the client's eyes? Some professionals may conduct assessment sessions in hospitals, clinics, prisons, schools, or office buildings in which the testing room is illuminated by florescent lights, which may cause headaches or visual problems for some individuals.

Hearing. If the assessment involves the individual's ability to hear (e.g., test instructions that are read aloud by the examiner or such tests as the Seashore Rhythm Test of the Halstead–Reitan Neuropsychological Test Battery), the professional needs to determine the degree to which the individual's ability to hear is attenuated to any significant degree. If a client customarily wears a hearing aid, is it in use and functioning properly throughout the examination? Are there any acoustical conditions in the room or external noises (e.g., loud noises in the hallway, construction work in an adjacent lot, or an air-conditioning unit producing an irritating rattle) that affect the individual's ability to hear clearly? As mentioned previously, the MMPI–2 may be administered using American Sign Language to those who cannot hear (Brauer, 1992); this method of administration should be noted in the forensic report.

Arm and hand movements. Some clients suffer from injuries to the hand or arm, carpal tunnel syndrome, neurological disorders affecting muscle control, diabetic nephropathy, and other conditions that may make the physical aspects of responding to some tests—especially those administered via computer—difficult or painful. Using three methods—asking the client directly, reviewing medical records, *and* observing the client during the assessment—helps the expert witness to make sure that such conditions are identified and do not undermine the assessment's validity. If one method does not work (e.g., the client denies a relevant condition), the others may.

Mobility and access. Clients may have special physical needs that can affect the validity of the assessment process. For example, a client may use a wheelchair. However, the office building, hospital, or other locale of the assessment may lack convenient access to the assessment room (e.g., the assessment room may be up three flights of stairs—with no working elevator—and have a very narrow door). The professional who conducts the assessment may be forced to consider alternative test sites (e.g., a cafeteria or lounge on the first floor) that may be extremely inappropriate for testing. Similarly, the assessment room's table on which the psychologist places the MMPI–2 or lays out the materials of the WAIS–III, Bender Gestalt Test, or Halstead–Reitan Neuropsychological Test Battery, may be constructed in such a way that its height and legs do not allow a person in a wheelchair to use it comfortably (or, in some cases, at all). The client may need to use the restroom before the testing and the only restroom in the building may not be wheelchair accessible.

Such circumstances require the professional conducting the assessment to confront two essential issues with care, candor, and integrity. First, do these conditions allow an adequate, valid, and fair assessment? Second, what responsibilities do professionals have to make sure the environment is accessible, convenient, and appropriate for all who seek (or are required to obtain) professional services?

Language, reading, and writing. Is the individual fluent in the relevant language? For example, the professional may be conducting the assessment in English, but English may be a second, third, or subsequent language—perhaps recently acquired—for some test takers. Obviously, if the test taker has trouble reading the instructions or the test itself, any results may be misleading at best.

Professionals who use the MMPI–2 need to make sure—although the inventory provides internal checks—that clients currently have at least a fifth-grade reading level (Butcher, Dahlstrom, Graham, Tellegen, & Kaemmer, 1989; Paolo, Ryan, & Smith, 1991; see also chaps. 2 and 9, this volume).

Physical illness or disorders. As anyone who has tried to do even the most routine work while suffering from a bad case of the flu will instantly understand, illness or physical pain and disorders can affect an individual's ability to perform a task. Those conducting psychological assessments must determine whether the individual is sick, in pain, or suffering from any physical disorder. The individual may not spontaneously volunteer such information. For example, the attorney may have told the client that the testing session is extremely important and that the client must by all means show up on time and complete the tests. Then the client shows up for testing while suffering an excruciating back spasm, debilitating arthritis attack, or migraine headache. The professional must determine whether tests administered under such conditions will have any real validity.

Professionals must also determine whether they can validly rule out neuropsychological impairment. Neuropsychological impairment may not, as discussed previously, be readily identifiable from an MMPI–2 profile but may, if undetected, lead to significantly misleading interpretations of the MMPI–2 and other test results. Reitan and Wolfson (1985), for example, reviewed a number of case

studies in which possible MMPI profile interpretations were *not* based on adequately validated research with neuropsychologically impaired individuals. In one case study, they noted a number of possible inferences that were based on a Conversion V profile, in which Hypochondriasis and Hysteria scores are higher than Depression scores.

> A Conversion V may have this significance in a psychiatric population, but there have been no studies of patients with neurological disorders that support the validity of this configuration in this group. There appear to be consistent indications that applying psychiatric criteria to neurological patients may have serious deficiencies. Researchers should investigate the possibly limited generality of the finding before recommending any clinical application and interpretation of a particular configuration of test data. . . .
>
> Although the items of the MMPI may be valid in terms of how they describe the feelings and complaints of this man, we must question their validity for interpretation within a psychiatric framework. For [the person evaluated], many of the items that contribute to the Hypochondriasis scale may represent valid problems which result from his brain disorder. (Reitan & Wolfson, 1985, pp. 285–286)

Drugs and medications. Has the person who is scheduled for assessment taken any legal or illegal drugs or other medications that might affect performance on the test? A variety of prescription as well as over-the-counter medications may cause drowsiness, irritability, difficulty concentrating, memory impairment, restlessness, hypervigilance, and other side effects that could produce misleading test results.

If the person regularly takes insulin, corticosteroids, anti-inflammatory agents, antianxiety agents, antidepressants, or Azidothymidine [AZT]), the professional needs to inquire if he or she failed to take the customary dosage in the time period leading up to and including the testing session or sessions, whether the person changed dosages recently, whether he or she is experiencing any symptoms from the medication, and whether the medication continues to be adequately effective.

Circumstances preceding the testing. Events leading up to the testing can profoundly affect testing results and undermine validity. As with other factors mentioned in this section, the client may not spontaneously disclose such events. A battered woman may have been threatened and perhaps assaulted by her partner immediately before the testing session. The partner may have threatened her with harm should she participate in the session. A client may have experienced a recent death in the family that makes it hard to concentrate, may have gotten caught in a traffic jam that created excruciating anxiety about whether he or she would miss the assessment session, or may be worried about the last-minute arrangements of child care because the regular child care provider cancelled at the last minute. Careful, sensitive, and comprehensive inquiry can help the professional find out about these factors.

Monitoring the Assessment

Forensic assessment sessions must always be carefully monitored. If the professional (or one of the professional's adequately trained and qualified assistants) is not present, there can be no assurance that the client filled out a self-report test such as the MMPI independently and under the standardized conditions required for validation (see the section on administration and scoring in chap. 9, this volume).

An unmonitored assessment can produce invalid and misleading results in many ways. One of the authors, for example,

> observed a patient taking the MMPI in an outpatient waiting room while the psychologist worked in his office. Frequently when the patient marked down a response, the patient's spouse, who was reading along, commented,

> "Now that's not you! That's not what you believe. Change that answer!" The patient would re-read the item, reconsider, and then dutifully change the answer. (Butcher & Pope, 1990, p. 39)

Professor Jack Graham described an interesting event at a psychiatric ward (cited in Butcher & Pope, 1992). A group of patients sat attentively in a large circle. At intervals, some of the patients would raise their hands. Graham became intrigued and asked a member of the group to tell him what was going on. The person explained that a psychologist had given an MMPI to one of the patients, asking him to return it to the psychologist's office later. The patient had asked the other residents for help. As the patient read aloud each MMPI–2 item, the residents raised their hands to vote whether the item should be answered true or false.

The Committee on Professional Standards of the American Psychological Association (1984) issued a formal ruling when a complaint was filed against a psychologist for failing to monitor administration of the MMPI–2 (see chap. 9, this volume, for the text of the committee's ruling). But there is another reason for avoiding unmonitored MMPI–2 administration aside from the extraneous influences (e.g., help from friends or family or the test taker consulting an MMPI–2 or MMPI–A book) that can lead a person to fill out the form differently than if he or she were monitored in accordance with the findings of the Committee on Professional Standards. The presence of an individual monitoring the testing is an element of standardization. As the Faschingbauer (1979) passage in chapter 9 vividly illustrates, self-administering the test unmonitored in a private office can drastically skew the results. Unless results of an unmonitored test were interpreted in light of validation studies conducted in an unmonitored setting, the assumptions of standardization would be violated.

> The assumption underlying standardized tests is that the test-taking situation and procedures are as similar as possible for everyone. When one departs from the procedures on which the norms are based, the standardized

norms lose their direct applicability and the "standard" inferences drawn from those norms become questionable. Standard 6.2 of the Standards for Educational and Psychological Testing (APA, 1985, p. 41) stated, "When a test user makes a substantial change in test format, mode of administration, instructions, language, or content, the user should revalidate the use of the test for the changed conditions or have a rationale supporting the claim that additional validation is not necessary or possible." (Pope & Vasquez, 1998, p. 149)

Careful monitoring of an assessment using standardized tests such as the MMPI–2 and MMPI–A is an essential requirement of forensic evaluation.

While monitoring the test administration, the professional should note the duration of the assessment, any signs of test-taker fatigue, any breaks or interruptions, and any behaviors that might be relevant to interpreting the test.

Remaining Alert to Critical or Urgent Situations

As noted earlier, the professional needs to disclose to the attorney and client the conditions under which the professional may need to take prompt action that may breach customary confidentiality. The professional must remain alert to any signs that the client is an immediate danger to self or others (i.e., is suicidal or homicidal), is becoming gravely disabled, or may be in immediate danger (e.g., a client discloses during an assessment that her partner, who has battered her in the past, has threatened to kill her).

Depending on the clinical circumstances and relevant law, the professional may be obligated to take certain steps to protect the client or identifiable third parties. Similarly, if the client reports child abuse, the professional may be legally required to make an immediate oral report and subsequent written report to child protective services or other legal agencies.

Ensuring Completeness and Considering Context

Conclusions on the basis of the MMPI–2 or MMPI–A alone must be viewed as hypotheses. These hypotheses can be evaluated in light of the support or contradiction provided by other sources of information about the individual. Psychologist Howard Garb (1988), for example, reviewed the available research studies "in which mental health professionals were given increasing amounts of information" (p. 442). He found a general increase in validity "when biographical, MMPI, or neuropsychological test data were added to demographic or psychometric information" (p. 442; see also Garb, 1984, 1992).

Without a structured interview and adequate review of records, it is easy to arrive at compelling but thoroughly misinformed, invalid, and misleading conclusions. Many clinicians, for example, may fail to inquire about a history of sexual abuse. In one research study, 50 charts of nonpsychotic female patients evaluated at a psychiatric emergency room (ER) were selected at random and reviewed. These charts were compared with 50 other charts of similar female patients; ER clinicians for the latter group of patients had been asked to include specific questions about possible child abuse in their structured interviews. The first group of charts recorded child abuse for only 6 of the 50 patients; the second group of charts recorded child abuse for 35 of the 50 patients (Briere & Zaidi, 1989).

Briere and Zaidi's (1989) research illustrates Harvard psychiatrist Judith Herman's (1992) observation that trauma victims or survivors will often be reluctant to volunteer their abuse history and have difficulty communicating it clearly.

> The ordinary response to atrocities is to banish them from consciousness. Certain violations of the social compact are too terrible to utter aloud: this is the meaning of the word unspeakable.
>
> Atrocities, however, refuse to be buried. Equally as powerful as the desire to deny atrocities is the conviction that denial does not work. . . .

This conflict between the will to deny horrible events and the will to proclaim them aloud is the central dialectic of psychological trauma. People who have survived atrocities often tell their stories in a highly emotional, contradictory, and fragmented manner which undermines their credibility and thereby serves the twin imperatives of truth-telling and secrecy. When the truth is finally recognized, survivors can begin their recovery. But far too often secrecy prevails, and the story of the traumatic event surfaces not as a verbal narrative but as a symptom. (p. 1)

Herman, Perry, and van der Kolk (1989), in a study of people suffering from borderline personality disorder who had also suffered traumatic abuse, found that what is customarily termed borderline symptomatology could obscure the original trauma and make a diagnosis of posttraumatic stress disorder (PTSD) difficult.

It appeared that memories of the abuse had become essentially ego syntonic. The subjects generally did not perceive a direct connection between their current symptoms and abusive experiences in childhood. This finding is compatible with observations from follow-up studies of trauma victims (30, 31) which indicate that fragments of the trauma may be transformed over time and relived in a variety of disguised forms, e.g., as somatic sensations, affect states, visual images, behavioral reenactments, or even dissociated personality fragments. (p. 494)

A history of abuse is one of many diverse factors that must be taken into account in arriving at an adequate understanding of test data and assessment results. Closed head injury, chronic medical conditions, and a history of previous involvement with the legal system exemplify other potentially critical factors in interpreting assessment findings. Expert witnesses must make sure that all relevant previous records and other sources of information have been taken into account. If sources of information that may be crucial to the context and meaning of test data are missing or otherwise unavailable, that should be explicitly noted in a forensic report and testimony.

Writing the Report

Putting the test findings and interpretations into an organized framework forces—or at least encourages—the professional to think through the various kinds of assessment data, to check hypotheses against other sources of data, and to communicate clearly the implications of the data for understanding the individual and his or her behavior. Chapter 8 focuses on writing the forensic report.

Releasing the Data

Professionals must know the current legal requirements for releasing information about their forensic work. The relevant legislation and case law vary from jurisdiction to jurisdiction.

Professionals must also know the relevant ethical standards. For example, the 2002 APA "Ethical Principles of Psychologists and Code of Conduct" presented a new approach to the release of test data.

9.04 Release of Test Data
(a) The term *test data* refers to raw and scaled scores, client/patient responses to test questions or stimuli, and psychologists' notes and recordings concerning client/patient statements and behavior during an examination. Those portions of test materials that include client/patient responses are included in the definition of *test data*. Pursuant to a client/patient release, psychologists provide test data to the client/patient or other persons identified in the release. Psychologists may refrain from releasing test data to protect a client/patient or others from substantial harm or misuse or misrepresentation of the data or the test, rec-

ognizing that in many instances release of confidential information under these circumstances is regulated by law. (See also Standard 9.11, Maintaining Test Security [APA, 2002].)

(b) In the absence of a client/patient release, psychologists provide test data only as required by law or court order.

What About the Health Insurance Portability and Accountability Act?

Some professionals have wondered whether the Health Insurance Portability and Accountability Act (HIPAA) applies to health information they handle in the course of forensic practice. Before we can answer this, let us look at the act. HIPAA requires that psychologists and other health professionals who transmit health information in electronic form (e.g., electronically submitting a claim for reimbursement) must use forms and procedures that comply with certain criteria. Extensive information is available online through the Department of Health and Human Services (2004) at http://www.cms.hhs.gov/hipaa and the Office of Civil Rights (2005) at http://www.hhs.gov/ocr.hipaa. The APA's Practice Organization and the APA's Insurance Trust have developed a HIPAA course that includes step-by-step strategies for compliance and an array of HIPAA-compliant forms for each of the states (i.e., the forms developed for each state were designed to comply with that state's relevant legislation and case law). Information about the course and about related HIPAA materials is available at the APA Web site (APA, 2005). Forensic practitioners may sometimes handle "protected health information," as it is defined under HIPAA, in the form of previous health records, but the complexity of determining in each case whether HIPAA applied and if so, how, is reflected in the introduction to an excellent article by forensic psychologists Mary Connell and Gerry Koocher (2003).

As of April 14, 2003 most of us had wrestled, at least superficially, with the HIPAA (45 CFR 160) notification issue and had attempted to determine whether we fell under the rubric of

"covered entities," who must comply in full with the regulations. Most of us probably at least filed for an extension to protract the painful process of trying to become compliant, hoping for divine guidance or at least word from some authoritative source that HIPAA does not apply to forensic practice.

Although the following attempt to explore the issue *does not represent an official position of any forensic governing authority*, we offer the product of our study in the hope that it will illuminate some relevant aspects of the question. Our disclaimer: do not rely upon our advice as the final word on the matter. Each practitioner must engage in a careful analysis of practice activities that might qualify as "health care" services. (p. 16)

Along with web sites cited earlier, the Cornell and Koocher article is an excellent starting point for expert witnesses trying to sort out HIPAA's implications for the materials they handle in the course of reviewing records, conducting assessments, and preparing reports in various jurisdictions. Other key articles include Erard (2004) and Fischer (2004).

TESTIFYING

The professional's fundamental responsibility when testifying is to respond to proper questions in a way that tells the truth, the whole truth, and nothing but the truth. As an expert witness, the professional offers information and opinions that help the triers-of-fact (i.e., the jury or judge) to understand issues that are considered beyond common or lay knowledge.

Many factors block the professional's attempts to fulfill this responsibility. The following sections identify major factors that tend to undermine clear, accurate communication.

Lack of Preparation

Lack of adequate preparation is a primary cause of disaster during depositions and courtroom testimony. Louis Nizer's (1961) fundamental rule of preparation, quoted in chapter 1, applies to the expert witness as much as to the attorney. Forensic psychiatrist Robert Sadoff (1975) painted a vivid picture of what inadequate preparation can do: "There is nothing more pitiful than to see a leading member of the community . . . brought to his knees under cross-examination because he is ill prepared. . . ." (p. 51). Brooten and Chapman (1987) estimated that "as a rule, at least four hours of preparation are required for any witness for every one hour to be spent in deposition or in court. In critical cases as much as six hours is advisable" (p. 176).

Setting aside enough time to prepare is essential. This includes the time it takes to gather all necessary documents for review.

A self-assessment can create justifiable confidence, identify areas of weakness, and serve as the final phase of adequate preparation. The self-assessment can include reviewing the deposition and cross-examination questions discussed in chapter 9. Reviewing the following factors can also help.

Lack of Familiarity With Forensic Settings and Procedures

Entering a new setting can be disorienting. Skills in one venue may not transfer easily to another. Readers are probably familiar with the clinical supervisor who describes clinical dynamics to a supervisee clearly but becomes tongue tied when standing in front of a packed lecture hall to deliver a lecture.

Something similar happens to many skilled professionals setting foot in a courtroom for the first time. The new rules, procedures, and terms can have a paralyzing effect. Professionals entering the forensic world can find out what the setting and process are like. Watching "Law and Order," "Boston Legal," and "Court TV" are not adequate preparation for the experience.

Talking with colleagues who have testified in court is one good way to learn about the process, as is observing a trial. Reading accounts of trial strategies often presents a more comprehensive, detailed, and coherent view of attorney preparation, discussions among attorneys, and the principals, legal briefs, and jury deliberations.

The following books can help expert witnesses learn what to expect. Each takes a different approach but shows how trials and the legal proceedings leading up to them operate in the real world.

Emily Couric's (1988) *The Trial Lawyers* is a good book to begin with for someone who has little or no experience in the courtroom. The author interviewed 10 prominent attorneys including Linda Fairstein, Arthur Liman, Richard "Racehorse" Haynes, James Neal, and Edward Bennett Williams. The attorneys describe the issues, the strategies, and the turning points of an important case. Brief excerpts of deposition and courtroom testimony illustrate key points.

A similar book is John Jenkin's (1989) *The Litigators*, an account of six trials that is based on interviews with high-profile attorneys. Alan Dershowitz's (1982) *The Best Defense* is similar to the others in that it provides accounts of 11 trials. Unlike the others, however, all of the trials involve the same attorney, who is telling the stories.

Each of the 51 chapters in *The Trial Masters: A Handbook of Strategies and Techniques That Win Cases* (Warshaw, 1984) focuses on individual aspects of a trial (e.g., conducting *voir dire* [examination of potential jurors] or direct examination of a medical expert). Some well-known attorneys (e.g., Louis Nizer, Vincent Bugliosi, Bruce Walkup, and Gerry Spence) provide a how-to-do-it (or at least a how-I-do-it) guide.

Grutman and Thomas's (1990) *Lawyers and Thieves* is a much shorter book (224 pages) that serves as a good supplement to *The Trial Masters*. Unlike the longer volume's focus on approaches that attorneys take in court, this account focuses more on the behind-the-scenes maneuvers—some of them questionable—attorneys use to try to gain advantage. As the title suggests, the book is more of an exposé.

Prompted by her experience as a juror in a capital case lasting 6 weeks, Robin Lakoff, professor of linguistics at the University of California, Berkeley, provides an excellent analysis of life and language in court in her book *Talking Power: The Politics of Language* (1990). Those preparing to serve for the first time as an expert witness may find her discussion of the subject extremely helpful. For example, she begins exploring the special nature of testimony by noting,

> The witness stand is not a place for comfortable conversation. Usually, the giver of information holds power, but a witness does not. A witness cannot control topics or their interpretation and has no say when the conversation begins and ends. . . . The lawyer–witness repartee may seem to an outside observer like especially snappy but otherwise normal conversation. But as in therapeutic discourse, its purpose and therefore its rules are different. To the observer, the discourse seems a dyad between lawyer and witness. But in terms of its function in a trial, both are in fact acting together as one participant, the speaker, with the jury as hearer. Without this understanding, much about the examination procedure would be unintelligible. (pp. 90–91)

The late John D. MacDonald provided a detailed account of a single trial (in which one of the attorneys was F. Lee Bailey) in *No Deadly Drug* (1968). Briefer accounts can provide the basic patterns, but a longer book-length account (656 pages) can show the ebb and flow of the long, complex sequence of events that can occur in a legal case. MacDonald, author of the Travis McGee detective stories and other novels, was an excellent writer. His descriptions of the extended direct and cross-examinations of the expert witnesses will be useful to virtually anyone preparing to serve in that role.

You Must Be Dreaming (Noel & Watterson, 1992) also focuses on a single case. The first-person account, coauthored by one of the parties to the case and a professional journalist, describes in detail the deposition process, how the issues in a civil case can interact with issues that come before a licensing board and a professional ethics committee, and the movements toward settling a case. Other books concentrating on a single case are *Defendant*

(Charles & Kennedy, 1985), *Betrayal* (Freeman & Roy, 1976), *Make No Law: The* Sullivan *Case and the First Amendment* (A. Lewis, 1991), and *The Sterilization of Carrie Buck* (J. D. Smith & Nelson, 1989), the latter two cases resulting in decisions by the U.S. Supreme Court. These books, by describing the individuals about whom the witnesses are testifying so vividly, serve as a crucial reminder of a witness's grave responsibilities. Expert testimony often affects individual lives in profound, sometimes permanent ways.

Expert witnesses will find it helpful to find out about the strategies, patterns, and dynamics of cross-examination. Francis Wellman's (1903/1936) *The Art of Cross-Examination*—especially his chapter on cross-examination of experts—is the classic text. This how-to book is extremely readable, illustrating the points with excerpts from trial transcripts. *The Trial Masters* contains a number of chapters on cross-examination, including the ominously titled "Cross-Examination of the Adverse Medical Witness: Keep the Jury Laughing" (Peters, 1984; see also Kassin, Williams, & Saunders, 1990; Marcus, 1987; Younger, 1986a, 1986b).

Effective cross-examination often depends on an effective deposition. David Boies has offered a vivid and instructive step-by-step account of his legendary deposing of Bill Gates in *Courting Justice* (Boies, 2004). Jay Ziskin wrote the classic text on cross-examining expert witnesses who testify regarding psychological assessment and related clinical matters: *Coping With Psychiatric and Psychological Testimony* (1969). Ziskin, a psychologist and attorney, created a densely referenced guide for attorneys on how to attack (this is not too strong a word) forensic experts in the mental health field. A continuing theme of the text is

> that movement toward a productive and valid law and behavioral science relationship can best be served by placing in the hands of lawyers, tools by which they can aid courts and juries to distinguish science from authoritarian pronouncement and validated knowledge from conjecture. (Ziskin, 1981a, p. 1)

Continuing to expand with each subsequent edition, *Coping With Psychiatric and Psychological Testimony* often causes considerable anxiety and perhaps panic for some expert witnesses while bringing an anticipatory smile to many attorneys preparing for cross-examination. If the anxiety and panic are not terminal, expert witnesses can prepare and improve by confronting challenges posed in these volumes. The text encourages a rethinking of the meaning of *expertise;* of the degree to which expert testimony is supported by independently conducted research appearing in peer-reviewed scientific and professional journals; and of the likelihood that expert opinions are biased, unsubstantiated, or vulnerable to attack. However stressful it is confronting these challenges in the privacy of one's study, it is far less stressful than confronting them for the first time during cross-examination, with a court reporter making a public, permanent record of one's responses.

An ideal companion to *Coping* is Stan Brodsky's (1991) *Testifying in Court: Guidelines and Maxims for the Expert Witness.* Brodsky, a psychologist who has testified as an expert in many trials, provides information, guidance, and support that can help restore the confidence of the expert witness who has been unable to cope with *Coping With Psychiatric and Psychological Testimony.* In a chapter titled "Ziskin & Faust Are Sitting on the Table," Brodsky observed that

> those of us who testify have a reason to be grateful for the impetus to reconsider the *whats* and *hows* of our work. It can be quite constructive to say this in court. I find that an overview of the field, acknowledging the contributions of Faust and Ziskin and speaking to how we have attended to their issues, disarms attorneys and is part of nondefensive, positive testimony. (Brodsky, 1991, p. 203)

This positive approach continues a theme he explored in another work.

> The testifying expert should know the research foundations and limitations of

every clinical procedure employed, and should be prepared to defend its use. If the expert is strongly attacked, the attack will serve the useful purpose of reminding him or her of the need to be accountable. The cross examination is a form of public examination and defense of what we know and how we know it. (Brodsky, 1989, p. 264)

Ron Rosenbaum's *Travels With Dr. Death* (1991; see also Tierney, 1982) describes three trials in which a psychiatrist known as "Dr. Death" testifies and is cross-examined. Rosenbaum notes that the doctor's "lopsided record over the past twenty years favors his chances: going into these three trials he has testified against 124 murderers, and acting on his advice, juries have sentenced 115 of them to death" (pp. 206–207).

To impose the death penalty, the judge or jury must find that the defendant constitutes a continuing risk to society because he or she is likely to commit future acts of violence. The nature of Dr. Death's assessments in such trials may trouble many readers and illustrates vital issues regarding the scientific basis of expert testimony and the adequacy of cross-examination. Rosenbaum summarizes the doctor's customary style of testimony.

> He'll take the stand, listen to a recitation of facts about the killing and the killer, and then—usually without examining the defendant, without ever setting eyes on him until the day of the trial—tell the jury that, *as a matter of medical science,* he can assure them the defendant will pose a continuing danger to society. (Rosenbaum, 1991, p. 210)

A stark contrast to the success of the doctor described by Rosenbaum is the psychiatrist who testified as an expert witness for the defense in the second trial (for spying) of Alger Hiss. The psychiatrist testified, on the basis of his psychological evaluation, that the major prosecution witness, Whittaker Chambers, had a personality disorder that included a propensity to lie.

The psychiatrist had never met Mr. Chambers but had observed his testimony in court, reviewed the facts of his life, and studied his published works. The psychiatrist testified *solely* from a study of Mr. Chambers's writings, a few facts about his life, and observation of him for awhile in the courtroom. The cross-examination of the defense psychiatrist has "frequently been described as the single most devastating cross-examination of an expert ever conducted" (Younger, 1986c, p. i). The verbatim transcript of this 3-day cross-examination was published as *Thomas Murphy's Cross-Examination of Dr. Carl A. Binger* (Younger, 1986c).

Trials of an Expert Witness (Klawans, 1991) presents a broad range of cases in which Harold Klawans testified as an expert witness. Unlike the previous two books, *Trials* provides first-person accounts of what it is like to be cross-examined.

McGill University professor Maggie Bruck provides a vivid account of the unexpected challenges and pressures an expert witness must survive in her chapter "The Trials and Tribulations of a Novice Expert Witness" (Bruck, 1998).

Finally, experts may find it helpful to consult books that present the statutory and case law criteria for serving as an expert, rules of evidence, and similar information specific to testifying in a particular state (e.g., R. Kennedy, 1983; R. Kennedy & Martin, 1987; J. C. Martin, 1985) as well as more comprehensive guides to a specific state's laws as they are relevant to mental health professionals, such as the APA's state-by-state series *Law and Mental Health Professionals* (e.g., Caudill & Pope, 1995; Charlton, Fowler, & Ivandick, 2006; M. O. Miller & Sales, 1986).

Passage of Time

An expert may assess a litigant and wait 3, 4, or 5 years before the deposition. Clinicians testifying as percipient or fact witnesses may face an even longer gap. They complete work with a therapy patient and 5, 10, or 15 years later open the morning mail to find a subpoena. The subpoena demands the therapy records and compels the therapist to testify in a civil or criminal case involving the former client.

Professionals preparing to testify after many years must take into account at least three major factors.

1. Professionals must review carefully the test report and all documents (e.g., therapy notes and raw test data) related to it. Memory can go gently or radically wrong, especially after years have gone by. Review the documents *before* arriving at the deposition.
2. Professionals must make sure that their knowledge and expertise in the relevant areas are up to date.
3. Professionals must clarify that the test data described the individual *at the time of the testing*. The passage of time may have qualified or invalidated some or all of the test findings. Professionals must also avoid unwarranted assumptions that a person's condition at the time of the testing necessarily reflected the individual's condition at an earlier time.

As Shapiro (1984) wrote,

> the forensic clinician must never assume that the symptom picture which occurs at the time of the evaluation is the same as the symptom picture present at the time of the offense. There may be deterioration, or restitution, with the patient appearing more disturbed, or more intact, than at some time in the past. (p. 182)

Carelessness

Professionals can discredit themselves needlessly but effectively through carelessness. MMPI–2 answer sheets and other test protocols should be carefully checked to ensure that they have been scored correctly, that any columns of numbers (e.g., for MMPI–A clinical scales, for the Wechsler Adult Intelligence Scale—III (WAIS–III) subscales, for Rorschach determinants, for Halstead–Reitan category test responses) accurately reflect the raw data, that the mathematical transformations of such numbers (e.g., adding them up for a scale or subscale value or using "correction" values) be performed without errors, that the proper norms or interpretive tables (e.g., for age on the WAIS–III) be applied, and so on. Opposing counsel (or their own experts) can easily check this information.

Attorneys can be exceptionally effective in using a mistake as a vivid example of the expert's fallibility, carelessness, or wrongness. Typical questions include the following.

- Knowing that this matter was so crucial for all parties involved in this unfortunate procedure and that you would be testifying under oath, you did not add that column of numbers carefully or even check to see if you'd made a mistake, did you?

- Did you use the same care in adding up this [incorrect] column of numbers that you did in carrying out your other so-called "assessment procedures"?

- Doctor, you have already reviewed the fees you charged for conducting the assessment. Did those fees not include payment for you to make an effort to ensure the accuracy of the assessment?

- You have discussed the motivations of the defendant whom you evaluated, doctor. What motives did you have to write down the wrong sum on a formal report that you knew you'd be submitting to this court?

- Do you believe that in conducting this assessment you took adequate steps to ensure that the information you would be presenting to the court would be correct? [This sort of question is designed to make experts particularly uncomfortable. If they answer "yes" (i.e., that they believe that they took adequate steps to ensure that the information was correct), then they are shown to be clearly wrong because the steps they took were not adequate to detect the error. If they answer "no" (i.e., that they do not believe that they took adequate steps to detect errors), then they are probably in for a long and painful series of questions regarding why they declined to take adequate steps to ensure that the information was correct.]

Impartial and Adversarial Roles

In a trial, a judge is expected to be objective. He or she is to be impartial, not an adversary or proponent of either side (e.g., civil plaintiff and defendant or state prosecutor and criminal defendant). The role of the expert may be compared to that of the judge in this respect. The expert testifies to help the jury and judge understand the issues at hand rather than to help one side or the other win the case. As forensic psychologist and clinical diplomate Herbert Weissman (1984) wrote,

> the expert's obligation is to present material objectively and accurately, consistent with the bounds of knowledge in the given area, and to share fully with the trier of fact all that has been relied upon in the derivation of opinions, including the reasoning process upon which opinions are founded. (p. 528)

And yet is this the type of expert that appears in court? Is this the type of expert that an attorney would actually hire to help win a case in an adversarial contest? Meier (1982; cited by Loftus, 1986) suggested otherwise: "I would go into a lawsuit with an objective, uncommitted, independent expert about as willingly as I would occupy a foxhole with a couple of noncombatant soldiers" (p. 1).

McCloskey, Egeth, and McKenna (1986) summarized the divisiveness of this issue as it was addressed in a conference on the psychologist as expert witness.

> Most of the conference participants agreed that the most desirable role for the expert is that of impartial educator, and some held that this is the only ethically defensible position. It is clear that the law defines the role of the expert as that of an impartial educator called to assist the trier of fact. . . . Therefore, it was argued, the psychologist has the ethical responsibility to present a complete and unbiased picture of the psychological research relevant to the case at hand. Many conference participants disagreed, however, contending that the educator role is difficult if not impossible to maintain,

both because of pressures toward advocacy from the attorneys who hire the expert, and because of a strong tendency to identify with the side for which one is working. Hence, they suggested, the psychologist should accept the realities of working within an adversary system, and seek to be a responsible advocate, presenting one side of an issue without distorting or misrepresenting the available psychological research. (p. 5; see also Hastie, 1986; Loftus, 1986)

Despite the lack of clear unanimity in the field, what is crucial is that the expert witness recognize intense, subtle pressures to distort facts and opinions. Some pressures are external. Successful trial attorneys tend to be skilled at persuasion and influence. An attorney may have an intuitive understanding of the principles of social psychology, decision making, and so on, that many psychologists may envy.

Some pressures are internal. Some witnesses, for example, may have a desire to please the attorney or to try to be helpful.

There is nothing inherently wrong with these external and internal pressures. What is crucial is that the expert acknowledge the pressures and make sure that they do not lead to a violation of the oath to tell the truth, the whole truth, and nothing but the truth. In their chapter "Therapist–Patient Sexual Intimacy on Trial: Mental Health Professionals as Expert Witnesses," Pope and Bouhoutsos (1986) wrote,

> The expert is not a hired gun, selling his or her "opinion" to the highest bidder. Nor can testimony be created or "shaped" in order to enrich a plaintiff, exonerate a defendant, or advance a purely personal point of view. The expert witness has a responsibility to fulfill the functions required by the court, and must resist all enticements— explicit or subtle, monetary, emotional, interpersonal, or ego-enhancing—to compromise this charge. (p. 137)

Wagenaar (1988) compared the role of the expert witness to that of a scientist presenting work in the context of peer-reviewed scientific journals.

> Scientists, publishing the results of their experimental studies, will not be allowed to omit relevant parts of the literature. They would be corrected by colleagues during the process of peer evaluation. If a biased representation of the literature did slip through, it would be an error, not a result of a defendable strategy. Expert witnesses who cannot present a balanced account of the literature are not really experts. (p. 508)

Finally, as emphasized in a previous section in this chapter on the clarification of tasks and clients, expert witnesses must avoid some situations altogether because they so clearly create a lack of objectivity and impartiality. The *American Bar Association Criminal Justice Mental Health Standards* (American Bar Association, 1989), for example, state clearly that a "professional who has been a defense or prosecution consultant in a given case ought not be called upon later to conduct an evaluation in that case. Under such circumstances, an objective evaluation would be impossible" (p. 12).

Words and Pictures

Professionals tend to think and speak in jargon. That is to say, professionals possess a psychological tendency to engage in complex cognitive activities and characteristic vocalizations centering on specialized terminology related to their professional field of endeavor.

Expert opinions are useless if the jury does not understand them. Consider this testimony, which clouds an MMPI–2-based assessment in jargon.

> The highest scales were 2 and 9. Both were at least two standard deviations above 50, but they were not statistically significantly different from each other so it is impossible to term this a 2–9 profile as opposed to a 9–2 profile—but the interpretations for the 2–9 and 9–2 would probably be

isomorphic, since we have no empirical way to distinguish them. They have
low profile definition. My professional
opinion would be that this individual
might be experiencing a unipolar or bipolar affective disorder, which may obscure or interact with or actually be the
symptoms of neuropsychological impairment, so that the hypomanic
symptomatology is due to somatopsy-
chic origins such as cerebral vascular
occlusions.

Trying out explanations with friends who are *not*
mental health professionals can help experts communicate in clear, everyday language.

Visual presentations can make testimony about
MMPI–2 scales, research foundations, and specific
profiles more understandable, vivid, and memorable. Displays can be examined by the judge and opposing attorney and marked for identification (as
evidence or exhibits). In some states, expert witnesses can use these displays in front of the jury if
they state that the displays would aid his or her testimony. This limited use is permitted in some states
even if the displays are not technically admissible
as evidence because they are not actually admitted
into evidence. They are used just to illustrate the
testimony and are not taken into the jury room
during deliberations.

Allowing judge and jury to see the array of validity, clinical, and content scales, the "average" responses of those in the normative groups as well as
those in specific populations (e.g., patients with
chronic pain, patients who have been hospitalized
for schizophrenia, or successful applicants for man-
agerial positions), and a specific individual's (e.g., a
plaintiff or defendant) profile for comparison and
contrast can provide a clarity and concreteness that
may not be possible through use of words alone.

If the witness can present the information in a
well-organized sequence, judge and jurors may be
fascinated to find out how a standardized psychological test works. The expert witness is fulfilling
the central responsibility of the testimony: helping
the triers-of-fact to understand facts and issues that
tend to lie outside the knowledge of the lay public.

Listening

Good cross-examiners tend to be good listeners
(e.g., Brodsky, 1991; Pope & Bouhoutsos, 1986).
They exploit the lack of precision that all of us display when we try to express ourselves without
reading from a script. They amplify and play with
ambiguity, the ambiguity in the expert's responses
and the ambiguity they use in wording their questions. They listen to what we say, not what we intended to say. They hear what we said, not what we
thought we said. As they pose a new question, they
repeat what we said just a few minutes earlier, but
the wording may be slightly different, the intona-
tion and implication sending the meaning off in a
different direction.

The person who testifies effectively and genu-
inely helps the judge and jury to understand the
facts and issues tends to be someone who listens
well during both direct and cross-examination. The
attorney and the expert may have discussed at
length exactly what the direct examination questions will be. The expert may have planned each response carefully. Yet the attorney may often wander
from the intended path during the direct examination. Sometimes it may be because he or she is
working from notes, and in rewording a question,
the intended meaning shifts. Sometimes unexpected developments force the attorney to cover
new ground with the expert, without having a
chance to discuss these matters in adequate detail
in advance. Sometimes the judge sustains objections to lines of questioning that had been planned
in advance, forcing the attorney to improvise.

In all instances, the expert witness must listen
carefully to each direct examination question. Re-
citing prepared answers to questions that no longer
quite fit confuses the jury and discredits the expert.
Experts may gain exceptional credibility in spontaneous moments during which an attorney conducting direct examination reformulates a prepared
question, unintentionally giving it a different meaning. The expert gives an answer that was not anticipated by the attorney, who registers, however subtly, surprise. In other instances, an attorney may try
to lead an expert to provide "stronger" (in the sense
of being favorable to the attorney's case) answers
than the expert can justify. In such spontaneous

moments, the expert may give the "wrong" answer (i.e., not the answer that the attorney wanted or expected), and the attorney and witness may appear to be arguing with one another, the attorney attempting to get the witness to acknowledge a point, the witness refusing to cooperate. When these moments are spontaneous, the jury can glimpse the independence and integrity of the witness

Similarly, the expert witness must listen with exceptional care to the questions during cross-examination. If the question is not clear, the witness must ask for the question to be repeated or for adequate clarification. An alternative approach is to respond along the following lines: "If I understand correctly that you are asking [clarification or restatement of the question], then my answer is. . . ." Shapiro (1991) provided an example of a witness who listens carefully to a question and recognizes the many meanings that the word *validity* can have.

Attorney: Now then, Doctor, hasn't research shown that the MMPI is invalid?

Expert: I really cannot answer that question; would you be able to define what you mean by validity?

Attorney: Come now, you're a doctor, don't you know what validity is?

Expert: Certainly, Counselor, but there is predictive validity, construct validity, and face validity, to name only a few. You will have to define your terms more precisely before I can respond to the question.

Attorney: I withdraw the question. (p. 215)

Logical Fallacies That Undermine Assessments and Testimony

Evaluating and pulling together the vast research literature on the MMPI and other assessment instruments, using this information to help understand an individual, and testifying about the results of an assessment in response to direct and cross-examination involves countless decisions.[1] These decisions are always vulnerable to logical fallacies that undermine our attempts to make logically sound decisions.

This section presents some of the most basic logical fallacies. This list of 18 logical fallacies is by no means comprehensive. But they seem to turn up repeatedly in the forensic and clinical literature, in assessment reports, and in deposition and courtroom testimony.

The fallacies are denying the antecedent, composition fallacy, affirming the consequent, division fallacy, golden mean fallacy, appeal to ignorance (*ad ignorantium*), disjunctive fallacy, false dilemma, mistaking deductive validity for truth, *post hoc ergo propter hoc* (after this, because of this), red herring, ad hominem, straw person, you too (*tu quoque*), naturalistic fallacy, false analogy, begging the question (*petitio principii*), and argument to logic (*argumentum ad logicam*).

The name of each fallacy is followed by a brief description and an example, often in exaggerated form, from the area of assessment and testimony.

Denying the antecedent. Denying the antecedent takes the form, "If *x*, then *y*. Not *x*. therefore, not *y*."

Example: "In my experience, when I'm conducting forensic assessments and the people I'm assessing don't want me to see their health care records, it usually means they're hiding something and I can't trust them. But this new person I'm evaluating let me see all her health care records, so I don't think she's hiding anything and I can trust her."

Composition fallacy. Composition fallacy takes the form of assuming that a group possesses the characteristics of its individual members.

Example: "Each of these standardized psychological tests is an efficient method of assessment with excellent levels of sensitivity and specificity. An assessment battery composed of these tests must be an efficient method of assessment with excellent sensitivity and specificity."

Affirming the consequent. Affirming the consequent takes the form of, "If *x*, then *y*. *y*. therefore, *x*."

Example: "Forensic psychologists who are smart, well-prepared, articulate, honest, and well-

[1] This section is adapted from "Fallacies and Pitfalls in Psychology," © by Kenneth S. Pope, and available at http://kspope.com.

respected are always in demand. The forensic psychologist my attorney hired for my case is always in demand, so he must be smart, well-prepared, articulate, honest, and well-respected."

Another example: "If this client is competent to stand trial, he will certainly know the answers to at least 80% of the questions on this standardized test. He knows the answers to 87% of the test questions. Therefore he is competent to stand trial."

Division fallacy. The division fallacy (also known as the decomposition fallacy) takes the form of assuming that the members of a group possess the characteristics of the group.

Example: "This MMPI–2 scale shows excellent validity and reliability in differentiating these two groups of litigants. Each item on the scale must be answered one way by one group of litigants and another way by the other group."

Golden-mean fallacy. The fallacy of the Golden Mean (also known as the fallacy of compromise or the fallacy of moderation) takes the form of assuming that the most valid conclusion is that which accepts the best compromise between two competing positions.

Example: "On one hand, I believe that administering an MMPI–2 is the best way to assess this particular forensic client for this particular case. On the other hand, I didn't schedule enough time in the session to administer an MMPI–2. So the best thing for me to do is administer an abbreviated form of the MMPI–2 that will fit into the available time limitation."

Another example: "The defense expert's test results suggested that the defendant's I.Q. is around 80. The prosecution expert's assessment battery suggested that the defendant's I.Q. was around 120. The best estimate of the defendant's I.Q. is therefore around 100."

Appeal to ignorance (*ad ignorantium*). The appeal to ignorance fallacy takes the form, "There is no (or insufficient) evidence establishing that x is false. Therefore, x is true."

Example: "The basic instrument in the test battery I use in custody cases is my own version of the MMPI–2, which I call M–Projective: I ask each par-

ent to pick their favorite MMPI–2 item and then draw a picture based on it. In the 12 years I've been using it, there has not been one published study showing that it has any weaknesses in reliability, validity, sensitivity, or specificity. My version of the MMPI–2 is clearly one of the best forensic assessment instruments ever devised for custody evaluations."

Disjunctive fallacy. This fallacy takes the form, "Either x or y. x. Therefore, not y."

Example: "I can see from my review of the records in this workers' compensation case that either the employee has become disabled due to her work or else she's exaggerating her condition. It's clear that she has sometimes been exaggerating. Therefore, she is not disabled."

False dilemma. Also known as the "either/or" fallacy or the fallacy of false choices, the false dilemma fallacy takes the form of only acknowledging two options (one of which is usually extreme) from a continuum or other array of possibilities.

Example: "Either I'll be able to remain calm and answer each cross-examination question clearly and persuasively or else I'm just not a good forensic psychologist."

Mistaking deductive validity for truth. Mistaking deductive validity for truth takes the form of assuming that because an argument is a logical syllogism, the conclusion must be true. It ignores the possibility that the premises of the argument may be false.

Example: "I just read a book that proves that that book's author knows the best way to identify malingering. He has a chart showing that every other method can fail sometimes but that his always works. That proves his method is best."

Post hoc, ergo propter hoc (after this, therefore on account of this).** The *post hoc, ergo propter hoc* fallacy takes the form of confusing correlation with causation and concluding that because y follows x, then y must be a result of x.

Example: "I'll never forget my first forensic assessment. The person was clearly a malingerer, and had been for years. That's what the jury decided. From the first time he walked into my office, he never could look me straight in the eye. It taught me quite a lesson: When people are malingering, it prevents them from looking you straight in the eye."

Red herring. The red herring fallacy takes the form of introducing or focusing on irrelevant information to distract from the valid evidence and reasoning. It takes its name from the strategy of dragging a herring or other fish across the path to distract hounds and other tracking dogs and to throw them off the scent of whatever they were searching for.

Example: "Some of you have objected to the new test batteries that I use in my forensic practice, alleging that they have no demonstrable validity, were not adequately normed for the kind of clients we see from various cultures, and are unusable for clients with physical disabilities. What you have conveniently failed to take into account, however, is that they cost less than a third of the price for the other tests I had been using, are much easier to learn, and can be administered and scored in less than half the time of the other tests I used to use."

Ad hominem. The *argumentum ad hominem* or *ad feminam* attempts to discredit an argument or position by drawing attention to characteristics of the person who is making the argument or who holds the position.

Example: "That attorney keeps telling me I should wear a suit when I testify as an expert witness, sit up a little straighter, speak in 'plainer' language, and all sorts of stuff that's just not me. But that attorney doesn't have a doctorate in psychology, isn't licensed as a psychologist, never testified as an expert witness, and never studied forensic psychology, so who does she think she is trying to tell me how to do my job?"

Straw person. The straw person, or straw man, or straw woman fallacy takes the form of mischaracterizing someone else's position in a way that makes it weaker, false, or ridiculous.

Example: "The idea that I should look up the validity, reliability, sensitivity, specificity, and so on about each test I administer is the kind of notion that assumes you can know everything about everything."

You too (*tu quoque*). The you too fallacy takes the form of distracting attention from error or weakness by claiming that an opposing argument, person, or position has the same error or weakness.

Example: "You accused me of not telling you the complete truth about myself before you hired me as an expert witness. I was hired. But you're not the most honest person in the world!"

Naturalistic fallacy. The naturalistic fallacy takes the form of logically deducing values (e.g., what is good, best, right, ethical, or moral) based only on statements of fact.

Example: "The Wechsler instruments are the most commonly used to estimate I.Q. in forensic settings, and no tests have more empirical support. It is clear that they are the right way to estimate I.Q. in forensic settings and they should always be used to estimate I.Q. in a forensic assessment."

False analogy. The false or faulty analogy fallacy takes the form of argument by analogy in which the comparison is misleading in at least one important aspect.

Example: "I know at least five very senior expert witnesses who barely look at the manual when administering one of the psychological tests in their standard forensic battery. It seems foolish for me to waste my time paying much attention to manuals, especially now when I'm just starting and have so many other things to think about when doing some initial forensic assessments."

Begging the question (*petitio principii*). Begging the question, one of the fallacies of circularity, takes the form of arguments or other statements that simply assume or restate their own truth rather than providing relevant evidence and logical arguments.

Examples: Sometimes this fallacy literally takes the form of a question, such as, "Have you stopped using that invalid assessment battery yet?" (The question assumes—and a "yes" or "no" response to the question affirms—that your assessment battery lacks validity.) Sometimes this fallacy takes the form of a statement such as, "No one can deny that my new psychological test is the only way to assess potential recidivism."

Argument to logic (*argumentum ad logicam*). The argument to logic fallacy takes the form of assuming that a proposition must be false because an argument offered in support of that proposition was fallacious.

Example: "I had started to question whether the method I've used for years to assess the presence of brain damage using the MMPI–2 might be wrong, but I just found out that the three colleagues who told me that it was an invalid method don't specialize in MMPI–2 assessments, aren't up on the MMPI–2 literature, and don't specialize in neuropsychology, so I think my method is sound after all."

Cognitive Processes That Undermine Assessments and Testimony

In addition to the logical fallacies, there are certain cognitive processes—typical ways that humans tend to think about or handle information—that encourage errors.

Many of these cognitive processes are versions of a human tendency to enter into what is known as a *cognitive set* and to view all additional information in terms of that set. A simple example of this tendency are the various series of childhood questions and answers in which the initial questions form a particular cognitive set and later lead to a wrong answer to an easy question. For instance, one elementary school child may ask another the following:

How do you pronounce [spelling the letters]: M-a-c-D-o-n-a-l-d?
How do you pronounce: M-a-c-H-e-n-r-y?
How do you pronounce: M-a-c-D-o-u-g-l-e?
How do you pronounce: M-a-c-H-i-n-e?

The other child, having formed, through answering the first three questions, a cognitive set in which the letters seem to spell a Scottish name with the prefix pronounced as if it were "mack" will often use the same "mack" pronunciation for the final word, at which time the questioner laughs and points out that he or she has spelled the common word "machine."

Clients who take the MMPI–2 may fall into such cognitive sets for responding. For example, some clients may tend to respond "no" to most questions, regardless of the content. For this reason, their profiles may not be valid, and the MMPI–2 scoring keys have ways of identifying such responders (see chap. 7, this volume).

Expert witnesses must also be aware of their own tendencies to form cognitive sets that promote errors in making inferences about the individual who is being assessed. Chanowitz and Langer (1981), for example, found research evidence supporting the concept of premature cognitive commitment. Psychologist Ellen Langer (1989; see also Langer & Piper, 1987) defined the concept as follows.

> Another way that we become mindless is by forming a mindset when we first encounter something and then clinging to it when we reencounter that same thing. Because such mindsets form before we do much reflection, we call them premature cognitive commitments. (p. 22)

Premature cognitive commitment is evident in the childhood question-and-answer example cited earlier: The first encounter with the prefix "mac" forms a mindset that words beginning with m-a-c are various Scottish proper names. The tendency to use such a small chunk of information as if it meant the same thing in all contexts—forgetting other possible alternatives—has profound implications for misdiagnosing individuals. Irving Weiner (1989), for example, noted the unfounded tendency of at least one professional to assume that a certain response to a certain Rorschach card inevitably indicates that the person is a victim of child sexual abuse (see the section on interpretation in chap. 9, this volume).

Describing similar examples, psychologist Robyn Dawes (1988b; see also Dickman & Sechrest, 1985) cited a university admissions committee's consideration of what seems to be an exceptionally well-qualified, highly sought applicant in engineering. One comment—in which a misspelling seems to be understood as a phenomenon that could only be a symptom of dyslexia—seemed to influence critically the view of this application.

Amy's high school loves her, and she wants to study engineering. Brown badly wants engineering students; unfortunately, Amy spells engineering wrong. "Dyslexia," says Jimmy Wren, a linguistics professor. After some debate, the committee puts her on the waiting list. (p. 152)

The potential power of cognitive sets to encourage error is magnified by the fact that in so many assessments, certain "facts" are known to the clinician that seem to offer a predetermined confirmation of a certain diagnosis or finding. As an extreme example, consider an expert witness reviewing records and providing testimony about a therapy client who committed suicide. Because the clinician already knows that the individual killed him- or herself, previous test and historical data may be interpreted retrospectively in light of this information, perhaps in a biased and unjustifiable manner (e.g., that the previous test results were clearly predictive of imminent suicide). Arkes, Saville, Wortmann, and Harkness (1981), for example, conducted research indicating that if professionals were given a symptom pattern, various alternative diagnoses, *and* the supposedly correct diagnosis, the professionals tended to overestimate significantly the probability that they would have chosen the correct diagnosis had they only known the symptom patterns and the diagnostic alternatives. This phenomenon is known as hindsight bias.

Those who know an event has occurred may claim that had they been asked to predict the event in advance, they would have been very likely to do so. In fact, people with hindsight knowledge do assign higher probability estimates to an event than those who must predict the event without the advantage of that knowledge. (Arkes et al., 1981, p. 252)

A fascinating example of how a "known fact" can—through hindsight—influence interpretation of a broad array of other information is Freud's application of the principles of psychoanalysis to understanding the life of Leonardo da Vinci (Coles, 1973a, 1973b; see also Fischoff, 1982). The key to Freud's analysis was da Vinci's account of how, as an infant, he was touched on the lips by a vulture that swooped down out of the sky.

Freud's astonishing breadth of knowledge led him to recognize that, in Egyptian, the hieroglyph for "vulture" is the same as that for "mother." From this fundamental observation, Freud conducted an incisive and insightful psychoanalysis of da Vinci, about whose younger years there was virtually no other illuminating information. The analysis seemed to spring from and cohere through da Vinci's recollection of an event that seemed to represent themes concerning an intimate relationship with his mother.

It was only later discovered that the translation Freud had been using had contained an error. The Italian word for "kite" had been mistakenly translated into the German word for "vulture"; it was a kite, rather than a vulture, that had caressed da Vinci's lips as he lay in his cradle.

The potential power of cognitive sets to encourage error is magnified not only by hindsight bias but also by social influence and group process. A clinician who has conducted a psychological assessment and is attempting to make sense of the findings may be consciously or unconsciously influenced by the knowledge, which is based on a review of previous records of assessment and treatment, that at least three other clinicians have all agreed that the individual is suffering from a particular disorder (e.g., borderline personality disorder or PTSD). The clinician may also be influenced by the fact that the individual and the individual's attorneys concur that a particular diagnosis or explanatory agent is relevant.

Solomon Asch (1956) was one of the first to conduct extensive research showing the sometimes uncanny ability of group pressure to influence individual decision making. Professor Irving Janis of Yale University (1972; see also Janis, 1982; Janis & Mann, 1979) explored the ways in which collaboration on certain types of decision making may tend to prematurely close off options and encourage a consensus that may not be warranted by the evidence.

A third factor—in addition to hindsight bias and social influences—that can magnify the power of cognitive sets to encourage errors is confirmation bias. If a professional begins an assessment with a particular understanding of the client (perhaps including the likely diagnosis and etiology) or reaches such an understanding early on, the subsequent aspects of assessment may be severely biased. The choice of subsequent tests, interviews, and other sources, as well as the ways in which the resulting data are interpreted, may be shaped by a clinician's hypothesis to such a degree that it is virtually impossible or at least highly unlikely that the clinician will not find confirming data.

> Confirmation bias is perhaps the best known and most widely accepted notion of inferential error to have come out of the literature on human reasoning. The claim . . . is that human beings have a fundamental tendency to seek information consistent with their current beliefs, theories or hypotheses and to avoid the collection of potentially falsifying evidence. (Evans, 1989, p. 41)

Judge Dennis Yule highlighted the issue of bias in seeking information when he wrote in regard to expert witness Richard Ofshe,

> Finally, Dr. Ofshe characterizes plaintiff's memories as a progress toward ritual, satanic cult images, which he states fits a pattern he has observed of false memories.
>
> It appears to the court, however, that in this regard, he is engaging in the same exercise for which he criticizes therapists dealing with repressed memory. Just as he accuses them of resolving at the outset defining repressed memories of abuse and then constructing them, he has resolved at the outset to find a macabre scheme of memories progressing toward satanic cult ritual and then creates them. (*Crook v. Murphy,* Case 91-2-0011-2-5 (1994);

see also Olio & Cornell, 1998; Pope, 1995, 1996, 1997)

Although potentially powerful, these cognitive processes that encourage error need not prevent an expert from reaching a valid opinion that is based on adequate evidence. What is crucial is that the expert remain constantly alert to these sources of bias and error and, when possible and appropriate, take steps to make sure that they are not interfering with fair and solidly based testimony.

Cognitive Processes That Undermine Ethical Behavior

Cognitive processes encouraging error are similar to cognitive processes encouraging unethical behavior. The discussion and examples throughout this book make clear that forensic work provides no shortage of temptations for behavior of the ethically questionable, ethically tainted, clearly unethical, and "how could you!" varieties. Although some may have no qualms about engaging in unethical behavior, for most of us the real challenge or temptation is to convince ourselves that what is unethical is actually ethical. For example, how can accepting a huge amount of money to testify in an area about which we know nothing—something that previously struck us as unethically working outside our area of competence—be redefined as altruistically coming to the aid of someone that no one else would help?

Common fallacies can be put to use justifying unethical behavior and quieting a noisy conscience. Pope and Vasquez (1998, 2005) called the cognitive processes used to rationalize unethical behavior *ethical substandards*, which are in no way ethical. Resourceful expert witnesses and attorneys can use these cognitive strategies to make even the most slimy, outrageous, and disgusting behaviors seem ethical, or at least insignificant. Being human (at least most of us are), all of us expert witnesses and attorneys have probably resorted to one or more of these, and some may have gone to the well more often.

Almost any reader can add to this list. If some of the following examples of these cognitive processes encouraging unethical behavior seem incomprehensible or funny to us, it is probably because we have yet to use these particular stratagies. Sometime in the future, facing an irresistible temptation, we may find that some assertion from the following list that once struck us as crazy now seems to express a deep and abiding human truth.

Pope and Vasquez (1998, 2005) provided the following 30 examples[2] of these ethical substandards.

1. It's not unethical as long as the attorney who retained us or the presiding judge required or suggested it.

2. It's not unethical if we can use the passive voice and look ahead. If it is discovered that our c.v. is full of degrees we never earned, positions we never held, and awards we never received, all we need do is nondefensively acknowledge that mistakes were made and it's time to move on.

3. It's not unethical if we're victims. If we need to justify our victim status, we can always use one of two traditional scapegoats: (a) our "anything-goes" society, lacking any clear standards, that lets what were once solid rules drift and leaves us all ethically adrift or, conversely, (b) our coercive, intolerant society, tyrannized by "political correctness"—that is always dumbing us down and keeping us down. Imagine, for example, we are arrested for speeding while drunk, and the person whose car we hit decides vengefully to press charges. We can show ourselves as the real victim by writing books and appearing on TV pointing out that the legal system has been hijacked by a vicious minority of politically correct, self-serving tyrants who refuse to acknowledge that most speeding while drunk is not only harmless but constructive, getting drivers to their destinations faster and in better spirits. Those who question our claims and reasoning are clearly intolerant, trying to silence us and destroy our right to do what is right.

4. It's not unethical as long as we can name others—some of them very prominent and influential—who do the same thing.

5. It's not unethical as long as there is no body of universally accepted, methodologically perfect (i.e., without any flaws, weaknesses, or limitations) studies showing—without any doubt whatsoever—that exactly what we did was the necessary and sufficient proximate cause of harm to the client and that the client would otherwise be free of all physical and psychological problems, difficulties, or challenges. This view was succinctly stated by a member of the Texas Pesticide Regulatory Board charged with protecting Texas citizens against undue risks from pesticides. In discussing Chlordane, a chemical used to kill termites, one member said, "Sure, it's going to kill a lot of people, but they may be dying of something else anyway" (Perspectives, 1990, p. 17).

6. It's not unethical if we acknowledge the importance of judgment, consistency, and context. For example, it may seem as if an expert witness who has given bogus testimony in a felony trial might have behaved "unethically." However, as attorneys and others representing such professionals often point out: It was simply an error in judgment, completely inconsistent with the high ethics manifest in every other part of the persons' life, and insignificant in the context of the unbelievable good that this person does.

7. It's not unethical as long as no law was broken.

8. It's not unethical if we can say any of the following about it (feel free to extend the list): "What else could I do?" "Anyone else would've done the same thing." "It came from the heart." "I listened to my soul." "I went with my gut." "It was the smart thing to do." "It was just common sense." "I just knew that's what needed to be done."

---

[2] From *Ethics in Psychotherapy and Counseling: A Practical Guide* (2nd ed.), by K. S. Pope and M. T. Vasquez, 1998, Hoboken, NJ: John Wiley & Sons. Copyright 1998 by John Wiley & Sons. Reprinted with permission John Wiley & Sons.

"I'd do the same thing again if I had it to do over."

"It worked before."

"I'm only human, you know!"

"What's the big deal?"

9. It's not unethical if the American Psychological Association, the American Psychiatric Association, or a similar organization allows it.

10. It's not unethical as long as we didn't mean to hurt anyone.

11. It's not unethical even if our acts have caused harm as long as the person harmed has failed to behave perfectly, is in some way unlikable, or is acting unreasonably.

12. It's not unethical if we have written an article, chapter, or book about it.

13. It's not unethical as long as we were under a lot of stress. No fair-minded person would hold us accountable for what we did when it is clear that it was the stress we were under—along with all sorts of other powerful factors—that must be held responsible.

14. It's not unethical as long as no one ever complained about it.

15. It's not unethical as long as the "system" makes it so hard to do our jobs that it is the system that elicited and is responsible for whatever it was we did (not, of course, to admit that we actually did anything).

16. It's not unethical as long as we don't talk about ethics. The principle of general denial is at work here. As long as no one mention ethical aspects of practice, no course of action could be identified as unethical.

17. It's not unethical as long as we don't know a law, ethical principle, or professional standard that prohibits it. This rationalization encompasses two principles: specific ignorance and specific literalization. The principle of specific ignorance states that even if there is, say, a law prohibiting an action, what we do is not illegal as long as we don't know about the law. The principle of literalization states that if we cannot find specific mention of a particular incident anywhere in legal, ethical, or professional standards, it must be ethical. In desperate times, when the specific incident is unfortunately mentioned in the standards and we are aware of it, it is still perfectly ethical as long as the standard does not mention our theoretical orientation. Thus, if the formal standard prohibits tailoring our testimony to whichever side will pay us the most, an expert witness who works from a behavioral, humanistic, or psychodynamic theoretical orientation may legitimately engage in this activity as long as the standard does not explicitly mention behavioral, humanistic, or psychodynamic frameworks.

18. It's not unethical as long as there are books, articles, or papers claiming that it is the right thing to do.

19. It's not unethical as long as a friend of ours knew someone who said an ethics committee somewhere once issued an opinion that it's okay.

20. It's not unethical as long as we know that legal, ethical, and professional standards were made up by people who don't understand the hard realities of psychological practice.

21. It's not unethical as long as we know that the people involved in enforcing standards (e.g., licensing boards or administrative law judges) are dishonest, stupid, destructive, and extremist; are unlike us in some significant way; or are conspiring against us.

22. It's not unethical as long as it results in a higher income or more prestige (i.e., is necessary).

23. It's not unethical as long as it would be really hard to do things another way.

24. It's not unethical as long as no one else finds out—or if whoever might find out probably wouldn't care anyway.

25. It's not unethical if we could not (or did not) anticipate the unintended consequences of our acts.

26. It's not unethical as long as we can find a consultant who says its OK.

27. It's not unethical as long as we believe strongly in what we're doing.

28. It's not unethical as long as we don't intend to do it more than once.

29. It's not unethical as long as we're very important and can consider ourselves beyond ethics. The criteria for importance in this context generally include being rich, well-known, extensively published, or tenured; having a large practice; having what we think of as a "following" of like-minded people; or having discovered and given clever names to at least five new diagnoses described on television talk shows as reaching epidemic proportions. Actually, if we just think we're important, we'll have no problem finding proof.

30. It's not unethical as long as we're busy. After all, given our workload and responsibilities, who could reasonably expect us to examine the validity, reliability, sensitivity, and specificity for the relevant population and assessment question of every assessment instrument we use, to keep up with all the relevant research, and to explore alternative explanations of the data?

Attempts to Be Funny

It is hard to be critical of humor. Gentle, self-deprecating humor can humanize an expert, showing that he or she—while taking the work seriously—does not take him- or herself too seriously. Humor can make a point in a pleasant, vivid, and memorable way. It can relieve the tension that has built up during vigorous adversarial cross-examination.

But attempts at humor during testimony often lead to disaster. One rule that expert witnesses may want to consider and possibly adopt is, "Never make a joke or a flip comment during a deposition." The temptation can be overwhelming. Opposing attorneys, sensing that an inexperienced witness may be naive, will do their best to create an informal atmosphere in which it appears that colleagues are just sitting around a table discussing various facts and opinions. What they hope that the witness does not recognize or eventually forgets is that all depositions are formal proceedings in which the witness is giving testimony under oath that will result in a written record. The witness may see an opportunity (often carefully and subtly created by the examining attorney) to make a joke, say

something witty, use a clever and ironic turn of phrase, or speak sarcastically.

However funny, ironic, or clever such spontaneous utterances may be at the time, they will almost certainly lack all humor when the attorney reads them back to the witness in the courtroom in front of the jury. Almost everyone recognizes the principle that transporting humor from one setting to another is a difficult task, as so many after-dinner raconteurs have defensively explained after telling what had seemed to them so funny: "Well, you had to be there." The jury will *not* have been there. They will not have been present in what may have *seemed* the casual and relaxed atmosphere of the deposition. The attorney can be trusted to read the witness's words back with minimal context and with a very different inflection. No witness needs to go through the ordeal of sitting in court and explaining what must seem an unwarranted, bizarre, or mystifying comment by saying something such as, "Oh, I was just making a joke."

Expert witnesses need to take special care to avoid irony or sarcasm during depositions. In conversation, irony or sarcasm is generally made clear through vocal inflection and physical demeanor, neither of which will come through when the cross-examining attorney reads verbatim from a deposition transcript. As an exaggerated example, an exasperated deponent, having spent hours enduring savage questioning about the apparent lack of care in conducting a forensic assessment, may exclaim in bitter sarcasm, "I was obviously *trying* to be careless!" Those words can never be called back but are now part of the permanent record of the trial and may, if the deponent frequently testifies, be made available by the opposing attorney to attorneys in future cases in which the expert is to participate.

Even in the courtroom, where the witness can assess the mood of the jury and the jury in turn can see the demeanor and hear the inflection of the witness, humor can be extremely risky. However gentle and well meaning a joke made by a witness seems at the time, a skilled attorney tends to have a varied arsenal for turning the spontaneous comment to his or her advantage. In a criminal trial, for example, an expert may make what seems a perfectly appropriate and innocuous humorous comment, and virtually everyone in the courtroom may laugh. The attorney conducting cross-examination may pause until all laughter has died away and then continue the pause. A *long* silence ensues. Finally, the attorney may ask the expert something along the lines of, "Do you think your assessment of the defendant is a fit subject for joking?"

Basically, the witness pondering this question has three options. First, he or she may answer "yes," an answer that will, when pursued by a skilled attorney, have some obvious disadvantages for the witness. Second, he or she may answer "no," inviting jurors and the attorney to reflect on his or her subsequent explanations about why, if the topic of the trial is not an occasion for joking, the expert used it as an occasion for joking. Third, the witness may attempt an elaborate and probably defensive explanation about how nothing was meant by the joke (which will probably be objected to by the attorney as nonresponsive to the question), about how humor has its place in even the most serious situations, and so on. Even if the witness offers a skilled theoretical exposition of justification, the attorney has succeeded in diverting attention from the expert's professional opinions. In other words, the attorney (with the help of the witness) has managed to change the subject.

Presenting clearly the results of a complex psychological and neuropsychological assessment is enough of a challenge for even the most skilled and seasoned expert witness without being forced to discuss unexpected and confusing side issues (e.g., the expert's joking about the case at hand) that are likely to make the task of helping the jury to understand difficult issues even more difficult. Trial attorney Louis Nizer provided a vivid case study of a professional comedian's attempts to be funny on the witness stand with disastrous results (see Nizer, 1961, pp. 233–286).

"I Don't Know"

Some expert witnesses find it all but impossible to say, "I don't know." Some do not want to undermine their testimony by acknowledging that they are not experts in all areas relevant to the case.

Some do not want to appear "dumb." Some allow themselves to be seduced and manipulated by a skilled and prepared attorney who as part of deposition and cross-examination subtly leads the expert farther and farther from an area of genuine expertise and toward more and more grandiose claims of omniscience and infallibility.

Attorney Melvin Belli of San Francisco wrote of one of his unsuccessful cross-examinations. He was facing a modest and unassuming cardiologist who had provided solid testimony during direct examination. Again and again, Belli tried to draw him into areas in which he was not an expert. Each time, the expert refused to take the bait. According to Belli,

> [the expert] refused to stray into any other field. When I asked him a question about gastroenterology, he replied, "I don't claim expertise in that area. I'm here as an expert on cardiology."
>
> "But you're an internist," I persisted. "Aren't all internists familiar with both cardiology and gastroenterology?"
>
> "Yes . . . but we don't claim to know all about them. . . ."
>
> "Well, . . . when you graduated from medical school . . . , didn't you think you knew all about medicine?"
>
> "Yes, I did . . . however, that was 30 years ago. Every medical student thinks he knows all about medicine when he graduates." (Belli & Carlova, 1986, p. 159)

Belli described how the modest, thoughtful manner of the expert won over the jury. The expert's lack of a know-it-all attitude kept Belli from scoring points with the jury. Belli noted that he (Belli) lost this case.

Constant Questioning

Expert witnesses who constantly question—and for whom nothing is off-limits for questioning—can catch errors before they make it into forensic reports and testimony. They can strengthen their findings and avoid getting caught off-guard during cross examination.

The questions begin with the most basic aspects of the case: "How do I know that the demographic information I received about this litigant is correct? How do I know that the litigant filled out this MMPI–2 form? How do I know that the WAIS, WMS [Wechsler Memory Scale] and other tests in the litigant's earlier medical record were correctly scored and interpreted? What if this diagnosis is wrong? Is there any important relevant information that's missing?" The process of questioning includes not only what we're unsure of but also our certainties, our basic assumptions, what we tend to take for granted.

This persistent questioning can be viewed as a basic of the scientific method, as the title of the *American Psychologist* article "Science As Careful Questioning" (Pope, 1997) suggests. The process of continuous questioning can also be understood as a basic ethic of the profession (Pope & Vasquez, 1998, p. 69). The questioning can extend from one's own work and the materials created or assembled for the case to the peer-reviewed literature. Even "facts" widely repeated in the peer-reviewed scientific literature may be demonstrably mistaken, and examining original sources on which they are based can be helpful.

> Examining original sources is necessary because all of us in this area, the tone of some of our writings to the contrary, are human and subject to error. It is likely that all of us have, at one time or another, made mistakes in characterizing an experiment, a legal case, an article, or some other source of information. Unfortunately, such mistakes may remain in the literature . . . , may be repeated in second and third hand articles, textbooks, legal cases, or courses, and may become widely accepted as accurate despite discordance with the original source on which it is based. . . . (Pope, 1998, p. 1175)

Olio and Cornell (1998), for example, compared original documents with a widely cited account of a prominent case and demonstrated the ways in which the "imperfect narrative of this case and pseudoscientific conclusions have been uncritically accepted and repeated in the literature, thus becoming an academic version of an urban legend" (p. 1182).

The constant openness to having made mistakes, overlooked important information, relied on inaccurate information, or misconstrued patterns of facts—and the persistent, active searching for errors, weaknesses, and alternative explanations—can be a key to fulfilling the responsibilities of the expert witness.

CHAPTER 6

THE ATTORNEY PREPARES
AND PRESENTS

This book emphasizes adequate preparation as a fundamental principle for attorneys and expert witnesses alike. Preparing to present and confront expert testimony about the Minnesota Multiphasic Personality Inventory (MMPI–2 or MMPI–A) requires the same diligence and work as any other aspect of the attorney's case. Commitment to the integrity of the case is essential. To achieve that commitment, attorneys must prepare so that they understand the evidence and arguments supporting their client's case but also anticipate and understand the opposition's assumptions, approach, and documentation.

To illustrate the essential elements of preparation, this chapter discusses preparation from the point of view of a plaintiff's attorney in personal injury litigation involving psychological damages and a jury trial. However, any litigation preparation—civil or criminal, prosecution or defense—requires the same fundamental understanding of and commitment to the strongest possible presentation of the case.

This chapter addresses preparation for hiring experts, pretrial motions, *voir dire* questions, opening statements, direct testimony, trial exhibits, and closing arguments. The chapter also discusses special problems inherent in the discovery in a criminal case. The first step in this preparation is pretrial research.

BACKGROUND RESEARCH

A hypothetical personal injury case involving psychological damages illustrates the extensive re-

search and discovery essential to cases involving the MMPI–2. After carefully obtaining the client's version of events and supportive documentation, the attorney must ensure that he or she understands the MMPI–2 as a standardized psychological test (see chaps. 2 and 3, this volume); its legal history and context (see chap. 4, this volume); and the principles of evaluating, administering, scoring, and interpreting psychological tests (see chaps. 5 and 8, this volume).

The attorney must be familiar with the MMPI–2—its nature, items, reliability, validity, and limitations. Taken alone and out of the context of the test (e.g., the MMPI–2 scales), a response to a single MMPI–2 item may be of questionable psychometric validity. The response to the item remains, however, a statement by the individual who took the MMPI–2. That statement may enhance or contradict other testimony. For example, the individual's responses to MMPI–2 items about nightmares or suicide attempts may contradict the individual's deposition testimony about these experiences. Some jurisdictions have ruled that cross-examination based on specific answers given to MMPI–A or MMPI–2 questions is inadmissible. The decision in *Hudgins v. Moore* (337 S.C. 333 (1999)), for example, reversed a death sentence based in large part on such improper cross-examination.

In most states, however, the admissibility of individual questions and responses from the MMPI remains an open question. Therefore, the lawyer reads the actual test items. Literally thousands of articles about the various forms of the MMPI have appeared in respected, peer-reviewed scientific and professional journals. Although this book provides fundamental information about MMPI–2 theory, research, and practice, the attorney (or an expert retained by the attorney) will need to conduct a literature search (perhaps beginning with some of the review articles cited in this book) to locate MMPI–2 articles directly relevant to the case at issue. Appendixes C through G present citations of works focusing on malingering, faking good, personal injury cases, child custody cases, and MMPIs administered in prison settings. The *Malingering Research Update* (Pope, 2005a) at http://kspope.com/assess/malinger.php may also be useful. The successful attorney reviews—perhaps working with an expert consultant—this literature and its application to the case. To the extent that the attorney is unfamiliar with the test and the relevant literature published in peer-reviewed journals, he or she is not yet ready to try a case involving the MMPI–2.

RETAINING AN EXPERT

Retaining an expert may make the task of conducting a review of the relevant MMPI–2 research much easier. Moreover, expert testimony may significantly influence the outcome of a trial.

The initial sections of chapter 9 (this volume) present areas of deposition and cross-examination questions for opposing experts, some of which focus on criteria for assessing competence. The attorney should evaluate the expert he or she is considering retaining in terms of these *same* criteria. The attorney needs to ensure that the professional has adequate education, training, credentials, and experience for the issues central to the case at hand (see also the section on competence in chap. 5, this volume). In addition, by reviewing chapter 5, the attorney supplements his or her understanding of the MMPI–2 with a detailed understanding of the steps an expert witness must take in preparing for and conducting a forensic examination. This understanding will be invaluable to the attorney in screening and communicating with potential expert witnesses.

If the potential expert witness is a psychologist, the attorney should determine whether he or she

obtained a doctorate from a graduate program accredited by the American Psychological Association (APA), whether an APA-accredited internship was completed, whether the individual is an APA fellow, and whether he or she is a diplomate of the American Board of Professional Psychology (again, see the section on competence in chap. 5, this volume; see also Appendix R).

If the potential expert is a psychiatrist, the attorney should determine if all medical training institutions, including internships and residencies, were fully accredited, if the expert is certified by the American Board of Psychiatry and Neurology, and if he or she is certified as an expert witness by the American Board of Forensic Psychiatry. The initial sections of chapter 9 (on deposing and cross-examining expert witnesses) set forth other criteria for the attorney to review in choosing his or her own expert (e.g., occupational history, record of research, and authorship of articles relevant to the case that have been published in peer-reviewed scientific and professional journals).

Most experts have a curriculum vitae or other summary of qualifications that can be submitted to the (potentially) hiring attorney as an aid in answering these questions. Any expert who wants to make him- or herself available to a specific attorney should be willing to give candid and fully detailed answers to the full range of questions outlined in the initial sections of chapter 9.

The careful attorney will take steps to verify independently some of this information. In cases in which the expert has been identified and endorsed by opposing counsel, transcripts may be subpoenaed from educational institutions; other documents can also be secured to verify the claims made by the expert. As noted in chapter 9, some "experts" have been known to exaggerate or simply invent qualifications. For example, one expert claimed to have been deemed by a prominent professional association to be one of the foremost authorities in a particular area. Careful research by the opposing attorney discovered that the professional association had made no such claim.

As this chapter was being written, the *Minnesota Star-Tribune* reported that an individual who had testified in a number of cases was charged . . . with three counts of perjury and three counts of practicing psychology without a license. . . . [The individual] who was paid $6,120 by the state for testifying [in one case], also lied about having a Ph.D. in clinical psychology from a correspondence school, Madison University, and a master of arts degree in clinical psychology from the University of St. Thomas, according to the charges. . . . He also said he graduated from the University of Wisconsin–Madison, but the school has no record that he ever attended. (Xiong, 2005, p. 7B)

Another expert claimed in court that the MMPI could fairly be used as a "lie detector." The appellate court criticized the expert's testimony and reversed the case (*Bentley v. Carroll,* 355 Md. 312 (1999)).

Chapter 5 quotes at length from the decision *United States v. Huberty* (50 M.J. 704 (A.F. Ct. Crim. App. 1999)) in which the appellate court upheld the trail court's decision to preclude the testimony by a prominent psychologist whose use of the MMPI–2 did not seem well-supported or widely accepted.

It is preferable to discover the reliability of an expert's curriculum vitae and other claims *before* deciding whether to hire (or at least before the other attorney shows the unreliability of such claims during a sworn deposition or in court testimony in front of the jury).

As emphasized in chapter 9, the fact that a professional has impressive credentials, is employed by a prestigious university or other institution, has a national or international reputation, or has testified frequently as an expert witness is no guarantee that claims about education, credentials, publications, and so on, are accurate.

Once credentials have been checked, the attorney needs to know if the expert can help the jury understand—on an emotional as well as an intellectual level—what happened to the client and how it relates to the issues before the court. Is the expert able to organize complex material and present it in everyday language? Can the expert help the jury to learn the connection between responses on an MMPI–2 protocol and the client's experience? Some experts may have a thorough understanding of psychometric theory and practice but are unable to put it into language understandable to those who have not won a Nobel prize in physics. Some may be able to talk about tests clearly but are unable to help jurors get to know and understand the client's condition. The expert who gives a vivid, specific, and compelling description will be much more likely to help the jury to follow the client's story and to understand the client's experience than the expert who may be able to cite the *Diagnostic and Statistical Manual of Mental Disorders, Fourth Edition* (*DSM–IV;* American Psychiatric Association, 1994) diagnostic data but provides only a general and ineffective description of the client.

If the attorney decides to retain an expert, the agreement should be adequately specific regarding such aspects as responsibilities, fees, scheduling, preparation of forensic reports, and so on. The agreement should also be written to help guard against misunderstandings or faulty memory (see Appendix L, this volume). There should be adequate discussion to prevent or at least minimize the chance that a conflict of interest (e.g., regarding the relationship of the expert to the opposing party or attorney in the case) is present or will emerge. Because the aspects of initial attorney–expert contacts and agreements are discussed in chapter 5, they are not repeated here.

The fact that an expert has been hired to evaluate MMPI–2 results does not mean that the expert should be called to testify. Fundamental questions to make this determination include the following.

1. Will the MMPI–2 results help the judge or jury understand facts or theories at issue in the case?
2. Are the MMPI–2 results consistent with the attorney's theory of the case?
3. If the MMPI–2 results are inconsistent, is there a reason for the inconsistency?
4. Will the MMPI–2 results confuse the judge or jury?

PREPARING FOR THE OPPOSING EXPERT

Chapter 9 on deposing and cross-examining the expert witness discusses sets of questions (about training, credentialing, formal complaints, publications, the nature and basis of expert opinions, etc.) that are useful in gathering information crucial to trying a case. What is easily overlooked, however, is the importance of verifying the claims made by the expert witness, and using the deposition material as a path to additional—sometimes pivotal—data.

For example, no matter how famous, influential, and respected the expert is, verify the degrees (do they exist at all and, if so, are they exactly as portrayed in the vitae and in deposition testimony?), the licensing status, the employment history, and so on. If possible, obtain deposition or trial transcripts of the expert's prior testimony. In some instances, one or two lines of previous testimony can, in proper context, discredit an expert. Has the expert honestly disclosed all instances of previous testimony or other involvement in legal proceedings, and candidly indicated for whom the work was done (e.g., plaintiff, prosecutor, defense, the court)? Does the percentage of work done for one side or the other suggest bias?

Obtain copies of all relevant articles, chapters, or books the expert has written and *read them carefully*. Showing that an expert's testimony in a current case is directly contradicted by the witness's own writings (or by a source cited in the witness's writings as authoritative) can be devastating cross-examination.

Conduct a Lexus/Nexus search, as well as other forms of Internet searching (e.g., Google,

PsycINFO, MedLine) using the expert's name as the search term. Try similar searches using the names of the expert's books, articles, and chapters.

The more information you gather about the expert, the more prepared you are to try the case well. *Any* documentation you find (from universities, credentialing programs, licensing boards, disciplinary bodies, deposition and trial transcripts, newspapers, books, articles, chapters, etc.) showing that the claims made by the expert (about training, accomplishments, experience, knowledge, the basis of expert opinions, etc.) are not completely accurate and honest goes directly against the expert's credibility.

If the opposing expert is to conduct an assessment, sometimes attorneys arrange for a forensic psychological assessment to be recorded. For example, when a defense expert witness is to conduct a forensic assessment of the plaintiff in a personal injury suit, the plaintiff attorney may attempt to arrange for a recording of the assessment. The recording may take the form of a videotape, an audiotape, or a court reporter who provides a transcript. In some instances the plaintiff may have a legal right to an observer or recorder. Expert witnesses, as described in chapter 5, may object to the presence of a third party.

The advantage for the attorney who has such a recording available is that judge and jury can examine for themselves the assessment process, the demeanor and behavior of both the expert witness conducting the assessment and the person being assessed. If there are departures—whether intentional or unintentional—from the standardized instructions or procedures for a test or assessment method, they can be identified. If the expert witness makes errors in a written assessment report about what a client actually said during an interview or in response to test questions, the mistakes can be identified. The jury can judge for itself whether the expert witness's assessment is biased or not accurately portrayed in the written assessment report.

PREFILING CONSIDERATIONS

In a civil injury case, consideration of the MMPI–2 precedes filing. Complaints must be drafted with an understanding of potential affirmative defenses. For example, an affirmative defense that has garnered significant attention in the last decade is the defense raised through statutes of limitations to claims founded on allegations of sexual abuse. If proven, the defense that the action was not brought in a timely way defeats the plaintiff's case. In *Doe v. Shults-Lewis Child & Family Servs,* (718 N.E.2d 738 (Ill. 1999)), an appellate court reversed the trial court, which had dismissed an action founded on childhood sexual abuse, finding that the statute of limitations had expired. The appellate court relied heavily on the MMPI–2 results, which supported the plaintiff's claim of repressed memory. Thus, even before an action is filed, a prepared attorney should consider potential uses for appropriate psychological testing.

DOCUMENT PRODUCTION

Once the attorney has a fundamental understanding of (a) the client's version of events, (b) all supportive documentation that the client is able to supply, (c) the nature and function of the MMPI–2 as it is relevant to the case, (d) the relevant diagnostic frameworks and categories, and (e) the expert's opinions and role (or roles, if one or more experts have been retained), he or she collects *all* remaining available information concerning the case that is the subject of the litigation through releases executed by the client, subpoenas, litigation procedures such as requests for production of documents, and depositions of the professionals involved.

All jurisdictions permit the parties to a civil litigation to inspect and copy any relevant designated documents that are not otherwise privileged. Some states require that the court order production of documents. Other states dictate that most routine document production occur without court intervention. Statutes or procedural rules of each jurisdiction control the timing of document production, inspection, and copying. Documents in control of people other than the parties involved are generally not subject to the same rules concerning production of documents. In those cases, the records are obtained through a *subpoena duces tecum,* more commonly called a "subpoena to produce."

In each case, the production request or subpoena lists both generally and specifically the documents requested. The term *document* is defined broadly to include any written material, correspondence, testing material, testing results (whether hand or computer scored), memoranda, audiotape recordings, videotape recordings, computer recordings (whether printed or otherwise stored), photographs, ledgers, and notes. Many of these documents are requested generally and then again specifically to ensure their production.

The documents requested of any expert who evaluates an MMPI–2 include a comprehensive list of possible original documents to be copied. In the following hypothetical case, Ms. Mary Smith is suing Dr. A. Acme. Dr. Jones was retained by Dr. Acme's attorney to conduct a psychological evaluation of Ms. Smith using an MMPI–2. The *subpoena duces tecum* asked for all materials related to the administration, scoring, and evaluation of the MMPI–2, as well as to all consultations. The subpoena specifically enumerated materials as follows.

1. Dr. Jones's entire original file pertaining to the psychological examination (evaluation) of Ms. Smith and any psychological testing, including but not limited to testing materials and results of the MMPI–2 or any version of the MMPI. (If Dr. Jones brings a copy instead of the original file, relocate the deposition to the location of the original file.)

2. All notes of conversations with any person, including Ms. Smith or any person consulted in connection with this case or the examination (evaluation) of Ms. Smith and any psychological testing, including but not limited to the MMPI–2 or any version of the MMPI.

3. All scorings, computerized scorings, and hand scorings of any and all psychological tests or assessment instruments, including but not limited to the MMPI–2 or any version of the MMPI.

4. All psychological testing documents for Ms. Smith, including the original completed examinations (i.e., the actual answer form), score sheets, and notes written by Ms. Smith or anyone else in connection with the testing.

5. All MMPI–2 testing documents for Ms. Smith, including the original completed examination, score sheets, and notes.

6. All documents that were reviewed in connection with your examination (evaluation) of Ms. Smith or any aspect of the case of *Smith v. Acme*.

7. All reports and drafts of reports prepared in connection with your examination (evaluation) of Ms. Smith or your evaluation in the case of *Smith v. Acme*.

8. A list of all documents, including computer-scored or computer-generated information, that you reviewed or wrote or that you discussed with any person in connection with your examination (evaluation) of Ms. Smith or the evaluation of her MMPI–2 testing, regardless of whether these documents are still in your possession.

9. The original file folders in which any information regarding Ms. Smith is or has been stored.

10. All calendars that refer to appointments with Ms. Smith or any person with whom you discussed the evaluation of Ms. Smith or the case of *Smith v. Acme*.

11. All billing statements and payment records.

12. All correspondence with any person in any way relating to the case of *Smith v. Acme*.

13. All videotape recordings or audio tape recordings of or pertaining to Ms. Smith.

14. The witness's curriculum vitae; a list of all articles, papers, chapters, books, or other documents he or she has written or published; a list of all articles, papers, chapters, books, or other documents, materials, or sources of information that he or she relied on in forming expert opinions regarding the matters at issue; transcripts from all institutions of higher learning attended by the expert; a list of all legal cases in which the expert has been endorsed in the past 5 years; a list of all attorneys and their addresses for each case in which the expert has been endorsed; and, in some cases, a copy of the expert's dissertation (thesis).

15. The originals of all correspondence, notes of conversations, and documents between and among the expert witness, attorneys (who re-tained the expert), representatives, and consultants of the attorneys in any way related to the case.

16. Access to all electronic messaging that in any way relates to the case including but not limited to e-mails.

The original file (see item 9), including the original file folder, is requested because short scribbled notes or notes on the reverse sides of documents can provide a wealth of information that might be missed when copies are requested. (See chap. 9, this volume, for deposition questions addressing the production, completeness, nature, and integrity of subpoenaed items.)

EXPERT ENDORSEMENT

Most states have adopted the Federal Rules of Civil Procedure, or some version of those rules. (See chap. 4, this volume, for discussion of rules concerning admissibility of MMPI–2 results). FED. R. CIV. P. 26(a)(2)(B) requires that material related to retained experts be disclosed to the other side in a timely manner. For decades many attorneys prided themselves on a "trial by ambush" tactic that included providing expert disclosures that included a minimum of information about what the expert intended to testify to. That scenario has changed. The rules require, and courts enforce, full disclosure of the expert's opinions, credentials, and previous testimony. Many courts refuse to allow experts to testify to any opinions that are not clearly set out in the expert's report. Indeed, FED. R. CIV. P. 37(c)(1) provides sanctions for nondisclosure that include total prohibition of the expert's testimony at trial. Thus, after *Daubert v. Merrell Dow Pharmaceuticals, Inc.* (509 U.S. 579 (1993), discussed in chap. 4, this volume), even the first expert report (the "disclosure" report) should show that the opinions are grounded in methods and procedures that are peer reviewed, generally accepted and reliable, and that the opinions are relevant to a fact at issue. Absent that information clearly set out in the first report, the expert may be placed on the defensive as the report is attacked or even precluded from testifying at trial.

Although counsel may need to guide an expert on the type of information necessary to survive a *Daubert* challenge, both the attorney and the expert should ensure and document that the expert, not the attorney, writes the disclosure report. Cross-examination of an expert based on a report written by an attorney is devastating to the expert's credibility. Nonetheless, the attorney should work with the expert to ensure that, pursuant to Rule 26, the disclosure report contains at a minimum the following.

- A "complete statement of all opinions" and the "basis and reasons therefore."
- A list of all "data or other information" that the expert has considered.
- All exhibits to be used. (If the MMPI–2 basic score profile may be used as an exhibit, it should be attached to the report.)
- The qualifications of the witness, including a list of publications authored in the past 10 years, and a list of other cases in which the expert has testified at trial or deposition within the previous 4 years.
- The compensation to be paid for document review, preparation and testimony.

In some cases, the Health Insurance Portability and Accountability Act (HIPAA) will be relevant to the issue of document production. HIPAA's potential implications will depend on such factors as the original purpose of the data (e.g., collected for medical purposes or part of a forensic assessment), the kind of case (e.g., civil or criminal), jurisdiction (if HIPAA constitutes the most stringent standard or state law is more stringent and consequently overrides HIPAA), the nature of the release, and so forth. Chapter 5 presents useful resources for determining HIPAA requirements.

DEPOSITIONS

In civil litigation proceedings, depositions generally follow production of documents. A deposition is testimony taken under oath before any trial. A structured guide to important areas of deposition questioning (which, if appropriate, may later become the basis of cross-examination in court) is presented in chapter 9. Although some attorneys may approach depositions and cross-examinations with the sole objective of, in Walter's (1982) words, "destroying the opponent's expert witness" (p. 10), a better strategy includes at least two alternative tasks: (a) learning from the expert in such a way that the opposing attorney can better understand his or her own client and case and (b) assessing whether the opposing expert's testimony might be beneficial to one's own case. Walter (1982) presented examples of this latter approach. If the expert's opinion is so ill-founded that an attorney can easily "destroy" it, better to gain additional information at deposition and save the destruction for trial.

With regard to the MMPI–2, the opposing attorney should be prepared to ask extensive questions about the results and about the test itself. The attorney should use the deposition to learn about the test and to then wed the expert to his or her opinions so that any later trial impeachment is crisp and clear. If there is a computer-generated report, the attorney should confirm at the deposition the limitations and weaknesses of such reports in general and of this report in particular. That way if any parts of the report are introduced at trial, the expert's earlier testimony can be used to mitigate negative impact.

PRETRIAL MOTIONS

To the extent practical, any questions about the admissibility of evidence are resolved before the jury is seated. If there is any question about the admissibility of test results because of novelty, that question should be addressed by a motion *in limine* before the jury is seated. (A motion *in limine* is made before the trial begins to limit certain types of evidence.) Interruptions, unless planned to alter the pace of the trial, are counterproductive. Virtually all *Daubert* challenges to the reliability and relevance of MMPI testing are raised and resolved before trial.

As discussed in chapter 4, the MMPI–2 and MMPI–A have all of the indicia of reliability required by *Daubert*. Nonetheless, counsel should include the testimony concerning that reliability at any *Daubert* hearing to educate any judge unfamiliar with the tests. However, the more disputed prong on the admissibility test will almost certainly revolve around the question of relevance. The attorney should be prepared to clearly answer this straightforward question in the affirmative: "Does the test result help to answer the question at issue?"

Pretrial motions have another benefit, particularly in criminal cases. In the states that allow formal discovery, including depositions in criminal cases, the procedure outlined in this chapter can be used to obtain the expert's opinion and foundation for that opinion. However, many states do not routinely allow discovery depositions to be taken in criminal cases. Where depositions are not allowed, other court proceedings can provide much of the information. For example, a defense attorney may attack the validity and admissibility of the MMPI–2 testing under FED. R. EVID. R. 702 and FED. R. EVID. R. 703 (see chap. 4 for a discussion of MMPI–2 admissibility).

The evidentiary hearing on the MMPI–2's validity allows an adequately prepared attorney to learn much of the information that could have been obtained through the civil discovery process. The subpoena *duces tecum* to the opposing expert witness should include all of the items identified in this chapter. The inquiry itself, however, is changed somewhat because the judge actually presides at the hearing, and the judge often severely restricts questioning. Therefore, the areas that seem most important (or least likely to be discovered through methods other than deposition) must be asked first. When the court restricts examination, the attorney, through offer of proof, explains on the record why the information is essential to adequately defend the client from the state's criminal allegations. A well-prepared, well-reasoned, and well-documented offer of proof may obtain extended inquiry.

The forensic use of any psychological testing requires that the attorney understand both the test administered and the results suggested by the test. A familiarity with the questions asked in the test as well as their general purpose in the evaluation process can help the attorney to understand, address, and exclude any incompatible testing results. For example, answering "true" to questions such as the following might be construed to suggest problems with alcohol or drug use. (Note: These are only examples and not actual MMPI items.)

- When I am at a party or get-together, sometimes I'll unexpectedly pass out. (*true*)
- Occasionally when coming home after dinner I'll stumble and fall down. (*true*)

This interpretation might be wrong. For example, the person may have a neurological disorder. The circumstances need to be considered by a competent clinician. This example highlights the difficulties in attempting to rely on a single response to an individual item and the crucial importance of obtaining and reviewing records of previous assessment and treatment. If a test interpretation is detrimental to the case, the attorney should ask the court before the trial to exclude the evidence because it is untrustworthy and likely to lead to confusion. Indeed, some courts have precluded cross-examination focusing on answers to single test questions. (See, e.g. *Hudgins v. Moore*, 337 S.C. 333 (1999).)

VOIR DIRE

The trial begins. Every well-tried case involves a morality play built on a few compelling themes. Themes allow a lawyer to simplify the evidence and to motivate the jurors to right a wrong; to protect our human family; to help someone who cannot help him- or herself. As noted earlier in this book, *voir dire* is the process of questioning potential jurors to determine which ones will be accepted as jurors for the trial and which ones will be excluded. This is conducted at the beginning of the trial, and it is the first time that the lawyer plants the seeds of the themes that are central to his or her case—the seeds that will be cultivated through argument, ripened with evidence, and harvested at closing. The theme of an effective case presentation is developed early and followed through *voir dire,* opening statement, direct and cross-examination of witnesses, and closing arguments.

The most powerful themes are simple, compelling, and consistent with and supported by the evidence—betrayal of trust, abuse of power, refusal to listen, protection of the vulnerable, rush to judgment. The themes central to the case are first discussed in *voir dire*. *Voir dire* also gives the jury its first impression of the lawyer and his or her case. Research has shown that first impressions with jurors are lasting and difficult to reverse (e.g., Kelven & Zeisel, 1966). Most federal court and many state courts preclude or severely limit the attorney's *voir dire*. In those jurisdictions that allow the attorneys to question the jury, the *voir dire* process gives attorneys the opportunity to create a strong first impression both for themselves and for their case.

Voir dire has three general purposes: (a) to establish rapport between the attorney and the jurors; (b) to obtain information from the jurors to separate those jurors who are most likely to accept the theme from those who should be challenged; and (c) to educate the jurors about the case. The second and third purposes are particularly important when MMPI–2 results or psychological testimony form an essential part of the case that the jury will hear.

In cases that involve substantial psychological testimony, the *voir dire* process is used by each side to identify the jurors who will accept the advocate's case. Many jurors distrust psychological testimony. Many distrust therapists and other clinicians, and they distrust the "mumbo-jumbo" testing on which some psychological testimony is based. The attorney needs to know who those jurors are. Closed-ended questions that are generally answered with "yes" or "no" are unlikely to generate answers that provide information. Open-ended questions that invite the jurors to openly share their feelings are more likely to obtain the information needed. Examples of closed-ended questions that will likely result in minimal information about the jurors include the following.

- This case may involve testimony from a psychologist about a test called the MMPI–2. Can you listen fairly to evidence from a psychologist?
- You will hear testimony about a test called the MMPI–2. Do you believe that psychological

testing can help a psychologist to evaluate the emotional health of someone?
- Do you understand that the MMPI–2 has been accepted in psychological communities for years?
- Do you understand that it is your responsibility to weigh the credibility of expert witnesses along with the credibility of any other witnesses in this case?

It is a rare juror who will respond to any of these questions with anything except "yes." The answers reveal little or nothing about the jurors.

Examples of open-ended questions that are more likely to elicit valuable information from the jurors include the following.

- What are your feelings about psychologists? Why?
- What do you think about testing that tries to evaluate a person's emotional condition?
- How do you feel about psychological or emotional damages?
- What sorts of evidence would you want to see to prove psychological damages?
- What do you think about a person who would go to a psychiatrist or psychologist for help?

The attorney may not like the answers he or she receives from the prospective juror, but it is better to learn those answers in *voir dire* than in an unfavorable verdict. Barton (1990) has provided additional examples of general open-ended questions intended to identify jurors who accept the idea of psychological damages.

THE OPENING STATEMENT AND CALLING WITNESSES

The opening statement is probably the most underestimated and poorly used phase in a jury trial. It is the first opportunity for the advocate to tell the client's story. It is difficult to overemphasize the importance of conveying a trial's complex evidence and information in the form of a coherent narrative. Cognitive psychologist Roger Schank (1990) summarized a wealth of research data into a basic principle.

People think in terms of stories. They understand the world in terms of stories that they have already understood. New events or problems are understood by reference to old previously understood stories and explained to others by the use of stories. We understand personal problems and relationships between people through stories that typify those situations. We also understand just about everything else this way as well. (p. 219)

(See also Schank, 1980; Schank & Abelson, 1977; Schank, Collins, & Hunter, 1986.)

In an article in the journal *Science*, Gordon Bower and Daniel Morrow of Stanford University (1990; see also Black & Bower, 1979; Bower & Clark, 1969; Morrow, Greenspan, & Bower, 1987) used much more technical language to describe the complex process by which people actively respond to stories.

We do not distinguish studies based on reading from those based on listening, since the input modality is irrelevant to the points at issue. Most researchers agree that understanding involves two major components. . . . First, readers translate the surface form of the text into underlying conceptual propositions. Second, they then use their world knowledge to identify referents (in some real or hypothetical world) of the text's concepts, linking expressions that refer to the same entity and drawing inferences to knit together the causal relations among the action sequences of the narrative. The reader thus constructs a mental representation of the situation and actions being described. This referential representation is sometimes called a mental model or situation model. Readers use their mental model to interpret and evaluate later statements in the text; they use incoming messages to update the elements of the model, including moving the characters from place to place and changing the state of the hypothetical story world. Readers tend to remember the mental model they constructed from the text, rather than the text itself. . . . The bare text is somewhat like a play script that the reader uses like a theater director to construct in imagination a full stage production. Throughout the story the narrator directs the reader's focus of attention to a changing array of topics, characters, and locations, thus making these elements temporarily more available for interpreting new information. (Bower & Morrow, 1990, p. 44)

Novelist Joan Didion (1979) put it this way: "We tell ourselves stories in order to live. . . . We interpret what we see, select the most workable of the multiple choices. We live . . . by the imposition of a narrative line upon disparate images" (p. 11).

For additional research and discussion regarding the nature and influence of narrative, see chapter 5 of this book; see also Bakan (1978); Chandler, Greenspan, and Barenboim (1973); Emery and Csikszentmihalyi (1981); Greenfield (1983–1984); H. C. Martin (1981–1982); Meringoff (1980); Pearson and Pope (1981–1982); Schafer (1992); Schank (1990); Steinberg (1982–1983).

The best litigators understand and use the power of narrative from the beginning of a trial to its conclusion. A few outstanding attorneys—Gerry Spence in Wyoming and (Judge) Christopher Munch in Colorado—have spent decades crafting opening statements into storytelling. Chicago litigator Patricia Bobb (1992) has argued that advocates can win their cases with opening statements. Recounting one of his trials, Gerry Spence described his typical opening: "I began my story like the old storyteller, setting the scene, creating the characters" (Spence & Polk, 1982, p. 298). In another trial, he actually used the words "once upon a time" in his opening statement: "'Ladies and gentlemen—my dear friends,' I began. 'Once upon a time . . .'" (Spence, 1983, p. 242). Nizer (1961, p. 37) described making long opening statements without notes, taking the opportunity to make eye contact with each juror, and letting the honesty and sincerity of the statement invite the jurors' involvement. For examples of compelling opening statements and guides to creating them, see Habush (1984), Julien (1984), LaMarca (1984), F. Levin (1984), and J. D. MacDonald (1968).

The storytelling technique can be fatal to those who use it if the story rings false in any way, if it is not fully supported by the evidence, or if the truthfulness of the witness's testimony and the attorney's statements is not apparent. This approach heightens either the veracity or the falsity of the attorney's case. If attorneys do not have a valid story to tell—one that represents the truth as accurately and vividly as possible—it is better, as the old joke has it, to simply "bang on the table." Nizer (1961) wrote compellingly of this principle: If the story does not make sense in terms of the evidence, the testimony, common sense, and the jurors' own experience, the false story will bring down the case.

The storytelling technique requires the attorney to discard legal terminology and concepts and, instead, to tell a story with word pictures and imagery that allow the listener to identify with the client, to make sense of what will likely be complex information, and to want to hear the testimony. Nowhere is the storytelling technique more valuable than in the opening statement of a case involving psychological damages. The advocate has the opportunity either to reinforce skepticism about psychological damages and psychological testing or to use those tests to paint a vivid picture of harm. Specific descriptions that evoke images replace general wording. Humanizing the client through use of his or her name replaces all reference to "my client." Concentrating on the facts of the case replaces the traditional (and ineffective) opening statement disclaimers.

The first minutes of the opening statement are critical to inviting the members of the jury into the case. Consider the first few minutes of two versions of the following opening statement.

Version 1: Ladies and gentlemen of the jury. It is a pleasure to have this opportunity to describe what I believe the evidence will show. This is a road map only. Nothing I say to you is evidence. The evidence in this case will come from that witness stand and from exhibits that the court accepts into evidence. The evidence in this case will include the testimony of a renowned psychologist. That psychologist examined my client and conducted several standard tests. He will testify that his conclusions, as confirmed by the psychological tests that he administered, show that my client was psychotic for more than a year. The expert witness will tell you that my client's psychosis was caused because she went to a therapist for counseling and that therapist instead had sex with her. You will also hear evidence that, as a direct and proximate cause of the therapist's abuse of my client, she continues to suffer from a posttraumatic stress disorder. You will hear testimony from a board-certified psychiatrist that the conduct of Dr. Jones fell below the standard of care required of therapists in the community.

Version 2: Since Gail's 2-year-old son died in April of 1986, there have been days she can't get out of bed. She cries for hours. Her little girl asks her mommy if she can help. Gail knows she has to do something to get better. She still has a daughter who needs her. She knows she can't do it alone. She turns for help to a person she believes she can trust. She turns to a counselor. This is a case about a betrayal of Gail's trust.

The first counseling session is April 23, 1986. The doctor gives Gail a psychological test that shows her therapist that Gail is depressed and vulnerable. By May of 1986, the counselor is holding her hand during sessions. By June, he is kissing her cheek. At each session, he holds her, repeating, "God loves you, your boy is in heaven." By July, Gail begins losing track of time. She finds herself in her car, not knowing where she is or how she got there. August 4, 1986, is the first time Gail has seen her little boy since his funeral four months before. He is dressed in the same navy shorts and yellow shirt he was wearing the day he died. She moves past the dining room table and reaches to touch her son. Her hand passes through the air that moments before had, to her, been a 2-year-old boy—her 2-year-old boy. She later tells her counselor how scared she was. He tells her not to worry. He can fix it. He holds her, fondles her, and repeats, "God loves you, your boy is in heaven." Later that week she begins seeing and hearing other persons who are not there. For 18 months, Gail never knows if the hand she reaches out to touch is real. Doctors will explain, and independent testing confirms, that Gail is psychotic for more than a year and a half because her counselor, the person she believes she can trust, so confuses her that she does not know what is real and what isn't.

These two opening statements are based on the same facts. The first story is weak. The second story is strong. A strong opening statement is vivid, compelling, and told in present tense. A strong opening statement cannot be made on the spur of the moment. It requires months of attention, thought, and structure. The opening statement should be drafted, revised, and delivered to any friend, associate, or secretary who will listen. They will tell you those areas that are unclear, repetitive, or boring. The story should also convey the theme. The first

story has no real theme. The second shows how the client's trust is betrayed.

Witnesses should be called and testimony elicited in such a way that adds support, clarity, detail, significance, and immediacy to the basic story that the attorney is trying to communicate to the jury. There is research supporting the notion that jurors may best organize the overwhelming information they encounter during a complex trial in terms of such narratives. Pennington and Hastie (1992; see also Pennington & Hastie, 1981, 1988, 1991), for example, described their explanation-based story model as an "empirically supported image of the juror decision process that can serve as the basis for a unified, coherent discussion of the behavior of jurors in practical and scientific analyses" (1992, p. 203). Their research supports the view that the "story structure was a mediator of decisions and of the impact of credibility evidence" and that judgments made at the conclusion of a case "followed the prescriptions of the Story Model, not of Bayesian or linear updating models" (p. 189).

Nizer (1961) linked the story told by the witness to the jurors' perceptions of the witness's credibility: "We talk of the credibility of witnesses, but what we really mean is that the witness has told a story which meets the tests of plausibility and is therefore credible" (p. 11).[1]

Conley, O'Barr, and Lind (1978) discussed in detail the differences between testimony in *narrative style* and testimony in *fragmented style*. They noted, for example, that

> if those hearing testimony believe that its style is determined by the lawyer, they may believe that use of a narrative style indicates the lawyer's faith in the witness' competence. Similarly, when the witness uses a fragmented style, presumably under the direction of the lawyer, the lawyer may be thought to

---

[1] The Pennington and Hastie research addressed how jurors arrive at decisions about guilt or innocence in a criminal trial. Costanzo and Costanzo (1992) discussed jury decision making during the penalty phase of such trials when "the question is no longer 'What happened?' but 'What punishment does this defendant deserve?'" (p. 197). V. L. Smith (1991) presented research concerning how jurors use a judge's instructions when the "judge's instructions are intended to educate untrained jurors in the legal concepts that apply to the case that they must decide" (p. 858; see also Elwork & Sales, 1985; Elwork, Sales, & Alfini, 1977, 1982; Luginbuhl, 1992). For some of the fundamental concepts and research regarding how juries arrive at decisions, see the landmark works, *The American Jury* (Kelven & Zeisel, 1966) and *Jury Verdicts* (Saks, 1977).

consider the witness incompetent.
(p. 1387)

Similarly, Bank and Poythress (1982) wrote, "Both experienced mental health witnesses and recent experimental findings emphasize the superiority of the narrative style of testimony" (p. 188).

Providing opening statements and testimony in narrative style is one way of making the story more vivid. Other aspects of language may have similar effects. Bell and Loftus (1985; see also Erickson, Lind, Johnson, & O'Barr, 1978; Lakoff, 1990), for example, noted,

> Vivid detailed testimonies are more likely to be more persuasive than pallid testimonies for a variety of reasons. Relative to pallid information, vivid information presented at trials may garner more attention, recruit more additional information from memory, cause people to spend more time in thought, be more available in memory, be perceived as having a more credible source, and have a greater affective impact. (p. 663)

DIRECT EXAMINATION OF THE EXPERT

Months, even years, of hard work by the attorney and the expert witness boil down to one question: "Can the expert effectively provide the judge or the jury with competent, understandable, and helpful information?" The direct examination is founded in a simple concept: The attorney asks the expert questions about crucial issues in the case; the witness answers those questions.

There are two phases to the direct testimony of an expert. The first involves "qualifying" the expert to give his or her testimony. Before any expert testimony is taken, the judge decides whether the expert should be allowed to give testimony. He acts as a "gatekeeper" to make sure that the expert's testimony will be both relevant and reliable, as discussed in chapter 4. Assuming the expert is allowed by the court to testify, the second phase involves the testimony actually given by the expert.

Qualifying the Expert for Direct Examination

The theory underlying expert testimony is that experts, because of special knowledge, training, and experience, are able to form better opinions on certain subjects than those who do not have that special knowledge. Under certain circumstances the law allows the expert to provide those opinions to the jury to assist it in resolving issues in the case. (The issue of admissibility is discussed in detail in chap. 4. For convenience, an abbreviated discussion follows.)

Expert witnesses are treated differently from lay witnesses in several ways. First, the litigant who calls the expert pays the expert without being subject to allegations of bribing a witness. Second, the expert witness may testify to opinions and to hearsay—statements that other people told him or her—which lay witnesses are generally precluded from testifying to in court. In many ways virtually everything the expert testifies to would be improper testimony from any other witness. Third, there is often an imprimatur of expertise that, critics contend, bestows inordinate weight to an expert who may have limited credentials or limited practical knowledge regarding the issue about which he or she testifies.

To have the right to testify to hearsay and opinions, the court needs to recognize the expert status, which, theoretically, makes that hearsay and those opinions of the witness, nonetheless, reliable.

We live in a time of daily, even hourly scientific change. A relatively short while ago, DNA testing was an untested theory, and testimony concerning DNA would not have been allowed into the courtroom. Discussion of cloning animals belonged in a "Star Trek" episode, not in a courtroom. Preliminary questions need to be answered before expertise is accepted in court. When does a person with knowledge become an "expert"? When does a "charlatan's" theory become special knowledge worthy of a jury's consideration?

As discussed at length in chapter 4, before 1993, the answers to the questions concerning predicate for expert testimony involved the concept of "general acceptance." In *Frye v. United States* (293 F. 1013 (D.C. Cir. 1923)), the court held,

Just when a scientific principle or discovery crosses the line between the experimental and demonstrable stages is difficult to define. Somewhere in this twilight zone the evidential force of the principle must be recognized, and while courts will go a long way in admitting testimony deduced from a well recognized scientific principle or discovery, the thing from which the deduction is made must be sufficiently established to have gained general acceptance in the particular field in which it belongs. (293 F. at 1014)

Now the Federal Rules of Evidence guide the courts in deciding when an expert may testify and to what an expert may testify. Rule 702 states that

if scientific, technical, or other specialized knowledge will assist the trier of fact to understand the evidence or to determine a fact in issue, a witness qualified as an expert by knowledge, skill, experience, training, or education, may testify thereto in the form of an opinion or otherwise.

In *Daubert v. Merrell Dow Pharmaceuticals, Inc.* (509 U.S. 579 (1993)), the court held that, to be qualified to testify as an expert, the attorney first must explain to the court how the testimony of the expert will likely be helpful and second must show the court that the witness is qualified to give the testimony. Many attorneys jump to the second question without properly addressing the first. The mistake can cost the case a crucial witness.

Judges want to know how the projected testimony fits into the case. What "fact at issue" will it help to clarify? A brief discussion between the lawyer and the expert in front of the judge concerning how the MMPI–2 results can clarify something at issue—competency, sanity, injury—lays a foundation that can be critical. Although this first hurdle looks simple, the problems encountered in matching experts with issues can be complex and subtle. Is a psychologist who has never treated a person for posttraumatic stress disorder (PTSD), but who

knows all of the literature, qualified to evaluate a party for that disorder? Can a doctor who limits her practice to research testify as to the standard of care owed by a psychologist to a client?

Having analyzed the issues that need to be addressed by the expert, the second part of qualifying an expert is generally simple and straightforward. It involves showing the court that the knowledge, skill, experience, training, or education that the witness possesses gives him or her special insight such that the testimony, even opinion testimony, should be allowed. In addition, as concerns admission of the results from psychological testing such as MMPI–2, it involves showing the court that the methods and procedures possess requisite validity to establish evidentiary reliability. Many of the questions asked in front of the judge to convince the judge to allow the expert testimony should be repeated later before the jury to let the jury know that the expert brings something to the case that will help the jurors to resolve an important issue.

The following is a sample list of questions to be asked by an attorney, which should result in the qualification of an expert, provided, of course that the expert really is qualified. The questions are suggestions only, and should not be read like a checklist. Rather, the attorney and the expert should strive to carry on a conversation, with the attorney asking questions not on the list as part of that normal conversation. The first questions should be broad and should give a judge or a jury a general sense of who the expert is and why she is going to testify. The qualification questions should, wherever feasible, relate to the issue that will be before the jury. The jury needs to develop confidence that the expert will help the jurors to decide an issue that has importance to the case. The more relevant the expert's experience and education is to the issue at hand, the more likely the jury is to rely on what he or she says.

- Tell the jury your name, doctor.
- What is your business?
- How long have you been a psychologist?
- Doctor, have you come to court prepared to state your expert opinion concerning whether or not Mrs. Jones has been hurt? (Note: The expert

should be prepared to simply answer "Yes, I have." The expert has not yet been qualified to give her opinion. However, this question early on tells the jury the reason that the expert is there. This question tells the jurors that they need to listen to the doctor's credentials because the credentials may be important to a crucial issue.)

- Before we get to your opinions, Dr. Smith, I would like you to tell the jury a little bit about yourself. Let's start with your education and training.
- Describe your educational background.
- What courses did you study that were particularly useful in your evaluation of Mrs. Jones?
- What is clinical psychology?
- Tell the jury your academic training in clinical psychology.
- Was that background particularly helpful for you in this case? (Note: Emphasize the importance of any background, training, education that the opposing expert lacks.)
- Have you had experience in teaching and administration in the field of clinical psychology?
- Describe that experience.
- Have you been involved in training other professionals in psychology?
- Describe that training to the jury.
- How long did you provide psychological care at the Free Clinic to children who had been abused by their parents? (Note: Emphasize any training or experience that undercuts potential prejudice against an expert as a "hired gun.")
- Tell us about any experiences that you had at Children's Hospital that relate to your evaluation of Mrs. Jones.
- What is the MMPI–2?
- What is the difference between a subjective test and the MMPI–2?
- How does the MMPI–2 relate to the work you did in assessing whether or not Mrs. Jones was hurt?
- Have you attended any workshops on the MMPI–2?
- Have you published any works in psychology? (Note: Questions should only be asked if the attorney knows before testimony that the answers

will support the special education and training required under Rule 702 of the Federal Rules of Evidence. If the answer to this question is, "No," the question should not be asked on direct examination unless intended to preempt cross-examination, in which case the next question should be, "Why not?" A good and modest answer, as long as it is truthful, might be, "I spend 10 hours a day treating trauma patients at the emergency room. I just haven't had time to attend any recent workshop on the MMPI–2.")

- Are you familiar with computer software that scores and interprets the MMPI–2?
- Have you developed any software to score and interpret the MMPI–2?
- How does the development of that software relate to your work in this case?
- Doctor, to what professional associations do you belong?
- How did you become a member?
- Does the American Psychological Association have any activities that relate specifically to evaluating the type of injuries that Mrs. Jones suffered?
- What was your role in that matter?
- Dr. Smith, I'm handing you a copy of Exhibit 18. Is that your current resume? Does it provide additional information about your education and work experience?
- Your Honor, I offer Plaintiff's Exhibit 18.
- Dr. Smith, on page 4, your resume describes an article you wrote for *Psychological Assessment* for the American Psychological Association. Please tell us what that journal is.
- What is a "peer-reviewed" journal?
- Is that a peer-reviewed journal?
- Did your work on that article help you in this case? How? (Note: Do not have the witness read every item on the resume. Rather, the attorney should highlight a few publications or education experiences that are particularly relevant to this case. Keep the discussion short.)
- Doctor, before forming an opinion in this case, what did you do? What materials did you review? What was the evaluation process? (Note: The expert's description of what he did in the case at hand brings the jury back to the connection between the expert's credentials

and the issues they will decide. In addition, the information gives weight and credibility to the subsequent testimony.)

- Your honor, I offer Dr. Smith as an expert in psychology and ask that she be allowed to testify as an expert in the area of psychological assessment and interpretation of psychological testing, including the MMPI–2. Dr. Smith is qualified by reason of her education and experience, particularly her work at Harvard at Children's Hospital, to provide expert testimony on the cause of Mrs. Jones's injury and on her diagnosis and her prognosis. (Note: This is the formal tender of the witness to the court as an expert. A tender is not required or allowed in all jurisdictions. Where permitted, the tender tells the court and the jury the areas that the lawyer expects the witness to address.)

Standard questions aimed at giving fundamental information to the jury are only part of a well-planned direct testimony. The bulk of the testimony should involve powerful and persuasive techniques. Often attorneys expect experts to provide testimony that is necessarily dry. However, that need not be the case. The use of metaphors and analogies and vivid details recognized as fundamental to telling any story are likewise central to testimony by experts. The most impressive credentials are worthless if the jury is unable or unwilling to hear the testimony provided. Every person who testifies wants to provide compelling testimony. Many just do not know how to do it. Failure of attorneys to encourage experts to provide testimony rich with active verbs and strong images is a disservice to the client. For example, even the use of jargon and acronyms such as "PTSD" or "DID" (Dissociative Identity Disorder) diminishes the power of the diagnosis that describes the illness. Words such as "traumatic," "stress," and "identity," even "disorder," all carry power and meaning that acronyms do not.

Consider the following testimony given by psychiatrist Dr. J. Gary May in a Colorado jury trial in 1998. It is a strong example of giving testimony in the present, rather than the past tense, and in using descriptive analogy. He was asked to explain the use of transference within psychotherapy. Other doctors had already defined transference in technical and colorless language. The power of the transference phenomenon had been lost to the jury through the use of powerless language. The eyes of the jury glazed over when the questioning began. Within minutes the entire jury leaned forward, eager to understand the concept.

Attorney: The first thing I'd like you to do is tell the jury what countertransference and transference are.

Expert: In spite of the sound of the words, I don't believe the concept is really very complicated. [A fairly standard definition of transference followed.] There was a terrific episode of "Star Trek" in which the group went down to a new planet, and there they are being seduced by incredible, beautiful people, and Captain Kirk falls in love with this extraordinary woman, and he is going to stay. He isn't going to go back. He just couldn't go back to the ship, and then something happens where the powers for the aliens are lost, and he finds out he was in love with a worm, and the worm had projected an image into his mind of what she was really like, that fit exactly what he had always hoped to find. I'm not saying that psychiatrists are usually or always worms, but the fact of the matter is that many of the same things happen to your patient, when they begin to idealize you . . . they are responding to this person in terms of their own distortions and their own wishes and their own altered beliefs. . . .

Of course, the use of analogy and metaphor must be carefully planned. A metaphor that seems flip or an analogy that is not on target can backfire in the hands of a skillful cross-examination. In the previous example, the timing was perfect and the humor appropriate. The analogy had been carefully considered, and it served its purpose—to effectively and concretely communicate a technical concept. The cross-examiner made the mistake of exploring the story. However, the power of the analogy actually grew during the cross-examination.

Attorney: It would be inappropriate, then, for Captain Kirk to engage in a sexual relationship with nurse Chapel (a member of his crew)?

Expert: I don't know what spaceship captains' codes of ethics are. I think this would be hazardous to both actually.

Attorney: Might it be damaging to nurse Chapel?

Expert: It might be.

Attorney: That's because of a perceived power differential?

Expert: That would be only one of the reasons. Also because of the distortion that takes place. The power differential seems to add greatly to the potential for a powerful transference distortion.

Direct Examination: Maximizing the Offense

The lawyer should let the jury know as soon as the witness is accepted by the court as an expert that this testimony is important. Start strong and immediately address the most important issues. Discuss potential weaknesses. If the defense theme claims that the client is malingering, the attorney might ask the doctor immediately whether the evaluation suggests that the client is "faking."

- What is your opinion about whether or not Mrs. Jones's life has been changed by the collision in this case?
- What is malingering?
- Is there any evidence to support the notion that Mrs. Jones is malingering?
- Why not?
- What is the evidence in the objective testing that supports your conclusion that this woman is really hurt?

If the main issue is whether or not the injury was caused by the event or was preexisting, the attorney should address it with the best evidence he or she has.

- Were you able to review an MMPI–2 test that was given to Mrs. Jones 2 years ago?
- Did you compare it with a test you gave her in April?
- What did you conclude?
- Tell the jury what in the testing helped you figure this out.

In general, each major opinion by the expert should be presented under a three-step approach. First, ask the expert whether he or she has an opinion on a specific topic. Second, have the expert tell the jury what the opinion is in one or two sentences. Third, ask the expert to explain the basis for the opinion.

- Doctor, do you have an opinion that you can state within a reasonable degree of psychological probability as to whether or not the injury to Mrs. Jones was caused by the actions of the defendant?
- What is that opinion?
- Tell the jury why you believe that she was injured in May of 1998 and not earlier.

The following types of direct questions specifically relate to the MMPI–2. If the test results are an important part of the case, the lawyer will want the jury to understand the fundamentals of the test.

- What is the MMPI–2?
- How was the test developed?
- What is the difference between the MMPI–2 and the MMPI.
- What are MMPI–2 scales?
- Are there "standard" interpretations for MMPI–2 scales? What does "standard" mean?
- Do the scales measure current problems or lasting personality features?
- Does the MMPI–2 have scales that evaluate a person's cooperation with the testing?
- How do the validity scales work in evaluating a client?
- Does Mrs. Jones have interpretable MMPI–2 profiles in the test she took?
- What personality statements can be made about Mrs. Jones on the basis of her MMPI–2 scores?
- What diagnostic statements can be made about Mrs. Jones on the basis of her MMPI–2 scores?
- Is there a scale designed to evaluate posttraumatic stress disorder?
- Is this scale of the MMPI–2 specifically applicable to evaluating a posttraumatic stress disorder?
- Is this scale applicable to Mrs. Jones? What does it tell us?

- Do the MMPI–2 profiles produced by Mrs. Jones clearly reflect a posttraumatic stress disorder?
- Describe to the jury what leads you to that conclusion.

Direct Examination: Preempting the Defense

Any good, direct examination will include a discussion of any weaknesses in the witness's expertise and in the opinion. Addressing weaknesses directly has two advantages. First, it takes the thunder out of the opponent's cross-examination; second, it tells the jury that you have nothing to hide.

In general, the best way to deal with a problem is to address it directly.

- Doctor, have you ever made mistakes scoring an MMPI–2?
- Did you originally make a mistake scoring Mrs. Jones's MMPI–2?
- How did the mistake happen?
- Does that mistake affect the conclusion here?
- Why (or why not)?

TRIAL EXHIBITS

Demonstrative evidence has played an increasingly important role in litigation in the past decade. Jurors want to *see* the evidence. Trial exhibits lend vividness to direct testimony: The visual symbol illustrates and reinforces the spoken word. The best exhibits usually contain a minimal amount of information and are strongly illustrative. The MMPI–2 lends itself to several types of exhibits.

One exhibit to consider is an enlargement of the MMPI–2 basic scale profile (see Appendix Z, this volume). To the extent that the profile peaks help to explain a significant aspect of the case, the exhibit will assist a jury in remembering and understanding the MMPI–2 evidence.

In the case that was the subject of the opening statements just described, if the offending doctor had administered an MMPI–2, enlargements of single questions taken directly from the MMPI–2, with the answers of the patient, might help to convince the jury that the doctor knew that his or her patient was vulnerable.

As previously discussed, lawyers and expert witnesses may have divergent views about singling out a response to an individual MMPI–2 item. The expert may view the individual response in light of its lack of psychometric validity when taken out of context. The attorney, on the other hand, may view an individual's response to a specific MMPI–2 item as a "statement" made by the individual, a statement that is relevant to the facts at issue before the court.

Another exhibit to consider, particularly in psychological damages cases, is an enlargement of the diagnostic criteria for those disorders suggested by the MMPI–2 or diagnosed by experts. The diagnostic criteria for posttraumatic stress disorder, for example, include re-experiencing a trauma through recurrent and intrusive recollections of the event, recurrent dreams and flashbacks, and psychological distress at exposure to events that symbolize or resemble the trauma. Each criterion that fits the case can be expanded by expert and lay witnesses from the general into a specific and compelling story through the details of the client's life.

Even the characteristics or symptoms of personality disorders can help form a compelling story in a case. For example, a formal chart or visual display of the diagnostic criteria for dependent personality disorder could be used to help a judge or jury understand that a therapist knew or should have known of the power that he or she possessed in the client's life.

Any exhibit that can help the jury to understand a complicated diagnosis should be considered.

SPECIAL JURY INSTRUCTIONS IN CIVIL CASES

A number of possible civil jury instructions address the unique problems associated with psychological damages cases.

A major defense in most civil claims involving psychological injury is that the person harmed was ill before the trauma occurred. This defense is often used in cases in which the litigation involves a defendant therapist who exploits a patient who has come to the therapist for help. Such a person usually seeks therapeutic help because he or she has a preexisting problem. In Colorado, as in many states, an approved jury instruction discusses the exacerbation of preexisting conditions. Colorado Jury Instruction 6:8 requires that a jury attempt to separate the amount of damages caused by the negligence of the defendant from the preexisting damages. The instruction goes on to say,

> If you are unable to separate the damages caused by the ailment or disability which existed before (the occurrence) and the damages caused by the (negligence) of the defendant, then the defendant is legally responsible for the entire amount of damages you find the plaintiff has incurred.

The concept of a preexisting condition or disability is different from the notion of a vulnerability or frailty. In most jurisdictions, the wrongdoer takes the plaintiff as he or she finds him or her. In *Fischer v. Moore* (183 Colo. 392, 517 P.2d 458 (1973)), the Colorado supreme court said that the wrongdoer "may not seek to reduce the amount of damages by spot-lighting the physical frailties of the injured party" (517 P.2d at 459). A specific instruction highlighting the premise that the defendant takes the plaintiff as he or she finds the plaintiff sets a background for a closing argument that includes an appeal to fundamental fairness: The vulnerable deserve protection. Colorado Jury Instruction 6:7 reads as follows.

> In determining the amount of plaintiff's actual damages, you cannot reduce the amount of damages or refuse to award any such damages because of any physical frailties (mental condition or illness) of the plaintiff that may have made him more susceptible to injury, disability or impairment.

Every set of standard jury instructions contains language telling the jury that it should not consider bias, sympathy, or prejudice in its deliberations. Defense attorneys use the instruction to argue that the jury should not feel sorry for the plaintiff. A skilled and prepared plaintiff's attorney can respond in closing, "It is not sympathy that Gail wants. She is not asking for a verdict based on sympathy. She is not asking for a verdict based on charity. She is asking only that your verdict compensate her for what she has lost."

CLOSING ARGUMENTS

Good closing arguments tend to share common elements (see, e.g., Cartwright, 1984). The story or theme, developed at every stage during the trial, is repeated in closing. The seeds planted and nurtured throughout the case are harvested. The closing is organized, simple, and based on the truth. Like the opening statement, the closing argument tells a vivid and compelling story. Unlike the opening statement, the closing argument may involve appropriate emotion and obvious persuasion techniques.

The closing argument should not be a recitation of the testimony of witnesses or a depiction of a time line. Most cases have a natural organization by major points. Argument by point is generally more effective than the stream-of-consciousness argument often used in closing arguments. A criminal defense closing argument, for example, may begin and conclude with the importance of the constitutional presumption of innocence. Other important points may include those facts that suggest that the wrong person is on trial because the wrong person was arrested or that the investigation that the police refused or failed to do could have uncovered facts that would have proved that the wrong person stands accused.

In a personal injury case, the points should include discussion of major issues such as liability, comparative negligence, economic damages, and noneconomic damages to the human spirit.

In any closing argument in which the application of MMPI–2 results is discussed, the descriptions used by the attorney should avoid legal or technical words to the extent that this is practical. The MMPI–2 results are used to help expand concepts that already make sense to the jury: A person's mental health is usually taken for granted; a person's mental health is one of the most important things he or she can possess.

To the extent that MMPI–2 results are particularly compelling, those results might form the basis of a complete point to be argued in closing. For example, use of the MMPI–2 might allow a graceful repetition in a liability argument in a case involving a doctor who abused his patient, as follows.

- Gail took this test because her doctor told her that it would help her get well.
- She did not know that her doctor would learn from the test those parts of her life that were hurting her and making her vulnerable to him.
- She did not know that her doctor would learn from this test how frightened and trusting she was.

- She did not know, she could not have known, that the doctor she trusted would use the information that he learned from this test to hurt her.

The degree to which the MMPI–2 results are compelling will rest to considerable degree on whether the jury accepts—with good reason on the basis of expert testimony—that the results represent the honest responses of the person who filled out the form and not an attempt to dissemble, distort, or deceive. This issue—malingering and other aspects of credibility—is discussed in the next chapter.

CHAPTER 7

ASSESSING MALINGERING AND OTHER ASPECTS OF CREDIBILITY

This chapter discusses a difficult forensic challenge: assessing credibility. Do the defendant's bizarre demeanor and incoherent speech reflect severe psychosis or acting talent? Does agonizing pain—or a plan to score a lot of money painlessly—prompt this personal injury claim? These custody applicants would make great parents—or are they faking it? The trier of fact—usually the jury, sometimes the judge—decides these questions. Expert testimony about credibility helps the trier-of-fact answer these questions.

The Minnesota Multiphasic Personality Inventory (MMPI–2), as previously noted studies have suggested, is the most widely used standardized personality test in forensic settings and has the most extensive research base in detecting malingering. Rogers, Sewell, Martin, and Vitacco (2003) wrote that "[T]he Minnesota Multiphasic Personality Inventory—2 (MMPI–2) is the most extensively researched psychological measure of feigned mental disorders. . . . These studies are heterogeneous, reflecting important differences in feigning indexes, types of feigned disorders, and simulation designs" (p. 160). Appendix C cites more than 350 articles on the MMPI/MMPI–2's performance in assessing malingering or faking bad. Appendix D cites almost 300 articles on the MMPI/MMPI–2's performance in assessing defensive responding or hiding symptoms. The *Malingering Research Update* (Pope, 2005a) at http://kspope.com/assess/malinger.php provides summaries of studies of the MMPI and other instruments from 2001 to the present.

The test's wide use, extensive research base, and different ways of correctly identifying attempts to fake or cheat help account for courts usually finding MMPI–2-based testimony to be admissible (see chap. 4 and Appendixes A and B, this volume; see also Adelman & Howard, 1984; Ogloff, 1995).

With so much riding on the outcome of a civil or criminal case, litigants may choose to shade the truth, withhold facts to make themselves look different than they really are, or downright lie. What happens when they fail to answer each MMPI–2 item honestly and try to create a false impression? What if someone coaches them in how to beat the test? What if they just do not care and randomly check off responses? Any psychological test that fails to take these natural response tendencies into account is likely to provide only limited, inaccurate, or misleading information. The following sections discuss those possibilities and the ways to identify invalid responding.

COACHING AND PREPARING TO TAKE PSYCHOLOGICAL TESTS

Some individuals are carefully briefed about the reason and rationale for the test, well beyond what the standard instructions for the test administration allow. Lees-Haley (1997a), for example, wrote, "Attorneys influence psychological data by a variety of means. They advise their clients how to respond to psychological tests, make suggestions of what to tell examining psychologists and what to emphasize, and lead patients not to disclose certain information important to psychologists" (p. 321). Forensic psychologists conducting personality evaluations must keep in mind that the client may have been warned about the MMPI validity scales or actually told the best strategy to respond to the items by an attorney who says, "Don't answer any questions that might incriminate you," or "You should be aware of the fact that there are questions on the test that are designed to trap you if you aren't careful." Some clients have actually received an MMPI–2 booklet to study before the assessment.

The extent to which attorneys brief their clients before they are assessed in a forensic evaluation may be considerable. Wetter and Corrigan (1995) conducted a survey of 70 attorneys and 150 law students with respect to whether they briefed their clients before they were administered psychological tests. They found "that almost 50% of the attorneys and over 33% of the students believe that clients referred for testing always or usually should be informed of validity scales on tests" (p. 474). It is unknown, however, what percentage of attorneys actually brief their clients and how much information about the MMPI–2 they actually provide.

Someone preparing to take a forensic examination can find information and coaching from other sources than attorneys. Information about psychological tests is widely available on the Internet. For example, Ruiz, Drake, Glass, Marcotte, and van Gorp (2002) searched the Web and found the following.

> On one site, a psychologist posted the test stimuli of many popular neuropsychological instruments (e.g., Dementia Rating Scale [DRS]; Mattis, 1988). Another site contained an accurate facsimile of the Rorschach Inkblot cards, with detailed information on how the results are interpreted and instructions on how to respond "appropriately." A set of Rorschach plates, which are generally restricted from unauthorized purchase, were also for sale on a popular Internet auction site. In another instance, a Web site provided explicit instructions on how to dissimulate on

certain psychological tests. For example, this site provided detailed information about the MMPI–2 and the Rorschach. This information included pictures of the inkblots as well as the detection strategies used on both instruments to identify pathology and malingering. Sites provided information about the purpose of the independent medical evaluation and provided advice to potential examinees on how to present themselves in a manner to obtain disability benefits. (pp. 296–297; see also Victor & Abeles, 2004)

Providing information or guidance that goes beyond the standard instructions that are actually printed on the face page of the answer booklet can lead to an invalid protocol.

COACHING AND THE VALIDITY SCALES

Can test takers successfully fake the results if they are informed in advance about the validity scales on the MMPI–2? Several studies have explored whether providing people with specific information about the role of the MMPI–2 validity scales influences the "fakability" of the tests. Rogers, Bagby, and Chakraborty (1993), for example, reported that clients can be instructed in strategies that will allow them to present a faked clinical pattern on the MMPI–2 and avoid detection by the MMPI–2 validity indicators such as the Infrequency scale (F). They found that coached simulators were better than uncoached simulators at faking results. The MMPI–2 F scale was ineffective at detecting coached simulators from genuine patients with schizophrenia. However, one measure, the revised Dissimulation Scale ($DsR2$; R. Greene, 2000), did show some effectiveness at detecting coached malingerers.

Lamb, Berry, Wetter, and Baer (1994) found that coaching participants on head injury symptoms tended to result in elevations on both the clinical and validity scales; however, coaching on the validity scales tended to lower the overall elevations on both the validity and clinical scales.

Storm and Graham (1998) designed a study to assess malingering of general psychopathology in coached malingerers, but were not able to replicate the findings of Rogers et al. (1993). Instead, Storm and Graham (1998) found that the $F(p)$ (Infrequency Psychiatric) scale was effective in detecting both uncoached and coached malingerers.

Some research suggests that coaching respondents about the MMPI–2 defensiveness scales can result in more moderate elevations on the standard validity scales. Studies by Fink and Butcher (1972); Butcher, Atlis, and Fang (2000); Butcher, Morfitt, Rouse, and Holden (1997); Cigrang and Staal (2001); and Gucker and McNulty (2004) have shown that providing information about the presence of validity scales (in settings such as personnel screening where defensiveness is common) can result in valid protocols with more pathology as reflected in elevations in clinical and content scales.

Research on the topic of fakability of the MMPI–2 to date suggests that briefings of clients with respect to the validity scales can affect the results of testing in unknown ways. Coaching symptoms does not appear to influence the detection of malingering. Moyer et al. (2002), for example, found that coaching test takers by telling them the diagnostic criteria for posttraumatic stress disorder (PTSD) before they took they test did not help them fool the test. The results suggested "that knowledge about the specific symptoms of PTSD did not create a more accurate profile, but rather was likely to produce more invalid ($F > T89$) profiles, detecting them as malingerers" (p. 81).

Similarly, Bagby, Nicholson, Bacchiochi, Ryder, and Bury (2002) studied the capacity of the MMPI–2 and the Personality Assessment Inventory (PAI; Morey, 2003) validity scales and indexes to detect coached and uncoached feigning. They found that "coaching had no effect on the ability of the research participants to feign more successfully than those participants who received no coaching. For the MMPI–2, the Psychopathology F scale, or $F(p)$, proved to be the best at distinguishing psychiatric patients from research participants instructed to malinger" (p. 69).

Bury and Bagby (2002) studied participants who were either uncoached or coached under several conditions about PTSD symptom information, about MMPI–2 validity scales, or about both symptoms and validity scales. Their MMPI–2 profiles were then compared with protocols of claimants who had workplace accident-related PTSD. Participants in the study who were given information about the validity scales were the most successful in avoiding detection as faking. However, the infrequency validity indicators (i.e., F, Infrequency-Back scale [$F(B)$], $F(p)$), particularly $F(p)$, produced consistently high rates of positive and negative predictive power. They noted the following.

Although FP [$F(p)$] showed a pattern of diminished predictive capacity in the context of validity-scale coaching, as did the other validity scales and indexes, this scale produced the largest effect size differences between the fake-PTSD groups and the claimants with bona fide PTSD and was a close second to $Ds2$ with respect to overall correct classification accuracy rates in distinguishing accurately faked protocols from bona fide protocols. Storm and Graham (2000) also reported FP to be effective in distinguishing research participants given information about the MMPI–2 validity scales and indexes from bona fide psychiatric patients. These authors suggested that one possible reason for the effectiveness of FP in their investigation was that no specific instruction on how to avoid detection on FP was provided, although such information was provided for some of the other validity scales (e.g., F and $Ds2$ [Dissimulation]). In the current study, we included specific information about how to avoid detection by FP and were still able to demonstrate the continued effectiveness of this scale. Storm and Graham also only included a single coached condition in their study (validity-scale information) and were therefore unable to examine the effectiveness of FP across other conditions. In this study we included a number of different conditions and were able to demonstrate the effectiveness of *FP* across a number of instructional sets. (p. 480)

Nicholson et al. (1997) noted that the "pattern of findings for the defensiveness indicators suggests that the discrimination of respondents who are faking good from psychologically healthy respondents is a more challenging task than is the discrimination of fake-bad responders from genuine patients" (see also Baer, Wetter, & Berry, 1992; Graham, Watts, & Timbrook, 1991; p. 476). Bagby and his colleagues (2006) also noted that "classification accuracy is typically higher for the fake-bad validity scales and indexes in detecting of overreporting than for underreporting validity scales and indexes in detecting fake-good" (p. 63).

The extent to which coaching has distorted test results can be difficult to determine. The client may give clues about having been helped, for example, by omitting items that seemingly relate to the case, and so forth; however, inquiring into this possibility can be problematic. A careful review of the validity scales can sometimes alert the expert witness that the client has produced an overly cautious or "managed" self-report. It might also be valuable for the professional who administers the MMPI–2 to conduct an inquiry after testing is completed to assess the extent to which previous instructions may have influenced responses, as long as there is no inquiry into privileged communication with attorneys. The expert should *never* intrude into privileged attorney–client communications.

MMPI–2-BASED MEASURES OF RESPONSE INVALIDITY

Hathaway and McKinley (1940, 1943), the original MMPI authors, carefully considered the idea that people responding to the MMPI might not endorse the items truthfully. The original instrument included several control scales or validity measures to assess profile validity. The following sections (a) review these measures, describe research that bears on their continued use in personality assessment

today, and summarize the ways in which these scales operate on the MMPI–2; (b) describe several more recent measures of protocol validity and illustrate their use; and (c) discuss some controversial measures.

THE CANNOT SAY SCORE

The Cannot Say (?) index is the total number of items that were either unanswered or answered both *true* and *false* at different points in the MMPI–2. In the original MMPI, *T* scores for the Cannot Say scale were actually provided on the profile sheet with an arbitrary mean score value of 30. This is probably because the original authors instructed participants that they could omit items—a practice that has not been followed.

This practice of providing *T* scores for the Cannot Say score was discontinued in the MMPI–2 because the *T* scores were neither psychometrically sound nor clinically appropriate. The shape of the distributions, in part because of the fact that people omit few and variable numbers of items, does not allow for the generation of meaningful *T* scores. The most appropriate use of the Cannot Say score is to make a rough determination of whether the person endorsed enough items to provide useful information. Omissions greater than or equal to 30 items reflect an excessive number of omitted items and will likely attenuate the profile.

Profiles with greater than 30 of Cannot Say items should *not* be interpreted. In an empirical evaluation of item omissions, Clopton and Neuringer (1977) reported that excessive item omissions (i.e., greater than 30) can alter the MMPI scores by lowering scale elevations and altering the code type. Berry et al. (1997) conducted an empirical evaluation of the impact of Cannot Say scores on the client's scale scores and profile pattern and found that even fewer than 30 items could result in attenuated profile patterns. However, they found that well-defined code types were less likely to be different from baseline than those that did not meet criteria of scale definition.

The traditional rule against interpreting profiles with high Cannot Say counts, of course, assumes that the omitted items are scattered throughout the

---

EXHIBIT 7.1

Summary of Cannot Say Interpretative Rules for the MMPI–2 and MMPI–A in Forensic Evaluations

Omitting items on personality scales is a relatively common means for test takers in forensic settings to attempt to control the test.

Cannot Say scores (*?*) ≥ 30 indicate that the individual has produced an invalid protocol that should not be interpreted except under circumstances noted below. No other MMPI–2/ MMPI–A scales should be interpreted.

Cannot Say scores between 11–29 suggest that some scales might be invalid; selective omission of items likely.

Berry, Adams, et al. (1997) pointed out that even lower levels of omitted items can impact scale scores.

If most of the omitted items occur toward the end of the booklet (after item 370 on MMPI–2 or 350 on MMPI–A), the validity and standard scales can be interpreted. However, the supplementary and content scales, which contain items toward the end of the booklet, should not be interpreted.

At the time of administration, if the individual has omitted items, the test should be returned with encouragement to try and complete all of the items.

Augmentation of profile scores by correcting for omitted items should be avoided.

Possible reasons for item omissions:

- Perceived irrelevance of items
- Lack of cooperation
- Defensiveness
- Indecisiveness
- Fatigue
- Low mood
- Carelessness
- Low reading comprehension

Note. See also discussion by Butcher et al. (2001) and Graham (2006).

---

booklet and thus affect all of the clinical scales. (Interpretations for high Cannot Say scores are shown in Exhibit 7.1.)

Expert witnesses can be somewhat more precise interpreting the Cannot Say score by evaluating where in the sequence of items the omissions occur or whether a particular scale is actually affected by item omission. If all omitted items appear at the end of the booklet, for example, the traditional MMPI validity and clinical scales are unaffected. That is, the first 370 items on the MMPI–2 and the first 350 items on the MMPI–A include all standard scale items. Items beyond these points influence

only scales such as the MacAndrew Scale—Revised (*MAC–R*) scale or the MMPI–2 content scales that contain items that appear toward the end of the booklet. However, it should be kept in mind that item deletions beyond item 370 *do* influence the *VRIN*, *TRIN*, and *F(p)* scales, which could make it difficult to interpret the profile.

If the individual responds to all items on a particular scale, even though the overall Cannot Say score numbers are high, then that particular scale might provide useful information. Knowing the actual response rate for the items composing each scale could add considerably to the expert witness's confidence in the interpretation of the scale. This information is available through some computer scoring programs. For example, the Minnesota Forensic Report for the MMPI–2 from Pearson Assessment Systems provides the percentage of items composing each scale that are actually endorsed by the individual (Butcher, 1998b). The expert witness can determine for each scale whether there has been a high percentage of items omitted.

In forensic settings, the Cannot Say score should be carefully evaluated because item omissions are a fairly common means for clients to distort patterns. Even five or six omitted items, if they occur on a particular scale, can undermine its reliability and validity.

Although some clinicians have augmented profiles in which a number of items have been omitted—that is, simply scored the items in the pathological direction as though the client answered them that way based on previous answers—*no* empirical data exist to justify these procedures (see, e.g., R. Greene, 1991). In fact, Graham (1963) has shown that one could not predict how people would answer the items the second time.

There are two methods some have used to adjust full-scale scores by estimating what the score would be if the individual had responded to all of the items. First, if the client was judged to have had time to complete the record but left out some items, then the items left unanswered that are scored on the scales are simply added to the total scale scores *as if* they had been endorsed in the deviant direction. Second, if the individual did not have time to complete the record, the full-scale score can be prorated by determining the proportion of endorsed items for those completed and applying this same proportion to the unanswered items on the scales.

There are many solid reasons that expert witnesses should *never* augment profiles in forensic settings. First, it is important to score standardized tests *as the individual actually responded to them* rather than changing the individual's responses or making up responses. Second, there is no research justifying this approach. As emphasized throughout this book, expert witnesses and attorneys must always ask whether research has established for a specific test, scale, scoring method, or interpretation rule adequate validity, reliability, sensitivity, and specificity for the relevant forensic use, relevant setting, and relevant population. Third, augmentation invites cross-examination along the lines of, "You actually made up those MMPI scores, didn't you, Doctor?" and "Will you explain to the jury which MMPI items the defendant filled out and which MMPI items you filled out; and then explain what the defendant's items tell us about the defendant and what your items tell us about you?"

THE LIE SCALE

One approach to detecting deception takes a cognitive rather than an affective perspective. As Lanyon (1997) described an "accuracy of knowledge" approach, "a person's success at deception regarding a particular characteristic depends on the extent of his or her knowledge of that characteristic" (p. 377). The original MMPI attempted to assess unrealistic claims about certain characteristics. Drawing on Hartshorne and May's (1928) work, Hathaway and McKinley developed a rational scale including statements proclaiming overly positive characteristics to assess the general characteristic that some individuals have to proclaim an unrealistic degree of personal virtue.

The Lie scale (*L*) was devised, according to Dahlstrom, Welsh, and Dahlstrom (1972), "to identify deliberate or intentional efforts to evade answering the test frankly and honestly" (p. 109). These items, asserting high moral value or an un-

usual quality of virtue, were scaled to provide an indication of whether the individual excessively asserts high virtue compared with other people in general. Individuals who claim more than a few of these unrealistically positive characteristics are considered to be presenting a favorable view of themselves that is unlikely to be accurate, even for individuals with model lifestyles.

A general tendency to endorse the MMPI *L* items suggests that the individual has likely responded to the other items in the inventory in a way that denies reasonable personal frailty and weakness and presents an unrealistically favorable image. High *L* scorers tend to deny even minor faults that most people would not object to endorsing in a self-report evaluation. (See Exhibit 7.2 for a description of high *L* characteristics.)

EXHIBIT 7.2

Summary of Interpretative Rules for the MMPI–2 *L* in Forensic Evaluations

T scores from 60–64, inclusive, indicate that the individual used a good impression response set to create the view that he or she is a virtuous person.

T scores from 65–69, inclusive, indicate possible profile invalidity due to an overly virtuous self-presentation. Person likely minimized psychological problems.

T scores ≥ 65 but < 74 suggest clear distortion of item responding to manipulate what others think of him or her. May be invalid.

T scores > = 75 Likely invalid.

Many individuals with high *L* scores produce low scores on the symptom scales. However, elevated *L* scale scores can be associated with other elevated MMPI–2 scale scores, particularly when the individual attempts to create a particular pattern of disability (e.g., physical problems).

The *TRIN* scale (inconsistent true or false responding) can aid the interpreter in determining whether an elevated *L* score is due to a false or nay-saying response set.

Descriptors associated with elevations of *L*:

- Unwilling to admit even minor flaws
- Unrealistic proclamation of virtue
- Claims near-perfect adherence to high moral standards
- Naive self-views
- Outright effort to deceive others about motives or adjustment
- Personality adjustment problems

Note. See also discussion by Butcher et al. (2001) and Graham (2006).

In general, an elevation on the *L* scale suggests that the client has failed to fully disclose problems on the MMPI–2. Such an approach to the MMPI–2 among compensation claimants suggests that the client may have a poor prognosis for successful treatment of injured workers. For example, an elevation on the *L* scale in claimants suffering chronic pain as a result of a work-related injury has been found to be associated with a failure to return to work after treatment through a work-hardening program (Alexy & Webb, 1999). It is worth noting at this point two themes emphasized throughout this book: *Valid MMPI interpretation requires expert witnesses* to maintain awareness of the full array of relevant research on aspects such as the *L* scale, and the nature of the MMPI as a standardized test requires initial findings from the instrument to be viewed as *actuarially based hypotheses*.

Bagby and Marshall (2004) found that the *L* scale consistently loaded on the impression-management factor in their study of indexes of underreporting on the MMPI–2. Historically, studies have supported the value of the *L* scale as an indicator of the "good impression" profile. Burish and Houston (1976) found that the *L* scale correlated with denial. Joe Matarazzo (1955), a former president of the American Psychological Association (APA) who has conducted extensive research in the area of psychological assessment, found that the *L* scale was associated with lower levels of manifest anxiety. Elevations on the *L* scale have also been reported among forensic patients who were paranoid and grandiose. Coyle and Heap (1965) concluded that some hospitalized patients were "pathologically convinced of their own perfection" (p. 729). Fjordbak (1985) found that high-*L* patients with normal profiles were often psychotic and showed paranoid features.

Vincent, Linsz, and Greene (1966) considered the usefulness of the *L* scale to be limited to unsophisticated clients, however. They reported that the *L* scale does not seem to detect the sophisticated individual who has been given instructions to falsify responses on the test. However, groups that tend to obtain higher scores on the *L* scale include college-educated applicants to airline flight jobs (Butcher, 1994) and parents being assessed in domestic court

to determine who gets custody of the minor children (Bathurst et al., 1997), because these individuals tend to be asserting that they possess many virtues and no faults, even minor ones.

Graham et al.'s (1991) research suggested that the *L* scale appears to work the same in the revised version of the inventory as in the original MMPI. The *L* scale is identical in item content in the MMPI and MMPI–2. The main difference between the two forms is that originally Hathaway and McKinley rationally set or estimated the *T*-score distribution. The MMPI–2's *T* scores were derived by a linear transformation based on the new normative samples. In practice, the *L*-scale distribution for the MMPI–2 provides a broader range of values than Hathaway and McKinley's distribution of *L* in the original MMPI. The same raw score on *L* would receive a slightly higher *T* score on MMPI–2 than the original distribution.

L is a valuable scale for assessing impression management (see, e.g., the discussion by Paulhus, 1986), which is often an important focus of forensic testimony. *L*-scale elevations between 60 and 64 (unless otherwise indicated, "scores" in this chapter refer to *T* scores) suggest that the individual has been less than frank in the assessment and has probably underreported psychological symptoms and problems. Scores between 65 and 69 tend to reflect a strong inclination to accentuate the positive side of one's adjustment and to deny or to suppress the possibility of personal frailty. Clinical profiles with scores in this range are less likely to provide a useful or accurate reflection of the individual's problem picture. Blatant distortion or conscious manipulation of the personality assessment process is associated with elevations above 70. This fake-good pattern is unlikely to provide much valid personality or symptomatic information.

Baer et al. (1992) conducted a meta-analysis of measures of underreporting psychopathology on the MMPI–2. They concluded that consistently effective cutting scores for many published indexes have yet to be established. However, they recommended that

> until such research becomes available, clinicians using the MMPI–2 may be

best advised to consider the *L* and *K* [Defensiveness] scales when making judgments about underreporting of psychopathology, as these scales showed reasonable mean effect sizes and have not been altered on the MMPI–2. (p. 523)

Appendix D contains an array of studies on the *L* scale.

THE DEFENSIVENESS SCALE

Paul Meehl and Starke Hathaway (1946) created the Defensiveness scale (*K*) scale for two purposes. The first was to detect the presence in some individuals of a tendency to present themselves in a socially favorable light—that is, to respond to items in a manner as to claim no personal weakness or psychological frailty. This tendency was observed to occur in some inpatients who had psychological problems but whose clinical profiles were normal. Moreover, the *L* scale did not appear to be effective in detecting their defensiveness.

The second reason, as noted in chapter 2, was to correct for test defensiveness in patients who had mental health problems but were defensive in their self-report descriptions. The scale developers assumed that the tendency some individuals have to present overly favorable self-views could be adequately scaled and used to correct their clinical profiles. If patients were defensive (produced high *K* scores), then points could be added to their clinical scale scores. As discussed in chapter 2, the *K* factor was thus derived as an empirical correction for improving the discrimination between individuals who were defensive and did not accurately report mental health problems in clinical settings and those who were not defensive (eight items on the scale were included as a correction for psychoticism).

Hathaway and Meehl originally determined the percentages of *K* scores that improved the identification of defensive patients using inpatient data. *K* correction for other settings have not been developed and validated.

The *K* score appears to be a valuable indicator of the tendency to present a favorable self-report (see

---

Exhibit 7.3 for a listing of the *K* scale correlates and interpretative guidelines) and can provide useful cautions for interpreting MMPI–2 profiles. However, factors such as socioeconomic class and education have been shown to influence *K* scores (Baer, Wetter, Nichols, Greene, & Berry, 1995; Butcher, 1990a; Dahlstrom et al., 1972). Interpretation of original MMPI *K*-corrected profiles required that adjustments be made for people with education levels surpassing high school because the original *K* score was based on people with an eighth- or ninth-grade education—depending on whether the arithmetic mean or median (see Glossary) is used. Because the average educational level in the United States today is higher than in the 1930s, when the original norms were collected, the original *K* scores are elevated above 60 for most people. The MMPI–2 *K* score, which is based on a more representative sample, is more relevant for the majority of people today. However, it is important to note that on average, *K* is slightly lower for those individuals with less than a high school education. Low *K* scores in this population could be a function of cultural factors.

As discussed in chapter 2, the *K* scale, as a correction factor, has not been without its critics. The MMPI Restandardization Committee considered dropping the *K* correction from the five corrected clinical scales. However, most external validity studies have been based on *K*-corrected scores. The *K* correction was maintained to preserve continuity on the clinical scales between the MMPI and MMPI–2. However, several researchers have noted that the *K* scale, as a correction factor for test defensiveness, does *not* improve classification in a uniformly successful manner (Colby, 1989; Hunt, 1948; Schmidt, 1948; Wrobel & Lachar, 1982). Early studies by Hunt, Carp, Cass, Winder, and Kantor (1947); Silver and Sines (1962); and a later study by Barthlow, Graham, Ben-Porath, Tellegen, and McNulty (2002) found that non–*K*-corrected scores worked as well as *K*-corrected scores in inpatient assessment. There also has been the suggestion that the *K* correction might actually *lower* external test validity (Weed, Ben-Porath, & Butcher, 1990; Weed & Han, 1992). As a consequence, a high *K* in a forensic assessment may prompt consideration that the *K*-corrected scores may, when compared with non–*K*-corrected scores, provide a *less* clear and *less* accurate understanding.

Chapter 2 discusses the challenges facing the expert witness who must decide whether to set aside the *K* correction when examining MMPI scores in a forensic assessment. As with each aspect of forensic assessment, expert witnesses and attorneys must ask if an adequate array of well-designed research has established the validity, reliability, sensitivity, and specificity for a particular measure, scoring method, or interpretive approach—in this case, using non–*K*-corrected scores—to be used for a particular purpose in a particular setting with a particular population.

THE SUPERLATIVE SELF-PRESENTATION SCALE

Test defensiveness or the set to present oneself on the MMPI–2 in a highly virtuous manner is a test-taking behavior that has been the focus of a great deal of research since the MMPI was first published in 1940. As noted earlier, the original test authors,

Hathaway and McKinley, developed the *L* scale to detect this disingenuous response approach tendency to better improve test discrimination. As also noted, a few years later, Meehl and Hathaway published an additional measure, the *K* scale, to measure the tendency of people to present themselves as unrealistically well adjusted and free of psychological flaws, even minor ones. Although these scales tend to provide useful information about "virtue claiming" and denying problems, they nevertheless do not serve to fully explore motivations for test defensiveness.

Researchers have attempted to develop other good-impression scales with the original MMPI, but none of the measures achieved broad acceptance and confident utility. The development of the MMPI–2 and its additional, novel test items enabled the creation of the Superlative Self-Presentation scale (*S*; see Exhibit 7.4 for a listing of the *S*-scale correlates and interpretative guidelines).

EXHIBIT 7.4

Summary of Interpretative Rules for the MMPI–2 *S* (Superlative Self-Presentation Scale) Score in Forensic Evaluations

T scores ≥ 65 suggest possible defensive responding. Elevations in this range are common in forensic evaluations in which the individual is motivated to present a favorable image (e.g., family custody evaluations).

T scores greater than *T* ≥ = 70 suggest invalidity.

As with the *K* scale, absence of psychopathology cannot be assumed for profiles with an elevated *K* score and normal limits scale scores.

Interpretive hypotheses with elevated *S* scores:

- Defensiveness
- Possessing a great need to present oneself as problem free
- Evaluation of the *S* scale subscales can provide clues as to the ways in which the client is being defensive
  - *S1 Belief in Human Goodness*
  - *S2 Serenity*
  - *S3 Contentment With Life*
  - *S4 Patience/Denial of Irritability/Anger*
  - *S5 Denial of Moral Flaws*

Note. See also discussion by Butcher and Han (1995); Butcher et al. (2001); and Williams and Graham (2000).

Development of the S Scale

The *S* scale was developed according to a refinement of the empirical scale development approach. Initially, items for the scale were empirically selected by including in the provisional scale only items that empirically separated a group of extremely defensive job applicants (airline pilot applicants) from the MMPI–2 normative sample (see study by Butcher, 1994, for a discussion of defensiveness among pilot applicants).

Item analysis and content analysis helped ensure that these initially selected items created a homogeneous scale. Then *T* scores were developed on the MMPI–2 normative sample to provide a means of comparing individual scores with a relevant norm group.

The initial publication (Butcher & Han, 1995) noted that the *S* scale is highly correlated with the *K* scale (.81), indicating that the scale addresses test defensiveness in a manner similar to the original *K* scale. However, the *S* scale is a longer scale that contains items scattered throughout the booklet, providing for a more reliable assessment of the client's response patterns throughout the test.

The length of the *S* scale also allowed for the development of a set of subscales to assess the several facets of test defensiveness. The subscales of *S* were developed as follows: The 50 items on the final version of the *S* scale were submitted to an item factor analysis to determine if reliable subscales would point to different content dimensions that appeared to make up MMPI–2 measured defensiveness. The five subdimensions of the *S* scale follow.

- *S1 Belief in Human Goodness*
- *S2 Serenity*
- *S3 Contentment With Life*
- *S4 Patience/Denial of Irritability/Anger*
- *S5 Denial of Moral Flaws*

Empirical evaluation studies have explored the *S* scale. Bagby and Marshall (2004), for example, pointed out that the *S* scale, like the *K* scale, primarily assesses self-deceptive responding and loads exclusively on the self-deceptive factor in their study of defensive response styles. Lim and Butcher

(1996) reported that the *S* scale showed "particular promise" at identifying fake-good profiles (both denial and claiming extreme virtues).

Baer et al. (1995) found that the *S* scale showed significant incremental validity over the *L* and *K* scales in the detection of symptom underreporting.

Findings from Bagby and colleagues (1997) suggested "that in situations where one is assessing 'nonclinical' individuals (e.g., personnel selection), the *Od* [Denial of Minor Faults] and *S* scales are best at detecting those normal individuals who might be presenting themselves in an overly favorable light" (p. 412).

Nicholson et al. (1997) found that "the *S* scale produced the farthest departure from the line of no information, followed in order by *CI, O–S, K, L, Mp,* and, finally, *F–K,* which produced the smallest departure from the diagonal." They also found that "the *S* scale yielded a significantly larger AUC [Receiver–Operator Curve] than did *K* and *F–K.* In addition, *CI* and *O–S* produced significantly larger AUCs than did *F–K.* However, no other differences among defensiveness indicators were statistically significant" (p. 474).

Baer and Miller's (2002) meta-analysis of underreporting symptoms found that the motivation to fake-good is associated with higher scores on both the standard and nonstandard validity scales of the *MMPI–2,* and that the *S* scale was associated with the mean largest effect size (Cohen's *d* = 1.51).

Butcher (1998a) compared the responses of two defensive groups on the *S* subscales. The differing *S* subscale responses from two rather different but typically defensive test applications were compared: These were airline pilot applicants and parents being seen in custody evaluations. Airline pilot applicants and parents involved in family custody disputes are equally defensive on the MMPI–2; however, their pattern of defensiveness differs somewhat according to the *S* subscales. Commercial pilots who were administered the MMPI–2 in pre-employment evaluations showed significantly higher scores (compared with the normative MMPI–2 sample) on all five subscales, whereas parents who were evaluated in family custody disputes as part of their court case to determine custody, visitation, or both had significantly higher scores on "Patience/Denial of Irritability" and on "Denial of Moral Flaws."

Uses of the *S* Scale in Forensic Assessment

The *S* scale can be of value in forensic evaluations in two ways. First, the scale provides a reliable measure for detecting test defensiveness. The full score on the *S* scale shows that the individual has claimed to have many positive attributes and fewer problems than people generally endorse when taking the MMPI–2. High scores ($T > 70$) strongly suggest that test takers are presenting themselves in an unrealistically favorable manner, in all likelihood so that they will be viewed favorably in the assessment.

Second, the *S* subscales provide a means of gaining insight into a client's form of defensive responding on the MMPI–2 or clues as to possible sources of unrealistic virtue claims. As noted, different defensive groups may manifest their defensiveness in somewhat different ways, as in the study of airline pilot applicants and family custody clients.

USING MODIFIED INSTRUCTIONS TO LOWER DEFENSIVENESS

As noted in chapter 2, research has demonstrated that defensive clients taking the MMPI (Fink & Butcher, 1972) or the MMPI–2 (Butcher, Morfitt, et al., 1997) will be more open and cooperative in the testing if they are informed about the presence of validity scales in the test. Moreover, Butcher, Morfitt, and colleagues (1997) have shown that airline pilot applicants who are provided information that the test contains effective measures of defensiveness will be less defensive and will frankly endorse more revealing personality characteristics than when the MMPI–2 is administered under standard instructions. Two recent studies have supported this procedure in personnel selection (Cigrang & Staal, 2001; Gucker & McNulty, 2004).

Butcher, Atlis, et al. (2000) conducted a study in which volunteer participants were administered the MMPI–2 with altered instructions as their only instructions to the testing. They found that women (but not men) produced lower *L* and *K* scale scores on the administration and showed no difference on the clinical scales to groups of people who took the test under standard instructions.

In light of these intriguing findings, why not simply administer the MMPI–2 with altered instructions when testing clients who tend to present themselves in overly positive ways? The problem is that we currently lack adequate research using the altered instructions to collect new norms (for the version of the test that uses the altered instructions) and to establish validity, reliability, sensitivity, and specificity for relevant forensic purposes, relevant settings, and relevant populations.

(Mis)using a standardized test in a nonstandard and unvalidated way for forensic assessments could produce misleading results in many ways. For example, researchers (e.g., Baer & Sekirnjak, 1997; Baer, Wetter, & Berry, 1995) have found that even low-detail feedback on fake-good scales may make underreporters more difficult to detect (particularly on the traditional validity indicators *L* and *K*).

THE INFREQUENCY SCALE

One of the most useful measures in forensic assessment is the *F* scale because many individuals in forensic evaluations tend to exaggerate symptoms to appear more psychologically disturbed than they actually are. The rationale for the development of the *F* scale was straightforward. Dahlstrom and Dahlstrom (1980) wrote,

> The *F* variable was composed of 64 items that were selected primarily because they were answered with a relatively low frequency in either the true or false direction by the main normal group; the scored direction of response is the one which is rarely made by unselected normals. Additionally, the items were chosen to include a variety

of content so that it was unlikely that any particular pattern would cause an individual to answer many of the items in the unusual direction. The relative success of this selection of items, with deliberate intent of forcing the average number of items answered in an unusual direction downward, is illustrated in the fact that the mean score on the 64 items runs between two and four points for all normal groups. The distribution curve is, of course, very skewed positively; and the higher scores approach half the number of items. In distributions of ordinary persons the frequency of scores drops very rapidly at about seven and is at the 2 or 3 percent level by score twelve. Because of this quick cutting off of the curve the scores seven and twelve were arbitrarily assigned T scored values of 60 and 70 in the original F table. (Dahlstrom & Dahlstrom, 1980, p. 94)

Berry, Baer, and Harris (1991) conducted the first meta-analysis on the ability of the original MMPI to detect malingering. Their analysis of 28 studies suggested that F, Ds, and $F–K$ produced the largest effect sizes.

The F scale was modified in the MMPI–2 and MMPI–A in several ways. First, in the MMPI–2, four items were dropped from the scale because of their objectionable item content. Second, the F scale was empirically normed using linear T scores as opposed to the rationally derived setting of scale values in the original MMPI. Third, an additional infrequency scale, the Infrequency-Back scale $F(B)$, was developed to provide a measure of infrequency for the items that appear in the back of the booklet, because the original F scale contains only items that occur in the front half of the booklet.

The F scale for the MMPI–A was further revised to address more fully the tendency of adolescents to endorse items differently than adults

(Butcher et al., 1992). Many of the items on the traditional F scale did not operate as infrequency items for younger people. Therefore, a new F scale for the MMPI–A, which was based on adolescent frequency tables, was developed for individuals between the ages of 14 and 18. A separate set of 66 infrequency items, covering the full range of the items in the booklet, was obtained. The 66 F items are scattered throughout the 478-item booklet in the MMPI–A. To assess responding toward the end versus toward the front of the item pool, the F scale was divided into two equal parts, $F1$ and $F2$, each containing 33 items.

The F and the $F(B)$ scales on the MMPI–2 and the F, $F1$, and $F2$ scales on the MMPI–A were developed by simply identifying the items that are infrequently endorsed in the general population. When individuals approach the items in an unselective way and attempt to present a picture of psychological disturbance, they usually obtain high scores on these scales. However, individuals with actual psychological problems tend to respond in a more selective and consistent manner to items.

People who feign mental health problems on the MMPI, unless they have a background in psychology or the MMPI, will usually be unaware as to which items actually appear on the scales and what is the scored direction of particular items. Dissimulators—those who try to feign mental health problems—tend to over-respond to many extreme items. For example, Berry et al. (1995) found that the F and $F(B)$ scales significantly differentiated patients seeking compensation for head injuries from closed head injury patients not seeking compensation in terms of greater scale elevation. Dearth et al. (2005) found that the MMPI–2 validity indicators, particularly the F scale, had robust values at differentiating people who feigned head injury from those with genuine head injury and concluded that the MMPI–2 validity indicators are sensitive to feigning in an analog forensic study. (See also Clark, Gironda, & Young, 2003.)

The infrequency scales are important forensic indicators because they provide an assessment of the extent to which the person has responded carefully and selectively to the content of the items. High F or $F(B)$ scores ($T > 90$) threaten the validity and interpretability of the MMPI–2. Thus, the F scale has been referred to as a fake-bad scale. Records with scores of 90 or higher should be considered problematic for a straightforward interpretation of the clinical scales until possible reasons for the extreme responding can be determined. Those with F or $F(B)$ scores higher than 100 T are likely malingered records. However, in inpatient samples, it would also be desirable to consider elevations on $F(p)$ as well as to confirm this assessment.

Each potentially invalid profile that is based on F or $F(B)$ should be carefully evaluated to determine the possible source of invalidity. The following sections suggest possible hypotheses that might explain an elevated F or $F(B)$ score (see Exhibit 7.5 for the F scale and Exhibit 7.6 for the $F(B)$ scale for a summary of possible meanings for F-scale elevations).

Careless Responding

Perhaps the individual got mixed up in responding to the items and marked responses in the wrong place on the answer sheet. Careful test administration can often eliminate this concern because proctoring of the exam could prevent such mix-ups in the instructions from occurring. (Some individuals, however, may still be "off" by one or two items when reading the booklet and marking responses on the answer sheet.)

Examining the answer sheet can sometimes determine if the client became confused and mixed up on the test—for example, if an entire page of questions or a column of the answer sheet bubbles have been missed. Another way to evaluate the possibility of careless responding involves examining the consistency of the individual's response. One can determine, using validity indicators (such as the $VRIN$ scale) if the person has responded selectively to the content of the items or has responded in an inconsistent manner.

EXHIBIT 7.5

Summary of Interpretative Rules for the MMPI–2 F in Forensic Evaluations

The MMPI infrequency scales indicate unusual response to the item pool through claiming excessive, unlikely symptoms.

T scores below 50 may be associated with a response pattern that minimizes problems.

T scores from 55–79, inclusive, reflect a problem-oriented approach to the items.

T scores from 80–89, inclusive, indicate an exaggerated response set, which probably reflects an attempt to claim excessive problems. $VRIN$ T scores ≤ 79 can be used to rule out inconsistent responding.

T scores from 100–109, inclusive, are possibly indicators of an invalid protocol. Some high F profiles are obtained in inpatient settings and reflect extreme psychopathology. $VRIN$ T scores ≥ 79 can be used to rule out inconsistent profiles.

T scores ≥ 110 indicate an uninterpretable profile because of extreme item endorsements.

Interpretive hypothesis for elevated F scores:

- Confusion, reading problems
- Random responding (refer to $VRIN$)
- Severe psychopathology
- Possible symptom exaggeration
- Faking psychological problems
- Malingering

Note. See also discussion by Butcher et al. (2001) and Graham (2006).

Random Responding

Random responding produces highly deviant clinical profiles. However, the F-scale score will be so extremely elevated that the interpreter should not make personality inferences from the MMPI–2. There are two valuable indicators of randomness that should be carefully evaluated: F scores greater than 90 (usually random response sets will produce F scores greater than 120; see the profile in Figure 7.1). However, conservative test interpretation standards suggest that any F or $F(B)$ scores of 80 or higher for adults or of 70 or higher for adolescents should be carefully evaluated for possible dissimulation.

The $VRIN$ scale, discussed more fully later in this chapter, produces a response consistency score that addresses the extent to which the individual has responded inconsistently to similar items. High

EXHIBIT 7.6

Summary of Interpretative Rules for the MMPI–2 F(B) in Forensic Evaluations

The MMPI–2 F(B) scale indicates unusual response to the item toward the end of the booklet through claiming excessive, unlikely symptoms, or exaggerated symptoms.

T scores below 50 may be associated with a response pattern that minimizes problems.

T scores from 55–79, inclusive, reflect a problem-oriented approach to the items.

T scores from 80–89, inclusive, indicate an exaggerated response set, which probably reflects an attempt to claim excessive problems. VRIN T scores ≤ 79 can be used to rule out inconsistent responding.

T scores from 100–109, inclusive, are possibly indicators of an invalid protocol. Some high F profiles are obtained in inpatient settings and reflect extreme psychopathology. VRIN T scores ≥ 79 can be used to rule out inconsistent profiles.

T scores ≥ 110 indicate an uninterpretable profile because of extreme item endorsements.

Note: There are instances in which the F(B) score is invalid but the F scale is within an interpretable range. In this situation, the clinical scales might be valid and interpretable; however, scales with items toward the end of the booklet such as the content scales or supplementary scales would not be interpretable.

Interpretive hypothesis for elevated F(B) scores:

- Confusion, reading problems; confusion toward the end of the booklet
- Random responding (refer to VRIN)
- Severe psychopathology
- Possible symptom exaggeration
- Faking psychological problems
- Malingering

Note. See also discussion by Butcher et al. (2001) and Graham (2006).

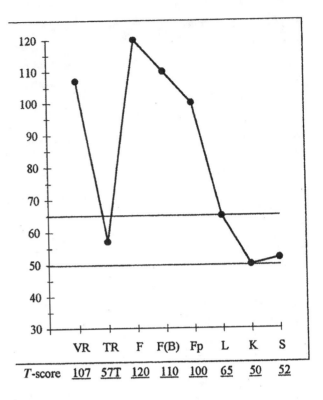

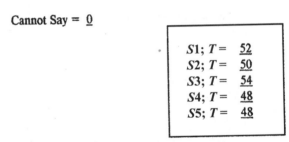

FIGURE 7.1. Random MMPI–2 basic profile.

VRIN scores are associated with random, careless, or noncontent-oriented responding. If the individual has a high F and a low to moderate VRIN, reasons other than a random response pattern may explain the high F (e.g., actual or feigned psychopathology).

Rogers, Harris, and Thatcher (1983) found a better than 90% accuracy rate for MMPI random-response indicators (F and T-R [Test–Retest] Index; R. Greene, 1979) in discriminating randomly generated profiles from profiles obtained in a forensic evaluation program. Berry, Wetter, et al. (1991); Berry et al. (1992); and Gallen and Berry (1996)

found that the F, F(B), and Variable Response Inconsistency scale (VRIN) scales were effective at detecting random responding on the MMPI–2.

Charter and Lopez's (2003) study provided "confidence interval bounds for random responding at the 95, 90, and 85% confidence levels for the F, F Back, and VRIN scales" (p. 985).

Archer, Handel, Lynch, and Elkins (2002) studied random responding on the MMPI–A. Their results suggested that "several MMPI–A validity scales are useful in detecting protocols that are largely random, but all of these validity scales are more limited in detecting partially random responding that involves less than half the total item pool located in the second half of the test booklet" (p. 417).

Stress or Distress

Stressful circumstances in the individual's life can influence infrequent item responding. Stressful life factors tend to be associated with elevated *F*-scale scores. Brozek and Schiele (1948; Schiele & Brozek, 1948) showed that increased *F*-scale elevation was associated with increased distress and an increase in neurotic symptomatology in individuals who were being systematically starved to 75% of their body weight in the Minnesota Experimental Semistarvation Studies during World War II (Keys, 1946).

Another obvious stressful circumstance that tends to produce extremely high *F* scores is admission to an inpatient psychiatric hospital or incarceration in a correctional facility. As a group, individuals in these settings tend to endorse a large number of extreme symptoms. Scheduling assessments after the individual has had time to acclimate usually results in more interpretable profiles. These findings reinforce the crucial importance, when interpreting a profile, of being aware of the circumstances at the time of testing (see chap. 5, this volume).

Cultural Background

Cultural factors sometimes lead to a high *F*. Cheung, Song, and Butcher (1991) found that some of the items on the *F* scale of the original MMPI did not work as infrequency items in China. For example, an item about belief in God was actually more frequently endorsed in the opposite direction in China than in the United States. (This item was dropped in MMPI–2.) A culturally specific *F* scale was subsequently developed using items that were infrequently endorsed in China. It is important that test protocols are scored using a culturally appropriate scoring key and set of norms when such cultural differences exist (see chap. 5, this volume).

Severe Psychological Disturbance

High *F* scores can reflect extreme psychopathology (Gynther, Altman, & Warbin, 1973). In an empirical evaluation of murderers in pretrial psychological evaluations, Holcomb, Adams, Ponder, and Anderson (1984) reported that high *F*-scale scores were more often associated with psychopathology than with test invalidity.

Faking Mental Health Problems

High scores on the *F* scale can also reflect the tendency to exaggerate adjustment problems or feign mental illness. This extreme pattern of self-reported psychological disturbance has been found when the individual is attempting to fake disability, perhaps to obtain compensation (Shaffer, 1981) or to escape punishment (Schretlen, 1988). Berry, Baer, and Harris (1991) performed a meta-analysis on the effectiveness of MMPI validity measures in 28 studies. Their results suggested that "these indices are good at detecting malingering, with the best scales being the *T*-scaled and raw i *F*, the original Dissimulation scale, and the *F–K* index" (p. 585). (See also the meta-analysis by Rogers, Sewell, & Saleken, 1994.)

Extensive research on the MMPI *F* scale has shown its effectiveness identifying tendencies to exaggerate or fake mental health symptoms over a wide variety of settings and conditions.[1] Graham, Watts, et al. (1991) found that a cut-off score of 100 correctly discriminated malingerers from genuine psychiatric patients but noted that the most effective cut-off of *F* for this purpose might vary for different settings. Iverson, Franzen, and Hammond (1995) found "that the MMPI–2 validity scales can differentiate with a high degree of accuracy inmates instructed to malinger mental illness from actual psychiatric patients.... The ... [*F(B)* scale] was found to be less accurate in classifying experimental malingers than the *F* scale. However, it did

---

[1] Anthony (1971); Bagby, Rogers, Buis, and Kalemba (1994); Bagby, Rogers, et al. (1997); Brunetti, Schlottman, Scott, and Hollrah (1998); Cofer, Chance, and Judson (1949); Dearth et al. (2005); Exner, McDowell, Pabst, Stackman, and Kirk (1963); Fairbank et al. (1985); R. Gallagher (1997); Gallucci (1984); Gendreau, Irvine, and Knight (1973); Grow, McVaugh, and Eno (1980); Hawk and Cornell (1989); Heaton, Smith, Lehman, and Vogt (1978); Iverson, Franzen, and Hammond (1995); Lundy, Geselowitz, and Shertzer (1985); McCaffrey and Bellamy-Campbell (1989); Pollack and Grainey (1984); Rathus and Siegel (1980); Rice, Arnold, and Tate (1983); Rogers, Dolmetsch, and Cavanaugh (1983); Rogers, Harris, et al. (1983); Roman, Tuley, Villanueva, and Mitchell (1990); Schretlen and Arkowitz (1990); Sivec, Hilsenroth, and Lynn (1995); Sivec, Lynn, and Garske (1994); Sweetland (1948); Walters, White, and Greene (1988); Wasyliw et al. (1988); Wetter et al. (1992); Wetter and Deitsch (1996); Wilcox and Dawson (1977).

identify 61% of the experimental malingerers who were faking on the second half of the test" (p. 120).

As noted earlier, the F scale works in detecting malingering because it is sensitive to the general tendency to overrespond—that is, to claim an extreme number of unrelated symptoms that people tend to show when they attempt to present a problem picture. The question as to whether people can be "taught" to claim more specific focused symptoms on the test and thereby avoid detection on scales such as F, F(B), and F(p) that detect symptom overresponding has been the subject of a number of studies. Wetter, Baer, Berry, Smith, and Larsen (1992) conducted a study with college students who were instructed to "moderate" their responding while at the same time attempting to claim psychological problems. They found that "instructed malingerers" could lower their clinical scale scores but were still detected by the F score falling in the malingering range. In a follow-up study, Wetter and her colleagues (Wetter, Baer, Berry, & Reynolds, 1994), using a community sample, evaluated whether people who were asked to fake borderline personality disorder and were told what the symptoms were would differ from "uninformed fakers" and from actual borderline personality disorder patients. Informing patients about the symptoms of borderline disorders was effective in producing clinical profiles resembling borderline personality disorder patients. However, the MMPI–2 F scale was just as effective at detecting "informed fakers" as well as "uninformed fakers," and the "results suggest that specific symptom information was of little help simulating a disturbance convincingly on the MMPI–2" (p. 199).

In similar studies, Bagby, Rogers, et al. (1997) informed participants of the specific symptom patterns in schizophrenia and depression and asked them to present themselves on the MMPI–2 as either depressed or schizophrenic. Although feigning normals did produce some differences in the clinical profile, the F scale, F(B), and F(p) worked well to differentiate malingering from patient profiles. Sivec, Hilsenroth, and Lynn (1994) found that the F scale was effective at detecting faking of paranoid symptoms but was less effective in discriminating faking of somatoform disorders.

Taken together, the diverse studies of feigning psychological problems seem to suggest that the MMPI–2 F scale is the single best predictor of malingering. The cut-off scores to detect malingering vary from setting to setting (Rogers & Cruise, 1998). However, F scores in the range of 100 or more are typically considered effective in detecting malingering of the MMPI–2. Coaching patients to take the MMPI–2 to present a particular psychological disorder tends not to be effective because the F scale is sensitive to faking, even among coached test takers. Coaching about the validity scales per se, however, may make detection difficult. Additional research on detecting feigned response sets is needed, preferably with research on known groups (Rogers & Cruise, 1998) as well as simulation studies, to further clarify the role that coaching plays in subverting detection efforts.

THE DISSIMULATION INDEX

To improve the detection of dissimulators on the MMPI, Gough (1947, 1950) developed an index using the relationship between the F and K scales. The F–K, or Dissimulation Index, tries to assess the extent to which an individual has claimed nonexistent problems or has exaggerated complaints. Gough considered that extremely high F elevations along with low K scores indicated an invalid or dissimulated performance. This measure, the F–K Index, is determined by subtracting the raw score of the K scale from the raw score of the F scale.

Gough originally recommended that an F–K score of 9 or higher would serve as an indication that the profile was invalid because of exaggerated symptoms. Others (e.g., Lachar, 1974) recommended that profiles with an F–K score of 12 or higher be considered invalid because the original score suggested by Gough was considered so low that it resulted in the elimination of too many valid, interpretable profiles. For discussions of norms and interpretations, and the influence of factors such as education and occupations, see Rothke, Friedman, Dahlstrom, and Greene (1994) and Brophy (1995).

The F–K Index in which the K score is greater than the F score (resulting in a negative number) that is used to detect a fake-good profile has not worked out well in practice and is not recommended for clinical use. Too many valid and interpretable protocols are rejected by this index when *K* is greater than *F*.

Empirical studies in forensic assessment have supported the *F–K* Index (e.g., Bagby, Nicholson, et al., 1997; Blanchard, McGrath, Pogge, & Khadivi, 2003; Hawk & Cornell, 1989). Berry, Baer, et al. (1991) conducted a meta-analysis to examine the effectiveness of MMPI-based measures in detecting faking. Their findings suggested that the *F–K* Index significantly differentiated people who were malingering from people who were not malingering: "These indices are good at detecting malingering, with the best scales being the *T*-scaled and raw *F*, the original Dissimulation scale, and the *F–K* Index. Effect sizes were much smaller for the revised Dissimulation index and the Subtle/Obvious scales, suggesting caution in their use" (p. 585; see also Schretlen & Arkowitz, 1990; Wasyliw et al., 1988).

Similarly, Graham, Timbrook, et al. (1991) found that the *F–K* Index significantly detected faking on the MMPI–2 with a sample of undergraduate students who were instructed to try to appear psychologically disturbed on the test. However, the Index did not work as well as using the *F* scale alone. Although the *F–K* Index appears to be effective in detecting faking on the MMPI and MMPI–2 (Wetzler & Marlowe, 1990), it does not appear to add incremental validity beyond use of the *F* scale alone.

THE *F(p)* SCALE

The *F* and *F(B)* scales are effective at detecting extreme endorsement; however, in moderate ranges they do not clearly differentiate symptom exaggeration from genuine psychopathology. That is, inpatients who are clearly disturbed psychologically can produce high scores on *F* and *F(B)*, even though they are *not* exaggerating. The confounding of symptom exaggeration with psychopathology results from the fact that these scales were made up from items that were infrequently endorsed in *nonclinical* populations. To detect exaggerated responding on personality items it is necessary to assess rare or extreme responses within a psychiatric population.

EXHIBIT 7.7

Summary of Interpretative Rules for the MMPI–2 *F(p)* in Forensic Evaluations

The MMPI–2 *F(p)* is an infrequency scale that indicates unusual response to the MMPI–2 items through claiming excessive, unlikely symptoms that are not typically endorsed by psychiatric patients.

T scores below 50 may be associated with a response pattern that minimizes problems.

T scores from 60–79, inclusive, reflect a problem-oriented approach to the items.

T scores from 70-99, inclusive, are possibly indicators of an invalid protocol as a result of claiming an extreme number of rare psychiatric symptoms.

T scores ≥ 100 indicate likely malingering of psychiatric symptoms and result in an uninterpretable profile because of extreme item endorsements.

Interpretive hypothesis for extremely elevated *F(p)* scores:

- Likely symptom exaggeration
- Faking psychological problems
- Malingering of mental health symptoms

Note. See also discussion by Arbisi and Ben-Porath (1995); Butcher et al. (2001); and Graham (2006).

Arbisi and Ben-Porath (1995, 1997) developed an extreme endorsement Symptom Exaggeration scale (*F(p)*) to assess extreme responding apart from two potential contributors to infrequency scale elevation—to be less influenced by severity of psychopathology and general maladjustment than *F* and *FB*. They used a more appropriate reference population—patients in an inpatient psychiatric facility—than the general normative sample for this purpose. Using a large sample of Veteran's Administration psychiatric patients and normal controls they found 27 MMPI–2 items that appeared to detect exaggerated responding in psychiatric inpatients. That is, these items reflected symptoms that were rarely endorsed by genuine psychiatric patients and normals. High scores (*T* > 80) reflect a tendency to endorse rare problems that are not usually endorsed by patients in a psychiatric setting and represent an overresponding or symptom exaggeration. However, the test is not considered invalid unless it is at a *T* score of 100 or greater. (See Exhibit 7.7 for a discussion of the interpretive meanings of the *F(p)* scale.)

There has been some suggestion that the $F(p)$ scale is confounded with fake-good responding because it includes four items from the L scale (e.g., Gass & Luis, 2001). However, other studies have reported that almost all the $F(p)$ items, including those contained on the L scale, contribute to identifying malingering (e.g., Strong, Greene, & Schinka, 2000). The $F(p)$ scale has performed well in empirical studies of malingering. For example, Blanchard and colleagues (2003) found that $F(p)$ was associated with the largest effect size among the standard scales when comparing students instructed to overreport and genuine psychiatric inpatients.

Recently, Megargee (2006) reported on the development of a similar specialized infrequency scale (Fc) for use in criminal populations, and Elhai and his colleagues (Elhai, Ruggiero, Frueh, Beckham, & Gold, 2002) developed an infrequency scale for veterans claiming PTSD (the $Fptsd$ scale).

CONSISTENCY MEASURES

Inconsistent responding threatens the validity of self-report. For test takers who endorse essentially identical MMPI items in opposite ways, their contradictory self-descriptions pose problems in interpreting the protocol.

The original MMPI contained 16 items that were repeated. Some investigators tried to use this artifact to appraise response consistency (Buechley & Ball, 1952; Dahlstrom et al., 1972; R. Greene, 1991). These repeated item pairs, if answered differently by an individual, were considered to be a clear indication that the person was not approaching the MMPI items with a consistent, cooperative response orientation. The resulting T-R Index (Test–Retest) was somewhat limited by the relatively small number of items. If a person endorsed more than four items in an inconsistent manner, he or she was considered to be producing a low credibility record (R. Greene, 1991). However, because many groups produce two or three inconsistent responses, an important determination hinges on small numbers.

The MMPI Restandardization Committee viewed the 16 repeated items as problematic and did not retain them in the MMPI–2. The lack of re-

peated items does *not* mean that response consistency cannot be evaluated, however. There are a number of items on the inventory that contain similar wording or possess content that reveal inconsistent responding. The $VRIN$ and $TRIN$ scales were developed from the revised item pool to assess response inconsistency in the MMPI–2.

The Variable Response Inconsistency Scale

The Variable Response Inconsistency ($VRIN$) scale is an empirically derived measure that is made up of pairs of items for which one or two of four possible configurations (*true–false, false–true, true–true, false–false*) would be considered semantically inconsistent. For example, answering *true* to "I buy new socks several times a week" and *false* to "I purchase new socks every couple of days or more often" represents semantically inconsistent responses.

The $VRIN$ score is based on the sum of inconsistent responses. As noted earlier, the $VRIN$ scale may be used to help interpret a high F score. For example, a high F score in conjunction with a low to moderate $VRIN$ score rules out the possibility that the former reflects random responding or confusion. (See Exhibit 7.8 for a summary of interpretive guidelines for $VRIN$.) Archer, Fontaine, and McCrae (1998) found that profiles with high $VRIN$ scores produced lower correlations with patient self-reports and ratings by clinicians than profiles that were found to be valid on the basis of the $VRIN$ score.

EXHIBIT 7.8

Summary of Interpretative Rules for the MMPI–2 and MMPI–A VRIN Scales in Forensic Evaluations

---

MMPI–2 *VRIN* T scores ≥ 80 or MMPI–A *VRIN* scores ≥ 75 indicate inconsistent random responding that invalidates the profile.

MMPI–2 *VRIN* scores from 65–79 or MMPI–A *VRIN* scores 70–74, inclusive, suggest a possibly invalid profile due to inconsistent responding. Careless responding can produce a VRIN in this range.

Note. See also discussion by Butcher et al. (2001) and Graham (2006).

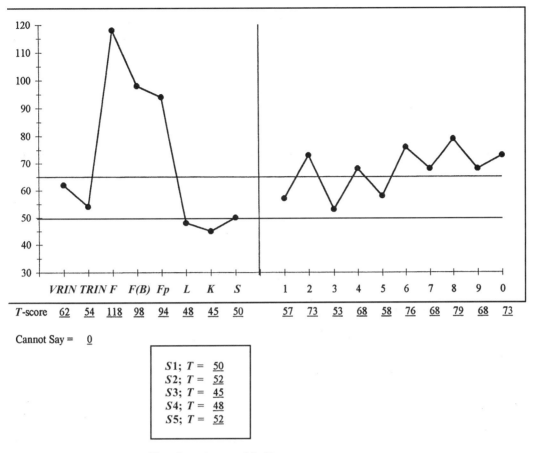

FIGURE 7.2. Basic MMPI–2 profile of a 36-year-old client.

Figure 7.2 illustrates the interpretative value of the *VRIN* scale. This MMPI–2 profile was produced by a 36-year-old man who had recently been admitted to an inpatient psychiatric unit of a general hospital. Examination of the *F* scale suggests that the profile is uninterpretable because the *T* score is 118 and indicates the possibility that he has answered the items in a random manner. However, the *VRIN*-scale score (*T* = 62) is in the valid range, signifying that he has not endorsed the items in a blatantly inconsistent manner. This rules out an interpretation that he has answered randomly (see research by Wetter et al., 1992). His clinical profile would be considered valid and interpretable. However, the large number of symptoms he has endorsed, either as a result of a psychotic process or as an effort to malinger, requires further consideration. Even though random or careless responding can be ruled out as an explanation of his high

F-scale elevation, it is still unclear at this point in the evaluation why he endorsed such broad-ranging, extreme symptoms.

The True Response Inconsistency Scale

The True Response Inconsistency (*TRIN*) scale was designed to assess the tendency to respond in an inconsistent manner by endorsing many items in the same direction (either true or false). The *TRIN* scale is made up of 20 pairs of items to which the same response is semantically inconsistent. Of the 20 item pairs, 11 are scored inconsistent only if the client responds *true* to both items. Six of the item pairs are scored inconsistent only if the client responds *false* to both items. Three are scored inconsistent if the client responds *true* to both or *false* to both (see Exhibit 7.9).

The scoring for *TRIN* is more complicated than the scoring of other MMPI–2 scales, and should be

Summary of Interpretative Rules for the MMPI–2 and MMPI–A *TRIN* Scales in Forensic Evaluations

MMPI–2 *TRIN* *T* scores ≥ 80 or MMPI–A *TRIN* scores ≥ 75 indicate inconsistent responding because of yea- or nay-saying. The profile is likely invalid.

MMPI–2 *TRIN* scores from 65–79 or MMPI–A *TRIN* scores 70–74, inclusive, are suspect and suggest possible inconsistent responding.

A yea-saying response set is found in a *TRIN* score in the inconsistent true direction and indicated by a (T) following the score.

A nay-saying response set is found by a *TRIN* score in the inconsistent false direction and indicated by a (F) following the score.

Note. For further discussion see Butcher et al. (2001) and Graham (2006).

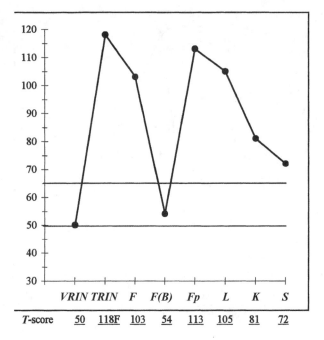

	VRIN	TRIN	F	F(B)	Fp	L	K	S
T-score	50	118F	103	54	113	105	81	72

Cannot Say = 0

*S*1; *T* =	69
*S*2; *T* =	71
*S*3; *T* =	63
*S*4; *T* =	68
*S*5; *T* =	53

FIGURE 7.3. An all-false response pattern on the MMPI–2.

carefully checked. Questions have been raised about the accuracy of the hand-scoring method for the consistency scales (Iverson & Barton, 1999). First, the number of *true* and *false* inconsistent responses to the item pairs is determined. One point is added to the person's score for each of the 14 item pairs in which a *true* response is inconsistent. One point is subtracted for each of the 9 item pairs if a *false* response is obtained. Next, a constant of 9 points is added to the scale to avoid negative raw score numbers. For example, if an individual endorsed four of the *true* item pairs and six of the *false* item pairs on *TRIN*, the score would be 4-6 + 9, or 7. The test scorer should then convert the *TRIN* raw score to a *T* score. The *T* scores for *TRIN* are constructed so that they will never be lower than 50. Any *T* score greater than 50 will be followed by either a "T," which denotes *true* response inconsistence ("yea saying"), or an "F," which denotes a *false* response inconsistency set ("nay saying"). Any *T* score greater than 80 indicates an extreme response set.

The *TRIN* score is particularly helpful in interpreting scores on scales *L* and *K* because all but one of the items on these scales is keyed *false*. An individual engaging in an inconsistent *false* response set may produce elevated scores on scales *L* and *K* that have nothing to do with defensiveness or faking

good. Conversely, an individual who answers the MMPI–2 items inconsistently *true* may produce low scores on *L* and *K* that have nothing to do with being excessively open, self-critical, or overwhelmed by stress. Whenever extreme scores appear on scales *L* and *K*, careful examination of the score on *TRIN* is essential.

Figure 7.3 presents an example of an MMPI forensic evaluation that was invalidated by inconsistent responding (an "all false" pattern).

AN ESSENTIAL KEY TO EVALUATING MALINGERING TESTS, SCALES, AND APPROACHES

Malingering is defined as the intentional production of false or greatly exaggerated physical or psychological symptoms motivated by external incentives (American Psychiatric Association, 1987).

Throughout this book we emphasize a fundamental principle: *Always* ask whether an adequate array of well-designed research published in peer-reviewed scientific and professional journals establishes the validity, reliability, sensitivity, and specificity of the test, scale, or approach for the relevant forensic question at issue, for the relevant setting, and for the relevant population.

Some measures may achieve remarkable results in virtually *never* failing to identify a certain characteristic (i.e., an extremely low false negative rate) but fail to adequately rule out the absence of that characteristic. Consider the extreme hypothetical: The Nevermiss Company markets a one-question self-report scale that, according to the press release, *never* fails to identify people who have been convicted of a crime. The sole question on the test is, "Have you ever breathed?" and all "*yes*" answer scores indicate, according to the test interpretation manual, that the person has a criminal record. Research supports the claim: The test never fails to identify those who turn out to have criminal records. It has false negative rate of zero. However, it is worthless because it fails to prevent false positives: It falsely classifies those who have no criminal records as criminals.

A competitor company, NOFALSERECORDS, markets a one-question self-report scale that, according to the press release, *never* falsely classifies those without criminal records as criminals. The sole question on their test is, "Are you alive right now?" and all "*yes*" answers indicate, according to the test interpretation manual, that the person has no criminal record. The test has no false positives but is worthless because of its high false negative rate: Those with criminal records are classified as not having criminal records.

Expert witnesses and attorneys must evaluate each test, scale, or approach in light of how well it accomplishes its function and does so consistently, without making mistakes, according to well-designed scientific research. It can be helpful—sometimes crucial—to read the original research reports rather than relying on review articles (see the section "Constant Questioning" in chap. 5, this volume). A key to evaluating the research supporting (or failing to support) any test, scale, or approach is, "What criteria and methodology were used to test the test? How was the test, scale, or approach's performance measured as successful or unsuccessful?" In the hypothetical examples, the criterion would be whether each person whom the test identified as having or not having a criminal record actually had a criminal record. Research validating these two hypothetical tests would supposedly check all available databases to determine whether each person had a criminal record. A key question to ask is, "Does each research study evaluating this test use well-designed methodology and adequate criteria?" For example, in a study evaluating the two tests, is it possible that the methodology used to gather criminal records might miss some, or that some of the records themselves might be inaccurate or misleading?

The question of whether a test, scale, or approach has demonstrated adequate validity, reliability, sensitivity, and specificity for forensic use becomes more complex when malingering is at issue because the basic criterion is harder to establish. It is often difficult to *know* that a person is malingering unless behavior clearly contradicts a litigant's self-report. For example, attorneys may hire private detectives to videotape plaintiffs who are claiming physical injury to try to catch them acting in a way that contradicts their claim.

An essential key to evaluating tests, scales, and approaches that purport to identify malingering is to examine the criteria and methodology of the research supporting their validity, reliability, sensitivity, and specificity. How *exactly* do the researchers *know* which people in the study are actually malingering and which are not malingering?

Some studies may rely on short-cuts, reasoning that because a group has characteristics that are supposedly highly correlated with malingering they are probably malingering. Some studies may go so far as to fail to operationally define how malingerers and nonmalingerers were identified. The lack of specific methodology and criteria makes any research report scientifically questionable. A hallmark of the scientific method is the transparency and replicability of the methodology itself. Research reports must enable colleagues to evaluate and (attempt to) replicate each step of the research.

An example of a shortcut that is sometimes used in research exploring the validity, reliability, sensitivity, and specificity of standardized psychological tests is to assume that complaints of symptoms occurring in the context of litigation are more likely to be malingered and therefore a group of patients who are involved in litigation are more likely to be (or might, in light of other short-cuts, be assumed to be) malingerers. Even if the probabilistic reasoning underlying this short-cut were sound for this purpose, the research findings of Rogers and colleagues' (2003) meta-analysis, however, suggests that the basic assumption is flawed.

> Researchers employing a differential prevalence design have often assumed that the litigation substantially increases the likelihood of feigning. The current data question both the assumption and the use of this design in feigning research. Beyond litigation per se, forensic groups (even with child custody cases removed) have lower scores on validity scales than the genuine patients in general. . . . Indirectly, these combined results for forensic status cast doubt about the *Diagnostic and Statistical Manual of Mental Disorders, Fourth Edition's* (*DSM–IV;* American Psychiatric Association, 1994) postulation that the mere context of forensic evaluation increases the likelihood of malingering. (p. 174)

When assessing malingering, as in all cases, expert witnesses and attorneys must evaluate the scientific soundness of each forensic test, scale, and approach—for the relevant forensic question, relevant setting, and relevant population rather than just accepting the "findings."

MMPI AND MMPI–2 INDICATORS OF MALINGERING

Richard Rogers (1984) presented a useful model for detecting deception in forensic evaluations. His model of malingering has received empirical support when applied in a forensic assessment setting (Berry, 1995; Berry & Butcher, 1997; Heilbrun, Bennett, White, & Kelly, 1990). This section focuses on the three major indexes of malingering that he originally suggested, along with a fourth approach that involves the evaluation of atypical patterns. The detection of faking on standardized psychological tests is an important consideration for the forensic psychologist not only for interpreting the particular test in question but also for better understanding the individual's general approach to the entire assessment process. Dalby (1988) wrote that "given the evidence for generalized response set, the validity scores on these standardized measures may be useful in interpreting scores from concurrently administered instruments which do not contain validity indicators" (p. 54).

Rare Responding

Research on MMPI scales and malingering has consistently shown that the *F* scale and, to some extent, the *F–K* Index are valuable indicators of the tendency to fake bad on the MMPI. Wasyliw et al. (1988) reported that MMPI indexes of malingering, particularly the *F* scale, were effective in discriminating insanity defendants from individuals judged insane but not standing trial. Schretlen (1988) reviewed the research evidence for the use of several psychological tests (MMPI, Rorschach, Bender–Gestalt, WAIS–R) in detection of malingering and concluded that "it is probably indefensible to render expert testimony regarding the likelihood of malingering without psychological test data bearing on this question" (p. 473). His evaluation of the MMPI, thought to be the one most valuable means of detecting faking, was quite positive.

Berry, Baer, et al. (1991) conducted a meta-analysis of 28 studies of faking bad or malingering on the MMPI. They found that most of the studies that have been conducted provided strong support for the MMPI's ability to detect malingering. They concluded, "The major finding of this review was that MMPI based scales for detecting faking are quite good at separating groups of subjects known or suspected of malingering from those completing the inventory honestly, with a mean overall effect size of 2.07" (p. 594).

Defensive Responding

In some settings, particularly in workers' compensation or personal injury litigation cases in which the individual is exaggerating or feigning physical injury or disability, the defensive profile pattern is a common harbinger of complaints without actual organic problems (Butcher & Miller, 1998). Individuals in these settings often respond to the test items by claiming a high degree of virtue and denying (or minimizing) faults, as shown by high *L* and *K* scores, so that their claims of physical problems will seem more credible.

Inconsistent Responding

As Richard Rogers (1984) and others have noted, inconsistent responding on the MMPI items can reflect a general pattern of malingering on the test. Individuals who attempt to endorse extreme symptoms in an unselected fashion, endorse randomly, or respond according to an all-true or all-false response set tend to answer items on clinical scales in an inconsistent manner. Indexes of inconsistency, such as *VRIN* and *TRIN* on MMPI–2, will help detect potential malingering or other invalidating response approaches.

Atypical MMPI and MMPI–2 Patterns

A fourth possible indicator of malingering on the MMPI–2 involves the presence of atypical response patterns. This approach is analogous to the reporting of incompatible physical symptoms such as "glove anesthesia" that cannot be explained by actual neural connections or other biological aspects. Those who malinger or dissimulate often give responses that are inconsistent with other clinical observations (see, e.g., J. M. MacDonald, 1976). This approach with the MMPI–2 involves the use of different sources of information within the test. That is, clients may present incompatible or inexplicable symptom patterns on the test that call into question the accuracy of the profile.

In this approach to detecting malingering, the expert witness matches behavior or symptoms from the client's responses to that of a modal or expected clinical pattern established by research on the particular sample involved or by the base rates for the relevant population (Butcher, 1997). Research has

established consistent or expected behavior patterns that can be evaluated through the various scales and indexes. Hypotheses about an individual's expected behavior on the MMPI–2 can be matched with features of actual behavior. Modal or expected MMPI–2 performances can be identified for a variety of clinical situations or phenomena. Clients who deviate from the expected performance, particularly with respect to the validity scale pattern, would be considered as possibly malingering. The following two examples illustrate instances in which the individual's MMPI–2 results are inconsistent with the expected MMPI–2 performance for the situation, suggesting that the client may have distorted the presentation of symptoms.

Example 1. In the first example, the MMPI–2 was used in a mental health treatment setting to determine treatment amenability and willingness to self-disclose (Butcher, 1990b). The expected validity pattern in this situation is that the individual presents honestly (low *L*) and openly (low *K*) and discusses mental health problems candidly (*F* between 60 and 89), as illustrated in Figure 7.4.

Example 2. In the second example, the MMPI–2 was administered in a medical clinic as part of an examination to determine if the individual was cooperating with the evaluation and presenting physical symptoms accurately. As the profile in Figure 7.5 shows, the individual has affirmed an excessive (relative to the expected) number of complaints.

COMMON FORENSIC VALIDITY PATTERNS

Case examples illustrating some of the more common prototypical validity patterns found in forensic evaluations show the relation among the various validity scales.

The Righteous Responder

Individuals with this validity pattern tend to project the most favorable social image possible, usually to create an impression that they are beyond reproach. The high *L* score is quite prominent and may be accompanied by an elevation on the *K* scale. *F*-scale scores are typically low (i.e., less than average). Test takers profess high moral values and

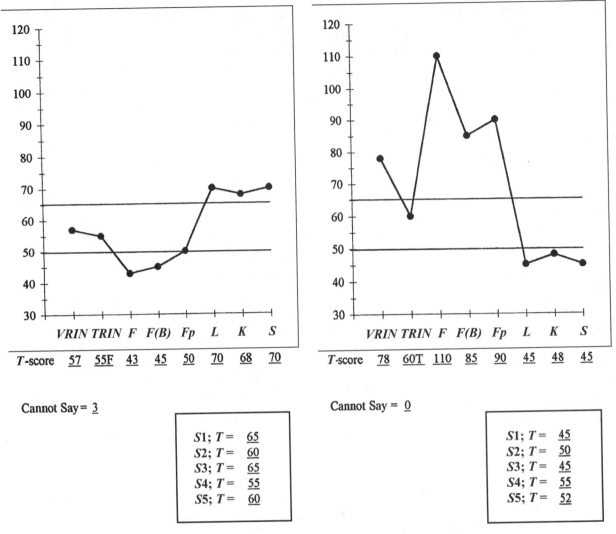

T-score	VRIN	TRIN	F	F(B)	Fp	L	K	S
	57	55F	43	45	50	70	68	70

Cannot Say = 3

S1; T =	65
S2; T =	60
S3; T =	65
S4; T =	55
S5; T =	60

FIGURE 7.4. An atypical validity pattern for a treatment-oriented patient.

T-score	VRIN	TRIN	F	F(B)	Fp	L	K	S
	78	60T	110	85	90	45	48	45

Cannot Say = 0

S1; T =	45
S2; T =	50
S3; T =	45
S4; T =	55
S5; T =	52

FIGURE 7.5. An unlikely validity profile.

assert that they have personal characteristics (e.g., high moral character) that they think will make their testimony credible. However, they seemingly claim too much virtue through asserting unrealistically extreme qualities that people who lead highly moral lives would not claim.

Figure 7.6 is an example of an individual (Mr. A.) who subscribed to an extreme and exaggerated positive self-view so that his claims of other symptoms would be given a high degree of credence. (Note: the original MMPI has been rescored on MMPI–2 norms.) The data suggest that Mr. A. engaged in conscious malingering of psychological and physical symptoms to convince the court of the legitimacy of his disability claims.

Mr. A., a 38-year-old litigant, claimed severe disability after *almost* being injured in a near-miss incident involving two airplanes. While taxiing a single engine airplane to depart on a charter flight, he was cleared to an active runway for takeoff by the air traffic controller. At the same time, a commercial jet airplane was cleared by a traffic control operator to land on the same runway. The jet plane scraped the smaller plane, producing minor damages but no physical injury. Several months later, the litigant filed a workers' compensation claim for retraining in another field. Later—after the workers' compensation was used up—he filed a lawsuit against the government for damages (lost income) because he claimed that he was not able to follow

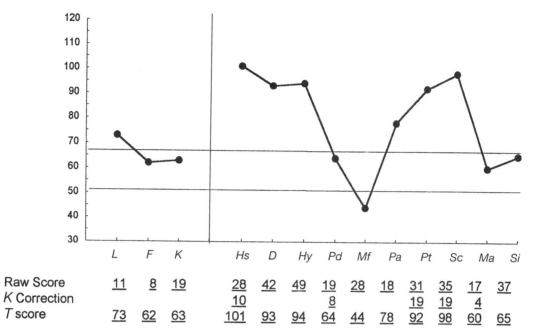

FIGURE 7.6. Basic MMPI profile (replotted on MMPI–2 norms) of Mr. A.

up on his original aviation career plans (as an airline pilot) as a result of his alleged impaired mental state resulting from the incident. He reportedly became so tense, depressed, and stressed that he had to change his goals to a less lucrative career rather than to follow the original aviation career plans he was pursuing at the time of the incident.

His profile on the original MMPI reflects an extreme tendency to present a highly virtuous picture of himself while at the same time asserting that he is suffering from extreme physical and mental fatigue and disability. Mr. A.'s apparent attempt to distort the MMPI personality appraisal, as reflected in the "good impression" validity pattern, was consistent with other attempts on his part to oversell himself. For example, he had previously completed job application forms for airline positions that contained false information about his flying background and qualifications. His MMPI validity pattern was consistent with that of an individual who was falsely describing himself to create a particular impression.

The Defensive Self-Protector

As noted earlier, parents who are being assessed in a domestic court case to determine custody or establish visitation rights often present an overly favorable self-portrait in their response to psycholog-

ical testing (Butcher, 1997). Figure 7.7 presents an MMPI–2 pattern typical of an individual (Mr. B.) who denies faults and asserts that he has no psychological problems or personal weaknesses. Even with his defensive profile, other aspects of his profile show a pattern of personality characteristics that probably reflect problem behavior.

The second hypothetical case study involves Brenda (age 38) and Mr. B. (age 41), who have been divorced for about 3 years and whose relationship continues to be troublesome. Brenda claims that Mr. B., her ex-husband, has been irregular with his alimony and child support payments and owes back alimony. Mr. B. claims that Brenda has not lived up to the visitation program established by the court and has recently refused to let him see their daughter.

A domestic court ordered a psychological assessment of Mr. B. to determine if his parental visitation rights should be suspended. Investigation is currently under way to determine if he is guilty of sexually abusing his 9-year-old daughter, as alleged by his ex-wife. His daughter has not acknowledged that the abuse occurred, but his ex-wife insists that she has observed him fondling their daughter in the past and believes that the abuse continues. She also alleges that Mr. B. has engaged extensively in

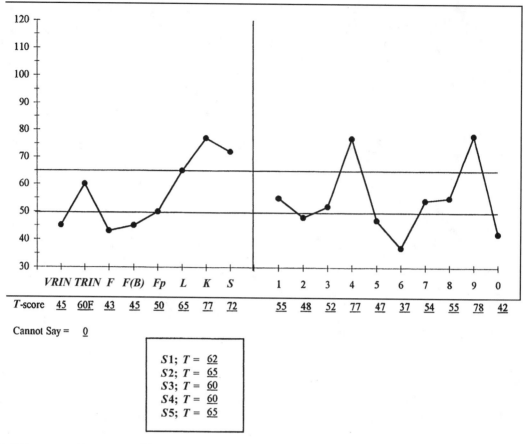

FIGURE 7.7. Basic MMPI–2 profile of Mr. B.

other irresponsible behavior—financial, legal, and interpersonal—and that she does not wish to expose her child to his deviant behavior. Mr. B. has a history of excessive drinking and problematic behavior, such as reckless driving and driving under the influence of alcohol. He told the psychologist that he agreed to the court-ordered MMPI–2 evaluation in an effort to clear his name and keep his visitation rights with his daughter.

Mr. B.'s MMPI–2 validity scale configuration shows a clear pattern of test defensiveness. He made an effort to place himself in the most favorable light, denying faults and projecting a positive self-image. Although he attempted to present himself as a problem-free and well-adjusted individual, his MMPI–2 clinical pattern reflected a number of possible problems such as poor impulse control, antisocial behavior, and poor judgment. His problems are probably more extreme than the clinical scales suggest.

The court-appointed psychologist conducting the evaluation concluded that Mr. B's long history of problematic behavior, along with his MMPI–2-based personality pattern, supports the possibility that his negative behavior could produce a deleterious influence on the child. Closer supervision and more restricted family visitation were recommended pending review of visitation rights by the court.

A Case of Malingering in a Not Guilty by Reason of Insanity Plea

The following case involves an evaluation of a 22-year-old, unemployed woman (Ms. C.) who pleaded that she was not guilty by reason of insanity after being arrested and charged with attempted aggravated murder following an incident in which she stabbed a taxi driver in the back. She was referred for psychological evaluation to determine her present condition and whether her present con-

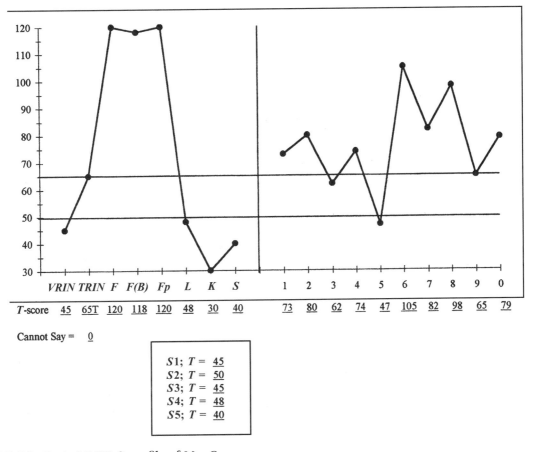

Cannot Say = 0

S1; T =	45
S2; T =	50
S3; T =	45
S4; T =	48
S5; T =	40

FIGURE 7.8. Basic MMPI–2 profile of Ms. C.

dition might bear on her allegation that she was insane at the time of the assault.

In the diagnostic interview, she appeared to be somewhat confused and seemed not to respond appropriately even to simple questions asked of her. She took the MMPI–2 as part of the forensic evaluation. Her MMPI–2 standard profile is shown in Figure 7.8.

Ms. C.'s MMPI–2 validity pattern shows a clear symptom exaggeration and a unlikely F-scale elevation, indicating that she claimed numerous, unrelated psychological problems and attitudes. According to her F-scale elevation, her clinical profile is likely to be an exaggerated and uninterpretable pattern of symptoms.

As noted earlier, several possible explanations can be found for profiles with this level of elevation on the MMPI–2 F scale. It is important to rule out the possibility that this is a random profile. Ms. C. has had limited education, and the examiner won-

dered if she could read well enough to complete a valid MMPI–2. Her low score on the VRIN scale (T = 45) indicates that she has endorsed similar items in a consistent manner, thus eliminating the possibility that she had responded in a noncontent-oriented or random fashion. If she simply had been confused, disoriented, or unable to read the items, she would have produced a higher VRIN-scale score. In addition, it is unlikely that she was experiencing a psychotic process at the time of the testing. Individuals with extreme psychological disorders do not generally produce this extreme level of F elevation; instead, they tend to respond more selectively to symptoms, producing lower F scores.

Her extremely high F-score elevation is more likely the result of a false claim of psychological problems on her part. Ms. C.'s validity pattern more closely resembles those extremely exaggerated profiles found by Graham, Watts, et al. (1991) in individuals who attempt to fake the MMPI–2 by claiming mental health problems that they do not have. Other information obtained in the interview and background evaluation added substance to the conclusion that her MMPI–2 profile represented an effort to fake the test to appear psychiatrically disturbed.

The effectiveness of computer-based MMPI–2 interpretation to detect invalid records following standard MMPI–2 invalidity indexes has been noted. Shores and Carstairs (1998) reported that the computer-based MMPI–2 system (Minnesota Reports) was effective in differentiating faked or malingered records from test protocols of individuals who were given the standard instructions. The Minnesota Report detected 94% of the fake-good records and 100% of the fake-bad (malingered) records, while classifying 78% of the standard records correctly. The authors noted that "the value of the Minnesota Report in identifying fake-bad response sets was amply demonstrated, and it is such performances that may be helpful in detecting malingering in forensic evaluations" (p. 101).

CONTROVERSIAL MEASURES OF INVALIDITY

One tradition in objective psychological assessment research has been to use the MMPI item pool as a source of items for the development of scales or indexes that could detect problems or symptom clusters of interest. An untold number of scales were developed for the original MMPI and published without ever becoming an "official" part of the instrument. For example, there were scales developed for such diverse attributes as "success in baseball," assessing "pharisaic virtue," and for "alixythimia," although these never became incorporated in standard interpretative approaches. The following sections focus on three controversial scales.

THE FAKE BAD SCALE

In a 1991 issue of the journal *Psychological Reports*, Lees-Haley, English, and Glenn (1991) presented "A Fake Bad Scale on the MMPI–2 for Personal Injury Claimants." The scale contains 43 items.

The Fake Bad Scale (FBS) became the focus of a spirited and still-unresolved controversy. For example, Butcher, Arbisi, Atlis, and McNulty (2003), in their article "The Construct Validity of the Lees-Haley Fake Bad Scale: Does This Scale Measure Somatic Malingering and Feigned Emotional Distress?" reported a study "to investigate the psychometric characteristics of the *FBS* using MMPI–2 profiles from six settings: Psychiatric Inpatient . . . ; Correctional Facility . . . ; Chronic Pain Program . . . ; General Medical . . . ; Veterans Administration Hospital Inpatient . . . ; and Personal Injury Litigation" (p. 473). They stated the following.

> The analyses presented in this study show that the *FBS* is not a psychometrically sound measure of somatic malingering but is more associated with the expression of psychopathology in which physical symptoms are experienced. The *FBS* does not reflect malingering in the way that other scales developed for the MMPI–2 do, such as the F, F(b), and F(p). The scale also does not assess "extreme" or rare symptoms but appears to reflect the presentation of a number of physical complaints. Medical conditions that are chronic and manifest a broad range of symptomatic content (such as multiple sclerosis or neuralgia) are also likely to produce extreme elevations on the *FBS* and thereby be considered "malingering." Further, mental health patients who have psychologically based disorders or have a chronic medical condition are likely to have high *FBS* scores. (p. 482)

Butcher, Arbisi, and colleagues concluded,

> The MMPI–2 is widely used in disability and personal injury evaluations because it is a well-validated and objective measure of psychopathology and contains validity scales that assess the test taker's approach to the instruments. The *FBS* does not meet the

standards set by the other MMPI–2 validity scales nor does it live up to the authors' claim that it can accurately detect malingering within the context of disability evaluations. Moreover the *FBS* is not likely to meet the legal criteria in forensic cases because of the lack of empirical validity and the low level of professional acceptance of it as a measure of malingering. (2003, p. 484)

Lees-Haley and Fox (2004) replied that these criticisms reflected a misunderstanding of the *FBS* and faulty assumptions about malingering.

> Their reasoning and methodology do not support their conclusions. Their methodology and reporting are very unusual for a research study. Not even basic descriptive statistics were reported, for example, means, standard deviations, or ranges. Five of their six samples were not in the setting for which the *FBS* was designed, and only one—their smallest sample—was personal injury litigants. (p. 333)

Arbisi and Butcher (2004a) responded to Lees-Haley and Fox's comments, adding that the comments did not "address the primary issue raised in our paper regarding the psychological construct measured by the *FBS*" (p. 341).

Others have joined in this controversy, exploring these and other questions that have been raised about the *FBS* on the basis of the research to date. Currently no apparent consensus has formed.

Research regarding *FBS* has produced mixed results. Larrabee (2003), for example, found in a study of 55 cases that the "Lees-Haley Fake Bad Scale (*FBS*) was the most sensitive MMPI–2 scale in discriminating the malingerers from the head-injured persons" (p. 54). Greiffenstein, Baker, Gola, Donders, and Miller (2002) found that

> the *FBS* was sensitive to both litigation status and nonconforming vs. conforming symptom courses. . . . *FBS* showed significant associations with various neuropsychological symptom

validity measures. *FBS* appears to capture a hybrid of infrequent symptom reporting styles with an emphasis on unauthentic physical complaints. However, *FBS* also correlated with documented abnormal neurological signs within a litigating moderate–severe brain-injury group. Its use as a symptom infrequency measure may have to be modified in more severe injury litigants, as some *FBS* items may reflect true long-term outcome in severe cerebral dysfunction. (p. 1591)

Iverson, Henrichs, Barton, and Allen (2002) conducted a study in which "cutoff scores proposed by P. R. Lees-Haley and colleagues were applied to inmate volunteers from a federal prison, medical outpatients, and patients from an inpatient substance abuse unit." They found that the "original cutoff scores correctly identified the majority of inmates instructed to malinger psychopathology, but these scores resulted in unacceptably high rates of false positive classifications. The revised cutoff scores resulted in fewer false positives, i.e., 8–24%" (p. 131).

Rogers and colleagues (2003), on the basis of a meta-analysis of 73 studies, discussed a possible reason for the *FBS*'s lack of success in the meta-analysis: "In stark contrast to *Ds*, *FBS* also tries to capitalize on erroneous stereotypes but was designed for only circumscribed referrals (i.e., personal injury cases). Its general lack of success (mean $d = .32$) is likely attributable to its narrow focus" (p. 172).

Whether any scale—including the *FBS*—is new or old, controversial or widely accepted, nothing can spare the expert witness and attorney the responsibility of reading carefully and with an open mind the full array of relevant research and commentary to determine *for a specific forensic question, setting, and population* whether an adequate array of well-designed research published in peer-reviewed journals clearly establishes the scale's validity, reliability, sensitivity, and specificity. Additional examples of works addressing the *FBS* include (but are not limited to) Bury and Bagby (2002); Dearth et al. (2005); Elhai et al. (2000); Elhai, Gold, Sellers, et al. (2001); Graham (2006, pp. 38–39); Greiffenstein, Baker, Axelrod, Peck, and Gervais (2004); Greve and Bianchini (2004); Larrabee (2003); Lees-Haley and Fox (2004); Martins, Donders, and Millis (2001); Ross, Millis, Krukowski, Putnam, and Adams (2004); Slick, Hopp, Strauss, and Spellacy (1996); and Tsushima and Tsushima (2001).

Careful evaluation of the full array of relevant research and commentary is key not only to deciding whether there is a clear scientific basis for using a scale in a specific situation but also in preparing for *Daubert* (*Daubert v. Merrell Dow Pharmaceuticals, Inc.*, 509 U.S. 579 (1993)) challenges, direct and cross-examination, and other aspects of forensic work.

Subtle–Obvious Scales

Socrates often challenged his pupils with an interesting dilemma. If you were suddenly given omniscient powers through wearing a special ring (Gyges ring) that allowed you to know what others were thinking without their knowledge, would it be proper to use such information to your advantage? Psychologists working in forensic settings might not wish to debate the ethics of having this phenomenal power, although many would find their work much easier with such a ring. To know other people's secrets and motives without their being aware that they had disclosed them to us might even be considered by some to be a forensic psychologist's dream.

Some psychologists have considered the MMPI "subtle" items to be just such a powerful technique—a way of assessing an individual without the test taker actually knowing that one has done so. We consider it important for psychologists to be aware of the flaws in this technology, and we caution against relying on these indicators in forensic assessments. Even though the so-called subtle scales have been officially dropped from the MMPI–2, these items still show up in historical documents of individuals who had been tested earlier with the MMPI.

In theory, it is possible to develop items for a personality measure that have strong predict-

ive validity but are not as obvious in content as other items on the scale (Jackson, 1971). A *subtle* item is defined as an item that predicts the criteria defining the scale but does not have an obvious content relationship to the construct in question. These items are thought to be subtle predictors and are believed by some to have special predictive properties.

Following the empirical scale construction doctrine underlying the MMPI (i.e., that all the items contained on an empirically derived scale are equally valid), Wiener and Harmon recognized that some items were less obviously related to content and were thought to be subtle predictors of the construct measured by the scale (Wiener, 1948b). The subtle items were thought to have special properties in that they allowed the clinician to assess people without their being consciously aware that they were providing important personal information in the assessment.

Wiener and Harmon (Wiener, 1948b) developed subtle and obvious subscales for several MMPI scales (*D*, Hysteria [*Hy*], Psychopathic Deviate [*Pd*], Paranoia [*Pa*], and Mania [*Ma*]). For a subtle item to work according to this premise, two item properties must be present: (a) the content of the item should not be obviously related to the construct being measured and (b) the item must predict the criterion as well as other items on the scale.

Unfortunately, the subtle subscales developed by Wiener and Harmon do not meet the second criterion. Two points should be considered. First, the subtle items on the Wiener–Harmon subscales are likely to be chance items. It is quite likely that the lack of content relevance in the subtle items results from the fact that they are imperfectly related to the criterion and were actually selected by chance as a result of incomplete validation procedures. (Hathaway and McKinley used relatively small samples in their original scale development.) For example, in developing a scale to assess characteristic "*x*" using 550 items, chance alone would place 27 items on the scale. We assume that cross-validation would eliminate the chance items, leaving only those items that are valid indicators of the characteristic being assessed.

Second, the research on the Wiener–Harmon subtle subscales shows that they are not valid predictors of the psychopathology they purportedly measure. Hathaway (1965), who championed the empirical method of scale construction and generally held the view that subtle items on the scales had the special powers described earlier, expressed doubts about the efficacy of subtle items when compared with face-valid items.

It is apparent that the response-set issue began with worry about the fact that face valid questions seemed to invite distortion by faking good or bad. Subtle items appeared to be an obvious way to control this, but McCall (1958) concluded from a study of the *D* scale of the MMPI "The 60 items of the depression scale of the MMPI were shown to be differentially effective in distinguishing depressive from a matched group of nondepressive psychotics in proportion to their face validity, as determined a priori." Such a finding supports the possibility that face validity is a central source of item validity. Wiener (1948b) approached the problem by forming separate subscales using the subtle and the obvious items from empirical scales. It will be apparent below that the very reality of many personality variables is tied to face validity. There could not be a subtle scale that would have much value for such a variable. (p. 468)

Several subsequent studies have shown that Hathaway's intuition was correct, at least with respect to the Wiener–Harmon subscales. The subtle subscales do not discriminate well enough in practice, and most studies show that they do not predict as clearly as the obvious items on the scale do.[2] In fact, Weed et al. (1990) found that the subtle items actually *lower* the validities of the full-scale score.

R. Greene (1991) reiterated the view that the subtle items give the interpreter a special way to evaluate invalid or unusual response attitudes. In his view, the difference in response to obvious as opposed to subtle items on a scale can be used as an indicator of test invalidity. In their article, "Failure of Wiener and Harmon Minnesota Multiphasic Personality Inventory (MMPI) Subtle Scales as Personality Descriptors and as Validity Indicators," Weed and colleagues reported research findings that "indicated that the addition of the subtle scales to the obvious scales attenuates validity to the same degree as the addition of a random variable. Likewise, results did not support the use of an index based on MMPI subtle scales designed to detect overreporting or underreporting of psychopathology" (1990, p. 281; see also Timbrook et al., 1991; Weed et al., 1990).

In most situations, personality and symptom scales work best for people who are willing to be assessed and are cooperative with the psychological evaluation. It is our own view that the Wiener–Harmon subtle subscales do not provide valid or useful information in any setting; however, they are especially problematic in forensic settings because they may tend to provide misleading information and detract from more valid and useful information that might be available in the test. As Graham (2006) concluded, "the Subtle–Obvious subscales do not permit very accurate differentiation of faked and valid profiles" (p. 216).

Adding Together the Raw Scores of the Validity Scales

R. Greene (1991) proposed adding together the absolute values of the MMPI–2 validity scales—such as *F*, *F*(*B*), and *VRIN* scores—reasoning that the sum of the raw scores of these scales would represent a more accurate estimate of inconsistency than each measure taken separately. Caution should be exercised in simply combining these scales because each scale has somewhat different psychometric properties. For example, although *F* and *F*(*B*) were

---

[2] Anthony (1971); Berry, Baer, et al. (1991); Grossman, Haywood, Ostrov, Wasyliw, and Cavanaugh (1990); Herkov, Archer, and Gordon (1991); Nelson (1987); Nelson and Cicchetti (1991); Nelson, Pham, and Uchiyama (1996); Rogers (1983); Schretlen (1990); Timbrook, Graham, Keiller, and Watts (1991); Wasyliw et al. (1988); Wrobel and Lachar (1982).

similarly derived scales, the number of items on each and the item response rates underlying the items differ. Ben-Porath and Tellegen (1992) wrote the following.

> We similarly caution users of the MMPI–2 against premature and uncritical reliance on various indices and ratios derived from the validity scales such as those recommended by Greene (1991) in his recent book. These indices may have the appeal of computational objectivity and the appearance of scientific rigor. In reality, however, they are subjectively derived composites that may discard or inappropriately weigh information contained in the validity scales themselves. In our assessment, an adequate empirical basis remains to be established for indices such as those proposed by Greene. (p. 8)

The essential question applies here, as it does to each test, scale, measure, and approach that the expert witness and attorney consider: Does the full array of well-designed, peer-reviewed, published research clearly support the validity, reliability, sensitivity, and specificity of this method for the relevant forensic issue, the relevant setting, and the relevant population?

The psychometric principles, research data, and legal contexts reviewed to this point in the book are the foundation of the written report of any forensic assessment that uses the MMPI–2. The next chapter focuses on the nature, content, and challenges of the forensic assessment report.

CHAPTER 8

WRITING FORENSIC REPORTS

The reasons for administering the Minnesota Multiphasic Personality Inventory (MMPI–2) shape the report's structure. Sometimes court cases focus on MMPI results even though the evaluation was conducted for purposes other than litigation (e.g., personnel screening). In other instances, attorneys or the court will request an evaluation to address the questions of psychological status, symptoms, diagnosis, prognosis, and competency. This chapter addresses the structure of reports communicating MMPI-based test results that are specifically prepared for forensic testimony in court cases.

In forensic assessment, the attorney often asks the psychologist to consult about the findings before writing a report because the attorney needs to know what the expert will say as a basis for deciding whether to call the psychologist to testify (see chap. 5, this volume). Most forensic psychologists have probably had the experience of providing expert consultation on a case only to find that the attorney chose to ignore the test results and not call the expert to testify.

Consider the following example: A man in his mid-40s consults a psychiatrist, reportedly for tension and sleeping difficulty. The psychiatrist administers an MMPI—but puts off scoring and interpreting it until later—interviews the client for 15 minutes, and prescribes medication to help him sleep. The man, a chronic alcoholic, fills the prescription, goes home, and kills himself using the medication provided by the psychiatrist. The patient's wife files a medical malpractice suit charging that the psychiatrist failed to conduct an adequate assessment and, as a result, her husband is dead. The psychiatrist's attorney contacts a psychologist to evaluate the patient's MMPI, administered on the day of his suicide, and to serve as a forensic witness on the case.

The results of computer-generated scoring and interpretation of the patient's MMPI clearly support the possibility that the psychiatrist failed to appropriately assess the client's high potential for suicide. The results of the computer-based report actually warned about the risk of suicide and the probability of abuse of prescription medications by the patient. The attorney chooses not to retain the psychologist as an expert witness in the case.[1] Psychologist Irving Weiner (1987) discussed the feelings that psychological consultants might have in such situations. He pointed out that

> being in effect dismissed from the case before a written report has been prepared—can raise some disturbing questions concerning proper practice. . . . The answers to these questions touch upon some ethical and realistic considerations in the practice of law and psychology. (p. 515)

---

[1] Clinicians, expert witnesses, and others using computerized services should ensure that the profiles *and* interpretations are empirically based on adequate research studies establishing validity and reliability for the specific forensic purpose(s) and the relevant population.

However, Weiner emphasized that

> the point is that it is entirely appropriate and consistent with prevailing practice for attorneys to question or reject the opinions of a consultant they have retained and to seek other consultants whose opinions will support more effectively the case they are trying to build. (p. 515)

USING COMPUTER-BASED MMPI REPORTS IN FORENSIC CASES

As noted in chapter 2, computer-based psychological assessment can serve an important role in a forensic evaluation. Computer reports are *preliminary* or *provisional* working papers, analogous to hypotheses that practitioners might collect by researching the published literature to find those that might be relevant to the profile at hand.

Those who use automated reports must be sufficiently familiar with the research literature to be able to cite the background sources if questioned in cross-examination. The late forensic psychologist Theodore Blau (1984a), former president of the American Psychological Association (APA), pointed out that "when relying on computer-based test interpretation, the forensic psychologist should be familiar with the rationale and validity of the interpretations and be prepared to justify their utilization in the judicial matter at hand" (p. 184; see also Appendix V, this volume).

Should the computerized report be submitted as evidence in the case or modified to suit the client? An important reason for the practitioner to be knowledgeable about the information incorporated in computer-based reports is that there may be hypotheses or descriptions in the report that do not apply to a particular case. In such instances, the practitioner may choose to use only those high-probability statements from the report that are deemed relevant to the case and ignore the others. This is appropriate because it is always the practitioner who has the final responsibility for deciding what elements of a psychological evaluation are appropriate for a particular client. However, if the opposing counsel conducts an adequate discovery, the computer-generated printout will be available as a basis for cross-examination. Therefore, as described below, the psychologist may wish to include in the written forensic report the reasoning process that led him or her to reject certain hypotheses set forth by the computer program.

Sometimes a computerized reports enters directly into evidence and serves as the focus of direct and cross-examination. In such cases, the attorney uses the computer-based report to support or challenge a practitioner's opinion. Because any notes or test materials used to arrive at decisions can be subpoenaed, computer reports are more frequently finding their way into evidence in court cases.

The psychologist may, at times, be faced with discordant test findings or with a computer-based report that includes statements that seem irrelevant or misleading in the present case.

As discussed, the practitioner may need to introduce in direct examination or defend in cross-examination the decision not to interpret seemingly discrepant findings or to include off target information that is printed out in a computerized report. Forensic psychologist David Shapiro (1991), a former president of the American Academy of Forensic Psychology, advised expert witnesses to anticipate controversial issues and deflate the impact of potentially weak points during direct examination. Shapiro emphasized the need to "take the wind out of the opposing side's sail" by confronting controversial points on direct examination.

> The expert needs to anticipate in advance what some of the challenges to the opinion will be, making a frank assessment of the weakest parts of the evaluation and opinion. One must attempt to deal with these in direct examination, rather than creating the impression that one is surprised by these questions when they arise on cross-examination. (pp. 206–207)

USING COMPUTERIZED REPORT LANGUAGE IN FORENSIC EVALUATIONS

The computerized personality description functions by design as a dictionary or a reference guide. Some psychologists bring the descriptive information from computer-based narratives into their final forensic reports by paraphrasing the text. Others use the text phrasing as it comes from the computer on grounds that "this is the most appropriate description of the client." Still others attach the computer report in an addendum to the evaluation. No clear-cut professional or ethical guidelines address this issue.

Do forensic evaluators make themselves vulnerable to cross-examination attacks for using the language of computer-based reports in their own evaluations? Can psychologists legitimately incorporate a computer-based report's language directly into their own reports without referring to the source? Is it considered to be plagiarism for a psychologist to incorporate the language of an empirical "cookbook" into his or her own forensic evaluation on a client? Here are some considerations in thinking through these complex issues.

Traditionally, MMPI interpretation has been based on using empirically supported behavioral descriptions stored in codebooks—reference sources that are referred to for given scale scores. Psychologists interpret scores on an elevated scale by referring to the established correlates for the scale—for example, "Scale 2 greater than a *T* score of 70 suggests extreme depression."

Computer-based MMPI–2 interpretation programs are, in large part, "electronic textbooks" or stored correlates for the various scale scores and indexes. They are developed as a professional-to-professional consultation—to look up established behavior–scale relationships. A sentence of text is a personality descriptor (e.g., "He is likely to be depressed at this time"), which is a prototype for the personality pattern obtained by the client. If the psychologist finds that the client being assessed matches the prototype closely, then using the hypothesis (i.e., that the person is probably depressed) seems not only permissible but appropriate (see Figure 8.1 and Exhibit 8.1).

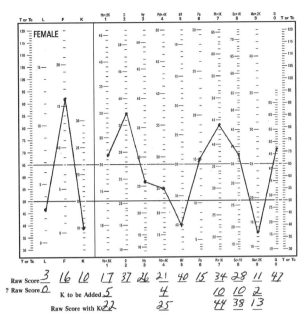

FIGURE 8.1. Computer-scored MMPI profile of Ms. Jones.

Sometimes statements from computerized reports need to be tailored to fit the particular situation. Sometimes changing the wording would cloud or change the meaning. Using the personality descriptors as they appear in the computerized report is legitimate and appropriate (a) if they are relevant to the case at hand, (b) if the source is clearly and explicitly noted, and (c) if quotation marks are used around any phrases from the report that are taken verbatim (as opposed to paraphrased).

PLANNING A FORENSIC REPORT

This section focuses on some general considerations for writing reports that might become the subject of forensic testimony. Readers interested in additional resources on writing reports can consult Harvey (1997), Ownby (1987), Tallent (1992, 1993), Williams and Boll (2000), and Witt (2003). Those interested in additional resources specifically on writing MMPI–2-based reports can consult Butcher (1999). Those interested in additional resources focusing on writing forensic reports can consult Clawar (1984), B. Hoffman (1986), B. Hoffman and Spiegel (1989), and J. Weiner (1995, 2006).

A clear and useful report, of course, depends on a carefully planned and conducted psychological

---

EXHIBIT 8.1

Computer-Generated Interpretation for Ms. Jones—The Minnesota Report: Adult Clinical System Interpretative Report

- Validity considerations. This client has reported a number of extreme symptoms. She may be experiencing a great deal of stress which she feels the need to express. She may also be experiencing low self-esteem and may feel that she is having difficulty managing daily routines. Although this MMPI profile is probably valid, it may reflect some exaggeration of symptoms due to her negative self-image. Individuals with this pattern are likely to be experiencing significant psychological problems.

- Symptomatic pattern. A pattern of chronic psychological maladjustment characterizes individuals with this MMPI profile. The client is overwhelmed by anxiety, tension, and depression. She feels helpless and alone, inadequate and insecure, and believes that life is hopeless and that nothing is working out right. She attempts to control her worries through intellectualization and unproductive self-analyses, but she has difficulty concentrating and making decisions.

- She is functioning at a low level of efficiency. She tends to overreact to even minor stress, and may show rapid behavioral deterioration. She also tends to blame herself for her problems. Her life-style is chaotic and disorganized, and she likely has a history of poor work and achievement. She may be preoccupied with obscure religious ideas.

- Interpersonal relations. Problematic personal relationships are also characteristic of such clients. She seems to lack basic social skills and is behaviorally withdrawn. She may relate to others ambivalently, never fully trusting or loving anyone. Many individuals with this profile have difficulty in intimate relationships.

- Behavioral stability. This is likely to be a rather chronic behavioral pattern. Individuals with this profile may live a disorganized and pervasively unhappy existence. They may have episodes of more intense and disturbed behavior resulting from an elevated stress level.

- Diagnostic considerations. Individuals with this profile show a severe psychological disorder and would probably be diagnosed as severely neurotic with anxiety disorder symptoms or mood disorder in a schizoid personality. The possibility of a more severe psychotic disorder, such as schizophrenic disorder, should also be considered, however.

- Treatment considerations. Inpatients with this MMPI profile usually receive psychotropic medications for their extreme depression or intense anxiety. Many individuals with this profile seek and require psychological treatment for their problems along with any medication that is given. Because many of their problems tend to be chronic ones, an intensive therapeutic effort might be required to bring about any significant change. Patients with this profile typically have many psychological and situational concerns; thus it is often difficult to maintain a focus in treatment.

- She probably needs a great deal of emotional support at this time. Her low self-esteem and feelings of inadequacy make it difficult for her to get energized toward therapeutic action. Her expectation for positive change in therapy may be low. Instilling a positive, treatment-expectant attitude is important for her if treatment is to be successful.

- Individuals with this profile tend to be overideational and given to unproductive rumination. They tend not to do well in unstructured, insight-oriented therapy and may actually deteriorate in functioning if they are asked to be introspective. She might respond more to supportive treatment of a directive, goal-oriented type.

Note. This MMPI–2 interpretation can serve as a useful source of hypotheses about clients. This report is based on objectively derived scale indexes and scale interpretations that have been developed in diverse groups of patients. The personality descriptions, inferences, and recommendations contained herein need to be verified by other sources of clinical information, as individual clients may not fully match the prototype. The information in this report should most appropriately be used by a trained, qualified test interpreter. The information contained in this report should be considered confidential.

---

assessment. Chapter 5 discussed steps in planning and conducting a forensic assessment, and many of these steps represent topics to be covered in a report. Following are seven additional aspects of a forensic report.

First, the report should be comprehensive in scope; that is, it should include the major relevant interpretive elements in the MMPI results that bear on the question or questions at issue.

Second, the report should include all relevant base-rate information. One of the most valuable

features of a widely used instrument such as the MMPI–2 is that extensive research data—including base rates—support its interpretation. These base-rates form an essential context for valid and meaningful interpretation. Sources of base-rate data on MMPI–2 patterns in different forensic settings include Bathurst et al. (1997); Butcher (1997); Butcher, Atlis, and Hahn (2003); Lees-Haley (1997b); and Megargee (1994, 1997). One computer-based interpretive program (The Minnesota Report, Pearson Assessments) provides base-rate information for the profile pattern (elevated *Pa* and *Pt* scales) as illustrated next for an individual evaluated in a child custody case.

PROFILE FREQUENCY

Profile interpretation can be greatly facilitated by examining the relative frequency of clinical scale patterns in various settings. The client's high-point clinical scale score (Paranoia [*Pa*]) occurs in 9.6% of the MMPI–2 normative sample of men. However, only 3% of the sample have *Pa* as the peak score at or above a *T* score of 65, and only 2.2% have well-defined *Pa* spikes. This elevated MMPI–2 pattern (6-7/7-6) is rare in samples of normals, occurring in fewer than 1% of the MMPI–2 normative sample of men. The relative frequency of this MMPI–2 high-point *Pa* score is high in various outpatient settings. In the large Pearson outpatient sample, this high-point clinical scale score (*Pa*) occurs in 13.6% of the men. Moreover, 8.1% of the male outpatients have this high-point scale spike at or above a *T* score of 65, and 5.2% have well-defined *Pa* high-point scores in that range. In a community mental health center population, Graham et al. (1997) found that male outpatients produced a *Pa* high-point score with a frequency of 12.0%. Like other studies of elevated profile types, 5.6% of male outpatients with well-defined high-point *Pa* spikes at or above a *T* score of 65 were obtained (Graham et al., 1999). This elevated MMPI–2 pattern (6-7/7-6) is found in 1.6% of the men in the Pearson outpatient sample. Graham et al. (1997) reported that fewer than 1% of male outpatients in a community-based outpatient study had a well-defined 6-7/7-6 code type. Only 1.7% of the cases showed this high code type pattern when elevation criteria were not applied. An examination of the relative frequency of high-point profile spikes in custody cases can provide the practitioner with useful information about families undergoing custody evaluations. In the large sample of men being assessed in custody cases (Butcher et al., 1997), this high-point clinical scale score (*Pa*) occurs in 29.4% of the men. This high point score is the most frequent well-defined peak above a *T* score of 65 in the profiles of men in custody evaluations,

with 8.5% of the sample having the *Pa* scale as a well-defined spike at or above a *T* score of 65. His elevated MMPI–2 two-point configuration (6-7/7-6) occurs in 2.9% of the sample of family custody cases compiled by Butcher et al. (1997). However, fewer than 1% of the sample of men had a well-defined 6-7/7-6 profile code above a *T* score of 65.

Third, the report should be balanced. It is important, for example, to honestly acknowledge and discuss significant aspects of the profile that appear to produce disparate conclusions or that are discounted in the report. Noting discrepant findings, of course, highlights seeming weaknesses that might serve as a focus of cross-examination. However, the expert witness's responsibility is not to win the case at all costs or to hide evidence but to present expert opinions and the basis for those opinions as truthfully, clearly, and fairly as possible. As noted elsewhere, the Golden Rule seems a useful guide. If you were a juror, would you want discrepant findings that are relevant to an expert witness's opinions and testimony to be hidden—through omission, misdirection, misinformation, or other means—from you or would you want them candidly disclosed? Openly acknowledging and explaining disparate information reflects an objective, scientific approach to test interpretation. Letting the court know about disparate information can also be viewed as required by the oath to tell the *whole* truth. It is crucial to avoid biased test interpretation and biased presentation of results.

Fourth, a forensic report should avoid misrepresenting what the MMPI–2 can and cannot do. In a hypothetical case, an attorney hires an expert witness to administer an MMPI–2 to a defendant before trial. No matter how skilled the expert witness, the MMPI–2 results cannot establish whether the defendant was psychotic at the time of the alleged crime, was sexually abused as a child, or currently has a brain tumor. Research has not validated the MMPI–2 for these purposes. The APA's "Ethical Principles for Psychologists and Code of Conduct" (2002) provides clear standards in this area.

> 9.02 Use of Assessments
> (a) Psychologists administer, adapt, score, interpret, or use assessment

techniques, interviews, tests, or instruments in a manner and for purposes that are appropriate in light of the research on or evidence of the usefulness and proper application of the techniques.

(b) Psychologists use assessment instruments whose validity and reliability have been established for use with members of the population tested. When such validity or reliability has not been established, psychologists describe the strengths and limitations of test results and interpretation.

The expert witness must be prepared to testify about the published research and other evidence supporting each statement in the report.

Fifth, a forensic report must communicate effectively—in clear, jargon-free language—to nonprofessionals who may be completely unfamiliar with the methods of psychological assessment (see, e.g., Ownby, 1987; Tallent, 1993).

Sixth, the report should make clear the degree of confidence that the psychologist has in the reliability of the interpretations and the basis of that confidence or lack of confidence. The jury or the judge should understand the extent to which the data and interpretations are credible, reliable, accurate, and relevant.

Seventh, the report should give some evidence of humility. Test-based psychological interpretations and conclusions are not perfect absolutes but probabilistic statements for specific situations made by fallible humans.

A CHECKLIST FOR REPORTS OF FORENSIC ASSESSMENT

A forensic report takes its form from the purpose, nature, and findings of the assessment. The structure depends on whether the report addresses one narrow question or an array of complex issues. It depends on whether the assessment was based on a single instrument or a battery. It depends on the nature of the background information, the assessment data, and other factors unique to the individual case.

Appendix P provides a checklist, drawing from the material presented in this book (especially chap. 5), that can help practitioners think through how to organize and present their findings and make sure that all important issues are addressed clearly.

SAMPLE FORENSIC REPORT

This section presents an example of MMPI-based forensic reports. This assessment—focusing on the MMPI–2 and a 90-minute interview—resulted in a relatively brief report. The report omitted demographic data, detailed history, and other information presented in other documents available to the court.

Report of Psychological Assessment Involving MMPI–2 and a 90-minute Interview conducted by James N. Butcher, PhD, on [date] from [time at start to time at end]

Case: Beatrice S.

Background and context. Beatrice S., a 47-year-old hourly worker in the garment industry, was walking on the sidewalk in a commercial district of a large city on her way to work when she tripped on slippery pavement and fell in front of a drugstore. She helped herself up (there were no witnesses to the fall) and went inside to complain and ask for assistance. An assistant manager drove her to a hospital emergency room, where she was treated and released after a relatively brief visit.

Claiming that her back and neck injuries prevented her from working and caused continuous head and neck pain, sleeplessness, nausea, tension, and mental strain, she sought additional treatment from her own physician and a doctor of chiropractic medicine. She was treated with several pain-relieving medications and chiropractic adjustments, but the pain allegedly persisted. She was finally hospitalized and placed in traction for about 10 days, but the pain reportedly became more intense after she was discharged. Following her discharge from the hospital, she filed a personal injury suit against the drugstore for negligence and sought damages for her intractable pain, loss of income, medical expenses, and mental suffering.

When she was evaluated by the physician selected by the drugstore's insurance carrier, consistent with the emergency room physician's initial re-

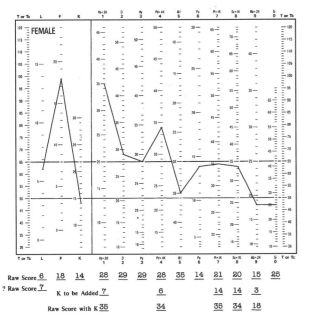

FIGURE 8.2. Basic MMPI–2 profile of Beatrice S.

port, her injuries were considered to be minimal and unlikely to result in the extent of disability she claimed. Her medical evaluation included a psychological examination to consider the extent of psychological distress and mental impairment she claimed from the alleged injury (see MMPI–2 profiles in Figures 8.2 and 8.3).

Psychological report.

Behavioral observations. Ms. S. was initially non-compliant with the psychological evaluation and re-

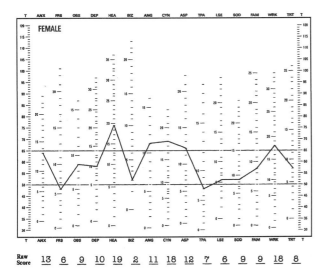

FIGURE 8.3. MMPI–2 content scale profile of Beatrice S.

fused to take the MMPI–2 at the request of the insurance carrier. After discussing the matter with her attorney, she rescheduled the appointment and complied with the evaluation. She was seen in a diagnostic interview for approximately an hour and a half and was administered the MMPI–2. She was generally hostile and brusque with the psychologist. During the interview, she presented herself as being in considerable pain, occasionally displaying pained mannerisms and facial expressions. She reportedly could not sit still to take the MMPI–2 in one sitting and got up several times and stretched. She complained at great length about her physical problems and how they had seemed to spread to other parts of her body after her traction treatment. During the interview, she was quite reluctant to explore areas of psychological conflict or past problems. She reluctantly acknowledged that she has seen mental health counselors in the past, had been in marital therapy at one time, and had been in an inpatient alcohol abuse treatment program 1 year earlier. She refused to acknowledge having mental health problems at this time and emphasized that her problems were purely physical.

Test-taking attitudes. Her lack of motivation to cooperate with the psychological evaluation was also reflected in her MMPI–2 performance. She did not complete the answer sheet as expected, leaving seven items blank. Moreover, she endorsed items in the extreme or rare direction regardless of content, as shown by her elevated score on the Variable Response Inconsistency scale (*VRIN*) and Infrequency scale (*F*).

Validity considerations. Ms. S.'s validity scale scores indicate that she responded to the MMPI–2 items in an extremely exaggerated manner, claiming many more problems and symptoms than others do, even patients in mental health treatment programs. Her tendency to endorse many symptoms produced an exaggerated pattern of scores commonly found among individuals who malinger or distort health problems. Consistent with research on feigning extreme symptoms, there is a strong possibility that her symptom pattern was exaggerated so that she would appear disabled.

Symptoms and behavior. Individuals with this MMPI–2 profile tend to present a pattern of chronic and extreme psychological maladjustment in which physical symptoms are the most prominent complaint. Apparently immature, moody, and rebellious, the client shows serious problems with self-control in which aggressive behavior and interpersonal problems are possible. Although she may attempt to deny responsibility for her problems and blame them on others, many individuals with this profile appear in treatment settings to escape responsibilities for problems that they have caused. Some may present small medical problems to gain attention or services. Because these physical complaints are less important in understanding her problem situation than are her personality problems, the possibility of personality maladjustment should be carefully evaluated.

She shows a low tolerance for frustration, and she may lose self-control easily. Her response content suggests that she has emotional control problems that could result in anger outbursts. Her immature behavior may be a part of a general tendency toward antisocial behavior. Beneath her vague and excessive medical complaints there appears to be an antisocial pattern of behavior that is probably of long-standing duration.

She appears to have problems in interpersonal situations. Her disregard for rules and her aggressive interpersonal style might create negative relationships with others.

Behavioral stability. Her MMPI–2 profile code is well defined; that is, her code type is more than 10 points higher than the next scale in the code. Her profile is likely to be similar on retest. In addition, this high profile definition suggests that the MMPI literature on the 1-4/4-1 personality type is likely to apply well in her case. This MMPI–2 profile suggests a long-standing tendency to act out and show impulse control problems.

Diagnostic considerations. Ms. S. is likely to have prominent features of a personality disorder. Her excess somatic symptoms may be viewed as an effort to manipulate others. In addition, Ms. S. appears likely to have problems of an addictive nature. She has endorsed items in a manner similar to individuals who are experiencing alcohol or drug abuse problems. She has acknowledged that she has had a problem with alcohol abuse in the past.

The extent to which alcohol abuse problems may have influenced other symptoms that she is reporting is not known.

Treatment or rehabilitation considerations. Her extreme somatic complaints may be secondary to long-standing personality problems. Possible secondary gain factors in her illness behavior should be carefully evaluated. Patients with this MMPI–2 profile are usually poor candidates for psychological intervention. They usually do not seek psychological treatment on their own. They tend to be only marginally cooperative in treatment programs. They are usually viewed as self-centered and immature and do not see much need for psychological therapy.

Her anger control problems are likely to adversely influence any rehabilitation efforts at this time. She is likely to terminate therapy early, possibly in anger. The manipulative behavior that patients with this pattern tend to show is likely to interfere with the development of trust in relationships, making the treatment relationship stormy.

She acknowledges having negative attitudes toward work and appears to view herself as unable to function productively in a work setting.

Case considerations. People with this pattern who are involved in personal injury claims tend to present with "excessive disability." Her extreme pattern of complaints is not internally consistent and appears to be an exaggerated effort to manipulate others to view her as disabled. Her pattern of symptom exaggeration is actually more extreme than one would expect from individuals who actually become physically disabled.

Case conclusions. In summary, Ms. S.'s scores on the MMPI–2 validity scales indicate that she responded to the MMPI–2 items in an extremely exaggerated manner, resembling individuals who are malingering rather than actual patients in distress. Her extreme pattern of physical complaints in the context of her MMPI–2 clinical profile reflects severe personality problems and suggests that her exaggerated symptom presentation is an effort to manipulate others to view her as disabled.

James N. Butcher, PhD
Licensed Psychologist

CHAPTER 9

DEPOSITION AND CROSS-EXAMINATION OF THE EXPERT WITNESS: BASIC QUESTIONS, WITH COMMENTARIES, IN 14 AREAS

This book emphasizes a fundamental theme: thorough preparation for attorney and expert witness alike. Few aspects of legal proceedings require more extensive, detailed preparation for both attorney and expert witness than discovery through deposition and subsequent cross-examination. Louis Nizer (1961) compared the task of the attorney to the painstaking work of the archaeologist, searching for, exhuming, and sifting through records of the past as they emerge in expert testimony and other evidence.

> How does he know where to search, and for what? This is the supreme test of preparation and . . . is the be all and end all of trial success. "The stupid man it will make bright, the bright, brilliant, and the brilliant, steady."
> (p. 8)

This chapter serves as a guide for the attorney who is conducting that search. It can also help expert witnesses prepare for depositions and cross-examination.

Earlier chapters presented a number of possible cross-examination questions. This chapter supplements those examples and provides a structured format that an attorney may use in exploring an expert witness's background, testimony, and the basis for that testimony.

We present basic questions (plus a few follow-up questions) created to help the attorney obtain information that is crucial to understanding assessment testimony. Obviously, expert witnesses preparing to testify about assessment must ensure that they understand both the nature of the questions and the answers relevant to a specific case.

Although attorneys conducting depositions or cross-examination may find it a useful strategy to jump occasionally from one topic to another (to determine how different aspects of the testimony fit together) and to return to a topic repeatedly (to assess the degree to which an expert's testimony is consistent during the long course of deposition and cross-examination), it is crucial that the attorney use a well-organized outline to ensure that all relevant questions are asked.

The outline that follows organizes the questions into 14 basic categories, moving from information about initial contacts, financial factors, and the expert's background to the details of the expert's professional opinions

1. initial contacts, relevant relationships, and subsequent meetings;
2. financial factors;
3. compliance with the subpoena;
4. education and training;
5. illegal, unethical, or unprofessional behavior;
6. occupational history;
7. research and publication history;
8. forensic history;
9. knowledge of general issues of tests and psychometrics;
10. method selection, validation, and research;
11. knowledge of the Minnesota Multiphasic Personality Inventory (MMPI);

169

12. administration and scoring;
13. interpretation; and
14. options and alternatives.

In this chapter, we make no distinction between questions to be put to the expert witness by opposing counsel during the deposition and during the trial. Generally speaking, there is not one set of questions to be asked during discovery and a distinctly different set of questions for the trial. The questions tend to be used in an exploratory manner during depositions or to verify information implied by other sources (e.g., the expert's curriculum vitae or a written report of forensic assessment). This process helps the attorney to identify areas of inquiry and information that are likely to be useful during the trial and to gather specific factual information or claims that can be researched in preparation for the trial.

Perhaps the major difference between deposition and cross-examination during the trial (aside from the much larger scope of deposition inquiry giving way to the much more focused cross-examination issues that the deposition indicated would be useful) is that deposition questions often take an open-ended form (inviting the witness to expand responses as much as possible). Cross-examination questions, on the other hand, tend to require a short, specific answer, often a "yes" or "no." However, even though the deposition questions may be phrased in an open-ended manner in an attempt to gather the maximum amount of information (and allow the expert to volunteer information), it is important for attorneys to ensure that they have obtained clear and specific answers to each question (if relevant) we describe.

The following questions, by no means exhaustive, exemplify ways that an attorney can explore and assess an expert's expertise and application of that expertise to the issues in dispute. Although each attorney has his or her own style, each case its own idiosyncrasies, and each expert a unique pattern of strengths and weaknesses, we recommend that the opposing attorney take advantage of the deposition to probe in *each* of the areas covered.

In some of the following sets of questions (e.g., illegal, unethical, or unprofessional behavior; ad-

ministration and scoring), it is probably worth asking each question in the series, even if the curriculum vitae, reputation, and previous trial experience of the expert give no hint of the expert's vulnerability in these areas (see chaps. 5 and 6, this volume). In other sections, a few questions of the type provided will likely give the attorney a fairly accurate assessment of the expert's strengths and weaknesses in those areas. Obviously, what is learned during the deposition can become the basis for research an attorney conducts before the trial as well as for cross-examination at the trial.

The rules of evidence and other relevant strictures vary, of course, from jurisdiction to jurisdiction. The attorney will need not only to adapt the questions in this chapter to his or her own personal style, the issues relevant to the case at hand, and so on, but also to ensure that the content and wording are acceptable for the relevant jurisdiction. In some jurisdictions, for example, the attorney may be generally precluded from inquiring about a history of misdemeanors, and even questions about a history of felony convictions may be limited (e.g., to the number of convictions but not to the nature of the crimes).

We intend this chapter to be helpful to experts who enjoy or endure cross-examination as well as to novice and experienced attorneys. Practicing answers to the types of questions in this chapter can enhance the expert's expertise by allowing him or her to identify and strengthen weaknesses. Practice can also enable experts to become more comfortable and articulate in responding to a carefully prepared, vigorous, informed cross-examination.

Commentary on the content or implications follows most of the questions we present. In some instances, attorneys may want to alter questions relating to the content and psychometric properties of the MMPI–2 or MMPI–A as a hedge against the possibility that a pseudo-expert may have been well coached or simply memorized answers to the questions listed in this book. If other tests, in addition to the MMPI–2 or MMPI–A, have been used, the attorney may want to adapt the questions focusing on the MMPI–2 (e.g., training in and understanding of the use of the instrument) so that they are applicable to each of the other tests. Thus, the attorney may ask all MMPI-specific questions, then adapt and ask them again for the Wechsler Adult Intelligence Scale—III (WAIS–III), then again for the Rorschach, and so on, for each standardized test or method of assessment.

INITIAL CONTACTS, RELEVANT RELATIONSHIPS, AND SUBSEQUENT MEETINGS

How did you first learn about this matter? Before this, had you ever met or had any contact with any of the principles in this case, with anyone else who was involved in the matter at issue, with any of their friends or family, with any of the other expert or fact witnesses, or with anyone associated with either of the law firms?

When deposing an expert witness, an attorney needs to find out exactly how the witness became involved in the matter (e.g., did the plaintiff or defendant contact the witness? Did the witness contact the attorney?) and the degree to which the witness may have known or had some relationship with anyone else involved in the case. Such information may lead to the discovery of additional facts that may be highly relevant to trying the case and that may reveal sources of bias. An attorney who fails to ask these questions may try a case, including cross-examination of the expert, completely unaware that the expert is the next-door neighbor, aunt, or former fraternity brother of the plaintiff or defendant.

At times, this questioning will reveal more subtle relationships. For example, an expert responding honestly to careful deposition questioning may disclose that the first discussion of this matter was with her life partner, who is the best friend of one of the litigants. At times, more complex information will emerge. For example, it may emerge that the attorney who retained the expert witness once sent letters on behalf of the expert (to represent his or her interests in a business matter) or had represented the expert in a separate legal matter.

After you first learned of this case, what meetings, contacts, or communications—whether face-to-face, via phone call, fax, email, or other modes—have you had with any of the litigants? . . . with any of the attorneys in this case or people working for or with the attorneys in this case? . . . with anyone else involved in this case? What was the time, date, duration, and purpose of each of these meetings, contacts, or communications? Who was present? Did you or anyone else keep notes or any other records of these meetings?

Learning about various meetings, as well as the purpose, timing, and patterns of these meetings, may provide the attorney with information that, although relevant to the case, may otherwise have gone undiscovered. The attorney may learn, for example, that all the expert witnesses testifying for the other side conferred with each other. Thus their complete agreement about the psychological condition of a litigant may not have been the result of independent psychological assessments but rather might have been influenced by consultation in which disagreements were resolved before writing a report or providing deposition testimony.

Do you have a history or relationship with anyone involved in this case—including the attorneys and their law offices, the principles, etc.—or their business partners, employees, or relatives—that might raise a question of bias, of conflict of interest, or similar issue? Have you discussed possible bias or conflict of interest or similar issues with anyone involved in this case, or with their business partners, employees, or relatives?

The "small world" phenomenon applies even when it comes to legal cases. If there are histories or relationships that may affect the outcome of a case, the attorney must find out about them so that they can be addressed.

FINANCIAL FACTORS

Have you had financial discussions, contracts, agreements, or arrangements with anyone involved in this case—or with their relatives or business partners—at any time in the past? Have there been financial transactions or discussions of finances at any time between you and anyone else involved in this case?

Learning about any financial relationships between the expert and others involved in the case may lead to the discovery of sources of bias. For example, the expert may at some time have been involved in a business arrangement with one of the litigants. It is not unusual for these questions to seemingly jog the memory of the expert, who will disclose previous financial arrangements or discussions with people involved in the case that the expert failed to mention in responding to the questions in the previous section. That is to say, the expert may have failed to mention having known anyone involved in the case before having been retained as an expert, but may, in response to these specific questions on financial relationships, acknowledge having engaged in some financial transactions with one or more people involved in the case at some time in the past.

Who is responsible for your fees and expenses in this case?

Finding out whether the expert's fees and expenses are to be covered by, for example, the attorney, a party to the case, the judge, or the expert (e.g., as a pro bono case) can help the attorney identify areas of potential, actual, or apparent bias.

What agreement do you have for coverage of your fees and expenses in this case?

The attorney may learn during this phase of questioning information that suggests rather clearly a potential bias or conflict of interest. For example, the person responsible for the expert witness's fees might be the plaintiff in a civil suit or the plaintiff's attorney, but the financial agreement might be written so that the only compensation is in the form of a lien against any settlement or jury award in the case. The more effectively this hypothetical expert might convince a jury that the plaintiff's MMPI–2 demonstrated that the plaintiff is an honest person, who would never exaggerate symptoms but is also someone who is suffering extreme psychological stress and disability (supposedly caused by the alleged tort), the more likely the expert is to be paid.

Are you aware of any written documents—e.g., draft or final contracts or agreements, correspondence, emails, notes, etc.—that describe, mention, or are relevant to your fees and expenses in this case? Do all such documents still exist or have any been lost or destroyed?

Attorneys should obtain and review copies of *all* of these documents.

Are you charging your usual and customary fees in this case? Do your financial arrangements differ in any way from those in previous cases you've participated in as an expert?

Any changes the expert has made in his or her usual and customary arrangements for fees and expenses should be carefully explored to see if they may reflect or introduce bias into the work.

If you were up to date in your billings, what would your total billings for fees and for expenses be from the start of your involvement in this case to the present? What do you anticipate your total billings and expenses will be for this case?

A clear and detailed understanding of exactly how much an expert is collecting serves many purposes. For example, the amount paid to an expert may strike some jurors as excessive and suggest potential bias.

How many hours have you spent on this case to date? Please specify how many hours you've spent consulting, how many in document review, how many administering tests or conducting the examination, how many scoring and interpreting the assessment instruments, how many writing and reviewing your written report, and so on.

It may surprise some attorneys—and some experts who are being deposed—how the responses to these questions may contradict the expert's billing records and other documents. Jurors may find some details about the expert's preparation relevant to evaluating the worth of the expert's testimony.

Of all the sources of gross professional income that you receive each year, approximately what percentage does your gross income from forensic work constitute?

Jurors may take the degree to which an expert's income is dependent on forensic testimony into account in weighing the worth of the testimony. Attorneys may find that in some cases experts will provide misleading deposition testimony in response to this line of questioning. Expert witnesses preparing for a deposition should make sure that they are able to provide candid, clear, and accurate responses to such questions.

COMPLIANCE WITH SUBPOENA DUCES TECUM

Have you complied fully with each and every element of the subpoena to produce? Are there any items that you did not make available?

As discussed in chapter 6, the attorney has generally subpoenaed all documents relevant to the case. The attorney has prepared areas of specific deposition questions on the basis of a previous review of these documents. It is worth asking the deponent to indicate under oath whether each element specified in the subpoena was produced. In some instances, such general questions are insufficient; the attorney may want to take the items mentioned in the subpoena one by one and ask if the deponent supplied all relevant documents. If documents were not supplied in a timely manner, the attorney may wish to consider suspending the deposition until the documents are delivered and deposition questions can be planned on the basis of a careful review. Alternatively, the attorney may wish to conduct part of the deposition immediately but reserve the right to complete the deposition once the missing documents have been made available.

Were any of these documents altered in any way? Were any of them recopied, erased, written over, enhanced, edited, or added to in any way since the time each was originally created? Are the photocopies made available true and exact replicas of the original documents without any revision?

Chart notes, original test forms, and other documents may have been copied over, rewritten, or otherwise altered. Obtaining the deponent's testimony under oath concerning the authenticity of the documents is important. In one case, for example, an expert, when questioned in detail about the completeness of assessment documents, acknowledged having submitted the MMPI–2 or MMPI–A answer sheet to a company that provided computer scoring and interpretation services. The expert had copied by hand the profile from the computer printout onto another form. Had the attorney not inquired specifically about these matters, he would not have known that the test had been scored and interpreted by computer. The expert's previous testimony about the meaning of the results had not been completely consistent with customary interpretations. Asked about the missing computer printout, the expert testified that the computer-generated profile and interpretation had somehow been misplaced. The expert's attempt to substitute a hand-copied replica of the computer-generated profile and to omit (until asked under oath) any mention of the original computer profile leads to the next set of questions.

Have any documents falling within the scope of the subpoena or otherwise relevant to the case been lost, stolen, misplaced, destroyed, or thrown away? Are any documents you made, collected, handled, or received that are within the scope of this subpoena or otherwise relevant to the case absent from the documents made available to me?

Depositions are part of the discovery process, and discovering that certain documents are missing or have otherwise become "unavailable" is crucial. This issue extends beyond expert witnesses and applies to a variety of percipient or fact witnesses as well.

If there is *any* question that some documents may be incomplete, changed, or missing, the attorney should learn in detail from the deponent his or her (or the institute's, company's, or business's for which he or she works) customary procedures for handling documents as well as the procedures for handling documents relevant to this case. Any discrepancies between the customary procedures and the procedures in this case should be carefully explored.

The deponent's testimony can later be verified by deposing other witnesses (clerical workers who prepared, filed, or otherwise handled or were familiar with the documents in question or the customary ways in which documents were handled; administrators who developed and monitored policies and procedures for document handling; and other professionals who may have reviewed the documents) and consulting relevant sets of documents *about* the documents in question. For example, customary or mandatory procedures for handling documents may be set forth in a policies and procedures manual, in written job descriptions for the expert (if he or she works within an organization), in governmental rules and regulations, in sets of standards maintained by accrediting agencies (e.g., the Joint Commission on Accreditation of Healthcare Organizations [JCAHO], located in Chicago, Illinois, sets forth specific requirements for a variety of documents to be maintained by hospitals, clinics, and other organizations that are JCAHO-accredited), and other sources.

Documents prepared by an expert witness specifically in connection with the forensic proceedings (e.g., "personal" notes and the other items that were specified for the initial subpoena in chap. 6, this volume) as well as a wide range of preexisting or collateral documents can play an influential (and sometimes determinative) role in trial preparation and in the trial itself. In a chapter in *Product Liability of Manufacturers 1988: Prevention and Defense*, Richard D. Williams (1988) reviewed issues faced by corporations about preserving or disposing of corporate records. He pointed out that documents that are retained by a corporation may be quite damaging. Understanding how an individual (e.g., expert witness) or organization created policies for keeping or eliminating documents, what those policies are (or were at the relevant time), the rationale for the policies, and the ways in which the policies were implemented and monitored can be essential to adequate preparation for trial.

EDUCATION AND TRAINING

Please list the degrees you've earned, identifying the type of degree, the awarding institution, and the year the degree was granted. Please also list the internships you've completed, including the type, institution, and year.

In most instances, the expert will have provided a curriculum vitae that lists this information. If so, the attorney can ask if the vitae is current, comprehensive, and completely accurate. If any of the information is lacking from the document itself, it should be elicited. See chapter 6 for items (such as transcripts, dissertations, etc.) relevant to this and many of the following questions that should be requested in the initial subpoena.

[For witnesses presenting themselves as psychologists] Do you meet all criteria of the American Psychological Association's educational requirements for the practice of psychology?

In some states, those who have no graduate or undergraduate degrees or other recognized formal training may term themselves *therapists, counselors, behavioral specialists*, or similar titles and conduct what they term *psychological services*. They may then come to refer to themselves (or to accept others referring to them) as *psychologists*. In some cases, the individual may have a bachelor's- or master's-level degree or other psychology degree but lack a doctorate in psychology (although he or she may possess a doctoral degree in some unrelated field).

The *General Guidelines for Providers of Psychological Services* (American Psychological Association [APA], 1987b), adopted by the APA Council of Representatives as a matter of formal policy for the Association, is applicable to all members of the Association who provide services.

> These General Guidelines apply to psychological service functions offered by psychologists, regardless of their specialty, of the setting, or of the form of remuneration given to them. Professional psychology has a uniform set of guidelines just as it has a common code of ethics. . . . These General Guidelines apply equally to individual practitioners and to those who work in

a group practice, an institutional agency, or another organizational setting. (p. 712)

The General Guidelines provide the following definition for the term *providers of psychological services.*

> This term subsumes two categories of providers of psychological services. The two categories are as follows:
>
> A. Professional psychologists. Psychologists have a doctoral degree in psychology from an organized, sequential program in a regionally accredited university or professional school. . . . Specific definitions of professional psychologists by each of the recognized specialties are provided in the Specialty Guidelines for the Delivery of Services.
>
> . . .
>
> B. Other persons who provide psychological services. Qualifications and supervision for these persons are commensurate with their responsibilities and are further delineated in these policies . . . and in the Specialty Guidelines for the Delivery of Services. (p. 713)

Similarly, as the "Model Act for State Licensure of Psychologists" (APA, 1987c) states,

> The Act recognizes the doctorate as the minimum educational requirement for entry into the professional practice as a psychologist.
>
> Applicants for licensure shall possess a doctoral degree in psychology from an institution of higher education. The degree shall be obtained from a recognized program of graduate study in psychology as defined by the rules and regulations of the board. (p. 698)

Both the General Guidelines and the Model Act reflect an APA policy decision made at its January 1977 meeting after considering the report of the Ad

Hoc Task Force on Master's-Level Issues and subsequent recommendations made by a meeting of the Executive Committees of the Board of Professional Affairs, the Education and Training Board, and representatives of the Board of Scientific Affairs (see J. J. Conger, 1977). The first segment of this policy decision follows.

RESOLUTION ON THE MASTER'S-LEVEL ISSUE

I. The title "Professional Psychologist" has been used so widely and by persons with such a wide variety of training and experience that it does not provide the information the public deserves.

As a consequence, the APA takes the position and makes it a part of its policy that the use of the title "Professional Psychologist," and its variations such as "Clinical Psychologist," "Counseling Psychologist," "School Psychologist," and "Industrial Psychologist" are reserved for those who have completed a Doctoral Training Program in Psychology in a university, college, or professional school of psychology that is APA or regionally accredited. In order to meet this standard, a transition period will be acknowledged for the use of the title "School Psychologist," so that ways may be sought to increase opportunities for doctoral training and to improve the level of the educational codes pertaining to the title.

The APA further takes the position and makes part of its policy that only those who have completed a Doctoral Training Program in Professional Psychology in a university, college, or professional school of psychology that is APA or regionally accredited are qualified independently to provide unsupervised direct delivery of professional services including preventive, assessment, and therapeutic services. The exclusions mentioned above pertaining to school psychologists do not apply to the independent, unsupervised, direct delivery of professional services discussed in this paragraph. (J. J. Conger, 1977, p. 426)

The "Ethical Principles of Psychologists and Code of Conduct" (APA, 2002) emphasize the importance of accurately representing one's credentials and other matters.

5.01 Avoidance of False or Deceptive Statements

(a) Public statements include but are not limited to paid or unpaid advertising, product endorsements, grant applications, licensing applications, other credentialing applications, brochures, printed matter, directory listings, personal resumes or curricula vitae, or comments for use in media such as print or electronic transmission, statements in legal proceedings, lectures and public oral presentations, and published materials. Psychologists do not knowingly make public statements that are false, deceptive, or fraudulent concerning their research, practice, or other work activities or those of persons or organizations with which they are affiliated.

(b) Psychologists do not make false, deceptive, or fraudulent statements concerning (1) their training, experience, or competence; (2) their academic degrees; (3) their credentials; (4) their institutional or association affiliations; (5) their services; (6) the scientific or clinical basis for, or results or degree of success of, their services; (7) their fees; or (8) their publications or research findings.

(c) Psychologists claim degrees as credentials for their health services only if those degrees (1) were earned from a regionally accredited educational institution or (2) were the basis

for psychology licensure by the state in which they practice.

The *Casebook on Ethical Principles of Psychologists* (APA, 1987a), which was written to "furnish precedents for the Association, for future APA Ethics Committees, and for state and local ethics committees of psychologists . . . [and] document the efforts of the Association to police its own house" (p. vii), described a relevant case.

An attorney, representing an insurance company that was contesting the payment of claims for an extensive psychological examination and therapy, charged that Psychologist A had falsely represented herself as a clinical psychologist trained in personality assessment. The attorney alleged that the psychologist, although licensed to practice in the state on the basis of having a master's degree in experimental psychology, had obtained clinical training and her Ph.D. from a nonaccredited university. Furthermore, her academic records indicated no evidence of coursework, training, or supervised experience in personality assessment. In addition, the attorney reported that their claims reviewer had observed that the mental health treatment reports the company received from Psychologist A were virtually identical to each other.

Ms. A responded to the Ethics Committee that she was an Associate of APA and that her application for that status clearly stated that her degree was a master's in psychology from a terminal program in a regionally accredited university. She had obtained further training through a nonaccredited Ph.D. clinical psychology program, which she realized APA did not recognize. (The program consisted primarily of reading projects with 6 weeks a year in residence.) She had, however, subsequently performed "postdoctoral" work through an internship at a local psychiatric hospital. She thought that so long as "Ph.D." did not appear on her stationery, she had not violated APA policy; however, Ms. A acknowledged that she did use the title "clinical psychologist" on her stationery to denote the area of her practice.

Adjudication: The Ethics Committee considered two issues. First, Ms. A was licensed and therefore legally able to practice in her state. Secondly, although she did not claim to have a Ph.D. in either the APA Membership Directory or on her stationery, she nonetheless presented herself to the public as a clinical psychologist. The Ethics Committee found Ms. A in violation of General Principle 2 and Principle 2.a. because her degree was from a nonaccredited university and from a psychology training program that did not meet minimal requirements for clinical training, a situation clearly at variance with the APA Specialty Guidelines criteria for the use of the title "clinical psychologist. . . ."

Ms. A's behavior was in serious violation of professional standards. . . . The Committee . . . recommended to the Board of Directors that she be dropped from membership in the Association. The Board approved this recommendation. (pp. 24–25)

It is useful for the attorney to have copies of the relevant ethics codes, casebooks, guidelines for providers of services, as well as any specialty guidelines and the laws and regulations governing licensure or certification in the state or states in which the deponent lives and works as well as (if different) the state in which the legal proceedings are occurring. More than 90 ethics codes, specialty guidelines, and similar documents for the various professions (psychology, psychiatry, social work, etc.) are on the Web in the section *Ethics Codes & Practice Guidelines for Assessment, Therapy, Counsel-*

ing, & Forensic Practice at http://kspope.com/ethcodes/index.php (2005).

The attorney can discover the extent to which the deponent meets—or fails to meet—the criteria in each domain. This information may be directly relevant to the deponent's qualifications and limitations to serve as an expert in the issues at hand and in the judicial jurisdiction. (See the section on competence in chap. 5, this volume; see also the "American Psychological Association Policy on Training for Psychologists Wishing to Change Their Specialty," which is reprinted in Appendix R, this volume.)

Which of these degrees or internships is relevant to your expertise and the testimony you will be providing?

Some experts have earned degrees (or, in rarer instances, have completed internships) in unrelated areas (see Appendix R, this volume). The degrees may nonetheless sound impressive to a judge or jury and may provide an unfounded aura of expertise for the issues at hand. Some experts will readily acknowledge that a degree in, say, nuclear physics or classical languages is irrelevant and does not add to their expertise in a particular case. Such a candid acknowledgment can be made part of the record and, if necessary, used at the trial (e.g., if the attorney who hired the expert dwells glowingly on this degree while attempting to qualify the witness as an expert).

Other experts, however, never wanting to concede *anything* to an opposing counsel, will, perhaps without thinking the response through clearly, give a vague affirmation of the potential relevance of a clearly irrelevant degree, imagining that all of his or her life experience adds to expertise and enhances judgment. Any such claims should be explored in detail during the deposition. In some instances, an expert will at some point back down and admit that the irrelevant degree is in fact irrelevant to any expertise involved in the case at hand. This honest acknowledgment of irrelevance can be contrasted, perhaps during the trial itself, with the expert's earlier claim of relevance. In other instances, an expert will never concede that an irrelevant degree (or training program, work experience, etc.) is in fact irrelevant. The more careful and detailed the questioning, the more strained and sometimes outlandish the rationales become. Such self-serving (i.e., in terms of the expert's attempts to falsely inflate the sources of his or her expertise) statements can often be useful at later points when quoted back to the expert. By attempting to stretch their expertise beyond its realistic limits, experts can discredit themselves in devastating ways, create mistrust for the content of their opinions, and offer a more effective form of rebuttal for their own testimony than could any other expert.

Which of your training programs and internships were fully accredited the full time you were in attendance?

Some schools may have impressive names (perhaps similar to the names of solid, reputable, and even "famous" institutions) but may have had (during the time the expert was enrolled) significant deficits, as noted by accrediting agencies. For psychologists serving as experts, it is worth asking specifically whether the graduate training program and the internship were approved by the APA and if not, why not. Lists of graduate training programs and internships that have been reviewed and approved can be obtained directly from APA's Office of Accreditation and are usually published on an annual basis in the December issue (with supplements sometimes appearing in the July issue) of the APA's journal of record, *American Psychologist.*

If the deponent affirms that the graduate program and internship were fully accredited, ask if they were fully accredited during the full time period that the individual participated.

If the deponent testifies that the university or professional school granting the doctorate or the internship was *not* fully accredited during the full time period that he or she participated, ask the deponent to describe the program's deficiencies that prevented accreditation. Ask also if the deponent has received subsequent training qualifying for a doctorate that did meet the standards set forth by the APA. If not, inquire as to the reasons that the deponent has either not sought or not been admitted to such a course of training.

Please give the full names, titles, and, if known, current addresses and telephone numbers of the directors of each graduate training program and internship at the time the expert was enrolled.

If it is assumed that not all people who offer themselves as experts always tell the complete truth about all matters relevant to their testimony, then it is worth checking the veracity of their deposition testimony. Asking for the name of the director of each graduate training program and internship serves at least three major purposes.

First, it gives the deposing attorney a way to check the veracity and completeness of the expert's testimony about his or her own training. A call to the director of a graduate program may lead to the discovery that, for example, contrary to the expert's testimony, the expert only attended a graduate program for 2 years and did not receive a doctoral degree; that the expert's training and graduate degree were actually in social psychology rather than clinical psychology, and thus the expert in fact had no training in psychological assessment generally or the MMPI instruments in particular; or that the expert failed courses or was formally censured. In some instances, an expert may have never had any connection whatsoever with a program from which he or she claimed to have a degree.

Second, the expert is put on notice that the attorney plans to ask detailed questions and to verify the expert's responses. A less-than-honest deponent may be disconcerted by the likelihood that the attorney will discover—through careful questioning and verification of claims—perjured testimony offered in previous cases and false testimony already given under oath in the current case (in previous affidavits and in testimony already given in this deposition). In light of this likelihood, the deponent may also respond to subsequent questions during the deposition and later at the trial in a different way than if he or she were confident that inflated or entirely bogus claims about training and other aspects of expertise would not be seriously scrutinized.

Third, even if the expert's testimony is completely accurate and contains no serious omissions or distortions to which graduate training and internship directors might be called to testify, the directors who trained the deponent may themselves be potentially impressive rebuttal witnesses (e.g., a judge or jury may tend to give more weight to a more senior professional who directed a training program than to that professional's student). Those who trained the expert may also be excellent sources of information about other potential expert witnesses who might offer rebuttal testimony.

Did you ever leave a doctoral degree-granting program without obtaining a doctoral degree or were you ever asked to leave a degree-granting program? Did you ever fail to complete successfully a clinical practicum, field placement, internship, or similar program, or were you ever asked to leave a practicum, field placement, internship, or similar program?

Unsuccessful experiences with training programs may not be listed on curriculum vitas but may be directly relevant to judgment and expertise. If, as the previous question and discussion note, the expert anticipates that the attorney will be checking the veracity of the testimony, he or she may tend to be more forthcoming about programs that were not completed.

If the expert acknowledges such experiences, the attorney should elicit detailed information and explanation. In some instances, the program that the expert was unable to complete successfully—and may have been asked to leave—may be directly relevant to his or her claimed expertise. The expert may, for example, have been asked to leave a program because of perceived incompetence in the area of assessment. Student evaluations, correspondence, and other material in the student's file at the school—which may still be kept in administrative offices and which may ultimately be accessible to the attorney (e.g., not protected by specific privilege)—may contain statements or information bearing specifically on the aptitude, stability, judgment, professionalism, ethics, or biases of the expert.

Please name each course, workshop, and so on, in psychological testing and assessment in which you actually enrolled, the institution at which it was offered, the year in which you took the course, the full name of the professor or other individual who taught the course, how many cumulative hours the course involved, whether you successfully completed the course and, if so, what your grade was.

A careful inquiry into specific courses in assessment enables an attorney to evaluate the expert's actual training in testing, diagnosis, and other aspects of psychological assessment. Formal training in testing is one of the prerequisites for basic competence and advanced expertise. Experts may hold impressive degrees, job titles, publication records, and similar indicants of expertise. They may have been admitted to testify as experts in numerous previous cases. They may view themselves as having a sort of generalized expertise: Whatever topic they turn their attention to is a topic for which they consider themselves experts.

And yet *no* expert is an expert in all areas. A world-famous therapist may have had no training whatsoever in psychological testing and other aspects of assessment. A renowned expert in anorexia nervosa, phobic fears of heights, or borderline personality disorder may have had no training in the administration, scoring, and interpretation of tests that might be useful in identifying the presence, absence, severity, or complications of such conditions. Only by careful inquiry into such factors as an expert's training and experience are the limits as well as the foundations of expertise revealed.

Taking a look at the expert's grades in assessment courses may be quite revealing. Some experts, of course, may claim to have received only A's in such courses; if a transcript obtained later by opposing counsel shows otherwise, the expert may have difficulty explaining why he or she inflated the grade while testifying under oath during the deposition. Experts who have failed or obtained low grades in assessment courses may also be legitimately challenged regarding the basis of their expertise.

If the attorney has subpoenaed the transcripts, as described in chapter 6, determining the accuracy of the deponent's responses will be an easier task and can be completed much more quickly.

How many hours in each of the previously listed courses, workshops, and so on, were devoted specifically to the MMPI instruments?

Once the extent of training in psychological testing and assessment has been established, it is important to determine the degree to which this training addressed the MMPI instruments. It is likely that general courses in testing and assessment devoted a minority of their total hours to the MMPI–2 or MMPI–A to cover an adequate range of basic assessment instruments (e.g., WAIS–III, Rorschach, Bender–Gestalt, etc.). If an expert has named only one assessment course that met for a total of 30 hours, the hours that such a course focused on the MMPI may be quite limited. The expert's description of the course content can be compared with a description provided by the instructor who taught the course or with a course catalog.

If the expert has taken coursework in the MMPI only recently, it is reasonable to inquire if genuine expertise can be acquired in so short a time (i.e., without a substantial number of years of experience in using the instrument). If the expert has taken coursework in the MMPI only in the distant past, it is reasonable to inquire whether, as described elsewhere in this volume (see chap. 5), the expert's training and knowledge base are current and up-to-date, namely with respect to the MMPI–2 or MMPI–A.

Have you received training in the MMPI–2 or MMPI–A? What recent books on the revised MMPI have you reviewed? What recent research articles on the revised MMPI have you reviewed? Which of these books and articles do you consider most relevant to your expert opinions in this case?

These questions will help the attorney discover the degree to which the expert witness is adequately aware of the revised instruments, knowledgeable about them, and trained in their use.

ILLEGAL, UNETHICAL, OR UNPROFESSIONAL BEHAVIOR

Has anyone ever filed a complaint against you with a licensing board in this or any other state, province, or jurisdiction?

This section of questions may seem pointless with experts possessing certain kinds of qualifications and reputations. The individual may in fact have served on a licensing board. Nevertheless, it is our strong recommendation that *each* question in this section be asked of a potential expert. There have been cases in which members of licensing boards, ethics committees, and so on have themselves been found to have violated formal standards. These findings of violation may not be widely known. Only by asking—and in some cases, by making an independent investigation—can an attorney find out whether an expert may have a record of engaging in questionable or even reprehensible acts that would be relevant to the credibility of his or her testimony.

It is probably best to avoid using the following form for the questions in this set: "Has any licensing board found you to have violated the licensing law?" No matter how carefully worded, such questions tend to allow the experts ways to conceal violations by semantic juggling. Experts may have reached some sort of stipulated settlement or similar carefully worded agreement with a licensing board that enables them to answer "no" to counsel's questions through some technicality in wording (e.g., it was not a violation of a licensing "law" but rather a licensing "regulation"; it was not the licensing "board" that found a violation but rather an administrative "tribunal"; it was technically not a "violation" but rather a "failure to comply"). Nevertheless, if the attorney learns of the settlement or other pertinent information, it may be a key component in shedding a more accurate light on the expert's "expertise." As a result, the best way to learn of the myriad ways in which a licensing board may have resolved a complaint against an expert is to ask if any complaints have been filed. If the expert answers "yes," then the nature and disposition of the complaint can be fully explored.

It is crucial to emphasize that even the most scrupulous expert may have been subjected to one or more invalid and entirely groundless complaints. In such cases, the honest expert answers a deposition question about whether a licensing complaint has been filed with a candid "yes." The importance of opposing counsel finding out all details regarding the disposition of such groundless complaints is obvious. Were opposing counsel to make such a groundless complaint a focus of cross-examination (i.e., assuming that the judge or jury will view the mere existence of a complaint as a discrediting fact), the attorney who originally called the expert could present in detail the licensing board's exculpatory findings, thus simultaneously "rehabilitating" an expert whose history has been cast in a false light *and* implicitly casting valid aspersions on the cross-examining attorney for presenting information in an incomplete, unfair, and misleading manner.

In cases in which there has been a complaint, it may be well worth the attorney's time to obtain all available documentation regarding the matter. Documents relating to formal complaints filed with licensing boards are often a matter of public record and may be obtained from the relevant board or governmental agency.

In some instances, documentation may reveal that an expert's characterization of the nature or disposition of the complaint does not match what actually happened. In other instances, the cross-examining attorney may learn additional information that may be extremely useful (e.g., that the expert did not comply with the licensing board's terms of probation).

Has anyone ever filed a complaint against you with any ethics committee, professional standards review committee, peer review board, or any other organization, association, institution, committee, or board—whether governmental, private, or other?

Aside from state licensing boards, a variety of review agencies receive and evaluate complaints against mental health professionals. These include local, state, or national ethics committees for the various mental health professional associations (e.g., the APA and the American Psychiatric Association), county or state patients' rights offices, hospital peer review boards, credentialing organizations (e.g., the American Board of Professional Psychology), community mental health center professional standards committees, and the quality assurance departments of clinics.

Have you ever been convicted of or pleaded nolo contendere to a crime or been a defendant or plaintiff in a malpractice or other civil suit?

Obviously, the fact that an expert witness has been convicted of or pleaded guilty or nolo contendere to or otherwise resolved criminal charges in such a way that might indicate guilt may be relevant to that witness's credibility and capacity to serve as an expert. Similarly, one or more findings that the witness committed malpractice or similar torts may bear directly on the case at hand.

Beyond the issues raised concerning criminal, unethical, or unprofessional behavior as determined by courts of law (or by licensing agencies, ethics committees, and the other boards or associations noted in the previous questions), however, is the issue of potential bias. If, for example, someone has participated in the legal system as a plaintiff and, regardless of the outcome of the case they initiated, always testifies for plaintiffs in similar suits, the question of potential bias is a legitimate one to raise and explore.

OCCUPATIONAL HISTORY AND PATTERNS

Please list all professional positions you have held since graduate school.

Like educational background, occupational history is often provided in the form of a resume or curriculum vitae. The attorney should always ask the expert if the information is comprehensive, correct, and current. It may be worth asking a follow-up question along the following lines: "Then there is no job or position that you omitted for any reason?" This follow-up question helps to prevent an expert from concealing a position and later claiming that it was omitted simply because "it didn't seem worth mentioning" or "it was not relevant to the case at hand." Any positions that the expert omits from the curriculum vitae and mentions at the deposition only when the attorney asks about omitted material deserve careful scrutiny. It may be that the expert was fired for cause or was otherwise found to have committed acts that might cast doubt on credibility or expertise.

The dates of each position should be examined to ensure that there are no gaps. When gaps appear, or when the expert has moved from one level to a seemingly lower level (e.g., from full-time tenured professor at a major university to full-time, untenured position at an unaccredited university within the same city), the attorney conducting the deposition should inquire fully. There may, of course, be a perfectly reasonable explanation, but the attorney needs to understand the explanation rather than simply assume that the expert's employment history is actually as glowing as it appears on the curriculum vitae.

Which of these positions involved your administering, scoring, or interpreting the MMPI–2 or MMPI–A?

This question will enable the attorney to begin understanding the extent of the expert's work experience with the MMPI–2 or MMPI–A. Some positions, such as clinical director or supervisor of interns, may be purely administrative and denote a time during which the expert had no day-to-day experience with the MMPI–2 or MMPI–A, although the position title might misleadingly imply otherwise to a judge or jury. As with the follow-up questions presented in the section on education and training, questions in this area can begin to focus with increasing precision on the extent of experience with the MMPI–2 or MMPI–A that each position provided. To develop additional sources of information, the attorney may also want to ask the following in relationship to some of the settings: "In that position, who was your immediate supervisor?" and "Do you know if that individual is still at the setting or how I can contact him or her?"

About how many hours—in the typical week, month, or year—do you devote to forensic cases and testimony, and how many hours to other professional work? What other professional work do you currently do and about how much time do you devote to it?

In evaluating an expert's qualifications, jurors may find it useful to consider whether testifying as an expert is a witness's sole occupation and whether significant time is devoted to other work that might be relevant to the expert's opinions.

RESEARCH AND PUBLICATION HISTORY

Have you conducted any research or published any books, chapters, articles, or other documents that involved the MMPI, MMPI–2, or MMPI–A?

This area of questioning serves at least two major purposes. First, it helps to define more clearly exactly what claim the deponent has to expertise regarding the MMPI–2 or MMPI–A. Careful questioning can help the attorney learn how the expert views the nature of and evidence for his or her expertise as they are reflected in a history of research and publication. Rationales for not submitting research to peer-reviewed journals and reputable publishers should be explored so that the attorney can understand and evaluate fully the expert's approach to these issues. Few experts will fail to present rationales for their approach. Only by learning these rationales during the deposition will the attorney be able to assess their persuasiveness, validity, and relevance.

As with some of the previous information in this chapter, research and publication are usually presented in the form of a curriculum vitae. If so, the attorney should, as with the previous areas of inquiry, ask if the curriculum vitae is complete, accurate, and up-to-date and then ask a follow-up question such as, "So there is no research study or any document you've presented publicly in the form of a book, chapter, article, monograph, or any other form concerning the MMPI–2 or MMPI–A that you have omitted from the curriculum vitae for any reason?"

When the expert has written articles and other documents, it is important for the attorney to learn the publisher, date of publication, and any other information necessary to locate the publication. Unless the attorney is familiar with journals in the field of psychological assessment, it is useful to inquire if any of the journals submitted the expert's work to peer review before publication. The process of peer review is important to the scientific process of ensuring the merit, accuracy, and integrity of new findings. Some journals do not provide peer review (i.e., do not send manuscripts to outside experts in the field who evaluate their scientific and professional worth and worthiness for publication) and even some that will, in exchange for payments by the author, publish manuscripts.

The attorney may also want to inquire if any of the journals are published by or in association with any scientific, academic, or professional organization. For example, *Psychological Assessment, American Psychologist*, and *Professional Psychology: Research and Practice* are among the journals published by the APA; *American Journal of Psychiatry* and *Psychiatric Services* are among the journals published by the American Psychiatric Association; *Psychological Science* and *Current Directions in Psychological Science* are journals published by the Association for Psychological Science, and *The Journal of Personality Assessment* is published by the Society for Personality Assessment.

An issue separate from publishing articles in reputable, peer-reviewed journals is that of publishing books. Judges and juries are often impressed by authorship of a technical book on a subject that is a focus of a trial. It is important for an attorney to discover, during the deposition, whether one or more books for which the deponent claims authorship were published by reputable publishers. In some instances, what are often called vanity presses will publish virtually any volume for an author, as long as the author pays the expenses. In other instances, an author may be claiming authorship of one or more books for whom the publisher was actually the author or the author's institute or corporation.

An example of this latter situation occurred in the trial of the police officers charged with using excess force to subdue Mr. Rodney King. The case received extensive publicity because when Mr. King was arrested in 1991, an amateur photographer captured part of the event on a home video camera, and the resulting videotape was shown repeatedly on television news programs. After the taping began, the film showed at least 56 baton swings by various police officers (Serrano, 1992). One former police officer called by the defense and appearing as an expert witness in police techniques

claimed that there were only about 20 instances in which Mr. King was actually hit, although the film showed at least 56 apparent hits. The judge "ordered the comments stricken from the court record" (Serrano, 1992, p. B3). The reason that the individual's testimony was disallowed may have been due in part to cross-examination focusing on the books he had written as the basis or evidence of his expertise. "Under cross-examination, [the expert witness] acknowledged that he published the two books he wrote about police techniques" (Serrano, 1992, p. B3).

If a clinician has no record of research or other work published in peer-reviewed scientific and professional journals or by reputable, independent publishing companies, the attorney may want to inquire more specifically if there is any evidence that the individual is recognized by his or her peers as a genuine expert with the instrument. Careful questioning can help the attorney learn how the expert views the nature of and evidence for his or her expertise as they are reflected in a history of research and publication. Rationales for not submitting research to peer-reviewed journals and reputable publishers should be explored so that the attorney can understand and evaluate fully the expert's approach to these issues.

The second major purpose for obtaining a complete list of all publications relevant to the MMPI, MMPI–2, or MMPI–A is to explore what the expert has publicly asserted in the past regarding the nature, uses, and implications of the MMPI. In other words, is the expert's testimony in the current case consistent with what the expert has previously written?

FORENSIC HISTORY

Have you previously testified as an expert witness regarding the MMPI, MMPI–2, or MMPI–A in any civil, criminal, or administrative procedure, or any other proceeding or setting?

As with the previous area of questioning, this line of inquiry will help the attorney to understand the deponent's basis for asserting expertise regarding the MMPI instruments (i.e., the extent to which other courts have admitted testimony from the clinician as an expert) and to obtain transcripts of previous deposition or court testimony to determine the degree to which it is consistent with the expert's testimony in the current case.

Have you previously testified as an expert witness in any cases not mentioned above?

This area of inquiry will help the attorney to understand the extent to which the expert has forensic experience.

Have there been any instances in which your name was submitted as a potential expert witness in a case and the court did not recognize you as an expert or that you were barred from testifying for any other reason?

This question may turn up flaws, shortcomings, or serious problems in the expert's forensic background.

If you've testified as an expert in any criminal cases, in how many were you called by the prosecution, how many by the defense, and how many by the judge?

This question allows the attorney to explore potential, actual, or apparent bias for the prosecution or defense.

If you were retained or appointed to testify as an expert in any criminal cases but did not subsequently testify, in how many were you called by the prosecution, how many by the defense, and how many by the judge?

This follow-up simply gathers additional data because experts may be retained to testify in many criminal trials that are settled before trial.

If you've testified as an expert in any civil or administrative cases, in how many were you called by each side (e.g., plaintiff or defense) or by the judge?

This line of questioning continues to explore patterns that may reveal potential, actual, or apparent bias.

If you were retained or appointed to testify as an expert in any civil or administrative cases but did not subsequently testify, in how many were you called by each side?

An expert may have no record of actual testimony, or perhaps only testified once or twice, yet a history of being called predominantly by one side raises the possible issues of potential bias that can be explored further.

KNOWLEDGE OF GENERAL ISSUES OF TESTS AND PSYCHOMETRICS

What is a psychological test?

It is surprising that those who administer, score, and interpret standardized psychological tests may never have thought carefully about what a test is. Initial inquiry at this fundamental level may help an attorney to begin assessing the degree to which an individual has genuine expertise and understands the nature of testing as opposed to following a cookbook method of test use or improvising opinions. The individual's response may also help the attorney to assess the degree to which the individual can communicate clearly and concretely to a judge or jury. Some individuals may be quite knowledgeable in the area of psychometrics and inferences from test data but may be incapable of putting their knowledge into words that can be understood by those without special training (see chap. 5, this volume).

One possible answer to this initial question was proposed by Cronbach in the original edition of his classic text (1960; see also Cronbach, 1990): "A test is a systematic procedure for comparing the behavior of two or more persons" (p. 21). Note that the "behavior" may be oral (e.g., repeating a series of numbers that the examiner has just spoken) or written (e.g., marking down *true* or *false* responses on the MMPI).

One of the most important aspects of the definition suggested by Cronbach is that the procedure for comparing behavior is *systematic*. For many tests, the system used to measure and compare behavior is *standardized*. The MMPI, like the WAIS–III and the Halstead–Reitan Neuropsychological Test Battery, is a standardized test. A standardized test presents a standardized set of questions or other stimuli (such as inkblots) under generally standardized conditions; responses from the individual are collected in a standardized format and scored and interpreted according to certain standardized norms or criteria. The basic idea is that all individuals who take the test take the same test under the same conditions. Obviously, not all aspects are exactly equivalent. One individual may take the test during the day in a large room; another may take the test at night in a small room. The assumption is, however, that in all essential respects (i.e., those that might significantly affect test performance), all individuals are taking the "same" test.

Because characteristics of the individual taking the test or the testing circumstances may significantly influence test results and interpretations, experts must be aware of the research literature that addresses these factors. For some tests, it may tend to make a difference whether the examiner and the examinee are similar or different in terms of gender, race, or age. For most popular tests, systematic investigations have indicated which factors need to be taken into account in the scoring or interpretation of the tests so that extraneous or confounding factors do not distort the results.

Later sections of this chapter focus in more detail on such aspects as administration (e.g., whether the expert followed the standard procedures for administering the test or whether special individual characteristics or testing circumstances were adequately taken into account and discussed in the forensic report); the basic issue in this section is assessing the deponent's understanding and ability to communicate the fundamental nature of a standardized test.

Are you able to distinguish retrospective accuracy from predictive accuracy?

(Alternative or follow-up questions could involve distinguishing sensitivity from specificity, or Type I error from Type II error, as noted in the Glossary of this book.)

This is a simple yes-or-no question. If the expert indicates understanding of these concepts, the at-

torney may want to ask a few follow-up questions to ensure that the answer is accurate.

If the expert replies "no," then the attorney may consider a subsequent question such as, "So would it be fair to say that you did not take these two concepts into account in your assessment?" If the witness has indicated inability to distinguish between the two concepts, he or she is in a particularly poor position to assert subsequently that the concepts were taken into account in the assessment.

If the witness does indicate that although he or she is unable to distinguish the two forms of accuracy, he or she nevertheless took them into account in the assessment, the attorney may ask the witness to explain the meaning of these two seemingly contradictory statements and how the two forms of accuracy were taken into account in the assessment.

On the other hand, if the witness testifies that it would be a fair statement that retrospective and predictive accuracy were not taken into account in the assessment, then the attorney may ask additional questions to clarify that the witness has no information to provide regarding the two forms of accuracy, cannot discuss any of his or her professional opinions in terms of these forms of accuracy, did not weigh (when selecting the test or tests to be administered) the types of available tests or evaluate the test results in light of these forms of accuracy, and so on.

The two concepts are simple but are crucial to understanding testing that is based on standardized instruments such as the MMPI–2 or MMPI–A. Assume that a hypothetical industrial firm announces that they have developed a way to use the MMPI–2 to identify employees who have shoplifted. According to their claims (which one should greet with skepticism), the MMPI–2, as they score and interpret it, is now a test of shoplifting.

Predictive accuracy begins with the test score. This hypothetical new MMPI–2 score (or profile) will be either positive (suggesting that the employee who took the test is a shoplifter) or negative (suggesting that the individual is not a shoplifter). The predictive accuracy of this new test is the probability, given a positive score, that the employee actually is a shoplifter, and the probability, if the employee has a negative score, that the individual is not a shoplifter. Thus, the predictive accuracy, as the name implies, refers to the degree (expressed as a probability) that a test is accurate in classifying individuals or in predicting whether or not they have a specific condition, characteristic, and so on.

Retrospective accuracy, on the other hand, begins not with the test but with the specific condition or characteristic that the test is purported to measure. In the example, the retrospective accuracy of this hypothetical MMPI–2 shoplifting test denotes the degree (expressed as a probability) that an employee who is a shoplifter will be correctly identified (i.e., caught) by the test.

Confusing the "directionality" of the inference (e.g., the likelihood that those who score positive on a hypothetical predictor variable will fall into a specific group versus the likelihood that those in a specific group will score positive on the predictor variable) is, in a more general sense, a cause of numerous errors in assessment and in testimony on assessment, assessment instruments, and assessment techniques. Cross-examination must carefully explore the degree to which testimony may be based on such misunderstandings.

Psychologist Robyn Dawes (1988a) provided a vivid example. Assume that the predictor is cigarette smoking (i.e., whether an individual smokes cigarettes) and that what is predicted is the development of lung cancer. Dawes observed that there is a 99% chance (according to the actuarial tables) that an individual who has lung cancer is a chronic smoker. This impressive statistic seems to indicate or imply that whether one is a chronic smoker might be an extremely effective predictor of whether he or she will develop lung cancer. But the chances that a chronic smoker will develop lung cancer are (again, according to the actuarial tables) only 10%.

Using these same statistics in another context, an expert witness might indicate reasonable certainty that, on the basis of a defendant's showing a particular MMPI profile, the defendant is a rapist. The witness's foundation for such an assertion might be that a research study of 100 rapists indicated that virtually all of them showed that particular MMPI profile (similar to the statistics indicating that virtually all people with lung cancer have been

smokers). The problem is in trying to make the prediction in the other direction: What percentage of all individuals (i.e., a comprehensive and representative sample that includes a full spectrum of nonrapists as well as rapists) showing that particular MMPI profile are *not* rapists? Without this latter information (that is based on solid, independently conducted research published in peer-reviewed scientific or professional journals), there is no way to determine whether the particular MMPI profile is effective in identifying rapists. To borrow again from the statistics on lung cancer, it may indeed be true that 99% or 100% of a sample of rapists showed the particular profile, but it may also be true that only about 10% of the individuals who show that profile are rapists. Thus, the evidence that the witness is presenting would actually suggest that there is a 90% chance that the defendant was *not* a rapist.

The confusion of predictive and retrospective accuracy may be related to the logical fallacy known as *affirming the consequent* (see chap. 5, this volume). In this fallacy, the fact that *x* implies *y* is erroneously used as a basis for inferring that *y* implies *x*. Logically, the fact that all versions of the MMPI are standardized psychological tests does *not* imply that all standardized psychological tests are versions of the MMPI.

When selecting a standardized psychological assessment instrument, what aspects of validity do you consider?

Expertise in MMPI–2 or MMPI–A administration, scoring, and interpretation requires at least a basic knowledge of validity issues (see, e.g., APA, 1985). Although follow-up questions—keyed to the content and detail of the initial response—are necessary, beginning inquiry in the area of validity by asking an open-ended question during the deposition can enable an attorney to obtain a general idea of how knowledgeable the deponent is in this area.

The attorney can assess the degree to which the deponent's initial response addresses the various kinds of validity. Although there are a variety of ways in which validity can be viewed and assessed, Cronbach (1960) set forth four basic types.

Predictive validity indicates the degree to which test results are accurate in forecasting some future outcome. For example, the MMPI–2 may be administered to all individuals who seek services from a community mental health center. The results may be used to predict which patients will be able to participate in and benefit from group therapy. Research to validate the MMPI–2's predictive validity for this purpose would explore possible systematic relationships between MMPI–2 profiles and patient responses to group therapy. The responses to group therapy might be measured in any number of ways, including the group therapist's evaluation of the patient's participation and progress, the patient's own self-report or self-assessment, and careful evaluation by independent clinicians.

Concurrent validity indicates the degree to which test results provide a basis for accurately assessing some other current performance or condition. For example, a clinician or researcher might develop the hypothesis that certain MMPI–2 profiles are pathognomonic signs of certain clinical diagnostic groups. (A pathognomonic sign is one whose presence always and invariably indicates the presence of a clinical diagnosis.) To validate (or invalidate) this hypothesis, MMPI–2 profiles might be compared with the diagnoses as currently determined in a clinic by more detailed, comprehensive, and time-consuming methods of assessment (e.g., extended clinical interviews conducted by independent clinicians in conjunction with a history of the individuals and a comprehensive battery of other psychological and neuropsychological tests). If the MMPI–2 demonstrates adequate concurrent validity in terms of this hypothesis, the MMPI–2 could be substituted—at least in certain situations—for the more elaborate and time-consuming methods of assessing diagnosis.

Content validity indicates the degree to which a test, as a subset of a wider category of performance, adequately or accurately represents the wider category of which it is a subset. For example, the bar examination and the psychology licensing examination supposedly measure some of the basic knowledge, skills, or abilities necessary to practice as an attorney or a psychologist. The degree to which such examinations ac-

curately reflect or represent this larger domain is the content validity.

Construct validity indicates the degree to which a test accurately indicates the presence of a presumed characteristic that is described (or hypothesized) by some theoretical or conceptual framework. For example, a researcher might develop a theory that there are four basic interpersonal styles that attorneys use in developing rapport with juries. According to this theory, each attorney uses the one basic style that is most consistent with his or her core personality. The researcher then hypothesizes that these styles can be identified according to an attorney's MMPI–2 profile (i.e., the researcher theorizes that one set of MMPI–2 profiles indicates a Type One core personality and a Type One interpersonal style for developing rapport with a jury, another set of MMPI–2 profiles indicates a Type Two core personality and a Type Two interpersonal style, etc.). Assessing the validity of such possible indicants of a theoretical construct is a complex task that involves attention to other external sources of information thought to be relevant to the construct, intercorrelations of test items, and examination of individual differences in responding to the test items (see APA, 1985).

Conceptualizations about test validity continue to emerge and constructs continue to evolve. Geisinger (1992) presented an interesting description of historic changes in our understanding of validation.

When selecting psychological assessment instruments, what aspects of reliability do you consider?

A basic knowledge of reliability issues is also—as with validity issues—fundamental to expertise in MMPI–2 or MMPI–A administration, scoring, and interpretation (see, e.g., APA, 1985). Again, an open-ended question may be the best approach to this area of inquiry during the deposition.

Reliability refers to the degree to which a test produces results that are free of measuring errors. If there were no measuring errors at all, then it is reasonable to assume that test results would be consistent.

Because reducing measuring errors increases a test's consistency, reliability is another way of describing how consistent the results of a test are. Consider the following hypothetical situation. For the purposes of the example, assume that there are two completely identical people. If they are completely identical and if a test (such as the MMPI–2 or MMPI–A) were completely reliable (i.e., free from any measuring errors), then both people should produce the same responses to the test. However, now assume that one of these two identical people takes the test at 9 a.m. when she is rested and alert. The other person takes the same test at 2 a.m. when she has just been awakened from a sound sleep and is tired and groggy. Differences in test results between these two otherwise identical people might be due purely to the times at which the test was administered. If the test were supposedly a measure of personality (such as the MMPI–2) and if the personalities of these hypothetically identical people were the same, then different test results do not actually represent a difference in personality but rather a difference or error in measurement (i.e., the time or conditions under which the test was administered).

Statistical techniques have been developed that indicate the degree to which a test is reliable. Such statistical analyses are often reported in the form of *reliability coefficients*. The coefficient will be a number that falls in the range of 0 (for no reliability) to 1 (indicating perfect reliability).

The coefficient may indicate the reliability between subsequent administrations of the same test (e.g., administering the MMPI–2 to a group of individuals and then administering the same MMPI–2 to the same group 1 week or 1 month later). Reports of this type of reliability will often refer to the *test–retest* reliability (or the coefficient of stability). They may indicate, using a coefficient of equivalence, the reliability between different forms of the same test. For example, a large group of individuals might be randomly divided in half. One half would be given the original MMPI, and the other half would be given the MMPI–2; 1 week later, the half that took the original MMPI would take the MMPI–2 and vice versa. Reliability between subsequent administrations (perhaps under different conditions) of the same test is often termed *stability*; reliability between different forms of the same test is often termed *equivalence* (Cronbach, 1960).

In some instances, test items will be divided independently into two halves as a way to estimate the reliability of the test. This method estimates the *split-half* reliability. The resulting coefficient, often measured using a statistical method known as the Spearman–Brown formula, is often termed the *coefficient of internal consistency*.

What types of scales were involved in the various tests and methods of assessment that you considered in selecting the instruments and diagnostic frameworks that you used in the case at hand?

Different forms of measurement use different scales. The scales can refer to scores on a test or to the categories into which test responses fall. There are four basic types of scales. The first type of scale is termed *nominal*. As the Latin root (*nomen*, meaning "name") from which we derive a number of similar English words (e.g., nominate, denomination, and nomenclature) implies, nominal scales simply provide names to two or more different categories, types, kinds, or classes. A two-category nominal scale might be invented to describe the various individuals in a courtroom: participants and observers. The same population might be described using a more detailed nominal scale with categories such as jurors, prosecution team, defense team, and so on. Note that the categories are listed in no particular order. Assigning an individual to a particular group on a nominal scale indicates only that the individual is in a group that is different from the others.

If placement of an individual (or object, verbal response, etc.) into a particular group indicates that an individual (or object, etc.) is in a different group from all others, then there can be no overlap among groups. That is to say, the groups must be *mutually exclusive*: Placement in one group indicates that the person, object, response, and so on, does not belong in any of the other groups. Thus, the four categories of mammals, living things, humans, and whales do not constitute a nominal scale in the sense used here because the categories are not mutually exclusive (i.e., a particular individual may be placed in more than one of the categories). Individuals who take the MMPI are asked to use a nominal scale in responding to each of the items; the scale has two values: *true* and *false*.

The second type of scale does place its categories in a particular order and is termed an *ordinal* scale. For example, an attorney might evaluate all the cases he or she has ever tried and sort them into three categories: easy, moderate, and difficult. The scale indicates that cases in the middle group were harder for the attorney to try than cases in the easy group, but there is no information about how much harder. The scale only places the items (in this instance, legal cases) in three ordered categories, each category having more (or less) of a particular attribute (such as difficulty) than the others.

The third type of scale is a particular kind of ordinal scale in which the interval between each group is the same. An example of an *interval* scale is any listing of the days of the week: Wednesday, Thursday, Friday, Saturday, Sunday, and so on. When events are classified according to this interval scale, it is clear that the temporal distance between Wednesday and Thursday is the same as that between Saturday and Sunday or any other two consecutive days. An important characteristic of an interval scale (that sets it apart from the fourth type of scale, described next) is that there is no absolute or meaningful zero point. Some people may begin their week on Mondays, others on Saturdays, still others on Sundays; from time to time a "3-day weekend" leads into a week that "begins" on Tuesday. The Fahrenheit scale for measuring temperature is an example of an interval scale: The zero on the scale is arbitrary.

The fourth type of scale is a scale of equal intervals in which the zero point is absolute, and it is termed a *ratio* scale. An example of a ratio scale is one's weight. The zero point is not arbitrary. As the name of the scale implies, the ratios may be meaningfully compared. For example, a person who weighs 100 pounds is twice as heavy as a person who weighs 50 pounds, and a person who weighs 200 pounds is twice as heavy as a person who weighs 100 pounds. Such ratios do *not* hold for the other three types of scales. For example, because the zero point on the Fahrenheit scale is arbitrary,

one cannot accurately state that 40 degrees is twice as hot as 20 degrees or that 200 degrees is twice as hot as 100 degrees.

The deponent's explanation of these different types of scales and their meaning for different assessment instruments that were considered (e.g., the MMPI–2 or MMPI–A, the WAIS–III, the Rorschach, a sentence-completion test) will indicate the degree to which he or she understands this aspect of psychological assessment and can communicate it effectively to a judge or jury.

What is an arithmetic mean? What is a median? What is a mode?

These concepts are central to understanding psychological assessment in general and the MMPI–2 or MMPI–A in particular. Without an understanding of these concepts, there can be no understanding of the T scores on which the MMPI–2 or MMPI–A is based. The mean is one of three major ways of describing the *central tendency* of a distribution of scores (i.e., the "center" around which all the other scores seem to cluster). The arithmetic *mean* can be defined statistically as the sum of all scores divided by the number of scores. In other words, the mean is the arithmetic average of the scores. The *median*, which is the second measure of central tendency, is that number that is in the "middle" of the distribution: half of the scores fall below the median, and the other half of the scores fall above the median. The third measure of central tendency is the *mode*, which indicates the score that appears most often. If there were seven IQ scores— 98, 100, 102, 102, 103, 103, and 103—then the mode would be 103 because it appears most often (i.e., three times out of seven).

These concepts are easily misunderstood. For example, an otherwise knowledgeable psychiatrist, Karl Menninger (1945), took other people to task for their statistical ignorance when he wrote,

> Fortunately for the world, and thanks to the statisticians (for this, of course, is a mathematically inevitable conclusion), there are as many people whose intelligence is above the average as there are persons whose intelligence is

below the average. Calamity howlers, ignorant of arithmetic, are heard from time to time proclaiming that two-thirds of the people have less than average intelligence, failing to recognize the self-contradiction of the statement. (p. 199)

While it is *possible* that the number of people whose intelligence is above average is exactly the same as the number of people whose intelligence is below average, there is no necessary self-contradiction in the statement that Menninger criticized. In the common IQ tests, the average IQ is 100. But this number, which is a mean, does not necessarily represent the median. Consider a population of three people: The first has an IQ of 90, the second has an IQ of 90, and the third has an IQ of 120. The average IQ for this population is 100 (i.e., 90 + 90 + 120 = 300, and 300 divided by 3 = 100), but two thirds of the population have less than average intelligence.

What is a standard deviation? What is variance?

The *standard deviation* is one way of describing the "scatter" of a distribution of scores—the degree to which the scores vary from the central tendency. These measures of scatter or dispersion are, like the concepts of central tendency described in the previous section, essential to understanding the *T* scores on which the MMPI instruments are based. The statistical formula for the standard deviation is somewhat complicated. Each score is subtracted from the mean to produce a deviation from the mean. Each of these deviations is squared. (A number is squared when the number is multiplied by itself. The square of 2—that is to say, 2 times 2—is 4; the square of 3—that is, 3 times 3—is 9; the square of 4 is 16.) These squared deviations are then added together into a total sum of squares. The total sum of squares is then divided by the number of scores.[1]

This total sum of squares divided by the number of scores (or the number of scores minus one) is the *variance* (i.e., the degree to which the scores vary from or vary around the mean). The *standard deviation* is the square root of the variance. The larger the standard deviation, the farther the scores tend to fall from the mean.

What is a T score, and what are its psychometric properties?

Understanding the nature of the *T* score is essential to understanding the MMPI instruments (see chap. 2, this volume). Both the original MMPI and the revised versions (MMPI–2 and MMPI–A) are based on *T* scores, although there are significant differences between the original and later versions that will serve as the focus of subsequent questions.

The raw scores (e.g., of the content scales) of the MMPI-based measures are translated—through statistical methods—into a *T-score* distribution. A *T scale* is a distribution of scores in which the mean, as previously described, is 50 and the standard deviation, described in the previous section, is 10.

If the *T* scale describes a normal distribution, the distribution is said to fall into a bell-shaped curve. In the normal distribution, 68% of the scores fall within one standard deviation of the mean; 95% fall within two standard deviations of the mean; and 99% fall within three standard deviations of the mean. These percentages apply only to a normal or normalized *T* scale and not necessarily to a linear *T* scale or a uniform *T* scale (for information about the *T* scale and its various forms, see chap. 2 and the Glossary, this volume).

Most of the original MMPI validity and clinical scales were derived according to the formula for linear *T* scores (Dahlstrom et al., 1972), except *L* and *F*, for which the mean values were arbitrarily set. Each of these scales was separately derived, and each has a slightly different skew. Thus, the distributions are not *uniform* nor are they normal. This is

---

[1] This is the formula for determining the variance or standard deviation in *descriptive* statistics. In *inferential* statistics, the sum of squares is divided not by the number of scores but rather by the number of scores minus one. In descriptive statistics, one is simply trying to describe the scores or numbers that are available (e.g., the IQ scores of the children in one sixth-grade classroom). In inferential statistics, one is trying to use the scores or numbers that are available—called the *sample*—as a basis for drawing inferences about a wider group of scores or numbers—called the *population* (e.g., attempting to use the IQ scores of the sample of children in one sixth-grade classroom to infer or estimate the IQ scores for the population of all sixth-grade students in the school system).

to say, a particular *T* score does not fall at the same percentile rank across all scales (Colligan, Osborne, & Swenson, 1983).

The original MMPI's lack of uniformity among the clinical scales has been somewhat problematic (e.g., when comparing scores on different scales). In MMPI–2 and MMPI–A, however, this lack of uniformity was resolved by developing linear *T* scores that did possess uniformity across given percentile values. This scale norming, referred to as uniform *T* scores, is described in the MMPI–2 manual (Butcher et al., 2001) and is discussed extensively by psychologists Auke Tellegen and Yossef Ben-Porath (1992).

SELECTING TESTS AND REPORTING RESULTS

For each test or assessment method that you selected to use in this case, was the test or method designed specifically for this forensic use with this population?

This question explores the expert witness's knowledge of the test's or method's origins. It provides information that will help determine whether the test or method was used appropriately or misused.

For each test or assessment method that you selected to use in this case, please tell me what scientific research, published in peer-reviewed journals, has established the test's or method's validity and reliability for this specific forensic use with this population.

This question helps determine whether the assessment met the requirements of sections 9.02(a) and 9.02(b) of the American Psychological Association's (2002) "Ethical Principles of Psychologists and Code of Conduct."

9.02 Use of Assessments
(a) Psychologists administer, adapt, score, interpret, or use assessment techniques, interviews, tests, or instruments in a manner and for purposes that are appropriate in light of the research on or evidence of the useful-

ness and proper application of the techniques.
(b) Psychologists use assessment instruments whose validity and reliability have been established for use with members of the population tested. When such validity or reliability has not been established, psychologists describe the strengths and limitations of test results and interpretation.

Have there been any claims in the literature that any of the tests or methods you used in this assessment are obsolete?

This question helps determine whether the assessment meets the requirement of section 9.08(b) of the American Psychological Association's (2002) "Ethical Principles of Psychologists and Code of Conduct:" "Psychologists do not base such decisions or recommendations on tests and measures that are obsolete and not useful for the current purpose."

Did your forensic report fully report each test or method that you used? Did you fail to mention any of them or not report all of their results fully?

Unfortunately, some forensic reports may omit mention of certain tests or the scores on certain tests. The attorney needs to know if there were omissions and the apparent rationale for the omissions.

KNOWLEDGE OF THE MMPI

To help me understand the MMPI and how it applies to this case, please tell me whether the person marked the first item true *or* false. *What did it mean that the person responded to the first item in this way? What is the meaning and importance of the first item? How did the person's response to this first MMPI item affect your professional opinion in regard to the issues in this case? If the person would have responded differently to the first item (i.e., responded* true *instead of* false *or vise versa), would it have changed your professional opinions or influenced them in any way in regard to the issues of this case? Is there any MMPI item which, if marked differently, would have led you to a different opinion in regard to any of the issues in this case?*

This line of questioning assesses the degree to which the expert adequately understands and can explain clearly the way in which the MMPI works. Responding clearly and effectively to questions about individual items can fall beyond the ability of even the most articulate expert who does not understand the role that individual items do—and do not—play in interpreting the MMPI.

Please describe the normative group for the original MMPI.

The basic group of individuals who served to define the original MMPI's psychometric standards of "normal" were 724 people, most of whom had accompanied patients to university hospitals in Minneapolis in the late 1930s (see chap. 2, this volume). That is to say, relatives, friends, and acquaintances who came to the hospital with patients (or to visit patients)—and a much smaller group of airline workers and Civilian Conservation Corps workers—were recruited to serve as "normals" for the purpose of scale construction (which provided in turn the "norms" for the test). People were excluded from the normative sample if they themselves were currently receiving medical care from a physician or hospital. As a result of such factors as time (the late 1930s) and circumstance (the demographics of the population in the area from which the normative sample was recruited), all of the normative sample were White (Dahlstrom, Welsh, & Dahlstrom, 1975). Thus, the "norms" of the original MMPI were defined by a sample that did not include individuals from Black, Asian American, Hispanic, American Indian, and certain other ethnic groups.

Some experts may find it difficult to explain the rationale for using a test that seems to equate, however unintentionally, the concept of "normal" or "normative" with being White. The more general demographic characteristics of the sample that provided the norms for the original MMPI may have clinical implications that the cross-examining attorney can explore. For example, Faschingbauer (1979) wrote the following.

> The original Minnesota group seems to be an inappropriate reference group for the 1980s. The median individual in that group had an eighth-grade education, was married, lived in a small town or on a farm, and was employed as a lower level clerk or skilled tradesman. None was under 16 or over 65 years of age, and all were white. As a clinician I find it difficult to justify comparing anyone to such a dated group. When the person is 14 years old, Chicano, and lives in Houston's poor fifth ward, use of original norms seems sinful. (p. 385)

Please describe the normative group for the MMPI–2.

The basic group of individuals who served to provide normative standards for the MMPI–2 was composed of 2,600 people (1,462 women and 1,138 men) drawn at random from seven states (California, Minnesota, North Carolina, Ohio, Pennsylvania, Virginia, and Washington state). The normative sample—which, unlike the normative sample for the original MMPI, includes individuals who are Black, Asian American, Hispanic, American Indian, and so on—is more generally reflective of the U.S. population in terms of age, gender, and minority representation (see chap. 2, this volume).

Is it true that the normative group for the MMPI–2 scored about half of one standard deviation above the mean on the clinical scales of the original MMPI? Doesn't this mean that the group was not really normal? Doesn't this mean that the means are "off" somehow?

Expert witnesses who use the MMPI–2 but are not adequately familiar with it may be unable to answer this question. It is true that the normative sample for the revised MMPI scored about one half of a standard deviation above the mean (both mean and standard deviation are explained in a previous section of this chapter) on the original MMPI. This would seem, in the absence of additional information, to suggest that there is something wrong with the sample or that pathology has increased among the supposedly "normal" population during the decades since the original norms were established.

However, those who are knowledgeable about the tests will be able to explain that the difference seems largely the result of differences in instructional sets and unanswered items. When the original norms were compiled, those who took the test were allowed to leave blank any items that they were unsure about or that they believed were inapplicable (Hathaway & McKinley, 1940). As a consequence, more than 30 items were typically unanswered on each form. The contemporary instructions for the MMPI and MMPI–2, however, encourage test takers to try to answer all items. As a result, only about two items are left unanswered on each form. Thus, more deviant items are, on average, endorsed on each form, and the normative sample for the MMPI–2 scored about a half of one standard deviation higher on the clinical scales of the original MMPI. As described previously (see chap. 2, this volume), when other groups of "normals" are scored on MMPI–2 norms, they tend to score around $T = 50$ (Butcher, Graham, Williams, & Ben-Porath, 1990).

On the original MMPI, at what level is a clinical score generally considered significant?

This question and the one that follows (i.e., clinical significance level for the MMPI–2) will be unnecessary if the deponent's previous responses have shown at least basic familiarity with the MMPI. The level of clinical significance is one of the first and most fundamental facts that people learn about the MMPI. The level is clearly marked on the profile sheet, so that even if the deponent played no role in administering or scoring the test, he or she can easily see the significance level. This question and the one that follows will be most useful if the deponent has shown little or no evidence of any education, experience, or knowledge regarding the MMPI. They will help reveal whether the deponent has even the most rudimentary understanding of

the instrument. On the original MMPI, a score on a clinical scale is generally considered significant when it reaches or exceeds 70.

On the MMPI–2, at what level is a clinical score generally considered significant?

The significance level for the MMPI–2 scales differs from that of the original MMPI (see chap. 2, this volume). On the MMPI–2, a score on a clinical scale is generally considered significant when it reaches or exceeds 65.

What scales on the MMPI or MMPI–2 indicate the degree to which a specific test protocol is valid? Please describe each scale.

This question is still relatively simple—the deponent may read the scales directly on the profile sheet—but does require an understanding of what each scale means (see chap. 7, this volume).

Four major validity scales are common to both the original MMPI and the MMPI–2. The Cannot Say (?) score—generally indicated by a question mark—is simply the number of items for which the test taker did not provide a clear answer. In some instances, the test taker may have left the item blank. In other instances, the test taker may have filled in both the *true* and the *false* response blank for a given item. As noted previously, most test takers leave no more than two items blank.

Any time a test taker fails to provide answers for more than, say, 5 or 10 items, there is the possibility that clinical and other scale scores may be distorted. Profiles that are based on tests in which at least 20 items have no clear answer should be interpreted with exceptional caution; profiles that are based on tests in which at least 30 items have no clear answer are invalid.

A significant elevation on the Lie scale (*L*) suggests that the test taker may have distorted answers to present him- or herself in a more favorable light. An individual who is trying to put up a "good front" may deny or minimize problems.

A significant elevation on the Infrequency scale (*F*) suggests that the test taker may have distorted answers to invent or exaggerate problems.

A significant elevation on the Subtle Defensiveness scale (*K*) suggests that the test taker may have distorted answers in a more subtle way than that measured by the *L* scale. In effect, the individual has responded defensively—in a more sophisticated way than those with elevated *L* scales—to present a more favorable image. The *K* scale is not only a measure of validity but also a basis for correcting for defensiveness. The deponent may describe the way in which the *K* score led to a statistical adjustment of the clinical scales known as a *K correction*. It is important that both social class and education be taken into account when considering the *K* scale.

In addition to these scales that are a part of both the original and the revised MMPI, three validity scales are only a part of the MMPI–2.

The Infrequency-Back [*F(B)*] scale is similar to the *F* scale. However, the *F* scale is based on items that appear within the first 370 items of the original MMPI. Thus, the *F* scale measures possible exaggeration of symptoms only in the early and middle parts of the test. The *F(B)* scale is composed of 40 items that appear in the second half of the MMPI–2. A significant elevation on the *F(B)* scale suggests possible exaggeration of symptoms.

The True Response Inconsistency scale (*TRIN*) measures inconsistency in responding to items. The *TRIN* scale is composed of pairs of items for which responding *true* to both items or *false* to both items constitutes a contradiction. For example, consider two items in a hypothetical test: (a) I always enjoy trying cases in which the MMPI–2 is the focus, and (b) I never enjoy trying cases in which the MMPI–2 is the focus. To answer *true* to both items would be contradictory, a likely indicant of indiscriminant acquiescence (or yea-saying). (In contrast to those who are indiscriminately acquiescent in their responses and who score high on *TRIN*, random responders tend to score around 50 on *TRIN*.)

The Variable Response Inconsistency scale (*VRIN*) is a measure of random responding. It comprises pairs of items for which some pattern of true–true, true–false, false–false, or false–true constitutes a contradiction.

These validity scales are discussed in more detail in chapter 7.

Are the clinical scales on the MMPI–2 based on K-corrected or non–K-corrected norms? If your interpretations are based on non–K-corrected clinical scores, what is the research support for your interpretations?

Most research and clinical applications of the MMPI–2 since the *K* scale was introduced to the test in 1948 have been conducted using *K*-corrected *T* scores (see discussion of non–*K*-corrected scores in chap. 2, this volume). Any interpretations based on non–*K*-corrected scores in forensic settings are questionable.

What reading level is required for the MMPI–2?

A fifth- or sixth-grade reading level is required (Paolo et al., 1991; see also Butcher, 1990a).

ADMINISTRATION AND SCORING

Did you administer the MMPI [MMPI–2 or MMPI–A]?

In some cases, the deponent may be testifying about one or more MMPI protocols that he or she personally administered (or that were administered under his or her supervision). In other cases, one or more of the protocols may have come from other sources (e.g., previous MMPIs—some perhaps years or decades old—that were part of the test taker's previous clinical records; MMPIs administered by an independent clinician appointed by the court; or MMPIs administered by the test taker's current therapist). It is important to clarify who was responsible for administration.

Whether the deponent or some third party was responsible for administering the test, it is also important to clarify whether the responsible party actually administered the test (e.g., gave the instructions, personally monitored the person during the entire time that he or she took the test, and then collected the completed form) or whether the responsible party delegated some or all of the administrative tasks to a supervisee, clerical worker, employee, or colleague. Because, as previously discussed, the validity of a standardized test such as the MMPI is dependent on a standardized method of administration, the way in which the test is administered and monitored becomes crucial.

If the person responsible for the administration delegated the task of administration to a third party, it is important to discover adequately detailed information about this third party. For example, consider the following questions.

- Who trained the person who actually administered the test?
- How much experience does the person have in administering MMPI–2s?
- How is that person supervised?
- How has that person's work (particularly in regard to MMPI–2 administration) been evaluated?
- Does that person have any formal clinical training?
- What information (about the MMPI–2 administration in the current case) did that person convey to the person who was responsible for test administration?
- Was that information in oral or written form?
- Does it appear in the formal report?
- Did the person who actually administered the MMPI–2 keep any written records of this particular administration?
- Did the test taker ask the person who administered the test any questions? If so, how did the person who actually administered the MMPI respond?
- Did the test taker make any comments while taking the test? If so, what were they?
- Did the test taker take any breaks while taking the MMPI–2? If so, for how long?

What instructions were given to the test taker?

The questions in this set are relevant regardless of whether the deponent, someone under the deponent's supervision, or some unrelated third party actually administered the test. The purpose of this set of questions is to discover the conditions under which the test was administered (and, for example, whether they adequately met the criteria for a standardized test), the deponent's extent of knowledge (which may be severely limited if the deponent did

not personally administer the test) about those conditions, and the deponent's understanding of the implications of those conditions. Did, for example, the person who administered the test include instructions regarding attempting to answer all items (an issue that, as previously noted, can affect validity)? If so, how were the instructions worded?

How was the test taker's reading level assessed?

If there is any question at all about the test taker's reading level (because of such factors as education, neuropsychological impairment affecting language processing, or reliance on English as a second or third language), it is useful to discover the degree to which the reading level was assessed. The MMPI–2 does have some internal checks, but if there is any reasonable question about the test taker's reading level, the deponent may be asked to explain the degree to which the internal checks have shown validity, the basis for deciding whether some other form of assessing reading level should have been included as part of a careful assessment process, and the full array of information on which his or her professional opinion about the reading level is based. (If the person taking the test does not have an adequate reading ability in English, the attorney may also want to inquire about any forms—such as those for informed consent for testing—that the deponent had the person "read" and sign.)

Was the test administration directly monitored?

If no one was with the test taker during the entire period that the test was taken, it is impossible to determine the degree to which the test taker may have relied on other sources for filling out the test. The test taker may, for example, have consulted written materials. Chapter 5 provides examples of settings in which third parties sometimes "helped" the test taker fill out the test by indicating which response blanks should be filled in. To administer the MMPI or MMPI–2 without adequate monitoring violates the published opinion of the APA's Committee on Professional Standards which held that whenever a psychologist does not have direct, firsthand information as to the condition under which the test is taken, he or she is forced (in the above instance, unnecessarily) to assume that the test responses were not distorted by the general situation in which the test was taken (e.g., whether the client consulted others about test responses). Indeed, the psychologist could have no assurance that this test was in fact completed by the client. In the instance where the test might be introduced as data in a court proceeding, it would be summarily dismissed as hearsay evidence. (Committee on Professional Standards, 1984, p. 664)

Was any phase of the assessment audiotaped, videotaped, or otherwise recorded?

If so, the taped record should have been produced in response to the *subpoena duces tecum*. The attorney may consider asking the deponent how audio- or videotaping might have affected the assessment (see the following question). For example, if a person is sensitive to being observed (e.g., becomes self-conscious or inhibited) or if he or she has paranoid traits, might not the sensitivity or the traits be exacerbated by the taping of an assessment session? The deponent might also be asked if he or she is aware of any published research or discussion regarding how recording an assessment session may affect the assessment process and results.

What conditions of test administration did you consider as potentially affecting the validity of this test?

As previously noted, a variety of factors can affect the validity or interpretation of a test, and psychologists are ethically required to explicitly note their reservations regarding validity in any test report. The attorney may want to explore this issue in detail. What sort of lighting was available in the room? Were there any extraneous noises or interruptions? Was the client taking any medication or suffering from any illness while taking the test?

Does the client require glasses or contact lenses for reading? If so, was the client wearing the glasses or contact lenses while taking the test?

Has anyone but you had access to the original completed response form?

This question addresses the integrity of the original test data and the security of the test form itself. If other people besides the test administrator handled the form or had access to it, the attorney may want to explore in detail the specific circumstances. Has the original completed test form been kept in a locked or otherwise secured locale?

Has the original completed response form been altered in any way by anyone? Did anyone except the test taker make marks on, erase, or change the original form in any way?

These questions also address the integrity of the original test data. The person who administered the test and is preparing to submit it for machine scoring may, for example, have worried that the test taker's pencil marks will not be sufficiently dark to register on the machine. He or she may decide to make the original marks darker to ensure proper scoring by the machine. If the administrator or anyone else has attempted to enhance the test in this way, a careful exploration of the process can be useful. How can the administrator be certain that the correct response slot for each item was enhanced?

There may be other instances in which the test taker left a large number of items blank. The administrator may have scanned the test form quickly, noticed the missing responses, and asked the test taker how he or she would answer these items.

Whatever the circumstances, the attorney should have a clear picture of exactly how the test was administered, the degree to which the requirements of standardization (in regard to administration) were met, and the possibility that the original, authentic responses may have changed in some manner.

Were any test data discarded, destroyed, recopied, or lost? Are all of the documents involved in the

administration and taking of the test present in their original form?

As a hypothetical example, a patient may be given an MMPI–2 immediately on admission to a hospital. However, because the patient appears to be psychotic, only half of the items are filled in. The patient is given some medication and, a few hours later, another MMPI–2 is administered. This time the patient fills in all the items but seems to have filled them in randomly (i.e., the *VRIN* scale is significantly elevated). Finally, the next day, the MMPI–2 is again administered. This time the patient seems sufficiently motivated, alert, and oriented to produce a valid profile. The psychologist who conducts psychological testing on the unit files the valid profile in the patient's chart, discarding the two previous protocols as incomplete, invalid, and useless. Only by asking directly about all documents relating to the administration and taking of psychological tests will an attorney likely discover the previous administrations of the test, information that may be key to understanding information relevant to the trial.

As another hypothetical example, a patient at a mental health clinic may sue the clinic and a number of staff members for malpractice. One of the staff members may fear that certain chart notes and test data may support the patient's case. At some point the staff member may surreptitiously go through the patient's file and weed out all documents that might significantly support the patient's charges. Again, only by asking specific questions of all those involved (while they are under oath) is an attorney most likely to discover that the test data that have been provided to him or her as part of the discovery process are somehow incomplete, changed, or supplemented with bogus data created after the fact.

Who scored this test?

In some instances, the test may have been hand scored. It is worth finding out whether the deponent or some third party did the actual calculations that converted the raw data (i.e., the marks that the test taker made in the *true* and *false* slots) into scale scores and an MMPI–2 or MMPI–A profile. In

other instances, the test may have been scored by machine. Other clinicians may send the raw data to an individual or institution that provides scoring and interpretation services.

Did the scoring differ in any way whatsoever from the scoring method set forth in the test manual?

As emphasized previously, the strength and validity of a standardized test is dependent on the standardization. To the degree that the standardized methods for scoring are altered (without additional validation and standardization), the test is no longer standardized. The reliability, validity, and interpretations that are associated with the standardized test do not automatically transfer to methods of scoring that deviate from those specified in the manual and the research literature.

What steps have you taken to ensure that the scoring of this test is accurate and free from error?

No matter how a test is scored, there may be errors. If the test was hand scored, the person doing the scoring may have misread some of the responses (e.g., scored a *true* as a *false* on a specific item), may have made mathematical errors in adding up the raw scores on each scale, may have made errors in translating the raw scores into scale scores, or may have made errors in plotting the profile on the form. If the individual who administered the test used a personal computer to score the test, he or she may have used an unauthorized scoring program with a bug in the software that reads and scores the responses. If the test was sent to a distant location for scoring, what assurance does the deponent have that the test was not incorrectly labeled in some way, that it was not somehow mixed up with one of the other test forms that was received by the facility, or that the report that was returned did not contain scoring or other errors?

By asking detailed questions, the attorney can discover the degree to which the deponent has taken appropriate and careful steps to verify that the scoring (and other) information is accurate. For example, has the deponent personally checked the scoring and the profile against the raw data? If not, why not? The failure to take such fundamental steps *may* (or may not) indicate a lack of care in reaching professional opinions. In any event, such information will help the attorney to discover the extent to which MMPI–2 or MMPI–A scores that are introduced into evidence (or that form a basis of an expert's opinion) are likely to be accurate and reliable.

Were there any changes made in the test format, mode of administration, instructions, language, or content?

This question is intended to be comprehensive in scope, picking up several themes that have been addressed in more limited form in previous questions. Again, the purpose is to discover the degree to which a standardized test was actually administered and scored in a standardized manner. The deponent needs to acknowledge, explain, and adequately justify any deviations from the standard instructions, content, administration, and so on.

> When a test user makes a substantial change in test format, mode of administration, instructions, language, or content, the user should revalidate the use of the test for the changed conditions or have a rationale supporting the claim that additional validation is not necessary or possible. (APA, 1985, p. 41)

INTERPRETATION

By what method were these interpretative statements derived from the MMPI–2 or MMPI–A scores and profiles?

The deponent may have hand scored the MMPI–2 or MMPI–A and looked up the relevant profiles in a set of actuarial tables or code book. The deponent may have used a computer-based scoring and interpretation service that provides a printout of the scores, profile, and interpretation. It is important for the attorney to discover the method or basis by which the scores and profile are translated into interpretative statements about the test taker. At this point, we are only addressing the general issues of personality assessment (e.g., "the person who took the test appears to be clinically depressed because of certain scale elevations"); more specific inferences and interpretation are addressed later in this chapter.

The use of a computer to score and interpret the test and the appearance of the test report in the form of a computer printout may lend an aura of authority, omniscience, and infallibility that is unwarranted (O'Dell, 1972). Section 9.09(a) of the "Ethical Principles of Psychologists and Code of Conduct" (APA, 2002) emphasizes, "Psychologists who offer assessment or scoring services to other professionals accurately describe the purpose, norms, validity, reliability, and applications of the procedures and any special qualifications applicable to their use."

Psychologists who rely on computer services as a component of forensic evaluations are responsible for choosing services that have shown demonstrable validity, according to section 9.09(b): "Psychologists select scoring and interpretation services (including automated services) on the basis of evidence of the validity of the program and procedures as well as on other appropriate considerations" (APA, 2002). Readers seeking a more extended discussion of the standards and rationale for linking interpretive statements clearly to raw data or standardized scores are referred to the "Ethical Principles of Psychologists and Code of Conduct" (APA, 2002) and *Standards for Educational and Psychological Testing* (APA et al., 1999).

Do you have any reservations or qualifications regarding the validity of the interpretations that you are presenting?

Few deponents are likely to assert that interpretations that are based on the MMPI–2 or MMPI–A are infallible. The attorney can obtain a clear and comprehensive explanation of the sources of possible error and the degree to which, and basis on which, the deponent believes the interpretations may be somewhat inaccurate, incomplete, misleading, or downright wrong.

What other documents or sources of information would you consider important or relevant to interpreting this MMPI–2 or MMPI–A profile?

This question invites the deponent to go on record—under oath—regarding the sources of information that could affect the interpretation of the MMPI–2 or MMPI–A. It is important to emphasize that statements about a specific MMPI–2 or MMPI–A test taker that are based on books, computer printouts, and so on, whether derived from actuarial tables (e.g., "92% of the individuals who were inpatients in psychiatric hospitals and who exhibited this profile on the MMPI–2 or MMPI–A showed the following personality characteristics") or other sources *must* be considered hypotheses. The degree to which these hypotheses are supported by, are consistent with, are modified by, or are seemingly contradicted by other sources of information is crucial to an informed understanding of the nature and strength of an MMPI-based interpretation.

Depending on the situation, other sources of information that might be relevant to evaluating the hypotheses derived from a specific MMPI–2 or MMPI–A profile could include previous or subsequent administrations of the MMPI–2 or MMPI–A, findings from other psychological or neuropsychological tests, assessments from clinical interviews or behavioral observation, medical records, school records, the personal history of the individual (e.g., significant life events and developmental influences), interviews with relatives or friends, employment records, previous or current court records or related legal documents, and current circumstances (e.g., those that might raise the possibility of malingering). If there are sources of information that seem relevant to the attorney but are not mentioned by the deponent, the attorney may want to ask about each source to discover the deponent's rationale for viewing it as relevant or irrelevant to interpreting the profile.

Have you carefully reviewed all of these documents or sources of information (i.e., those named by the deponent in responding to the previous question) that you consider important or relevant to interpreting this MMPI–2 or MMPI–A profile?

Unless the deponent gives a comprehensive "yes" in responding to this question, the attorney may wish to mention each of the sources of information to discover whether the deponent carefully reviewed it, the rationales for instances in which documents from other sources of information were not reviewed, and the possible impact that failure to consider specific sources of information may have on the interpretation of the MMPI–2 or MMPI–A.

[For a written assessment report or other document submitted by the expert witness] Which MMPI scales did you consider in ruling out malingering or other forms of responding in a less than completely honest manner?

This line of questioning begins exploring the degree to which the expert considered and was able to address questions of malingering and related misleading responding. It also taps the expert's knowledge of the MMPI in this area—some experts may be unaware of the various ways in which the MMPI is sensitive to faking bad or faking good.

[If the expert omits some of the relevant scales] Would you please explain why you did not consider the scales that you omitted?

Some experts may lack expertise in the MMPI and simply not know or understand the scales. Others may have not considered the full range of data in evaluating questions of faking good or bad.

What other measures or data did you consider— in addition to the MMPI—in assessing whether this individual might have been faking good or bad?

This question continues to assess the expert's care and comprehensiveness in addressing possible faking or exaggeration.

Were you aware of any indications suggesting that the individual might have been faking or exaggerating? If you concluded that the person was not malingering, were you able to rule out faking or exaggerating with 100% certainty? If not, what are the sources of your doubts?

These questions clarify the expert's stance and reasoning regarding possible faking or exaggeration. Cites and summaries of each research article from January 2001 to the present on malingering for over 50 psychological tests and assessment methods are on the Web at http://kspope.com/assess/malinger.php (Pope, 2005a).

At any point in your written report did you present the work, conclusions, or words of others without honestly acknowledging that these came from other sources?

Those who hand score an MMPI–2 or MMPI–A may look up published descriptions of the relevant profiles and copy these descriptions verbatim without indicating the source. Those who submit MMPI–2 or MMPI–A forms to a computerized scoring and interpretation service may copy the service's report verbatim, as part of the clinician's own report without acknowledging that these words came from a different source. While preparing forensic reports that are based on the MMPI–2 or MMPI–A, other standardized psychological tests, or other sources, the expert may copy passages word for word from published articles or clinical textbooks on psychopathology without providing the proper reference.

Imwinkelried (1982, pp. 289–290) cited Schwartz's account of the trial in which Sirhan Sirhan was charged with killing Robert Kennedy. The prosecutor noticed that a defense psychiatrist had apparently copied passages from a variety of published works into his report with no acknowledgment of the source material. The prosecutor asked the expert witness to read the relevant passages from his report and then presented the original sources for the passages. The prosecutor then subjected the witness to a series of cross-examination questions about whether he had been taught in college to indicate clearly (e.g., through quotation marks, footnotes, or explicit statements) any instances in his own writing when the words he was using were not his own, the customary ways in which he had acknowledged using the ideas and words of others in his previous writings, whether in writing his papers for various courses he had

indicated when he had copied from the works of others, and so on. Imwinkelried emphasized that such unreferenced verbatim copying may approach plagiarism, that the prosecutor in the Sirhan trial had condemned the defense psychiatrist for this unacknowledged usage in his closing argument, and that the defense attorney "virtually apologized" (p. 290) for this expert witness's testimony.

It is important for expert witnesses to make appropriate acknowledgment of source material. For example, a computerized interpretation of an MMPI–2 or MMPI–A is generally considered a professional-to-professional consultation. If the expert has used a computerized interpretation service, that fact should be noted in the forensic report. Similarly, if the expert quotes verbatim from the report (or from other sources), those verbatim quotations should be placed within quotation marks.

OPTIONS AND ALTERNATIVES

Having discovered and inquired in systematic detail about an expert witness's opinions and their foundation, the attorney needs now to discover the scope of the expert's examinations and considerations.

In arriving at your diagnosis (or other conclusion), what alternatives did you consider?

If, for example, the expert witness asserts that a comprehensive psychological and neuropsychological assessment indicates that the individual is suffering from bipolar affective disorder (i.e., manic–depressive mood syndrome), what other possible diagnostic categories (or explanations for the individual's behavior) did the expert consider or rule out? In some cases, the attorney may want to list possible alternatives and ask the expert to explain why he or she did not arrive at each alternative diagnosis.

Few events should arouse the attorney's interest as much as an expert who sets forth firm opinions but gives no evidence of having considered alternative explanations, let alone reasons for rejecting the alternatives. Even when experts name a few seemingly obvious alternative explanations, attorneys should see if they themselves or anyone among their consultants can imagine plausible alternative explanations that seem consistent with the data. The ease with which an alternative explanation can be overlooked is exemplified by a *Newsweek* (Garson, 1965) discussion of the early suffragette movement that had occurred more than 3 decades before the article was published. The *Newsweek* review of a book about the suffragette movement ended by asking what the early suffragettes such as Susan B. Anthony might have thought about a survey, conducted almost a half century after women had finally achieved the right to vote, which found that only about 1 wife out of every 22 voted differently than her husband. Although the review implied that this was obviously a disappointing finding that would have been cause for disappointment among the early suffragettes, a letter to the editor pointed out that there was an alternative way of viewing the data: "I feel that they would have been quite pleased. The feminist movement must have come a long way, if after fewer than 50 years since the enfranchisement of American women, only one husband out of 22 has the courage to vote against his wife" (Garson, 1965, p. 2).

Is there any other source of information that you did not take into account (e.g., because it was not available or because the expert chose not to administer a particular test) that might be relevant or that might change your opinion?

If the expert acknowledges that there might be some source of information that would be relevant to forming an accurate diagnosis (or other conclusion), the attorney can then ask (a) how such a source of information might alter the expert's opinion, (b) whether the expert is less certain of his or her opinion in the absence of this information, and (c) why the information was not obtained. In most cases, the attorney will find it useful to inquire about the steps that the expert took (or failed to take) to discover whether there were previous records of assessment, previous records of treatment, school records, legal records, and so on, and to ask in each case of a step not taken *why* the expert did not take the step to obtain relevant information. In some instances, the attorney may discover that the opposing attorney who retained the expert had possession of (or access to) such records or information but did not make them available to the expert; if so, this situation and its implications should be carefully explored.

CHAPTER 10

SOME FINAL THOUGHTS

This book draws together a great diversity of information, issues, and questions that can be intimidating to expert witnesses and attorneys alike. Those who are new to this area—psychologists who have never set foot in court and attorneys who have never heard of the Minnesota Multiphasic Personality Inventory (MMPI)—must confront complex, unfamiliar information and procedures. Those who are experienced in this area—expert witnesses who are seasoned and attorneys who may know more than some psychologists about the MMPI—know how many ways that a trial's twists and turns, clashing personalities, unanticipated evidence, and sequences of testimony and cross-examination can create surprises, dilemmas, and confrontations in the courtroom. As a consequence, the material in this book can seem overwhelming. At least that is how it seemed to us when we were deciding what to include and how to organize it.

Throughout the book, we have suggested possible guidelines or approaches that may be helpful in coping with complex, sometimes contradictory information and feelings of being overwhelmed. For example, chapter 9 offers a sequence of basic questions and commentaries that both attorneys and expert witnesses can use in planning for cross-examination, and the appendixes include checklists that expert witnesses and attorneys can use in preparing for trial.

In this final chapter, we return to four fundamental rules that we have found helpful coping with the sometimes vast array of facts, tasks,

and standards involved in the use of the MMPI, MMPI–2, and MMPI–A in court.

PREPARE

One fundamental principle applies equally to expert witnesses and attorneys: prepare. As emphasized throughout the book, thorough preparation is crucial. Expert witnesses and attorneys who walk into court unprepared invite disaster and do a disservice to their profession and to everyone involved in or affected by the legal proceeding. Adequate preparation requires time, effort, and self-discipline. Before accepting any case, expert witnesses and attorneys must make sure that they have adequate time to prepare, as well as personal resources (e.g., motivation, energy, and eagerness) and professional resources (e.g., access to relevant information and consultation) to prepare adequately. Reviewing the suggested steps for preparation in this book as well as the possible cross-examination questions can help expert witnesses and attorneys to monitor and assess the degree to which they accomplish the task of preparation.

LET THE OBJECTIVE TEST RESULTS SPEAK FOR THEMSELVES

A second fundamental principle, particularly relevant for expert witnesses, is this: Let the objective test results speak for themselves. As discussed in previous chapters, the MMPI (particularly the revised versions) can provide invaluable information if the results can be communicated clearly to the jury. If expert witnesses maintain a good working knowledge *in practical terms* of what the scales mean, the test's database, and the relevant research, they can present the findings with such clarity that the jury can "see" (particularly if appropriate exhibits are used; see, for example, chap. 6) what the test reveals about the individual and the questions at issue before the court.

A major pitfall is the tendency to mislead others by portraying hunches and guesses lacking empirical support as if they were conclusively demonstrated. Expert witnesses must state honestly and clearly what testimony is based solidly on well-accepted, adequately validated, and sufficiently standardized assessment instruments. Perhaps another way of stating this principle (with a slightly different focus) is this: Stick with the data. Of course, professionals may be called on to give opinions with greater and lesser degrees of certainty. But the jury has a right to know when the expert is speculating, using psychological constructs that have not been empirically validated, or relying on a *nonstandardized* method of administering (e.g., using a shortened form of the MMPI that has not been adequately validated), scoring, or interpreting a standardized test. Many of the questions presented in chapter 9 will help clarify these issues for attorneys who are confronting such testimony and for expert witnesses who are preparing to testify.

In some cases, the only relevant information from an MMPI is that the protocol is invalid. This fact alone may help everyone involved to understand the situation better (i.e., that the test results suggest that the individual was not accurately responding to the items) and may provide a perspective not readily available from other tests or testimony. In such cases, the expert witness must refrain from any temptation to abandon the principle of sticking with the data. Although expert opinions may derive from a variety of sources, expert opinion that purports to be based on the MMPI should *never involve interpretation of clinical or content scales* when the validity scales show that the profile is clearly invalid.

TELL THE TRUTH

A third fundamental principle is especially useful for expert witnesses: Tell the truth. Regardless of whether one is making initial contact with an attorney, talking with an individual who is being assessed, writing a forensic report, or testifying, telling the truth is essential. In this book, we have explored some factors that make this task difficult: the adversarial nature of the courtroom process, the potential role conflicts and conflicts of interest, tendencies not to admit that one does not know the answer to this or that question, and so on. During cross-examination, expert witnesses are likely, at least occasionally, to be baffled and caught off guard, to find it hard to admit that we overlooked something important (e.g., reviewing previous records or keeping up with the current professional literature in relevant areas) and as a result to go blank.

Regardless of the circumstances, the basic rule is always: Tell the truth. The whole truth. And nothing but the truth. It is easy to forget this fundamental principle, but the oath we take right before we testify is a good reminder.

TRUST THE JURY

The fourth fundamental principle is especially useful for attorneys: Trust the jury. No case is perfect. An attorney's handling of a case, before and during the trial, always has weaknesses as well as strengths. No attorney's work has ever been completely free of blunders. And trials almost always contain the unexpected. In the midst of even the most difficult circumstances, trusting the jury is crucial. While preparing and trying a case, the attorney must present the evidence as clearly as possible in a way that conveys a direct and immediate sense of the story of *what happened* and *how it is relevant* to the claims at issue. The process of *voir dire* and jury selection attempts to produce the best, most open, and most unbiased jury possible. To respect and trust those jurors to make a fair decision on the basis of the evidence and arguments can be the central and organizing principle for attorneys in even the most difficult trials.

THE EXPERT WITNESS VERSUS THE ATTORNEY

Addressed to two separate readerships, this book may seem at times to express contradictory views. For example, one section suggests "avoid focusing on, emphasizing, or relying on responses to an individual item," but another section advises "inquire about responses to and meanings of individual items." These apparent contradictions result from addressing a volume to two groups of professionals whose roles are sometimes in conflict because of the adversarial nature of the American judicial system.

We believe that the psychometric properties of individual items make it unwise to attempt actuarial interpretations on the basis of responses to an individual item. It is unlikely that the witness will be able to produce or refer to adequately validated actuarial databases for such individual item responses that have been published in peer-reviewed scientific or professional journals. Although at times an expert witness might consider using an individual item response to *illustrate* a general trend that has been identified by a more general actuarial method and supported by other sources of data, such use may—depending on context, qualification, and clarification—seem to imply that the individual item response itself warrants interpretation and is supported by actuarial tables or interpretive rules. If this implication is subjected to vigorous and informed cross-examination, the witness is likely to be in for a rough time.

Although expert witnesses should avoid highlighting responses to individual items, attorneys conducting discovery and cross-examination would do well to obtain and explore the expert's knowledge of, understanding of, use of, and professional opinions about the meaning of responses to individual items and the degree to which such responses are a valid source of inference about the person who was assessed. The attorney's questions will help show whether the expert uses this standardized test appropriately.

This adversarial process of careful, detailed discovery and vigorous cross-examination can show whether expert witnesses are genuine experts. Expert witnesses must be able to explain clearly how a test works *and* how it does not work (i.e., unjustified or inappropriate uses), even when responding to adversarial questioning. Anticipating tough questions can help experts learn more about the tests that they are using and prepare to testify. Covert rehearsal (e.g., Singer & Pope, 1978) of responses to the types of questions in chapters 2, 5, and 9, as well as trying out answers in front of friends and colleagues (while allowing them to comment on the responses and ask questions) can help experts to identify problem areas in their knowledge of tests. These steps can also help them say what they mean in clear, everyday language—rather than vocalizing, articulating, and jargonizing their thought processes in seemingly endless and aimless clouds of multisylabic associations of terminology that—well, you get the idea.

This process of discovery and cross-examination can also help the trier of fact understand uses and misuses of standardized psychological tests. Only when jurors (or the judge in nonjury trials) adequately understand how a test works can they know how much weight to give to test results and the expert opinions that are based on those test results. Watching the expert witness respond to vigorous, informed, and carefully planned cross-examination can also help the jurors to evaluate the expert's knowledge, credibility, and integrity.

THE EXPERT WITNESS AND THE ATTORNEY

Although the very nature of trials creates at least a *seeming* (but not necessarily actual) adversarial relationship between expert witnesses and the attorneys who depose and cross-examine them, experts and the attorneys who use them can form a collaborative relationship. Each has a responsibility to help educate and prepare the other. The expert witness can help educate the attorney regarding the use of psychological tests. The attorney can help educate the expert in trial procedures and the specifics of a particular case. Each also has a responsibility to educate the other regarding the ethics of their respective domains and to help ensure that all matters related to the endeavor are handled ethically.

The collaborative relationship creates dangers. The adversarial nature of trials can exert pressures—both subtle and powerful—leading the expert to be "for" the attorney who employs him or her and "against" the attorney who conducts discovery and cross-examination. The understandable impulse to want to help the employing attorney may, in fact, be a more profound threat to the expert's objectivity and responsibility to tell the truth than the potentially adversarial relationship with the other attorney. Chapter 5 explores these issues. Both experts and employing attorneys must monitor such factors to avoid eroding their own integrity and the integrity of their work.

THE EXPERT WITNESS IS *NOT* THE ATTORNEY

Any discussion of the complex interrelationship between the roles of witness and attorney is incomplete without emphasizing that the witness is *not* functioning as an attorney. Both expert and fact witnesses must respect the limitations of their knowledge and must, when appropriate, seek qualified legal guidance. Too often, the naive or arrogant witness will, as chapter 5 describes, "play attorney" in regard to one of the litigants. But even more often, an expert or fact witness will make unjustified assumptions or reach faulty conclusions about the witness's own legal duties, rights, or options. Responding to a subpoena for raw data or other client records is an area in which witnesses may, acting on faulty legal understandings, cause problems for their clients and themselves. *Sexual Involvement With Therapists: Patient Assessment, Subsequent Therapy, Forensics* (Pope, 1994) summarizes a case that provides an example.

> The clinician who has been asked or subpoenaed to testify must also ensure that both clinician and patient clearly understand how issues of confidentiality and privilege—reviewed with the patient at the beginning of therapy as part of the informed consent process—come into play in light of the impending testimony. When a patient files any formal complaint—even if sexual involvement is not part of the complaint—with a licensing board, civil court, or other authority, health care professionals who have provided services to the patient must take care to avoid violating confidentiality, privilege, and related rights on the reflexive and unexamined assumption that the patient has inevitably waived all rights of notification or challenge in regard to disclosure of his or her records. According to the published opinion in one case, a woman complained to the Board of Psychology of the State of California about . . . a licensed clinical psychologist. The Board initiated disciplinary action against [the psychologist] and a hearing was set before an administrative law judge. . . . In anticipation of the hearing, [the psychologist] served 17 or more subpoenas duces tecum on [the woman's] past and present physicians and psychotherapists and her former attorneys. Copies of the subpoenas were served on the Board but no notice of any kind was given to [the woman]. The records were produced to the ALJ [administrative law judge] at a prehearing conference and the ALJ gave them to [the psychologist's] attorney.
>
> When [the woman] discovered the disclosure, she filed a petition for a writ of mandate to compel the Department of General Services to quash the subpoenas and return the documents. The Board of Psychology (as one real party in interest) did not oppose the petition and disclaimed any interest in [the woman's] personal records. [The psychologist] (the other real party in interest) claimed the petition was moot because the disciplinary action had been settled but nevertheless insisted the records had been properly subpoenaed. . . .

The trial court granted the petition, finding service of the subpoenas without prior notice to [the woman] violated her rights of privacy, and ordered [the psychologist] to pay [the woman's] attorneys' fees of $70,830. (*Sehlmeyer v. Department of General Servs.,* 1993, p. 1075, as cited in Pope, 1994, p. 159–160)

* * *

The appellate court noted that "Stempf contends his subpoenas comply with the literal letter of the law as expressed in the Government Code" (p. 1076). The appellate court further noted: "According to Stempf, the Legislature's failure to mention Code of Civil Procedure section 1985.3 in subdivision (a) of section 11510 of the Government Code demonstrates a specific intent to exclude administrative subpoenas from the operation of section 1985.3. We do not engage in the somewhat sticky statutory analysis required to resolve this point—because even if Stempf is correct, there still exists a constitutional and common law right to privacy which resolves the underlying issue against Stempf" (p. 1077). The appellate court affirmed the trial court's judgment and order, holding that "before confidential third-party records may be disclosed in the course of an administrative proceeding, the subpoenaing party must take reasonable steps to notify the third-party of the pendency and nature of the proceedings and to afford the third-party a fair opportunity to assert her interests by objecting to disclosure, by seeking an appropriate protective order from the administrative tribunal, or by instituting other legal proceedings to limit the scope or nature of the matters sought to be discovered" (pp. 1080–1081). Because this particular case focused solely on the issue of notice, the court

stated, "We do not address [the woman's] rights, if any, against the health-care providers who turned over records without her consent. (Pope, 1994, pp. 160–161; see also EVID. CODE 995 [physician required to claim privilege], p. 1080)

Expert and fact witnesses must avoid playing the role of attorney and reaching unjustified conclusions about legal requirements emerging from legislation and case law. However certain a witness may be about the legal duties to disclose or withhold records, the wisest course is almost always to consult with the witness's own attorney (not relying solely on advice provided by attorneys of other parties in the case) before responding to a subpoena for records.

FEAR AND TREMBLING IN THE COURTROOM

Expert witnesses and attorneys—despite some reports, stereotypes, and well-known jokes to the contrary—are human. So it is not surprising that we may feel anxious or even panic-stricken at the prospect of walking into the adversarial atmosphere of the courtroom. All three of the authors of this book have, at least on occasion, felt nervous before and during court appearances. It is important to acknowledge that this is a normal and understandable human reaction to what can be an extremely challenging experience.

Part of the rationale for this book is to help people prepare for court experiences. Adequate preparation can help reduce uncomfortable—sometimes debilitating—anxiety. Of course, for some people, a little anxiety before any demanding task such as a court appearance may be adaptive and useful. It may help motivate them to prepare and remain alert. But excessive anxiety is more likely to hurt preparation and presentation and make life miserable for the individual. It tends to make some people lock up, freeze, and go blank in court; it makes others talk in a forced or stilted manner; it makes still others babble almost uncontrollably. In almost all instances, it makes it hard to concentrate, listen carefully, remember accurately, think creatively, and speak clearly.

Paradoxically, reading this book may stir up anxiety in many readers. Attorneys may find it hard to believe that they can ever learn enough about psychological tests and the principles of psychometrics, research, theory, and practice to conduct an adequately informed discovery and cross-examination. Expert witnesses may wonder if they can survive a vigorous cross-examination by someone who is knowledgeable about kurtosis, contrast errors, Lambda, reliability coefficients, dyscalculia, peer-reviewed journals, beta errors, and the social discomfort content scale. Part of the framework and content of this book evolved from the workshops conducted by the authors on forensic assessment and related psychological, legal, and professional issues. During parts of such workshops, the nervousness of some participants became both visible and audible.

It is crucial to recognize that such anxiety, when confronting detailed information in an important area of professional practice, is completely normal and understandable. Appearing in court—as an expert witness or an attorney—is demanding, challenging work that requires extensive knowledge, expertise, and preparation. Confronting the areas in which we may be less than adequately knowledgeable, expert, and prepared is likely to evoke some anxiety. Responding appropriately to the anxiety involves a reasonably simple task, although one that may require considerable time and effort: becoming familiar with the material.

Anxiety about acknowledging and exploring areas of complex information with which we are unfamiliar (and *all* expert witnesses and attorneys, no matter how knowledgeable, how experienced, or how widely known, published, or respected, encounter such areas) but which are relevant to our work can also elicit less adaptive responses such as denial, resentment, anger, paralyzing fear, and rationalization (e.g., pretending that one already knows this information or that it will never be relevant or important in forensic settings).

Alertness to the possibility of these less adaptive impulses can help prevent them from controlling our behavior. If the less adaptive responses continue to be tempting, the following consideration may be helpful. No matter how uncomfortable it is to read about the complex, detailed information relevant to forensic assessments, it tends to be much less uncomfortable for the expert witness to become adequately familiar with the material during trial preparation than to encounter the material for the first time during cross-examination. And it is generally less agonizing for an attorney to work through this material adequately during preparation than to encounter it for the first time from an expert witness called by opposing counsel.

BROADER ETHICAL RESPONSIBILITIES

In closing, perhaps the most useful perspective is to step back and take a look at the forensic context in which MMPI-based testimony and cross-examination occur. Throughout this book we have discussed ethical responsibilities of both expert witnesses and attorneys as they deal with each other, with the principle participants in the case (e.g., the individual who is being assessed), with their colleagues, and with the judge and jury in a particular trial. We have also tried to highlight some of the major ethical pitfalls and dilemmas (e.g., conflicting roles and responsibilities) that arise from time to time.

To the extent that ethical dilemmas or violations are made more likely or are intensified by the larger systems, individual expert witnesses, attorneys, and other readers must consider the degree to which they bear an ethical responsibility to attempt to address those issues. Are there laws, rules of evidence, or courtroom procedures, for example, that seem unjust or likely to create error, confusion, or misconduct, or that fail to specify clearly the responsibilities and standards to which expert witnesses and attorneys should be and can be held accountable? Do graduate training programs in law, psychology, and other relevant disciplines provide adequate training in forensic practice, ethical issues, and professional standards? Do professional associations adequately fulfill their responsibilities to provide clear standards, adequate involvement of the membership in developing those standards, workable procedures for ensuring adequate accountability to those standards, and sufficient education and open discussion of those standards? Are there unnecessary, unjustifiable, or unexamined conflicts among ethical, legal, professional, and related standards or responsibilities (see, e.g., Pope, 2003; Pope & Bajt, 1988; Pope & Vasquez, 1998)?

Experience with these larger systems in which we work makes it hard to claim that they lack serious problems or that the problems have been adequately discussed and addressed. The work of expert witnesses and attorneys and the larger systems in which they function exerts a profound effect on the lives of so many people, not only those who appear as plaintiffs or defendants in civil, criminal, and administrative cases but also those who represent the more general society. To the extent that the system of justice does not operate as well as it should, or at least as well as it can or might, we are negligent as a society, as responsible members of that society, and as professionals who work within the legal system. To ignore problems with this system helps ensure that such problems continue and likely worsen.

None of us practices in a vacuum. Each of us is affected by and shares responsibility for the broader context. Continuing appreciation of the context—or rather, contexts—in which we attempt to fulfill our responsibilities as expert witnesses and attorneys is crucial to our professional ability and integrity. Acknowledging and responding to problems in the system are no less important.

Society has entrusted expert witnesses and attorneys with the responsibility to help make the system of justice work. If we have anything to profess, it begins with this: We must take our work—and all its inescapable responsibilities—seriously.

Federal Cases Involving the MMPI

This appendix lists federal appellate decisions that mention the MMPI. The citations are listed in reverse chronological order, so that the most recent case appears first. Each citation is accompanied by a brief statement showing the relation of the MMPI to the case. This brief statement is not intended to provide a complete description of the case or of issues unrelated to the MMPI. All significant issues raised in any case should be examined through review of the full case opinions and subsequent appellate opinions that affirm or reject the legal precedent set out in the original case.

Northern District of Alabama

Mitchell v. Crowell, 966 F. Supp. 1071 (N.D. Ala. 1996). In a disability discrimination action, the MMPI was given to an employee before reactivating his security clearance.

Western District of Arkansas

Gray v. University of Arkansas, 658 F. Supp. 709 (W.D. Ark. 1987). An MMPI evaluation of a coach was used in a sex discrimination case.

Eastern District of Arkansas

United States. v. Lee, 89 F. Supp. 2d 1017 (E.D. Ark. 2000). The prosecutor presented evidence that the MMPI showed an elevated paranoia scale. Because the defendant had not opened that door, his rights were prejudiced by its introduction.

Fairchild v. Lockhart, 744 F. Supp. 1429 (E.D. Ark. 1989). The MMPI was used in evaluation of the petitioner.

Northern District of California

Allen v. Barnhart, 2003 WL 21848190 (N.D. Cal. 2003). The MMPI was discussed in a reversal of denial of benefits.

Turner v. Apfel, 1998 WL 289288 (N.D. Cal. 1998). The MMPI–2 was given to an applicant for disability insurance who hit a stalled vehicle and suffered injuries. Test results were consistent with subjective complaints of the applicant and showed evidence of cognitive deficits involving memory loss and verbal tasking.

Hernandez v. Heckler, 621 F. Supp. 439 (N.D. Cal. 1985). MMPI tests were used in evaluation of the plaintiff.

District of Colorado

Clausen v. Standard Ins. Co., 961 F. Supp. 1446 (D. Colo. 1997). The MMPI–2 was discussed in footnote 2 as given to the claimant, who participated in an Employment Retirement Income Security Act (ERISA) plan.

Reighley v. International Playtex, Inc., 604 F. Supp. 1078 (D. Colo. 1985). A reference article pertaining to the MMPI is listed in footnote 4.

District of Delaware

Parsons v. Barnhart, 2003 WL 22136299 (D. Del. 2003). An application for childhood disability benefits was denied. The MMPI–2 test was found invalid because questions were answered randomly.

Southern District of Florida

United States v. Sullivan, 28 F. Supp. 2d 1365 (S.D. Fla. 1998). On trial for embezzlement and obstruction of justice, validity patterns of the MMPI test and the defendant's 5-year period of criminal activity suggested conscious and volitional manipulation, as opposed to reduced mental capacity.

Barnes v. Cochran, 944 F. Supp. 897 (S.D. Fla. 1996). A pre-employment psychological examination (including MMPI testing) violated the Americans With Disability Act (ADA).

Stockett v. Tolin, 791 F. Supp. 1536 (S.D. Fla. 1992). In a sexual harassment action, the plaintiff's MMPI was consistent with severe emotional distress resulting from harassment.

Gant v. Sullivan, 773 F. Supp. 376 (S.D. Fla. 1991). The MMPI could not be administered because of the individual's extreme inability to read or write.

Middle District of Florida

Brown v. Bell South Telecommunications, Inc., 73 F. Supp. 2d 1308 (M.D. Fla. 1999). The MMPI is mentioned.

Northern District of Georgia

United States v. Battle, 264 F. Supp. 2d 1088 (N.D. Ga. 2003). An attempt to set aside the federal death sentence was rejected. The MMPI–2 results were unremarkable. The defendant unsuccessfully argued that rescored MMPI–2 results would have made a difference in the insanity defense.

United States v. Battle, 979 F. Supp. 1442 (N.D. Ga. 1997). A death sentence was affirmed where MMPI results showed no elevation of schizophrenia or paranoia scales.

Fields v. Harris, 498 F. Supp. 478 (N.D. Ga. 1980). The MMPI was used in evaluation of a claimant.

Central District of Illinois

Karraker v. Rent-A-Center, Inc., 316 F. Supp. 2d 675 (C.D. Ill. 2004). An employee claimed that the MMPI test requirement and the employer's treat-ment of results of the test violated the ADA. The parties disputed whether the MMPI was entitled to ADA "medical examination" confidentiality.

Southern District of Illinois

Wilson v. Lane, 697 F. Supp. 1500 (S.D. Ill. 1988). The MMPI was used to evaluate whether the plaintiff was an alcoholic.

Northern District of Illinois, Eastern Division

Cuevas v. Barnhart, 2004 WL 1588277 (N.D. Ill. 2004). The plaintiff responded "no" or "I don't know" to the first 78 MMPI items and refused to answer the rest. The case was remanded because the administrative law judge (ALJ) failed to support the denial of benefits.

Gardner v. Barnhart, 2004 WL 1470244 (N.D. Ill. 2004). The plaintiff was not entitled to disability benefits after MMPI–2 results were determined to be "invalid" and "suggested malingering as well as a serious adjustment disorder."

Lowe v. Barnhart, 2004 WL 2203424 (N.D. Ill. 2004). MMPI results suggested "faking bad" in a Social Security case.

Baker v. Barnhart, 2003 WL 21058544 (N.D. Ill. 2003). A decision denying benefits was reversed. The MMPI–2 was mentioned.

Blackwell v. Barnhart, 258 F. Supp. 2d 851 (N.D. Ill. 2003). The denial of Social Security Insurance benefits was reversed. MMPI–2 results suggested a bipolar disorder. Parties disagreed about the test's value because of a scaled score of 79 on the Infrequency (F) scale.

Hawkins v. Barnhart, 2003 WL 1717076 (N.D. Ill. 2003). Benefits were denied. MMPI–2 results helped neither party.

Jones-Ward v. Barnhart, 2003 WL 22839821 (N.D. Ill. 2003). The MMPI was administered. Disability benefits were disallowed.

Winfield v. Barnhart, 269 F. Supp. 2d 995 (N.D. Ill. 2003). Social Security Insurance benefits were denied. The MMPI–2 indicated fake-bad results.

Flood v. Long Term Disability Plan for First Data Corp., 2002 WL 31155099 (N.D. Ill. 2002). An MMPI–2 test was administered along with others in an ERISA case challenging denial of long-term benefits.

Hert v. Barnhart, 234 F. Supp. 2d 832 (N.D. Ill. 2002). Benefits were denied. Test scores produced an exaggerated profile.

Ishmael v. Barnhart, 212 F. Supp. 2d 865 (N.D. Ill. 2002). Social Security Insurance benefits were denied. The MMPI–2 results suggested over-reporting.

Raud v. Barnhart, 2002 WL 1793744 (N.D. Ill. 2002). A denial of benefits was remanded. The MMPI–2 results showed malingering.

Traum v. Equitable Life Assurance Society of U.S., 240 F. Supp. 2d 776 (N.D. Ill. 2002). A psychologist gave the MMPI–2 in an action against an insurance company for terminating depression disability benefits.

Far Fan v. Apfel, 1998 WL 677169 (N.D. Ill. 1998). The ALJ's denial of Social Security Insurance was reversed because the ALJ improperly disregarded the psychological test report (including the MMPI–2 results) and improperly concluded, without authority, that the MMPI–2 showed malingering.

Johnson v. Charter, 969 F. Supp. 493 (N.D. Ill. 1997). A Social Security Insurance benefits' claimant with a history of back pain and depression was given the MMPI.

Jabczynski v. Shalala, 882 F. Supp. 742 (N.D. Ill. 1995). The MMPI–2 was administered in connection with a worker's compensation claim held invalid because of elevated validity scores.

Winters v. Iowa State University, 768 F. Supp. 231 (N.D. Ill. 1991). The MMPI was relied on in a negative recommendation to the Chicago Police Department.

Mitchell v. Heckler, 590 F. Supp. 131 (N.D. Ill. 1984). The MMPI was improperly ignored by the ALJ in a disability benefits dispute.

Northern District of Indiana

Carradine v. Barnhart, 2002 WL 32083071 (N.D. Ind. 2002). MMPI–2 results showed an intense, anxious person.

Behymer v. Apfel, 45 F. Supp. 2d 654 (N.D. Ind. 1999). The MMPI results supported pain disability.

Matheney v. Anderson, 60 F. Supp. 2d 846 (N.D. Ind. 1999). The MMPI was mentioned.

McGraw v. Apfel, 87 F. Supp. 2d 845 (N.D. Ind. 1999). The MMPI results supported chronic fatigue syndrome.

Shidler v. Bowen, 651 F. Supp. 1291 (N.D. Ind. 1987). The MMPI was used in evaluation of the claimant.

Lee v. Heckler, 568 F. Supp. 456 (N.D. Ind. 1983). The MMPI was used in evaluation of the plaintiff.

Stokes v. U.S., 538 F. Supp. 298 (N.D. Ind. 1982). The MMPI was used in evaluation of the appellant in a competency case.

Southern District of Indiana

Routes v. Henderson, 58 F. Supp. 2d 959 (S.D. Ind. 1999). The court found that an employer cannot require a "fitness for duty" psychological exam of an employee who has been certified able to return to work unless postleave behavior justifies it.

United States v. Danser, 110 F. Supp. 2d 807 (S.D. Ind. 1999). The MMPI was administered in connection with an insanity defense to criminal sexual abuse charges.

Gossett v. Chater, 947 F. Supp. 1272 (S.D. Ind. 1996). The MMPI was administered to a claimant seeking disability benefits.

Northern District of Iowa

Engling v. Barnhart, 2004 WL 1212106 (N.D. Iowa 2004). In an appeal of denial of Social Security Insurance and disability benefits, the MMPI results suggested depression and exaggeration of symptoms.

Foell v. Mathes, 310 F. Supp. 2d 1020 (N.D. Iowa 2004). A murder conviction and sentence were upheld. The MMPI was administered.

Muckey v. Barnhart, 2004 WL 1725524 (N.D. Iowa 2004). In denying an application for disability benefits, the court found that the "MMPI results indicate he (claimant) would not be a good surgical candidate."

Raven v. Barnhart, 2004 WL 1683123 (N.D. Iowa 2004). The MMPI–2 was given and application for Social Security Insurance and disability was denied.

United States v. Taylor, 2004 WL 97653 (N.D. Iowa 2004). The MMPI was among a battery of tests given in request for Social Security Insurance benefits.

Anderson v. Barnhart, 2003 WL 22047389 (N.D. Iowa 2003). Denial of Social Security Insurance benefits was reversed because the ALJ ignored subjective complaints. The MMPI test results showed a shy and passive person.

Bates v. Apfel, 69 F. Supp. 2d 1143 (N.D. Iowa 1999). The MMPI supported pain disability.

Stone v. Harris, 492 F. Supp. 278 (N.D. Iowa 1980). The MMPI was administered to the plaintiff in a disability benefits request.

Southern District of Iowa

Gaudet v. Barnhart, 249 F. Supp. 2d 842 (S.D. Iowa 2003). A denial of benefits was reversed. The MMPI showed the claimant had a poor ability to cope with pain.

Horton v. Barnhart, 266 F. Supp. 2d 971 (S.D. Iowa 2003). MMPI results were mentioned in a reversal of a benefits' denial.

Rivera v. Massanari, 176 F. Supp. 2d 892 (S.D. Iowa 2001). A denial of Social Security Insurance benefits was reversed. The MMPI results suggested schizophrenia.

District of Kansas

Roney v. Barnhart, 2004 WL 1212049 (D. Kan. 2004). A denial of benefits was reversed because the ALJ disregarded the psychologist's examination, including the MMPI–2 test and diagnosis of schizoaffective disorder.

Miller v. Barnhart, 296 F. Supp. 2d 1269 (D. Kan. 2003). The court reversed a denial of benefits. The MMPI–2 was among the tests given.

Frazee v. Barnhart, 259 F. Supp. 2d 1182 (D. Kan. 2003). A denial of Social Security Insurance benefits was reversed. The MMPI profile was 2-8.

Conrad v. Board of Johnson County Commissioners, 237 F. Supp. 2d 1204 (D. Kan. 2002). In an employment discrimination case, the plaintiff was required to take the MMPI–2 test before a return to work. The MMPI–2 testing was job-related and therefore did not violate the ADA. In response to the plaintiff's main challenge, the court held that the MMPI questions concerning sexual matters and sexual deviancy are not covered by the ADA's prohibition against mental exams.

Kent v. Apfel, 75 F. Supp. 2d 1170 (D. Kan. 1999). The MMPI results supported pain disability.

Hoffman v. Apfel, 62 F. Supp. 2d 1204 (D. Kan. 1999). The MMPI was given in a disability examination.

Wright v. Wyandotte County Sheriff's Department, 963 F. Supp. 1029 (D. Kan. 1997). In a sex, race, and age discrimination suit, the MMPI was given to the plaintiff, who handled her duty weapon in an unsafe manner.

Burnett v. Shalala, 883 F. Supp. 565 (D. Kan. 1995). The claimant sought review of the denial of disability benefits. Evidence showed he exaggerated low back pain, and the MMPI profile may have been affected by an attempt to present an exaggerated version of his condition.

Elbrader v. Blevins, 757 F. Supp. 1174 (D. Kan. 1991). The MMPI was used in the evaluation.

Ringer v. Sullivan, 772 F. Supp. 548 (D. Kan. 1991). The plaintiff completed the MMPI in a disability case.

Ash v. Sullivan, 748 F. Supp. 804 (D. Kan. 1990). The MMPI was one of the tests used in the evaluation of the plaintiff.

Caldwell v. Sullivan, 736 F. Supp. 1076 (D. Kan. 1990). The MMPI was one of several tests used in evaluation of the plaintiff.

Durflinger v. Artiles, 563 F. Supp. 322 (D. Kan. 1981). The MMPI was used to evaluate the alleged perpetrator in a wrongful death action.

Western District of Kentucky

Slaughter v. Parker, 187 F. Supp. 2d 755 (W.D. Ky. 2001). Based in large part on the failure to administer the MMPI and lawyers' presentation of evidence around that failure, the death sentence was vacated and a new penalty hearing was ordered. The attorney had been ineffective in examining an expert who failed to give the defendant an MMPI because of a reading disability.

Canterino v. Wilson, 546 F. Supp. 174 (W.D. Ky. 1982). Results of 30 MMPI tests were used by defendants to show lack of psychological injury to plaintiffs.

Eastern District of Louisiana

Bertaut v. U.S., 852 F. Supp. 523 (E.D. La. 1994). The MMPI was administered and deemed by a doctor as the most accepted psychological test because it is largely objective, requiring little subjective interpretations.

District of Maine

McKay v. Barnhart, 2003 WL 1092746 (D. Me. 2003). A denial of Social Security Insurance benefits was reversed. The judgment was not supported by the MMPI results.

Taylor v. Heckler, 605 F. Supp. 407 (D. Me. 1984). Two MMPI tests were used in evaluation of the plaintiff and in testimony for the plaintiff.

District of Maryland

Baucom v. Potter, 225 F. Supp. 2d 585 (D. Md. 2002). Refusal to take the MMPI was found insufficient reason to dismiss disparate treatment or failure to accommodate claims in an employment discrimination case at the summary judgment stage.

United States v. Rigatuso, 719 F. Supp. 409 (D. Md. 1989). MMPI test results produced an invalid profile, but the results did show evidence of malingering.

Union Trust Co. of Maryland v. Charter Medical Corp., 663 F. Supp. 175 (D. Md. 1986). A condition of the acquisition of a medical group included extension of a sublicense to use the MMPI.

District of Massachusetts

United States v. Sampson, 335 F. Supp. 2d 166 (D. Mass. 2004). The first death sentence imposed in Massachusetts or the First Circuit since Congress and the president reinstated the death penalty in 1988. (This case is an instruction manual on how to keep psychological testing, including MMPI results, that may later be used during a penalty phase from being provided to the prosecution during the guilt phase of trial.)

Western District of Michigan

Simonds v. Blue Cross-Blue Shield of Michigan, 629 F. Supp. 369 (W.D. Mich. 1986). The MMPI used in evaluation of a plaintiff was found invalid.

District of Minnesota

Dornack v. Apfel, 49 F. Supp. 2d 1129 (D. Minn. 1999). The MMPI was used in support of chronic fatigue syndrome disability.

Leitzke v. Callahan, 986 F. Supp. 1216 (D. Minn. 1997). The MMPI was administered to the claimant, who was diagnosed with alcoholism in a Social Security benefits action.

Regents of the University of Minnesota v. Applied Innovations, Inc., 685 F. Supp. 698 (D. Minn. 1987). The MMPI was the subject of copyright dispute.

Doe v. Hennepin County, 623 F. Supp. 982 (D. Minn. 1985). The family's psychologist claimed that the court-approved psychologist improperly administered and interpreted MMPI tests.

Southern District of Mississippi

Kirksey v. City of Jackson, Miss., 461 F. Supp. 1282 (S.D. Miss. 1978). Use of the MMPI in police candidate testing was mentioned in this civil rights action.

Northern District of Mississippi

Hill v. Thigpen, 667 F. Supp. 314 (N.D. Miss. 1987). The MMPI was used in evaluation of the defendant. The defense was not given adequate time to use the results.

Eastern District of Missouri

Quaite v. Barnhart, 312 F. Supp. 2d 1195 (E.D. Mo. 2004). In request for disability, the MMPI–2 results of the plaintiff suggested moderate depression.

Maddox v. Massanari, 199 F. Supp. 2d 928 (E.D. Mo. 2001). Denial of disability and Social Security benefits was affirmed in a case in which MMPI results suggested an attempt to fake good.

Kovach v. Apfel, 119 F. Supp. 2d 943 (E.D. Mo. 2000). A judgment denying disability benefits was affirmed. The MMPI showed a "propensity for conversion of psychological distress into physical problems."

Stanfield v. Charter, 970 F. Supp. 1440 (E.D. Mo. 1997). The ALJ improperly discredited the medical opinion of the psychologist who administered the MMPI to a Social Security benefits claimant.

Russell v. Sullivan, 758 F. Supp. 490 (E.D. Mo. 1991). The MMPI was used in evaluation of the plaintiff.

Western District of Missouri

Harbour v. Bowen, 659 F. Supp. 732 (W.D. Mo. 1987). The MMPI was used in evaluation of the plaintiff.

Smith v. Armontrout, 632 F. Supp. 503 (W.D. Mo. 1986). The MMPI was mentioned as one of the tests directed to be given to Smith.

May v. United States, 572 F. Supp. 725 (W.D. Mo. 1983). The MMPI was mentioned. It was used in evaluation of the plaintiff.

Mikel v. Abrams, 541 F. Supp. 591 (W.D. Mo. 1982). The MMPI was mentioned in the case.

District of Montana

Marmon v. Califano, 459 F. Supp. 369 (D. Mont. 1978). The ALJ's treatment of a doctor's statements about MMPI results was reversed.

District of Nebraska

Perez v. Barnhart, 2004 WL 613051 (D. Neb. 2004). The denial of disability and Social Security Insurance benefits was affirmed. The MMPI–2 results suggested an "anti-social personality makeup."

Isaacs v. Barnhart, 196 F. Supp. 2d 934 (D. Neb. 2001). The court affirmed the ALJ opinion that the claimant was a malingerer and not entitled to benefits based, in part, on the MMPI *L* scale.

United States v. Calek, 48 F. Supp. 2d 919 (D. Neb. 1999). The MMPI was mentioned.

United States v. Follette, 990 F. Supp. 1172 (D. Neb. 1998). A previously administered MMPI was used as evidence of the defendant's diminished capacity in a motion to depart from sentencing guidelines.

United States v. Peterson, 25 F. Supp. 2d 1021 (D. Neb. 1998). A defendant who pled guilty to receiving child pornography through his computer unsuccessfully sought sentence departure partly due to an earlier MMPI–2.

United States v. Shasky, 939 F. Supp. 695 (D. Neb. 1996). The MMPI was required as a prerequisite to admission to the University of Minnesota Medical School program for treatment of sex offenders.

United States v. McMurray, 833 F. Supp. 1454 (D. Neb. 1993). The MMPI administered by a court-appointed psychiatrist found objective evidence that warranted downward departure of the sentencing guidelines for a conspiracy to distribute cocaine conviction.

District of New Jersey

LaCorte v. Bowen, 678 F. Supp. 80 (D.N.J. 1988). The MMPI was one of tests given to the plaintiff at a therapeutic center.

McKenna v. Fargo, 451 F. Supp. 1355 (D.N.J. 1978). There was discussion of a constitutional challenge to psychological testing.

District of New Mexico

United States v. Dennison, 652 F. Supp. 211 (D.N.M. 1986). The MMPI was one of the tests used in evaluation of the defendant.

Eastern District of New York

United States v. Nelson, 921 F. Supp. 105 (E.D.N.Y. 1996). The MMPI–2 was given to a juvenile defendant before the case was transferred to try the defendant as an adult.

Southern District of New York

United States v. Dupree, 339 F. Supp. 2d 534 (S.D.N.Y. 2004). The court refused to allow the defendant to invoke the belief that she was guided by God as an affirmative defense. The MMPI–2 was among the tests given.

United States v. Doe No. 3, 113 F. Supp. 2d 604 (S.D.N.Y. 2000). A minor defendant was transferred to stand trial as an adult in a murder case. The MMPI–2 results revealed an angry, defensive, and anxious person.

United States v. Doe, 74 F. Supp. 2d 310 (S.D.N.Y. 1999). A juvenile was transferred to adult jurisdiction because rehabilitation was deemed unlikely. MMPI testing was part of the evidence.

Batista v. Charter, 972 F. Supp. 211 (S.D.N.Y. 1997). The MMPI was quoted as being useful in establishing the existence of a mental disorder because the process of taking the test requires concentration, persistence, and pace.

Bartlett v. New York State Bd. of Law Examiners, 970 F. Supp. 1094 (S.D.N.Y. 1997). The MMPI was administered to the claimant asking for an extended time to take the state bar exam as a result of a learning disability.

Longin by Longin v. Kelly, 875 F. Supp. 196 (S.D.N.Y. 1995). The plaintiff's section 1983 claim failed where an off-duty defendant corrections officer shot the plaintiff during an altercation in a neighborhood park. The defendant's preemployment screening of eligible candidates included the MMPI. The doctor said no testing system can reliably predict the likelihood that an eligible candidate will use deadly force inappropriately while on or off duty.

Guardsmark, Inc. v. Pinkerton's, Inc., 739 F. Supp. 173 (S.D.N.Y. 1990). Advertising use of the MMPI in evaluating security personnel sparked a suit of false advertising and unfair competition.

Eastern District of North Carolina

Edwards v. Bowen, 672 F. Supp. 230 (E.D.N.C. 1987). The MMPI was one of the tests used in evaluation of the plaintiff.

Western District of North Carolina

United States v. Mason, 935 F. Supp. 745 (W.D.N.C. 1996). A comparison of MMPI profile results was used for retrospective determination of the defendant's competency during the first phase of trial.

District of North Dakota

United States v. Belgarde, 285 F. Supp. 2d 1080 (D.N.D. 2003). The defendant was found competent to stand trial. The testing included the MMPI–2.

Southern District of Ohio

Madden v. Commissioner of Social Security, 184 F. Supp. 2d 700 (S.D. Ohio 2001). Social Security Insurance benefits were denied. The MMPI results were found to be invalid.

DePew v. Anderson, 104 F. Supp. 2d 879 (S.D. Ohio 2000). The court ruled that there had been no ineffective assistance of counsel, even though the psychologist had erroneously scored the MMPI.

Henderson v. Collins, 101 F. Supp. 2d 866 (S.D. Ohio 1999). The MMPI was discussed.

Isaac v. Sullivan, 782 F. Supp. 1215 (S.D. Ohio 1992). The MMPI scores suggested somatic concerns that a doctor interpreted as indicating a personality disorder.

Tourlakis v. Morris, 738 F. Supp. 1128 (S.D. Ohio 1990). The defendant proffered testimony of a doctor who was prepared to testify that the MMPI scores showed a profile of battered woman's syndrome.

Northern District of Ohio

Lingo v. Secretary of Health and Human Services, 658 F. Supp. 345 (N.D. Ohio 1986). The MMPI was used in the evaluation of the plaintiff.

Northern District of Ohio, Eastern Division

Mason v. Mitchell, 95 F. Supp. 2d 744 (N.D. Ohio 2000). The MMPI was mentioned in denial of a habeas corpus request.

Burns v. Republic Sav. Bank, 25 F. Supp. 2d 809 (N.D. Ohio 1998). In a gender discrimination lawsuit, both the plaintiff and defense experts administered the MMPI to the plaintiff; however, there were conflicting results and difficulties with actual scoring of the tests.

Palmer v. Sullivan, 770 F. Supp. 380 (N.D. Ohio 1991). The MMPI was used in the evaluation of the claimant. There was no evidence of malingering.

Western District of Oklahoma

United States v. Barnes, 551 F. Supp. 22 (W.D. Okla. 1982). The MMPI was one of the tests used to evaluate the defendant.

Northern District of Oklahoma

Tolbert v. Apfel, 106 F. Supp. 2d 1217 (N.D. Okla. 2000). A denial of benefits was sustained. The MMPI–2 results showed depression.

District of Oregon

Snow v. Hill, 2004 WL 1201269 (D. Or. 2004). The MMPI–2 indicated a fake-good profile. The release date of a convicted sex offender was deferred.

Strauss v. Apfel, 45 F. Supp. 2d 1043 (D. Or. 1999). The MMPI was used in denial of benefits.

Pell v. Apfel, 990 F. Supp. 1259 (D. Or. 1998). The MMPI was given to the claimant, who challenged the denial of application for Social Security Insurance benefits.

Bergstad v. Commissioner of Social Security Admin., 967 F. Supp. 1195 (D. Or. 1997). In a Social Security Insurance benefits case, MMPI–2 findings were discounted by a doctor because the claimant's score on the validity scale indicated a "marked tendency to endorse items suggestive of severe personal problems."

Stark v. Shalala, 886 F. Supp. 565 (D. Or. 1995). A denial of Social Security Insurance and disability benefits was reversed because the MMPI supported disability.

Middle District of Pennsylvania

Michael v. Horn, 2004 WL 438678 (M.D. Pa. 2004). A prisoner sentenced to death was found competent to waive collateral challenge to his conviction and sentence. The MMPI–2 results showed a "normal" personality profile.

Siegel v. Abbottstown Borough, 2004 WL 230892 (M.D. Pa. 2004). A police officer plaintiff "failed" the MMPI. The report was held not privileged because the plaintiff knew that the results would be disclosed. Nonetheless, results were sealed because the test lacked relevance.

Rosenberry v. Barnhart, 2003 WL 21848190 (M.D. Pa. 2003). The plaintiff appealed denial of disability benefits in part on the court's interpretation that MMPI–2 scores with a high Defensiveness (*K*) scale reflected negatively on credibility. The appellate court held that the test results could be properly used to judge credibility.

Eastern District of Pennsylvania

Demeter v. Buskirk, 2003 WL 22416082 (E.D. Pa. 2003). Prisoners brought an action for violation of constitutional rights based, in part, on a requirement that prisoners "pass" the MMPI before getting a work release. The court held the requirement did not violate due process.

Koschoff v. Henderson, 109 F. Supp. 2d 332 (E.D. Pa. 2000). The MMPI results showed hypersensitivity in an unsuccessful employment discrimination challenge.

United States v. Kosma, 749 F. Supp. 1392 (E.D. Pa. 1990). The defendant was unable to complete the MMPI because of concentration problems.

Western District of Pennsylvania

Gardiner v. Mercyhurst College, 942 F. Supp. 1050 (W.D. Pa. 1995). In an ADA action, results of a first MMPI were deemed invalid by the administering doctor because the patient did not disclose previous psychological problems.

Ross v. Shalala, 865 F. Supp. 286 (W.D. Pa. 1994). The ALJ's determination that the claimant was not disabled was not supported by substantial evidence; the MMPI results suggested a mentally disordered condition.

Commonwealth of Pennsylvania v. Flaherty, 760 F. Supp. 472 (W.D. Pa. 1991). The MMPI–2 was used in selecting police officers; the effectiveness of the MMPI was questioned.

United States v. Slayman, 590 F. Supp. 962 (W.D. Pa. 1984). Two separate MMPI tests were used to evaluate the defendant.

District of Puerto Rico

Kerr-Selgas v. American Airlines, Inc., 977 F. Supp. 100 (D. Puerto Rico 1997). In a sex discrimination case, the plaintiff's doctor administered the MMPI earlier the same day that the defendant's doctor administered the MMPI. Administration of two tests in tandem contaminated the results of both tests.

United States v. R.I.M.A., 963 F. Supp. 1264 (D. Puerto Rico 1997). The MMPI was administered to a juvenile in connection with transfer of the juvenile for trial as an adult on bank robbery charges.

Diaz v. Secretary of Health and Human Services, 791 F. Supp. 905 (D. Puerto Rico 1992). The ALJ erred in denying an application for disability benefits. Psychiatric evaluations that included psychological testing showed evidence of problems, including depression, sleep problems, and motor retardation, which the judge ignored.

District of South Carolina

Alexander S. By and Through Bowers v. Boyd, 876 F. Supp. 773 (D.S.C. 1995). This relates to a study done at the South Carolina Department of Juvenile Justice where the MMPI is given to juveniles shortly before admission and shortly before release. Comparison showed juveniles had more hostility and aggressive tendencies after confinement.

Kay v. Secretary of Health and Human Services, 683 F. Supp. 136 (D.S.C. 1988). The MMPI was one of several tests used in evaluation of the plaintiff.

District of South Dakota

Holmberg v. Bowen, 687 F. Supp. 1370 (D.S.D. 1988). The MMPI was used in evaluation of the plaintiff.

Western District of Tennessee

Sterling v. Velsicol Chemical Corp., 647 F. Supp. 303 (W.D. Tenn. 1988). The MMPI was used to evaluate one man in an extensive personal injury case involving a chemical waste burial site.

Middle District of Tennessee

Williams v. Barnhart, 338 F. Supp. 2d 849 (M.D. Tenn. 2004). The MMPI–2 was administered in a Social Security Insurance case.

Grubbs v. Bradley, 552 F. Supp. 1052 (M.D. Tenn. 1982). The MMPI was one of the tests listed as part of an inmate classification process.

Eastern District of Texas

Vanderbilt v. Lynaugh, 683 F. Supp. 1118 (E.D. Tex. 1988). The MMPI was one of the tests listed as administered to the petitioner.

Northern District of Texas

Knight v. Dretke, 2004 WL 2026809 (N.D. Tex. 2004). An appeal of a death sentence was denied. The MMPI was administered.

Green v. Shalala, 852 F. Supp. 558 (N.D. Tex. 1994). The MMPI was administered to the claimant in denial of a disability benefits claim.

Southern District of Texas

Dowthitt v. Johnson, 180 F. Supp. 2d 832 (S.D. Tex. 2000). The MMPI–2 indicated psychological problems such that the defendant "may not have been able to assist his attorney in his defense." Nonetheless, the claim for habeas corpus relief in the death penalty case was denied.

Ruiz v. Estelle, 503 F. Supp. 1265 (S.D. Tex. 1980). The MMPI was the sole test given to evaluate or diagnose personality abnormalities of the inmates in the Texas Department of Corrections. The court concluded the test was useless for evaluating inmates who read at low levels because the test required sixth-grade reading ability. The court also discussed the lack of qualified personnel to supervise and evaluate diagnostic testing.

Western District of Virginia

Hensley v. Eastman Long-Term Disability Plan, 2002 WL 731765 (W.D. Va. 2002). The plaintiff was denied benefits in an ERISA case. The MMPI–2 was found not useful because the plaintiff was guarded when taking it.

Hughes v. Barnhart, 206 F. Supp. 2d 771 (W.D. Va. 2002). A denial of benefits was vacated. The MMPI–2 results were found invalid.

Brown v. Bowen, 682 F. Supp. 858 (W.D. Va. 1988). The MMPI was used to evaluate the plaintiff. The court reversed where the ALJ discredited evidence of a psychologist who administered the MMPI.

Eastern District of Washington

Molesky v. Walter, 931 F. Supp. 1506 (E.D. Wash. 1996). An inmate brought a section 1983 action against the prison, claiming he was compelled to undergo psychological evaluation (including MMPI testing) in violation of his constitutional rights.

Ware on Behalf of Ware v. Shalala, 902 F. Supp. 1262 (E.D. Wash. 1995). The MMPI was given to a child after Social Security Insurance was denied.

Carr v. Sullivan, 772 F. Supp. 522 (E.D. Wash. 1991). MMPI was used to evaluate a claimant.

Northern District of West Virginia

Dubois v. Alderson-Broaddus College, Inc., 950 F. Supp. 754 (N.D. W. Va. 1997). A learning-disabled student sued under the ADA for failure to make reasonable accommodations. The plaintiff refused to take the MMPI, which was a preapproved test, and failed to establish a specific learning disability.

Southern District of West Virginia

Black v. Rhone-Poulenc, Inc., 19 F. Supp. 2d 592 (S.D. W. Va. 1998). In footnote 7, the MMPI is described as one of the tests the plaintiffs took in an effort to show emotional effects of a fire and exposure to chemicals.

Gentry v. Ashland Oil, Inc., 938 F. Supp. 349 (S.D. W. Va. 1996). The MMPI was given to a former employee, who sued to recover disability benefits.

United States v. Kokoski, 865 F. Supp. 325 (S.D. W. Va. 1994). The defendant entered a guilty plea, then requested a competency hearing. MMPI results were extremely elevated, beyond psychotic. Second MMPI results were even more disturbing. The results were deemed so extreme that the defendant was malingering or exaggerating.

Eastern District of Wisconsin

Lechner v. Barnhart, 321 F. Supp. 2d 1015 (E.D. Wis. 2004). An application for disability was denied. The MMPI–2 was administered verbally because of deficient reading ability.

Worzalla v. Barnhart, 311 F. Supp. 2d 782 (E.D. Wis. 2004). A denial of disability was reversed. The MMPI–2 results suggested "poor tolerance for stress and pressure, a poor self-concept and self-dissatisfaction in a personality with deteriorated defenses." The court criticized the government's expert because he concluded that the MMPI profile may have been invalid "likely due to his attempt to exaggerate his symptoms" but used the same test result to substantiate a diagnosis.

Western District of Wisconsin

Corbecky v. Heckler, 588 F. Supp. 882 (W.D. Wis. 1984). The MMPI was used in evaluation of the plaintiff.

District of Wyoming

Poindexter v. Bowen, 685 F. Supp. 1545 (D. Wyo. 1988). The MMPI was one of the tests used to evaluate the claimant, as ordered by the ALJ.

District of Columbia

United States v. Klat, 213 F.3d 697 (D.C. Cir. 2000). A competency finding was affirmed. The defendant refused to take the MMPI.

United States v. Klat, 59 F. Supp. 2d 47 (D.C. Cir. 1999). The defendant had the right to counsel at a competency hearing despite having refused to take the MMPI.

Does I–IV v. District of Columbia, 962 F. Supp. 202 (D.C. Cir. 1997). The MMPI–2 was administered to all applicants. Plaintiff applicants were denied employment as firefighters on mental disqualification grounds.

Poulin v. Bowen, 817 F.2d 865 (D.C. Cir. 1987). The French version of the MMPI was used early in the evaluation of the plaintiff and mentioned in footnote 79 of the case.

United States v. Byers, 740 F.2d 1104 (D.C. Cir. 1984). The MMPI was one of several tests used to examine the defendant. The MMPI was mentioned in footnote 20 of the dissent.

United States v. Alexander, 471 F.2d 923 (D.C. Cir. 1973). The MMPI was one of the tests used to evaluate the defendant. The case contains a short discussion of testimony.

Second Circuit

Daley v. Koch, 892 F.2d 212 (2d Cir. 1989). The MMPI was one of the tests used in the psychological evaluation of a police officer candidate.

Berry v. Schweiker, 675 F.2d 464 (2d Cir. 1982). The MMPI was used as part of an examination of the appellant.

Third Circuit

Rompilla v. Horn, 355 F.3d 233 (3d Cir. Pa. 2004). The court granted a writ of habeas corpus on a death sentence because of the ineffective assistance of counsel based, in part, on the counsel's not obtaining and integrating mitigating information, including psychological testing.

Skretvedt v. E.I. DuPont de Nemours and Co., 268 F.3d 167 (3d Cir. Del. 2001). The case reversed a summary judgment for an employer on a claim that the plaintiff had been denied disability benefits. Psychological testimony and testing showed a "prominent anxiety disorder" that began in a work situation.

Zettlemoyer v. Fulcomer, 923 F.2d 284 (3d Cir. 1991). The MMPI was one of several tests used to evaluate the defendant.

Fourth Circuit

Beaver v. Thompson, 93 F.3d 1186 (4th Cir. 1996). The MMPI was performed on a defendant accused of shooting a state trooper. Results suggested that the defendant would explode with violent behavior.

Murphy v. Bowen, 810 F.2d 433 (4th Cir. 1987). In an action challenging denial of Social Security disability benefits, results of two psychological examinations conflicted. The MMPI was administered orally in the first examination because the individual could not read. In a second psychological assessment, the evaluator "administered a Rorschach test rather than the MMPI." The second evaluator maintained that the MMPI was only 65% effective when given orally.

Gross v. Heckler, 785 F.2d 1163 (4th Cir. 1986). The MMPI was mentioned in the case and used to evaluate the claimant.

United States v. Burgess, 691 F.2d 1146 (4th Cir. 1982). The MMPI was one of the tests used to evaluate the defendant and was mentioned in footnote 18.

Jacobs v. United States, 350 F.2d 571 (4th Cir. 1965). The MMPI was used to evaluate the defendant on entering a correctional facility. The doctor opined that the defendant was feigning illness.

Fifth Circuit

Styron v. Johnson, 262 F.3d 438 (5th Cir. Tex. 2001). A death sentence was affirmed. The MMPI results suggested hostility and aggression.

Lockett v. Anderson, 230 F.3d 695 (5th Cir. Miss. 2000). A death sentence was reversed because the counsel performed inadequate investigation, including failure to follow up or understand why the psychologist considered the MMPI results invalid.

Guilbeau v. W.W. Henry Co., 85 F.3d 1149 (5th Cir. 1996). The MMPI administered to a plaintiff claiming chronic toxic encephalopathy allegedly caused by an adhesive used by the defendant revealed the plaintiff was a somaticizer and had elevated hypochondriac scales.

United States v. Dockins, 986 F.2d 888 (5th Cir. 1993). The defendant was suspected of faking or exaggerating symptoms to appear more disturbed at the competency hearing. The MMPI was used because of two safeguards to detect faking.

United States v. Doe, 871 F.2d 1248 (5th Cir. 1989). The defendant claimed that the MMPI tests results were of questionable validity. The court upheld use of the results.

Harrell v. Bowen, 862 F.2d 471 (5th Cir. 1988). The MMPI was mentioned in the case.

Lowenfield v. Butler, 843 F.2d 183 (5th Cir. 1988). The MMPI was used to evaluate the defendant, who was denied a stay of execution.

Dawsey v. Olin Corp., 782 F.2d 1254 (5th Cir. 1986). The MMPI was used in evaluation of the plaintiff. The clinical interview did not bear out results of the MMPI.

Rumbaugh v. Procunier, 753 F.2d 395 (5th Cir. 1985). Validity of the MMPI test results were questioned because of the extremity of the defendant's score. The MMPI was mentioned in the dissent.

Gray v. Lucas, 677 F.2d 1086 (5th Cir. 1982). MMPI results were used to support the theory of mental disturbance in the defendant. The MMPI was mentioned in the case.

United States v. Harper, 450 F.2d 1032 (5th Cir. 1971). The MMPI was used to evaluate the defendant.

Sixth Circuit

Thompson v. Bell, 373 F.3d 688 (6th Cir. Tenn. 2004), 315 F.3d 566 (6th Cir. Tenn. 2003). MMPI test results used in a death penalty phase of a trial reflected malingering "in the mental illness direction." Later treatment, which documented psychotic features, ruled out malingering. The record was supplemented with subsequent treatment information and the execution was stayed pending further hearing.

McDonald v. Western-Southern Life Ins. Co., 347 F.3d 161 (6th Cir. Ohio 2003). The court held that disability benefits were wrongfully stopped based on exams that included the MMPI–2.

Smith v. Mitchell, 348 F.3d 177 (6th Cir. 2003). A writ of habeas corpus was refused. The MMPI was one of many tests given.

United States v. Cockett, 330 F.3d 706 (6th Cir. Mich. 2003). The court affirmed a downward departure from the sentencing guidelines in a criminal tax case in which psychological illness was supported by MMPI–2 results with $F(p)$ scale scores within normal limits.

Gonzales v. National Bd. of Medical Examiners, 225 F.3d 620 (6th Cir. Mich. 2000). The court affirmed denial of injunctive relief by a medical student asking for accommodations in taking a medical examination based on a disability because the applicant was not disabled within the definitions of the ADA. The MMPI was one of the tests administered.

Davis v. Secretary of Health and Human Services, 915 F.2d 186 (6th Cir. 1990). The MMPI was used to evaluate the claimant.

Young v. Secretary of Health and Human Services, 925 F.2d 146 (6th Cir. 1990). The MMPI was one of the tests used to evaluate the claimant.

Atterberry v. Secretary of Health and Human Services, 871 F.2d 567 (6th Cir. 1989). The MMPI was used by the consulting (not treating) physician to evaluate the claimant.

Allen v. Redman, 858 F.2d 1194 (6th Cir. 1988). The MMPI was used as part of an evaluation of the defendant.

Mullen v. Bowen, 800 F.2d 535 (6th Cir. 1986). The MMPI was used in evaluation of the claimant.

Williamson v. Secretary of Health and Human Services, 796 F.2d 146 (6th Cir. 1986). The MMPI was used in evaluation of the claimant, whose doctor believed he was taking the test with a "bad faith effort."

Seventh Circuit

Carradine v. Barnhart, 360 F.3d 751 (7th Cir. Ind. 2004). A denial of Social Security Insurance benefits based on pain disability was reversed because the ALJ based the determination on two errors in reasoning. The first involved testing. He noted that results of the MMPI–2 "did not indicate invalid responses or exaggeration, but did suggest 'somatization.'" The ALJ then reasoned that the MMPI performance "implies she exaggerates the severity of symptoms." The appellate court disagreed: "It (somatization) implies no such thing. It implies merely that the source of Carradine's pain is psychological."

United States v. Rettenberger, 344 F.3d 702 (7th Cir. Ill. 2003). The MMPI test results were consistent with malingering in criminal conviction.

Griffith v. Callahan, 138 F.3d 1150 (7th Cir. 1998). The MMPI used to evaluate the plaintiff showed her to have clear signs of stability, with long-standing problems of anxiety and depression. The ALJ concluded the plaintiff was not disabled and not entitled to Social Security Insurance benefits.

Anderson v. Sullivan, 925 F.2d 220 (7th Cir. 1991). The MMPI was used to evaluate the plaintiff.

Daniels v. Pipefitters Association Local Union No. 597, 945 F.2d 906 (7th Cir. 1991). The plaintiff had to take the MMPI because the union would not send a pro forma letter of recommendation in a racial discrimination case.

United States ex rel. Securities and Exchange Commission v. Billingsley, 766 F.2d 1015 (7th Cir. 1985). The MMPI was used to evaluate the defendant.

United States v. Bohle, 445 F.2d 54 (7th Cir. 1971). The MMPI was used to evaluate the defendant. The discussion concerned admissibility of MMPI results that were given over the telephone.

Eighth Circuit

Ryan v. Clarke, 387 F.3d 785 (8th Cir. Neb. 2004). In a case involving the death penalty, experts said that the MMPI, "a respected objective psychological test . . . showed that while Ryan had an odd personality, he had no mental illness that would cause him to be incompetent." The judge found defense experts not credible and the MMPI test results and state experts credible.

Osborne v. Barnhart, 316 F.3d 809 (8th Cir. Mo. 2003). The MMPI was one of several tests given in denial of Social Security Insurance benefits.

Haley v. Massanari, 258 F.3d 742 (8th Cir. Ark. 2001). A denial of disability benefits was affirmed. The MMPI was mentioned.

Muncy v. Apfel, 247 F.3d 728 (8th Cir. Mo. 2001). The case was remanded on insufficient evidence of mental status to discontinue Social Security Insurance benefits. The MMPI was mentioned.

Morstad v. Dep't of Corrections and Rehabilitation, 147 F.3d 741 (8th Cir. 1998). The MMPI–2 was given as part of a medical examination of a defendant convicted of gross sexual imposition against his 9-year-old daughter.

Branscomb v. Norris, 47 F.3d 258 (8th Cir. 1995). The MMPI results of a defendant were considered invalid by state evaluators because the defendant likely could not read the questions and answered them randomly.

McAlinney v. Marion Merrell Dow, Inc., 992 F.2d 839 (8th Cir. 1993). In a national origin employment discrimination claim by the plaintiff, the defendant cross-examined the plaintiff concerning the results of his MMPI.

Pratt v. Sullivan, 956 F.2d 830 (8th Cir. 1992). The plaintiff took the MMPI three different times. The results showed progressive intensification of symptoms over time.

Kenley v. Armontrout, 937 F.2d 1298 (8th Cir. 1991). The MMPI was used to evaluate the defendant.

Lubinski v. Sullivan, 952 F.2d 214 (8th Cir. 1991). The MMPI was used to evaluate the claimant.

Coffin v. Sullivan, 895 F.2d 1206 (8th Cir. 1990). The MMPI was used to evaluate the claimant.

Applied Innovations, Inc. v. Regents of the University of Minnesota, 876 F.2d 626 (8th Cir. 1989). The university was sued for copyright infringement against the company for exclusive ownership of the MMPI. The case contains an extensive discussion, history, and description of the MMPI.

Bryant v. Bowen, 882 F.2d 1331 (8th Cir. 1989). The MMPI was one evaluation used to test the claimant.

Buck v. Bowen, 885 F.2d 451 (8th Cir. 1989). The MMPI was one of many tests used to evaluate the claimant.

Freels v. United States Railroad Retirement Board, 879 F.2d 335 (8th Cir. 1989). The MMPI was used in evaluating the claimant.

United States v. Barta, 888 F.2d 1220 (8th Cir. 1989). The MMPI was used to evaluate the defendant.

Wheeler v. Sullivan, 888 F.2d 1233 (8th Cir. 1989). The MMPI profile was rendered invalid because the claimant "endorsed most test items in a pathological direction."

Bland v. Bowen, 861 F.2d 533 (8th Cir. 1988). The MMPI was used to evaluate the claimant.

Rush v. Secretary of Health and Human Services, 738 F.2d 909 (8th Cir. 1984). The MMPI was used to evaluate the claimant.

McDonald v. Schweiker, 698 F.2d 361 (8th Cir. 1983). The MMPI was used to evaluate the claimant.

Houghton v. McDonnell Douglas Corp., 627 F.2d 858 (8th Cir. 1980). The MMPI was mentioned as one of the tests used by the Mayo Clinic for pilots. The MMPI was mentioned in footnote 8.

Doe v. Department of Transportation, Federal Aviation Administration, 412 F.2d 674 (8th Cir. 1969). The MMPI was used to evaluate the applicant.

Marion v. Gardner, 359 F.2d 175 (8th Cir. 1966). The MMPI was used to evaluate the ward of a petitioner in request for Social Security benefits.

Ninth Circuit

Davis v. Woodford, 384 F.3d 982, 333 F.3d 982 (9th Cir. Cal. 2003). The death sentence was affirmed. The MMPI was one of the tests given.

Jensen v. Lane County, 222 F.3d 570 (9th Cir. Or. 2000). The MMPI was mentioned in a civil action against county officials and medical providers.

Kearney v. Standard Ins. Co., 175 F.3d 1084 (9th Cir. Cal. 1999). The appellate court reinstated disability benefits that had been denied in part based on "normal" MMPI test results.

Wallace v. Stewart, 184 F.3d 1112 (9th Cir. Ariz. 1999). The death penalty was reversed because the mental health examiner was not given mitigating information, such as MMPI results and the defendant's difficult family history.

Smith v. Apfel, 1998 WL 833621 (9th Cir. 1998). MMPI scores revealed that the appellant, who was denied disability benefits, might have been faking her impairment.

United States v. Rahm, 993 F.2d 1405 (9th Cir. 1993). The defendant who claimed to have no knowledge that the U.S. currency she tried to use was counterfeit was given the MMPI.

Mathis v. Pacific Gas and Electric Co., 891 F.2d 1429 (9th Cir. 1989). Two plaintiffs were denied access to a nuclear plant because they "failed" the MMPI.

Fife v. Heckler, 767 F.2d 1427 (9th Cir. 1985). The MMPI was used to evaluate the claimant.

Gallant v. Heckler, 753 F.2d 1450 (9th Cir. 1984). The MMPI was mentioned in dissent as to the mental state of the claimant.

United States v. Harris, 534 F.2d 1371 (9th Cir. 1976). The MMPI was used to evaluate the key prosecution witness.

Tenth Circuit

Humphreys v. Gibson, 261 F.3d 1016 (10th Cir. Okla. 2001). A death sentence was affirmed despite testimony that MMPI results had changed over several years.

United States v. Benally, 215 F.3d 1068 (10th Cir. N.M. 2000). A downward sentencing departure based on psychological mitigation was reversed. The MMPI–2 results indicated the defendant "may be rather amoral . . . and unpredicatable."

Carter v. Chater, 73 F.3d 1019 (10th Cir. 1996). The MMPI was used to evaluate the claimant in a Social Security Insurance benefits case in which the plaintiff complained of "job stress." Test results confirmed depression.

Winfrey v. Chater, 92 F.3d 1017 (10th Cir. 1996). The MMPI–2 was used to evaluate the plaintiff to determine mental status and impairment.

Miles v. Dorsey, 61 F.3d 1459 (10th Cir. 1995). An MMPI given to a criminal defendant indicated intentional malingering in an evaluation to determine mental competency to stand trial.

United States v. Denny-Shaffer, 2 F.3d 999 (10th Cir. 1993). Footnote 8 noted that in some multiple personality disorder victims, alters can be so different that alters score differently on tests such as the MMPI.

Casias v. Secretary of Health and Human Services, 933 F.2d 799 (10th Cir. 1991). The MMPI was mentioned in the case and used to evaluate the claimant.

Hays v. Murphy, 663 F.2d 1004 (10th Cir. 1981). The MMPI was mentioned in footnote 14 as a standard psychological test.

Eleventh Circuit

Hardwick v. Crosby, 320 F.3d 1127 (11th Cir. Fla. 2003). Habeas corpus relief was granted in a death penalty case because the counsel provided inadequate mitigation, which included results of MMPI testing.

Brownlee v. Haley, 306 F.3d 1043 (11th Cir. Ala. 2002). The court found ineffective assistance of counsel in a capital case. The MMPI was administered.

Grayson v. Thompson, 257 F.3d 1194 (11th Cir. Ala. 2001). The MMPI results showed no evidence of a major mental illness in a death penalty appeal.

Bryan v. Singletary, 140 F.3d 1354 (11th Cir. 1998). Two MMPI exams given to a convicted murderer revealed invalid profiles, suggesting the defendant was faking bad. A third MMPI showed some evidence of an organic brain syndrome, but it did not establish that the defendant had the inability to distinguish right from wrong. Because of the test results, the defense counsel's decision not to call a mental health expert did not rise to the level of ineffective counsel.

Freeman v. Continental Ins. Co., 996 F.2d 1116 (11th Cir. 1993). The plaintiff suffered from post-concussion syndrome resulting from an accident. The MMPI given to the plaintiff indicated he had longstanding hypochondriac tendencies.

Card v. Singletary, 963 F.2d 1440 (11th Cir. 1992). The defendant's capital murder conviction had been affirmed by the Florida supreme court, and he then sought to be released through a federal habeas corpus writ. The court held that neither the MMPI results suggesting psychotic disturbance nor other evaluation data were sufficient to set aside the conviction.

United States v. Manley, 893 F.2d 1221 (11th Cir. 1990). The MMPI was used in one evaluation of the defendant.

Smith v. Zant, 855 F.2d 712 (11th Cir. 1988). The MMPI was used to evaluate the defendant in a case that was vacated on a grant of rehearing.

Messer v. Kemp, 831 F.2d 946 (11th Cir. 1987). The MMPI was one of several tests used to evaluate the defendant. The MMPI was mentioned in footnote 10.

MacGregor v. Bowen, 786 F.2d 1050 (11th Cir. 1986). The MMPI was used to evaluate the claimant.

Moon v. Bowen, 794 F.2d 1499 (11th Cir. 1986). The MMPI was used to evaluate the claimant.

Popp v. Heckler, 779 F.2d 1497 (11th Cir. 1986). The MMPI scores were rendered invalid because the claimant attempted to appear in an unfavorable light.

United States v. Lindstrom, 698 F.2d 1154 (11th Cir. 1983). The MMPI was used to evaluate the witness in the case.

Military Court

United States v. Huberty, 50 M.J. 704 (A.F. Ct. Crim. App. 2000). The judge in a military prosecution of dishonorable indecent exposure properly precluded a psychologist from testifying that exhibitionists produce consistent MMPI–2 results, that the defendant did not produce such results, and that the defendant was, therefore, not an exhibitionist. The judge reasoned that the expert's theory did not have widespread support.

Y.R. v. West, 11 Vet. App. 393 (Vet. App. 1998). The appellant claimed that she was raped during military service 20 years earlier. As a result of the rape she consistently complained of PTSD. In 1994, MMPI–2 results suggested chronic symptomology of PTSD. As a result, the ALJ's denial of benefits was vacated.

State Cases Involving the MMPI

This appendix lists state appellate decisions that mention the MMPI. The citations are listed in reverse chronological order, with the most recent case presented first. Each citation is accompanied by a brief statement showing the relation of the MMPI to the case. This brief statement is not intended to provide a complete description of the case or of issues unrelated to the MMPI. All significant issues raised in any case should be examined through review of the full case opinions and subsequent appellate opinions that affirm or reject the legal precedent set out in the original case.

Alabama

C.J.L. v. M.W.B., 879 So.2d 1169 (Ala. Civ. App. 2003). Sole custody was awarded to a father despite allegations of abuse. The parties disagreed about the value of the MMPI test based on a scaled sore of 79 on the Infrequency Scale (*F* scale).

Lewis v. State, 2003 WL 21246584 (Ala. Crim. App. 2003). A death sentence was affirmed. The MMPI was found invalid but suggested faking bad.

State Employees Injury Compensation Trust Fund v. Shade, 869 So.2d 1136 (Ala. Civ. App. 2003). The MMPI–2 was one of several tests that suggested somatization and depression.

Wood v. State, 2003 WL 1949784 (Ala. Crim. App. 2003). A death sentence was affirmed. Testimony about the MMPI from a nonpsychologist was allowed.

Smith v. Smith, 836 So.2d 893 (Ala. Civ. App. 2002). In an appeal of a divorce decree, the MMPI was administered.

Ex parte Loggins, 771 So.2d 1093 (Ala. 2000). Capital murder convictions were affirmed. Two MMPIs indicated schizophrenia and antisocial behavior.

Hammonds v. State, 777 So.2d 750 (Ala. Crim. App. 1999). The MMPI suggested asocial and antisocial behavior. Conviction and the death sentence were affirmed.

K.A.C. v. Jefferson County DHR, 744 So.2d 938 (Ala. Civ. App. 1999). The MMPI results indicated "normal" in termination of parental rights.

Perkins v. State, 808 So.2d 1041 (Ala. Crim. App. 1999). A kidnapping and murder death sentence was affirmed. The MMPI was among tests mentioned.

R.D. v. State, 706 So.2d 770 (Ala. Crim. App. 1997). The MMPI administered to a defendant convicted of sexual abuse showed that the defendant did not manifest the symptoms of a sexual abuser. The trial court's decision to exclude test results was affirmed despite testimony that the test was valid and reliable.

Brown v. State, 686 So.2d 385 (Ala. Crim. App. 1995). In a murder case, the prosecution granted the defense expert's computerized MMPI results that were relied on in the insanity defense.

Hogan v. State, 663 So.2d 1017 (Ala. Crim. App. 1994). The MMPI was administered to a juvenile defendant convicted of murder.

Clark v. Blackwell, 624 So.2d 610 (Ala. Civ. App. 1993). The MMPI was administered to a father accused of locking his children out of his house. A doctor testified that the MMPI–2 was a preferred test for those in clinical practice.

Ex parte Henderson, 616 So.2d 348 (Ala. 1992). The death sentence was overturned where the MMPI and other tests showed a low level of intelligence. Because the defendant took tests with no glasses while handcuffed, mitigating circumstances should have been allowed into evidence.

C.M.B. v. State, 594 So.2d 695 (Ala. Crim. App. 1991). The MMPI results in "lower normal range" considered in effective waiver of rights by the 15-year-old defendant.

D.J. v. State Dep't of Human Resources, 578 So.2d 1351 (Ala. Civ. App. 1991). MMPI results were used as evidence of a mother's mental state.

Prince v. State, 584 So.2d 889 (Ala. Crim. App. 1991). The MMPI results referred to in testimony of a psychologist were about the mental capability of the defendant.

Brannon and the B.F. Goodrich Company v. Sharp, 554 So.2d 951 (Ala. 1989). The MMPI was used to evaluate the plaintiff. Test validity was not an issue.

Carter v. Reid, 540 So.2d 57 (Ala. 1989). The MMPI was used to evaluate the plaintiff.

Ex Parte Brown, 540 So.2d 740 (Ala. 1989). The MMPI was one of three tests used to evaluate the defendant's ability to stand trial as an adult.

McGahee v. State, 554 So.2d 454 (Ala. Crim. App. 1989). An expert was allowed to rebut the allegation that the MMPI was defective.

Wesley v. State, 575 So.2d 108 (Ala. Crim. App. 1989). Testimony of MMPI results was limited to the administering doctor.

Ford v. State, 515 So.2d 34 (Ala. Crim. App. 1986). The court allowed testimony that results of the MMPI could have been affected by the defendant's malingering or faking bad.

McCrory v. State, 505 So.2d 1272 (Ala. Crim. App. 1986). The MMPI taken by the victim and the defendant was held to be outside the scope of the case.

Musgrove v. State, 519 So.2d 565 (Ala. Crim. App. 1986). The MMPI was used in the testimony of a doctor to disprove claims of the defendant's insanity.

Bailey v. Gold Kist, Inc., 482 So.2d 1224 (Ala. Civ. App. 1985). A doctor was allowed to use results of an MMPI administered by another psychologist to testify as to the plaintiff's behavioral patterns.

Bailey v. State, 421 So.2d 1364 (Ala. Crim. App. 1982). The witness was found to be not qualified as an expert and thus not allowed to testify to results of the MMPI.

Smith v. State, 411 So.2d 839 (Ala. Crim. App. 1981). A psychologist found no major disorder at the time of testing, but testified that the defendant was suffering from psychosis during the commission of the crime.

Abex Corporation v. Coleman, 386 So.2d 1160 (Ala. Civ. App. 1980). The MMPI was one of three tests used to support the diagnosis of the plaintiff's psychological injuries.

Kyzer v. State, 399 So.2d 317 (Ala. Crim. App. 1979). Evidence of MMPI results was presented by the defense in the mitigation phase of a death penalty action.

Luster v. State, 221 So.2d 695 (Ala. Ct. App. 1969). Undisputed expert testimony, including MMPI data suggesting psychotic pathology, was found to be insufficient evidence of insanity to disturb the jury's finding.

Alaska

In re Reinstatement of Wiederholt, 89 P.3d 771 (Alaska 2004). Request for reinstatement to practice law was denied. The MMPI results reflected hostility.

In re Adoption of L.E.K.M., 70 P.3d 1087 (Alaska 2003). Granting legal and physical custody of children to family friends instead of grandparents was upheld. The MMPI was mentioned.

Gustafson v. State, 854 P.2d 751 (Alaska Ct. App. 1993). The MMPI–2 was administered to a defendant convicted of second-degree murder.

Adamson v. University of Alaska, 819 P.2d 886 (Alaska 1991). The MMPI was mentioned in evaluation of the plaintiff.

Wade v. Anchorage School District, 741 P.2d 634 (Alaska 1987). The MMPI was used to diagnose the patient. Its validity was not questioned.

Martin v. State, 664 P.2d 612 (Alaska Ct. App. 1983). Defense of diminished capacity largely centered on results of an MMPI test.

Alto v. State, 565 P.2d 492 (Alaska 1977). MMPI results consistent with psychosis supported reversing a determination of sanity.

Arizona

State ex rel. Romley v. Gaines, 67 P.3d 734 (Ariz. App. Div. 1st 2003). An appellate court reversed the trial court's suppression of statements made during a sex offender diagnosis and treatment that included the MMPI.

State v. Pandeli, 26 P.3d 1136 (Ariz. 2001). A death sentence was affirmed. The MMPI results suggested psychotic symptoms.

State v. Hoskins, 14 P.3d 997 (Ariz. 2000). Murder conviction and death sentences were affirmed. The MMPI indicated that the defendant was immature, passive, and dependent.

State v. Kayer, 194 Ariz. 423 (1999). The MMPI "found some unusual results." Murder conviction and death sentence were affirmed.

State v. Winters, 160 Ariz. 143, 771 P.2d 468 (1989). The MMPI results had no merit in the case and its use was not probative.

State v. McMurtry III, 151 Ariz. 105, 726 P.2d 202 (1986). The MMPI test results were found relevant to the defendant's habitual criminalism and sanity.

Makinson v. Industrial Commission of Arizona, 134 Ariz. 246, 655 P.2d 366 (1982). A psychiatrist based his diagnosis of the plaintiff on the MMPI and two personal visits.

Arkansas

Engram v. State, 2004 WL 2904678 (Ark. 2004). Conviction and death sentence were affirmed. Several tests were administered.

Hunt v. Perry, 2004 WL 907578 (Ark. 2004). MMPI examinations were given in a grandparents' visitation case.

Wren v. Saunders Plumbing Supply, 117 S.W.3d 657 (Ark. App. 2003). Denial of worker's compensation benefits was affirmed. The MMPI was found invalid because the applicant's wife helped fill it out.

Patterson v. Arkansas Dep't of Health, 33 S.W.3d 151 (Ark. 2000). Disability benefits were allowed through the "odd-lot doctrine." The MMPI profile was found to be valid and honest.

Akers v. Acco, Inc., 1999 Arkansas Workers' Compensation Commission 341 (Ark. 1999). The MMPI–2 was found to be valid and indicated overreported symptoms. The claimant failed to prove permanent total disability but did prove the need for some benefits.

Baker v. Pulaski County Special School Dist., 1998 WL 746229 (Ark. Ct. App. 1998). One reason for denial of disability benefits was refusal of the appellant to submit to MMPI testing, claiming she had a seventh-grade education and could not read well enough to take the test.

Miller v. State, 942 S.W.2d 825 (Ark. 1997). A defendant convicted of murder used a state doctor to administer the MMPI–2 and retained his own experts to double-check the results. The court denied a motion to continue to allow the defendant to retain additional experts.

Mitchell v. State, 913 S.W.2d 264 (Ark. 1996). A first-degree murder conviction was affirmed in which the MMPI administered to the defendant claiming demonic possession indicated the defendant's fitness to stand trial.

CDI Contractors v. McHale, 848 S.W.2d 941 (Ark. App. 1993). An employer unsuccessfully challenged a temporary total disability award. The MMPI–2 results were deemed invalid based on exaggeration of answers.

Willmon v. Allen Canning Co., 828 S.W.2d 868 (Ark. Ct. App. 1992). The appellate court reversed a decision that had denied benefits to the employee. MMPI results that showed an "abnormal profile" helped convince the court that physical trauma was prolonged by a psychological conflict and was compensable.

Freemen v. City of DeWitt, 787 S.W.2d 658 (Ark. 1990). The MMPI was used by a psychiatrist in recommendations for police officer candidates. The validity of the MMPI was not in question.

Wade v. Mr. C. Cavenaugh's and Cigna Ins. Co., 768 S.W.2d 521 (Ark. 1989). The MMPI was mentioned.

Garibaldi v. Deitz, 752 S.W.2d 771 (Ark. 1988). The MMPI results were noted in the dissenting opinion as one of the tests used to evaluate the plaintiff.

Wade v. Mr. C. Cavenaugh's and Cigna Ins. Co., 756 S.W.2d 923 (Ark. Ct. App. 1988). The MMPI results suggested a "normal profile."

Boyd v. General Industries and Aetna Life & Casualty, 733 S.W.2d 750 (Ark. Ct. App. 1987). The MMPI was recognized as an "objective" test. Results were not "negative."

Allen v. State, 488 S.W.2d 712 (Ark. 1973). The MMPI was one of several tests administered in a criminal forensic setting.

California

People v. Carter, 70 P.3d 981 (Cal. 2003). A death sentence was affirmed. The MMPI results suggested hypomania but no "significant mental disorder."

People v. Therrian, 113 Cal. App. 4th 609 (Cal. App. 3d Dist. 2003). Recommitment of a sexual offender was affirmed. No test, including the MMPI, gives infallible truth on risk of re-offending.

People v. Bolden, 58 P.3d 931 (Cal. 2002). A death sentence was affirmed. The MMPI revealed no major mental disorder.

People v. Lucero, 3 P.3d 248 (Cal. 2000). A death sentence was affirmed after remand. The MMPI reflected "fake" PTSD symptoms.

People v. Dacayana, 91 Cal. Rptr. 2d 121, *rev. granted* (Cal. App. 2d Dist. 1999). The MMPI–2 was used in prosecution under Sexually Violent Predators Act.

Sprague v. City of Los Angeles, 78 Cal. Rptr. 2d 525 (Cal. App. 2d Dist. 1998). A police officer was administered a psychological evaluation that included the MMPI–2.

People v. Davis, 896 P.2d 119 (Cal. 1995). The MMPI was administered and the defense's expert was cross-examined on MMPI results.

People v. Kelly, 1 Cal. 4th 495, 3 Cal. Rptr. 2d 677, 822 P.2d 385 (1992). In appeal from judgment of death, the court discussed evidence from the three phases (guilt, sanity, and penalty) of the criminal prosecution. In the sanity phase, the defense presented an expert psychologist who had administered the MMPI and opined that the defendant had a "psychotic-like disturbance."

Gootee v. Lightner, 224 Cal. App. 3d 587, 274 Cal. Rptr. 697 (Cal. App. 4th Dist. 1990). The MMPI was used to evaluate a family in a custody dispute.

In re Rodrigo S., San Francisco Dep't of Social Services v. Joan R., 225 Cal. App. 3d 1179, 276 Cal. Rptr. 183 (Cal. App. 1st Dist. 1990). The MMPI results of the father were used in testimony.

People v. Kelly, 51 Cal. 3d 931, 800 P.2d 516 (1990). The MMPI was used to evaluate the defendant.

People v. Ruiz, 220 Cal. App. 3d 537, 269 Cal. Rptr. 465 (1990). The MMPI and other accepted test results were deemed admissible to show that an individual was not likely to commit a crime. The MMPI was not subject to *Kelly/Frye* test.

People v. Ruiz, 222 Cal. App. 3d 1241, 272 Cal. Rptr. 368 (Cal. App. 1st Dist. 1990). A psychologist may give an opinion about the character of the defendant, based partly on MMPI results, but may not testify that the defendant did not possess characteristics shared by pedophiles, unless the material used was a reliable basis for such an opinion.

People v. Stoll, 49 Cal. 3d 1136, 265 Cal. Rptr. 111, 783 P.2d 698 (1989). The court recognized the validity of the MMPI as evidence of the defendant's good character. There is extensive discussion of the MMPI.

People v. Jackson, 193 Cal. App. 3d 875, 238 Cal. Rptr. 633 (1987). The MMPI was one of several tests scheduled to be given to the defendant. The trial court did not err in allowing time for tests.

People v. John W., 185 Cal. App. 3d 801, 229 Cal. Rptr. 783 (Cal. App. 1st Dist. 1986). The court discusses the test as it relates to determining sexual deviance. The MMPI was found not standardized in regard to a sexually deviant population.

People v. Coleman, 38 Cal. 3d 69, 211 Cal. Rptr. 102, 695 P.2d 189 (1985). Use of the MMPI in forming an opinion as to defendant's past mental state was questioned.

People v. Moore, 166 Cal. App. 3d 540, 211 Cal. Rptr. 856 (Cal. App. 2d Dist. 1985). The defendant attempted to have the MMPI "fixed" to show insanity.

In the Matter of Cheryl H., Dennis H. v. Los Angeles County Dep't of Social Services, 153 Cal. App. 3d 1098, 200 Cal. Rptr. 789 (Cal. App. 2d Dist. 1984). The MMPI was used to evaluate the family.

Ballard v. State Bar of California, 35 Cal. 3d 274, 197 Cal. Rptr. 556, 673 P.2d 226 (1983). MMPI results previously read into evidence were sufficient after the state bar misplaced the original results.

Insurance Company of North America v. Workers' Compensation Appeals Board of the State of California, 122 Cal. App. 3d 905, 176 Cal. Rptr. 365 (1981). The MMPI was used to diagnose an employee.

People v. Nicholas, 112 Cal. App. 3d 249, 169 Cal. Rptr. 497 (Cal. App. 1st Dist. 1980). Gross exaggeration on tests rendered the results invalid. Doctors considered it medically improper to draw any conclusions from the results.

Gay v. Workers' Compensation Appeals Board of the State of California, 96 Cal. App. 3d 555, 158 Cal. Rptr. 137 (1979). The MMPI was used to evaluate the claimant.

People v. Phillips, 90 Cal. App. 3d 356, 153 Cal. Rptr. 359 (1979). The MMPI was one of the tests used to evaluate the defendant/appellant.

People v. Arbuckle, 150 Cal. Rptr. 778, 587 P.2d 220 (1978). The MMPI was one of several tests administered to the defendant. The MMPI was mentioned in footnote 1.

People v. Cox, 82 Cal. App. 3d 211, 147 Cal. Rptr. 73 (1978). The MMPI was used by a psychiatric social worker to evaluate the defendant.

People v. Humphrey, 45 Cal. App. 3d 32, 119 Cal. Rptr. 74 (1975). The MMPI was administered orally in evaluation of the defendant.

People v. Coogler, 71 Cal. 2d 153, 454 P.2d 686 (1969). The MMPI was used by a clinical psychologist to evaluate the defendant.

Colorado

People v. Ickler, 877 P.2d 863 (Colo. 1994). The MMPI was administered to a sex offender to determine if he was eligible to participate in a sex offender counseling program as a condition of probation.

B.B. v. People, 785 P.2d 132 (Colo. 1990). The MMPI was one of the tests used to evaluate B.B.

People v. Roark, 643 P.2d 756 (Colo. 1982). The MMPI was not used as a basis for assessing the defendant's mental condition. The defendant's faking bad rendered the results unreliable.

District of Columbia

Charles P. Young Co. v. District of Columbia Dep't of Employment Serv., 681 P.2d 451 (D.C. 1994). Expert opinion that the worker's compensation applicant had a drinking history was confirmed by the MMPI results, which indicated a long-standing personality disorder with alcohol and drug use.

In re Woodward, 636 A.2d 969 (D.C. 1994). The MMPI was administered to determine whether an attorney with a substance abuse problem possessed the ability to practice law without supervision.

McEvily v. District of Columbia Dep't of Employment Services, 500 A.2d 1022 (D.C. 1985). The MMPI was administered to the claimant.

Connecticut

Cobb v. Commissioner of Correction, 2004 WL 2943129 (Conn. Super. 2004). A death sentence was affirmed. Testimony alluded to "invalid MMPI tests."

State v. Lapointe, 678 A.2d 942 (Conn. 1996). The MMPI showed that the defendant had little ability to control or check angry or disagreeable feelings, but the result was insufficient to render his confession involuntary.

Delaware

Martin v. Martin, 820 A.2d 410 (Del. Fam. Ct. 2002). Parties were given the MMPI in a custody dispute.

Joiner v. Raytheon Constructors, Inc., 2001 WL 880089 (Del. Super. Ct. 2001). In denial of worker's compensation benefits, MMPI results suggested a "false claim of mental illness."

Knott-Ellis v. State, 2000 WL 33113800 (Del. Super Ct. 2000). Worker's compensation was affirmed for a back sprain but not for PTSD. The MMPI results showed an exaggeration of symptoms.

Sowell v. Townsends, Inc., 2000 WL 305502 (Del. Super. Ct. 2000). The MMPI–2 "is not a valid indication of the individual's personality or symptoms; it can just help to determine credibility."

Fisher v. Fisher, 691 A.2d 619 (Del. Super. Ct. 1997). Custody was granted to the father after the MMPI and other psychological tests showed the mother's reaction to the children to be erratic.

State v. Shields, 593 A.2d 986 (Del. 1990). The MMPI was one of many tests used to evaluate the defendant.

Richardson v. State, 436 A.2d 1127 (Del. Super. Ct. 1981). Newly discovered psychological evidence did not warrant a new trial. The defendant's expert, relying on diagnosis from the MMPI, did not refute the state expert's diagnosis.

Florida

Alston v. State, 2004 WL 2297848 (Fla. 2004). A death row inmate was found competent despite MMPI–2 results that reflected "psychotic disturbance."

Kimbrough v. State, 886 So.2d 965 (Fla. 2004). Habeas corpus relief was denied. The MMPI had a "spike on scale four."

Phillips v. State, 2004 WL 2297824 (Fla. 2004). A death sentence was affirmed. The MMPI was mentioned.

Sochor v. State, 883 So.2d 766 (Fla. 2004). Conviction and death sentence were affirmed. The fake-bad findings on the MMPI were found invalid.

Caballero v. State, 851 So.2d 655 (Fla. 2003). A death sentence was affirmed. The MMPI–2 results were found to be invalid based on exaggeration.

Cole v. State, 841 So.2d 409 (Fla. 2003). Habeas corpus relief was denied in a death penalty case. The MMPI was used in mitigation.

Jones v. State, 845 So.2d 55 (Fla. 2003). A death sentence was affirmed despite the fact that the MMPI was used in mitigation.

Olges v. Dougherty, 856 So.2d 6 (Fla. App. 1st Dist. 2003). The plaintiff in an automobile accident was required to submit to psychological testing, including the MMPI, because the plaintiff's mental condition was in controversy.

Barnhill v. State , 834 So.2d 836 (Fla. 2002). A death sentence was affirmed. "Poor performance" on the MMPI was noted.

Caroll v. State, 815 So.2d 601 (Fla. 2002). A petition for habeas corpus was denied to a prisoner sentenced to death. The MMPI was administered.

Philmore v. State, 820 So.2d 919 (Fla. 2002). A death sentence was affirmed. An older version of the MMPI overestimated the degree of mental illness in Black males by as much as 90%.

Schwab v. State, 814 So.2d 402 (Fla. 2002). A death sentence was affirmed. The MMPI–2 supported a diagnosis of pedophilia.

Sweet v. State, 810 So.2d 854 (Fla. 2002). The court affirmed a murder conviction and death sentence. The MMPI was not administered at the penalty phase because nothing suggested a "severe form of mental illness. . . ."

Ragsdale v. State, 798 So.2d 713 (Fla. 2001). A death sentence was affirmed. The MMPI–2 was administered.

Rogers v. State, 783 So.2d 980 (Fla. 2001). A death sentence was affirmed. The MMPI was discussed.

Hitchcock v. State, 755 So.2d 638 (Fla. 2000). No error was found in admitting a three-page narrative report concerning the MMPI on rebuttal. The sentence of death was affirmed.

Mangum v. State, 765 So.2d 192 (Fla. App. 4th Dist. 2000). A murder conviction and life sentence was affirmed. The MMPI suggested hallucinations and delusions.

Mann v. State, 770 So.2d 1158 (Fla. 2000). A death sentence was affirmed. The MMPI was administered.

Westerheide v. State, 767 So.2d 637 (Fla. App. 5th Dist. 2000). Involuntary commitment of a sexually violent predator was affirmed. The MMPI was used for "background information."

Zack v. State, 753 So.2d 9 (Fla. 2000). A death sentence was affirmed. The "malingering scale" of the MMPI was found to be "outside of the normal limits," rendering the test results useless.

Evans v. State, 737 So.2d 1167 (Fla. App. 2d Dist. 1999). The sentence was reversed based on ineffective assistance of counsel where the defendant was given the wrong answer sheet for the MMPI–2, and his counsel did not inquire about ramifications of the mistake.

J.H.C. v. State, 642 So.2d 601 (Fla. App. 2d Dist. 1994). In a case involving sexual battery on a child under 12 years old, expert testimony that maintained that the daughter fit a "sexually abused child profile" based on results of the MMPI should have been excluded. Because the victim, at the time of the trial, was able to relate events, testimony on the sexual abuse profile was little more than opinion of the expert that the victim was telling the truth. Further, when the victim admits to engaging in other consensual sexual conduct, psychological exams cannot reliably identify individuals who have been subjected to sexual abuse.

DuBois v. DuBois, 586 So.2d 423 (Fla. App. 4th Dist. 1991). The MMPI was used to evaluate the appellant. The results were used in testimony.

Flanagan v. State, 586 So.2d 1085 (Fla. App. 1st Dist. 1991). The MMPI was mentioned in a case regarding controversy over whether test results can reliably exclude a person from a "profile" of a sexual deviant.

Grey v. Eastern Airlines, Inc., 480 So.2d 1341 (Fla. App. 1st Dist. 1985). The MMPI was one of the tests used to evaluate the appellant.

Valle-Axelberd and Associates, Inc. v. Metropolitan Dade County, 440 So.2d 606 (Fla. App. 3d Dist. 1983). Civil action was allowed based on a refusal of the institution to use the MMPI when witnesses testified it was perceived by the community to be racially skewed.

Georgia

Alpharetta First United Methodist Church v. Stewart, 472 S.E.2d 532 (Ga. App. 1996). In a nonconsensual sexual relation claim between the victim claiming transference and negligent hiring and the church claiming statute of limitations defense, the MMPI administered to the minister before his employment gave only generalities and not enough information to put the church on notice of propensity for sexual misconduct.

Christenson v. State, 261 Ga. 80, 402 S.E.2d 41 (1991). The MMPI was used to evaluate the defendant.

Stripling v. State, 261 Ga. 1, 401 S.E.2d 500 (1991). The MMPI was used to evaluate the defendant.

Jacobs v. Pilgrim, 186 Ga. App. 260, 367 S.E.2d 49 (1988). The MMPI was used to diagnose the plaintiff and to show a causal relationship between the injury and the accident.

Patillo v. State, 258 Ga. 255, 368 S.E.2d 493 (1988). The court denied a continuance to research MMPI results.

In re D.H., 178 Ga. App. 119, 342 S.E.2d 367 (1986). Evaluations of parents included the MMPI.

Ford v. State, 255 Ga. 81, 335 S.E.2d 567 (1985). Results of the short form of the MMPI were invalidated by the claimant's faking sick.

Idaho

State v. Siegel, 50 P.3d 1033 (Idaho App. 2002). Conviction for lewd conduct with a minor was affirmed. The MMPI was administered.

Cooper v. Board of Professional Discipline of Idaho State Bd. of Medicine, 4 P.3d 561 (Idaho 2000). A 6-month suspension of a medical license after alleged sex with a patient was reversed. The MMPI was administered.

Perry v. Magic Valley Regional Medical Center, 995 P.2d 816 (Idaho 2000). A medical malpractice judgment was affirmed. The MMPI–2 was administered but not "relied upon."

State v. Stradley, 899 P.2d 416 (Idaho 1995). The defendant's attorney failed to disclose a subsequently administered MMPI and the interpretive report.

O'Loughlin v. Circle A. Construction, 112 Idaho 1048, 739 P.2d 347 (1987). The MMPI was used to evaluate the appellant. The MMPI was mentioned briefly.

Illinois

In re Detention of Hughes, 805 N.E.2d 725 (Ill. App. 2d Dist. 2004). The denial of disability benefits was remanded; the MMPI–2 showed either deliberate exaggeration or failure to understand the test.

In re Detention of Sveda, 2004 WL 2715502 (Ill. App. 1st Dist. 2004). The MMPI–2 was given in a civil commitment of a convicted sexual abuser.

People v. Lee, 803 N.E.2d 552 (Ill. App. 1st Dist. 2004). The defendant was convicted of sexual assault. The victim was given the MMPI.

In re Detention of Hughes, 346 Ill. App. 677, *rev'g* 788 N.E.2d 370 (Ill. App. 2d Dist. 2003). The MMPI showed that the respondent minimized problems and it supported pedophile diagnosis. The case was remanded for proceeding on a commitment under the sexual offender statute.

People v. Gilford, 784 N.E.2d 841 (Ill. App. 1st Dist. 2002). The MMPI–2 and other tests suggested paraphilia. The case was remanded to determine if the mental condition of the defendant justified sexually dangerous commitment.

People v. Haynes, 737 N.E.2d 169 (Ill. 2000). A death sentence was affirmed. The MMPI results suggested paranoid schizophrenia.

People v. Robin, 728 N.E.2d 736 (Ill. App. 1st Dist. 2000). The defendant was found not guilty by reason of insanity and committed in 1989. In 1999 the defendant was granted conditional release. The MMPI showed the defendant to be defensive but not psychotic.

People v. Robles, 733 N.E.2d 438 (Ill. App. 2d Dist. 2000). An expert testified that the minor defendant should have been given the MMPI–A rather than the MMPI–2 and that the MMPI–2 results suggested either "4-8" or "4-6," which is inconsistent as "apples and oranges." The guilty but mentally ill verdict was reversed because the court denied the expert psychological rebuttal.

People v. Sizemore, 726 N.E.2d 204 (Ill. App. 4th Dist. 2000). The defendant was committed as a sexually dangerous person. The MMPI was unfinished and therefore not valid.

People v. Hill, 697 N.E.2d 316 (Ill. App. 1st Dist. 1998). The MMPI–2 was discussed as having scales "built into" it "as sort of truth detector."

People v. Kinkead, 695 N.E.2d 1255 (Ill. 1998). The state gave the defendant the MMPI–2, but did not register the use of psychotropic drugs. The defendant later appealed his own guilty plea. The guilty plea and death sentence were remanded to determine circumstances surrounding the defendant's ingestion of psychotropic medication during the time of his guilty plea and sentencing.

Doe v. Lutz, 668 N.E.2d 564 (Ill. App. 1st Dist. 1996). A priest, school principal, bishop, and archbishop were charged with child abuse. A defense expert testified that MMPI results refuted posttraumatic stress disorder.

People v. Haynes, 673 N.E.2d 318 (Ill. 1996). The MMPI–2 was administered and analyzed by a defense expert where the defendant claimed he was unfit to waive his right to a jury.

People v. Kinkead, 660 N.E.2d 852 (Ill. 1995). The MMPI was administered to a defendant to determine if the court should accept guilty plea before the defendant was sentenced to death. (See also *People v. Kinkead*, 695 N.E.2d 1255 (Ill. 1998).)

In re Marriage of Willis, 599 N.E.2d 179 (Ill. App. 3d Dist. 1992). Testimony about a mother's MMPI profile from a nonexpert was deemed not prejudicial.

Iwanski v. Steamwood Police Pension Board, 596 N.E.2d 691 (Ill. App. 1st Dist. 1992). Psychological testing, including MMPI results, showed depression, anxiety, and dysfunction but did not support disability.

Johnson v. May, 223 Ill.App.3d 477, 165 Ill. Dec. 828, 585 N.E.2d 224 (Ill. App. 5th Dist. 1992). Psychological examination, including MMPI testing, supported diagnosis of severe posttraumatic stress disorder. The jury's award of nothing for disability was therefore wrong, and results of the examination warranted new trial on damages.

People v. Gilyard, 602 N.E.2d 1335 (Ill. App. 2d Dist. 1992). MMPI results of a defendant convicted of felony murder were used to rule out personality disorder and depression. Little reliance was given to the MMPI in diagnosing the defendant because MMPI results indicated overadmission or high-distress profile.

People v. Scott, 148 Ill.2d 479, 594 N.E.2d 217 (Ill. 1992). A death sentence was affirmed. MMPI testing showed no evidence of thought disorder that would affect the defendant's ability to work with his attorney.

Amoco Oil Company v. Industrial Commission, 218 Ill. App. 3d 737, 161 Ill. Dec. 397, 578 N.E.2d 1043 (1991). The MMPI was used to evaluate the claimant.

People v. Camden, 219 Ill. App. 3d 124, 161 Ill. Dec. 565, 578 N.E.2d 1211 (1991). The MMPI was used to evaluate the defendant.

Illinois Mutual Ins. Co. v. Industrial Commission, 201 Ill. App. 3d 1018, 147 Ill. Dec. 679, 559 N.E.2d 1019 (1990). The MMPI was used to evaluate the claimants.

In re L.M., 205 Ill. App. 3d 497, 150 Ill. Dec. 872, 563 N.E.2d 999 (1990). The MMPI was mentioned in the case, but not used to evaluate the parents.

May v. Industrial Commission, 195 Ill. App. 3d 468, 141 Ill. Dec. 890, 552 N.E.2d 258 (1990). The MMPI was used to evaluate the claimant.

McDaniel v. Industrial Commission, 197 Ill. App. 3d 981, 145 Ill. Dec. 442, 557 N.E.2d 212 (1990). The MMPI was used to evaluate the claimant.

People v. Beekn, 205 Ill. App. 3d 533, 151 Ill. Dec. 101, 563 N.E.2d 1207 (1990). The MMPI was used to evaluate the defendant.

People v. Boclair, 129 Ill. 2d 458, 136 Ill. Dec. 29, 544 N.E.2d 715 (1989). MMPI test results were used in a doctor's testimony concerning evaluation of the defendant.

People v. Britz, 123 Ill. 2d 446, 124 Ill. Dec. 15, 528 N.E.2d 703 (1988). The MMPI was used to evaluate the defendant. Results indicated exaggeration and were deemed invalid.

People v. Thompson, 166 Ill. App. 3d 909, 117 Ill. Dec. 795, 520 N.E.2d 1146 (1988). The MMPI was administered to a defendant in the U.S. Navy. Results were read into testimony and accepted.

People v. Eckhardt, 156 Ill. App. 3d 1077, 109 Ill. Dec. 349, 509 N.E.2d 1361 (1987). MMPI results were used to refute malingering.

People v. Littlejohn, 144 Ill. App. 3d 813, 98 Ill. Dec. 555, 494 N.E.2d 677 (1986). The state entered the MMPI results against the defendant.

Roulette v. Department of Central Management Services, 141 Ill. App. 3d 394, 95 Ill. Dec. 587, 490 N.E.2d 60 (1986). When a rejected police officer candidate requested all documents, his MMPI profile was not included. He brought action to retrieve it.

People v. Gacy, 103 Ill. 2d 1, 82 Ill. Dec. 391, 468 N.E.2d 1171 (1984). The defendant attempted to use the MMPI to make his condition look worse than it actually was.

Aronson v. North Park College, 94 Ill. App. 3d 211, 49 Ill. Dec. 756, 418 N.E.2d 776 (1981). A student was required to take the MMPI. The results and her refusal of counseling led to dismissal from school, which provided the basis of litigation.

People v. Cooper, 64 Ill. App. 3d 880, 381 N.E.2d 1178 (1978). MMPI results confirmed insecurity and hostility and supported the conclusion that the defendant was "sexually dangerous."

Indiana

Patrick v. State, 2004 WL 2965848 (Ind. App. 2004). No Sixth Amendment violations were found in a 93-year sentence for murder. The MMPI–2 was administered.

Watson v. State, 784 N.E.2d 515 (Ind. App. 2003). MMPI results were admitted in a criminal trial over the objection of physician–patient privilege. The judge found defense experts not credible and prosecution experts, as well as the MMPI tests, to be credible.

Dunlop v. State, 724 N.E.2d 592 (Ind. 2000). The MMPI was administered in the sentencing phase of a criminal action.

Carter v. State, 711 N.E.2d 835 (Ind. 1999). Review of a sentence requires reexamining appropriate aggravating and mitigating circumstances, including psychological testing.

City of Fort Wayne v. Moore, 706 N.E.2d 605 (Ind. App. 1999). Civil action clarifies the employer's responsibility for employee acts. The MMPI was mentioned.

Doe v. Shults-Lewis Child & Family Svcs., 718 N.E.2d 738 (Ind. 1999). MMPI results on "regression subindex" raised a genuine issue concerning repressed memory. The court should not have dismissed the case at summary judgment because there was an issue as to whether repression had caused the plaintiffs to delay filing until after the statutory deadline.

Trueblood v. State, 715 N.E.2d 1242 (Ind. 1999). An appeal of a death sentence was denied despite extreme emotional disturbance shown, in part, through the MMPI–2.

Ridgeway v. Teshoian, 699 N.E.2d 1156, 1998 WL 644842 (Ind. App. 1998). The plaintiff claimed both physical and mental injuries resulting from a low-speed, rear-end collision. No evidence supported the physical injury claim, and the MMPI–2 results revealed that the claimant was resilient and capable of dealing with stressful events.

Ross v. Delaware County Dep't of Public Welfare, 661 N.E.2d 1269 (Ind. Ct. App. 1996). The MMPI was administered to a parent in a termination of the parent–child relationship hearing.

Tipton v. Marion County Dep't of Public Welfare, 629 N.E.2d 1262 (Ind. App. 1st Dist. 1994). The defendant recommended termination of parental rights based in part on MMPI results.

Byrd v. State, 593 N.E.2d 1183 (Ind. 1992). Results of the MMPI were held inadmissible to prove that the defendant's character was inconsistent with committing intentional murder.

Byrd v. State, 579 N.E.2d 457 (Ind. App. 1st Dist. 1991). The issue of whether a doctor should be allowed to give expert opinion about MMPI results already entered into evidence was discussed.

Ellis v. State, 567 N.E.2d 1142 (Ind. 1991). The MMPI was mentioned in the case.

Ulrich v. State, 550 N.E.2d 114 (Ind. App. 3d Dist. 1990). A doctor was not allowed to answer whether he believed that allegations of sexual activity by the defendant were consistent with the MMPI profile and results.

In the Matter of John L. Hudgins, 540 N.E.2d 1200 (Ind. 1989). The MMPI was used to evaluate an attorney in a disciplinary proceeding.

Isom v. Isom, 538 N.E.2d 261 (Ind. App. 3d Dist. 1989). MMPI results were used in testimony to decide a child custody dispute.

Sullivan v. Fairmont Homes, Inc., 543 N.E.2d 1130 (Ind. App. 1st Dist. 1989). MMPI computer-generated interpretation was deemed hearsay and properly excluded.

Van Cleave v. State, 517 N.E.2d 356 (Ind. 1987). A psychologist used results of the MMPI as the basis for the opinion that the defendant was an excellent candidate for vocational rehabilitation.

City of Greenwood v. Dowler, 492 N.E.2d 1081 (Ind. App. 1st Dist. 1986). MMPI test results were used to evaluate a police officer candidate.

Iowa

In re A.T., 665 N.W.2d 442 (Iowa App. 2003). A mother's parental rights were terminated. The MMPI showed the mother to be anxious and manipulative.

In re Marriage of Graham, 2001 WL 487999 (Iowa App. 2001). Modification of custody included MMPI–2 testing for parents and stepparents.

Terwilliger v. Snap-On Tools Corp., 529 N.W.2d 267 (Iowa 1995). The MMPI profile showed that a worker's compensation claimant developed physical symptoms of carpal tunnel syndrome as a reaction to mental or environmental stress.

State v. Randle, 484 N.E.2d 220 (Iowa Ct. App. 1992). A sexual abuse victim waived her physician–patient privilege when she authorized release of documents to the Department of Criminal Investigations, and, therefore, the victim's MMPI results were admissible to show that she experienced little stress 5 days after the alleged offense.

State ex rel. LEAS in Interest of O'Neal, 303 N.W.2d 414 (Iowa 1981). The MMPI was one of the tests used to evaluate parents in a parental rights termination case.

Gosek v. Garmer Stiles Co., 158 N.W.2d 731 (Iowa 1968). The MMPI was used in discussion of a worker's disability.

Kansas

In re Marriage of Phillips, 58 P.3d 680 (Kan. 2002). The MMPI was given to a husband who was not the biological father in custody litigation.

State v. Kleypas, 40 P.3d 139 (Kan. 2001). A death sentence was remanded. The MMPI was administered.

State v. Ordway, 934 P.2d 94 (Kan. 1997). The MMPI was administered to a defendant requesting voluntary manslaughter jury instruction.

West v. Martin, 11 Kan. App. 2d 55, 713 P.2d 957 (1986). MMPI admissibility was discussed.

Rund v. Cessna Aircraft Co., 213 Kan. 812, 512 P.2d 518 (1974). The MMPI was one of the tests used to evaluate the claimant.

State of Kansas v. Kilpatrick, 201 Kan. 6, 439 P.2d 99 (1968). The MMPI was one of several tests used to evaluate the defendant.

Kentucky

St. Clair v. Community, 140 S.W.3d 510 (Ky. 2004). An expert asked about four questions taken from the MMPI that had arguable relevance in a prison setting. A death sentence was reversed and a new penalty phase ordered on grounds unrelated to the MMPI.

Caudill v. Community, 120 S.W.3d 635 (Ky. 2003). A death sentence was affirmed. The MMPI–2 results reflected a submissive personality.

Staples, Inc. v. Konvelski, 56 S.W.3d 412 (Ky. 2001). The ALJ's determination of total disability was affirmed. The MMPI was not administered.

Commonwealth v. Jarboe, 464 S.W.2d 287 (Ky. 1971). The MMPI was given to potential adoptive parents.

Louisiana

Phillips v. Diocese of Lafayette, 869 So.2d 313 (La. App. 3d Cir. 2004). Worker's compensation benefits for psychotherapy, and penalties for denial of benefits, was granted. The MMPI–2 supported the finding that pain was related to psychological issues.

Flick v. Fischer Environmental Services, Inc., 853 So.2d 1 (La. App. 1st Cir. 2003). Pest control technician was doused with chemicals in the course of employment. The MMPI–2 results showed a long-term pattern of somatization.

Ranel v. McDonalds, 858 So.2d 843 (La. App. 3d Cir. 2003). Worker's compensation denial of benefits was reversed. The MMPI was mentioned.

Louis v. State ex rel. Dep't of Transp. and Development, 819 So.2d 379 (La. App. 5th Cir. 2002). In a maritime case, fault of an accident was found to be 90% state responsibility. The plaintiff was unable to complete the MMPI because he could not comprehend its statements.

Rayborn v. Diamond Offshore Co., 832 So.2d 1052 (La. App. 4th Cir. 2002). In a personal injury action, the MMPI showed an adjustment disorder and no malingering. The court reduced the jury's verdict.

State v. Carmouche, 872 So.2d 1020 (La. 2002). Sentence was remanded for consideration of a mental retardation prohibition to the death penalty. The MMPI was mentioned.

State v. Louviere, 833 So.2d 885 (La. 2002). Conviction and the death sentence were affirmed. The MMPI–2 results suggested sexual identity problems.

Weems v. Dixie Lion Warehouse & Cartige Co., 809 So.2d 305 (La. App. 1st Cir. 2001). Worker's compensation benefits were denied. The MMPI results indicated exaggerated response.

Baker v. Libbey Glass, Inc., 759 So.2d 1007 (La. App. 2d Cir. 2000). In a worker's compensation case, the MMPI results were not valid because the responses exaggerated pathology.

Billiot v. K-Mart Corp., 764 So.2d 329 (La. App. 1st Cir. 2000). The MMPI administered in a personal injury action indicated "hysteria, hypochondriasis, depression, schizophrenia, paresthesis and psychopathic deviant."

Dennis v. The Finish Line, Inc., 781 So.2d 12 (La. App. 1st Cir. 2000). Personal injury judgments were reduced. The MMPI results were found to be "normal."

McIntosh v. McIntosh, 768 So.2d 219 (La. App. 2d Cir. 2000). The father was awarded custody. The mother's MMPI results showed histrionic and narcissistic traits.

State ex rel. Hair, 757 So.2d 754 (La. App. 3d Cir. 2000). Maternal rights were terminated. The MMPI results "demonstrated normality."

Thibodeaux v. Bernard, 772 So.2d 897 (La. App. 3d Cir. 2000). The MMPI results revealed a psychological overlay and somatoform disorder in a personal injury case. The appellate court reversed the jury finding against the husband and awarded $10,000 for loss of consortium.

Metrejean v. Prudential, 99CA1148 (La. App. 1st Cir. 1999). The plaintiffs unsuccessfully appealed a personal injury verdict. The MMPI revealed chronic long-standing psychological problems and attempts to look sick.

Chateau v. City of Kenner, 712 So.2d 256 (La. App. 5th Cir. 1998). An employer successfully appealed a worker's award of full supplemental earnings benefits after MMPI–2 results refuted earlier findings that the employee had sustained psychological injury from a work-related injury.

Jones v. Trendsetter Production Co., Inc., 707 So.2d 1341 (La. App. 3d Cir. 1998). The MMPI was administered in a worker's compensation case.

Kuhl v. Kuhl, 715 So.2d 740 (La. App. 3d Cir. 1998). The MMPI–2 given to the mother who alleged the father was sexually abusing the daughter supported the proposition that the mother's motivation was rooted in vindictiveness and not a desire to protect the child.

Raney v. Wren, 1998 WL 781856 (La. Ct. App., 1998). In a custody trial, a clinical psychologist's testimony regarding the MMPI test scores of the parents were found admissible because the expert was not asked to comment on the mental health of the parties or give a recommendation as to custody.

Myers v. Broussard, 696 So.2d 88 (La. App. 3d Cir. 1997). The MMPI administered to an auto accident victim suffering from depression and physical complaints revealed a valid profile, and thus the jury verdict for pain and suffering was affirmed.

State v. Koon, 704 So.2d 756 (La. 1997). The MMPI was administered before a murder trial. The defense expert testified that the defendant was truthful about being passive and not aggressively violent. The state rebutted each defense point and commented on MMPI results. Because the defense "opened the door," rebuttal evidence regarding the MMPI results was allowed.

Creel v. Concordia Elec. Co-op., Inc., 670 So.2d 406 (La. App. 3d Cir. 1996). A burned employee alleged emotional and physical distress as a result of a workplace accident. Truthful MMPI results showed extreme distress.

Morris v. Ferriss, 669 So.2d 1316 (La. App. 4th Cir. 1996). The plaintiff sued for medical malpractice for partial paralysis and loss of some speaking ability after brain surgery to correct seizures. The case was dismissed because the MMPI administered as part of the psychological workup before surgery contained "red flags" that the patient suffered psychogenic seizures rather than true organic seizures.

Danzey v. Evergreen Presbyterian Ministries, 657 So.2d 491 (La. App. 3d Cir. 1995). The MMPI was administered, along with a disability evaluation for an on-the-job injury.

Howell v. Service Merchandise Co., Inc., 663 So.2d 96 (La. App. 3d Cir. 1995). The MMPI administered in a worker's compensation case indicated that the worker's depression and chronic pain syndrome was related to the workplace accident.

State v. Green, 655 So.2d 272 (La. 1995). Discussed in footnote 10, the defense expert used MMPI results to unsuccessfully rebut testimony that a juvenile was intelligent and knowingly waived his *Miranda* rights, resulting in a life sentence for murder.

State v. Green, 634 So.2d 503 (La. App. 4th Cir. 1994). In support of defense that the defendant did not knowingly and intelligently waive *Miranda* rights, the defendant presented expert testimony that the MMPI and other tests showed a low-level IQ and mild retardation.

Cheramie v. J. Wayne Plaisance, Inc., 595 So.2d 619 (La. 1992). The plaintiff was evaluated by a psychologist using the MMPI.

Bankston v. Alexandria Neurosurgical Clinic, 583 So.2d 1148 (La. App. 3d Cir. 1991). The plaintiff alleged that doctors destroyed the MMPI test results, along with other tests, "with conspiracy to deny plaintiff due course of justice."

Castille v. Great Atlantic & Pacific Tea Co., 591 So.2d 1299 (La. App. 3d Cir. 1991). The MMPI was used to evaluate the plaintiff.

Miley v. Landry, 582 So.2d 833 (La. 1991). The MMPI was used to evaluate the plaintiff.

State v. Widenhouse, 582 So.2d 1374 (La. App. 2d Cir. 1991). The MMPI was used to evaluate the defendant.

Utz v. Kienzle, 574 So.2d 1288 (La. App. 3d Cir. 1991). The MMPI was used, along with interviews, in a custody battle to evaluate two sets of parents.

Ward v. Commercial Union Ins. Co., 591 So.2d 1286 (La. App. 3d Cir. 1991). The MMPI was used to evaluate the plaintiff.

Broussard v. Grey Wolf Drilling Company, 562 So.2d 1006 (La. App. 3d Cir. 1990). The MMPI was part of the evaluation of the plaintiff.

Whatley v. Regional Transit Authority, 563 So.2d 1194 (La. App. 4th Cir. 1990). The MMPI was used to evaluate the plaintiff.

Cronier v. Cronier, 540 So.2d 1160 (La. App. 1st Cir. 1989). The MMPI was part of the evaluation of a husband in a custody dispute.

Valin v. Barnes, 550 So.2d 352 (La. App. 3d Cir. 1989). The MMPI was used to evaluate the plaintiff in a personal injury suit.

Miles v. Dolese Concrete Co., 518 So.2d 999 (La. 1988). The MMPI was used to evaluate a worker's compensation plaintiff. There is some discussion of the MMPI.

Miles v. Dolese Concrete Co., 507 So.2d 2 (La. App. 1st Cir. 1987). The MMPI was used to evaluate a worker's compensation plaintiff.

State v. Bowman, 491 So.2d 1380 (La. App. 3d Cir. 1986). The MMPI was used to evaluate the defendant. Portions of the results were read into testimony pertaining to plea of insanity.

Bunch v. Bunch, 469 So.2d 1191 (La. App. 3d Cir. 1985). The MMPI was used to evaluate the wife in a custody dispute.

Droddy v. Cliff's Drilling, Inc., 471 So.2d 223 (La. 1985). The MMPI was given to the plaintiff three different times to determine whether he was being truthful.

Laborde v. Velsicol Chemical Corp., 474 So.2d 1320 (La. App. 3d Cir. 1985). The MMPI was one of many evaluations used with the plaintiff.

Lewis v. East Feliciana Parish School Board, 452 So.2d 1275 (La. App. 1st Cir. 1984). The MMPI was one of several tests used to evaluate the plaintiff.

State v. Felde, 422 So.2d 370 (La. 1982). The MMPI was used to evaluate the defendant, who was characterized as having posttraumatic stress disorder (PTSD).

State v. Freeman, 409 So.2d 581 (La. 1982). MMPI was used by the state to establish the defendant's ability to aid and participate in her own defense.

Walton v. William Wolf Baking Co., Inc., 406 So.2d 168 (La. 1981). The MMPI was used to evaluate the plaintiff on three occasions.

Smith v. Angelle, 339 So.2d 922 (La. App. 3d Cir. 1976). The MMPI was one of the tests used to evaluate the claimant.

Maine

State v. Bridges, 413 A.2d 937 (Me. 1980). The MMPI was not used to evaluate the defendant because doctors believed it would prove inconclusive. There is a brief discussion of the MMPI.

State of Maine v. Howard, 405 A.2d 206 (Me. 1979). The defendant attempted to introduce a report that contained MMPI results but did not lay proper foundation for such admission.

State v. Buzynski, 330 A.2d 422 (Me. 1974). The defendant unsuccessfully attempted to have a doctor's testimony concerning MMPI results stricken.

Maryland

In re Adoption/Guardianship Nos. J9610436 and J9711031, 796 A.2d 778 (Md. 2002). Parents who are disabled were found to have the same right to a parent–child relationship as others. The MMPI was not given because parents were unable to read. Termination of parental rights was reversed.

Bentley v. Carroll, 355 Md. 312 (1999). The MMPI showed no evidence of depression or PTSD. Despite an order prohibiting its introduction at trial, an expert also discussed the test as "sort of, I hate to use the word, mini-truth, or lie detector." Because of the improper "attack on the veracity of Appellant," the judgment for the defendant was reversed.

Scott v. Prince George's County Dep't of Social Services, 76 Md. App. 357, 545 A.2d 81 (1988). The MMPI was used to evaluate the appellant in a parental rights dispute.

Bremer v. State, 18 Md. App. 291, 307 A.2d 503 (1973). The MMPI was one of several tests used to evaluate the defendant/appellant.

Massachusetts

Michael v. Trustmark Ins. Co., 2003 WL 21030177 (Mass. Super. 2003). Employment disability benefits were provided. The MMPI and MMPI–2 results showed depression and anxiety.

Commissioner v. Morasse, 2001 WL 1566407 (Mass. Super. 2001). In a competency finding, MMPI–2 results suggested psychiatric problems.

Lambley v. Kameny, 682 N.E.2d 907 (Mass. App. Ct. 1997). A job applicant sued a psychiatrist who examined the applicant at the request of a prospective employer. The MMPI was part of the evaluation.

Commonwealth v. LaCaprucia, 671 N.E.2d 984 (Mass. App. Ct. 1996). MMPI profiles were mentioned in footnote 3.

Commonwealth v. Kappler, 625 N.E.2d 513 (Mass. 1993). In rebuttal to the defendant's assertion that he lacked criminal responsibility, the defendant's MMPI–2 code did not suggest active psychosis. MMPI testing was discussed in footnote 5.

Commonwealth v. Goulet, 402 Mass. 299, 522 N.E.2d 417 (Mass. 1988). The MMPI was administered to the defendant, whom doctor opined was faking bad.

Commonwealth v. Meech, 403 N.E.2d 1174 (Mass. 1980). The MMPI was used to evaluate the defendant on behalf of the defense.

Michigan

People v. Lloyd, 590 N.W.2d 738 (Mich. 1999). The MMPI–2 showed "mental confusion or real psychopathology" despite exaggerated symptomology. The case was remanded on other grounds for a competency hearing.

Adkerson v. MK-Ferguson Co., 191 Mich. App. 129, 477 N.W.2d 465 (1991). An employee who was terminated because of MMPI scores brought an action for damages.

In the Matter of Farley, 469 N.W.2d 295 (Mich. 1991). The mother in a parental rights dispute was given the MMPI twice to help indicate progress through therapy.

People v. Bowman, 141 Mich. App. 390, 367 N.W.2d 867 (1985). The MMPI was used to evaluate the defendant.

People v. Arroyo, 138 Mich. App. 246, 360 N.W.2d 185 (1984). The expert witness for the defense testified that the defendant was legally insane based on an interview and MMPI results.

People v. Murphy, 331 N.W.2d 152 (Mich. 1982). The state relied on MMPI results to show the defendant was sane, where the defendant gave an unusual number of extremely rare responses.

Minnesota

In re Civil Commitment of Linn, 2003 WL 22234642 (Minn. App. 2003). The denial of release from civil commitment was affirmed. MMPI results could not detect "rambling thought" disorder because a person must be able to "think in an organized fashion" to complete the test.

In re Disciplinary Action Against Jellinger, 655 N.W.2d 312 (Minn. 2002). MMPI results suggested depression. The respondent was disbarred for unethical acts.

In Re Petition for Reinstatement Kadrie, 602 N.W.2d 868 (Minn. 1999). The lawyer's petition for reinstatement was denied. MMPI results showed depression and possible personality disorder that would be resistant to rehabilitation.

Matter of Knops, 536 N.W.2d 616 (Minn. 1995). The defendant charged with sexual assault on a child was deemed mentally ill and dangerous after MMPI results indicated depression, pessimism, anxiety, tension, nervousness, guilt-ridden feelings, and characteristics of a perfectionist.

Loveland v. Kremer, 464 N.W.2d 306 (Minn. App. 1990). The MMPI was mentioned in the case.

In re Miera, 426 N.W.2d 850 (Minn. 1988). The MMPI was used to evaluate a judge and his employee in sexual harassment dispute.

J.E.P. v. J.C.P., 432 N.W.2d 483 (Minn. App. 1988). The MMPI was used to evaluate both a husband and a wife in a protective order hearing.

Matter of Reinstatement of Williams, 433 N.W.2d 104 (Minn. 1988). The MMPI was used to evaluate the lawyer and in petition for reinstatement.

State v. Jurgens, 424 N.W.2d 546 (Minn. App. 1988). The MMPI was given to the defendant three times over a number of years. All three test results were relevant to the sanity issue.

Bjerke v. Wilcox, 401 N.W.2d 97 (Minn. App. 1987). The MMPI was used to evaluate the father, mother, father's fiancee, and mother's new husband in a custody dispute.

In re Bolen, 416 N.W.2d 449 (Minn. 1987). The lawyer used the MMPI to reinforce mitigating circumstances in suspension of a probation hearing.

Matter of Welfare of J.A.R., 408 N.W.2d 692 (Minn. App. 1987). The MMPI was used to evaluate a juvenile while he was incarcerated.

Petersen v. Kidd, 400 N.W.2d 413 (Minn. App. 1987). The MMPI was used as part of the evaluation of the plaintiff.

Hoffa v. Hoffa, 382 N.W.2d 522 (Minn. App. 1986). The MMPI was used to evaluate both parents in a custody dispute.

Hreha v. Hreha, 392 N.W.2d 914 (Minn. App. 1986). The petitioner filed for a change of custody. The MMPI was used to evaluate the respondent.

Jorschumb v. Jorschumb, 390 N.W.2d 806 (Minn. App. 1986). The MMPI was used to evaluate both parents in a custody dispute. The appellant claimed that his being denied access to psychological tests rendered the testing psychologist's testimony inadmissible.

Matter of Welfare of P.L.C. and D.L.C., 384 N.W.2d 222 (Minn. App. 1986). The MMPI was used to evaluate the father in a guardianship dispute against the grandfather.

Novotny v. Novotny, 394 N.W.2d 256 (Minn. App. 1986). The MMPI was used to evaluate both parents in a custody dispute.

Riewe v. Arnesen, 381 N.W.2d 448 (Minn. App. 1986). Disclosure of use of MMPI test results to the defense counsel on the afternoon before the trial was ruled not for purpose of taking advantage of defense.

Rosen v. Rosen, 398 N.W.2d 38 (Minn. App. 1986). Disputed MMPI results for both parents were used in a custody dispute.

Application for Discipline of McCallum, 366 N.W.2d 100 (Minn. 1985). A lawyer was required to take the MMPI and other psychiatric examinations as a condition of petitioning for reinstatement.

Matter of Welfare of D.D.K., 376 N.W.2d 717 (Minn. App. 1985). The MMPI was used as part of the evaluation of both parents in a hearing to terminate all parental rights.

Matter of Welfare of R.B. and B.B., 369 N.W.2d 353 (Minn. App. 1985). The father was required, as part of a visitation order, to submit to MMPI testing in a neglect due to sexual abuse proceeding.

Newmaster v. Mahmood, 361 N.W.2d 130 (Minn. App. 1985). The plaintiff was evaluated with the MMPI to help determine the "economic impact" of her injuries.

State v. Cermak, 365 N.W.2d 238 (Minn. 1985). The MMPI was used to evaluate the codefendant.

Enebake v. Noot, 353 N.W.2d 544 (Minn. 1984). The MMPI was used as part of an evaluation of the plaintiff in review of committal to a mental facility.

Halper v. Halper, 348 N.W.2d 360 (Minn. App. 1984). The MMPI was used to evaluate both parents in a custody dispute.

Matter of Welfare of A.K.K., 356 N.W.2d 337 (Minn. App. 1984). The MMPI was used to evaluate the mother in a termination of parental rights hearing.

State v. Bouwman, 354 N.W.2d 1 (Minn. 1984). The MMPI had been used in evaluation and treatment of the defendant before the commission of the crime.

Wills v. Red Lake Municipal Liquor Store, 350 N.W.2d 452 (Minn. App. 1984). The MMPI was mentioned.

McClish v. Pan-O-Gold Baking Co., 336 N.W.2d 538 (Minn. 1983). A rehabilitation psychologist testified that McClish was unemployable in a competitive labor market, based partly on MMPI scores.

Cornfeldt v. Tongen, 262 N.W.2d 684 (Minn. 1977). The MMPI was mentioned in a medical malpractice case.

Hagen v. Swenson, 306 Minn. 257, 236 N.W.2d 161 (1975). Qualifications of the expert testifying as to MMPI results were challenged and upheld.

Haynes v. Anderson, 304 Minn. 185, 232 N.W.2d 196 (1975). The plaintiff appealed an order requiring her to submit to an MMPI test. There was discussion of the MMPI.

Ritchie v. Children's Home Soc'y of St. Paul, 216 N.W.2d 900 (Minn. 1974). A petition for adoption was denied after the child was found to have excessive bruises on his body, and the MMPI indicated that the petitioner "could not deal well with extremely stressful or emotional situations."

Saholt v. Northwest Airlines, Inc., 290 Minn. 393, 188 N.W.2d 772 (1971). The MMPI was used to evaluate a worker's compensation claimant.

Mississippi

Chase v. State, 873 So.2d 933 (Miss. 2004). There is discussion of the 2002 U.S. Supreme Court decision that execution of the mentally retarded constitutes cruel and unusual punishment and is therefore prohibited by the Eighth Amendment. The MMPI–2 provides a clear threshold standard to be used by Mississippi in determining mental retardation.

Doss v. State, 882 So.2d 176 (Miss. 2004). A capital murder conviction was sustained, but a hearing was allowed on the issue of ineffective assistance of counsel at sentencing. The MMPI–2 was held to be the best test to detect malingering of mental retardation because it provides a "clear standard."

Public Employee's Retirement System v. Smith, 880 So.2d 348 (Miss. App. 2004). Hurt-on-the-job disability benefits were denied. The MMPI was mentioned as the test that detects malingering.

Scott v. State, 878 So.2d 933 (Miss. 2004). A death sentence was affirmed. The defendant was "unwilling" to take the MMPI–2.

Wiley v. State, 2004 WL 1902428 (Miss. 2004). A death sentence was affirmed. The MMPI–2 or "similar testing" is required before a defendant can be adjudged mentally retarded and constitutionally protected from being executed.

Foster v. State, 848 So.2d 172 (Miss. 2003). A death sentence was remanded for determination of mental retardation. The MMPI–2 was found to be the best test suited to detect malingering.

Goodin v. State, 856 So.2d 267 (Miss. 2003). Because the MMPI–2 detects malingering, it is "difficult to cheat on without getting caught." A death sentence was reversed and remanded for determination of mental retardation.

Russell v. State, 849 So.2d 95 (Miss. 2003). A death sentence was remanded for determination of mental retardation. The court requires the MMPI be given as a prerequisite to remand in death penalty cases in Mississippi.

Schuck v. State, 865 So.2d 1111 (Miss. 2003). A murder conviction was affirmed. The defendant had high schizophrenia and paranoia readings on the MMPI.

Illinois Central Railroad v. Gandy, 750 So.2d 527 (Miss. 1999). Damages awarded for debilitating PTSD as a result of a fatal collision and derailment were sustained. The MMPI that could have ascertained malingering was not given.

Billiot v. State, 655 So.2d 1 (Miss. 1995). The MMPI was administered in a case where the defendant was found competent to be executed.

Williams v. Williams, 656 So.2d 325 (Miss. 1995). The MMPI administered to a father in a custody case who was accused of violence and inhumane treatment revealed a normal personality.

Tyler v. State, 618 So.2d 1306 (Miss. 1993). The MMPI revealed that the defendant knew right from wrong and therefore the murder conviction was affirmed

King v. State, 503 So.2d 271 (Miss. 1987). The MMPI was mentioned in a concurring opinion.

Bethany v. Stubbs, 393 So.2d 1351 (Miss. 1981). The MMPI was used to evaluate a mental patient petitioning for habeas corpus.

Missouri

In re Care and Treatment of Burgess, 147 S.W.3d 822 (Mo. App. S.D. 2004). In a civil commitment of a "sexually violent predator," the MMPI results were unusable because of unanswered questions.

Wainwright v. State, 143 S.W.3d 681 (Mo. App. W.D. 2004). The MMPI–2 was given by state's experts to "make sure" that the psychologist's hypothesis was "on target." The appellate court reversed and remanded the murder conviction based on ineffective assistance of counsel because counsel had not presented available testimony that the state's MMPI–2 testimony was substandard and a "misrepresentation of (Appellant's) psychological state." The defense at trial had been diminished capacity.

Henderson v. State, 111 S.W.3d 537 (Mo. App. 2003). A murder conviction was affirmed. The MMPI results were invalidated by exaggerated responses.

In re Coffel, 117 S.W.3d 116 (Mo. App. E.D. 2003). Determination that the defendant was a sexually violent predator was unsupported where no MMPI was given. The case was reversed.

Elliott v. Kansas City, Mo., School Dist, 71 S.W.3d 652 (Mo. App. W.D. 2002). The finding of 75% permanent partial disability in a worker's compensation setting was reversed and remanded. The MMPI–2 was given.

In re N.B., 64 S.W.3d 907 (Mo. App. S.D. 2002). The court remanded a case in which a child had been placed with social services. The MMPI results showed that the mother presented herself in an overly favorable light.

Chatmon v. St. Charles County Ambulance Dist., 55 S.W.3d 451 (Mo. App. E.D. 2001). The court found total disability in a worker's compensation case. The MMPI was administered.

Johnson v. State, 58 S.W.3d 496 (Mo. 2001). The sentence as a sexually violent predator was reversed. The MMPI was mentioned.

Tracy v. Tracy, 961 S.W.2d 855 (Mo. App. S.D. 1998). In an effort to win full custody of his children, a father presented the favorable results of his MMPI–2 evaluation.

State v. Elbert, 831 S.W.2d 646 (Mo. App. W.D. 1992). An expert's testimony that, based on the results of the MMPI, the defendant did not fit the profile of a sex offender, was properly excluded. Although the MMPI was generally accepted for purposes of diagnosis and treatment, it had not achieved general acceptance for purposes of determining whether a criminal fits a profile of a sex offender.

In Interest of S.A.J. and S.L.J., 818 S.W.2d 690 (Mo. App. 1991). The appellant was evaluated with the MMPI during a series of parental rights hearings.

Bussell v. Leat, 781 S.W.2d 97 (Mo. App. 1989). The MMPI was used by the defendant to evaluate the plaintiff's mental condition. There was discussion of the administering doctor's qualifications.

State v. Kennedy, 726 S.W.2d 884 (Mo. App. 1987). The MMPI was mentioned in the case.

State v. Taylor, 745 S.W.2d 173 (Mo. App. 1987). The MMPI was mentioned. The defendant claimed the trial court erred in overruling his objection to the state's cross-examination of the administering psychologist.

State v. Quillar, 683 S.W.2d 656 (Mo. App. 1986). The MMPI was used to evaluate the appellant on three separate occasions.

Juvenile Office of Cape Girardeau County v. M.E.J., 666 S.W.2d 957 (Mo. App. 1984). The MMPI was used to evaluate the appellant in a parental rights termination.

In Interest of C.L.M., 625 S.W.2d 613 (Mo. 1981). The MMPI was one of several tests used to evaluate a mother in a parental rights hearing.

Montana

In re A.N., 995 P.2d 427 (Mont. 2000). Parental rights were terminated. The MMPI–2 "indicated a defensive profile with a paranoid scale."

State v. Turner, 12 P.3d 934 (Mont. 2000). The request to withdraw a guilty plea to murder charges was denied. The MMPI profile was "remarkably normal."

State v. Smith, 931 P.2d 1272 (Mont. 1996). The MMPI was administered to the defendant, whose conviction resulted in a death sentence.

In re Custody of J.M.D., 857 P.2d 708 (Mont. 1993). A social worker conducted an evaluation of a mother, father, and father's new wife by administering the MMPI in a custody and visitation determination action.

Mason v. Ditzel, 842 P.2d 707 (Mont. 1992). The MMPI administered to an automobile accident victim revealed PTSD.

State v. Brodniak, 221 Mont. 212, 718 P.2d 322 (Mont. 1986). The MMPI was used as part of the evaluation of the victim.

Nebraska

In re Interest of Headrick, 532 N.W.2d 643 (Neb. Ct. App. 1995). The court ruled that the respondent was a substantial risk to herself or others based on her high MMPI scores for addiction, paranoia, and sociopathy, and low MMPI scores for depression.

Van Winkle v. Electric Hose & Rubber Co., 214 Neb. 8, 332 N.W.2d 209 (Neb. 1983). The MMPI was used to evaluate the plaintiff two different times.

Davis v. Western Electric, 210 Neb. 771, 317 N.W.2d 68 (Neb. 1982). The plaintiff refused to take the MMPI.

State v. Alvarez, 154 N.W.2d 746 (Neb. 1967). The defendant's high schizophrenic score on the MMPI, which was uncorroborated by other psychological tests, led the expert to believe that the defendant was faking incompetence.

New Hampshire

State v. Cavaliere, 663 A.2d 96 (N.H. 1995). Expert testimony was offered to show that the defendant's MMPI psychological profile was inconsistent with that of a sex offender was inadmissible.

New Jersey

In re Commitment of R.S., 773 A.2d 72 (N.J. Super. A.D. 2001). The respondent's civil commitment under the sexual predator act was affirmed. The MMPI–2 was consistent with anger, hostility, and antisocial personality.

Matter of Vey, 639 A.2d 718 (N.J. 1994). The MMPI was administered to determine whether a candidate for appointment as a police officer was mentally fit to effectively perform police duties.

State v. Martini, 619 A.2d 1208 (N.J. Super. Ct. 1993). The probative value of a defendant's answers to MMPI questions outweighed any prejudicial effect because the questions were part of a basis for the defense expert opinions.

New Jersey State Parole Board v. Cestari, 224 N.J. Super. 534, 540 A.2d 1334 (A.D. 1988). The MMPI was used to evaluate the defendant.

New Mexico

Matter of Ayala, 112 N.M. 109, 812 P.2d 358 (N.M. 1991). The MMPI was mentioned in the case. A psychologist testified that Ayala faked test answers.

New York

People v. Harris, 98 N.Y.2d 452 (N.Y. 2002). In the first sentence of death in New York in 20 years, MMPI–2 results were found to be "normal." The sentence was affirmed.

People v. Berrios, 150 Misc. 2d 229, 568 N.Y.S.2d 512 (Sup. Ct. 1991). The MMPI was one of four standardized tests used to evaluate the defendant.

H. Jon Geis, P.C. v. Landau, 117 Misc. 2d 396, 458 N.Y.S.2d 1000 (N.Y. Civ. Ct. 1983). The MMPI was mentioned in the case under "Brown and Dunbar, 'MMPI Difference Between Fee-Paying and Non-fee-paying Psychotherapy Clients,' *Journal of Clinical Psychology,* October 1978, Vol. 54, No. 4."

Buehler v. New York Telephone Co., 89 A.D.2d 664, 453 N.Y.S.2d 105 (App. Div. 3d Dist. 1982). Case was brought because the claimant refused to take the MMPI because her disability was orthopedic.

North Carolina

State v. Jones, 595 S.E.2d 124 (N.C. 2004). In a capital case, the defendant's expert was cross-examined on a specific MMPI question. The death sentence was affirmed.

Barringer v. Mid Pines Development Group, LLC, 568 S.E.2d 648 (N.C. App. 2002). The verdict in the civil action was reversed because the MMPI summary contained terms such as *psychopathic deviate, hypochondriasis,* and *hysteria,* which prejudiced the plaintiff.

In re Hayes, 564 S.E.2d 305 (N.C. App. 2002). The jury found the defendant not guilty by reason of insanity in an earlier proceeding. Recommitment was affirmed when the MMPI–2 results showed he was angry, impulsive, egocentric, and irresponsible.

State v. Davis, 539 S.E.2d 243 (N.C. 2000). The death sentence was affirmed. The computer-scored MMPI results generated possible interpretations that the defendant was manipulative, aggressive, resentful, and threatening toward women.

State v. Locklear, 505 S.E.2d 277 (N.C. 1998). Although the defendant, in his capital murder trial, asserted improper cross-examination of his expert witness regarding administration of the MMPI to the defendant, nothing in the record suggested such abuse.

State v. Bronson, 423 S.E.2d 772 (N.C. 1992). The defendant convicted of first-degree murder unsuccessfully claimed that certain questions asked of his expert witness permitted the expert to express an opinion on the defendant's credibility, which invaded the fact-finding process of the jury. The expert testified that the lie scale of the defendant's MMPI indicated that he took the test honestly. Because the defendant did not object there was no reversible error.

State v. Holder, 418 S.E.2d 197 (N.C. 1992). The MMPI was administered to a defendant claiming he lacked necessary intent to be convicted of first-degree murder.

Matter of Kennedy, 103 N.C. App. 632, 406 S.E.2d 307 (N.C. App. 1991). The MMPI was used to evaluate an entire family in a juvenile neglect case.

State v. Huff, 325 N.C. 1, 381 S.E.2d 635 (N.C. 1989). Results of the MMPI were discounted by a psychologist because the validity scale indicated that the answers were not accurate measures of the defendant's condition.

In re Parker, 90 N.C. App. 423, 368 S.E.2d 879 (1988). The MMPI was mentioned in the case.

State v. Mancuso, 321 N.C. 464, 364 S.E.2d 359 (N.C. 1988). The MMPI was one of the tests used to evaluate the defendant.

State v. Hoyle, 49 N.C. App. 98, 270 S.E.2d 582 (1980). The MMPI test results were ruled hearsay and highly prejudicial. The administering psychologist was not present to be cross-examined.

North Dakota

In Interest of C.K.H., 458 N.W.2d 303 (N.D. 1990). Termination of parental rights of the mother and both her husband and ex-husband to five children was upheld. The MMPI was used to support a finding that the second husband was "self-centered, selfish and egocentric."

Kopp v. North Dakota Workers' Compensation Bureau, 462 N.W.2d 132 (N.D. 1990). The MMPI was used to evaluate the plaintiff.

Oberlander v. Oberlander, 460 N.W.2d 400 (N.D. 1990). MMPI results were used extensively to evaluate both parents in a custody dispute.

State v. Skjonsby, 417 N.W.2d 818 (N.D. 1987). The MMPI test results were refuted. Three MMPIs were administered.

Sexton v. J.E.H., 355 N.W.2d 828 (N.D. 1984). The MMPI was used to evaluate the mother in a parental rights' termination.

Gramling v. North Dakota Workers' Compensation Bureau, 303 N.W.2d 323 (N.D. 1981). The plaintiff claimed violation of due process with respect to MMPI test results.

Ohio

State v. Mink, 805 N.E.2d 1064 (Ohio 2004). A death sentence was affirmed. The MMPI–2 was administered.

Ashcraft v. Univ. Cincinnati Hosp., 2003 WL 22827536 (Ohio App. 10th Dist. 2003). A medical negligence action was dismissed. The MMPI was mentioned. ·

State ex rel. Kohl's Dep't Stores v. Industry Commission, 784 N.E.2d 1251 (Ohio App. 10th Dist. 2003). Psychological conditions reached maximum improvement and temporary total disability compensation was terminated. MMPI results indicated "compensatory factors are contributing to the clinical picture. . . ."

State v. Hughbanks, 792 N.E.2d 1081 (Ohio 2003). Convictions and a death sentence were affirmed. The MMPI–2 was given.

State v. Robertson, 768 N.E.2d 1207 (Ohio App. 3d Dist. 2002). A finding of "sexual predator" status was affirmed. The MMPI–2 profile type indicated that the defendant "tend[ed] to harbor deviant religious and/or political views, and their behavior is erratic, unpredictable and impulsive."

Smith v. Smith, 780 N.E.2d 221 (Ohio 2002). A death sentence was affirmed. MMPI–2 tests suggested depression and alcohol abuse.

Beaver v. Beaver, 757 N.E.2d 41 (Ohio App. 4th Dist. 2001). Despite an MMPI–2 profile of the father in a child custody case indicating resentment, hostility and egocentricity, a custody finding for the mother was reversed and remanded.

State v. Hardie, 749 N.E.2d 792 (Ohio App. 4th Dist. 2001). The determination of a woman's sexual predator status was affirmed. The MMPI–2 showed the defendant as anxious, tense, fearful, and lacking insight.

State v. Murphy, 747 N.E.2d 765 (Ohio 2001). A death sentence was affirmed. The MMPI results were "consistent with impulsiveness and anger."

State v. Bays, 87 Ohio St. 3d 15 (1999). The MMPI–2 was administered. Conviction and sentence of death was affirmed.

In the Matter of Doyle G., 1998 WL 735320 (Ohio Ct. App. October 23, 1998). The MMPI administered to a mother who lost custody of her children to the Children's Services Board revealed that she suffered from dysthymia but did not have a borderline personality disorder.

State v. Goff, 694 N.E.2d 916 (Ohio 1998). The murder conviction and death sentence were affirmed despite mitigating evidence from the defendant's childhood MMPI.

State v. Howard, 1998 WL 801364 (Ohio. Ct. App. 1998). MMPI test results of a defendant convicted of sexual assault indicated that he was personality disordered, lacked insight and self-understanding, and therefore established that the defendant was a sexual predator.

State v. Berry, 686 N.E.2d 1079 (Ohio 1997). The MMPI was administered to the defendant to determine if he was mentally competent when he decided to terminate his death sentence appeal and submit to execution.

State v. Dennis, 683 N.E.2d 1096 (Ohio 1997). The MMPI was administered to a defendant sentenced to death.

Elling v. Graves, 640 N.E.2d 1156 (Ohio App. 6th Dist. 1994). The MMPI administered to a husband by his own doctor in a divorce and custody proceeding contradicted the court-appointed psychologist's evaluation of the husband.

State v. Daws, 662 N.E.2d 805 (Ohio App. 2d Dist. 1994). The MMPI was administered to a woman claiming battered woman's syndrome.

State v. Haight, 649 N.E.2d 294 (Ohio App. 10th Dist. 1994). A prison psychologist administered the MMPI to the defendant convicted of capital murder and sentenced to death.

State v. Martens, 629 N.E.2d 462 (Ohio App. 3d Dist. 1993). The MMPI administered to a rape victim revealed PTSD.

State v. Jones, 615 N.E.2d 713 (Ohio App. 2d Dist. 1992). The MMPI was administered 2 months after a rape for unrelated reasons.

Cleveland Civil Service Commission v. Ohio Civil Rights Commission, 57 Ohio St. 3d 62, 565 N.E.2d 579 (1991). The MMPI was used to evaluate a police department applicant. The MacAndrew Alcoholism Scale was mentioned.

State v. Ambrosia, 587 N.E.2d 892 (Ohio App. 6th Dist. 1990). The results of the MMPI were not allowed as character evidence in a rape case.

Pinger v. Behavioral Science Center, Inc., 52 Ohio App. 3d 17, 556 N.E.2d 209 (1988). The plaintiff sued a company retained by his employer to conduct psychological testing. The MMPI was one of the tests administered.

In re Barnes, 31 Ohio App. 3d 201, 510 N.E.2d 392 (1986). The MMPI was mentioned in the case.

Oklahoma

Frederick v. State, 37 P.3d 908 (Okla. Crim. App. 2001). A 1992 death sentence was remanded for resentencing trial in 1995. The MMPI–2 was administered. The second death sentence was affirmed.

Alverson v. State, 983 P.2d 498 (Okla. Crim. 1999). The MMPI–2 was administered by a person not qualified to do so in a murder and robbery case.

Davis v. Medical Arts Laboratory, 952 P.2d 52 (Okla. Civ. App. 1997). The MMPI was administered to a claimant alleging injury arising out of employment with the defendant when the Alfred P. Murrah Federal Building was bombed. MMPI results indicated the claimant's psychological condition preexisted the bombing.

In the Matter of L.S., 805 P.2d 120 (Okla. App. 1990). The MMPI was not given orally by a doctor because the patient could not read.

Haworth v. Central National Bank of Oklahoma City, 769 P.2d 740 (Okla. 1989). The MMPI was mentioned in the case.

State ex rel. Oklahoma Bar Association v. Colston, 777 P.2d 920 (Okla. 1989). The MMPI was one of several tests used to evaluate an attorney in a disciplinary proceeding.

Reynolds v. State, 717 P.2d 608 (Okla. Crim. 1986). Testimony of an expert who administered the MMPI was disallowed.

Faulkenberry v. Kansas City Southern Railway Co., 661 P.2d 510 (Okla. 1983). Two separate MMPI test results were used.

Jones v. State, 648 P.2d 1251 (Okla. Crim. 1982). The MMPI was used to evaluate the defendant.

Oregon

State ex rel. Dep't of Human Services v. Williams, 94 P.3d 131 (Or. App. 2004). The MMPI was mentioned.

Cunningham v. Thompson, 71 P.3d 110 (Or. App. 2003). The MMPI results suggested antisocial behavior. The conviction was affirmed.

State ex rel. State Office for Services to Children and Families v. Mellor, 47 P.3d 19 (Or. App. 2002). A judgment denying termination of parental rights was reversed. The mother answered the MMPI questions without reading them.

State ex rel. Juvenile Department v. DeVore, 108 Or. App. 426, 816 P.2d 647 (1991). The MMPI was used to evaluate a mother in a parental rights termination.

Gasper v. Adult and Family Services Division, 77 Or. App. 209, 712 P.2d 167 (1986). The MMPI was one of the tests used to evaluate the claimant.

Short v. State Accident Insurance Fund Corporation, 79 Or. App. 423, 719 P.2d 894 (1986). The MMPI was used several times to evaluate the claimant.

State v. Huntley, 302 Or. 418, 730 P.2d 1234 (1986). The MMPI was used to evaluate the defendant.

Berwick v. Adult and Family Services Division, 74 Or. App. 460, 703 P.2d 994 (1985). The MMPI was used to evaluate the petitioner.

Ferguson v. Industrial Indemnity Co., 70 Or. App. 46, 687 P.2d 1130 (1984). The MMPI was used to evaluate the claimant.

State ex rel. Juvenile Department v. Grannis, 67 Or. App. 565, 680 P.2d 660 (1984). Results of the MMPI were used in testimony against a mother in parental rights termination.

Matter of Swartzfager, 290 Or. 799, 626 P.2d 882 (1981). The MMPI test given to a mother was rendered invalid because she had preconceived notions of the test.

Pennsylvania

Commissioner v. Mitchell, 839 A.2d 202 (Pa. 2003). A death sentence was affirmed. The MMPI–2 was mentioned.

Curran v. Commissioner, Dep't of State, Bd. of Psychology, 766 A.2d 907 (Pa. Commw. 2001). Revocation of a license to practice psychology was reversed because of improper commingling of adjudicative and prosecutorial functions. The psychologist had administered the MMPI, which contains both "sexually related and non-sexually related matters" and had placed his hands on a female client's shoulders while asking about sexually related matters.

Paxos v. WCAB (Frankford-Quaker Grocery), 631 A.2d 826 (Pa. Commw. 1993). The MMPI was administered to determine whether a worker's compensation claimant was able to perform gainful employment.

In re Adoption of B.G.S., 614 A.2d 1161 (Pa. Super. 1992). A birth mother's psychological records and MMPI test results were deemed relevant and material in termination proceedings.

Marsico v. Workmen's Compensation Appeal Board (Dep't of Revenue), 588 A.2d 984 (Pa. Commw. 1991). Two MMPI tests were used to evaluate the claimant.

Moore v. Unemployment Compensation Board of Review, 578 A.2d 606 (Pa. Commw. 1990). The MMPI was mentioned in the case.

In re Adoption of Stunkard, 551 A.2d 253 (Pa. Super. 1988). The MMPI was used to evaluate a father in a parental rights termination case.

Wool v. Workmen's Compensation Appeal Board, 450 A.2d 1081 (Pa. Commw. 1982). The MMPI was used to evaluate the claimant.

Rhode Island

State v. Gardner, 616 A.2d 1124 (R.I. 1992). It was an error for the trial court to exclude MMPI results because the results were neither equivocal nor unreliable.

South Carolina

Von Dohlen v. State, 602 S.E.2d 738 (S.C. 2004). A new sentencing hearing was granted based on ineffective assistance of counsel where newly discovered evidence, including a 1990 MMPI, would have changed the expert's testimony.

Hudgins v. Moore, 337 S.C. 333 (1999). A juvenile defendant was convicted and sentenced to death for killing a police officer. During trial, he was questioned about specific answers he gave to MMPI–A items, but his attorney did not object to these questions. The death sentence was reversed based on ineffective assistance of counsel because the attorney did not object to the line of questioning.

Estridge v. Joslyn Clark Controls, Inc., 482 S.E.2d 577 (S.C. App. 1997). The MMPI was administered to a successful appellant of denial of benefits for psychological injuries that resulted from compensable physical injuries.

Howle v. PYA/Monarch, Inc., 288 S.C. 586, 344 S.E.2d 157 (S.C. App. 1986). The MMPI was used to evaluate the plaintiff.

South Dakota

Streeter v. Canton School Dist., 677 N.W.2d 221 (S.D. 2004). The MMPI showed no malingering in a worker's compensation case.

Wiedmann v. Merillat Industries, 623 N.W.2d 43 (S.D. 2001). Denial of worker's compensation benefits was affirmed where the worker refused to participate in a pain management program. The MMPI–2 results suggested significant depression.

Johnson v. Albertson's, 610 N.W. 2d 449 (S.D. 2000). A work-related injury was found to be not causally related to mental disability. The MMPI–2 F scale had an elevated score of 82.

State v. Anderson, 604 N.W.2d 482 (S.D. 2000). The trial court failed to establish a factual basis for finding the defendant mentally ill.

Jones v. Jones, 542 N.W.2d 119 (S.D. 1996). In a custody suit, the MMPI and other psychological tests were administered to parents. Both the father and mother demonstrated adequate parental capacities despite the father's history of alcoholism and abuse.

State v. Titus, 426 N.W.2d 578 (S.D. 1988). The MMPI was used to diagnose the defendant.

People in Interest of M.J.B., 364 N.W.2d 921 (S.D. 1985). The MMPI was used to evaluate parents in therapy to correct the domestic situation in a parental rights termination case.

Tennessee

Leavy v. State, 2004 WL 42220 (Tenn. Crim. App. 2004). A murder conviction and life sentence was affirmed. The MMPI results did not indicate antisocial or aggressive tendencies.

State v. Robbins, 2004 WL 2715334 (Tenn. Ct. App. 2004). A mother's parental rights were terminated. The MMPI–2 results suggested impulse disorder.

State v. Rogers, 2004 WL 1462649 (Tenn. Crim. App. 2004). A death sentence was affirmed. The MMPI results suggested exaggeration, a cry for help, or malingering.

State v. Flake, 114 S.W.3d 487 (Tenn. 2003). An insanity verdict was reversed. The MMPI is not a "medical examination" as defined in and given special confidential status under the Americans With Disabilities Act (ADA).

State v. Reid, 2003 WL 23021393 (Tenn. Crim. App. 2003), 91 S.W.3d 247 (Tenn. 2002). A death sentence was affirmed. The MMPI–2 was mentioned.

State v. Torres, 82 S.W.3d 236 (Tenn. 2002). A death sentence was reversed and remanded where the jury had said it was deadlocked. The MMPI–2 results were found to be "of questionable validity."

State v. Coulter, 67 S.W.3d 3 (Tenn. Crim. App. 2001). A murder conviction was affirmed. The MMPI–2 was administered.

Coe v. State, 17 S.W.3d 193 (Tenn. 2000). A prisoner was found competent to be executed. The MMPI showed malingering.

Irick v. State, 973 S.W.2d 643 (Tenn. Crim. App. 1998). A conviction and death sentence was affirmed when the court denied postconviction relief based in part on high MMPI–2 fake scale scores.

Skelton v. Robertshaw Controls Co., 1998 WL 740852 (Tenn. 1998). A woman who was denied worker's compensation benefits was administered the MMPI, and as a result, she was diagnosed with PTSD caused by her work-related back injury.

State v. Jackson, 890 S.W.2d 436 (Tenn. 1994). The MMPI was administered to the defendant, whose first-degree murder conviction was reversed because the state failed to prove that the defendant was capable of knowing right from wrong even though he suffered mental illness.

State v. Payne, 791 S.W.2d 10 (Tenn. 1990). The MMPI was used to evaluate the defendant.

Wade v. Aetna Casualty and Surety Co., 735 S.W.2d 215 (Tenn. 1987). The MMPI was mentioned in the case.

State v. Dicks, 615 S.W.2d 126 (Tenn. 1981). The MMPI was one of several tests used to evaluate the appellant. Testimony of a psychologist who administered the tests was not allowed in the trial in the guilt phase.

Texas

Commitment of Fisher v. State, 123 S.W.3d 828 (Tex. Ct. App. Corpus Christi 2003). A commitment under the sexual predator act was reversed. The due process rights of the defendant not capable of reading the MMPI were violated.

Campbell v. State, 125 S.W.3d 1 (Tex. Ct. App. Houston 2002). An involuntary commitment extension was reversed and remanded. MMPI results alone were found insufficient for involuntary commitment.

Muhammad v. State, 46 S.W.3d 493 (Tex. Ct. App. El Paso 2001). A life sentence was reversed and remanded because the court excluded the testimony of an expert psychologist, whose testimony included MMPI–2 results that showed "no signs of antisocial personality."

S.V. v. R.V., 933 S.W.2d 1 (Tex. 1996). A daughter made a tort claim against her father for sexual abuse. The MMPI administered to the daughter showed a classic profile shared by many survivors of sexual abuse, but was not conclusive of abuse. The MMPI given to the father showed traits similar to sex offenders but did not show him to be a sex abuser.

Garza v. State, 878 S.W.2d 213 (Tex. Ct. App. 1994). The MMPI administered while the defendant was in custody was unsuccessfully offered as evidence of immediate influence and sudden passion defense for murder.

Hernandez v. State, 885 S.W.2d 597 (Tex. Ct. App. 1994). The MMPI testing before a guilty plea did not reveal evidence to support an insanity defense; thus the plea was valid.

In Interest of A.V., 849 S.W.2d 393 (Tex. Ct. App. 1993). A mother successfully petitioned to terminate a father's parental rights due to alleged child sexual abuse. The MMPI administered to the father revealed no indications of sexual problems, but no psychosexual evaluation could prove or disprove guilt.

Nolte v. State, 854 S.W.2d 304 (Tex. Ct. App. 1993). The exclusion of expert testimony that a sex abuser's profile has high scores on certain scales and the defendant's MMPI scores were not elevated was deemed a harmless error.

Johnson v. King, 821 S.W.2d 425 (Tex. Ct. App. Fort Worth 1991). The MMPI was used to evaluate the plaintiff.

City of Dallas v. Cox, 793 S.W.2d 701 (Tex. Ct. App. Dallas 1990). There was extensive discussion of an officer's grid sheet, which contained MMPI information. There was also discussion of the MMPI testing procedure.

Davis v. Davis, 794 S.W.2d 930 (Tex. Ct. App. Dallas 1990). The MMPI was used to evaluate a father in a custody dispute.

Ochs v. Martinez, 789 S.W.2d 949 (Tex. Ct. App. San Antonio 1990). The MMPI was mentioned in a footnote.

Moss v. State, 704 S.W.2d 939 (Tex. Ct. App. 3d Dist. 1986). MMPI results showed the defendant to be normal. The defendant was taking antipsychotic drugs at the time of testing.

Matter of Franklin, 699 S.W.2d 689 (Tex. Ct. App. 6th Dist. 1985). The MMPI was one of the tests used to evaluate the claimant.

Williams v. State, 649 S.W.2d 693 (Tex. Ct. App. 7th Dist. 1983). A psychologist explained the MMPI, used the results on a chart, and gave his opinion of the appellant based on test results.

Utah

State v. Blubaugh, 904 P.2d 688 (Utah Ct. App. 1995). Testifying about an MMPI administered to a defendant convicted of depraved manslaughter of his girlfriend's child, an expert said, "When crimes are committed by individuals who score high on the MMPI they tend to be vicious and assaultive and often appear as senseless, poorly planned and poorly executed."

J.H. By and Through D. H. v. West Valley City, 840 P.2d 115 (Utah 1992). In a negligent hiring action where a police officer sexually abused a child, the MMPI was mentioned in footnote 36 as a test that was available for the defendant to use on its applicants.

State v. Bryan, 709 P.2d 257 (Utah 1985). The MMPI was mentioned in footnote 2 as one of two tests administered to the defendant by a psychologist.

Vermont

In re B.M., 682 A.2d 477 (Vt. 1996). Parental rights were terminated after MMPI results revealed that the father possessed a "pervasive lack of empathy" and "egocentric approach" to parenting.

Virginia

M.E.D. v. J.P.M., 3 Va. App. 391, 350 S.E.2d 215 (1986). The MMPI was one of several tests used to evaluate the father in a child custody case.

Washington

State v. Oliva, 73 P.2d 1016 (Wash. App. Div. 3d 2003). The court's denial of a sex offender sentencing was upheld. MMPI results showed an antisocial personality makeup.

In re Combs, 19 P.3d 469 (Wash. App. Div. 3d 2001). The trial court improperly refused to consider the mother's wish to move out of state when it granted custody to the mother. MMPI–2 results were defensive and "more defensive."

Mazzi v. Mazzi, 1998 WL 729687 (Wash. Ct. App., 1998). In a child custody trial, a forensic psychologist relied on MMPI results and parenting questionnaires to determine that the mother's personality issues would interfere with childrearing tasks.

State v. Sagastegui, 954 P.2d 1311 (Wash. 1998). The MMPI–2 given to the defendant convicted of three counts of murder supported the finding that the defendant knowingly and voluntarily waived his right to appeal.

In re Dependency of C. B., 904 P.2d 1171 (Wash. Ct. App. 1995). A doctor's testimony regarding the MMPI administered to a father supported the court's termination of parental rights.

State v. Pirtle, 904 P.2d 245 (Wash. 1995). The MMPI was administered to the defendant, who appealed his conviction and death sentence penalty.

In re Marriage of Luckey, 868 P.2d 189 (Wash. Ct. App. 1994). The MMPI was administered to a father because the mother accused him of child sex abuse. Although his scaled score matched the profiles of known child molesters, use of profile testing was found to be unfairly prejudicial.

In re Rice, 828 P.2d 1086 (Wash. 1992). The MMPI administered to the defendant after arrest indicated no mental disorder; therefore the death sentence was affirmed.

State v. Rice, 110 Wash. 2d 577, 757 P.2d 889 (1988). The MMPI was discussed in evaluation of the defendant and in the argument that the defendant had time to fabricate evidence of mental disease while incarcerated.

DeHaven v. Gant, 42 Wash. App. 666, 713 P.2d 149 (1986). Admissibility of MMPI results were argued.

State v. Harris, 106 Wash. 2d 784, 725 P.2d 975 (1986). An unscored MMPI was administered to evaluate the defendant. A request for a new trial based on new evidence including the scored MMPI was denied.

State v. Walker, 40 Wash. App. 658, 700 P.2d 1168 (1985). The MMPI was used to evaluate the defendant.

State v. Despenza, 38 Wash. App. 645, 689 P.2d 87 (1984). The MMPI was used to evaluate the victim. Testimony of those results was refused.

In re Mosley, 34 Wash. App. 179, 660 P.2d 315 (1983). The MMPI was used to evaluate the mother in a parental rights termination appeal.

Bertsch v. Brewer, 96 Wash. 2d 973, 640 P.2d 711 (1982). Admission of MMPI tests results, without laying a proper foundation, was found prejudicial and necessitated a new trial.

West Virginia

Keith A. v. Jennifer J. A., 500 S.E.2d 552 (W. Va. 1997). The MMPI was given to the mother, father, children, and paternal grandfather, where the paternal grandfather and father were accused of sexually abusing children. Based on the grandfather's MMPI–2 results, the expert suggested supervised contact with grandchildren.

Weece v. Cottle, 352 S.E.2d 131 (W. Va. 1986). The MMPI was used to evaluate the mother in a custody dispute.

State v. Duell, 332 S.E.2d 246 (W. Va. 1985). MMPI test results were rendered invalid because they were scored with the wrong gender scale.

Wisconsin

Shultz v. State, 274 N.W.2d 614 (Wis. 1979). The MMPI profile of a chronic undifferentiated schizophrenic was allowed as evidence of the defendant's mental defect but did not warrant a verdict of not guilty by reason of insanity.

Goetsch v. State, 172 N.W.2d 688 (Wis. 1969). Based on MMPI results, the state's expert testified to the strong probability that the defendant had significant psychopathology and should be criminally committed under the Sex Crimes Act.

Wyoming

Page v. State, 949 P.2d 466 (Wyo. 1997). The MMPI administered to an incarcerated defendant showed that the defendant suffered from schizophrenia requiring transfer to a state hospital despite his objections to transfer.

McGinn v. State, 928 P.2d 1157 (Wyo. 1996). An expert was allowed to rely on the MMPI results administered to the defendant.

May v. Southeast Wyoming Mental Health Center, 866 P.2d 732 (Wyo. 1993). The MMPI was administered to a father accused of sexually abusing his daughter. The father then brought action against state agencies responsible for investigating suspected child abuse.

Zabel v. State, 765 P.2d 357 (Wyo. 1988). The same expert whose testimony was allowed in *Brown v. State* (discussed in the following case) testified in this case. The case was reversed because the expert expanded her testimony beyond discussing the validity scoring as she had in *Brown v. State* (see below) and into improper evaluation of and comment on credibility.

Brown v. State, 736 P.2d 1110 (Wyo. 1987). An expert testified that MMPI validity scales suggested that an alleged sexual assault victim had approached the test truthfully, neither exaggerating nor covering up. Testimony was held not to be an inappropriate comment on the witness's truthfulness.

Malingering or Faking Bad References

This appendix lists published works on malingering or faking bad; symptom exaggeration; unusual responding that invalidates the record; and coached malingering. For an annotated lists of research articles addressing malingering not only on the MMPI but also on other psychological assessment instruments and approaches, please see the *Malingering Research Update* at http://kspope.com/assess/malinger.php.

Adams, S. V. (2001). MMPI frequency scale using a Hispanic population: An ethnic validity study. *Dissertation Abstracts International: Section B: The Sciences and Engineering, 61*(5-B), 2742.

Adelman, R. M., & Howard, A. (1984). Expert testimony on malingering: The admissibility of clinical procedures for the detection of deception. *Behavioral Sciences and the Law, 2,* 5–19.

Anthony, N. (1971). Comparison of clients' standard, exaggerated, and matching MMPI profiles. *Journal of Consulting and Clinical Psychology, 36,* 100–103.

Anthony, N. (1976). Malingering as role taking. *Journal of Clinical Psychology, 32,* 32–41.

Arbisi, P. A., & Ben-Porath, Y. S. (1995). An MMPI–2 infrequent response scale for use with psychopathological populations: The Infrequency–Psychopathology Scale, *F(p)*. *Psychological Assessment, 4,* 424–431.

Arbisi, P. A., & Ben-Porath, Y. S. (1997). Characteristics of the *F(p)* scale as a function of diagnosis in an inpatient sample of veterans. *Psychological Assessment, 9,* 102–105.

Arbisi, P. A., & Ben Porath, Y. S. (1998). The ability of the Minnesota Multiphasic Personality Inventory–2 validity scales to detect fake-bad responses in psychiatric inpatients. *Psychological Assessment, 10,* 231–228.

Arbisi, P. A., Ben-Porath, Y. S., & McNulty, J. (2003). Refinement of the *F(p)* Scale is not necessary: A response to Gass and Luis. *Assessment, 10,* 123–128.

Arbisi, P. A., & Butcher, J. N. (2004). Failure of the FBS to predict malingering of somatic symptoms: Response to critiques by Greve and Bianchini and Lees Haley and Fox. *Archives of Clinical Neuropsychology, 19*(3), 341–345.

Arbisi, P. A., & Butcher, J. N. (2004). Psychometric perspectives on detection of malingering of pain: The use of the MMPI–2. *Clinical Journal of Pain, 20,* 383–398.

Arbisi, P., & Butcher, J. N. (2004). Relationship between personality and health symptoms: Use of the MMPI–2 in medical assessments. *International Journal of Health and Clinical Psychology, 4,* 571–595.

Arce, R., del Carmen Pampillon, M., & Farina, F. (2002). *Desarrollo y evaluacion de un procedimiento empirico para deteccion de la simulacion de enajenacion mental en el contexto legal* [Development and assessment of an empirical procedure for detecting simulated mental insanity in the legal context]. *Anuario de Psicologia, 33*(3), 385–408.

Archer, R. P., & Elkins, D. E. (1999). Identification of random responding on the MMPI–A. *Journal of Personality Assessment, 73,* 407–421.

Archer, R. P., Fontaine, J., & McCrae, R. R. (1998). Effects of two MMPI–2 validity scales on basic scale relations to external criteria. *Journal of Personality Assessment, 70,* 87–102.

Archer, R. P., Handel, R. W., Greene, R. L., Baer, R. A., & Elkins, D. E. (2001). An evaluation of the usefulness of the MMPI–2 F(p) scale. *Journal of Personality Assessment, 76,* 282–295.

Archer, R. P., Handel, R. W., Lynch, K. D., & Elkins, D. E. (2002). MMPI–A validity scale uses and limitations in detecting varying levels of random responding. *Journal of Personality Assessment, 78,* 417–431.

Austin, J. S. (1990). The detection of malingering in forensic inpatients: A look at the MMPI and MCMI. *Dissertation Abstracts International, 50,* 1981.

Austin, J. S. (1992). The detection of fake good and fake bad on the MMPI–2. *Educational and Psychological Measurement, 52,* 669–674.

Bacchiochi, J. R., & Bagby, R. M. (2003, June). *Development of the malingering discriminant function index (M–DFI).* Paper presented at the 38th annual Workshop and Symposium on the MMPI–2 and MMPI–A, Minneapolis, MN.

Bacchiochi, J. R., & Bagby, R. M. (2004, March). *Validation of the Malingering Discriminant Function (MDFI) for the MMPI–2.* Paper presented at the 2004 Midwinter Meeting of the Society for Personality Assessment, Miami, FL.

Baer, R. A., Ballenger, J., Berry, D. T. R., & Wetter, M. W. (1997). Detection of random responding on the MMPI–A. *Journal of Personality Assessment, 68,* 139–151.

Baer, R. A., Kroll, L. S., Rinaldo, J., & Ballenger, J. (1999). Detecting and discriminating between random responding and overreporting on the MMPI–A. *Journal of Personality Assessment, 72,* 308–320.

Bagby, R. M. (1998). Utility of the Deceptive–Subtle items in the detection of malingering. *Journal of Personality Assessment, 70,* 405–415.

Bagby, R. M., Buis, T., & Nicholson, R. A. (1995). Relative effectiveness of the standard validity scales in detecting fake-bad and fake-good responding: Replication and extension. *Psychological Assessment, 7,* 84–92.

Bagby, R. M., Marshall, M. B., Bury, A. S., & Bacchiochi, J. R. (2006). Assessing underreporting and overreporting response style on the MMPI. In J. N. Butcher (Ed.), *MMPI–2: A practitioner's guide* (pp. 39–69). Washington, DC: American Psychological Association.

Bagby, R. M., Nicholson, R. A., Bacchiochi, J. R., Ryder, A. G., & Bury, A. S. (2002). The predictive capacity of the MMPI–2 and PAI validity scales and indexes to detect coached and uncoached feigning. *Journal of Personality Assessment, 78,* 69–86.

Bagby, R. M., Nicholson, R. A., & Buis, T. (1998). Utility of the Deceptive–Subtle items in the detection of malingering. *Journal of Personality Assessment, 70,* 405–415.

Bagby, R. M., Rogers, R., & Buis, T. (1994). Detecting malingered and defensive responding on the MMPI–2 in a forensic inpatient sample. *Journal of Personality Assessment, 62,* 191–203.

Bagby, R. M., Rogers, R., Buis, T., & Kalemba, V. (1994). Malingered and defensive response styles on the MMPI–2: An examination of validity scales. *Assessment, 1,* 31–38.

Bagby, R. M., Rogers, R., Nicholson, R., & Buis, T. (1997). Does clinical training facilitate feigning schizophrenia on the MMPI–2? *Psychological Assessment, 9,* 106–112.

Bagby, R. M., Rogers, R., Nicholson, R. A., Buis, T., Seeman, M. V., & Rector, N. A. (1997). Effectiveness of the MMPI–2 validity indicators in the detection of defensive responding in clinical and nonclinical samples. *Psychological Assessment, 9,* 406–413.

Bagdade, P. S. (2004). Malingering on the MMPI–A: An investigation of the standard validity scales and the Infrequency–Psychopathology Scale—Adolescent version (*Fp–A*). *Dissertation Abstracts International: Section B: The Sciences and Engineering, 64*(7-B), 3513.

Bannatyne, L. A., Gacono, C. B., & Greene, R. L. (1999). Differential patterns of responding among three groups of chronic, psychotic, forensic outpatients. *Journal of Clinical Psychology, 55,* 1553–1565.

Barrick, M. R., & Mount, M. K. (1996). Effects of impression management and self-deception on the predictive validity of personality constructs. *Journal of Applied Psychology, 81,* 261–272.

Beal, D. (1989). Assessment of malingering in personal injury cases. *American Journal of Forensic Psychology, 7,* 59–65.

Ben-Porath, Y. (1994). The ethical dilemma of coached malingering research. *Psychological Assessment, 6,* 14–15.

Berry, D. T. R. (1995). Detecting distortion in forensic evaluations with the MMPI–2. In Y. S. Ben-Porath, J. R. Graham, G. C. N. Hall, R. D. Hirschman, & M. S. Zaragoza (Eds.), *Forensic applications of the MMPI–2* (pp. 82–103). Thousand Oaks, CA: Sage.

Berry, D. T. R., Adams, J. J., Clark, C. D., Thacker, S. R., Burger, T. L., Wetter, M., et al. (1996). Detection of a cry for help on the MMPI–2: An analog investigation. *Journal of Personality Assessment, 67,* 26–36.

Berry, D. T. R., Adams, J. J., Smith, G. T., Greene, R. L., Sekirnjak, G. C., Weiland, G., et al. (1997). MMPI–2 clinical scales and 2-point code types: Impact of varying levels of omitted items. *Psychological Assessment, 9,* 158–160.

Berry, D. T. R., Baer, R. A., & Harris, M. J. (1991). Detection of malingering on the MMPI: A meta-analysis. *Clinical Psychology Review, 11,* 585–598.

Berry, D. T. R., Baer, R. A., Rinaldo, J. C., & Wetter, M. W. (2002). Assessment of malingering. In J. N. Butcher (Ed.), *Clinical personality assessment: Practical approaches* (2nd ed., pp. 271–302). New York: Oxford University Press.

Berry, D. T. R., & Butcher, J. N. (1998). Detection of feigning of head injury symptoms on the MMPI–2. In C. Reynolds (Ed.), *Detection of malingering in head injury litigation* (pp. 209–238). New York: Plenum Press.

Berry, D. T., R., Cimono, C. R., Chong, N. K., LaVelle, S. H., Ivy, K., Morse, T. L., et al. (2001). MMPI–2 fake-bad scale: An attempted cross-validation of proposed cutting scores for outpatients. *Journal of Personality Assessment, 76,* 296–314.

Berry, D. T. R., Lamb, D., Wetter, M., Baer, R., & Widiger, T. (1994). Ethical considerations in research on coached malingering. *Psychological Assessment, 6,* 16–17.

Berry, D. T. R., Wetter, M. W., & Baer, R. A. (1995). Assessment of malingering. In J. N. Butcher (Ed.), *Clinical personality assessment: Practical approaches* (pp. 236–248). New York: Oxford University Press.

Berry, D. T. R., Wetter, M. W., Baer, R. A., Larsen, L., Clark, C., & Monroe, K. (1992). MMPI–2 random responding indices: Validation using a self-report methodology. *Psychological Assessment, 4,* 340–345.

Berry, D. T. R., Wetter, M. W., Baer, R. A., Widiger, T. A., Sumpter, J. C., Reynolds, S. K., et al. (1991). Detection of random responding on the MMPI–2: Utility of *F, back F,* and *VRIN* scales. *Psychological Assessment, 3,* 418–423.

Berry, D. T. R., Wetter, M. W., Baer, R. A., Youngjohn, J. R., Gass, C. S., Lamb, D. G., et al. (1995). Overreporting of closed-head injury symptoms on the MMPI–2. *Psychological Assessment, 76,* 517–523.

Blanchard, D. D., McGrath, R. E., Pogge, D. L., & Khadivi, A. (2003). A comparison of the PAI and MMPI–2 as predictors of faking bad in college students. *Journal of Personality Assessment, 80,* 197–205.

Blazer, J. (1965). MMPI interpretation in outline: III. The *F* scale. *Psychology, 2,* 2–9.

Blumbert, S. (1967). MMPI *F* Scale as an indicator of severity of psychopathology. *Journal of Clinical Psychology, 23,* 96–99.

Boone, D. (1994). Reliability of the MMPI–2 subtle and obvious scales with psychiatric inpatients. *Journal of Personality Assessment, 62,* 346–351.

Boone, D. (1995). Differential validity of the MMPI–2 subtle and obvious scales with psychiatric inpatients: Scale 2. *Journal of Clinical Psychology, 51,* 526–531.

Boone, K. B., & Lu, P. H. (1999). Impact of somatoform symptomatology on credibility of cognitive performance. *Clinical Neuropsychologist, 13*(4), 414–419.

Brems, C., & Harris, K. (1996). Faking the MMPI–2: Utility of the Subtle–Obvious scales. *Journal of Clinical Psychology, 52,* 525–533.

Brems, C., & Johnson, M. E. (1991). Subtle–Obvious scales of the MMPI: Indicators of profile validity in a psychiatric population. *Journal of Personality Assessment, 56,* 536–544.

Brophy, A. L. (1995). Educational level, occupation, and the MMPI–2 *F–K* index. *Psychological Reports, 77*(1), 175–178.

Brophy, A. L. (1995). *F–K* Dissimulation Index on the MMPI–2. *Psychological Reports, 76*(1), 158.

Brozek, J. H., & Schiele B. (1948). Clinical significance of the Minnesota Multiphasic *F* scale evaluated in experimental neurosis. *American Journal of Psychiatry, 105,* 259–266.

Brunnetti, D. G. (1995). The effects of faking instructions of MMPI–2 response latencies. *Dissertation Abstracts International, 56,* 2316.

Brunetti, D. G., Schlottmann, R. S., Scott, A. B., & Hollrah, J. L. (1998). Instructed faking and MMPI–2 response latencies: The potential for assessing response validity. *Journal of Clinical Psychology, 54,* 143–153.

Buechley, R., & Ball, H. (1952). A new test of "validity" for the group MMPI. *Journal of Consulting Psychology, 16,* 299–301.

Burkhart, B. R., Christian, W. L., & Gynther, M. D. (1978). Item subtlety and faking on the MMPI: A paradoxical relationship. *Journal of Personality Assessment, 42,* 76–80.

Burkhart, B. R., Gynther, M. D., & Christian, W. L. (1978). Psychological mindedness, intelligence, and item subtlety endorsement patterns on the MMPI. *Journal of Clinical Psychology, 34,* 76–79.

Burkhart, B. R., Gynther, M. D., & Fromuth, M. E. (1980). The relative predictive validity of subtle vs. obvious items on the MMPI depression scale. *Journal of Clinical Psychology, 36,* 748–751.

Bury, A. S., & Bagby, R. M. (2002). The detection of feigned uncoached and coached posttraumatic stress disorder with the MMPI–2 in a sample of workplace accident victims. *Psychological Assessment, 14,* 472–484.

Butcher, J. N., Arbisi, P. A., Atlis, M. M., & McNulty, J. L. (2003). The construct validity of the Lees-Haley Fake Bad Scale. Does this scale measure somatic malingering and feigned emotional distress? *Archives of Clinical Neuropsychology, 18,* 473–485.

Campbell, J. E. (2003). Predictive variables for invalid Minnesota Multiphasic Personality Inventory—2 profiles: An inpatient sample. *Dissertation Abstracts International: Section B: The Sciences and Engineering, 63*(11–B), 5507.

Cassisi, J. E., & Workman, D. E. (1992). The detection of malingering and deception with a short form of the MMPI–2 based on the *L, F,* and *K* scales. *Journal of Clinical Psychology, 48,* 54–58.

Charles, T. L., Jr. (2000). Usefulness of the Minnesota Multiphasic Personality Inventory—2 in detection of deception in a personal injury type forensic population. *Dissertation Abstracts International: Section B: The Sciences and Engineering, 60*(10–B), 5221.

Cheung, F. M., Song, W. Z., & Butcher, J. N. (1991). An infrequency scale for the Chinese MMPI. *Psychological Assessment, 3,* 648–653.

Christian, W. L., Burkhart, B. R., & Gynther, M. D. (1978). Subtle–obvious ratings of MMPI items:

New interest in an old concept. *Journal of Consulting and Clinical Psychology, 46,* 1178–1186.

Clark, M. E., Gironda, R. J., & Young, R. W. (2003). Detection of back random responding: Effectiveness of MMPI–2 and Personality Assessment Inventory validity indices. *Psychological Assessment, 15,* 223–234.

Cofer, C. N., Chance, J., & Judson, A. J. (1949). A study of malingering on the MMPI. *Journal of Psychology, 27,* 491–499.

Cohn, T. S. (1952). Is the *F* scale indirect? *Journal of Abnormal and Social Psychology, 47,* 732.

Cohn, T. S. (1956). The relation of the *F* Scale to a response set to answer positively. *Journal of Social Psychology, 44,* 129–133.

Colligan, R. C. (1976). Atypical response sets and the automated MMPI. *Journal of Clinical Psychology, 32*(1), 76–78.

Comrey, A. L. (1958). A factor analysis of items on the *F* scale of the MMPI. *Educational and Psychological Measurement, 18,* 621–632.

Conkey, V. A. (2000). Determining the sensitivity of the MMPI–A to random responding and malingering in adolescents (Minnesota Multiphasic Personality Index, validity scales). *Dissertation Abstracts International, 60,* 3608.

Cooke, G., & Robey, A. (1971). The MMPI: A case study in dissimulation. *Journal of Consulting and Clinical Psychology, 36,* 355–359.

Corrigan, S. K. (1997). Malingering on the MMPI–2: An analogue investigation of the coached simulation of posttraumatic stress disorder. *Dissertation Abstracts International, 57,* 7221.

Costa, L. D., London, P., & Levita, E. (1963). A modification of the *F* scale of the MMPI. *Psychological Reports, 12,* 427–433.

Cramer, K. M. (1995). Comparing three new MMPI–2 randomness indices in a novel procedure for random profile derivation. *Journal of Personality Assessment, 65,* 514–520.

Cramer, K. M. (1995). The effects of description clarity and disorder type on the MMPI–2 fake-bad indices. *Journal of Clinical Psychology, 51,* 831–840.

Cukrowicz, K. C., Reardon, M. L., Donohue, K. F., & Joiner, T. E., Jr. (2004). MMPI–2 *F* scale as a predictor of acute versus chronic disorder classification. *Assessment, 11,* 145–151.

Cumella, E. J., Wall, A. D., & Kerr-Almeida, N. (2000). MMPI–2 in inpatient assessment of women with eating disorders. *Journal of Personality Assessment, 75,* 387–403.

Dahlstrom, W. G., Brooks, J. D., & Peterson, C. D. (1990). The Beck Depression Inventory: Item order and the impact of response sets. *Journal of Personality Assessment, 55,* 224–233.

Dalby, J. (1988). Detecting faking in the pretrial psychological assessment. *American Journal of Forensic Psychology, 6,* 49–55.

Dannenbaum, S. E., & Lanyon, R. I. (1993). The use of subtle items in detecting deception. *Journal of Personality Assessment, 61,* 501–510.

Dearth, C. S., Berry, D. T., Vickery, C. D., Vagnini, V. L., Baser, R. E., Orey, S. A., et al. (2005). Detection of feigned head injury symptoms on the MMPI–2 in head injured patients and community controls. *Archives of Clinical Neuropsychology, 20,* 95–110.

Deutschle, J. J., Jr. (1998). The development and use of subscales for the *F* and *FB* scales on the MMPI–2 to aid in the comparison of response styles in depressed vs. psychotic and informed vs. uninformed dissimulators. *Dissertation Abstracts International: Section A: Humanities and Social Sciences, 58*(10-A), 3844.

DiLalla, D. L., Gottesman, I. I., Carey, G., & Bouchard, T. J. (1999). Heritability of MMPI Harris–Lingoes and Subtle–Obvious subscales in twins reared apart. *Assessment, 6,* 353–366.

DuAlba, L., & Scott, R. L. (1993). Somatization and malingering for workers' compensation applicants: A cross-cultural MMPI study. *Journal of Clinical Psychology, 49,* 913–917.

Dubinsky, S., Gamble, D. J., & Rogers, M. L. (1985). A literature review of subtle–obvious items on the MMPI. *Journal of Personality Assessment, 49,* 62–68.

Dubinsky, S., Rogers, M. L., & Karman, R. (1983). *Ability and subtle–obvious items endorsement patterns on the MMPI.* Unpublished study, Biola University, Rosemead School of Psychology.

Duff, F. L. (1955). Item subtlety in personality inventory scales. *Journal of Consulting Psychology, 29,* 565–570.

Dush, D. M., Simons, L. E., Platt, W., Nation, P. C., & Ayres, S. Y. (1994). Psychological profiles distinguishing litigating and nonlitigating pain patients: Subtle, and not so subtle. *Journal of Personality Assessment, 62,* 299–313.

Echols, M. A. (1999). The relative contributions of the F–Psychopathology scale and MMPI–2 validity scales in the assessment of MMPI–2 protocol validity of African-American and Caucasian dual-diagnosis patients. *Dissertation Abstracts International: Section B: The Sciences and Engineering, 60*(2-B), 0825.

Elhai, J. D., & Frueh, B. C. (2001). Subtypes of clinical presentations in malingerers of posttraumatic stress disorder: An MMPI–2 cluster analysis. *Assessment, 8,* 75–84.

Elhai, J. D., Frueh, B. C., Gold, P. B., Gold, S. N., & Hamner, M. B. (2000). Clinical presentations of posttraumatic stress disorder across trauma populations: A comparison of MMPI–2 profiles of combat veterans and adult survivors of child sexual abuse. *Journal of Nervous and Mental Disease, 188,* 708–713.

Elhai, J. D., Gold, P. B., Frueh, B. C., & Gold, S. N. (2000). Cross-validation of the MMPI–2 in detecting malingered posttraumatic stress disorder. *Journal of Personality Assessment, 75,* 449–463.

Elhai, J. D., Gold, S. N., Sellers, A. H., & Dorfman, W. I. (2001). The detection of malingered posttraumatic stress disorder with MMPI–2 fake bad indices. *Assessment, 8,* 217–232.

Elhai, J. D., Naifeh, J. A., Zucker, I. S., Gold, S. N., Deitsch, S. E., & Frueh, B. C. (2004). Discriminating malingered from genuine civilian posttraumatic stress disorder: A validation of three MMPI–2 infrequency scales (*F, Fp,* and *Fptsd*). *Assessment, 11,* 139–144.

Elhai, J. D., Ruggiero, K. J., Frueh, B. C., Beckham, J. C., Gold, P. B., & Feldman, M. E. (2002). The Infrequency–Posttraumatic Stress Disorder Scale (*Fptsd*) for the MMPI–2: Development and initial validation with veterans presenting with combat-related PTSD. *Journal of Personality Assessment, 79,* 531–549.

Esser, C., & Schneider, J. F. (1998). Differentielle Reaktionslatenzzeiten beim Bearbeiten von Persönlichkeitsfragebogen als möglicher indicator für Verfäischungstendenzen [Differential response latencies as a possible indicator for detecting faking on personality test items]. *Zeitschrift für Differentielle und Diagnostische Psychologie, 19,* 246–257.

Evans, R. G. (1984). The Test–Retest Index and high F MMPI profiles. *Journal of Clinical Psychology, 40*(2), 516–518.

Evans, R. G., & Dinning, W. D. (1983). Response consistency among high F scale scorers on the MMPI. *Journal of Clinical Psychology, 39*(2), 246–248.

Exner, J., McDowell, E., Pabst, J., Stackman, W., & Kirk, L. (1963). On the detection of willful falsification in the MMPI. *Journal of Consulting Psychology, 27,* 91–94.

Fairbank, J. A., McCaffrey, R. J., & Keane, T. M. (1985). Psychometric detection of fabricated symptoms of posttraumatic stress disorder. *American Journal of Psychiatry, 42*(4), 501–503.

Fernandez, E. C. (1999). Detecting malingering in a federal pretrial sample. *Dissertation Abstracts International, 59,* 5575.

Fliter, J. M. K., Elhai, J. D., & Gold, S. N. (2003). MMPI–2 F scale elevations in adult victims of child sexual abuse. *Journal of Traumatic Stress, 16*(3), 269–274.

Forey, W. F. (1997). MMPI–2 dissimulation with an American Indian sample. *Dissertation Abstracts International: Section B: The Sciences and Engineering, 58*(5–B), 2746.

Fox, D. D., Gerson, A., & Lees-Haley, P. R. (1995). Interrelationship of the MMPI–2 validity scales in personal injury claims. *Journal of Clinical Psychology, 51*, 42–47.

Franklin, C. L., Repasky, S. A., Thompson, K. E., Shelton, S. A., & Uddo, M. (2002). Differentiating overreporting and extreme distress: MMPI–2 use with compensation-seeking veterans with PTSD. *Journal of Personality Assessment, 79*, 274–285.

Franklin, C. L., Repasky, S. A., Thompson, K. E., Shelton, S. A., & Uddo, M. (2003). Assessment of response style in combat veterans seeking compensation for posttraumatic stress disorder. *Journal of Traumatic Stress, 16*, 251–255.

Frueh, B. (1994). The susceptibility of the Rorschach inkblot test to malingering of combat-related PTSD. *Journal of Personality Assessment, 62*, 280–298.

Frueh, B. C., Elhai, J. D., Gold, P. B., Monnier, J., Magruder, K. M., Keane, T. M., et al. (2003). Disability compensation seeking among veterans evaluated for posttraumatic stress disorder. *Psychiatric Services, 54*, 84–91.

Frueh, B. C., & Kinder, B. N. (1994). The susceptibility of the Rorschach inkblot test to malingering of combat-related PTSD. *Journal of Personality Assessment, 62*, 280–298.

Frueh, B. C., Smith, D. W., & Barker, S. E. (1996). Compensation seeking status and psychometric assessment of combat veterans seeking treatment for PTSD. *Journal of Traumatic Stress, 9*, 427–439.

Gallagher, R. W. (1997). Detection of malingering at the time of intake in a correctional setting with the MMPI–2 validity scales. *Dissertation Abstracts International: Section B: The Sciences and Engineering, 58*(11-B), 6233.

Gallen, R. T., & Berry, D. T. R. (1996). Detection of random responding in MMPI–2 protocols. *Assessment, 3*(2), 171–178.

Gallen, R. T., & Berry, D. T. R. (1997). Partially random MMPI–2 protocols: When are they interpretable? *Assessment, 4*(1), 61–68.

Gallucci, N. T. (1984). Prediction of dissimulation on the MMPI in a clinical field setting. *Journal of Consulting and Clinical Psychology, 52*, 917–918.

Gallucci, N. T. (1987). The influence of elevated F scales on the validity of adolescent MMPI profiles. *Journal of Personality Assessment, 51*, 133–139.

Gandolfo, R. (1995). MMPI–2 profiles of worker's compensation claimants who present with claims of harassment. *Journal of Clinical Psychology, 51*, 711–715.

Ganellen, R. J., Wasyliw, O. E, Haywood, T. W., & Grossman, L. S. (1996). Can psychosis be malingered on the Rorschach? An empirical study. *Journal of Personality Assessment, 66*, 65–80.

Gass, C. S., & Luis, C. A. (2001). MMPI–2 scale $F(p)$ and symptom feigning: Scale refinement. *Assessment, 8*, 425–429.

Gendreau, P. M., Irvine, M., & Knight, S. (1973). Evaluating response set styles on the MMPI with prisoners faking good adjustment and maladjustment. *Canadian Journal of Abnormal Psychology, 82*, 139–140.

Gillis, J. R., Rogers, R., & Dickens, S. E. (1990). The detection of faking bad response styles on the MMPI. *Canadian Journal of Behavioural Science, 22*(4), 408–416.

Gloye, E. E., & Zimmerman, I. L. (1967). MMPI item changes by college students under ideal self response set. *Journal of Projective Techniques and Personality Assessment, 31*, 63–69.

Gomez, J., F., & Sanchez Crespo, G. (2002). Sensibilidad al fingimiento de la Escala Psiquiatrica Fp de Arbisi y Ben-Porath (1995, 1998) en la adaptacion espanola del MMPI–2 [Sensitivity to faking in Arbisi and Ben-Porath's psychiatric Fp scale (1995, 1998) in the Spanish adoption of the MMPI–2]. *Revista Iberoamericana de Diagnostico y Evaluacion Psicologica, 14*(2), 119–134.

Gough, H. G. (1947). Simulated patterns on the Minnesota Multiphasic Personality Inventory. *Journal of Abnormal and Social Psychology, 42*, 215–225.

Gough, H. G. (1950). The *F* minus *K* dissimulation index for the MMPI. *Journal of Consulting Psychology, 14*, 408–413.

Graham, J. R., Watts, D., & Timbrook, R. E. (1991). Detecting fake-good and fake-bad MMPI–2 profiles. *Journal of Personality Assessment, 57*, 264–277.

Grant, J. G. (1967). *A study of deliberate faking in the MMPI with seminarians.* Chicago: Loyola University Press.

Gravitz, M. A. (1987). An empirical study of MMPI *F* scale validity. *Psychological Reports, 60*(2), 389–390.

Greene, R. L. (1978). An empirically derived MMPI Carelessness Scale. *Journal of Clinical Psychology, 34*, 407–410.

Greene, R. L. (1979). Response consistency on the MMPI: The *T–R* index. *Journal of Personality Assessment, 43*, 69–71.

Greene, R. L. (1988). Assessment of malingering and defensiveness by objective personality inventories. In R. Rogers (Ed.), *Clinical assessment of malingering and deception* (pp. 123–158). New York: Guilford Press.

Greene, R. L. (1988). The relative efficacy of *F–K* and the obvious and subtle scales to detect overreporting of psychopathology on the MMPI. *Journal of Clinical Psychology, 44*, 152–159.

Greene, R. L. (1997). Assessment of malingering and defensiveness by multiscale inventories. In R. Rogers (Ed.), *Clinical assessment of malingering and deception* (2nd ed., pp. 169–207). New York: Guilford Press.

Greiffernstein, M. F., Baker, J., Axelrod, B., Peck, E., & Gervais, R. (2004). Fake Bad Scale and MMPI–2 Family in detection of implausible psychological trauma claims. *Neuropsychologist, 18*, 573–590.

Greiffenstein, M. F., Baker, W. J., Gola, T., Donders, J., & Miller, L. (2002). The Fake Bad Scale in atypical and severe closed head injury litigants. *Journal of Clinical Psychology, 58*, 1591–1600.

Greiffenstein, M. F., Baker, W. J., & Johnson-Greene, D. (2002). Actual versus self-reported scholastic achievement of litigating postconcussion and severe closed head injury claimants. *Psychological Assessment, 14*, 202–208.

Greiffenstein, M. F., Gola, T., & Baker, W. J. (1995). MMPI–2 validity scales versus domain specific measures in detection of factitious traumatic brain injury. *Clinical Neuropsychologist, 9*, 230–240.

Greve, K. W., & Bianchini, K. J. (2004). Response to Butcher et al., The construct validity of the Lees-Haley Fake-Bad Scale. *Archives of Clinical Neuropsychology, 19*(3), 337–339.

Greve, K. W., Bianchini, K. J., Love, J. M., Brennan, A., & Heinly, M. (in press). Sensitivity and specificity of MMPI–2 validity scales and indicators to malingered neurocognitive dysfunction in traumatic brain injury. *Clinical Neuropsychologist.*

Griffin, G. A. E., Normington, J., May, R., & Glassmire, D. (1996). Assessing dissimulation among Social Security disability income claimants. *Journal of Consulting and Clinical Psychology, 64*, 1425–1430.

Grillo, J., Brown, R. S., Hilsabeck, R., & Price, J. R. (1994). Raising doubts about the claims of malingering: Implications of relationships between MCMI–2 and MMPI performance. *Journal of Clinical Psychology, 50*, 651–655.

Gross, L. R. (1959). MMPI *L–F–K* relationships with criteria of behavioral disturbance and social adjustment in a schizophrenic population. *Journal of Consulting Psychology, 23*, 319–323.

Gross, S. Z. (1964). A normative study and cross-validation of MMPI subtle and obvious scales for parents seen at a child guidance clinic. *Psychology, 1*, 5–7.

Grossman, L. S., & Wasyliw, O. E. (1988). A psychometric study of stereotypes: Assessment of malingering in a criminal forensic group. *Journal of Personality Assessment, 52,* 549–563.

Grow, R., McVaugh, W., & Eno, T. D. (1980). Faking and the MMPI. *Journal of Clinical Psychology, 36,* 910–917.

Gynther, M. D., Altman, H., & Warbin, R. (1973). Interpretation of uninterpretable MMPI profiles. *Journal of Clinical Psychology, 40,* 78–83.

Gynther, M. D., Burkhardt, B. R., & Hovanitz, C. (1979). Do face valid items have more predictive validity than subtle items? The case of the MMPI *Pd* scale. *Journal of Consulting and Clinical Psychology, 47,* 295–300.

Gynther, M. D., & Petzel., T. P. (1967). Differential endorsement of MMPI *F* Scale items by psychotics and behavior disorders. *Journal of Clinical Psychology, 23,* 185–188.

Hahn, J. (2001, March). *Faking and defensive responding in Korean MMPI–2.* Paper presented for 36th Annual symposium on MMPI–2/MMPI–A, Tampa, FL.

Hahn, J. (2003). Faking and defensive responding in Korean MMPI–2. *Dissertation Abstracts International: Section B: The Sciences and Engineering, 64*(6-B), 2971.

Hahn, J. (2005). Faking bad and faking good by college students on the Korean MMPI–2. *Journal of Personality Assessment, 85,* 65–73.

Hanley, C. (1957). Deriving a measure of test-taking defensiveness. *Journal of Consulting Psychology, 21,* 391–397.

Hanlon-Klang, L. M. (1989). Personality assessment: An investigation of the ability of the subtle and obvious scales to improve the diagnostic validity of Scale 6 of the MMPI. *Dissertation Abstracts International, 49,* 4592.

Harper, J. W. (1976). An investigation of the faking scales of the MMPI and their use in differential diagnosis. *Dissertation Abstracts International, 37,* 2506.

Harvey, M. A., & Sipprelle, C. N. (1976). Demand characteristics effects on the subtle and obvious subscales of the MMPI. *Journal of Personality Assessment, 40,* 539–544.

Hathaway, S. R., & McKinley, J. C. (1940). A multiphasic personality schedule (Minnesota): I. Construction of the schedule. *Journal of Psychology, 10,* 249–254.

Hawk, G. L., & Cornell, D.G. (1989). MMPI profiles of malingerers diagnosed in pretrial forensic evaluations. *Journal of Clinical Psychology, 45,* 673–678.

Heaton, R. K., Smith, H. H., Lehman, R. A., & Vogt, A. T. (1978). Prospects for faking believable deficits on neuropsychological testing. *Journal of Consulting and Clinical Psychology, 46,* 892–900.

Heilbrun, K., Bennett, W. S., White, A. J., & Kelly, J. (1990). An MMPI-based empirical model of malingering and deception. *Behavioral Sciences and the Law, 8,* 45–53.

Heinze, M. (2003). Developing sensitivity to distortion: Utility of psychological tests in differentiating malingering and psychopathology in criminal defendants. *Journal of Forensic Psychiatry and Psychology, 14,* 151–177.

Heinze, M. C., & Purisch, A. D. (2001). Beneath the mask: Use of psychological tests to detect and subtype malingering in criminal defendants. *Journal of Forensic Psychology Practice, 1,* 23–52.

Herkov, M. J. (1991). Adolescent MMPI subtle–obvious ratings: Influences of age and race in a forensic population. *Dissertation Abstracts International, 51,* 5575.

Hiner, D. L, Ogren, D. J., & Baxter, J. C. (1969). Ideal self responding on the MMPI. *Journal of Projective Techniques and Personality Assessment, 33,* 389–396.

Hinojosa, L. (1993). The MMPI–2 and malingering: A study aimed at refining the detection of deception. *Dissertation Abstracts International, 54,* 2203.

Hoffman, R. G., Scott, J. G., Emick, M. A., & Adams, R. L. (1999). The MMPI–2 and closed-head injury: Effects of litigation and head injury severity. *Journal of Forensic Neuropsychology, 1,* 3–13.

Holcomb, W. R., Adams, W. P., Ponder, H. M., & Anderson, W. (1984). Cognitive and behavioral predictors of MMPI scores in pretrial psychological evaluations of murderers. *Journal of Clinical Psychology, 40,* 592–597.

Hunt, H. F. (1948). The effects of deliberate deception on MMPI performance. *Journal of Consulting Psychology, 12,* 396–402.

Hyer, L., Fallon, J. H., Harrison, W. R., & Boudewyns, P. A. (1987). MMPI overreporting by Vietnam combat veterans. *Journal of Clinical Psychology, 43*(1), 79–83.

Inman, T. H., Vickery, C. D., Berry, D. T. R., Lamb, D. G., Edwards, C. L., & Smith, G. T. (1998). Development and initial validation of a new procedure for evaluating adequacy of efforts given during neuropsychological testing: The Letter Memory Test. *Psychological Assessment, 10,* 128–139.

Iverson, G. L., & Barton, E. (1999). Interscorer reliability of the MMPI–2: Should *TRIN* and *VRIN* be computer scored? *Journal of Clinical Psychology, 55*(1), 65–69.

Iverson, G. L., Franzen, M. D., & Hammond, J. A. (1995). Examination of inmates' ability to malinger on MMPI–2. *Psychological Assessment, 4,* 111–117.

Jacobson, E. J. (2004). The utility of response latencies in detecting malingering using a clinical sample. *Dissertation Abstracts International: Section B: The Sciences and Engineering, 64*(7-B), 3527.

Jana, Y. A. (2001). The effectiveness of the MMPI–2 in detecting malingered schizophrenia in adult female inmates in Puerto Rico who receive coaching on diagnostic-specific criteria. *Dissertation Abstracts International: Section B: The Sciences and Engineering, 62*(2-B), 1084.

Jiménez, G., & Sanchez, C. G. (2001). La contribucion de las subescalas Obvio–Sutil del MMPI–2 en la deteccion del fingimiento [The contribution of the Obvious–Subtle scales of the MMPI on the detection of faking]. *Revista Iberoamericana de Diagnostico y Evaluacion Psicologica, 11*(1), 111–130.

Johnson, J. H., Klingler, D. E., & Williams, T. A. (1977). An external criterion study of the MMPI validity indices. *Journal of Clinical Psychology, 33*(1), 154–156.

Johnson, P. L. (1983). Black–White differences on the faking indexes of the MMPI in a prison sample. *Dissertation Abstracts International, 43,* 2709.

Johnston, S. W. (2003). The training of malingering assessment and detection strategies in clinical psychology programs: A survey of American Psychological Association graduate student affiliates. *Dissertation Abstracts International: Section B: The Sciences and Engineering, 64*(5-B), 2391.

Jones, A. (2001). An examination of the MMPI–2 Wiener–Harmon subtle subscales for *D* and *Hy*: Implications for parent scale and neurotic triad interpretation. *Journal of Personality Assessment, 77,* 105–121.

Kataoka, G., Ono, N., & Shindo, H. (1968). A discussion relative to the *F* scale of the MMPI: Clinical figures of juvenile delinquents with high *F* score. *Japanese Journal of Criminal Psychology, 6,* 28.

King, F. W. (1967). The MMPI *F* scale as a predictor of lack of adaptation to college. *Journal of the American College Health Association, 15,* 261–269.

Klotz Flitter, J. M., Elhai, J. D., & Gold, S. N. (2003). MMPI–2 *F* scale elevations in adult victims of child sexual abuse. *Journal of Traumatic Stress, 16,* 269–274.

Kodman, F., Jr., & McDaniel, E. (1960). Further investigation of the reliability of an MMPI scale for auditory malingerers. *Journal of Clinical Psychology, 16*(4), 451.

Kodman, F. J., Sedlacek, G., & McDaniel, E. (1960). Performance of suspected auditory malingerers on the subtle–obvious keys of MMPI. *Journal of Clinical Psychology, 16,* 193–195.

Kroger, R. O. (1974). Faking in interest measurement: A social–psychological perspective. *Measurement and Evaluation in Guidance, 7,* 130–134.

Kucharski, L. T., Johnsen, D., & Procell, S. (2004). The utility of the MMPI–2 infrequency psychopathology *F(p)* and the revised infrequency psychopathology scales in the detection of malingering. *American Journal of Forensic Psychology, 22*(1), 33–40.

Kurtz, R. A. (1993). The vulnerability of the MMPI–2, *M* Test, and *SIRS* to two strategies of malingering psychosis in a forensic setting. *Dissertation Abstracts International, 54,* 129–130.

Ladd, J. S. (1998). The *F(p)* Infrequency–Psychopathology scale with chemically dependent inpatients. *Journal of Clinical Psychology, 54,* 665–671.

Lally, S. (2003). What tests are acceptable for use in forensic evaluations? A survey of experts. *Professional Psychology: Research and Practice, 34,* 491–498.

Lamb, D. G. (1992). Malingering closed head injury on the MMPI–2: Effect of information about symptoms and validity scales. *Dissertation Abstracts International, 53,* 1611.

Lamb, D. G., Berry, D. T. R., Wetter, M. W., & Baer, R. A. (1994). Effects of two types of information on malingering of closed head injury on the MMPI–2: An analog investigation. *Psychological Assessment, 6,* 8–13.

Lambert, J. B. (2000). Analysis of the Rey 15-item memory test as a measure of malingering in a litigating, mildly brain-injured sample. *Dissertation Abstracts International, 60,* 4231.

Lanyon, R. I., Almer, E. R., & Curran, P. (1993). Use of biographical and case history data in the assessment of malingering during examination for disability. *Bulletin of the American Academy of Psychiatry and the Law, 21,* 495–503.

Lanyon, R. I., & Lutz, R. W. (1984). MMPI discrimination of defensive and nondefensive felony sex offenders. *Journal of Consulting and Clinical Psychology, 52,* 841–843.

Larrabee, G. (1998). Somatic malingering on the MMPI and MMPI–2 in personal injury litigants. *Clinical Neuropsychologist, 12,* 179–188.

Larrabee, G. (2003). Detection of malingering using atypical performance patterns on standard neuropsychological tests. *Clinical Neuropsychologist, 17,* 410–425.

Larrabee, G. (2003). Detection of symptom exaggeration with the MMPI–2 in litigants with malingered neurocognitive dysfunction. *Clinical Neuropsychologist, 17,* 54–68.

Larrabee, G. (2003). Exaggerated MMPI–2 symptom report in personal injury litigants with malingered neurocognitive deficit. *Archives of Clinical Neuropsychology, 18,* 673–686.

Lawton, M. P. (1963). Deliberate faking on the psychopathic deviate scale of the MMPI. *Journal of Clinical Psychology, 19,* 327–330.

Lawton, M. P., & Kleban, M. H. (1965). Prisoners' faking on the MMPI. *Journal of Clinical Psychology, 21,* 269–271.

Lees-Haley, P. R. (1984). Detecting the psychological malingerer. *American Journal of Forensic Psychology, 2*(4), 165–169.

Lees-Haley, P. R. (1986). How to detect malingerers in the workplace. *Personnel Journal, 65,* 106, 108, 110.

Lees-Haley, P. R. (1989). Malingering post-traumatic stress disorder on the MMPI. *Forensic Reports, 2,* 89–91.

Lees-Haley, P. R. (1989). MMPI *F* and *F–K* scales: Questionable indices of malingering. *American Journal of Forensic Psychology, 7,* 81–84.

Lees-Haley, P. R. (1991). Ego strength denial on the MMPI–2 as a clue to simulation of personal injury in vocational neuropsychological and emotional distress evaluations. *Perceptual and Motor Skills, 72,* 815–819.

Lees-Haley, P. R. (1991). MMPI–2 *F* and *F–K* scores of personal injury malingerers in vocational neuropsychological and emotional distress claims. *American Journal of Forensic Psychology, 9,* 5–14.

Lees-Haley, P. R. (1992). Efficacy of MMPI–2 validity scales and MCMI–II modifier scales for detecting spurious PTSD claims: *F, F–K,* Fake Bad scale, Ego Strength, Subtle–Obvious subscales, *DIS,* and *DEB. Journal of Clinical Psychology, 48,* 681–689.

Lees-Haley, P. R. (1997). MMPI–2 base rates for 492 personal injury plaintiffs: Implications and challenges for forensic assessment. *Journal of Clinical Psychology, 53,* 745–755.

Lees-Haley, P. R., English, L. T., & Glenn, W. J. (1991). A fake-bad scale on the MMPI–2 for personal injury claimants. *Psychological Reports, 68,* 203–210.

Lees-Haley, P. R., & Fox, D. D. (1990). MMPI subtle–obvious scales and malingering: Clinical versus simulated scores. *Psychological Reports, 66,* 907–911.

Lees-Haley, P. R., & Fox, D. D. (2004). Commentary on Butcher, Arbisi, Atlis, and McNulty (2003) on the Fake Bad Scale. *Archives of Clinical Neuropsychology, 19*(3), 333–336.

Lees-Haley, P. R., Iverson, G. L., Lange, R. T., Fox, D. D., & Allen, L. M., III (2002). Malingering in forensic neuropsychology: *Daubert* and the MMPI–2. *Journal of Forensic Neuropsychology, 3*(1–2), 167–203.

LePage, J. P., & Mogge, N. L. (2001). Validity rates of the MMPI–2 and PAI in a rural inpatient psychiatric facility. *Assessment, 8,* 67–74.

Lewis, J. L., Simcox, A. M., & Berry, D. T. R. (2002). Screening for feigned psychiatric symptoms in a forensic sample by using the MMPI–2 and the Structured Inventory of Malingered Symptomatology. *Psychological Assessment, 14,* 170–176.

Lim, J. (1994). Detection of faking on the MMPI–2 profiles: Differentiation between faking-bad, denial, and claiming extreme virtue. *Dissertation Abstracts International, 55,* 2430.

Lim, J., & Butcher, J. N. (1996). Detection of faking on the MMPI–2: Differentiating among faking-bad, denial, and claiming extreme virtue. *Journal of Personality Assessment, 67,* 1–25.

Linbald, A. D. (1994). Detection of malingered mental illness within a forensic population: An analogue study. *Dissertation Abstract International, 54-B,* 4395.

Long, B., Rouse, S. V., Nelson, R. O., & Butcher, J. N. (2004). The MMPI–2 in sexual harassment and discrimination cases. *Journal of Clinical Psychology, 60,* 643–658.

Lopez, M. N., & Charter, R. A. (2001). Random responding to the MMPI–2 *F* Scale. *Psychological Reports, 88*(2), 398.

Lucio, E., Duran, C., Graham, J. R., & Ben-Porath, Y. S. (2002). Identifying faking bad on the Minnesota Multiphasic Personality Inventory—Adolescent with Mexican adolescents. *Assessment, 9*(1), 62–69.

Lundy, R., Geselowitz, L., & Shertzer, C. (1985). Role-played and hypnotically induced simulation of psychopathology on the MMPI: A partial replication. *International Journal of Clinical and Experimental Hypnosis, 33,* 302–309.

Maclean, A. G., Tait, A. T., & Catterall, C. D. (1953). The *F* minus *K* index on the MMPI. *Journal of Applied Psychology, 37,* 315–316.

Maloney, M. P., Duvall, S. W., & Friesen, J. (1980). Evaluation of response consistency on the MMPI. *Psychological Reports, 46*(1), 295–298.

Mann, C. A. (2003). Diagnostic practices in determining malingered mental illness: A survey of psychological test usage by forensic psychologists. *Dissertation Abstracts International: Section B: The Sciences and Engineering, 64*(3-B), 1499.

Martens, M., Donders, J., & Millis, S. R. (2001). Evaluation of invalid response sets after traumatic head injury. *Journal of Forensic Neuropsychology, 2,* 1–18.

Matarazzo, J. D. (1955). MMPI validity scores as a function of increasing levels of anxiety. *Journal of Consulting Psychology, 19,* 213–217.

McAnulty, D. P., Rappaport, N. B., & McAnulty, R. D. (1985). An a posteriori investigation of standard MMPI validity scales. *Psychological Reports, 57*(1), 95–98.

McCaffrey, R., & Bellamy-Campbell, R. (1989). Psychometric detection of fabricated symptoms of combat-related PTSD: A systematic replication. *Journal of Clinical Psychology, 45,* 76–79.

McCann, J. T. (1998). *Malingering and decepetion in adolescents.* Washington, DC: American Psychological Association.

McCusker, P. J., Moran, M. J., Serfass, L., & Peterson, K. H. (2003). Comparability of the MMPI–2 *F(p)* and *F* scales and the *SIRS* in clinical use with suspected malingerers. *International Journal of Offender Therapy and Comparative Criminology, 47,* 585–596.

McGrath, R. E., Pogge, D. L., Stein, L. A. R., Graham, J. R., Zaccario, M., & Piacentini, T. (2000). Development of an Infrequency–Psychopathology scale for the MMPI—A: The *Fp–A* scale. *Journal of Personality Assessment, 74,* 282–295.

McKegney, F. P. (1965). An item analysis of the MMPI *F* scale in juvenile delinquents. *Journal of Clinical Psychology, 21,* 201–205.

McNulty, J., Forbey, J., Graham, J., Ben-Porath, Y., Black, M., Anderson, S., et al. (2003). MMPI–2 validity scale characteristics in a correctional sample. *Assessment, 10,* 288–298.

Meisner, S. (1988). Susceptibility of Rorschach distress corrrelates to malingering. *Journal of Personality Assessment, 52,* 564–571.

Mercer, J. (1970). Faking ability on the MMPI and prognosis in a state hospital population. *Dissertation Abstracts International, 31,* 3710–3711.

Meyer, R. G., & Deitsch, S. M. (1995). The assessment of malingering in psychodiagnostic evaluations: Research-based concepts and methods for consultants. *Consulting Psychology Journal: Practice and Research, 47,* 234–245.

Meyers, J. E., Millis, S. R., & Volkert, K. (2002). A validity index for the MMPI–2. *Archives of Clinical Neuropsychology, 17,* 157–169.

Mittenberg, W., Tremont, G., & Rayls, K. R. (1996). Impact of cognitive function on MMPI–2 validity in neurological impaired patients. *Assessment, 3,* 157–163.

Moran, P. J. (2000). MMPI–2 profiles of students instructed to overreport depressive and manic psychopathology using either specific symptom information or symptom stereotypes. (malingering). *Dissertation Abstracts International, 60,* 3609.

Morel, K. R. (1998). Development and preliminary validation of a forced-choice test of a response bias for posttraumatic stress disorder. *Journal of Personality Assessment, 70*(2), 299–314.

Morgan, C. D., Shoenberg, R., Dorr, D., & Burke, M. J. (2002). Overreport on the MCMI–III: Concurrent validation with the MMPI–2 using a psychiatric inpatient sample. *Journal of Personality Assessment, 78,* 288–300.

Moskowitz, J. L., Lewis, R. J., Ito, M. S., & Ehrmentraut, J. (1999). MMPI–2 profiles of NGRI and civil patients. *Journal of Clinical Psychology, 55,* 659–668.

Moyer, D. M., Burkhardt, B., & Gordon, R. M. (2002). Faking PTSD from a motor vehicle accident on the MMPI–2. *American Journal of Forensic Psychology, 20*(2), 81–89.

Munley, P. H., Bains, D. S., & Bloem, W. D. (1993). *F* Scale elevation and PTSD MMPI profiles. *Psychological Reports, 73*(2), 363–370.

Myer, G. J., Finn, S. E., Eyde, L. D., Kay, G. G., Moreland, K. L., Dies, R. R., et al. (2001). Psychological testing and psychological assessment: A review of evidence and issues. *American Psychologist, 56,* 128–165.

Nelson, L. D., & Cicchetti, D. (1991). Validity of the MMPI Depression scale for outpatients. *Psychological Assessment, 3,* 55–59.

Nelson, L. D., Pham, D., & Uchiyama, C. (1996). Subtlety of the MMPI–2 Depression Scale: A subject laid to rest? *Psychological Assessment, 8,* 331–333.

Nichols, D. S., & Greene, F. L. (1991, March). *New measures for dissimulation on the MMPI/MMPI–2.* Paper presented at the 26th annual symposium on

Recent Developments in the Use of the MMPI, St. Petersburg Beach, FL.

Nichols, D. S., & Greene, R. L. (1997). Dimensions of deception in personality assessment: The example of the MMPI–2. *Journal of Personality Assessment, 68,* 251–266.

Nichols, D. S., Greene, R. L., & Schmolck, P. (1989). Criteria for assessing inconsistent patterns of item endorsement on the MMPI: Rationale, development, and empirical trials. *Journal of Clinical Psychology, 45,* 239–250.

Nicholson, R. A., Mouton, G. J., Bagby, R. M., Buis, T., Peterson, S. A., & Buigas, R. A. (1997). Utility of MMPI–2 indicators of response distortion: Receiver operating characteristic analysis. *Psychological Assessment, 9,* 471–479.

Osberg, T. M., & Harrigan, P. (1999). Comparative validity of the MMPI–2 Wiener–Harmon subtle–obvious scales in male prison inmates. *Journal of Personality Assessment, 72,* 36–48.

Osborne, D., Colligan, R. C., & Offord, K. P. (1986). Normative tables for the *F–K* index of the MMPI based on a contemporary normal sample. *Journal of Clinical Psychology, 42,* 593–595.

Owens, R. G. (1995). The psychological signatures of malingering: Assessing the legitimacy of claims. *American Journal of Forensic Psychology, 13,* 61–75.

Palermo, G. B. (2004). Editorial: A look at malingering. *International Journal of Offender Therapy and Comparative Criminology, 48*(3), 265–267.

Paolo, A. M., & Ryan, J. J. (1992). Detection of random response sets on the MMPI–2. *Psychotherapy in Private Practice, 11*(4), 1–8.

Parwatikar, S. D., Holcomb, W. R., & Menninger, K. A. (1985). The detection of malingered amnesia in accused murderers. *Bulletin of the American Academy of Psychiatry and the Law, 13,* 97–103.

Pensa, R., Dorfman, W. I., Gold, S. N., & Schneider, B. (1996). Detection of malingered psychosis with the MMPI–2. *Psychotherapy in Private Practice, 14,* 47–63.

Perconte, S. T., & Goreczny, A. J. (1990). Failure to detect fabricated posttraumatic stress disorder with the use of the MMPI in a clinical population. *American Journal of Psychiatry, 147,* 1057–1060.

Pflaum, J. (1964). Development and evaluation of equivalent forms of the *F* scale. *Psychological Reports, 15,* 663–669.

Pinsoneault, T. B. (1998). A Variable Response Inconsistency Scale and a True Response Inconsistency Scale for the Jesness Inventory. *Psychological Assessment, 10,* 21–32.

Pinsoneault, T. B. (1999). Efficacy of the three randomness validity scales for the Jesness Inventory. *Journal of Personality Assessment, 73,* 395–406.

Pizitz, T. D. (2001). Detection of malingered mild head injury using the tripartite conceptual model of malingering and the Inventory of Problems. *Dissertation Abstracts International: Section B: The Sciences and Engineering, 61*(11-B), 6145.

Pollock, P. H. (1996). A cautionary note on the determination of malingering in offenders. *Psychology Crime and Law, 3,* 97–110.

Poole, E. D. (1996). MMPI assessment of malingered emotional distress in head-trauma patients. *Dissertation Abstracts International: Section B: The Sciences and Engineering, 57*(5-B), 3419.

Post, R. D., & Gasparikova-Krasnec, M. (1979). MMPI validity scales and behavioral disturbance in psychiatric inpatients. *Journal of Personality Assessment, 43*(2), 155–159.

Ray, J. J. (1983). Psychopathy, anxiety and malingering. *Personality and Individual Differences, 4,* 351–353.

Reynolds, C. (1998). *Detection of malingering in head injury litigation.* New York: Plenum Press.

Rice, M. E., Arnold, L. S., & Tate, D. L. (1983). Faking good and bad adjustment on the MMPI and overcontrolled-hostility in maximum security psychiatric patients. *Canadian Journal of Behavioural Science, 15,* 43–51.

Rissmiller, D. A., Steer, R. A., Friedman, M., & DeMercurio, R. (1999). Prevalence of malingering in suicidal psychiatric inpatients: A replication. *Psychological Reports, 84,* 726–730.

Rissmiller, D. J., Wayslow, A., Madison, H., Hogate, P., Rissmiller, F. R., & Steer, R. A. (1998). Prevalence of malingering in inpatient suicide ideators and attempters. *Crisis, 19,* 62–66.

Rogers, R. (1983). Malingering or random? A research note on obvious vs. subtle subscales of the MMPI. *Journal of Clinical Psychology, 39*(2), 257–258.

Rogers, R. (1988). Researching dissimulation. In R. Rogers (Ed.), *Clinical assessment of malingering and deception* (pp. 309–327). New York: Guilford Press.

Rogers, R., Bagby, R. M., & Chakraborty, D. (1993). Feigning schizophrenic disorder on the MMPI–2: Detection of coached simulators. *Journal of Personality Assessment, 60,* 215–226.

Rogers, R., Dolmetsch, R., & Cavanaugh, J. L. (1983). Identification of random responders on MMPI protocols. *Journal of Personality Assessment, 47,* 364–368.

Rogers, R., & Gillis, J. (1991). Detection of malingering on the Structured Interview of Reported Symptoms (SIRS): A study of coached and uncoached simulators. *Psychological Assessment, 3,* 673–677.

Rogers, R., & Gillis, J. (1991). Standardized assessment of malingering: Validation of the Structured Interview of Reported Symptoms. *Psychological Assessment, 3,* 89–96.

Rogers, R., Hinds, J. D., & Sewell, K. W. (1996). Feigning psychopathology among adolescent offenders: Validation of the SIRS, MMPI–A, and SIMS. *Journal of Personality Assessment, 67,* 244–257.

Rogers, R., Kropp, P., Bagby, R. M., & Dickens, S. E. (1992). Faking specific disorders: A study of the Structured Interview of Reported Symptoms (SIRS). *Journal of Clinical Psychology, 48,* 643–648.

Rogers, R., Sewell, K. W., Martin, M. A., & Vitacco, M. J. (2003). Detection of feigned mental disorders: A meta-analysis of the MMPI–2 and malingering. *Assessment, 10,* 160–177.

Rogers, R. R., Sewell, K. W., & Ustad, K. L. (1995). Feigning among chronic outpatients on the MMPI–2: A systematic examination of fake-bad indicators. *Assessment, 2,* 81–89.

Roman, D. D., Tuley, M. R., Villanueva, M. R., & Mitchell, W. E. (1990). Evaluating MMPI validity in a forensic psychiatric population: Distinguishing between malingering and genuine psychopathology. *Criminal Justice and Behavior, 17,* 186–198.

Ross, S. R., Millis, S. R., Krukowski, R. A., Putnam, S. H., & Adams, K. M. (2004). Detecting incomplete effort on the MMPI–2: An examination of the Fake-Bad Scale in mild head injury. *Journal of Clinical and Experimental Neuropsychology, 26*(1), 115–124.

Rothke, S. E., & Friedman, A. F. (1994). Response to Fox: Comment and clarification. *Assessment, 1*(4), 421–422.

Rothke, S. E., Friedman, A. F., Dahlstrom, W. G., & Greene, R. L. (1994). MMPI–2 normative data for the *F–K* index: Implications for clinical, neuropsychological, and forensic practice. *Assessment, 1*(1), 1–15.

Rothke, S. E., Friedman, A. F., Jaffe, A. M., Greene, R. L., Wetter, M. W., Cole, P., et al. (2000). Normative data for the *F(p)* Scale of the MMPI–2: Implications for clinical and forensic assessment of malingering. *Psychological Assessment, 12,* 335–340.

Ruiz, M. Z., Drake, E., Glass, A., Marcotte, D., & van Gorp, W. (2002). Trying to beat the system: Misuse of the Internet to assist in avoiding detection of psychological symptom dissimulation. *Professional Psychology: Research and Practice, 33,* 294–299.

Sari, D. J. (2001). MMPI–2 and neuropsychological indicators of malingering in traumatic brain injury litigants. *Dissertation Abstracts International: Section B: The Sciences and Engineering, 61*(12-B), 6720.

Schaugaard, M. J. (1999). Detection of MMPI–2 faked, honest response, and archival comparison group membership. *Dissertation Abstracts International: Section B: The Sciences and Engineering, 60*(3-B), 1314.

Schiele, B. C., & Brozek, J. (1948). "Experimental neurosis" resulting from semistarvation in man. *Psychosomatic Medicine, 10,* 31–50.

Schinka, J., Elkins, D. E., & Archer, R. P. (1998). Effects of psychopathology and demographic characteristics on MMPI–A scale scores. *Journal of Personality Assessment, 71,* 295–305.

Schretlen, D. (1988). The use of psychological tests to identify malingered symptoms of mental disorder. *Clinical Psychology Review, 8,* 451–476.

Schretlen, D. (1990). A limitation of using Wiener and Harmon Obvious and Subtle Scales to detect faking on the MMPI. *Journal of Clinical Psychology, 46,* 1090–1095.

Schretlen, D., & Arkowitz, H. (1990). A psychological test battery to detect prison inmates who fake insanity or mental retardation. *Behavioral Sciences and the Law, 8*(1), 75–84.

Schretlen, D., Wilkins, S. S., Van Gorp, W. G., & Bobholz, J. H. (1992). Cross-validation of a psychological test battery to detect faked insanity. *Psychological Assessment, 4,* 77–83.

Scott, A. B. (1997). Response latencies and faking on the MMPI–2: Implications for elevated versus nonelevated profiles. *Dissertation Abstracts International, 58,* 2176.

Scronce, C. A. (1995). The use of the MMPI–2 to detect malingered psychosis in a criminal forensic setting. *Dissertation Abstracts International: Section B: The Sciences and Engineering, 55*(9-B), 4133.

Seeman, W. (1952). "Subtlety" in structured personality tests. *Journal of Clinical Psychology, 16,* 278–283.

Seeman, W. (1953). Concept of "subtlety" in structured psychiatric and personality tests: An experimental approach. *Journal of Abnormal and Social Psychology, 48,* 239–247.

Shaffer, J. W. (1981). Using the MMPI to evaluate mental impairment in disability determination. In

J. N. Butcher, G. Dahlstrom, M. Gynther, & W. Schofield (Eds.), *Clinical notes on the MMPI* (pp. 1–12). Nutley, NJ: Hoffman-La Roche Laboratories/NCS.

Shapiro, D. L. (1993). Detection of malingering and deception. In L.VandeCreek (Ed.), *Innovations in clinical practice: A source book* (pp. 5–13). Sarasota, FL: Professional Resource Press/Professional Resource Exchange.

Shondrick, D. D., Ben-Porath, Y. S., & Stafford, K. (1992, May). *Forensic assessment with the MMPI–2: Characteristics of individuals undergoing court-ordered evaluations.* Paper presented at the 27th Annual Symposium on Recent Developments in the Use of the MMPI (MMPI–2), Minneapolis, MN.

Shores, E. A., & Carstairs, J. R. (1998). Accuracy of the MMPI–2 Computerized Minnesota Report in identifying fake-good and fake-bad response sets. *Clinical Neuropsychologist, 12,* 101–106.

Siem, F. M. (1996). The use of response latencies to enhance self-report personality measures. *Military Psychology, 8*(1), 15–27.

Sinnett, E. R., Holen, M. C., & Albott, W. L. (1999). Profile validity standards for MMPI and MMPI–2 *F* scales. *Psychological Reports, 84*(1), 288–290.

Sivec, H. J., Hilsenroth, M. J., & Lynn, S. J. (1995). Impact of simulating borderline personality disorder on the MMPI–2: A costs-benefits analysis. *Journal of Personality Assessment, 64,* 295–311.

Sivec, H. J., Lynn, S. J., & Garske, J. P. (1994). The effect of somatoform disorder and paranoid psychotic role-related dissimulations as a response set on the MMPI–2. *Assessment, 1,* 69–81.

Slick, D. J., Hopp, G., Strauss, E., & Spellacy, F. J. (1996). Victoria Symptom Validity Test: Efficiency for detecting feigned memory impairment and relationship to neuropsychological tests and MMPI–2 validity scales. *Journal of Clinical and Experimental Neuropsychology, 18,* 911–922.

Smith, C. P. (1980). Behavioral correlates for the MMPI standard *F* scale and a modified *F* scale for

Black and White psychiatric patients. *Dissertation Abstracts International, 41*(4-B), 1528.

Smith, C. P., & Burger, G. K. (1997). Detection of malingering: Validation of the Structured Inventory of Malingered Symptomatology (SIMS). *Bulletin of the American Academy of Psychiatry and the Law, 25,* 183–189.

Smith, C. P., & Graham, J. R. (1981). Behavioral correlates for the MMPI standard *F* scale and for a modified *F* scale for Black and White psychiatric patients. *Journal of Consulting and Clinical Psychology, 49,* 455–459.

Smith, D. W., & Frueh, B. (1996). Compensation seeking, comorbidity, and apparent exaggeration of PTSD symptoms among Vietnam combat veterans. *Psychological Assessment, 8,* 3–6.

Smith, D. W., Frueh, B. C., Sawchuk, C. N., & Johnson, M. R. (1999). Relationship between symptom over-reporting and pre- and post-combat trauma history in veterans evaluated for PTSD. *Depression and Anxiety, 10,* 119–124.

Snoke, M., & Ziesner, N. (1946). *Relationship between subtle–obvious keys and* K *scale of the MMPI.* Minneapolis, MN: Regional Veterans Administration Office.

Snyter, C. M., & Graham, J. R. (1984). The utility of subtle and obvious MMPI subscales based on scale-specific ratings. *Journal of Clinical Psychology, 40,* 981–985.

Sprock, J. (2000). Invalid response sets in MMPI and MMPI–2 profiles of college students. *Educational and Psychological Measurement, 60,* 956–964.

Steffan, J. S., Clopton, J. R., & Morgan, R. D. (2003). An MMPI–2 scale to detect malingered depression (*Md*). *Assessment, 10,* 382–392.

Stein, L. A. R., Graham, J. R., & Williams, C. L. (1995). Detecting fake-bad MMPI–A profiles. *Journal of Personality Assessment, 65,* 415–427.

Storm, J. (2003). The development of a scale to detect coached malingering on the MMPI–2. *Dissertation Abstracts International: Section B: The Sciences and Engineering, 63*(10-B), 4926.

Storm, J., & Graham, J. R. (1998, March). *The effects of validity scale coaching on the ability to malinger psychopathology.* Paper presented at the 33rd Annual Symposium on Recent Developments in the Use of the MMPI–2, Clearwater, FL.

Storm, J., & Graham, J. R. (2000). Detection of coached general malingering on the MMPI–2. *Psychological Assessment, 12,* 158–165.

Strong, D. R., Greene, R. L., & Schinka, J. A. (2000). A taxometric analysis of MMPI–2 infrequency scales [*F* and *F(p)*] in clinical settings. *Psychological Assessment, 12,* 166–173.

Stukenberg, K., Brady, C., & Klinetob, N. (2000). Use of the MMPI–2's VRIN scale with severely disturbed populations: Consistent responding may be more problematic than inconsistent responding. *Psychological Reports, 86,* 3–14.

Timbrook, R. E., Graham, J. R., Keiller, S. W., & Watts, D. (1993). Comparison of the Weiner–Harmon subtle–obvious scales and the standard validity scales in detecting valid and invalid MMPI–2 profiles. *Psychological Assessment, 5,* 53–61.

Timmons, L. A., Lanyon, R. I., Almer, E. R., & Curran, P. J. (1993). Development and validation of Sentence Completion Test indices of malingering during examination for disability. *American Journal of Forensic Psychology, 11,* 23–38.

Tolin, D. F., Maltby, N., Weathers, F. W., Litz, B. T., Knight, J., & Keane, T. M. (2004). The use of the MMPI–2 infrequency–psychopathology scale in the assessment of posttraumatic stress disorder in male veterans. *Journal of Psychopathology and Behavioral Assessment, 26*(1), 23–29.

Tsushima, W. T., & Tsushima, V. G. (2001). Comparison of the Fake Bad Scale and other MMPI–2 validity scales with personal injury litigants. *Assessment, 8,* 205–212.

Turin, C. M. (1986). Detecting malingering with the MMPI and the PST. *Dissertation Abstracts International, 47,* 2190.

Turnbull, W. (1971). *A role theory of faking: The case of the MMPI.* Unpublished master's thesis, University of North Carolina, Chapel Hill.

Vaughan, A. E. (1995). Detecting malingering among federal inmates using the MMPI–2. *Dissertation Abstracts International, 56,* 2936.

Veith, W. T. (1995). Use of the MMPI malingering indices to differentiate type of claim and employment status in workers' compensation claimants. *Dissertation Abstracts International, 56,* 0539.

Vesprani, G. J., & Seeman, W. (1974). MMPI X and Zero items in a psychiatric outpatient group. *Journal of Personality Assessment, 38,* 61–64.

Viglione, D. J., Fals-Stewart, W., & Moxham, E. (1995). Maximizing internal and external validity in MMPI malingering research: A study of a military population. *Journal of Personality Assessment, 65,* 502–513.

Viglione, D. J., Wright, D. M., Dizon, N. T., Moynihan, J. E., DuPuis, S., & Pizitz, T. D. (2001). Evading detection on the MMPI–2: Does caution produce more realistic patterns of responding? *Assessment, 8*(3), 237–250.

Vincent, K. R., Linsz, N. L., & Greene, M. I. (1966). The scale of the MMPI as an index of falsification. *Journal of Consulting and Clinical Psychology, 22,* 214–215.

Wales, B., & Seeman, W. (1969). What do MMPI zero items really measure: An experimental investigation. *Journal of Clinical Psychology, 25,* 420–424.

Wallace, G. D. (1995). The development and cross-validation of a malingering scale for the Minnesota Multiphasic Personality Inventory—2. *Dissertation Abstracts International, 55,* 3030.

Walters, G. L. (1998). The effect of symptom information and validity scale information on the malingering of depression on the MMPI—2. *Dissertation Abstracts International, 59,* 1381.

Walters, G. L., & Clopton, J. R. (2000). Effect of symptom information and validity scale information on the malingering of depression on the MMPI–2. *Journal of Personality Assessment, 75,* 183–199.

Walters, G. D., White, T. W., & Greene, R. L. (1988). Use of the MMPI to identify malingering and exaggeration of psychiatric symptomatology in male prison inmates. *Journal of Consulting and Clinical Psychology, 56,* 111–117.

Wasyliw, O. E., Grossman, L. S., Haywood, T. W., & Cavanaugh, J. L. (1988). The detection of malingering in criminal forensic groups: MMPI validity scales. *Journal of Personality Assessment, 52,* 321–333.

Webb, L. M. (1999). Clinical assessment of malingering utilizing the Minnesota Multiphasic Personality Inventory—II (MMPI–II), Millon Clinical Multiaxial Inventory—III (MCMI–III), and Dissociative Experiences Scale. *Dissertation Abstracts International, 59,* 4362.

Weed, N., Ben-Porath, Y. S., & Butcher, J. N. (1990). Failure of Weiner and Harmon Minnesota Multiphasic Personality Inventory (MMPI) subtle scales as personality descriptors and as validity indicators. *Psychological Assessment, 2,* 281–285.

Welburn, K. R., Fraser, G. A., Jordan, S. A., Cameron, C., Webb, L. M., & Raine, D. (2003). Discriminating dissociative identity disorder from schizophrenia and feigned dissociation on psychological tests and structured interview. *Journal of Trauma and Dissociation, 4,* 109–130.

Wetter, M., Baer, R., Berry, D., & Reynolds, S. (1994). The effect of symptom information on faking on the MMPI–2. *Assessment, 1,* 199–207.

Wetter, M. W., Baer, R. A., Berry, D. T., Robinson, L. H., & Sumpter, J. (1993). MMPI–2 profiles of motivated fakers given specific symptom information: A comparison to matched patients. *Psychological Assessment, 5,* 313–323.

Wetter, M. W., Baer, R. A., Berry, D. T. R., Smith, G. T., & Larsen, L. H. (1992). Sensitivity of MMPI-validity scales to random responding and malingering. *Psychological Assessment, 4,* 369–374.

Wetter, M. W., & Corrigan, S. K. (1995). Providing information to clients about psychological tests: A survey of attorney's and law students' attitudes. *Professional Psychology: Research and Practice, 26,* 1–4.

Wetter, M. W., & Deitsch, S. E. (1996). Faking specific disorders and temporal response consistency on the MMPI–2. *Psychological Assessment, 8,* 39–47.

Wetzler, S., & Marlowe, D. B. (1990). "Faking bad" on the MMPI, MMPI–2, and Millon–II. *Psychological Reports, 67,* 1117–1118.

Wiener, D. N. (1948). Selecting salesmen with subtle–obvious keys for the Minnesota Multiphasic Personality Inventory. *American Psychologist, 3,* 364.

Wiener, D. N. (1948). The subtle–obvious factor in vocational and educational success. *American Psychologist, 3,* 299.

Wiggins, J. S. (1959). Interrelationships among the MMPI measures of dissimulation under standard and social desirability instructions. *Journal of Consulting Psychology, 23,* 419–427.

Wiggins, J. S. (1964). Convergences among stylistic response measures from objective personality tests. *Educational and Psychological Measurement, 24,* 551–562.

Wilcox, P., & Dawson, J. G. (1977). Role-played and hypnotically induced simulation of psychopathology on the MMPI. *Journal of Clinical Psychology, 33*(3), 743–745.

Wise, E. A. (2002). Relationships of personality disorders with MMPI–2 malingering, defensiveness, and inconsistent response scales among forensic examinees. *Psychological Reports, 90,* 760–766.

Wong, J. L., Lerner-Poppen, L., & Durham, J. (1998). Does warning reduce obvious malingering on memory and motor tasks in college samples? *International Journal of Rehabilitation and Health, 4,* 153–165.

Woychyshyn, C. A., McElheran, W. G., & Romney, D. M. (1992). MMPI validity measures: A comparative study of original with alternative indices. *Journal of Personality Assessment, 58,* 138–148.

Wright, P., Nussbaum, D., Lynett, E., & Buis, T. (1997). Forensic MMPI–2 profiles: Normative limitations impose interpretive restrictions with both males and females. *American Journal of Forensic Psychology, 15,* 19–37.

Wrobel, T. A., & Lachar, D. (1982). Validity of the Wiener subtle and obvious scales for the MMPI: Another example of the importance of inventory-item content. *Journal of Consulting and Clinical Psychology, 50,* 469–470.

Youngjohn, J. R., Burrows, L., & Erdal, K. (1995). Brain damage or compensation neurosis? The controversial post-concussion syndrome. *Clinical Neuropsychologist, 9*(2), 112–123.

Youngjohn, J. R., Davis, D., & Wolf, L. (1997). Head injury and the MMPI–2: Paradoxical effects and the influence of litigation. *Psychological Assessment, 9,* 177–184.

Youngjohn, J. R., Lees-Haley, P. R., & Binder, L. M. (1999). Comment: Warning malingerers produces more sophisticated malingering. *Archives of Clinical Neuropsychology, 14,* 511–515.

Youngjohn, J. R., Spector, J., & Mapou, R. L. (1997). Neuropsychological findings in silicone breast-implant complainants: Brain damage, somatization, or compensation neuroses? *Clinical Neuropsychologist, 11*(2), 132–141.

Zielinski, J. J. (1994). Malingering and defensiveness in the neuropsychological assessment of mild traumatic brain injury. *Clinical Psychology—Science and Practice, 1,* 169–184.

Defensiveness or Faking Good References

This appendix lists published works on faking-good, defensiveness, overly virtuous responding, symptom underreporting, and socially desirable responding.

Abramowitz, S. I., Carroll, J., & Schaffer, C. B. (1984). Borderline personality disorder and the MMPI. *Journal of Clinical Psychology, 40*(2), 410–413.

Adams, J. (1972). Defensiveness on the MMPI as a function of the warmth of test introduction. *Journal of Consulting and Clinical Psychology, 36*, 444.

Alexy, W. D., & Webb, P. M. (1999). Utility of the MMPI–2 in work-hardening rehabilitation. *Rehabilitation Psychology, 44*(3), 266–273.

Alperin, J. J., Archer, R. P., & Coates, G. D. (1996). Development and effects of an MMPI–A K-correction procedure. *Journal of Personality Assessment, 67*, 155–168.

Anderson, T., & Leitner, L. M. (1991). The relationship between the Defense Mechanisms Inventory and reported symptomatology in college females. *Personality and Individual Differences, 12*, 967–969.

Archer, R. P., Fontaine, J., & McCrae, R. R. (1998). Effects of two MMPI–2 validity scales on basic scale relations to external criteria. *Journal of Personality Assessment, 70*, 87–102.

Archer, R. P., Handel, R. W., & Couvadelli, B. (2004). An evaluation of the incremental validity of the MMPI–2 Superlative (S) Scale in an inpatient psychiatric sample. *Assessment, 11*(1), 102–108.

Archer, R. P., White, J. L., & Orvin, G. H. (1979). MMPI characteristics and correlates among adolescent psychiatric inpatients. *Journal of Clinical Psychology, 35*(3), 498–504.

Audubon, J. J. (1986). Cognitive traps to detect hidden schizophrenia. *Journal of Clinical Psychology, 42*(1), 123–125.

Audubon, J. J., & Kirwin, B. R. (1982). Defensiveness in the criminally insane. *Journal of Personality Assessment, 46*, 304–311.

Austin, J. S. (1992). The detection of fake good and fake bad on the MMPI–2. *Educational and Psychological Measurement, 52*(3), 669–674.

Back, S. M., Post, R. D., & D'Arcy, G. (1982). A study of battered women in a psychiatric setting. *Women and Therapy, 1*(2), 13–26.

Baer, R. A., Ballenger, J., & Kroll, L. S. (1998). Detection of underreporting on the MMPI–A in clinical and community samples. *Journal of Personality Assessment, 71*(1), 98–113.

Baer, R. A., & Miller, J. (2002). Underreporting of psychopathology on the MMPI–2: A meta-analytic review. *Psychological Assessment, 14*, 16–26.

Baer, R. A., & Sekirnjak, G. (1997). Detection of underreporting on the MMPI–2 in a clinical population: Effects of information about validity scales. *Journal of Personality Assessment, 69*, 555–567.

Baer, R. A., Wetter, M. W., & Berry, D. T. R. (1992). Detection of underreporting of psychopathology on the MMPI: A meta-analysis. *Clinical Psychology Review, 12,* 509–525.

Baer, R. A., Wetter, M. W., & Berry, D. T. R. (1995). Effects of information about validity scales on underreporting of symptoms on the MMPI–2: An analogue investigation. *Assessment, 2,* 189–200.

Baer, R. A., Wetter, M. A., Berry, D. T. R., & Nichols, D. S. (1993, August). *Sensitivity of MMPI–2 validity scales to underreporting of symptoms.* Paper presented at the 101st Annual Convention of the American Psychological Association, Toronto, Ontario, Canada.

Baer, R. A., Wetter, M. W., Nichols, D. S., Greene, R., & Berry, D. T. R. (1995). Sensitivity of MMPI–2 validity scales to underreporting of symptoms. *Psychological Assessment, 7,* 419–423.

Bagby, R. M., & Marshall, M. B. (2004). Assessing underreporting response bias on the MMPI–2. *Assessment, 11,* 115–126.

Bagby, R. M., Marshall, M. B., Bury, A. S., & Bacchiochi, J. R. (2006). Assessing underreporting and overreporting response style on the MMPI. In J. N. Butcher (Ed.), *MMPI–2: A practitioner's guide* (pp. 36–69). Washington, DC: American Psychological Association.

Bagby, R. M., Nicholson, R. A., Buis, T., Radovanovic, H., & Fidler, B. J. (1998, March). *Defensive responding on the MMPI–2 in family custody and access evaluations.* Paper presented at the 33rd Annual Symposium on Recent Developments in the Use of the MMPI–2/MMPI–A Workshop and Symposia, Clearwater Beach, FL.

Bagby, R. M., Nicholson, R. A., Buis, T., Radovanovic, H., & Fidler, B. J. (1999). Defensive responding on the MMPI–2 in family custody and access evaluations. *Psychological Assessment, 11,* 24–28.

Bagby, R. M., Rogers, R., & Buis, T. (1994). Detecting malingered and defensive responding on the MMPI–2 in a forensic inpatient sample. *Journal of Personality Assessment, 62,* 191–203.

Bagby, R. M., Rogers, R., Buis, T., & Kalemba, V. (1994). Malingered and defensive response styles on the MMPI–2: An examination of validity scales. *Assessment, 1*(1), 31–38.

Bagby, R. M., Rogers, R., Nicholson, R. A., Buis, T., Seeman, M. V., & Rector, N. A. (1997). Effectiveness of the MMPI–2 validity indicators in the detection of defensive responding in clinical and nonclinical samples. *Psychological Assessment, 9,* 406–413.

Baker, J. N. (1967). Effectiveness of certain MMPI dissimulation scales under "real-life" conditions. *Journal of Counseling Psychology, 14,* 286–292.

Baldwin, K., & Roys, D. T. (1998). Factors associated with denial in a sample of alleged adult sexual offenders. *Sexual Abuse: Journal of Research and Treatment, 10*(3), 211–226.

Bannatyne, L. A. (1997). The effects of defensiveness on select MMPI–2 and Rorschach variables for schizophrenic forensic patients. *Dissertation Abstracts International: Section B: The Sciences and Engineering, 57,* 4773.

Bannatyne, L. A., Gacono, C. B., & Greene, R. L. (1999). Differential patterns of responding among three groups of chronic, psychotic, forensic outpatients. *Journal of Clinical Psychology, 55,* 1553–1565.

Barthlow, D., Graham, J. R., Ben-Porath, Y. S., Tellegen, A., & McNulty, J. L. (2002). The appropriateness of the MMPI–2 K correction. *Assessment, 9*(3), 219–229.

Bartol, C. R. (1991). Predictive validation of the MMPI for small-town police officers who fail. *Professional Psychology: Research and Practice, 22,* 127–132.

Bathurst, K., Wisdom, J. M., Barter, A., & Gottfried, A. W. (1996, June). *Comparison of scales developed to facilitate interpretation of underreporting on the MMPI–2 in a sample of child custody litigants.* Paper presented at the 31st Annual Symposium on Recent Developments in the Use of the MMPI–2/MMPI–A Workshop and Symposia, Minneapolis, MN.

Bendig, A. M. (1959). An inter-item factor analysis of two "Lie" scales. *Psychological Newsletter, New York University, 10,* 299–303.

Bendig, A. W. (1962). A factor analysis of "social desirability," "defensiveness," "lie," and "acquiescence" scales. *Journal of General Psychology, 66,* 129–166.

Bennett, L. A. (1970). Test taking "insight" of prison inmates and subsequent parole adjustment. *Correctional Psychologist, 4,* 27–34.

Ben-Porath, Y. (1994). The ethical dilemma of coached malingering research. *Psychological Assessment, 6,* 14–15.

Ben-Porath, Y. S., & Arbisi, P. A. (2000, May). *The ability of the MMPI–2 to detect fake good responding in psychiatric inpatients.* Paper presented at the 35th Annual Symposium on Recent Developments in the Use of the MMPI–2/MMPI–A, Minneapolis, MN.

Bieliauskas, L. A. (1980). Life events, 17-OHCS measures, and psychological defensiveness in relation to aid seeking. *Journal of Human Stress, 6*(1), 28–36.

Binder, J., Mayman, M., & Doehrman, S. (1974). Self-ideal–self discrepancy as a defensive style. *Comprehensive Psychiatry, 15,* 335–343.

Biondi, M., Peronti, M., Pacitti, F., Pancheri, P., Pacifici, R., Paris, L., et al. (1994). Personality, endocrine and immune changes after eight months in healthy individuals under normal daily stress. *Psychotherapy and Psychosomatics, 62,* 176–184.

Blazer, J. A. (1966). MMPI interpretation in outline: IV. The *K* scale. *Psychology: A Journal of Human Behavior, 3*(2), 4–11.

Block J. (1965). *The challenge of response sets: Unconfounding meaning, acquiescence, and social desirability in the MMPI.* New York: Appleton-Century-Crofts.

Boe, E. E., & Kogan, W. S. (1964). Effect of social desirability instructions on several MMPI measures of social desirability. *Journal of Consulting Psychology, 28*(3), 248–251.

Boehme, H., & Teusch, L. (1997). *Abwehr in ratingskalen und therapieerfolg* [Defense in rating scales and therapy]. *Nervenarzt, 68,* 896–902.

Borum, R., & Stock, H. V. (1993). Detection of deception in law enforcement applicants: A preliminary investigation. *Law and Human Behavior, 17*(2), 157–166.

Brophy, A. L. (2000). Desirability of old and new MMPI–2 items. *Psychological Reports, 87*(3, Pt 1), 928.

Brophy, A. L. (2003). MMPI–2 *L+K* and *L+K—F* indexes of underreporting: Normative and desirable responding. *Psychological Reports, 92*(1), 223–227.

Browning, J. A. (2003). An exploratory investigation into faking good on the adult attachment interview. *Dissertation Abstracts International: Section B: The Sciences and Engineering, 64*(2-B), 956.

Burish, T. G., & Houston, B. K. (1976). Construct validity of the Lie scale as a measure of defensiveness. *Journal of Clinical Psychology, 32*(2), 310–314.

Burns, D., & Ohayv, R. J. (1980). Psychological changes in meditating Western monks in Thailand. *Journal of Transpersonal Psychology, 12*(1), 11–24.

Burns, J. W. (2000). Repression predicts outcome following multidisciplinary treatment of chronic pain. *Health Psychology, 19*(1), 75–84.

Bush, M. (1975). Relationship between color–word test interference and MMPI indices of psychoticism and defensive rigidity in normal males and females. *Journal of Consulting and Clinical Psychology, 43,* 926.

Butcher, J. N. (1994). Psychological assessment of airline pilot applicants with the MMPI–2. *Journal of Personality Assessment, 62,* 31–44.

Butcher, J. N. (1998, March). *Analysis of MMPI–2 S-scale subscales to refine interpretation of "good impression."* Paper presented at the 34th Annual Conference of Recent Developments in the Use of the MMPI/MMPI–2, Clearwater, FL.

Butcher, J. N., Atlis, M. M., & Fang, L. (2000). Effect of altered instructions on the MMPI–2 profiles of college students who are not motivated to distort their responses. *Journal of Personality Assessment, 75*, 492–501.

Butcher, J. N., & Han, K. (1995). Development of an MMPI–2 scale to assess the presentation of self in a superlative manner: The *S* Scale. In J. N. Butcher & C. D. Spielberger (Eds.), *Advances in personality assessment* (Vol. 10, pp. 25–50). Hillsdale, NJ: Erlbaum.

Butcher, J. N., Morfitt, R., Rouse, S., & Holden, R. (1996, June). *Reducing MMPI–2 defensiveness for a job applicant sample: The effect of special instructions on retest validity*. Paper presented at the 31st Annual Symposium on Recent Developments in the Use of the MMPI–2/MMPI–A Workshop and Symposia, Minneapolis, MN.

Butcher, J. N., Morfitt, R. C., Rouse, S. V., & Holden, R. R. (1997). Reducing MMPI–2 defensiveness: The effect of specialized instructions on retest validity in a job applicant sample. *Journal of Personality Assessment, 68*, 385–401.

Butcher, J. N., & Tellegen, A. (1978). MMPI research: Methodological problems and some current issues. *Journal of Consulting and Clinical Psychology, 46*, 620–628.

Caldwell-Andrews, A. A. (2001). Relationships between MMPI–2 validity scales and *NEO PI–R* experimental validity scales in police candidates. *Dissertation Abstracts International: Section B: The Sciences and Engineering, 61*(7-B), 3833.

Calvin, A. D., & Hanley, C. (1957). An investigation of dissimulation on the MMPI means of the "lie detector." *Journal of Applied Psychology, 41*, 312–316.

Carsky, M., Selzer, M. A., Terkelsen, K. G., & Hurt, S. W. (1992). The PEH: A questionnaire to assess acknowledgment of psychiatric illness. *Journal of Nervous and Mental Disease, 180*, 458–464.

Chyatte, C., & Goldman, I. J. (1961). The willingness of actors to admit to socially undesirable behavior on the MMPI. *Journal of Clinical Psychology, 17*(1), 44.

Cigrang, J. A., & Staal, M. A. (2001). Readministration of the MMPI–2 following defensive invalidation in a military job applicant sample. *Journal of Personality Assessment, 76*, 472–481.

Cloak, N. L., Kirklen, L. E., Strozier, A., & Reed, J. R. (1997). Factor analysis of Minnesota Multiphasic Personality Inventory—1 (MMPI–1) Validity Scale items. *Measurement and Evaluation in Counseling and Development, 30*(1), 40–49.

Clopton, J. R., & Neuringer, C. (1977). MMPI Cannot Say scores: Normative data and degree of profile distortion. *Journal of Personality Assessment, 41*, 511–513.

Clopton, J. R., Shanks, D. A., & Preng, K. W. (1987). Classification accuracy of the MacAndrew scale with and without *K* corrections. *International Journal of Addictions, 22*, 1049–1051.

Cofer, C. N., Chance, J., & Judson, A. J. (1949). A study of malingering on the MMPI. *Journal of Psychology, 27*, 491–499.

Colby, F. (1989). Usefulness of the *K* correction in MMPI profiles of patients and nonpatients. *Psychological Assessment, 1*, 142–145.

Colligan, R. C., & Offord, K. P. (1991). Adolescents, the MMPI, and the issue of *K* correction: A contemporary normative study. *Journal of Clinical Psychology, 47*, 607–631.

Comrey, A. L. (1958). A factor analysis of items on the *K* scale of the MMPI. *Educational and Psychological Measurement, 18*, 633–639.

Cook, M., Young, A., Taylor, D., & Bedford, A. P. (1996). Personality correlates of psychological distress. *Personality and Individual Differences, 20*(3), 313–319.

Costello, R. M., Schneider, S. L., & Schoenfeld, L. S. (1993). Applicants' fraud in law enforcement. *Psychological Reports, 73*, 179–183.

Costello, R. M., & Schoenfeld, L. S. (1981). Time-related effects on MMPI profiles of police academy recruits. *Journal of Clinical Psychology, 37*(3), 518–522.

Couch, A., & Keniston, K. (1960). Yeasayers and naysayers: Agreeing response set as a personality variable. *Journal of Abnormal and Social Psychology, 60,* 151–174.

Couch, A., & Keniston, K. (1961). Agreeing response set and social desirability. *Journal of Abnormal and Social Psychology, 62,* 175–179.

Coyle, W. C., & Heap, R. F. (1965). Interpreting the MMPI *L* scale. *Psychological Reports, 17,* 722.

Cramer, P. (1988). The Defense Mechanism Inventory: A review of research and discussion of the scales. *Journal of Personality Assessment, 52,* 142–164.

Crespo, G. S., & Gomez, F. J. (2003). Le Escala Superlative S de Butcher y Han (1995): El fingimiento en la adaptación española del MMPI–2 [The superlative scale *S* of Butcher and Han (1995): The "fake-good" in the Spanish adaptation of the MMPI–2]. *Revista de Psicologia, 21*(1), 5–39.

Cruse, D. B. (1966). Some relations between minimal content, acquiescent–dissentient, and social desirability scales. *Journal of Personality and Social Psychology, 3,* 112–119.

Dahl, D. F. (2001). The predictive validity of the *K* correction on Scale 4 of the MMPI in the assessment of antisocial personality. *Dissertation Abstracts International: Section B: The Sciences and Engineering, 61*(8-B), 4397.

Dahlstrom, W. G., Brooks, J. D., & Peterson, C. D. (1990). The Beck Depression Inventory: Item order and the impact of response sets. *Journal of Personality Assessment, 55,* 224–233.

Dahlstrom, W. G., Welsh, G. S., & Dahlstrom, L. E. (1972). *An MMPI handbook: Vol. I. Clinical interpretation.* Minneapolis: University of Minnesota Press.

Dannenbaum, S. E., & Lanyon, R. I. (1993). The use of subtle items in detecting deception. *Journal of Personality Assessment, 61,* 501–510.

Darkangelo, D. D., Ben-Porath, Y. S., & Stafford, K. P. (1996, June). *Defensive MMPI–2 profiles in a forensic diagnostic center.* Paper presented at the 31st Annual Symposium on Recent Developments in the Use of the MMPI–2/MMPI–A Workshop and Symposia, Minneapolis, MN.

Dean, R. S., & Jacobson, B. P. (1982). MMPI characteristics for parents of emotionally disturbed and learning-disabled children. *Journal of Consulting and Clinical Psychology, 50,* 775–777.

Dempsey, P. (1964). Overall performance on the MMPI as it relates to test-taking attitudes and clinical scale scores. *Journal of Clinical Psychology, 20*(1), 154–156.

Detrick, P., Chnibnall, J. T., & Rosso, M. (2001). Minnesota Multiphasic Personality Inventory—2 in police officer selection: Normative data and relation to the Inwald Personality Inventory. *Professional Psychology: Research and Practice, 32,* 484–490.

Dicks, R. H., & McHenry, J. D. (1985). Predictors of outcomes in a performance ladder program. *Journal of Offender Counseling, Services and Rehabilitation, 9,* 57–70.

Dietz, C. B. (2000). Effects of underreporting of psychopathology on MMPI–2 substance abuse scales among college students. *Dissertation Abstracts International: Section B: The Sciences and Engineering, 60*(8-B), 4215.

Duckworth, J., & Levitt, E. (1985). Personality analysis of a swingers' club. *Lifestyles, 8*(1), 35–45.

Duris, M. C. (2003). Religiousness as a motivation response characteristic for the MMPI–2 lie scale. *Dissertation Abstracts International: Section B: The Sciences and Engineering, 64*(4-B), 1940.

Edwards, A. (1957). *The social desirability variable in personality assessment and research.* New York: Dryden.

Edwards, A. E., & Husted, J. R. (1976). Penile sensitivity, age, and sexual behavior. *Journal of Clinical Psychology, 32*(3), 697–700.

Eisen, M. L., Morgan, D. Y., & Mickes, L. (2002). Individual differences in eyewitness memory and suggestibility: Examining relations between acquiescence, dissociation and resistance to misleading information. *Personality and Individual Differences, 33*, 553–572.

Elder, R. L., & Johnson, D. C. (1989). Varying relationships between adaption–innovation and social desirability. *Psychological Reports, 65*(3, Pt. 2), 1151–1154.

Eschenbach, A. E., & Dupree, L. (1959). The influence of stress on MMPI scale scores. *Journal of Clinical Psychology, 15*, 42–45.

Evans, J. H., Fabry, J. J., Sternitzke, M. E., & Bischoff, R. A. (1992). Validity of MMPI profiles with chemically dependent adolescents. *Journal of Adolescent Chemical Dependency, 2*(2), 9–22.

Exner, J., McDowell, E., Pabst, J., Stackman, W., & Kirk, L. (1963). On the detection of willful falsification in the MMPI. *Journal of Consulting Psychology, 27*, 91–94.

Fink, A., & Butcher, J. N. (1972). Reducing objections to personality inventories with special instructions. *Educational and Psychological Measurements, 27*, 631–639.

Finney, J. C. (1965). Effects of response sets on new and old MMPI scales. *Psychological Reports, 17*, 907–915.

Fisher, G. (1967). The performance of male prisoners on the Marlowe–Crowne Social Desirability Scale: II. Differences as a function of race and crime. *Journal of Clinical Psychology, 23*, 473–475.

Fisher, G. M., & Parsons, T. H. (1962). The performance of male prisoners on the Marlowe–Crowne social desirability scale. *Journal of Clinical Psychology, 18*, 140–141.

Fjordbak, T. (1985). Clinical correlates of high Lie scale elevations among forensic patients. *Journal of Personality Assessment, 49*, 252–255.

Florian, V., Mikulincer, M., & Green, E. (1993). Fear of personal death and the MMPI profile of middle-age men: The moderating impact of personal losses. *Omega: Journal of Death and Dying, 28*(2), 151–164.

Fordyce, W. E. (1956). Social desirability in the MMPI. *Journal of Consulting Psychology, 20*, 171–175.

Fricke, B. G. (1956). Response set as a suppressor variable in the OAIS and MMPI. *Journal of Consulting Psychology, 20*, 161–169.

Fukunishi, I., Nakagawa, T., Nakamura, H., Ogawa, J., & Nakagawa, T. (1993). A comparison of Type A behaviour pattern, hostility and *typus melancholicus* in Japanese and American students: Effects of defensiveness. *International Journal of Social Psychiatry, 39*(1), 58–63.

Fulkerson, S. C., Freud, S. L., & Raynor, G. H. (1958). The use of the MMPI in the psychological evaluation of pilots. *Journal of Aviation Medicine, 29*, 122–129.

Ganellen, R. J. (1994). Attempting to conceal psychological disturbance: MMPI defensive response sets and the Rorschach. *Journal of Personality Assessment, 63*, 423–437.

Gendreau, P., Irvine, M., & Knight, S. (1973). Evaluating response set styles on the MMPI with prisoners: Faking good adjustment and maladjustment. *Canadian Journal of Behavioural Science, 5*, 183–194.

Goodwin, R., & Andersen, A. E. (1984). The MMPI in three groups of patients with significant weight loss. *Hillside Journal of Clinical Psychiatry, 6*(2), 188–203.

Gough, H. G. (1947). Simulated patterns on the Minnesota Multiphasic Personality Inventory. *Journal of Abnormal and Social Psychology, 42*, 215–225.

Gough, H. G. (1950). The *F* minus *K* dissimulation index for the MMPI. *Journal of Consulting Psychology, 14*, 408–413.

Gowan, J. C. (1955). Relation of the "*K*" scale of the MMPI to the teaching personality. *California Journal of Educational Research, 6*, 208–212.

Graham, J. R. (1963). *The meaning of Cannot Say scores on the MMPI*. Unpublished master's thesis, University of North Carolina, Chapel Hill.

Graham, J. R., Watts, D., & Timbrook, R. E. (1991). Detecting fake-good and fake-bad MMPI–2 profiles. *Journal of Personality Assessment, 57,* 264–277.

Grayson, H. M., & Olinger, L. B. (1957). Simulation of "normalcy" by psychiatric patients on the MMPI. *Journal of Consulting Psychology, 21,* 73–77.

Greene, R. L. (1988). Assessment of malingering and defensiveness by objective personality inventories. In R. Rogers (Ed.), *Clinical assessment of malingering and deception* (pp. 123–128). New York: Guilford Press.

Greiffenstein, M. F., & Baker, W. J. (2001). Comparison of premorbid and postinjury MMPI–2 profiles in late post-concussion claimants. *Clinical Neuropsychologist, 15*(2), 162–170.

Grossman, L. S., & Cavanaugh, J. L. (1989). Do sex offenders minimize psychiatric symptoms? *Journal of Forensic Sciences, 34,* 881–886.

Grossman, L. S., Haywood, T. W., Ostrov, E., Wasyliw, O., & Cavanaugh, J. L. (1990). Sensitivity of MMPI validity indicators to motivational factors in psychological evaluations of police officers. *Journal of Personality Assessment, 55,* 549–561.

Gucker, D., & McNulty, J. (2004, May). *The MMPI–2, defensiveness, an analytic strategy.* Paper presented at the 39th Annual Symposium on Recent Developments in the Use of the MMPI–2, Minneapolis, MN.

Gurman, E. B., & Balban, M. (1990). Self-evaluation of physical attractiveness as a function of self-esteem and defensiveness. *Journal of Social Behavior and Personality, 5,* 575–580.

Hahn, J. (2001, March). *Faking and defensive responding in Korean MMPI–2.* Paper presented at the 36th Annual Symposium on Recent Developments in the Use of the MMPI–2/MMPI–A, Safety Harbor, FL.

Hahn, J. (2003). Faking and defensive responding in Korean MMPI–2. *Dissertation Abstracts International: Section B: The Sciences and Engineering, 64*(6-B), 2971.

Hall, G. C. N. (1989). Self-reported hostility as a function of offense characteristics and response style in a sexual offender population. *Journal of Consulting and Clinical Psychology, 57,* 306–308.

Hanley, C. (1957). Deriving a measure of test-taking defensiveness. *Journal of Consulting Psychology, 21,* 391–397.

Hartshorne, H., & May, M. A. (1928). *Studies in deceit.* New York: Macmillan.

Heilbrun, A. B., Jr. (1961). The psychological significance of the MMPI *K* scale in a normal population. *Journal of Consulting Psychology, 25,* 486–491.

Heilbrun, A. B., Jr. (1963). Revision of the MMPI *K* correction procedure for improved detection of maladjustment in a normal college population. *Journal of Consulting Psychology, 27*(2), 161–165.

Heilbrun, K., Bennett, W. S., White, A. J., & Kelly, J. (1990). An MMPI-based empirical model of malingering and deception. *Behavioral Sciences and the Law, 8*(1), 45–53.

Hilts, D., & Moore, J. M., Jr. (2003). Normal Range MMPI–A Profiles Among Psychiatric Inpatients. *Assessment, 10*(3), 266–272.

Himelstein, P., & Lubin, B. (1966). Relationship of the MMPI *K* scale and a measure of self-disclosure in a normal population. *Psychological Reports, 19*(1), 166.

Holland, T. R., & Boik, R. J. (1978). Impression management in the ethical self-presentation of offenders undergoing presentence evaluation. *Criminal Justice and Behavior, 5*(3), 259–270.

Hollender, J. W. (1978). College clients: Replication of MMPI differences between vocational and personal clients and findings of defensiveness in vocational clients. *Catalog of Selected Documents in Psychology, 8,* 1649.

Hopkins, L. C. (1999). The role of the *K*-scale as a validity measure in court-ordered child custody MMPIs. *Dissertation Abstracts International, 60,* 3010.

Horn, J. L., Adams, D. K., & Levy, G. (1968). On the concept validity of MMPI scales. *Journal of Educational Measurement, 5*(1), 79–90.

Houston, B. K. (1973). Viability of coping strategies, denial, and response to stress. *Journal of Personality, 41*(1), 50–58.

Hsu, L. M. (1986). Implications of differences in elevations of *K*-corrected and non-*K*-corrected MMPI *T* scores. *Journal of Consulting and Clinical Psychology, 54*, 552–557.

Hunt, H. F. (1948). The effect of deliberate deception on MMPI performance. *Journal of Consulting Psychology, 12*, 396–402.

Isenhart, C. E., & Silversmith, D. J. (1996). MMPI–2 response styles: Generalization to alcoholism assessment. *Psychology of Addictive Behaviors, 10*(2), 115–123.

Ismir, A. A., & Kleban, M. H. (1962). The applicability of the Marlowe–Crowne Social Desirability Scale to a psychiatric hospital population. *Journal of Clinical Psychology, 18*(2), 144–146.

Jamner, L. D., Shapiro, D., Goldstein, I. B., & Hug, R. (1991). Ambulatory blood pressure and heart rate in paramedics: Effects of cynical hostility and defensiveness. *Psychosomatic Medicine, 53*, 393–406.

Jansen, D. G., & Johnson, L. E. (1975). Patients who schedule meetings with a state hospital review board. *Psychological Reports, 36*(1), 283–286.

Jenkins, G. (1984). *Response sets and personality measures: The K scale of the MMPI.* Unpublished doctoral dissertation, Texas Tech University, Lubbock.

Ji, S., Gao, C., Li, M., Ji, Y., Guo, C., & Fang, M. (1999). Effect of *K* correction on the profile of the MMPI. *Chinese Journal of Clinical Psychology, 7*(1), 12–15.

Joiner, T. E., Jr., Schmidt, N. B., Lerew, D. R., Cook, J. H., Gencoz, T., & Gencoz, F. (2000). Differential roles of depressive and anxious symptoms and gender in defensiveness. *Journal of Personality Assessment, 75*, 200–211.

Kania, W. (1966). An investigation of the *K* scale of the MMPI as a measure of defensiveness in Protestant theological seminary students. *Dissertation Abstracts, 26*, 6169–6170.

Karle-Brueck, H. R. (2003). Denial in convicted sex offenders: A preliminary examination. *Dissertation Abstracts International: Section B: The Sciences and Engineering, 63*(12-B), 6097.

Keddy, P. J., Erdberg, P., & Sammon, S. D. (1990). The psychological assessment of Catholic clergy and religious referred for residential treatment. *Pastoral Psychology, 38*(3), 147–159.

Kelly, D. B. (1985). Detection of faking good on the MMPI in a psychiatric inpatient population. *Dissertation Abstracts International, 45*, 3074.

Kelly, D. B., & Greene, R. L. (1989). Detection of faking good on the MMPI in a psychiatric inpatient population. *Psychological Reports, 65*, 747–750.

Kimball, H. C., & Cundick, B. F. (1977). Emotional impact of videotape and reenacted feedback on subjects with high and low defenses. *Journal of Counseling Psychology, 24*, 377–382.

King, G. F., & Schiller, M. (1958). Note on ego-strength, defensiveness, and acquiescence. *Psychological Reports, 4*, 434.

King, G. F., & Schiller, M. (1959). A research note on the *K* scale of the MMPI and "defensiveness." *Journal of Clinical Psychology, 15*, 305–306.

Knoff, R. H. (1984). MMPI som "logndetektor": Erfaringer fra fengselspraksis [The MMPI used as a "Lie detector": Prison data]. *Tidsskrift for Norsk Psykologforening, 21*, 345–352.

Koch, D. A., Chandler, M. J., Harder, D. W., & Paget, K. F. (1982). Parental defense style and child competence: A match–mismatch hypothesis. *Journal of Applied Developmental Psychology, 3*(1), 11–21.

Kornfeld, A. D. (1995). Police officer candidate MMPI–2 performance: Gender, ethnic, and normative factors. *Journal of Clinical Psychology, 51*, 536–540.

Lachar, D., & Alexander, R. S. (1978). Veridicality of self-report: Replicated correlates of the Wiggins MMPI content scales. *Journal of Consulting and Clinical Psychology, 46,* 1349–1356.

Langevin, R., Wright, P., & Handy, L. (1990). Use of the MMPI and its derived scales with sex offenders: II. Reliability and criterion validity. *Annals of Sex Research, 3,* 453–486.

Lanyon, R. I. (1967). Simulation of normal and psychopathic MMPI personality patterns. *Journal of Consulting Psychology, 31,* 94–97.

Lanyon, R. I. (1993). Validity of MMPI sex offender scales with admitters and nonadmitters. *Psychological Assessment, 5,* 302–306.

Lanyon, R. I. (1997). Detecting deception: Current models and directions. *Clinical Psychology Science and Practice, 4,* 377–387.

Lanyon, R. I. (2001). Dimensions of self-serving misrepresentation in forensic assessment. *Journal of Personality Assessment, 76,* 169–179.

Lanyon, R. I., & Almer, E. R. (2002). Characteristics of compensable disability patients who choose to litigate. *Journal of the American Academy of Psychiatry and the Law, 30,* 400–404.

Lanyon, R. I., Dannenbaum, S. E., & Brown, A. R. (1991). Detection of deliberate denial in child abusers. *Journal of Interpersonal Violence, 6*(3), 301–309.

Lanyon, R. I., Dannenbaum, S. E., Wolf, L. L., & Brown, A. (1989). Dimensions of deceptive responding in criminal offenders. *Psychological Assessment, 1,* 300–304.

Lanyon, R. I., & Lutz, R. W. (1984). MMPI discrimination of defensive and nondefensive felony sex offenders. *Journal of Consulting and Clinical Psychology, 52,* 841–843.

Laxminarayan, C. S., & Murthy, H. N. (1970). Development of K Scale. *Transactions of All-India Institute of Mental Health, 10,* 127–130.

Layne, C. (1978). Relationship between the Barnum Effect and personality inventory responses. *Journal of Clinical Psychology, 34*(1), 94–97.

Lewinsohn, P. M. (1956). Personality correlates of duodenal ulcer and other psychosomatic reactions. *Journal of Clinical Psychology, 12,* 296–298.

Lim, J. (1994). Detection of faking on the MMPI–2 profiles: Differentiation between faking-bad, denial, and claiming extreme virtue. *Dissertation Abstracts International, 55,* 2430.

Lim, J. (1994, May). *Empirical evaluation of the effectiveness of the S scale in detection of symptom underreporting.* Paper presented at the 29th Annual Symposium on Recent Developments in the Use of the MMPI–2/MMPI–A Workshop and Symposia, Minneapolis, MN.

Lim, J., & Butcher, J. N. (1996). Detection of faking on the MMPI–2: Differentiation among faking-bad, denial, and claiming extreme virtue. *Journal of Personality Assessment, 67,* 1–25.

Lipovsky, J. A., Finch, A. J., & Belter, R. W. (1989). Assessment of depression in adolescents: Objective and projective measures. *Journal of Personality Assessment, 53,* 449–458.

Long, B., Rouse, S. V., Nelson, R. O., & Butcher, J. N. (2004). The MMPI–2 in sexual harassment and discrimination cases. *Journal of Clinical Psychology, 60,* 643–658.

Louks, J. L., Freeman, C. W., & Calsyn, D. A. (1978). Personality organization as an aspect of back pain in a medical setting. *Journal of Personality Assessment, 42,* 152–158.

Magarey, C. J., Todd, P. B., & Blizard, P. J. (1977). Psycho-social factors influencing delay and breast self-examination in women with symptoms of breast cancer. *Social Science and Medicine, 11*(4), 229–232.

Maloney, E. R. (1998). Faking good on the MMPI–2: A quantitative study. *Dissertation Abstracts International, 59,* 1906.

Manners, K. O. (1997). Faking good, social desirability, and the MMPI–A. *Dissertation Abstracts International, 58,* 1538.

Matarazzo, J. D. (1955). MMPI validity scores as a function of increasing levels of anxiety. *Journal of Consulting Psychology, 19,* 213–217.

Match, J., & Wiggins, N. (1974). Individual viewpoints of social desirability related to faking good and desirability estimation. *Educational and Psychological Measurement, 34,* 591–606.

Mayo, G. D., & Guttman, I. (1959). Faking in a vocational classification situation. *Journal of Applied Psychology, 43,* 117–121.

McAnulty, D. P., Rapaport, N. B., & McAnulty, R. D. (1985). An aposteriori investigation of standard MMPI validity scales. *Psychological Reports, 57,* 95–98.

McCann, J. T. (1998). *Malingering and deception in adolescents.* Washington, DC: American Psychological Association.

McCrae, R., Costa, P. T., Dahlstrom, W. G., & Barefoot, J. C., Siegler, I. C., & Williams, R. B. (1989). A caution on the use of the MMPI *K*-correction in research on psychosomatic medicine. *Psychosomatic Medicine, 51*(1), 58–65.

McGrath, R. E., Sweeney, M., O'Malley, W. B., & Carlton, T. K. (1998). Identifying psychological contributions to chronic pain complaints with the MMPI–2: The role of the *K* scale. *Journal of Personality Assessment, 70,* 448–459.

McKinley, J. C., Hathaway, S. R., & Meehl, P. E. (1948). The Minnesota Multiphasic Personality Inventory: VI. The *K* Scale. *Journal of Consulting Psychology, 12,* 20–31.

Medoff, D. (1999). MMPI–2 validity scales in child custody evaluations: Clinical versus statistical significance. *Behavioral Sciences and the Law, 17*(4), 409–411.

Meehl, P. E., & Hathaway, S. R. (1946). The *K* factor as a suppressor variable in the Minnesota Multiphasic Personality Inventory. *Journal of Applied Psychology, 30,* 525–564.

Meikle, S., Robinson, C., & Brody, H. (1977). Recent changes in the emotional reactions of therapeutic abortion applicants. *Canadian Psychiatric Association Journal, 22*(2), 67–70.

Messick, S., & Jackson, D. (1961). Desirability scale values and dispersions for MMPI items. *Psychological Reports, 8,* 409–414.

Monts, J. K., Zurcher, L. A., & Nydegger, R. V. (1977), Interpersonal self-deception and personality correlates. *Journal of Social Psychology, 103,* 91–99.

Moore, R. T., & Davies, J. A. (1984). Predicting GED scores on the bases of expectancy, valence, intelligence, and pretest skill levels with the disadvantaged. *Educational and Psychological Measurement, 44*(2), 483–490.

Morrell, J. S., & Rubin, L. J. (2001). The Minnesota Multiphasic Personality Inventory—2, posttraumatic stress disorder, and women domestic violence survivors. *Professional Psychology: Research and Practice, 32,* 151–156.

Moyer, D. M., Burkhardt, B., & Gordon, R. M. (2002). Faking PTSD from a motor vehicle accident on the MMPI–2. *American Journal of Forensic Psychology, 20*(2), 81–89.

Mrad, D. F., & Krasnoff, A. G. (1976). Use of MMPI and demographic variables in predicting dropouts from a correctional therapeutic community. *Offender Rehabilitation, 1*(2), 193–201.

Muller, B. P. (1994, May). *To tell the truth: Assessing underreporting of symptoms on the MMPI–2 by police applicants.* Paper presented at the 29th Annual Symposium on Recent Developments in the Use of the MMPI–2/MMPI–A Workshop and Symposia, Minneapolis, MN.

Nakamura, C. Y. (1960). Validity of *K* scale (MMPI) in college counseling. *Journal of Counseling Psychology, 7,* 108–115.

Nichols, D. S., & Greene, R. L. (1997). Dimensions of deception in personality assessment: The example of the MMPI–2. *Journal of Personality Assessment, 68,* 251–266.

Nicholson, R. A., Mouton, G. J., Bagby, R. M., Buis, T., Peterson, S. A., & Buigas, R. A. (1997). Utility of MMPI–2 indicators of response distortion: Receiver operating characteristic analysis. *Psychological Assessment, 9,* 471–479.

O'Hara, C. (1988). Emotional adjustment following minor head injury. *Cognitive Rehabilitation, 6*(2), 26–33.

Olander, R. (2004). Defensive styles and other factors that differentiate between two types of child molesters: Use of the MCMI–II, MMPI–2, and the 16PF. *Dissertation Abstracts International: Section B: The Sciences and Engineering, 64*(7-B), 3537.

Osborne, D. (1970). A moderator variable approach to MMPI validity. *Journal of Clinical Psychology, 26*(4), 486–490.

Otto, R. K., Lang, A. R., Megargee, E. I., & Rosenblatt, A. I. (1988). Ability of alcoholics to escape detection by the MMPI. *Journal of Consulting and Clinical Psychology, 56*, 452–457.

Papciak, A. S., Feuerstein, M., Belar, C. D., & Pistone, L. (1986). Alexithymia and pain in an outpatient behavioral medicine clinic. *International Journal of Psychiatry in Medicine, 16*(4), 347–357.

Patrick, J. (1988). Personality characteristics of work-ready workers' compensation clients. *Journal of Clinical Psychology, 44*, 1009–1012.

Paulhus, D. L. (1984). Two-component models of socially desirable responding. *Personality and Individual Differences, 46*, 598–609.

Paulhus, D. L. (1986). Self-deception and impression management in test responses. In A. Angleitner & J. S. Wiggins (Eds.), *Personality assessment via questionnaires: Current issues in theory and measurement* (pp. 143–165). Berlin, Germany: Springer-Verlag.

Paulhus, D. L. (1991). Measurement and control of response bias. In J. P. Robinson, R. Phillip, & L. S. Wrightman (Eds.), *Measures of personality and social psychological attitudes* (pp. 17–59). San Diego, CA: Academic Press.

Perry, W., Viglione, D., & Braff, D. (1992). The Ego Impairment Index and schizophrenia: A validation study. *Journal of Personality Assessment, 59*, 165–175.

Peters, P. K., Swenson, W. M., & Mulder, D. W. (1978). Is there a characteristic personality profile in amyotrophic lateral sclerosis? A Minnesota Multiphasic Personality Inventory study. *Archives of Neurology, 35*(5), 321–322.

Peterson, S. A., Mouton, G. J., Nicholson, R. A., & Bagby, R. M. (1995, March). *Detecting simulated defensiveness on the MMPI–2: Receiver operating characteristic (ROC) analysis.* Paper presented at the 30th Annual Symposium on Recent Developments in the Use of the MMPI–2/MMPI–A, St. Petersburg, FL.

Pickens, M. S. (2003). MMPI–2 scales of defensiveness: Are they measuring defensiveness? *Dissertation Abstracts International: Section B: The Sciences and Engineering, 63*(11-B), 5532.

Pierloot, R. A., Wellens, W., & Houben, M. E. (1975). Elements of resistance to a combined medical and psychotherapeutic program in anorexia nervosa: An overview. *Psychotherapy and Psychosomatics, 26*(2), 101–117.

Plante, T. G., Manuel, G., & Bryant, C. (1996). Personality and cognitive functioning among hospitalized sexual offending Roman Catholic priests. *Pastoral Psychology, 45*(2), 129–139.

Plante, T. G., Manuel, G., & Tandez, J. (1996). Personality characteristics of successful applicants to the priesthood. *Pastoral Psychology, 45*(1), 29–40.

Post, R. D., & Gasparikova-Krasnec, M. (1979). MMPI validity scales and behavioral disturbance in psychiatric inpatients. *Journal of Personality Assessment, 43*, 155–159.

Posthuma, A. B., & Harper, J. F. (1998). Comparison of MMPI–2 responses of child custody and personal injury litigants. *Professional Psychology: Research and Practice, 29*, 437–443.

Putzke, J. D., Williams, M. A., & Boll, T. J. (1998). A defensive response set and the relation between cognitive and emotional functioning: A replication. *Perceptual and Motor Skills, 86*(1), 251–257.

Putzke, J. D., Williams, M. A., Daniel, F. J., & Boll, T. J. (1999). The utility of *K*-correction to adjust for a defensive response set on the MMPI. *Assessment, 6*(1), 61–70.

Putzke, J. D., Williams, M. A., Millsaps, C. L., McCarty, H. J., Azrin, R. I., LaMarche, J. A., et al. (1997). The impact of a defensive response set on the relationship between MMPI and cognitive tests among heart transplant candidates. *Assessment, 4*(4), 365–375.

Redfering, D. L., & Jones, J. G. (1978). Effects of defensiveness on the State-Trait Anxiety Inventory. *Psychological Reports, 43*(1), 83–89.

Rhue, J. W., & Lynn, S. J. (1987). Fantasy proneness and psychopathology. *Journal of Personality and Social Psychology, 53*, 327–336.

Rice, M. E., Arnold, L. S., & Tate, D. L. (1983). Faking good and bad adjustment on the MMPI and overcontrolled-hostility in maximum security psychiatric patients. *Canadian Journal of Behavioural Science, 15*, 43–51.

Richwerger, D. C. (1990). A quantitative investigation of "faking good" on the MMPI. *Dissertation Abstracts International, 50*, 3754.

Ries, H. A. (1966). The MMPI *K* scale as a predictor of prognosis. *Journal of Clinical Psychology, 22*(2), 212–213.

Rios-Garcia, L. R., & Cook, P. E. (1975). Self-derogation and defense style in college students. *Journal of Personality Assessment, 39*, 273–281.

Rogers, A. H., & Walsh, T. M. (1959). Defensiveness and unwitting self-evaluation. *Journal of Clinical Psychology, 15*, 302–304.

Rogers, R., & Nussbaum, D. (1991). Interpreting response styles of inconsistent Minnesota Multiphasic Personality Inventory profiles. *Forensic Reports, 4*(4), 361–366.

Rosen, E. (1956). Self-appraisal, personal desirability, and perceived social desirability of personality traits. *Journal of Abnormal and Social Psychology, 52*, 151–158.

Rosenheim, H., & Dunn, R. W. (1977). The effectiveness of rational behavior therapy in a military population. *Military Medicine, 142*, 550–552.

Ruch, F. L., & Ruch, W. W. (1967). The *K* Factor as a (validity) suppressor variable in predicting success in selling. *Journal of Applied Psychology, 51*(3), 201–204.

Samuel, S. E., DeGirolamo, J., Michals, T. J., & O'Brien, J. (1994). Preliminary findings on MMPI "Cannot Say" responses with personal injury litigants. *American Journal of Forensic Psychology, 12*, 5–18.

Sappington, A., & Grizzard, R. (1975). Self-discrimination responses in Black school children *Journal of Personality and Social Psychology, 31*, 224–231.

Sappington, J. (1975). Psychometric correlates of defensive style in process and reactive schizophrenics. *Journal of Consulting and Clinical Psychology, 43*(2), 154–156.

Sarason, I. G. (1956). The relationship of anxiety and "lack of defensiveness" to intellectual performance. *Journal of Consulting Psychology, 20*, 220–222.

Saunders, B. T., & Fenton, T. (1975). MMPI profiles of child care applicants at a children's residential treatment center. *Devereux Forum, 10*(1), 16–19.

Scafidi, F. A., Field, T., Prodromidis, M., & Abrams, S. M. (1999). Association of fake-good MMPI–2 profiles with low Beck Depression Inventory scores. *Adolescence, 34*, 61–68.

Schwartz, M. M., Cohen, B. D., & Pavlik, W. B. (1964). Effects of subject- and experimenter-induced defensive response sets on picture-frustration test reactions. *Journal of Projective Techniques and Personality Assessment, 28*(3), 341–345.

Severin, D. A. (2003). A taxometric analysis of MMPI–2 impression management and self-deception scales in clergy. *Dissertation Abstracts International: Section B: The Sciences and Engineering, 64*(6-B), 2939.

Shapiro, D., Goldstein, I. B., & Jamner, L. D. (1995). Effects of anger/hostility, defensiveness, gender, and family history of hypertension on cardiovascular reactivity. *Psychophysiology, 32*, 425–435.

Siegel, J. C. (1996). Traditional MMPI–2 validity indicators and initial presentation in custody evaluations. *American Journal of Forensic Psychology, 14,* 55–63.

Siegel, J. C., & Langford, J. S. (1998). MMPI–2 validity scales and suspected parental alienation syndrome. *American Journal of Forensic Psychology, 16*(4), 5–14.

Silver, R., & Sines, L. K. (1962). Diagnostic efficiency of the MMPI with and without *K* correction. *Journal of Clinical Psychology, 18,* 312–314.

Simms, L. J., & Clark, L. A. (2001). Detection of deception on the Schedule for Nonadaptive and Adaptive Personality: Validation of the validity scales. *Assessment, 8*(3), 251–266.

Sines, L. K., Baucom, D. H., & Gruba, G. H. (1979). A validity scale sign calling for caution in the interpretation of MMPIs among psychiatric inpatients. *Journal of Personality Assessment, 43,* 604–607.

Sirigatti, S., & Giannini, M. (2000). *Identificazione del comportamento distorsivo (faking good) con il MMPI–2: Caratteristiche psicometriche della scala* S [Detection of faking good on the MMPI–2: Psychometric characteristics of the S scale]. *Bollettino di Psicologia Applicata, 232,* 61–69.

Smith, E. E. (1959). Defensiveness, insight, and the *K* scale. *Journal of Consulting Psychology, 23,* 275–277.

Snyder, S., & Pitt, W. M. (1985). Characterizing anger in the *DSM–III* borderline personality disorder. *Acta Psychiatrica Scandinavica, 72,* 464–469.

Stansell, V., Beutler, L. E., Neville, C. W., & Johnson, D. (1975). MMPI correlates of extreme field independence and field dependence in a psychiatric population. *Perceptual and Motor Skills, 40,* 539–544.

Stava, L. (1984). The use of hypnotic uncovering techniques in the treatment of pedophilia. *International Journal of Clinical and Experimental Hypnosis, 32,* 350–355.

Stein, L. A. R., & Graham, J. R. (1999). Detecting fake-good MMPI–A profiles in a correctional facility. *Psychological Assessment, 11,* 386–395.

Stevens, M. J., Kwan, K., & Graybill, D. F. (1993). Comparison of MMPI–2 scores of foreign Chinese and Caucasian-American students. *Journal of Clinical Psychology, 49*(1), 23–27.

Strong, D. R., Greene, R. L., Hoppe, C., Johnston, T., & Olesen, N. (1999). Taxometric analysis of impression management and self-deception on the MMPI–2 in child custody litigants. *Journal of Personality Assessment, 73,* 1–18.

Strong, D. R., Greene, R. L., & Kordinak, S. T. (2002). Taxometric analysis of impression management and self-deception in college student and personnel evaluation settings. *Journal of Personality Assessment, 78,* 161–175.

Stroupe, M. A. (1999). The effects of *K*-correction on the validity of MMPI–A. *Dissertations International: Section B: The Sciences and Engineering, 59*(10-B), 5615.

Sweetland, A., & Quay, H. (1953). A note on the *K* scale of the Minnesota Multiphasic Personality Inventory. *Journal of Consulting Psychology, 17,* 314–316.

Tamkin, A. S., & Hyer, L. (1983). Defensiveness in psychiatric elderly persons: Fact or fiction. *Psychological Reports, 52*(2), 455–458.

Thorndike, R. M. (1972). On scale correction in personality measurement. *Measurement and Evaluation in Guidance, 4*(4), 238–241.

Thumin, F. J. (1969). MMPI scores as related to age, education and intelligence among male job applicants. *Journal of Applied Psychology, 53,* 404–407.

Thumin, F. J. (1994). Correlations for a new personality test with age, education, intelligence, and the MMPI–2. *Perceptual and Motor Skills, 79,* 1383–1389.

Thumin, F. J. (2002). Comparison of the MMPI and MMPI–2 among job applicants. *Journal of Business and Psychology, 17*(1), 73–86.

Timbrook, R. E., Graham, J., Keiler, S. W., & Watts, D. (1993). Comparison of the Wiener–Harman Subtle–Obvious scales and the standard validity scales in detecting valid and invalid

MMPI–2 profiles. *Psychological Assessment, 5,* 53–61.

Todd, P. B., & Magarey, C. J. (1978). Ego defenses and affects in women with breast symptoms: A preliminary measurement paradigm. *British Journal of Medical Psychology, 51*(2), 177–189.

Tyler, F. T., & Michaelis, J. U. (1953). *K*-scores applied to MMPI scales for college women. *Educational and Psychological Measurement, 13,* 459–466.

Vandereycken, W., & Vanderlinden, J. (1983). Denial of illness and the use of self-reporting measures in anorexia nervosa patients. *International Journal of Eating Disorders, 2*(4), 101–107.

Van Deventer, J., & Webb, J. T. (1974). Manifest hostility as modified the *K* and *SO–R* scales of the MMPI. *Journal of Psychology, 87,* 209–211.

Vaughan, R. P. (1963). The effect of stress on the MMPI scales *K* and *D*. *Journal of Clinical Psychology, 19,* 432.

Vincent, K. R., Linsz, N. L., & Greene, M. I. (1966). The *L* scale on the MMPI as an index of falsification. *Journal of Clinical and Consulting Psychology, 12,* 214–215.

Walder, J. N. (1962). An examination of the role of the experimentally determined response set in evaluating Edwards' Social Desirability scale. *Journal of Consulting Psychology, 26*(2), 162–166.

Wales, B., & Seeman, W. (1968). A new method for detecting the fake-good response set on the MMPI. *Journal of Clinical Psychology, 24,* 211–216.

Walters, G. D. (1988). Assessing dissimulation and denial on the MMPI in a sample of maximum security, male inmates. *Journal of Personality Assessment, 52,* 465–474.

Walters, G. D., Greene, R. L., & Jeffrey, T. B. (1984). Discriminating between alcoholic and non-alcoholic Blacks and Whites on the MMPI. *Journal of Personality Assessment, 48,* 486–488.

Walters, G. D., Solomon, G. S., & Walden, V. R. (1982). Use of the MMPI in predicting psychotherapeutic persistence in groups in male and female

outpatients. *Journal of Clinical Psychology, 38*(1), 80–83.

Waniek, W., Hampel, R., & Bohme, H. (1976). Investigation of factorial communality and specificity of FPI and MMPI scales. *Zeitschrift für Experimentelle und Angewandte Psychologie, 23*(2), 310–319.

Wasyliw, O. E., Benn, A. F., Grossman, L., & Haywood, T. W. (1988). Detection of minimization of psychopathology on the Rorschach in cleric and noncleric alleged sex offenders. *Assessment, 5*(4), 389–397.

Watson, C. G., Tilleskjor, C., & Jacobs, L. (1990). The construct validity of an aftereffect-based subtyping system for alcoholics. *Journal of Clinical Psychology, 46,* 507–517.

Watson, D. (1982). Neurotic tendencies among chronic pain patients: An MMPI item analysis. *Pain, 14,* 365–385.

Weed, N. C. (1993). An evaluation of the efficacy of MMPI–2 indicators of validity. *Dissertation Abstracts International, 53,* 3800.

Weed, N., & Han, K. (May, 1992). *Is K correct?* Paper presented at the 27th Annual Symposium on Recent Developments in the Use of the MMPI, Minneapolis, MN.

Wennerholm, M. A., & Zarle, T. H. (1976). Internal–external control, defensiveness, and anxiety in hypertensive patients. *Journal of Clinical Psychology, 32*(3), 644–648.

Wexler, H. K., & de Leon, G. (1977). The therapeutic community: Multivariate prediction of retention. *American Journal of Drug and Alcohol Abuse, 4*(2), 145–151.

Weybrew, B. B., & Noddin, E. M. (1979). The mental health of nuclear submariners in the United States Navy. *Military Medicine, 144,* 188–191.

Wiggins, J. S. (1966). Social desirability estimation and "faking good" well. *Educational and Psychological Measurement, 26,* 329–341.

Wiggins, J. S. (1959). Interrelationships among MMPI measures of dissimulation under standard and social desirability instructions. *Journal of Consulting Psychology, 23*, 419–427.

Williams, M. A., Putzke, J. D., LaMarche, J. A., Bourge, R. C., Kirklin, J. K., McGiffin, D. C., et al. (2000). Psychological defensiveness among heart transplant candidates. *Journal of Clinical Psychology in Medical Settings, 7*, 167–174.

Wink, P. (1991). Two faces of narcissism. *Journal of Personality and Social Psychology, 61*, 590–597.

Wise, E. A. (2002). Relationships of personality disorders with MMPI–2 malingering, defensiveness, and inconsistent response scales among forensic examinees. *Psychological Reports, 90*(3, Pt. 1), 760–766.

Wooten, A. J. (1984). Effectiveness of the *K* correction in the detection of psychopathology and its impact on profile height and configuration among young adult men. *Journal of Consulting and Clinical Psychology, 52*, 468–473.

Wright, P., Nussbaum, D., Lynett, E., & Buis, T. (1997). Forensic MMPI–2 profiles: Normative limitations impose interpretive restrictions with both

males and females. *American Journal of Forensic Psychology, 15*(4), 19–37.

Yen, S., & Siegler, I. C. (2003). Self-blame, social introversion, and male suicides: Prospective data from a longitudinal study. *Archives of Suicide Research, 7*(1), 17–27.

Yonge, G. D. (1966). Certain consequences of applying the *K* factor to MMPI scores. *Educational and Psychological Measurement, 26*, 887–893.

Ze-Ping, X., Ming-Dao, Z., & Zhen, W. (2003). A study of the psychology and biology difference between obsessive–compulsive disorder patients with or without inherited history. *Chinese Journal of Clinical Psychology, 11*(2), 89–91.

Zhang, J. (1992). A study of *K* corrections used in Scale 8 and Scale 9 of the Chinese normative version of the MMPI. *Acta Psychologica Sinica, 24*, 429–435.

Zielinski, J. J. (1994). Malingering and defensiveness in the neuropsychological assessment of mild traumatic brain injury. *Clinical Psychology: Science and Practice, 1*(2), 169–184.

Personal Injury References

This appendix lists published works on personal injury litigation, compensation, traumatic brain injury, chronic pain, and posttraumatic stress disorder.

Abrams, K. R. (1994). An assessment of the impact of excessive medication use on the psychological functioning of chronic pain patients and the MMPI–2's ability to detect substance abuse among chronic pain patients, inpatient substance abusers and a normal control group. *Dissertation Abstracts International, 55,* 6704.

Adams, K. M. (1981). Use of the MMPI with patients who report chronic back pain. *Psychological Reports, 48,* 855–866.

Adams, K. M., Heilbronn, M., & Blumer, D. P. (1986). A multimethod evaluation of the MMPI in a chronic pain patient sample. *Journal of Clinical Psychology, 42,* 878–886.

Ahern, D. K., & Follick, M. J. (1985). Distress in spouses of chronic pain patients. *International Journal of Family Therapy, 7,* 247–257.

Akerlind, I., HornQuist, J. O., & Bjurulf, P. (1992). Psychological factors in the long-term prognosis of chronic low back pain patients. *Journal of Clinical Psychology, 48,* 596–605.

Albrecht, N. N., Talbert, F. S., Albrecht, J. W., Boudewyns, P. A., Hyer, L. A., Touze, J., et al. (1994). A comparison of MMPI and MMPI–2 in PTSD assessment. *Journal of Clinical Psychology, 50,* 578–585.

Alexy, W. D., & Webb, P. M. (1999). Utility of the MMPI–2 in work-hardening rehabilitation. *Rehabilitation Psychology, 44*(3), 266–273.

Alfano, D. P., & Finlayson, M. (1987). Comparison of standard and abbreviated MMPIs in patients with head injury. *Rehabilitation Psychology, 32,* 67–76.

Alfano, D. P., Neilson, P. M., Paniak, C. E., & Finlayson, M. (1992). The MMPI and closed-head injury. *Clinical Neuropsychologist, 6,* 134–142.

Alfano, D. P., Paniak, C., & Finlayson, M. (1993). The MMPI and closed head injury: A neurocorrective approach. *Neuropsychiatry, Neuropsychology and Behavioral Neurology, 6,* 111–116.

Alyman, C. A. (1999). The relationship of personality disorders and persistent post-concussive syndrome in mild head injury. *Dissertation Abstracts International, 59,* 6482.

Andreetto, U., & de Bertolini, C. (1999). Personality tests in the assessment of head traumas. *Medicina Psicosomatica, 44,* 199–221.

Ansher, L. S. (2003). Use of the pain presentation inventory in comparing personality traits with symptom presentation. *Dissertation Abstracts International: Section B: The Sciences and Engineering, 63*(12-B), 6084.

Arbisi, P. A., Ben-Porath, Y. S., & McNulty, J. (2005). *The ability of the MMPI–2 to detect feigned PTSD in the context of disability evaluation: An analogue study contrasting mental health professional feigning PTSD and veterans undergoing disability evaluation for PTSD*. Unpublished manuscript.

Arbisi, P. A., & Butcher, J. N. (2004). Failure of the FBS to predict malingering of somatic symptoms: Response to critiques by Greve and Bianchini and Lees Haley and Fox. *Archives of Clinical Neuropsychology, 19*(3), 341–345.

Arbisi, P. A., & Butcher, J. N. (2004). Psychometric perspectives on detection of malingering of pain: The use of the MMPI–2. *Clinical Journal of Pain, 4*, 571–595.

Arbisi, P. A., Murdoch, M., Fortier, L., & McNulty, J. (2004). The relationship between MMPI–2 validity and award of service connection for PTSD during the compensation and pension evaluation. *Psychological Services, 1*, 56–67.

Archambault, D. L. (1990). MMPI scale scores and demographic variables as predictors of medication dependency in chronic pain patients: A discriminative analysis. *Dissertation Abstracts International, 51*, 2666.

Archibald, H. C. (1955). Referred pain in headache. *California Medicine, 82*, 186–187.

Armentrout, D. P. (1982). Pain–patient MMPI subgroups: The psychological dimensions of pain. *Journal of Behavioral Medicine, 5*, 201–211.

Aronoff, G. M., & Evans, W. O. (1982). The prediction of treatment outcome at a multidisciplinary pain center. *Pain, 14*, 67–73.

Atkinson, J. H., Ingram, R. E., Kremer, E. F., & Saccuzzo, D. P. (1986). MMPI subgroups and affective disorder in chronic pain patients. *Journal of Nervous and Mental Disease, 174*, 408–413.

Axelrod, B, N., & Lees-Haley, P. (2002). Construct validity of the PCSQ as related to the MMPI–2. *Archives of Clinical Neuropsychology, 17*(4), 343–350.

Bachiocco, V., Morselli, A. M., & Carli, G. (1993). Self-control expectancy and postsurgical pain: Relationships to previous pain, behavior in past pain, familial pain tolerance models, and personality. *Journal of Pain and Symptom Management, 8*, 205–214.

Bailles, E., Pintor, L., Fernandez-Egea, E., Torres, X., Matrai, S., de Pablo, J., et al. (2004). Psychiatric disorders, trauma, and MMPI profile in a Spanish sample of nonepileptic seizure patients. *General Hospital Psychiatry, 26*(4), 310–315.

Baldrachi, R., Hilsenroth, M., Arsenault, L., Sloan, P., & Walter, C. (1999). MMPI-2 assessment of varying levels of posttraumatic stress in Vietnam combat veterans. *Journal of Psychopathology and Behavioral Assessment, 21*, 109–116.

Barnes, D., Gatchel, R. J., Mayer, T. G., & Barnett, J. (1990). Changes in MMPI profile levels of chronic low back pain patients following successful treatment. *Journal of Spinal Disorders, 3*(4), 353–355.

Barnett, J. (1987). The comparative effectiveness of the Millon Behavioral Health Inventory (MBHI) and the Minnesota Multiphasic Personality Inventory (MMPI) as predictors of treatment outcome in a rehabilitation program for chronic low back pain. *Dissertation Abstracts International, 48*, 869–870.

Beal, D. (1989). Assessment of malingering in personal injury cases. *American Journal of Forensic Psychology, 7*, 59–65.

Beausoleil, R., & Rioux, S. (1983). Traitement multi-dimensionnel pour patients souffrant de maux de dos chroniques: Une etude comparative [Multi-dimensional treatment for patients suffering from chronic low-back pain: A comparative study]. *Revue de Modification du Comportement, 13*, 107–116.

Beckham, J. C., Crawford, A. L., Feldman, M. E., Kirby, A. C., Hertzberg, M. A., Davidson, J. R. T., et al. (1997). Chronic posttraumatic stress disorder and chronic pain in Vietnam combat veterans. *Journal of Psychosomatic Research, 43*, 379–389.

Beniak, T., Heck, D., & Erdahl, P. E. (1992, May). *Intractable epilepsy: MMPI and MMPI–2 profiles.* Paper presented at the 27th Annual Symposium on Recent Developments in the Use of the MMPI (MMPI–2), Minneapolis, MN.

Bernstein, I. H., & Gabin, C. P. (1983). Hierarchical clustering of pain patients' MMPI profiles: A replication note. *Journal of Personality Assessment, 47,* 171–172.

Berry, D. T. (1995). Overreporting of closed-head injury symptoms on the MMPI–2. *Psychological Assessment, 7,* 517–523.

Berry, D., & Butcher, J. N. (1998). Detection of feigning of head injury symptoms on the MMPI–2. In C. Reynolds (Ed.), *Detection of malingering in head injury litigation* (pp. 209–238). New York: Plenum Press.

Bigos, S. J., Battie, M. C., Spengler, D. M., Fisher, L. D., W.E. F., Hansson, T. H., Nachemson, A. L., et al. (1991). A prospective study of work perceptions and psychosocial factors affecting the report of back injury. *Spine, 16,* 1–6.

Binder, L. M., & Rohling, M. L. (1996). Money matters: A meta-analytic review of the effects of financial incentives on recovery after closed head injury. *American Journal of Psychiatry, 153,* 7–10.

Block, A. R. (1999). Presurgical psychological screening in chronic pain syndromes: Psychosocial risk factors for poor surgical results. In R. J. Gatchel (Ed.), *Psychosocial factors in pain: Critical perspectives* (pp. 390–400). New York: Guilford Press.

Boccaccini, M. T., & Brodsky, S. L. (1999). Diagnostic test usage by forensic psychologists in emotional injury cases. *Professional Psychology: Research and Practice, 30,* 253–259.

Bowler, R. M., Rauch, S. S., Becker, C. H., Hawes, A., & Cone, J. D. (1989). Three patterns of MMPI profiles following neurotoxin exposure. *American Journal of Forensic Psychology, 7,* 15–31.

Bradley, L. A., Prieto, E. J., Hopson, L., & Prokop, C. K. (1978). Comment on "Personality organization as an aspect of back pain in a medical setting." *Journal of Personality Assessment, 42,* 573–578.

Bradley, L. A., & Van der Heide, L. H. (1984). Pain-related correlates of MMPI profile subgroups among back pain patients. *Health Psychology, 3,* 157–174.

Brandwin, M. A., & Kewman, D. G. (1982). MMPI indicators of treatment response to spinal epidural stimulation in patients with chronic pain and patients with movement disorders. *Psychological Reports, 51,* 1059–1064.

Brennan, A. F., Barrett, C. L., & Garretson, H. D. (1986). The prediction of chronic pain outcome by psychological variables. *International Journal of Psychiatry in Medicine, 16,* 373–387.

Brennan, A. F., Barrett, C. L., & Garretson, H. D. (1987). The utility of McGill Pain Questionnaire subscales for discriminating psychological disorder in chronic pain patients. *Psychology and Health, 1,* 257–272.

Brophy, A. L. (1996). Provisional statistics for MMPI–2 dependency, prejudice, social status, control, and low back pain scales. *Psychological Reports, 78,* 1075–1078.

Brozek, J. H., & Schiele, B. (1948). Clinical significance of the Minnesota Multiphasic *F* scale evaluated in experimental neurosis. *American Journal of Psychiatry, 105,* 259–266.

Brulot, M. M., Strauss, E., & Spellacy, F. (1997). Validity of the Minnesota Multiphasic Personality Inventory–2 correction factors for use with patients with suspected head injury. *Clinical Neuropsychologist, 11,* 391–401.

Burchiel, K. J., Anderson, V. C., Wilson, B. J., Denison, D. B., Olson, K. A., & Shatin, D. (1995). Prognostic factors of spinal chord stimulation for chronic back and leg pain. *Neurosurgery, 36,* 1101–1111.

Burns, J. W. (2000). Repression predicts outcome following multidisciplinary treatment of chronic pain. *Health Psychology, 19*(1), 75–84.

Burton, L. A., & Volpe, B. T. (1994). Depression after head injury: Do physical and cognitive sequelae have similar impact? *Journal of Neurologic Rehabilitation, 8,* 63–67.

Bury, A. S., & Bagby, R. M. (2002). The detection of feigned uncoached and coached posttraumatic stress disorder with the MMPI–2 in a sample of workplace accident victims. *Psychological Assessment, 14,* 472–484.

Butcher, J. N. (1985). Assessing psychological characteristics of personal injury or worker's compensation litigants. *Clinical Psychologist, 38,* 84–87.

Butcher, J. N. (1995). Personality patterns of personal injury litigants: The role of computer-based MMPI–2 evaluations. In Y. S. Ben-Porath, J. R. Graham, G. C. N. Hall, R. D. Hirschman, & M. S. Zaragoza (Eds.), *Forensic applications of the MMPI–2* (pp. 179–201). Thousand Oaks, CA: Sage.

Butcher, J. N. (1997). *Base-rate information for the personal injury samples in the Minnesota forensic study.* Unpublished study.

Butcher, J. N. (1997). Frequency of MMPI–2 scores in forensic evaluations. *MMPI–2 News and Profiles, 8,* 4–5.

Butcher, J. N. (1997). *User's guide to the Minnesota Report: Forensic system.* Minneapolis, MN: National Computer systems.

Butcher, J. N., & Ben-Porath, Y. S. (2004). Use of the MMPI–2 in medico legal evaluations: An alternative interpretation for the Senior & Douglas (2001) critique. *Australian Psychologist, 39,* 44–50.

Butcher, J. N., & Harlow, T. C. (1987). Personality assessment in personal injury cases. In I. B. Weiner & A. K. Hess (Eds.), *Handbook of forensic psychology* (pp. 128–154). New York: Wiley.

Butcher, J. N., & Miller, K. B. (1999). Personality assessment in personal injury litigation. In A. K. Hess & I. B. Weiner (Eds.), *The handbook of forensic psychology* (2nd ed., pp. 104–126). New York: Wiley.

Byers, A. P. (1995). Neurofeedback therapy for a mild head injury. *Journal of Neurotherapy, 1,* 22–37.

Cairns, D., Mooney, V., & Crane, P. (1984). Spinal pain rehabilitation: Inpatient and outpatient treatment results and development of predictors for outcome. *Spine, 9,* 91–95.

Caldirola, D. (1983). Incest and pelvic pain: The social worker as part of a research team. *Health and Social Work, 8,* 309–319.

Caldwell, A. B., & Chase, C. (1977). Diagnosis and treatment of personality factors in chronic low back pain. *Clinical Orthopaedics and Related Research, 129,* 141–149.

Calsyn, D. A., Spengler, D. M., & Freeman, C. W. (1977). Application of the Somatization factor of the MMPI–168 with low back pain patients. *Journal of Clinical Psychology, 33,* 1017–1020.

Cannon, D. S., Bell, W. E., Andrews, R. H., & Finkelstein, A. S. (1987). Correspondence between MMPI PTSD measures and clinical diagnosis. *Journal of Personality Assessment, 51,* 517–521.

Carr, J. E., Brownsberger, C. N., & Rutherford, R. C. (1966). Characteristics of symptom-matched psychogenic and "real" pain patients on the MMPI. *Proceedings of the Annual Convention of the American Psychological Association,* 215–216.

Carracher, J. C. (1984). Analysis of the internal consistency of the three special MMPI low back pain scales. *Dissertation Abstracts International, 45,* 1008.

Carragee, E. J. (2001). Psychological screening in the surgical treatment of lumbar disc herniation. *Clinical Journal of Pain, 17,* 215–219.

Caslyn, D. A., Louks, J., & Freeman, C. W. (1976). The use of the MMPI with chronic low back pain patients with a mixed diagnosis. *Journal of Clinical Psychology, 32,* 532–536.

Castelnuovo-Tedesco, P., & Kraut, B. M. (1970). Psychosomatic aspects of chronic pelvic pain. *Psychiatry in Medicine, 1,* 109–126.

Caston, J., Cooper, L., & Paley, H. (1970). Psychological comparison of patients with cardiac neurotic chest pain and angina pectoris. *Psychosomatics, 11,* 543–550.

Catchlove, R. F., Cohen, K. R., Braha, R. E., & Demers-Desrosiers, L. A. (1985). Incidence and implications of alexithymia in chronic pain patients. *Journal of Nervous and Mental Disease, 173,* 246–248.

Cattelani, R., Gugliotta, M., Maravita, A., & Mazzucchi, A. (1996). Post-concussive syndrome: Paraclinical signs, subjective symptoms, cognitive functions and MMPI profiles. *Brain Injury, 10*, 187–195.

Chaney, H. S., Williams, S. G., Cohn, C. K., & Vincent, K. R. (1984). MMPI results: A comparison of trauma victims, psychogenic pain, and patients with organic disease. *Journal of Clinical Psychology, 40*, 1450–1454.

Chapman, S. L., & Brena, S. F. (1982). Learned helplessness and responses to nerve blocks in chronic low back pain patients. *Pain, 14*, 355–364.

Charles, T. L. (2000). Usefulness of the Minnesota Multiphasic Personality Inventory—2 in detection of deception in a personal injury type forensic population. *Dissertation Abstracts International: Section B: The Sciences and Engineering, 60*(10-B), 5221.

Chervinsky, A. B., Ommaya, A. K., deJonge, M., Spector, J., Schwab, K., & Salazar, A. M. (1998). Motivation for traumatic brain injury rehabilitation questionnaire (MOT–Q): Reliability, factor analysis, and relationship to MMPI–2 variables. *Archives of Clinical Neuropsychology, 13*, 433–446.

Chibnall, J. T., & Tait, R. C. (1999). Social and medical influences on attributions and evaluations of chronic pain. *Psychology and Health, 14*, 719–729.

Chodak, M. (1989). *Zastosowanie MMPI w ortopevii* [Application of MMPI to patients with low back pain]. *Przeglad Psychologiczny, 32*, 793–806.

Clark, M. E. (1996). MMPI–2 Negative Treatment Indicators Content and Content Component Scales: Clinical correlates and outcome prediction for men with chronic pain. *Psychological Assessment, 8*, 32–38.

Clark, S. A., Velasquez, R. J., & Callahan, W. J. (1993). MMPI–ER differences among Hispanic worker's compensation applicants by psychiatric diagnosis. *Journal of Applied Rehabilitation Counseling, 24*, 15–18.

Cohen, M. J., McArthur, D. L., Vulpe, M., & Schandler, S. L. (1988). Comparing chronic pain from spinal cord injury to chronic pain of other origins. *Pain, 35*, 57–63.

Cohen, N. J. (1987). The response of chronic pain patients to the original and revised versions of the Minnesota Multiphasic Personality Inventory. *Dissertation Abstracts International, 48*, 259.

Collet, L., Cottraux, J. A., & Juenet, C. (1986). Tension headaches: Relation between MMPI paranoia score and pain and between MMPI hypochondriasis score and frontalis EMG. *Headache, 26*, 365–368.

Collins, L. (1966). Family structure and pain reactivity. *Journal of Clinical Psychology, 22*, 33.

Collins, L. J. (1999). Select MMPI–2 scales and consistency of physical effort during trunk extension exercise as predictors of treatment outcome for functional restoration rehabilitation in chronic back pain patients. *Dissertations International: Section B: The Sciences and Engineering, 59*(10-B), 5573.

Colotla, V. A., Bowman, M. L., & Shercliffe, R. J. (2001). Test–retest stability of injured workers' MMPI–2 profiles. *Psychological Assessment, 13*, 572–576.

Comer-Hilbert, D. R. (1993). The use of the Minnesota Multiphasic Personality Inventory in chronic pain patients suffering from headaches: Cluster analysis. *Dissertation Abstracts International, 53*, 5474.

Constans, J. I., Lenhoff, K., & McCarthy, M. (1997). Depression subtyping in PTSD patients. *Annals of Clinical Psychiatry, 9*, 235–240.

Costello, R. M., Hulsey, T. L., Schoenfeld, L. S., & Ramamurthy, S. (1987). P-A-I-N: A four-cluster MMPI typology for chronic pain. *Pain, 30*, 199–209.

Cripe, L. I. (1999). Use of the MMPI with mild closed head injury. In N. R. Varney (Ed.), *The evaluation and treatment of mild traumatic brain injury* (pp. 291–314). Mahwah, NJ: Erlbaum.

Cripe, L. I., Maxwell, J. K., & Hill, E. (1995). Multivariate discriminant function analysis of neurologic, pain, and psychiatric patients with the MMPI. *Journal of Clinical Psychology, 51*, 258–268.

Crowe, D. V. (1996). Efficacy of MMPI–2 content scales in the prediction of chronic pain treatment outcome. *Dissertation Abstracts International, 57,* 692.

Curtiss, G., Kinder, B. N., Kalichman, S., & Spana, R. (1988). Affective differences among subgroups of chronic pain patients. *Anxiety Research, 1,* 65–73.

Davidson, P. O., & McDougall, C. (1969). The generality of pain tolerance. *Journal of Psychosomatic Research, 13,* 83–89.

Deardorff, W. W. (2000). The MMPI–2 and chronic pain. In R. J. Gatchel (Ed.), *Personality characteristics of patients with pain* (pp. 109–125). Washington, DC: American Psychological Association.

Deardorff, W. W., Chino, A. F., & Scott, D. W. (1993). Characteristics of chronic pain patients: Factor analysis of the MMPI–2. *Pain, 54,* 153–158.

Dearth, C. S., Berry, D. T., Vickery, C. D., Vagnini, V. L., Baser, R. E., Orey, S. A., et al. (2005). Detection of feigned head injury symptoms on the MMPI–2 in head injured patients and community controls. *Archives of Clinical Neuropsychology, 20,* 95–110.

Demers-Desrosiers, L. A., & Cohen, K. (1983). The measure of symbolic function in alexithymic pain patients. *Psychotherapy and Psychosomatics, 39,* 65–76.

Denny, A. S. (1998). Predictors of return to work following a chronic pain rehabilitation program. *Dissertation Abstracts International, 59*(5-B), 2466.

Dersh, J., Polatin, P. B., & Gatchel, R. J. (2002). Chronic pain and psychopathology: Research findings and theoretical considerations. *Psychosomatic Medicine, 64,* 773–786.

Dhanens, T. P., & Jarrett, S. R. (1984). MMPI Pain Assessment Index: Concurrent and predictive validity. *Clinical Neuropsychology, 6,* 46–48.

Dikmen, S., Reitan, R. M., Temkin, N. R., & Machamer, J. E. (1992). Minor and severe head injury emotional sequelae. *Brain Injury, 6,* 477–478.

Dolce, J. J., Crocker, M. F., & Doleys, D. M. (1986). Prediction of outcome among chronic pain patients. *Behaviour Research and Therapy, 24,* 313–319.

Donham, G. W., & Mikhail, S. (1984). Value of consensual ratings in differentiating organic and functional low back pain. *Journal of Clinical Psychology, 40,* 432–439.

Dorris, G. G. (1993). The relationship between MMPI typology and compensation in chronic pain patients. *Dissertation Abstracts International, 54,* 1661.

Dowdy, W. M. (1990). Pain as a symptom of depression. *Dissertation Abstracts International, 50,* 4450.

DuAlba, L., & Scott, R. L. (1993). Somatization and malingering for workers' compensation applicants: A cross-cultural MMPI study. *Journal of Clinical Psychology, 49,* 913–917.

Duckro, P. N., Margolis, R. B., & Tait, R. C. (1985). Psychological assessment in chronic pain. *Journal of Clinical Psychology, 41,* 499–504.

Dufton, B. D. (1990). Depression and the mediation of chronic pain. *Journal of Clinical Psychiatry, 51,* 248–250.

Dunn, J. T., & Lees-Haley, P. R. (1995). The MMPI–2 correction factor for closed-head injury: A caveat for forensic cases. *Assessment, 2,* 47–51.

Dush, D. M., Simons, L. E., Platt, M., & Nation, P. C. (1994). Psychological profiles distinquishing litigating and nonlitigating pain patients: Subtle, and not so subtle. *Journal of Personality Assessment, 62,* 299–313.

Dzioba, R. B., & Doxey, N. C. (1984). A prospective investigation into the orthopaedic and psychologic predictors of outcome of first lumbar surgery following industrial injury. *Spine, 9,* 614–623.

Dzwierzynski, W. W., Grunert, B. K., Rusch, M. D., Zader, G., & Keller, D. (1999). Psychometric assessment of patients with chronic upper extremity pain attributed to workplace exposure.

Journal of Hand Surgery—American Volume, 24, 46–52.

Eberly, R. E., Harkness, A. R., & Engdahl, B. E. (1991). An adaptational view of trauma response as illustrated by the prisoner of war experience. *Journal of Traumatic Stress, 4,* 363–380.

Edwards, D. W., Dahmen, B. A., Wanlass, R. L., Holmquist, L. A., Wicks, J. J., Davis, C., et al. (2003). Personality assessment in neuropsychology: The nonspecificity of MMPI–2 neurocorrection methods. *Assessment, 10*(3), 222–227.

Egle, U. T., Schwab, R., Porsch, U., & Hoffmann, S. O. (1991). Ist eine frühe Differenzierung psychogener von organischen Schmerzpatienten möglich? Literaturuebersicht und Ergebnisse einer Screening studie (Is an early differentiation between psychogenic and organic pain possible? Review of literature and results of a screening study). *Nervenarzt, 62,* 148–157.

Elhai, J. D., Frueh, B. C., Gold, P. B., Gold, S. N., & Hamner, M. B. (2000). Clinical presentations of posttraumatic stress disorder across trauma populations: A comparison of MMPI–2 profiles of combat veterans and adult survivors of child sexual abuse. *Journal of Nervous and Mental Disease, 188,* 708–713.

Elhai, J. D., Gold, P. B., Frueh, B. C., & Gold, S. N. (2000). Cross-validation of the MMPI–2 in detecting malingered posttraumatic stress disorder. *Journal of Personality Assessment, 75,* 449–457.

Elhai, J. D., Gold, S. N., Mateus, L. F., & Astaphan, T. A. (2001). Scale 8 elevations on the MMPI–2 among women survivors of childhood sexual abuse: Evaluating posttraumatic stress, depression, and dissociation as predictors. *Journal of Family Violence, 16,* 47–58.

Elhai, J. D., Gold, S. N., Sellers, A. H., & Dorfman, W. I. (2001). The detection of malingered posttraumatic stress disorder with MMPI–2 fake-bad indices. *Assessment, 8,* 217–232.

Elhai, J. D., Klotz Flitter, J. M., Gold, S. N., & Sellers, A. H. (2001). Identifying subtypes of women survivors of childhood sexual abuse: An MMPI–2

cluster analysis. *Journal of Traumatic Stress, 14,* 153–169.

Elhai, J. D., Naifeh, J. A., Zucker, I. S., Gold, S. N., Deitsch, S. E., Frueh, B. C., et al. (2004). Discriminating malingered from genuine civilian posttraumatic stress disorder: A validation of three MMPI–2 infrequency scales (*F, Fp,* and *Fptsd*). *Assessment, 11*(2), 139–144.

Elkins, G. R., & Barrett, E. T. (1984). The MMPI in evaluation of functional versus organic low back pain. *Journal of Personality Assessment, 48,* 259–264.

Engdahl, B. E., Eberly, R. E., & Blake, J. D. (1996). Assessment of posttraumatic stress disorder in World War II veterans. *Psychological Assessment, 8,* 445–449.

Engdahl, B. E., Speed, N., Eberly, R. E., & Schwartz, J. (1991). Comorbidity of psychiatric disorders and personality profiles of American World War II prisoners of war. *Journal of Nervous and Mental Disease, 179,* 181–187.

Ercolani, M., & Erroi, G. (1990). Componenti organiche e psicologiche del dolore cronico: Possibilità di discriminazione attraverso il linguaggio e l test psicometrici [Organic and psychologic components of chronic pain: Differential diagnosis using language psychometric tests]. *Medicina Psicosomatica, 35,* 3–11.

Etscheidt, M. A., Steger, H. G., & Braverman, B. (1995). Multidimensional Pain Inventory profile classifications and psychopathology. *Journal of Clinical Psychology, 51,* 29–36.

Evans, R. W. (1994). The effects of litigation on treatment outcome with personal injury patients. *American Journal of Forensic Psychology, 12*(4), 19–34.

Fairbank, J. A., Keane, T. M., & Malloy, P. F. (1983). Some preliminary data on the psychological characteristics of Vietnam veterans with posttraumatic stress disorders. *Journal of Consulting and Clinical Psychology, 51,* 912–919.

Fairbank, J. A., McCaffrey, R., & Keane, T. M. (1985). Psychometric detection of fabricated symptoms of post-traumatic stress disorder. *American Journal of Psychiatry, 142,* 501–503.

Feuerstein, M., & Thebarge, R. W. (1991). Perceptions of disability and occupational stress as discriminators of work disability in patients with chronic pain. *Journal of Occupational Rehabilitation, 1,* 185–195.

Finlayson, R. E., Maruta, T., Morse, R. M., & Swenson, W. M. (1986). Substance dependence and chronic pain: Profile of 50 patients treated in an alcohol and drug dependence unit. *Pain, 26,* 167–174.

Fisher, R. E. (1990). Diagnostic accuracy of the MMPI Depression Scale and a proposed subscale in a chronic pain population. *Dissertation Abstracts International, 50,* 4769–4770.

Flamer, S., & Buch, W. (1992, May). *Differential diagnosis of post-traumatic stress disorder in injured workers; Evaluating the MMPI–2.* Paper presented at the 27th Annual Symposium on Recent Developments in the Use of the MMPI (MMPI–2), Minneapolis, MN.

Follick, M. J., Smith, T. W., & Ahern, D. K. (1985). The Sickness Impact Profile: A global measure of disability in chronic low back pain. *Pain, 21,* 67–76.

Forbes, D., Creamer, M., Allen, N., McHugh, T., Debenham, P., & Hopwood, M. (2003). MMPI–2 as a predictor of change in PTSD symptom clusters: A further analysis of the Forbes et al. (2002) data set. *Journal of Personality Assessment, 81,* 183–186.

Forbes, D., Creamer, M., & McHugh, T. (1999). MMPI–2 data for Australian Vietnam veterans with combat-related PTSD. *Journal of Traumatic Stress, 12,* 371–378.

Fordyce, W. E. (1978). Relationship of patient semantic pain descriptions to physician diagnostic judgments, activity level measures and MMPI. *Pain, 5,* 293–303.

Fordyce, W. E., Bigos, S. J., Batti'e, M. C., & Fisher, L. D. (1992). MMPI scale 3 as a predictor of back injury report: What does it tell us? *Clinical Journal of Pain, 8*(3), 222–226.

Forfar, C. S. (1993). Keane's MMPI–PTSD scale: A false positive analysis. *Dissertation Abstracts International, 54,* 1664.

Fow, N. R., Dorris, G., Sittig, M., & Smith-Seemiller, L. (2002). An analysis of the influence of insurance sponsorship on MMPI changes among patients with chronic pain. *Journal of Clinical Psychology, 58,* 827–832.

Fow, N. R., Sittig, M., Dorris, G., & Breisinger, G. (1994). An analysis of the relationship of gender and age to MMPI scores of patients with chronic pain. *Journal of Clinical Psychology, 50,* 537–554.

Fox, D. D., Gerson, A., & Lees-Haley, P. R. (1995). Interrelationship of MMPI–2 validity scales in personal injury claims. *Journal of Clinical Psychology, 51,* 42–47.

Frixione, S. K. (1993). MMPI profile validity among workers' compensation claimants. *Dissertation Abstracts International, 54*(5-B), 2748.

Franklin, C. L., Repasky, S. A., Thompson, K. E., Shelton, S. A., & Uddo, M. (2002). Differentiating overreporting and extreme distress: MMPI–2 use with compensation-seeking veterans with PTSD. *Journal of Personality Assessment, 79,* 274–285.

Franklin, C. L., Repasky, S. A., Thompson, K. E., Shelton, S. A., & Uddo, M. (2003). Assessment of response style in combat veterans seeking compensation for posttraumatic stress disorder. *Journal of Traumatic Stress, 16,* 251–255.

Franz, C., Paul, R., Bautz, M., & Chorba, B. (1986). Psychosomatic aspects of chronic pain: A new way of description based on MMPI item analysis. *Pain, 26,* 33–43.

Fredrickson, B. E., Trief, P. M., VanBeveren, P., Yuan, H. A., & Baum, G. (1988). Rehabilitation of the patient with chronic back pain: A search for outcome predictors. *Spine, 13*(3), 351–353.

Freeman, C., Calsyn, D., & Louks, J. (1976). The use of the Minnesota Multiphasic Personality Inventory with low back pain patients. *Journal of Clinical Psychology, 32,* 294–298.

Freeman, C. W., Calsyn, D. A., Paige, A. B., & Halar, E. M. (1980). Biofeedback with low back pain patients. *American Journal of Clinical Biofeedback, 3,* 118–122.

Frueh, B. (1994). The susceptibility of the Rorschach inkblot test to malingering of combat-related PTSD. *Journal of Personality Assessment, 62,* 280–298.

Frueh, B. (1995). Interrelationship between MMPI–2 and Rorschach variables in a sample of Vietnam veterans with PTSD. *Journal of Personality Assessment, 64,* 312–318.

Frueh, B. (1995). Self-administered exposure therapy by a Vietnam veteran with PTSD. *American Journal of Psychiatry, 152,* 1831–1832.

Frueh, B. (1996). Compensation seeking status and psychometric assessment of combat veterans seeking treatment for PTSD. *Journal of Traumatic Stress, 9,* 427–440.

Frueh, B. (1996). Racial differences on psychological measures in combat veterans seeking treatment for PTSD. *Journal of Personality Assessment, 66,* 41–53.

Frueh, B. (1997). A racial comparison of combat veterans evaluated for PTSD. *Journal of Personality Assessment, 68,* 692–702.

Frueh, B. (1997). Symptom overreporting in combat veterans evaluated for PTSD: Differentiation on the basis of compensation seeking status. *Journal of Personality Assessment, 68,* 369–384.

Frueh, B. C., Elhai, J. D., Hamner, M. B., Magruder, K. M., Sauvageot, J. A., & Mintzer, J. (2004). Elderly veterans with combat-related posttraumatic stress disorder in specialty care. *Journal of Nervous and Mental Disease, 192,* 75–79.

Frueh, B. C., Elhai, J. D., Monnier, J., Hamner, M. B., & Knapp, R. G. (2004). Symptom patterns and service use among African American and Caucasian veterans with combat-related PTSD. *Psychological Services, 1,* 22–30.

Frueh, B., Hamner, M. B, Cahill, S. B., Gold, P. B., & Namlin, K. L. (2000). Apparent symptom overreporting in combat veterans evaluated for PTSD. *Clinical Psychology Review, 20,* 853–885.

Gagliese, L., Schiff, B. B., & Taylor, A. (1995). Differential consequences of left- and right-sided chronic pain. *Clinical Journal of Pain, 11,* 201–207.

Gallagher, R. M., Rauh, V., Haugh, L. D., Milhous, R., Callas, P. W., Langelier, R., et al. (1989). Determinants of return-to-work among low back pain patients. *Pain, 39,* 55–67.

Gallagher, R. M., Williams, R. A., Skelly, J., & Haugh, L. D. (1995). Workers' compensation and return-to-work in low back pain. *Pain, 61,* 299–307.

Gandolfo, R. (1995). MMPI–2 profiles of worker's compensation claimants who present with complaints of harassment. *Journal of Clinical Psychology, 51*(5), 711–715.

Garron, D. C., & Leavitt, F. (1983). Chronic low back pain and depression. *Journal of Clinical Psychology, 39,* 486–493.

Garron, D. C., & Leavitt, F. (1983). Psychological and social correlates of the Back Pain Classification Scale. *Journal of Personality Assessment, 47,* 60–65.

Gasquoine, P. G. (2000). Postconcussional symptoms in chronic back pain. *Applied Neuropsychology, 7,* 83–89.

Gass, C. S. (1991). MMPI–2 interpretation and closed head injury: A correction factor. *Psychological Assessment, 3,* 27–31.

Gass, C. S. (1992). MMPI–2 interpretation of patients with cerebrovascular disease: A correction factor. *Archives of Neuropsychology, 7,* 17–27.

Gass, C. (1996). MMPI–2 variables in attention and memory test performance. *Psychological Assessment, 8,* 135–138.

Gass, C. S., & Apple, C. (1997). Cognitive complaints in closed-head injury: Relationship to memory test performance and emotional disturbance. *Journal of Clinical and Experimental Neuropsychology, 19,* 290–299.

Gass, C., & Brown, M. C. (1992). Neuropsychological test feedback to patients with brain dysfunction. *Psychological Assessment, 4*, 272–277.

Gass, C. S., & Wald, H. S. (1997). MMPI–2 interpretation and closed-head trauma: Cross-validation of a correction factor. *Archives of Clinical Neuropsychology, 12*, 199–205.

Gaston, L., Brunet, A., Koszycki, D., & Bradwejn, J. (1996). MMPI profiles of acute and chronic PTSD in a civilian sample. *Journal of Traumatic Stress, 9*, 817–832.

Gatchel, R. J. (2000). How practitioners should evaluate personality to help manage patients with chronic pain. In R. J. Gatchel (Ed.), *Personality characteristics of patients with pain* (pp. 241–257). Washington, DC: American Psychological Association.

Gatchel, R. J. (2000). *Personality characteristics of patients with pain.* Washington, DC: American Psychological Association.

Gatchel, R. J., & Gardea, M. A. (1999). Psychosocial issues: Their importance in predicting disability, response to treatment, and search for compensation. *Neurologic Clinics, 17*, 149–166.

Gatchel, R. J., Polatin, P. B., & Kinney, R. K. (1995). Predicting outcome of chronic back pain using clinical predictors of psychopathology: A prospective analysis. *Health Psychology, 14*, 415–420.

Gatchel, R. J., Polatin, P. B., & Mayer, T. G. (1995). The dominant role of psychosocial risk factors in the development of chronic low back pain disability. *Spine, 20*, 2702–2709.

Gentry, W. D., Shows, W. G., & Thomas, M. (1974). Chronic low back pain: A psychological profile. *Psychosomatics, 15*, 174–177.

Glassmire, D. M., Kinney, D. I., Greene, R. L., Stolberg, R. A., Berry, D. T. R., & Cripe, L. (2003). Sensitivity and specificity of MMPI–2 neurologic correction factors: Receiver operating characteristic analysis. *Assessment, 10*(3), 299–309.

Gold, P. B., & Frueh, C. B. (1999). Compensation-seeking and extreme exaggeration of psychopathology among combat veterans evaluated for posttraumatic stress disorder. *Journal of Nervous and Mental Disease, 187*, 680–684.

Golden, Z., & Golden, C. J. (2003). The differential impacts of Alzheimer's dementia, head injury, and stroke on personality dysfunction. *International Journal of Neuroscience, 113*, 869–878.

Goldstein, G., Van Kammen, W., Shelly, C., & Miller, D. J. (1987). Survivors of imprisonment in the Pacific theater during World War II. *American Journal of Psychiatry, 144*, 1210–1213.

Goodman-Delahunty, J., & Foote, W. E. (1995). Compensation for pain and suffering and other psychological injuries: The impact of *Daubert* on employment discrimination claims. *Behavioral Sciences and the Law, 13*, 183–206.

Graves, G. J. (1996). The back pain classification scale and the Minnesota Multiphasic Personality Inventory: A comparative analysis. *Dissertation Abstracts International, 56*, 5767.

Greenblatt, R. L., & Davis, W. E. (1999). Differential diagnosis of PTSD, schizophrenia, and depression with the MMPI–2. *Journal of Clinical Psychology, 55*(2), 217–223.

Greiffenstein, M. F., & Baker, W. J. (2001). Comparison of premorbid and postinjury MMPI–2 profiles in late postconcussion claimants. *Clinical Neuropsychologist, 15*, 162–170.

Greiffenstein, M. F., Baker, W. J., Gola, T., Donders, J., & Miller, L. J. (2002). The FBS in a typical and severe closed head injury litigants. *Journal of Clinical Psychology, 58*, 1591–1600.

Grubman, J. A. (1984). A cluster analysis of MMPI profiles of low back pain patients. *Dissertation Abstracts International, 45*, 1286.

Grushka, M., Sessle, B. J., & Miller, R. (1987). Pain and personality profiles in burning mouth syndrome. *Pain, 28*, 155–167.

Guck, T. P., Meilman, P. W., & Skultety, F. (1987). Pain Assessment Index: Evaluation following multidisciplinary pain treatment. *Journal of Pain and Symptom Management, 2,* 23–27.

Guck, T. P., Meilman, P. W., & Skultety, F. (1988). Pain–patient Minnesota Multiphasic Personality Inventory (MMPI) subgroups: Evaluation of long-term treatment outcome. *Journal of Behavioral Medicine, 11,* 159–169.

Haley, W. E., Turner, J. A., & Romano, J. M. (1985). Depression in chronic pain patients: Relation to pain, activity, and sex differences. *Pain, 23,* 337–343.

Hansen, F. R., Biering-Sorensen, F., & Schroll, M. (1995). Minnesota Multiphasic Personality Inventory profiles in persons with or without low back pain. *Spine, 20,* 2716–2720.

Hanvik, L. J. (1949). *Some psychological dimensions of low back pain.* Minneapolis: University of Minnesota.

Hanvik, L. J. (1951). MMPI profiles in patients with low-back pain. *Journal of Consulting Psychology, 15,* 350–353.

Hare, R. D. (1965). Psychopathy, fear arousal and anticipated pain. *Psychological Reports, 16,* 499–502.

Hart, R. R. (1984). Chronic pain: Replicated multivariate clustering of personality profiles. *Journal of Clinical Psychology, 40,* 129–133.

Hasemann, D. M. (1998). Practices and findings of mental health professionals conducting workers' compensation evaluations. *Dissertation Abstracts International, 58,* 6236.

Hasenbring, M., Marienfeld, G., Kuhlendahl, D., & Soyka, D. (1994). Risk factors of chronicity in lumbar disc patients: A prospective investigation of biologic, psychologic, and social predictors of therapy outcome, *Spine, 19,* 2759–2765.

Hastie, B. A. (2002). Comparisons of validity and pain treatment outcome measures in the multidimensional pain inventory and the MMPI–2 in a chronic headache and orofacial pain population. *Dissertation Abstracts International: Section B: The Sciences and Engineering, 63*(2–B), 1028

Haven, G. A., & Cole, K. M. (1972). Psychological correlates of low back pain syndrome and their relationship to the effectiveness of low back pain program. *Newsletter for Research in Psychology, 14,* 31–33.

Heaton, R. K., Chelune, G. J., & Lehman, R. A. W. (1978). Using neuropsychological and personality tests to assess the likelihood of patient employment. *Journal of Nervous and Mental Disease, 166,* 408–416.

Heine, B. J. (1996). Exploring the utility of the MMPI–2 content scales with chronic pain patients. *Dissertation Abstracts International, 57,* 1442.

Hendler, N. (1985). A comparison between the MMPI and the "Mensana Clinic Back Pain Test" for validating the complaint of chronic back pain in women. *Pain, 23,* 243–251.

Henrichs, T. F. (1981). Using the MMPI in medical consultations. In W. Schofield (Ed.), *Clinical notes on the MMPI* (Vol. 6). Minneapolis, MN: National Computer Systems.

Henrichs, T. F. (1987). MMPI profiles of chronic pain patients: Some methodological considerations that concern clusters and descriptors. *Journal of Clinical Psychology, 43,* 650–660.

Herman, D. S., Weathers, F. W., Litz, B. T., & Keane, T. M. (1996). Psychometric properties of the embedded and stand-alone versions of the MMPI–2 Keane PTSD scale. *Assessment, 3,* 437–442.

Hersch, P. D., & Alexander, R. W. (1990). MMPI profile patterns of emotional disability claimants. *Journal of Clinical Psychology, 46,* 795–799.

Hickling, E. J., Sison, G. F., & Holtz, J. L. (1985). Role of psychologists in multidisciplinary pain clinics: A national survey. *Professional Psychology: Research and Practice, 16,* 868–880.

Hiley-Young, B., Blake, D. D., Abueg, F. R., & Rozynko, V. (1995). Warzone violence in Vietnam: An examination of premilitary, military, and postmilitary factors in PTSD in-patients. *Journal of Traumatic Stress, 8,* 125–141.

Hillary, B. E., & Schare, M. L. (1993). Sexually and physically abused adolescents: An empirical search for PTSD. *Journal of Clinical Psychology, 49,* 161–165.

Hodges, W. F. (1968). Effects of ego threat and threat of pain on state anxiety. *Journal of Personality and Social Psychology, 8,* 364–372.

Hoffman, R. G., Scott, J. G., Emick, M. A., & Adams, R. L. (1999). The MMPI–2 and closed head injury: Effects of litigation and head injury severity. *Journal of Forensic Neuropsychology, 1,* 3–13.

Holland, J. L. (1952). A study of measured personality variables and their behavioral correlates as seen in oil paintings. *Dissertations Abstract, 12,* 380.

Hollingsworth, D. K., & Watson, D. D. (1980). Chronic low back pain and the rehabilitation process: A multiple regression analysis. *Journal of Applied Rehabilitation Counseling, 11,* 90–93.

Holmes, G. E., Williams, C. L., & Haines, J. (2001). Motor vehicle accident trauma exposure: Personality profiles associated with posttraumatic diagnoses. *Anxiety, Stress and Coping: An International Journal, 14,* 301–313.

Holroyd, K. A., Holm, J. E., Keefe, F. J., & Turner, J. A. (1992). A multi-center evaluation of the McGill Pain Questionnaire: Results from more than 1700 chronic pain patients. *Pain, 48,* 301–311.

Hovanitz, C. A., & Kozora, E. (1989). Life stress and clinically elevated MMPI scales: Gender differences in the moderating influence of coping. *Journal of Clinical Psychology, 45,* 766–777.

Hovens, J. (1994). The assessment of posttraumatic stress disorder: With the Clinician Administered PTSD Scale: Dutch results. *Journal of Clinical Psychology, 50,* 325–340.

Hubbard, K. M. (1983). Patient response to pain treatment: Personality variables associated with the use of transcutaneous electrical nerve stimulation. *Dissertation Abstracts International, 43,* 2708.

Hudgens, A. J. (1979). Family-oriented treatment of chronic pain. *Journal of Marital and Family Therapy, 5,* 67–78.

Hyer, L. A., Boudewyns, P. A., O'Leary, W. C., & Harris, W. R. (1987). Key determinants of the MMPI—PTSD subscale: Treatment considerations. *Journal of Clinical Psychology, 43,* 337–340.

Hyer, L., Leach, P., Boudewyns, P. A., & Davis, H. (1991). Hidden PTSD in substance abuse inpatients among Vietnam veterans. *Journal of Substance Abuse Treatment, 8,* 213–219.

Hyer, L. A., Walker, C., Swanson, G., & Speer, S. (1992). Validation of PTSD measures for older combat veterans. *Journal of Clinical Psychology, 48,* 579–588.

Hyer, L. A., Woods, M. G., & Boudewyns, P. A. (1991). A three tier evaluation of PTSD among Vietnam combat veterans. *Journal of Traumatic Stress, 4,* 165–194.

Iezzi, A., Stokes, G. S., Adams, H. E., & Pilon, R. N. (1994). Somatothymia in chronic pain patients. *Psychosomatics, 35,* 460–468.

Iverson, G. L., King, R. J., Scott, J. G., & Adams, R. L. (2001). Cognitive complaints in litigating patients with head injuries or chronic pain. *Journal of Forensic Neuropsychology, 2,* 19–30.

Jarvis, P. E., & Hamlin, D. (1984). Avoiding pitfalls in compensation evaluations. *International Journal of Clinical Neuropsychology, 6,* 214–216.

Jordan, R. G., Nunley, T. V., & Cook, R. R. (1992). Symptom exaggeration in a PTSD inpatient population: Response set or claim for compensation. *Journal of Traumatic Stress, 5,* 633–642.

Juhr, G. D. (1980). Development of an MMPI subscale predicting outcome of multidisciplinary treatment for chronic low back pain. *Dissertation Abstracts International, 41,* 1112–1113.

Keane, T. M., Mallyo, P. F., & Fairbank, J. A. (1984). Empirical development of an MMPI subscale for the assessment of posttraumatic stress disorder. *Journal of Consulting and Clinical Psychology, 52,* 888–891.

Keane, T. M., Weathers, F. W., & Kaloupek, D. G. (1992). Psychological assessment of post-traumatic stress disorder. *PTSD Research Quarterly, 3,* 1–3.

Keane, T. M., Wolfem, J., & Taylor, K. L. (1987). Post-traumatic stress disorder: Evidence for diagnostic validity and methods of psychological assessment. *Journal of Clinical Psychology, 43,* 32–43.

Keller, L. S. (1989). Characteristics and correlates of the revised Minnesota Multiphasic Personality Inventory (MMPI–2) in a chronic pain patient population. *Dissertation Abstracts International, 50*(3-B), 1111.

Keller, L. S., & Butcher, J. N. (1991). *Assessment of chronic pain patients with the MMPI–2.* Minneapolis: University of Minnesota Press.

Kendall, P. C., Edinger, J., & Eberly, C. (1978). Taylor's MMPI correction for spinal cord injury: Empirical endorsement. *Journal of Consulting and Clinical Psychology, 46,* 370–371.

Kenderdine, S. K., Phillips, E. J., & Scurfield, R. M. (1992). Comparison of the MMPI–PTSD subscale with PTSD and substance abuse patient populations. *Journal of Clinical Psychology, 48,* 136–139.

Kiluk, D. J. (1986). Cross validation of a chronic pain scale of the MMPI across four patient populations. *Dissertation Abstracts International, 47,* 360.

Kinder, B. N., & Curtiss, G. (1990). Alexithymia among empirically derived subgroups of chronic back pain patients. *Journal of Personality Assessment, 54,* 351–362.

Kinder, B. N., Curtiss, G., & Kalichman, S. (1986). Anxiety and anger as predictors of MMPI elevations in chronic pain patients. *Journal of Personality Assessment, 50,* 651–661.

King, S. A., & Snow, B. R. (1989). Factors for predicting premature termination from a multidisciplinary inpatient chronic pain program. *Pain, 39,* 281–287.

Kirz, J. L., Drescher, K. D., Klein, J. L., Gusman, F. D., & Schwartz, M. F. (2001). MMPI–2 assessment of differential post-traumatic stress disorder patterns in combat veterans and sexual assault victims. *Journal of Interpersonal Violence, 16,* 619–639.

Kleinke, C. L. (1991). How chronic pain patients cope with depression: Relation to treatment outcome in a multidisciplinary pain clinic. *Rehabilitation Psychology, 36,* 207–218.

Kleinke, C. L. (1994). MMPI scales as predictors of pain-coping strategies preferred by patients with chronic pain. *Rehabilitation Psychology, 39,* 123–128.

Kleinke, C. L., & Spangler, A. S. (1988). Predicting treatment outcome of chronic back pain patients in a multidisciplinary pain clinic: Methodological issues and treatment implications. *Pain, 33,* 41–48.

Korgeski, G. P., & Leon, G. R. (1983). Correlates of self-reported and objectively determined exposure to Agent Orange. *American Journal of Psychiatry, 140,* 1443–1449.

Koretzky, M. B., & Peck, A. H. (1990). Validation and cross-validation of the PTSD subscale of the MMPI with civilian trauma victims. *Journal of Clinical Psychology, 46,* 296–300.

Kramlinger, K. G., Swanson, D. W., & Maruta, T. (1983). Are patients with chronic pain depressed? *American Journal of Psychiatry, 140,* 747–749.

Krusen, E. M. (1968). Cervical pain syndromes. *Archives of Physical Medicine, 49,* 376–382.

Kubany, E. S., Gino, A., Denny, N. R., & Torigoe, R. Y. (1994). Relationship of cynical hostility and PTSD among Vietnam veterans. *Journal of Traumatic Stress, 7,* 21–31.

Kubiszyn, T. (1984, August). *The MMPI, litigation, and back pain treatment: A curvilinear relationship.* Paper presented at the 92nd Annual Convention of the American Psychological Association, Toronto, Ontario, Canada.

Kuperman, S. K., Golden, C. J., & Blume, H. G. (1979). Predicting pain treatment results by personality variables in organic and functional patients. *Journal of Clinical Psychology, 35,* 832–837.

Kvale, A., Ellertsen, B., & Skouen, J. S. (2001). Relationships between physical findings (GPE–78) and psychological profiles (MMPI–2) in patients with long lasting musculoskeletal pain. *Nordic Journal of Psychiatry, 55,* 177–184.

Lacroix, J. (1986). Predictors of biofeedback and relaxation success in multiple-pain patients: Negative findings. *International Journal of Rehabilitation Research, 9,* 376–378.

Lakehomer, J. B. (1985). Chronic pain and the prediction of outcome: Towards validation of the MMPI as a predictor. *Dissertation Abstracts International, 46,* 1691.

Lally, S. J. (2003). What tests are acceptable for use in forensic evaluations? A survey of experts. *Professional Psychology: Research and Practice, 34,* 491–498.

Lamb, D. G. (1992). Malingering closed head injury on the MMPI–2: Effect of information about symptoms and validity scales. *Dissertation Abstracts International, 53,* 1611.

Lamb, D. G., & Berry, D. T. (1994). Effects of two types of information on malingering of closed head injury on the MMPI–2: An analog investigation. *Psychological Assessment, 6,* 8–13.

Lanyon, R. I., & Almer, E. R. (2002). Characteristics of compensable disability patients who choose to litigate. *Journal of the American Academy of Psychiatry Law, 30*(3), 400–404.

Larrabee, G. J. (1998). Somatic malingering on the MMPI and MMPI–2 in personal injury litigants. *Clinical Neuropsychologist, 12,* 179–188.

Larrabee, G. J. (2000, February 11). *Exaggerated MMPI–2 symptom report in probable malingerers.* Paper presented at the 28th Annual Meeting of the International Neuropsychological Society, Denver, CO.

Larrabee, G. (2003). Detection of malingering using atypical performance patterns on standard neuropsychological tests. *Clinical Neuropsychologist, 17,* 410–425.

Larrabee, G. (2003). Detection of symptom exaggeration with the MMPI–2 in litigants with malingered neurocognitive dysfunction. *Clinical Neuropsychologist, 17,* 54–68.

Laurie, B. W. (1998). Use of the MMPI and the Beck Depression Inventory to determine correlation of anxiety and depression in workers' compensation claimants. *Dissertation Abstracts International, 59,* 2423.

Leavitt, F. (1982). Comparison of three measures for detecting psychological disturbance in patients with low back pain. *Pain, 13,* 299–305.

Leavitt, F. (1985). The value of the MMPI conversion "V" in the assessment of psychogenic pain. *Journal of Psychosomatic Research, 29,* 125–131.

Leavitt, F. (2001). The development of the Somatoform Dissociation Index (SDI): A screening measure of dissociation using MMPI–2 items. *Journal of Trauma and Dissociation, 2*(3), 69–80.

Leavitt, F., & Garron, D. C. (1979). The detection of psychological disturbance in patients with low back pain. *Journal of Psychosomatic Research, 23,* 149–154.

Leavitt, F., & Garron, D. C. (1980). Validity of a Back Pain Classification Scale for detecting psychological disturbance as measured by the MMPI. *Journal of Clinical Psychology, 36,* 186–189.

Leavitt, F., & Garron, D. C. (1982). Patterns of psychological disturbance and pain report in patients with low back pain. *Journal of Psychosomatic Research, 26,* 301–307.

Leavitt, F., & Garron, D. C. (1982). Rorschach and pain characteristics of patients with low back pain and "conversion V" MMPI profiles. *Journal of Personality Assessment, 46,* 18–25.

Lee, H. C., Cheung, F. M., Man, H. M., & Hsu, S. Y. (1992). Psychological characteristics of Chinese low back pain patients: An exploratory study. *Psychology and Health, 6,* 119–128.

Lee-Riordan, D. L. (1990). Comparisons between the Millon Behavioral Health Inventory and the MMPI in the assessment of pain patients. *Dissertation Abstracts International, 50,* 4775.

Lee-Riordan, D., & Sweet, J. J. (1994). Relationship between the Millon Behavioral Health Inventory and the Minnesota Multiphasic Personality Inventory (MMPI) in low-back pain patients. *Journal of Clinical Psychology in Medical Settings, 1,* 387–398.

Lees-Haley, P. R. (1986). How to detect malingerers in the workplace. *Personnel Journal, 65,* 106, 108, 110.

Lees-Haley, P. R. (1986, February 28–31). Personal injury malingering. *For the Defense,* n.p.

Lees-Haley, P. R. (1991). Ego strength denial on the MMPI–2 as a clue to simulation of personal injury in vocational neuropsychological and emotional distress evaluations. *Perceptual and Motor Skills, 72,* 815–819.

Lees-Haley, P. R. (1991). MMPI–2 *F* and *F–K* scores of personal injury malingerers in vocational neuropsychological and emotional distress claims. *American Journal of Forensic Psychology, 9,* 5–14.

Lees-Haley, P. R. (1992). Efficacy of MMPI–2 validity scale and MCMI–II modifier scales for detecting spurious PTSD claims: *F, F–K,* Fake Bad Scale, Ego Strength, Subtle-Obvious subscales, *DIS,* and *DEB. Journal of Clinical Psychology, 48,* 681–689.

Lees-Haley, P. R. (1997). MMPI–2 base rates for 492 personal injury plaintiffs: Implications and challenges for forensic assessment. *Journal of Clinical Psychology, 53,* 745–755.

Lees-Haley, P. R. (2001). Commentary on "Misconceptions and misuse of the MMPI–2 in assessing personal injury claimants." *NeuroRehabilitation, 16*(4), 301–302.

Lees-Haley, P. R., English, L. T., & Glenn, W. J. (1991). A fake bad scale on the MMPI–2 for personal injury claimants. *Psychological Reports, 68,* 203–210.

Lees-Haley, P. R., Smith, H. H., Williams, C. W., & Dunn, J. T. (1995). Forensic neuropsychological test usage: An empirical survey. *Archives of Clinical Neuropsychology, 11,* 45–51.

Lehmann, T. S. (1990). An empirical test of a clinically derived system for classifying chronic pain patients with the MMPI. *Dissertation Abstracts International, 50,* 3704.

Leister, S. C. (1991). The assessment of depression in chronic back pain patients using the MMPI and the Beck Depression Inventory—Short Form. *Dissertation Abstracts International, 51,* 3608.

Lemmon, K. W. (1983). Chronic lower back pain differentiation of the real and imagined. *Medical Hypnoanalysis, 4,* 17–30.

Levenson, H., Glenn, N., & Hirschfeld, M. L. (1988). Duration of chronic pain and the Minnesota Multiphasic Personality Inventory: Profiles of industrially injured workers. *Journal of Occupation Medicine, 30,* 809–812.

Levenson, H., Hirschfeld, M. L., & Hirschfeld, A. H. (1985). *Duration of chronic pain and the MMPI: Profiles of industrially-injured workers.* Paper presented at the 20th Symposium on Recent Developments in the Use of the MMPI, Honolulu, HI.

Levine, J. B., Weisgerber, K., Nehme, A. M., & Mitra, N. (1994). Symptom laterality and psychological presentation in chronic pain syndrome. *Stress Medicine, 10,* 197–202.

Lewis, J. L., Simcox, A. M., & Berry, D. T. R. (2002). Screening for feigned psychiatric symptoms in a forensic sample by using the MMPI–2 and the Structured Inventory of Malingered Symptomatology. *Psychological Assessment, 14,* 170–176

Lewis, J. M., Kraus, W. L., Gossett, J. T., & Phillips, V. A. (1971). Chest pain, personality and coronary arteriography: A preliminary study. *Southern Medical Journal, 64,* 467–471.

Li, S. M., Li, L. M., & Rodriguez de Souza, L. F. (1991). Uso do MMPI (Minnesota Multiphasic Personality Inventory) na avaliaçăo de pacientes com syndrome de dor crönica [Use of MMPI (Minnesota Multiphasic Personality Inventory) on the assessment of the chronic pain syndrome patients]. *Arquivos de Neuro-Psiquiatria, 49,* 426–429.

Lichtenberg, P. A., Skehan, M. W., & Swensen, C. H. (1984). The role of personality, recent life stress and arthritic severity in predicting pain. *Journal of Psychosomatic Research, 28,* 231–236.

Light, K. C., Herbst, M. C., Bragdon, E. E., & Hinderliter, A. L. (1991). Depression and Type A behavior pattern in patients with coronary artery disease: Relationships to painful versus silent myocardial ischemia and β-endorphin responses during exercise. *Psychosomatic Medicine, 53,* 669–683.

Litz, B. T., Penk, W., Walsh, S., Hyer, L., Blake, D. D., Marz, B., et al. (1991). Similarities and differences between Minnesota Multiphasic Personality Inventory (MMPI) and MMPI–2 applications to the assessment of post-traumatic stress disorder. *Journal of Personality Assessment, 57,* 238–254.

Loganovsky, K. N. (2003). Psychophysiological features of somatosensory disorders in victims of the Chernobyl accident. *Human Physiology, 29*(1), 122–130.

Long, B., Rouse, S. V., Nelson, R. O., & Butcher, J. N. (2004). The MMPI–2 in sexual harassment and discrimination cases. *Journal of Clinical Psychology, 60,* 643–658.

Long, C. J. (1981). The relationship between surgical outcome and MMPI profiles in chronic pain patients. *Journal of Clinical Psychology, 37,* 744–749.

Lorentz, R. P. (1995). Back pain and mental distress workers' compensation claimants: A Rorschach and MMPI study of emotional regulation. *Dissertation Abstracts International, 56,* 1113.

Louks, J. L., Freeman, C. W., & Calsyn, D. A. (1978). Personality organization as an aspect of back pain in a medical setting. *Journal of Personality Assessment, 42,* 152–158.

Lousberg, R., Greonman, N., & Schmidt, A. (1996). Profile characteristics of the MPI–DLV clusters of pain patients. *Journal of Clinical Psychology, 52,* 161–167.

Love, A. W. (1987). Depression in chronic low back pain patients: Diagnostic efficiency of three self-report questionnaires. *Journal of Clinical Psychology, 43,* 84–89.

Love, A. W., & Peck, C. L. (1987). The MMPI and psychological factors in chronic low back pain: A review. *Pain, 28,* 1–12.

Lucenko, B. A., Gold, S. N., Elhai, J. D., Russo, S. A., & Swingle, J. M. (2000). Relations between coercive strategies and MMPI–2 scale elevations among women survivors of childhood sexual abuse. *Journal of Traumatic Stress, 13,* 169–177.

Lumley, M. A., Asselin, L. A., & Norman, S. (1997). Alexithymia in chronic pain patients. *Comprehensive Psychiatry, 38,* 160–165.

Lupton, D., & Johnson, D. L. (1973). Myofascial pain-dysfuntion syndrome: Attitudes and other personality characteristics related to tolerance for pain. *Journal of Prosthetic Dentistry, 29,* 323–329.

Lyons, J. A., & Keane, T. M. (1992). Keane PTSD Scale: MMPI and MMPI–2 update. *Journal of Traumatic Stress, 5,* 111–117.

Lyons, J. A., & Wheeler-Cox, T. (1999). MMPI, MMPI–2 and PTSD: Overview of scores, scales, and profiles. *Journal of Traumatic Stress, 12,* 175–183.

MacNiven, E., & Finlayson, M. (1993). The interplay between emotional and cognitive recovery after closed head injury. *Brain Injury, 7,* 241–246.

Magnani, B., Johnson, L. R., & Ferrante, F. (1989). Modifiers of patient-controlled analgesia efficacy: II. Chronic pain. *Pain, 39,* 23–29.

Main, C. J., & Waddell, G. (1987). Personality assessment in the management of low back pain. *Clinical Rehabilitation, 1,* 139–142.

Malec, J. F. (1983). Relationship of the MMPI–168 to outcome of a pain management program at long-term follow-up. *Rehabilitation Psychology, 28,* 115–119.

Marcos, T. (1985). *Proceso de validación de la escala NF/F para la evaluación de la psicogeneidad dei dolor* [Structural validation of the NF/F scale to evaluate the psychological factors involved in pain]. *Revista del Departamento de Psiquiatria de la Facultad de Medicina de Barcelona, 12,* 239–248.

McArthur, D. L., Cohen, M. J., Gottlieb, H. J., & Naliboff, B. D. (1987). Treating chronic low back pain: I. Admissions to initial follow-up. *Pain, 29,* 1–22.

McCaffrey, R., & Bellamy-Campbell, R. (1989). Psychometric detection of fabricated symptoms of combat-related PTSD: A systematic replication. *Journal of Clinical Psychology, 45,* 76–79.

McCreary, C. P. (1985). Empirically derived MMPI profile clusters and characteristics of low back pain patients. *Journal of Consulting and Clinical Psychology, 53,* 558–560.

McCreary, C. P., & Colman, A. (1984). Medication usage, emotional disturbance, and pain behavior in chronic low back pain patients. *Journal of Clinical Psychology, 40,* 15–19.

McCreary, C. P., & Turner, J. (1983). Psychological disorder and pain description. *Health Psychology, 2,* 1–10.

McCreary, C. P., & Turner, J. A. (1984). Locus of control, repression-sensitization, and psychological disorder in chronic pain patients. *Journal of Clinical Psychology, 40,* 897–901.

McCreary, C. P., Turner, J., & Dawson, E. (1979). The MMPI as a predictor of response to conservative treatment for low back pain. *Journal of Clinical Psychology, 35,* 278–284.

McCreary, C. P., Turner, J., & Dawson, E. (1980). Emotional disturbance and chronic low back pain. *Journal of Clinical Psychology, 36,* 709–715.

McFall, M. E., Smith, D. E., Roszell, D. K., & Tarver, D. J. (1990). Convergent validity of measures of PTSD in Vietnam combat veterans. *American Journal of Psychiatry, 147,* 645–648.

McGill, J. C. (1980). Relationship of MMPI profile clusters to pain behaviors. *Dissertation Abstracts International, 40,* 5820.

McGill, J. C. (1983). The relationship of Minnesota Multiphasic Personality Inventory (MMPI) profile clusters to pain behaviors. *Journal of Behavioral Medicine, 6,* 77–92.

McGrath, R. E., Sweeney, M., O'Malley, W. B., & Carlton, T. K. (1998). Identifying psychological contributions to chronic pain complaints with the MMPI–2: The role of the *K* Scale. *Journal of Personality Assessment, 70*(3), 448–459.

Meikle, J. (1987). The Minnesota Multiphasic Personality Inventory (MMPI) and back pain. *Clinical Rehabilitation, 1,* 143–145.

Meldolesi, G. (2000). Personality and psychopathology in patients with temporomandibular joint pain-dysfunction syndrome: A controlled investigation. *Psychotherapy and Psychosomatics, 69,* 328.

Melzack, R., Katz, J., & Jeans, M. E. (1985). The role of compensation in chronic pain: Analysis using a new method of scoring the McGill Pain Questionnaire. *Pain, 23,* 101–112.

Mendelson, G. (1982). Alexithymia and chronic pain: Prevalence, correlates and treatment results. *Psychotherapy and Psychosomatics, 37,* 154–164.

Mesholam, R. I. (1999). The West Haven–Yale Multidimensional Pain Inventory as a predictor of outcome in chronic pain patients who undergo spinal cord stimulator or infusion pump implantations. *Dissertation Abstracts International, 60,* 2974.

Michalek, J. E., Barrett, D. H., Morris, R. D., & Jackson, W. G., Jr. (2003). Serum dioxin and psychological functioning in U.S. Air Force veterans of the Vietnam war. *Military Medicine, 168*(2), 153–159.

Middleton, T. P. (1987). A study of the effects of physical sequelae of head injury on MMPI scale elevations. *Dissertation Abstracts International, 48,* 344.

Milhous, R. L., Haugh, L. D., Frymoyer, J. W., Ruess, J. M., Gallagher, R. M., Wilder, D. G., et al. (1989). Determinants of vocational disability in patients with low back pain. *Archives of Physical Medicine and Rehabilitation, 70,* 589–593.

Millard, R. W. (1995). Assessment of pain and pain behavior. In L. A. Cushman (Ed.), *Psychological assessment in medical rehabilitation* (pp. 237–273). Washington, DC: American Psychological Association.

Miller, H. R., Goldberg, J. O., & Streiner, D. L. (1995). What's in a name? The MMPI–2 PTSD scales. *Journal of Clinical Psychology, 51,* 626–631.

Miller, T. W. (1990). *Chronic pain* (Vols. 1 & 2) Madison, CT: International Universities Press.

Miller, T. W., & Kraus, R. F. (1990). An overview of chronic pain. *Hospital and Community Psychiatry, 41,* 433–440.

Mittenburg, W., Patton, C., Canycock, E. M., & Condit, D. C. (2002). Base rates of malingering and symptom exaggeration. *Journal of Clinical and Experimental Neurosychology, 24,* 109–114.

Mittenberg, W., Tremont, G., & Rayls, K. R. (1996). Impact of cognitive function on MMPI–2 validity in neurological impaired patients. *Assessment, 3,* 157–163.

Monsen, K., & Monsen, J. T. (2000). Chronic pain and psychodynamic body therapy: A controlled outcome study. *Psychotherapy, 37,* 257–259.

Monsen, K., & Havik, O. E. (2001). Psychological functioning and bodily conditions in patients with pain disorder associated with psychological factors. *British Journal of Medical Psychology, 74,* 183–195.

Moody, D. R., & Kish, G. B. (1989). Clinical meaning of the Keane PTSD Scale. *Journal of Clinical Psychology, 45,* 542–546.

Moore, J. E., Armentrout, D. P., Parker, J. C., & Kivlahan, D. R. (1986). Empirically derived pain–patient MMPI subgroups: Prediction of treatment outcome. *Journal of Behavioral Medicine, 9,* 51–63.

Moore, J. E., & Chaney, E. F. (1985). Outpatient group treatment of chronic pain: Effects of spouse involvement. *Journal of Consulting and Clinical Psychology, 53,* 326–334.

Moore, J. E., McFall, M. E., Kivlahan, D. R., & Capestany, F. (1988). Risk of misinterpretation of MMPI Schizophrenia scale elevations in chronic pain patients. *Pain, 32,* 207–213.

Morrell, J. S., & Rubin, L. J. (2001). The Minnesota Multiphasic Personality Inventory—2, Posttraumatic stress disorder, and women domestic violence survivors. *Professional Psychology: Research and Practice, 32,* 151–156.

Moyer, D. M., Burkhardt, B., & Gordon, R. M. (2002). Faking PTSD from a motor vehicle accident on the MMPI–2. *American Journal of Forensic Psychology, 20*(2), 81–89.

Mullins, W. H. (1988). Chronic pain: A study of treatment outcome as it relates to coping behaviors, assertiveness, spiritual well-being, and MMPI scores. *Dissertation Abstracts International, 48,* 3689.

Munley, P. H., Bains, D. S., & Bloem, W. D. (1993). F Scale elevation and PTSD MMPI profiles. *Psychological Reports, 73*(2), 363–370.

Munley, P. H., Bains, D. S., Bloem, W. D., & Busby, R. M. (1995). Post-traumatic stress disorder and the MMPI–2. *Journal of Traumatic Stress, 8,* 171–178.

Munley, P. H., Bains, D. S., Frazee, J., & Schwartz, L. T. (1994). Inpatient PTSD treatment: A study of pretreatment measures, treatment dropout, and therapist ratings of response to treatment. *Journal of Traumatic Stress, 7,* 319–325.

Murphy, J. K., Sperr, E. V., & Sperr, S. J. (1986). Chronic pain: An investigation of assessment instruments. *Journal of Psychosomatic Research, 30,* 289–296.

Murray, J. B. (1982). Psychological aspects of low back pain: Summary. *Psychological Reports, 50,* 343–351.

Myer, G. J., Finn, S. E., Eyde, L. D., Kay, G. G., Moreland, K. L., Dies, R. R., et al. (2001). Psychological testing and psychological assessment: A review of evidence and issues. *American Psychologist, 56,* 128–165.

Naliboff, B. D. (1985). Comprehensive assessment of chronic low back pain patients and controls: Physical abilities, level of activity, psychological adjustment and pain perception. *Pain, 23,* 121–134.

Naliboff, B. D., Cohen, M. J., & Yellen, A. N. (1982). Does the MMPI differentiate chronic illness from chronic pain? *Pain, 13,* 333–341.

Naliboff, B. D., McCreary, C. P., McArthur, D. L., & Cohen, M. J. (1988). MMPI changes following behavioral treatment of chronic low back pain. *Pain, 35,* 271–277.

Neal, L. A., Busuttil, W., Rollins, J., Herepath, R., Strike, P., & Turnbull, G. (1994). Convergent validity of measures of post-traumatic stress disorder in a mixed military and civilian population. *Journal of Traumatic Stress, 7*(3), 447–455.

Neal, L. A., Hill, N., Hughes, J., & Middleton, A. (1995). Convergent validity of measures of PTSD in an elderly population of former prisoners of war. *International Journal of Geriatric Psychiatry, 10,* 617–622.

Neighbours, J. S. (1991). The use of the MMPI and a cross-validation of the Keane PTSD subscale in the differential diagnosis of posttraumatic stress disorder in workers' compensation patients. *Dissertation Abstracts International, 51,* 6147.

Nelson, D. V., Novy, D. M., Averill, P. M., & Berry, L. A. (1996). Ethnic comparability of the MMPI in pain patients. *Journal of Clinical Psychology, 52,* 485–497.

Nelson, D. V., Turner, J. A., & McCreary, C. P. (1991). MMPI short forms as predictors of response to conservative treatment for low back pain. *Journal of Clinical Psychology, 47,* 533–537.

Nesbit, M. (1979). The treatment of chronic pain patients via a structured group counseling approach. *Dissertation Abstracts International, 39,* 5331.

Newnan, O. S., Heaton, R. S., & Lehman, R. A. W. (1978). Neuropsychological and MMPI correlates of patient's future employment characteristics. *Perceptual and Motor Skills, 46,* 635–642.

Nickel, J. A. (1994). Multivariate clustering of chronic pain patients: A replication using the MMPI–2. *Dissertation Abstracts International, 54,* 2470.

Nieberding, R. J. (1995). MMPI–2 correlates of chronic pain: An examination of the role of anger. *Dissertation Abstracts International, 55,* 4128.

Novack, T. A., Daniel, M. S., & Long, C. J. (1984). Factors related to emotional adjustment following head injury. *International Journal of Clinical Neuropsychology, 6,* 139–142.

Novy, D. M., Nelson, D. V., Berry, L. A., & Averill, P. M. (1995). What does the Beck Depression Inventory measure in chronic pain?: A reappraisal. *Pain, 61,* 261–270.

Nyagu, A., & Privalova, N. N. (1988). Clinico–psychological mechanisms of compensations of brain dysfunctions in patients with traumatic lesions of polar-basal regions of frontal lobes. *Zhurnal Nevropatologii i Psikhiatrii Imeni–S.S. Korsakova, 88,* 40–45.

O'Hara, C. (1988). Emotional adjustment following minor head injury. *Cognitive Rehabilitation, 6,* 26–33.

Oleske, D. M., Andersson, G. B. J., Lavender, S. A., & Hahn, J. J. (2000). Association between recovery outcomes for work-related low back disorders and personal, family, and work factors. *Spine, 25,* 1259–1265.

O'Maille, P. S. (2001). The impact of compensation on symptom distortion in chronic pain patients: An examination of MMPI–2 symptom distortion measures. *Dissertation Abstracts International: Section B: The Sciences and Engineering, 62*(5-B), 2496.

Onorato, V. A., & Tsushima, W. T. (1983). EMG, MMPI, and treatment outcome in the biofeedback therapy of tension headache and posttraumatic pain. *American Journal of Clinical Biofeedback, 6,* 71–81.

Oostdam, E. (1981). Predictive value of some psychological tests on the outcome of surgical intervention in low back pain patients. *Journal of Psychosomatic Research, 25,* 227–235.

Oostdam, E. (1983). Predictability of the result of surgical intervention in patients with low back pain. *Journal of Psychosomatic Research, 27,* 273–281.

Oostdam, E. (1987). Description of pain and the relationship with psychological factors in patients with low back pain. *Pain, 28,* 357–364.

Ornduff, S. R., & Brennan, A. (1988). The Minnesota Multiphasic Personality Inventory (MMPI) Hysteria (*Hy*) Scale: Scoring bodily concern and psychological denial subscales in chronic back pain patients. *Journal of Behavioral Medicine, 11,* 131–146.

Owen, R. C. (1989). MMPI assessment of surgical vs nonsurgical chronic pain patients. *Dissertation Abstracts International, 49,* 2869.

Palav, A., Ortega, A., & McCaffrey, R. J. (2001). Incremental validity of the MMPI–2 content scales: A preliminary study with brain-injured patients. *Journal of Head Trauma Rehabilitation, 16*(3), 275–283.

Pancheri, L., Pancheri, P., di Cesare, G., & Marini, S. (1987). Correlati psiconeuroendocrini dell'effetto placebo nel dolore cronico [Psychoneuroendocrine correlates of the placebo effect in chronic pain]. *Rivista di Psichiatria, 22,* 110–129.

Papciak, A. S., Feuerstein, M., Belar, C. D., & Pistone, L. (1986). Alexithymia and pain in an outpatient behavioral medicine clinic. *International Journal of Psychiatry in Medicine, 16,* 347–357.

Papciak, A. S., Feuerstein, M., Belar, C. D., & Pistone, L. (1987). Alexithymia and pain in an outpatient behavioral medicine clinic. *International Journal of Psychiatry in Medicine, 16,* 347–357.

Parker, J. C., Doerfler, L. A., Tatten, H. A., & Hewett, J. E. (1983). Psychological factors that influence self-reported pain. *Journal of Clinical Psychology, 39,* 22–25.

Patrick, J. (1988). Personality characteristics of work-ready workers' compensation clients. *Journal of Clinical Psychology, 44,* 1009–1012.

Peniston, E. G., & Hughes, R. B. (1986). Use of the MMPI and PAT as evaluative measures of chronic pain. *Clinical Biofeedback and Health: An International Journal, 9,* 15–21.

Peniston, E. G., Hughes, R. B., & Kulkosky, P. J. (1986). EMG biofeedback-assisted relaxation training in the treatment of reactive depression in chronic pain patients. *Psychological Record, 36,* 471–481.

Penk, W. E., Rierdan, J., Losardo. M., & Robinowitz, R. (2006). Using the MMPI–2 for assessing post-traumatic stress disorder (PTSD). In J. N. Butcher (Ed.), *MMPI–2: A practitioner's guide* (pp. 121–142). Washington, DC: American Psychological Association.

Penk, W. E., Robinowitz, R., Black, J., & Dolan, M. P. (1989). Co-morbidity: Lessons learned about post-traumatic stress disorder (PTSD) from developing PTSD scales for the MMPI. *Journal of Clinical Psychology, 45,* 709–717.

Penk, W. E., Robinowitz, R., Black, J., & Dolan, M. P. (1989). Ethnicity: Post-traumatic stress disorder (PTSD) differences among Black, White, and Hispanic veterans who differ in degrees of exposure to combat in Vietnam. *Journal of Clinical Psychology, 45,* 729–735.

Penk, W. E., Robinowitz, R., Dorsett, D., Black, J., Dolan, M. P., & Bell, W. (1989). Co-morbidity: Lessons learned about post-traumatic stress disorder (PTSD) from developing PTSD scales for the MMPI. *Journal of Clinical Psychology, 45,* 709–717.

Perconte, S. T., & Goreczny, A. J. (1990). Failure to detect fabricated posttraumatic stress disorder with the use of the MMPI in a clinical population. *American Journal of Psychiatry, 147,* 1057–1060.

Perl, J. L., & Kahn, M. W. (1983). The effects of compensation on psychiatric disability. *Social Science and Medicine, 17,* 439–443.

Perrin, S., Van Hasselt, V. B., Basilio, I., & Hersen, M. (1996). Assessing the effects of violence on women in battering relationships with the Keane MMPI–PTSD Scale. *Journal of Traumatic Stress, 9,* 805–816.

Perrin, S., Van Hasselt, V. B., & Hersen, M. (1997). Validation of the Keane MMPI–PTSD Scale against *DSM–III–R* criteria in a sample of battered women. *Violence and Victims, 12,* 99–104.

Peters, J. F., Benjamin, B., Helvey, W. M., & Albright, G. A. (1963). A study of sensory deprivation, pain, and personality relationships for space travel. *Aerospace Medicine, 34,* 830–837.

Petrovich, D. V. (1958). The Pain Apperception Test: Psychological correlates of pain perception. *Journal of Clinical Psychology, 14,* 367–374.

Pichot, P. (1972). MMPI evaluation of personality characteristics of subjects with chronic functional low back pain. *Revue de Psychologie Appliquee, 22,* 145–172.

Pichot, P., Perse, J., Lebeauzx, M.O., Dureau, J. L., Perez, C., & Ryckewaert, A. (1972). MMPI evaluation of personality characteristics of subjects with chronic functional low back pain. *Revue de Psychologie Appliquee, 22,* 145–172.

Pilling, L. F., Brannick, T. L., & Swenson, W. M. (1967). Psychologic characteristics of psychiatric patients having pain as a presenting symptom. *Canadian Medical Association Journal, 97,* 387–394.

Piotrowski, C., (1998). Assessment of pain: A survey of practicing clinicians. *Perceptual and Motor Skills, 86,* 181–192.

Poitrenaud, J. P. S. (1967). The role of pain in the psychology of the ulcer patient. *Encéphale, 56,* 510–529.

Pollack, D. R. (1992, May). *Assessment of brain trauma personal injury litigants.* Paper presented at the 27th Annual Symposium on Recent Developments in the Use of the MMPI–2/MMPI–A Workshop and Symposia, Minneapolis, MN.

Pollack, D. R., & Grainey, T. F. (1984). A comparison of MMPI profiles for state and private disability insurance applicants. *Journal of Personality Assessment, 48,* 121–125.

Porzelius, J. (1995). Memory for pain after nerve-block injections. *Clinical Journal of Pain, 11,* 112–120.

Posthuma, A. B., & Harper, J. F. (1998). Comparison of MMPI–2 responses of child custody and personal injury litigants. *Professional Psychology: Research and Practice, 29,* 437–443.

Postone, N. (1986). Alexithymia in chronic pain patients. *General Hospital Psychiatry, 8,* 163–167.

Prokop, C. K. (1986). Hysteria scale elevations in low back pain patients: A risk factor for misdiagnosis? *Journal of Consulting and Clinical Psychology, 54,* 558–562.

Prokop, C. K., Bradley, L. A., Margolis, R., & Gentry, W. (1980). Multivariate analysis of the MMPI profiles of patients with multiple pain complaints. *Journal of Personality Assessment, 44,* 246–252.

Putnam, S. H., Kurtz, J. E., Millis, S. R., & Adams, K. M. (1995, March). *Prevalence and correlates of MMPI–2 codetypes in patients with traumatic brain injury.* Paper given at the 30th Annual Symposium on Research Developments in the Use of the MMPI–2, St. Petersburg, FL.

Quick, D. M. (1997). Empirically derived MMPI–2 profile clusters: Prediction of pain rehabilitation program outcome. *Dissertation Abstracts International, 57,* 5929.

Rayls, K. R., Mittenburg, W., Burns, W. J., & Therous, S. (2000). Prospective study of the MMPI–2 correction factor after mild head injury. *Clinical Neuropsychologist, 14,* 546–550.

Reich, J., Steward, M. S., Tupin, J. P., & Rosenblatt, R. M. (1985). Prediction of response to treatment in chronic pain patients. *Journal of Clinical Psychiatry, 46,* 425–427.

Repko, G. R., & Cooper, R. (1983). A study of the average workers' compensation case. *Journal of Clinical Psychology, 39,* 287–295.

Repko, G. R., & Cooper, R. (1985). The diagnosis of personality disorder: A comparison of MMPI profile, Millon inventory and clinical judgment in a workers' compensation population. *Journal of Clinical Psychology, 41,* 867–881.

Reynolds, C. (1998). *Detection of malingering in head injury litigation.* New York: Plenum Press.

Riley, J. L. (1998). Validity of MMPI–2 profiles in chronic back pain patients: Differences in path models of coping and somatization. *Clinical Journal of Pain, 14,* 324–335.

Riley, J. L., Robinson, M. E., Geisser, M. E., Wittmer, V. T., & Smith, A. G. (1995). Relationship between MMPI–2 cluster profiles and surgical outcome in low-back pain patients. *Journal of Spinal Disorders, 8,* 213–219.

Roberts, K. A. (2000). Trauma recovery in military veterans with chronic PTSD: An emphasis on the problem of guilt. A treatment outcomes study. *Dissertation Abstracts International, 60,* 4249.

Roberts, L. C. (1997). Post-traumatic stress disorder in adolescent sex offenders as measured by elevations on the MMPI–2 PTSD *PK* subscale. *Dissertation Abstracts International, 58,* 1544.

Robinson, M. E., O'Connor, P. D., MacMillan, M., & Shirley, F. R. (1992). Physical and psychosocial correlates of test-retest isometric torque variability in patients with chronic low back pain. *Journal of Occupational Rehabilitation, 2,* 11–18.

Robinson, R. C. (1999). Occupational and health outcomes of polymorphous pain individuals: Briquet's syndrome revisited. *Dissertation Abstracts International, 59,* 4528.

Robinson, R. C. (2000). Psychometric testing: The early years and the MMPI. In R. J. Gatchel (Ed.), *Personality characteristics of patients with pain* (pp. 37–58). Washington, DC: American Psychological Association.

Romano, J. M., Turner, J. A., & Moore, J. E. (1989). Psychological evaluation. In C. D. Tollison (Ed.), *Handbook of chronic pain management* (pp. 38–51). Baltimore: Williams & Wilkins.

Ronnei, M. A. (1995). An evaluation of the PTSD subscales of the MMPI–2 with female civilian trauma victims. *Dissertation Abstracts International, 56,* 2379.

Rosen, J. C., Grubman, J. A., Bevins, T., & Frymoyer, J. W. (1987). Musculoskeletal status and disability of MMPI profile subgroups among patients with low back pain. *Health Psychology, 6,* 581–598.

Rosenblum, A., Joseph, H., Fong, C., Kipnis, S., Cleland, C., & Portenoy, R. K. (2003). Prevalence and characteristics of chronic pain among chemically dependent patients in methadone maintenance and residential treatment facilities. *Journal of American Medical Association, 289,* 2370–2378.

Rosenthal, R. H., Ling, F. W., Rosenthal, T. L., & McNeeley, S. (1984). Chronic pelvic pain: Psychological features and laparoscopic findings. *Psychosomatics, 25,* 833–841.

Ross, S. R., Millis, S. R., Krukowski, R. A., Putnam, S. H., & Adams, K. M. (2004). Detecting incomplete effort on the MMPI–2: An examination of the Fake-Bad scale in mild head injury. *Journal of Clinical and Experimental Neuropsychology, 26*(1), 115–124.

Ross, S. R., Putnam, S. H., Gass, C. S., Bailey D. E., & Adams, K. M. (2003). MMPI–2 indices of psychological disturbance and attention and memory test performance in head injury. *Archives of Clinical Neuropsychology, 18,* 905–916.

Rothke, S. E., Friedman, A. F., Jaffe, A. M., Greene, R. L., Wetter, M. W., Cole, P., et al. (2000). Normative data for the *F(p)* scale of the MMPI–2: Implications for clinical and forensic assessment of malingering. *Psychological Assessment, 12,* 335–340.

Ruttan, L. A., & Henrichs, R. W. (2003). Depression and neurocognitive functioning in mild traumatic brain injury patients referred for assessment. *Journal of Clinical and Experimental Neuropsychology, 25,* 407–419.

Samuel, S. E., DeGirolamo, J., Michals, T. J., & O'Brien, J. (1994). Preliminary findings on MMPI "Cannot Say" responses with personal injury litigants. *American Journal of Forensic Psychology, 12,* 5–18.

Sapp, M., Farrell, W. C., Johnson, J. H., & Ioannidis, G. (1997). Utilizing the *PK* scale of the MMPI–2 to detect posttraumatic stress disorder in college students. *Journal of Clinical Psychology, 53,* 841–846.

Scarpetti, W. (1973). The repression–sensitization dimension in relation to impending painful stimulation. *Journal of Consulting and Clinical Psychology, 40,* 377–382.

Severin, D. A. (2003). A taxometric analysis of MMPI–2 impression management and self-deception scales in clergy. *Dissertation Abstracts International: Section B: The Sciences and Engineering, 64*(6–B), 2939.

Shaffer, J. W. (1981). Using the MMPI to evaluate mental impairment in disability determination. In J. N. Butcher, G. Dahlstrom, M. Gynther, & W. Schofield (Eds.), *Clinical notes on the MMPI* (pp. 1–12). Nutley, NJ: Hoffman-La Roche Laboratories/National Computer Systems.

Shaffer, J. W., Nussbaum, K., & Little, J. M. (1972). MMPI profiles of disability insurance claimants. *American Journal of Psychiatry, 129,* 63–67.

Scheibe, S., Bagby, R. M., Miller, L. S., & Dorian, B. J. (2001). Assessing posttraumatic disorder with the MMPI–2 in a sample of workplace accident victims. *Psychological Assessment, 13,* 369–374.

Schein, E., Hill, W., Williams, H., & Lubin, A. (1957). Distinguishing characteristics of collaborators and resisters among American prisoners of war. *Journal of Abnormal and Social Psychology, 55,* 197–201.

Schiff, B. B., & Gagliese, L. (1994). The consequences of experimentally induced and chronic unilateral pain: Reflections of hemispheric lateralization of emotion. *Cortex, 30,* 255–267.

Schmidt, J. P., & Wallace, R. W. (1982). Factorial analysis of the MMPI profiles of low back pain patients. *Journal of Personality Assessment, 46,* 366–369.

Schnurr, P. P., Friedman, M. J., & Rosenberg, S. D. (1993). Preliminary MMPI scores as predictors of combat-related PTSD symptoms. *American Journal of Psychiatry, 150,* 479–483.

Schnurr, P. P., Friedman, M., & Rosenberg, S. D. (1994). "Predicting post-combat PTSD by using premilitary MMPI scores": Reply. *American Journal of Psychiatry, 151,* 156–157.

Schulman, J. H. (1960). The relationship of manifest anxiety to the pain reaction in low stress and high stress situations. *Dissertation Abstracts International, 21,* 963.

Schwartz, D. P., & DeGood, D. E. (1984). Global appropriateness of pain drawings: Blind ratings predict patterns of psychological distress and litigation status. *Pain, 19,* 383–388.

Scotti, J. R., Sturges, L. V., & Lyons, J. A. (1996). The Keane PTSD Scale extracted from the MMPI:

Sensitivity and specificity with Vietnam veterans. *Journal of Traumatic Stress, 9,* 643–650.

Seltzer, S., Dewart, D., Pollack, R. L., & Jackson, E. (1983). The effects of dietary tryptophan on chronic maxillofacial pain and experimental pain tolerance. *Journal of Psychiatric Research, 17,* 181–186.

Senior, G., & Douglas, L. (2001). Misconceptions and misuse of the MMPI–2 in assessing personal injury claimants. *Neurorehabilitation, 16*(4), 203–213.

Shaffer, J. W., Nussbaum, K., & Little, J. M. (1972). MMPI profiles of disability insurance claimants. *American Journal of Psychiatry, 129,* 64–67.

Shearer, D. S. (2001). The Minnesota Multiphasic Personality Inventory—2 and low back pain surgery outcome. *Dissertation Abstracts International: Section B: The Sciences and Engineering, 62*(1-B), 532.

Sherman, E. S., Strauss, E., Slick, D. J., & Spellacy, F. (2000). Effects of depression on neuropsychological functioning in head injury: Measurable but minimal. *Brain Injury, 14,* 621–632.

Sherman, R. A., Camfield, M. R., & Arena, J. G. (1995). The effect of presence or absence of low back pain on the MMPI's conversion V. *Military Psychology, 7,* 29–38.

Shipman, W. G., Greene, C. S., & Laskin, D. M. (1974). Correlation of placebo responses and personality characteristics in myofascial pain-dysfunction (MPD) patients. *Journal of Psychosomatic Research, 18,* 475–483.

Shiri, S., Tsenter, J., Livai, R., Schwartz, I., & Vatine, J. (2003). Similarities between the psychological profiles of complex regional pain syndrome and conversion disorder patients. *Journal of Clinical Psychology in Medical Settings, 10*(3), 193–199.

Shoenberg, B., Carr, A. C., Kutscher, A. H., & Zegarelli, E. V. (1971). Chronic idiopathic orolingual pain: Psychogenesis of burning mouth. *New York State Journal of Medicine, 71,* 1832–1837.

Shulman, E. (1994). Predicting postcombat PTSD by using premilitary MMPI scores. *American Journal of Psychiatry, 151*, 156.

Shulman, R., Turnbull, I. M., & Diewold, P. (1982). Psychiatric aspects of thalamic stimulation for neuropathic pain. *Pain, 13,* 127–135.

Sillanpaa, M. C., Agar, L. M., & Axelrod, B. N. (1999). Minnesota Multiphasic Personality Inventory—2 validity patterns: An elucidation of gulf war syndrome. *Military Medicine, 164,* 261–263.

Silver, S. M., & Salamone-Genovese, L. (1991). A study of the MMPI clinical and research scales for post-traumatic stress disorder diagnostic utility. *Journal of Traumatic Stress, 4*(4), 533–548.

Singer, D. C. (1992). Chronic pain and workers' compensation: An MMPI study. *Dissertation Abstracts International, 52,* 6690–6691.

Singer, M. T., & Schein, E. (1958). Projective test responses of prisoners of war following repatriation. *Psychiatry, 21,* 375–385.

Sinnett, E. R. (1994). Note on the PTSD–S scale of the MMPI. *Psychological Reports, 74,* 1041–1042.

Sinnett, E. R. (1996). Does the MMPI *PTSD–PK* scale measure robustness? *Psychological Reports, 79,* 211–217.

Sivik, T. M. (1991). Personality traits in patients with acute low-back pain: A comparison with chronic low-back pain patients. *Psychotherapy and Psychosomatics, 56,* 135–140.

Sivik, T. M., Gustafsson, E., & Olsson, K. K. (1992). Differential diagnosis of low back pain patients: A simple quantification of the pain drawing. *Nordisk Psykiatrisk Tidsskrift, 46,* 55–62.

Sivik, T. M., Roejvall, S., Gustafsson, E., & Klingberg-Olsson, K. (1992). Relationship between back pain and personality: Psychologic vulnerability as risk factor for the development of chronic back pain. *Nordic Journal of Psychiatry, 46,* 189–193.

Slesinger, D. (2001). Minnesota Multiphasic Personality Inventory–2: Correlates in a chronic pain population. *Dissertation Abstracts International: Section B: The Sciences and Engineering, 62*(3-B), 1633.

Slesinger, D., Archer, R. P., & Duane, D. (2002). MMPI–2 characteristics in a chronic pain population. *Assessment, 9*(4), 406–414.

Slick, D. J., Hopp, G., Strauss, E., & Spellacy, F. J. (1996). Victoria Symptom Validity Test: Efficiency for detecting feigned memory impairment and relationship to neuropsychological tests and MMPI–2 validity scales. *Journal of Clinical and Experimental Neuropsychology, 18,* 911–922.

Small, E. W. (2001). *An investigation into the incidence of psychogenic factors underlying the temporomandibular joint pain/dysfunction syndrome.* Norfolk, VA: Old Dominion University.

Smith, D. P. (1969). A psychiatric study of atypical facial pain. *Canadian Medical Association Journal, 100,* 286–291.

Smith, D. W., & Frueh, B. (1996). Compensation seeking, comorbidity, and apparent exaggeration of PTSD symptoms among Vietnam combat veterans. *Psychological Assessment, 8,* 3–6.

Smith, D. W., Frueh, B. C., Sawchuk, C. N., & Johnson, M. R. (1999). Relationship between symptom over-reporting and pre- and post-combat trauma history in veterans evaluated for PTSD. *Depression and Anxiety, 10,* 119–124.

Smith, E. D. (2000). The Minnesota Multiphasic Personality Inventory (MMPI–2) and mild traumatic brain injury: Analysis of a neurocorrection factor in a litigation sample. *Dissertation Abstracts International: Section B: The Sciences and Engineering, 61*(6–B), 3293.

Smith, R. J. (1990). Correlational study of the UNT Neuropsych-screen, the MMPI and time among chronic pain patients. *Dissertation Abstracts International, 50,* 4274.

Smith, T. W., Aberger, E. W., Follick, M. J., & Ahern, D. K. (1986). Cognitive distortion and psychological distress in chronic low back pain. *Journal of Consulting and Clinical Psychology, 54,* 573–575.

Smith, T. W., Follick, M. J., & Ahern, D. K. (1985). Life-events and psychological disturbance in chronic low back pain. *British Journal of Clinical Psychology, 24,* 207–208.

Smith, W. L. (1979). Personality and the relief of chronic pain: Predicting surgical outcome. *Clinical Neuropsychology, 1,* 35–38.

Snibbe, J. R., Peterson, P. J., & Sosner, B. (1980). Study of psychological characteristics of a worker's compensation sample using the MMPI and Millon Clinical Multiaxial Inventory. *Psychological Reports, 47,* 959–966.

Snyder, D. K. (1990). Assessing chronic pain with the Minnesota Multiphasic Personality Inventory (MMPI). In T. W. Miller (Ed.), *Chronic pain* (pp. 215–257). Madison, CT: International Universities Press.

Snyder, D. K., & Power, D. G. (1981). Empirical descriptors of unelevated MMPI profiles among chronic pain patients: A typological approach. *Journal of Clinical Psychology, 37,* 602–607.

Solbakk, A. K., Reinvang, I., & Nielsen, C. S. (2000). ERP indices of resource allocation difficulties in mild head injury. *Journal of Clinical and Experimental Neuropsychology, 22,* 743–760.

Solberg, W., Flint, R., & Brantner, J. (1972). Temporomandibular joint pain and dysfunction: A clinical study of emotional and occlusal components. *Journal of Prosthetic Dentistry, 28,* 412–422.

Spaulding, R. C., & Ford, C. V. (1972). The Pueblo incident: Psychological reactions to the stresses of imprisonment and repatriation. *American Journal of Psychiatry, 129,* 17–26.

Sperr, E. V., Sperr, S. J., & Craft, R. (1990). MMPI profiles and post-traumatic symptomatology in former prisoners of war. *Journal of Traumatic Stress, 3,* 369–378.

Steffen, L. J. (1999). MMPI–2 indicators of return to work following injury and participation in a chronic pain program. *Dissertations International: Section B: The Sciences and Engineering, 59*(7-B), 3716.

Stein, N., Fruchter, H. J., & Trief, P. M. (1983). Experiences of depression and illness behavior in patients with intractable chronic pain. *Journal of Clinical Psychology, 39,* 31–33.

Sternbach, R. A., Wolf, S. R., Murphy, R. W., & Akeson, W. H. (1973). Traits of pain patients: The low back "loser." *Psychosomatics, 14,* 226–229.

Stevens, R. R. (1967). Sex differences and personality correlates of pain experience. *Dissertation Abstracts International, 28,* 2633B.

Stone, R. K., & Pepitone-Arreola-Rockwell, F. (1983). Diagnosis of organic and functional pain patients with the MMPI. *Psychological Reports, 52,* 539–548.

Strassberg, D. S. (1981). The MMPI and chronic pain. *Journal of Consulting and Clinical Psychology, 49,* 220–226.

Strassberg, D. S., & Russell, S. W. (2000). MMPI–2 content scales validity within a sample of chronic pain patients. *Journal of Psychopathology and Behavioral Assessment, 22*(1), 47–61.

Strassberg, D. S., Tilley, D., Bristone, S., & Oei, T. P. (1992). The MMPI and chronic pain: A cross-cultural view. *Psychological Assessment, 4,* 493–497.

Sullivan, M., Toshima, M., Lynn, P., & Roy-Byrne, P. (1993). Phenobarbital versus clonazepam for sedative-hypnotic taper in chronic pain patients: A pilot study. *Annals of Clinical Psychiatry, 5,* 123–128.

Summers, M. N., Hyer, L. A., Boyd, S., & Boudewyns, P. A. (1996). Diagnosis of later-life PTSD among elderly combat veterans. *Journal of Clinical Geropsychology, 2,* 103–115.

Sutker, P. B., & Allain, A. N. (1996). Assessment of PTSD and other mental disorders in World War II and Korean conflict POW survivors and combat veterans. *Psychological Assessment, 8,* 18–25.

Sutker, P. B., Allain, A. N., & Johnson, J. L. (1993). Clinical assessment of long-term cognitive and emotional sequelae to World War II prisoner-of-war confinement: Comparison of pilot twins. *Psychological Assessment, 5,* 3–10.

Sutker, P. B., Allain, A. N., & Motsinger, P. (1988). Minnesota Multiphasic Personality Inventory (MMPI)-derived psychopathology subtypes among former prisoners of war (POWs): Replication and extension. *Journal of Psychopathology and Behavioral Assessment, 10,* 129–140.

Sutker, P. B., Bugg, B. F., & Allain, A. (1991). Psychometric prediction of PTSD among POW survivors. *Psychological Assessment, 3,* 105–110.

Sutker, P. B., Winstead, D. K., & Galena, Z. (1991). Cognitive deficits and psychopathology among former prisoners of war and combat veterans of the Korean conflict. *American Journal of Psychiatry, 148,* 67–72.

Sutker, P. B., Winstead, D. K., Goist, K. C., & Malow, R. M. (1986). Psychopathology subtypes and symptom correlates among former prisoners of war. *Journal of Psychopathology and Behavioral Assessment, 8,* 89–101.

Swanson, D. W., Maruta, T., & Wolff, V. A. (1986). Ancient pain. *Pain, 25,* 383–387.

Swanson, D. W., Swenson, E. M., Maruta, T., & McPhee, M. C. (1976). Program for managing chronic pain. *Mayo Clinic Proceedings, 51,* 401–408.

Sweet, J. J. (1981). The MMPI in evaluation of response to treatment of chronic pain. *American Journal of Clinical Biofeedback, 4,* 121–130.

Sweet, J. J. (1985). The Millon Behavioral Health Inventory: Concurrent and predictive validity in a pain treatment center. *Journal of Behavioral Medicine, 8,* 215–226.

Talbert, F. S., Albrecht, N. N., Albrecht, J. W., Boudewyns, P. A., Hyer, L. A., Touze, J. H., et al. (1994). MMPI profiles in PTSD as a function of comorbidity. *Journal of Clinical Psychology, 50,* 529–537.

Takaishi, N. (1967). Psychological features of pregnant women under training for painless delivery. *Journal of the Japanese Psychosomatic Society, 7,* 371–372.

Tapp, J. T. (1989). A multisystems perspective on chronic pain. *Psychotherapy in Private Practice, 7,* 1–15.

Tatrow, K., Blanchard, E. B., Hickling, E. J., & Silverman, D. J. (2003). Posttraumatic headache: Biopsychosocial comparisons with multiple control groups. *Headache, 43,* 755–766.

Taylor, M. L. (1988). The relationship between M.M.P.I. profile cluster subgroup membership and self-report of treatment effect from a multidisciplinary chronic pain treatment program. *Dissertation Abstracts International, 48,* 3427.

Terelak, J., Tarnowski, A., & Kwasucki, J. (1993). Psychometryczna uzytecznosc kwestionariuszy Zunga I Hendlera sluzacych do oceny psychologicznego komponentu bólu krzyza [Psychometric utility of the Zung and Hendler Tests for the estimation of a psychological component of low-back pain]. *Przeglad Psychologiczny, 36,* 87–97.

Thomas, M. R., & Lyttle, D. (1976). Development of a diagnostic checklist for low back pain patients. *Journal of Clinical Psychology, 32,* 125–129.

Thomas, M. R., & Lyttle, D. (1980). Patient expectations about success of treatment and reported relief from low back pain. *Journal of Psychosomatic Research, 24,* 297–301.

Thrift, R. D. (1990). The use of the MMPI in identifying personality factors affecting maximum voluntary effort in a chronic low back pain rehabilitation program. *Dissertation Abstracts International, 51,* 2665.

Timmermans, G., & Sternbach, R. A. (1974). Factors of human chronic pain: An analysis of personality and pain reaction variables. *Science, 184,* 806–808.

Tippery, M. A. (1987). Development of an MMPI subscale and a 3-item rating scale to predict outcome of inpatient multidisciplinary treatment of pain. *Dissertation Abstracts International, 47,* 4339.

Toomey, T. C., Ghia, J. N., Mao, W., & Gregg, J. M. (1977). Acupuncture and chronic pain mechanisms: The moderating effects of affect, personality, and stress on response to treatment. *Pain, 3,* 137–145.

Torre, E., Ancona, M., Nattero, G., & de Lorenzo, C. (1987). Cefalee idiopatiche: Profili di personalita. Indagini sulla popolazione maschile e femminile ed effetti del dolore cronico (Idiopathic headaches: Personality profiles: Studies on male and female populations and the effects of chronic pain). *Medicina Psicosomatica, 32,* 97–117.

Trabin, T., Rader, C., & Cummings, C. (1987). A comparison of pain management outcomes for disability compensation and non-compensation patients. *Psychology and Health, 1,* 341–351.

Trief, P. M., & Yuan, H. A. (1983). The use of the MMPI in a chronic back pain rehabilitation program. *Journal of Clinical Psychology, 39,* 46–53.

Tsushima, W. T., & Tsushima, V. G. (1993). Relation between headaches and neuropsychological functioning among head injury patients. *Headache, 33,* 139–142.

Tsushima, W. T., & Tsushima, V. G. (2001). Comparison of the fake bad scale and other MMPI–2 validity scales with personal injury litigants. *Assessment, 8,* 205–211.

Tsushima, W. T., & Newbill, W. (1996). Effects of headaches during neuropsychological testing of mild head injury patients. *Headache, 36,* 613–615.

Tsushima, W. T., Pang, D. B., & Stoddard, V. M. (1987). Sex similarities and differences in the biofeedback treatment of chronic pain. *Clinical Biofeedback and Health: An International Journal, 10,* 45–50.

Tsushima, W. T., & Stoddard, V. M. (1990). Ethnic group similarities in the biofeedback treatment of pain. *Medical Psychotherapy: An International Journal, 3,* 69–75.

Tsushima, W. T., & Wong, J. M. (1992). Comparison of legal and medical referrals to neuropsychological examination following head injury. *Forensic Reports, 5,* 359–366.

Tsytsareva, I. V. (1986). The role of the patients' personality–psychological peculiarities in mental decompensations in late depressions. *Trudy Leningradskogo Nauchno-Issledovatel'skogo Psikhonevrologicheskogo Instituta im V M Bekhtereva, 114,* 40–47.

Turk, D. C., & Rudy, T. E. (1992). Classification logic and strategies in chronic pain. In D. C. Turk

(Ed.), *Handbook of pain assessment* (pp. 409–428). New York: Guilford Press.

Turner, J. A., Calsyn, D. A., Fordyce, W. E., & Ready, L. (1982). Drug utilization patterns in chronic pain patients. *Pain, 12,* 357–363.

Turner, J. A., Herron, L., & Weiner, P. (1986). Utility of the MMPI Pain Assessment Index in predicting outcome after lumbar surgery. *Journal of Clinical Psychology, 42,* 764–769.

Turner, J., & McCreary, C. P. (1978). Short forms of the MMPI with back pain patients. *Journal of Consulting and Clinical Psychology, 46,* 354–355.

Turner, J. A., & Romano, J. M. (1984). Self-report screening measures for depression in chronic pain patients. *Journal of Clinical Psychology, 40,* 909–913.

Ursano, R. J., Wheatley, R., Sledge, W., & Rahe, A. (1986). Coping and recovery styles in the Vietnam era prisoner of war. *Journal of Nervous and Mental Disease, 174,* 707–714.

Van Hoof, E., De Meirleir, K., Cluydts, R., & Coomans, D. (2003). The symptoms and psychiatric status of the Bijlmermeer plane crash disaster: Similarities with chronic fatigue syndrome and gulf war syndrome. *Journal of Chronic Fatigue Syndrome, 11*(3), 3–21.

Vander Kolk, C. J., & Stewart, W. W. (1988). Characteristics of injured persons involved in litigation. *Vocational Evaluation and Work Adjustment Bulletin, 21,* 103–106.

Vanderploeg, R. D., Sison, G. F., & Hickling, E. J. (1987). A reevaluation of the use of the MMPI in the assessment of combat-related posttraumatic stress disorder. *Journal of Personality Assessment, 51,* 140–150.

Vando, A. (1970). A personality dimension related to pain tolerance. *Dissertation Abstracts International, 31,* 2292–2293.

Veith, W. T. (1995). Use of the MMPI malingering indices to differentiate type of claim and employment status in workers' compensation claimants. *Dissertation Abstracts International, 56*(1-B), 539.

Vendrig, A. A. (1999). *The prediction of outcome in the multimodal treatment of chronic back pain: The role of emotional distress and personality*. Doctoral Dissertation, University of Nijmegen, Nijmegen, the Netherlands.

Vendrig, A. A. (1999). Prognostic factors and treatment-related changes associated with return to work in the multimodal treatment of chronic back pain. *Journal of Behavioral Medicine, 22,* 217–232.

Vendrig, A. A. (2000). The Minnesota Multiphasic Personality Inventory and chronic pain: A conceptual analysis of a long-standing but complicated relationship. *Clinical Psychology Review, 20,* 533–559.

Vendrig, A. A., de Mey, H. R., Derksen, J. L., & van Akkerveeken, P. F. (1998). Assessment of chronic back pain patient characteristics using factor analysis of the MMPI-2: Which dimensions are actually assessed? *Pain, 76,* 179–188.

Vendrig, A. A., & Derksen, J. J. (1999). Utility of selected MMPI-2 scales in the outcome prediction for patients with chronic back pain. *Psychological Assessment, 11,* 381–385.

Vendrig, A. A., Derksen, J. L., & de Mey, H. R. (1999). Utility of selected MMPI-2 scales in the outcome prediction for patients with chronic back pain. *Psychological Assessment, 11,* 381–385.

Vendrig, A. A., Derksen, J. J. L., & de Mey, H. R. (2000). MMPI-2 Personality Psychopathology Five (PSY-5) and prediction of treatment outcome for patients with chronic back pain. *Journal of Personality Assessment, 74,* 423–438.

Veraldi, D. M. (1992). Assessing PTSD in personal injury cases. *American Journal of Forensic Psychology, 10,* 5–13.

Volpini, M. (1992). Cassa Integrazione e salute mentale. Ricerca presso I lavoratori in Cassa Integrazione Guadagni della Società SIT-Stampaggio di Terni [Unemployment and mental health: Research on the workers of the SIT Printing Company of Terni receiving unemployment compensation]. *Medicina Psicosomatica, 37,* 235–245.

von Baeyer, C. L., Bergstrom, K. J., Brodwin, M. G., & Brodwin, S. K. (1983). Invalid use of pain drawings in psychological screening of back pain patients. *Pain, 16,* 103–107.

von Baeyer, C. L., & Wyant, G. M. (1988). Tension in opposing muscle groups and psychopathology: The "spring response" in chronic pain patients and normal subjects. *Pain Clinic, 2,* 7–14.

Wade, J. B., Dougherty, L. M., Hart, R. P., & Cook, D. B. (1992). Patterns of normal personality structure among chronic pain patients. *Pain, 48,* 37–43.

Wade, J. B., Price, D. D., Hamer, R. M., & Schwartz, S. M. (1990). An emotional component analysis of chronic pain. *Pain, 40,* 303–310.

Wang, Y., Wu, C., &, Wu, A. (2000). The MMPI results in patients with chronic pain. *Chinese Mental Health Journal, 14,* 321–322.

Watson, C. G., Herder, J., Kucala, T., & Hoodecheck-Schow, E. (1987). Intellectual deterioration and personality decompensation in schizophrenia. *Journal of Clinical Psychology, 43,* 447–455.

Watson, C. G., Juba, M., Anderson, P. E., & Manifold, V. (1990). What does the Keane et al. PTSD scale for the MMPI measure? *Journal of Clinical Psychology, 46,* 600–606.

Watson, C. G., Plemel, D., DeMotts, J., & Howard, M. T. (1994). A comparison of four PTSD measures' convergent validities in Vietnam veterans. *Journal of Traumatic Stress, 7,* 75–82.

Watson, C. G., Plemel, D., DeMotts, J., Howard, M. T., Tuorila, J., Moog, R., et al. (1994). A comparison of four PTSD measures' convergent validities in Vietnam veterans. *Journal of Traumatic Stress, 7,* 75–82.

Watson, D. (1982). Neurotic tendencies among chronic pain patients: An MMPI item analysis. *Pain, 14,* 365–385.

Wehrlin, M. G. (1993). The efficacy of the MMPI-2 PTSD scale in identifying past abuse. *Dissertation Abstracts International, 53,* 4972.

Weisberg, J. N., & Vaillancourt, P. D. (1999). Personality factors and disorders in chronic pain. *Seminars in Clinical Neuropsychiatry, 4,* 155–166.

Wetzel, R. D., Clayton, P. J., Cloninger, C., Robert, B. J., Martin, R. L., Guze, S. B., et al. (2000). Diagnosis of posttraumatic stress disorder with the MMPI: *PK* scale scores in somatization disorder. *Psychological Reports, 87(2),* 535–541.

Wheatley, R. D. (1984). Psychometric evaluation of head injury among fliers referred to the USAF School of Aerospace Medicine. *United States Air Force School of Aerospace Medicine Technical Report, Technical Report, 84,* 21.

White, G. A. (1996). A descriptive study of the MMPI profiles of chronic pain patients following successful rehabilitation. *Dissertation Abstracts International, 56,* 7087.

Wilcoxson, M. A., Zook, A., & Zarski, J. J. (1988). Predicting behavioral outcomes with two psychological assessment methods in an outpatient pain management program. *Psychology and Health, 2,* 319–333.

Williams, R. B. (1986). Psychosocial and physical predictors of anginal pain relief with medical management. *Psychosomatic Medicine, 48,* 200–210.

Williams, S. C. (1979). MMPI assessment of the chronic low-back pain syndrome: The "conversion V" as an iatrogenic profile. *Dissertation Abstracts International, 39,* 6151.

Wise, E. A. (1996). Diagnosing posttraumatic stress disorder with the MMPI clinical scales: A review of the literature. *Journal of Psychopathology and Behavioral Assessment, 18,* 71–82.

Wittenauer, D. A. (1988). Psychological and demographic variables related to duration of pain in chronic pain syndrome. *Dissertation Abstracts International, 49,* 1414.

Wright, A. R. (1998). Psychosocial factors involved in the progression from acute to chronic low back pain disability. *Dissertation Abstracts International, 58,* 4479.

Wyermann, A. G., Norris, F. H., & Hyer, L. A. (1996). Examining comorbidity and posttraumatic stress disorder in a Vietnam veteran population using the MMPI–2. *Journal of Traumatic Stress, 9(2),* 353–360.

Youngjohn, J. R., Burrows, L., & Erdal, K. (1995). Brain damage or compensation neurosis? The controversial post-concussion syndrome. *Clinical Neuropsychologist, 9,* 112–123.

Youngjohn, J. R., Davis, D., & Wolf, I. (1997). Head injury and the MMPI–2: Paradoxical severity effects and the influence of litigation. *Psychological Assessment, 9,* 177–184.

Youngjohn, J. R., Spector, J., & Mapou, R. L. (1997). Neuropsychological findings in silicone breast-implant complainants: Brain damage, somatization, or compensation neuroses? *Clinical Neuropsychologist, 11,* 132–141.

Zaretsky, H. H., Lee, M. H., & Rubin, M. (1976). Psychological factors and clinical observations in acupuncture analgesia and pain abatement. *Journal of Psychology, 93,* 113–120.

Zierhoffer, D. M. (1997). Validity of the *Pk* and *Ps* scales of the MMPI–2: PTSD and incest. *Dissertation Abstracts International, 57,* 3835.

Ziesat, H. A. (1978). Are family patterns related to the development of chronic back pain? *Perceptual and Motor Skills, 46,* 1062.

Ziesat, H. A., & Gentry, W. (1978). The Pain Apperception Test: An investigation of concurrent validity. *Journal of Clinical Psychology, 34,* 786–789.

Child Custody-Related References

This appendix contains published works on child custody forensic evaluations, family litigation, parental behavior, and child–parent relationships.

Ackerman, M. J. (1995). *Clinician's guide to child custody evaluations.* New York: Wiley.

Ackerman, M. J., & Ackerman, M. C. (1997). Custody evaluation practices: A survey of experienced professionals (revisited). *Professional Psychology: Research and Practice, 28,* 137–145.

Ackerman, M. J., & Kane, A. W. (1996). *Psychological experts in divorce, personal injury, and other civic actions* (2nd ed., Vol. 2, 1996 Cum. Suppl.). New York: Wiley.

Adams, E. B., & Sarason, I. G. (1964). Relation between anxiety in children and their parents. *Child Development, 34,* 237–246.

Adrian, R. J. (1957). The relationship of parental personality structures to child adjustment and adoption selection. *Dissertation Abstracts International, 17,* 1386.

Albarracin, M., Albarracin, D., Sacchi, C., & Torres, G. (1996). Divorcia y resolucion de conflictos: Un modelo policausado complejo de determinación ambiental [Divorce and conflict resolution: A complex multicausal model of environmental effects]. *Revista Interamericana de Psicologia, 30,* 15–25.

Alley, G. R., Snider, B., Forsyth, R. A., & Opitz, E. (1974). Comparative parental MMPI protocols of children evaluated at a child development clinic. *Psychological Reports, 35,* 1147-1154.

Anagnostis, C. J. (2003). The development of a comprehensive biopsychosocial measure of disability for chronic musculoskeletal disorders: The pain dysfunction questionnaire. *Dissertation Abstracts International: Section B: The Sciences and Engineering, 63*(10-B), 4888.

Anderson, L. M. (1969). Personality characteristics of parents of neurotic, aggressive, and normal preadolescent boys. *Journal of Consulting and Clinical Psychology, 33,* 575–581.

Archer, R. P., Stolberg, A. L., Gordon, R. A., & Goldman, W. (1986). Parent and child MMPI responses: Characteristics among families with adolescents in inpatient and outpatient settings. *Journal of Abnormal Child Psychology, 14,* 181–190.

Archer, R. P., Sutker, P. B., White, J. L., & Orvin, G. H. (1978). Personality relationships among parents and adolescent offspring in inpatient treatment. *Psychological Reports, 42,* 207–214.

Armentrout, J. A. (1975). Repression-sensitization and MMPI correlates of retrospective reports of parental child-rearing behaviors. *Journal of Clinical Psychology, 31,* 444–448.

Arnold, P. D. (1970). *Recurring MMPI two-point codes of marriage counselors and "normal" couples with implications for interpreting marital interaction behavior.* Unpublished doctoral dissertation, University of Minnesota, Minneapolis.

Austin, J. S. (1992). The detection of fake good and fake bad on the MMPI–2. *Educational and Psychological Measurement, 52,* 669–674.

Baer, R. A., Wetter, M. A., & Berry, D. T. R. (1992). Detection of underreporting of psychopathology on the MMPI: A meta-analysis. *Clinical Psychology Review, 12,* 509–525.

Baer, R. A., Wetter, M. A., Berry, D. T. R., & Nichols, D. S. (1993, August). *Sensitivity of MMPI–2 validity scales to underreporting of symptoms.* Paper presented at the 101st Annual Convention of the American Psychological Association, Toronto, Ontario, Canada.

Bagby, R. M., Nicholson, R. A., Buis, T., Radovanovic, H., & Fidler, B. J. (1998, March). *Defensive responding on the MMPI–2 in family custody and access evaluations.* Paper presented at the 33rd Annual Symposium on Recent Developments in the Use of the MMPI–2/MMPI–A Workshop and Symposia, Clearwater Beach, FL.

Bagby, R. M., Nicholson, R. A., Buis, T., Radovanovic, H., & Fidler, B. J. (1999). Defensive responding on the MMPI–2 in family custody and access evaluations. *Psychological Assessment, 11,* 24–28.

Bagby, R. M., Nicholson, R. A., Rogers, R., Buis, T., Seeman, M. V., & Rector, N. A. (1997). Effectiveness of the MMPI–2 validity indicators in the detection of defensive responding in clinical and nonclinical samples. *Psychological Assessment, 9,* 406–413.

Bagby, R. M., Rogers, R., Buis, T., & Kalemba, V. (1994). Malingered and defensive response styles on the MMPI–2: An examination of validity scales. *Assessment, 1,* 31–38.

Barrett, R. K. (1973). *Relationship of emotional disorder to marital maladjustment and disruption.* Unpublished doctoral dissertation, Kent State University, Kent, OH.

Barry, J. R., Anderson, H. E., & Thomas, O. R. (1967). MMPI characteristics of alcoholic males who are well and poorly adjusted to marriage. *Journal of Clinical Psychology, 23,* 355–360.

Bathurst, K., Gottfried, A. W., & Gottfried, A. E. (1997). Normative data for the MMPI–2 in child custody litigation. *Psychological Assessment, 9,* 205–211.

Beier, E. G., & Ratzeburg, F. (1953). The parental identifications of male and female college students. *Journal of Abnormal and Social Psychology, 48,* 569–572.

Ben-Porath, Y. (1994). The ethical dilemma of coached malingering research. *Psychological Assessment, 6,* 14–15.

Ben-Porath, Y., & Graham, J. (1995). Scientific bases of forensic applications of the MMPI–2. In Y. S. Ben-Porath, J. Graham, G. Hall, R. Hirschman, & M. Zaragosa (Eds.), *Forensic applications of the MMPI–2* (pp. 1–17). Thousand Oaks, CA: Sage.

Ben-Porath, Y., Graham, J., Hall, G., Hirschman, R., & Zaragoza, M. (1995). *Forensic applications of the MMPI–2.* Thousand Oaks, CA: Sage.

Berry, D. T. R. (1995). Detecting distortion in forensic evaluations with the MMPI–2. In Y. S. Ben-Porath, J. Graham, G. Hall, R. Hirschman, & M. Zaragosa (Eds.), *Forensic applications of the MMPI–2* (pp. 82–102). Thousand Oaks, CA: Sage.

Berry, D., Baer, R., & Harris, M. J. (1991). Detection of malingering on the MMPI: A meta-analysis. *Clinical Psychology Review, 11,* 585–598.

Berry, D., Lamb, D., Wetter, M., Baer, R., & Widiger, T. (1994). Ethical considerations in research on coached malingering. *Psychological Assessment, 6,* 16–17.

Birtchnell, J. (1978). Early parent death and the clinical scales of the MMPI. *British Journal of Psychiatry, 132,* 574–579.

Birtchnell, J. (1979). Some MMPI characteristics of psychiatric patients whose breakdown followed recent parent death. *Social Psychiatry, 14,* 181–186.

Block, J. H. (1969). Parents of schizophrenic, neurotic, asthmatic, and congenitally ill children: A comparative study. *Archives of General Psychiatry, 20,* 659–664.

Block, J., Patterson, V., Block, J., & Jackson, D. D. (1958). A study of the parents of schizophrenic and neurotic children. *Psychiatry, 21,* 387–397.

Bloomquist, M. L., & Harris, W. G. (1984). Measuring family functioning with the MMPI: A reliability and concurrent validity study of three MMPI family scales. *Journal of Clinical Psychology, 40,* 1209–1214.

Bonieskie, L. M. (2000). An examination of personality characteristics of child custody litigants on the Rorschach. *Dissertation Abstracts International: Section B: The Sciences and Engineering. 61*(6-B), 3271.

Borkhuis, G. W. (1990). Developmental effects of divorce on children: An MMPI perspective of adolescent personality. *Dissertation Abstracts International, 50,* 4243.

Borkhuis, G. W., & Patalano, F. (1997). MMPI personality differences between adolescents from divorced and non-divorced families. *Psychology—A Quarterly Journal of Human Behavior, 34,* 37–41.

Bosquet, M., & Egeland, B. (2000). Predicting parenting behaviors from Antisocial Practices content scale scores of the MMPI–2 administered during pregnancy. *Journal of Personality Assessment, 74,* 146–162.

Bradley, P. E. (1974). Parental MMPIs and certain pathological behaviors in children. *Journal of Clinical Psychology, 30,* 379–382.

Bresse, P., Stearns, G. B., Bess, B. H., & Packer, L. S. (1986). Allegations of child sexual abuse in child custody disputes: A therapeutic assessment model. *American Journal of Orthopsychiatry, 56,* 550–559.

Browning, J. A. (2003). An exploratory investigation into faking good on the adult attachment interview. *Dissertation Abstracts International: Section B: The Sciences and Engineering, 64*(2-B), 956.

Buikhuisen, W., Plas-Korenhoff, C., & Bontekoe, E. H. (1985). Parental home and deviance. *International Journal of Offender Therapy and Comparative Criminology, 29,* 201–210.

Burger, G. K., Armentraut, J. A., & Rapfogel, R. G. (1975). Recalled parental behavior and objective personality measures: A canonical analysis. *Personality Assessment, 39,* 514–522.

Butcher, J. N. (1965). Manifest aggression: MMPI correlates in normal boys. *Journal of Consulting Psychology, 29,* 446–455.

Butcher, J. N. (1965). Manifest aggression: MMPI correlates in normal boys and their parents. *Dissertation Abstracts International, 25,* 6755–6756.

Butcher, J. N., & Messick D. M. (1966). Parent–child profile similarity and aggression: A preliminary study. *Psychological Reports, 18,* 440–442.

Butcher, J. N., & Pope, K. S. (1992). Forensic psychology: Psychological evaluation in family custody cases—Role of the MMPI-2 and MMPI–A. *Family Law News, 15,* 25–28.

Butcher, J. N., Williams, C. L., Graham, J. R., Tellegen, A., Ben-Porath, Y. S., Archer, R. P., et al. (1992). *Manual for administration, scoring, and interpretation of the Minnesota Multiphasic Personality Inventory for Adolescents: MMPI–A.* Minneapolis: University of Minnesota Press.

Chen, S., Wang, Y., Liu, J., Ji, J., et al. (1992). A preliminary assessment of the personality of parents of learning disabled children and children with attention deficit disorder with hyperkinesias. *Chinese Mental Health Journal, 6,* 246–249.

Clark-Sly, J. B. (1985). The effect of divorce on inpatient psychiatric adolescents: A multivariate analysis of family systems and the ten Minnesota Multiphasic Personality Inventory (MMPI) clinical scales. *Dissertation Abstracts International, 45,* 2681.

Climent, C. E., Plutchik, R., Ervin, F. R., & Rollins, A. (1977). Parental loss, depression and violence: III. Epidemiological studies of female prisoners. *Acta Psychiatrica Scandinavica, 55,* 261–268.

Cohler, B. J., & Grunebaum, H. (1982). Children of parents hospitalized for mental illness: II. The evaluation of an intervention program for mentally ill mothers of young children. *Journal of Children in a Contemporary Society, 15,* 57–66.

Cole, S., Williams, R. L., & Moore, C. H. (1969). Parental interpretation of Rorschach Cards IV and VII among adjusted and maladjusted subjects. *Journal of General Psychology, 81,* 131–135.

Cookerly, J. R. (1974). The reduction of psychopathology as measured by the MMPI clinical scales in three forms of marriage counseling. *Journal of Marriage and Family, 36,* 332.

Cooper, B. (1963). Parents of schizophrenic children compared with the parents of non-psychotic emotionally disturbed and well children: A discriminant function analysis. *Dissertation Abstracts Internation, 24,* 1694.

Cunningham, G. B. (1966). Prediction of staff ratings from personality variables of counselors in training and prediction of intelligence test scores of children from personality variables of parents. *Dissertation Abstracts International, 33BA.*

Da Silva, M. S. (1984). *Presença de Ansiedade em Adolescentes, Relacionada à Searação de Pais Biológicos* [The presence of anxiety in adolescents, related to separation from biological parents]. *PSICO, 9,* 9–65.

Dasteel, J. C. (1982). Stress reactions to marital dissolution as experienced by adults attending courses on divorce. *Journal of Divorce, 5,* 37–47.

David, K. H. (1968). Ego-strength, sex differences, and description of self, ideal and parents. *Journal of General Psychology, 79,* 79–81.

Davids, A. (1970). Personality and attitudes of child care workers, psychotherapists, and parents of children in residential treatment. *Child Psychiatry and Human Development, 1,* 41–49.

Dean, R. S., & Jacobson, B. P. (1982). MMPI characteristics for parents of emotionally disturbed and learning-disabled children. *Journal of Consulting and Clinical Psychology, 50,* 775–777.

Dee, C., & Dee, H. L. (1972). MMPIs of parents of emotionally disturbed, motor dysfunctional, and normal children. *Journal of Consulting and Clinical Psychology, 38,* 464.

Deed, M. L. (1991). Court-ordered child custody evaluations: Helping or victimizing vulnerable families. *Psychotherapy, 28,* 76–84.

Diehl, S. K. (2003). Adult attachment patterns: The relationship between security of attachment and adjustment to prison and separation from loved ones. *Dissertation Abstracts International: Section B: The Sciences and Engineering, 63*(9-B), 4365.

Dietrich, D. R. (1984). Psychological health of young adults who experienced early parent death: MMPI trends. *Journal of Clinical Psychology, 40,* 901–908.

Dixit, R. C., & Mathur, M. B. (1973). Loving and punishing parental behaviour and masculinity-femininity development in school girls. *Journal of Psychological Researches, 17,* 47–49.

Egeland, B., Erickson, N., Butcher, J. N., & Ben Porath, Y. S. (1991). MMPI–2 profiles of women at risk for child abuse. *Journal of Personality Assessment, 57,* 254–263.

Erickson, M. T. (1968). MMPI comparisons between parents of young emotionally disturbed and organically retarded children. *Journal of Consulting and Clinical Psychology, 32,* 701–706.

Erickson, M. T. (1969). MMPI profiles of parents of young retarded children. *American Journal of Mental Deficiency, 73,* 728–732.

Eyberg, S. M., & Robinson, E. A. (1982). Parent–child interaction training: Effects on family functioning. *Journal of Clinical Child Psychology, 11,* 130–137.

Faller, K. C. (1991). Possible explanations for child sexual abuse allegations in divorce. *American Journal of Orthopsychiatry, 61,* 552–557.

Fillion, D. T. (2003). Theoretical taxonomies of child molesters. *Dissertation Abstracts International: Section B: The Sciences and Engineering, 64*(2-B), 961.

Finch, A. (1975). Application of Faschingbauer's abbreviated MMPI to parents of emotionally disturbed children. *Psychological Reports, 37,* 571–574.

Finch, A. (1975). Utility of the Mini-Mult with parents of emotionally disturbed children. *Journal of Personality Assessment, 39,* 146–150.

Finch, A. J., Jr., Griffin, J. L., Jr., & Edwards, G. L. (1974). Abbreviated *Mf* and *Si* scales: Efficacy with parents of emotionally disturbed children. *Journal of Clinical Psychology, 30.*

Firestone, P., & Witt, J. E. (1982). Characteristics of families completing and prematurely discontinuing a behavioral parent-training program. *Journal of Pediatric Psychology, 7,* 209–222.

Fitzelle, G. T. (1959). Personality factors and certain attitudes toward child rearing among parents of asthmatic children. *Psychosomatic Medicine, 21,* 208–217.

Follette, W. C., Naugle, A. E., & Follette, V. M. (1997). MMPI–2 profiles of adult women with child sexual abuse histories: Cluster-analytic findings. *Journal of Consulting and Clinical Psychology, 65,* 858–866.

Gardner, R. A. (1969). The guilt reaction of parents of children with severe physical disease. *American Journal of Psychiatry, 126,* 636–644.

Garrido, M. (1996, June). *Integrating the MMPI–2 and the Thematic Apperception Test for culturally competent evaluations of Latinos: Three cases of Latino parents undergoing child custody evaluations.* Paper presented at the 31st Annual Symposium on Recent Developments in the Use of the MMPI–2/MMPI–A Workshop and Symposia, Minneapolis, MN.

Garrido, M. (2001, March). *The MMPI–2 (Spanish) as indicator of parenting stress among Latinos.* Paper presented at the 36th Annual Symposium on Recent Developments in the Use of the MMPI–2/MMPI–A, Safety Harbor, FL.

Garrido, M., Velasquez, R. J., Reimann, J. O., Parsons, J. P., & Salazar, J. (1997, June). *MMPI–2 performance of Hispanic and White abusive and neglectful parents.* Paper presented at the 32nd Annual Symposium on Recent Developments in the Use of the MMPI–2/MMPI–A Workshop and Symposia, Minneapolis, MN.

Gjerde, C. M. (2001). *Parent–child resemblances in vocational interests and personality traits.* Minneapolis: University of Minnesota Press.

Goodstein, L. D. (1956). MMPI profiles of stutterers' parents: A follow-up study. *Journal of Speech Disorders, 21,* 430–435.

Goodstein, L. D. (1960). MMPI differences between parents of children with cleft palates and parents of physically normal children. *Journal of Speech and Hearing Research, 3,* 31–38.

Goodstein, L. D. (1960). Personality test differences in parents of children with cleft palates. *Journal of Speech and Hearing Research, 3,* 39–43.

Goodstein, L. D., & Dahlstrom, W. G. (1956). MMPI differences between parents of stuttering and nonstuttering children. *Journal of Consulting Psychology, 20,* 365–370.

Goodstein, L. D., & Rowley, V. N. (1961). A further study of MMPI differences between parents of disturbed and nondisturbed children. *Journal of Consulting Psychology, 25,* 460.

Gottheil, E., Paredes, A., & Exline, R. V. (1968). Parental schemata in emotionally disturbed women. *Journal of Abnormal Psychology, 73,* 416–419.

Gregg, P. A. (1998). The effect of impression management on correlations between Rorschach and MMPI–2 variables. *Dissertation Abstracts International: Section B: The Sciences and Engineering, 58*(9-B), 5185.

Gregory, I. (1965). Anterospective data following childhood loss of a parent: Delinquency and high school dropout. *Archives of General Psychiatry, 13,* 99–109.

Gregory, I. (1966). Retrospective data concerning childhood loss of a parent: II. Category of parental loss by decade of birth, diagnosis, and MMPI. *Archives of General Psychiatry, 15,* 362–367.

Griffin, J. (1976). MMPI/Midi–Multi correspondence with parents of emotionally disturbed children. *Journal of Clinical Psychology, 32,* 54–56.

Gross, S. Z. (1964). A normative study and cross-validation of MMPI subtle and obvious scales for parents seen at a child guidance clinic. *Psychology, 1,* 5–7.

Grossman, D. J. (1952). A study of the parents of stuttering and non-stuttering children using the Minnesota Multiphasic Personality Inventory and the Minnesota Scale of Parents' Opinions. *Speech Monographs, 19,* 193–194.

Hackney, G. R., & Ribordy, S. C. (1980). An empirical investigation of emotional reactions to divorce. *Journal of Clinical Psychology, 36,* 105–110.

Hafner, A. J., Butcher, J. N., Hall, M. D., & Quast, W. (1969). Comparisons of MMPI studies of parents. In J. N. Butcher (Ed.), *Recent developments in the use of the MMPI* (pp. 297–322). New York: McGraw-Hill.

Hafner, A. J., Butcher, J. N., Hall, M. D., & Quast, W. (1969). Parent personality and childhood disorder: A review of MMPI findings. In J. N. Butcher (Ed.), *MMPI: Research developments and clinical applications* (pp. 181–189). New York: McGraw Hill.

Hall, G. C., Maiuro, R., Vitaliano, P., & Proctor, W. (1986). The utility of the MMPI with men who have sexually assaulted children. *Journal of Consulting and Clinical Psychology, 54,* 111–112.

Hall, G. C., Shepherd, J. B., & Mudrak, P. (1992). MMPI taxonomies of child sexual and nonsexual offenders: A cross-validation and extension. *Journal of Personality Assessment, 58,* 127–137.

Hall, M. D. (1966). *Personality characteristics of parents with children with learning problems.* Unpublished work.

Han, K., Weed, N. C., & Butcher, J. N. (2003). Dyadic agreement on the MMPI–2. *Personality and Individual Differences, 35,* 603–615.

Hanvik, L. J. B. M. (1959). MMPI profiles of parents of child psychiatric patients. *Journal of Clinical Psychology, 15,* 427–431.

Hartman-Crouch, T. S. (2000). The Minnesota Multiphasic Personality Inventory–2 in the context of child custody litigation. *Dissertation Abstracts International: Section B: The Sciences and Engineering, 61*(5-B), 2762.

Heilbrun, A. B. (1964). Social value: Social behavior consistency, parental identification, and aggression in late adolescence. *Journal of Genetic Psychology, 104,* 135–146.

Heilbrun, A. B., Jr., Orr, H. K., & Harrell, S. N. (1966). Patterns of parental childrearing and subsequent vulnerability to cognitive disturbance. *Journal of Consulting Psychology, 30,* 51–59.

Heinicke, C. M., Diskin, S. D., Ramsey-Klee, D. M., & Given, K. (1983). Pre-birth parent characteristics and family development in the first year of life. *Child Development, 54,* 194–208.

Hill, M. S., & Hill, R. N. (1973). Hereditary influence on the normal personality using the MMPI: I. Age-corrected parent–offspring resemblances. *Behavior Genetics, 3,* 133–144.

Hjemboe, S., Almagor, M., & Butcher, J. N. (1992). Empirical assessment of marital distress: The Marital Distress Scale (MDS) for the MMPI–2. In C. D. Spielberger & J. N. Butcher (Eds.), *Advances in personality assessment* (Vol. 9, pp. 141–152). Hillsdale, NJ: Erlbaum.

Hjemboe, S., & Butcher, J. N. (1991). Couples in marital distress: A study of demographic and personality factors as measured by the MMPI–2. *Journal of Personality Assessment, 57,* 216–237.

Holmes, G. R., Sabalis, R. F., Chestnut, E., & Khoury, L. (1984). Parent MMPI critical item and clinical scale changes in the 1970s. *Journal of Clinical Psychology, 40,* 1194–1198.

Holmes, G. R., Sabalis, R. F., Chestnut, E., & Sheppard, B. (1986). Comparison of MMPI clinical scale and critical item changes of adult outpatients and parents of child psychiatry outpatients during the 1970s. *Journal of Clinical Psychology, 42,* 913–916.

Hooker, E. (1969). Parental relations and male homosexuality in patient and nonpatient samples. *Journal of Consulting and Clinical Psychology, 33,* 140–142.

Hopkins, L. C. (1999). The role of the *K*-scale as a validity measure in court-ordered child custody MMPIs. *Dissertation Abstracts International, 60,* 3010.

Hunt, M. E. (1999). A comparison between MMPI and CPI adult profiles of children of alcoholics and nonalcoholics. *Substance Use and Misuse, 34,* 921–933.

Hunter, J. A., Childers, S. E., & Esmaili, H. (1990). An examination of variables differentiating clinical sub-types of incestuous child molesters. *International Journal of Offender Therapy and Comparative Criminology, 34,* 95–104

Kalhorn, J. (1947). Personality and parent behavior. *American Psychologist, 2,* 425,

Kalichman, S. C., & Henderson, M. C. (1991). MMPI profile subtypes of nonincarcerated child molesters. *Criminal Justice and Behavior, 18,* 379–396.

Keilin, W. G., & Bloome, L. J. (1986). Child custody evaluation practices: A survey of experienced professionals. *Professional Psychology: Research and Practice, 17,* 338–346.

Kennelly, J. J. (2002). Rorschach responding and response sets in child custody evaluations. *Dissertation Abstracts International: Section B: The Sciences and Engineering, 63*(6-B), 3034.

Khan, F. I., Welch, T., & Zilmer, E. (1993). MMPI–2 profiles of battered women in transition. *Journal of Personality Assessment, 60,* 100–111.

Klinge, V. (1983). A comparison of parental and adolescent MMPIs as related to substance use. *International Journal of the Addictions, 18,* 1179–1185.

Knisely, J. S., Barker, S. B., Ingersoll, K. S., & Dawson, K. S. (2000). Psychopathology in substance abusing women reporting childhood sexual abuse. *Journal of Addictive Diseases, 19*(1), 31–44.

Koch, D. A., Chandler, M. J., Harder, D. W., & Paget, K. F. (1982). Parental defense style and child competence: A match–mismatch hypothesis. *Journal of Applied Developmental Psychology, 3,* 11–21.

Koegel, R. L., Schreibman, L., O'Neill, R. E., & Burke, J. C. (1983). The personality and family-interaction characteristics of parents of autistic children. *Journal of Consulting and Clinical Psychology, 51,* 683–692.

Kordinak, S. T. (1995, March). *Marital distress in dual career law enforcement couples.* Paper presented at the 30th Annual Symposium on Recent Developments in the Use of the MMPI–2/MMPI–A Workshop and Symposia, St. Petersburg, FL.

Krinke, A., Krinkova, L., & Moll, I. (1987). Srovnáni osobnostnich charackteristik partneru z funkcnich a psychologicky soudne znalecky rešenych (následne rozvedenych) manzelstvi ve vysledcich MMPI [Comparison of personality traits of spouses from functional marriages and marriages resolved by psychological and legal processes (and ending in divorce) based on MMPI results]. *Ceskoslovenska Psychologie, 31,* 333–336.

Kwall, D. S., & Lackner, F. M. (1966). Ability, sociometric and parent–child relationship variables in the prediction of elementary school achievement. *Proceedings of the Annual Convention of the American Psychological Association,* 273–274.

L'Abate, L. (1956). The personality of problem parents. *American Psychologist, 11,* 415.

Lahey, B. B., Russo, M. F., Walker, J. L., & Piacentini, J. C. (1989). Personality characteristics of mothers of children with disruptive behavior disorders. *Journal of Consulting and Clinical Psychology, 57,* 512–515.

Lauterbach, C. G., London, P., & Bryan, J. (1961). MMPI's of parents of child guidance cases. *Journal of Clinical Psychology, 17,* 151–154.

Lauterbach, C. G., Schafer, E. S., & Vogel, W. (1964). Reports of parents' behavior and the MMPIs of psychiatrically disturbed soldiers. *American Psychologist, 19,* 186.

Lauterbach, C. G., Vogel, W., & Hart, J. (1962). Comparison of the MMPI's of male problem adolescents and their parents. *Journal of Clinical Psychology, 18,* 485–487.

Lefkowitz, M. M., & Huesmann, L. (1978). Parental punishment: A longitudinal analysis of effects. *Archives of General Psychiatry, 35,* 186–191.

Levitt, E. E. (1959). A comparison of parental and self-evaluations of psychopathology in children. *Journal of Clinical Psychology, 15,* 402–404.

Lichtman, H. (1984). Parental communication of Holocaust experiences and personality characteristics among second-generation survivors. *Journal of Clinical Psychology, 40,* 914–924.

Lipson, K. J., Stevens, M. J., Graybill, D., & Mark, K. I. (1995). MMPI–2 and family environment differences between bulimic and nonbulimic women and their parents. *Assessment, 2,* 203–218.

Liverant, S. (1959). MMPI differences between parents of disturbed and nondisturbed children. *Journal of Consulting Psychology, 23,* 256–260.

Loeb, J. (1966). The personality factor in divorce. *Journal of Consulting Psychology, 30,* 562.

Loeb, J., & Price, J. R. (1966). Mother and child personality characteristics related to parental marital status in child guidance cases. *Journal of Consulting Psychology, 30,* 112–117.

Lund, S. N. (1975). *Personality and personal history factors of child abusing parents.* Unpublished doctoral dissertation, University of Minnesota, Minneapolis.

Martin, C. V., & Channell, L. H. (1964). Personality and social history characteristics of delinquents and their parents. *Corrective Psychiatry and Journal of Social Therapy, 10,* 93–107.

Marzoff, S. (1965). Parent behavior as reported by college students. *Journal of Clinical Psychology, 21,* 360–366.

McAdoo, W. G. (1974). The application of Goldberg's classification rules to parents in a child guidance clinic and in an adult psychiatric clinic. *Journal of Community Psychology, 2,* 174–175.

McAdoo, W. G., & Connolly, F. J. (1975). MMPIs of parents in dysfunctional families. *Journal of Consulting and Clinical Psychology, 43,* 270.

McCann, J. T. (1998). *Malingering and deception in adolescents.* Washington, DC: American Psychological Association.

McConaghy, N., & Clancy, M. (1968). Familial relationships of allusive thinking in university students and their parents. *British Journal of Psychiatry, 114,* 1079–1087.

McCranie, E. W., & Kahan, J. (1986). Personality and multiple divorce: A prospective study. *Journal of Nervous and Mental Disease, 174,* 161–164.

McDonald, R. L. (1965). Ego control patterns and attribution of hostility to self, parents, and others. *Perceptual and Motor Skills, 21,* 340–348.

Medoff, D. (1999). MMPI–2 validity scales in child custody evaluations: Clinical versus statistical significance. *Behavioral Sciences and the Law, 17,* 409–411.

Miller, W. (1974). Predicting behavioral treatment outcome in disturbed children: A preliminary report of the Responsivity Index of Parents (RIP). *Behavior Therapy, 5,* 210–214.

Miller, W. H., & Kerin, W. C. (1978). Personality measurement in parents of retarded and emotionally disturbed children: A replication. *Journal of Clinical Psychology, 34,* 686–690.

Minor, K. I., Karr, S. K., & Jain, S. K. (1987). An examination of the utility of the MMPI in predicting male prison inmates' abusive parenting attitudes *Psychological Record, 37,* 429–436.

Mlott, S. R. (1972). Some significant relationships between adolescents and their parents as revealed by the Minnesota Multiphasic Personality Inventory. *Adolescence, 7,* 169–182.

Morrell, J. S., & Rubin, J. L. (2001). The Minnesota Multiphasic Personality Inventory—2, posttraumatic stress disorder, and women domestic violence survivors. *Professional Psychology: Research and Practice, 32,* 151–156.

Mosby, D. V. P. (1966). Maternal "identification" and perceived similarity to parents in adolescents as a function of grade placement. *Dissertation Abstracts, 26,* 6841.

Mrazek, D. A., Klinnert, M. D., Mrazek, P., & Macey, T. (1991). Early asthma onset: Consideration of parenting issues. *Journal of the American Academy of Child and Adolescent Psychiatry, 30,* 277–282.

Murstein, B. I. (1967). The relationship of mental health to marital choice and courtship progress. *Journal of Marriage and the Family, 29,* 447–451.

Murstein, B. I., & Glaudin, V. (1968). The use of the MMPI in the determination of marital adjustment. *Journal of Marriage and Family, 30,* 651–655.

Nelson, C., & Valliant, P. (1993). Personality dynamics of adolescent boys where the father was absent. *Perceptual and Motor Skills, 76*(2), 435–443.

Ollendick, D. G. (1984). Scores on three MMPI alcohol scales of parents who receive child custody. *Psychological Reports, 55,* 337–338.

Ollendick, D. G., & Otto, B. J. (1984). MMPI characteristics of parents referred for child-custody studies. *Journal of Psychology, 117,* 227–232.

Olsinski, P. K. (1980). A study of the effect of some Minnesota Multiphasic Personality characteristics on the adjustment of married, marriage counseled and divorced individuals. *Dissertation Abstracts International, 41,* 539.

O'Reilly, B. P., Graham, J. R., Hjemboe, S. M., & Butcher, J. N. (2003, June). *The construct validity of the MMPI–2 marital distress scale.* Paper presented at the 38th MMPI–2 Conference on Recent Developments in the Use of the MMPI–2 and MMPI–A Workshop and Symposia, Minneapolis, MN.

Osborne, D. (1971). An MMPI index of disturbed marital interaction. *Psychological Reports, 29,* 851–854.

Otto, R. K., & Butcher, J. N. (1995). Computer-assisted psychological assessment in child custody evaluations. *Family Law Quarterly, 29,* 79–96.

Otto, R. K., & Collins, R. P. (1995). Use of the MMPI–2/MMPI–A in child custody evaluations. In Y. S. Ben-Porath, J. Graham, G. Hall, R. Hirschman, & M. Zaragosa (Eds.), *Forensic applications of the MMPI–2* (pp. 222–252). New York: Wiley.

Patterson, G. R. (1965). Parents as dispensers of aversive stimuli. *Journal of Personality and Social Psychology, 2,* 844–851.

Paulson, M. J. (1975). A MMPI scale for identifying "at risk" abusive parents. *Journal of Clinical Child Psychology, 4,* 22–24.

Paulson, M. J., Afifi, A., Chaleff, A., Thomason, M., & Lui, V. (1975). An MMPI scale for identifying at risk abusive parents. *Journal of Clinical Child Psychology, 4,* 22–24.

Paulson, M. J., Afifi, A. A., Thomason, M. L., & Chaleff, A. (1974). The MMPI: A descriptive measure of psychopathology in abusive parents. *Journal of Clinical Psychology, 30,* 387–390.

Paulson, M. J., Schwemer, G. T., & Bendel, R. B. (1976). Clinical application of the *Pd, Ma* and (*OH*) experimental MMPI scales to further understanding of abusive parents. *Journal of Clinical Psychology, 32,* 558–564.

Perr, H. M. (1958). Criteria distinguishing parents of schizophrenic and normal children: An initial study with the interpersonal diagnostic system. *Archives of Neurology and Psychiatry, 79,* 217–224.

Peyrot, M. (1995). Psychological testing and forensic decision making: The properties-in-use of the MMPI. *Social Problems, 42*(4), 574–586.

Plotkin, R. C., Twentyman, C. T., & Perri, M. G. (1982). The utility of a measure of aggression in differentiating abusing parents from other parents who are experiencing familial disturbance. *Journal of Clinical Psychology, 38,* 607–610.

Posthuma, A. (2003). A new MMPI–2 scale for custody disputes. *American Journal of Forensic Psychology, 21,* 51–64.

Posthuma, A. B., & Harper, J. F. (1998). Comparison of MMPI–2 responses of child custody and personal injury litigants. *Professional Psychology: Research and Practice, 29,* 437–443.

Rangel, S. J., Yanez, E. M., Jaghab, K., & Velasquez, R. J. (2001, March). *MMPI–2 correlates for neglectful/abusive Latino and non-Latino parents: Preliminary results.* Paper presented at the 36th Annual Symposium on Recent Developments in the Use of the MMPI–2/MMPI–A, Safety Harbor, FL.

Ray, J. J., & Ray, J. A. (1982). Some apparent advantages of subclinical psychopathy. *Journal of Social Psychology, 117,* 135–142.

Remschmidt, H., Strunk, P., Methner, C., & Tegeler, E. (1973). Children of endogenically depressive parents: An investigation in the frequency of behavior disturbances and of personality structure. *Fortschritte der Neurologie, Psychiatrie und Ihrer Grenzgebiete, 41*, 326–340.

Ritzler, B. (1981). Predicting offspring vulnerability to psychopathology from parents' test data. *Journal of Personality Assessment, 45*, 600–607.

Roeder, V. (1996). Differences in MMPI–2 and MMPI scales *Hs, Hy, Pa,* and *R* of parents making unfounded allegations of child sexual abuse while involved in child custody disputes. *Dissertation Abstracts International, 57*, 4041.

Rosenstein, A. (1960). A comparative study of the role conflict, marital adjustment, and personality configuration of private adoptive and agency adoptive parents. *Dissertation Abstracts International, 20*, 4208.

Schmidtgall, K., King, A., Zarski, J. J., & Cooper, J. E. (2000). The effects of parental conflict on later child development. *Journal of Divorce and Remarriage, 33*, 157.

Schubert, D. (1969). Decrease of rated adjustment on repeat DAP tests apparently due to lower motivation. *Journal of Projective Techniques and Personality Assessment, 33*, 34.

Schubert, D. S. (1973). Increase of apparent adjustment in adolescence by further ego identity formation and age. *College Student Journal, 7*, 3–6.

Schulte, S., Anderson, U., & Velasquez, R. J. (2001, March). *Socio-demographic and MMPI–2 characteristics of foster parent applicants.* Paper presented at the 36th Annual Symposium on Recent Developments in the Use of the MMPI–2/MMPI–A, Safety Harbor, FL.

Schultz, J. P., Firetto, A., & Walker, R. E. (1969). The relationship of parental assessment and anxiety in high school freshmen. *Psychology in the Schools, 6*, 311–312.

Scott, R., & Stone, D. (1986). Measures of psychological disturbance in adolescent and adult victims of father–daughter incest. *Journal of Clinical Psychology, 42*, 251–269.

Scott, R., & Stone, D. (1986). MMPI profile constellations in incest families. *Journal of Consulting and Clinical Psychology, 54*, 364–368.

Shane, D. S. (1980). Joint Parental Personality Inventory profiles related to adolescent psychopathology. *Dissertation Abstracts International, 41*, 1526.

Shapiro, T. H. (1978). A comparison of counseling MMPI profiles of couples who remain married with those who divorce. *Dissertation Abstracts International, 38*, 3965–3966.

Sharp, J. R. (1979). The relationship between parental MMPIs and the dimensions of child problem behavior. *Dissertation Abstracts International, 40*, 1914–1915.

Sher, K. J., & McCrady, B. S. (1984). The Mac-Andrew Alcoholism Scale: Severity of alcohol abuse and parental alcoholism. *Addictive Behaviors, 9*, 99–102.

Siegel, J. C. (1996). Traditional MMPI–2 validity indicators and initial presentation in custody evaluations. *American Journal of Forensic Psychology, 14*, 55–63.

Siegel, J. C., & Langford, J. S. (1998). MMPI–2 validity scales and suspected parental alienation syndrome. *American Journal of Forensic Psychology, 16*, 5–14.

Simon, W., & Lumry, G. K. (1970). Suicide of the spouse as a divorce substitute. *Diseases of the Nervous System, 31*, 608–612.

Sklar, A. D., & Harris, R. F. (1985). Effects of parent loss: Interaction with family size and sibling order. *American Journal of Psychiatry, 142*, 708–714.

Slater, P. E. (1962). Parental behavior and the personality of the child. *Journal of Genetic Psychology, 101*, 53–68.

Smith, D. W., & Frueh, B. (1996). Compensation seeking, comorbidity, and apparent exaggeration of PTSD symptoms among Vietnam combat veterans. *Psychological Assessment, 8*, 3–6.

Snortum, J. (1970). The relationship of self-concept and parent image to rule violations in a women's prison. *Journal of Clinical Psychology, 26*, 284–287.

Snyder, D. K., Cozzi, J. J., & Baucom, D. H. (1998, March). *Replicated MMPI subtypes of couples entering marital therapy.* Paper presented at the 33rd Annual Symposium on Recent Developments in the Use of the MMPI–2/MMPI–A Workshop and Symposia, Clearwater Beach, FL.

Snyder, D., & Regts, J. M. (1990). Personality correlates of marital satisfaction: A comparison of psychiatric, maritally distressed, and nonclinic samples. *Journal of Sex and Marital Therapy, 16,* 34–43.

Snyder, D. K., Velasquez, J. M., Clark, B. L., & Means-Christensen, A. J. (1997). Parental influence on gender and marital role attitudes: Implications for intervention. *Journal of Marital and Family Therapy, 23,* 191–201.

Somera, M., Schulte, S., & Velasquez, R. J. (2001, March). *Personality disorders and MMPI–2: Foster parent applicants.* Paper presented at the 36th Annual Symposium on Recent Developments in the Use of the MMPI–2/MMPI–A, Safety Harbor, FL.

Sopchak, A. L. (1952). Parental "identification" and "tendency toward disorders" as measured by the Minnesota Multiphasic Personality Inventory. *Journal of Abnormal and Social Psychology, 47,* 159–165.

Sopchak, A. L. (1952). *Personality and identification with parents.* Unpublished dissertation, Syracuse University, Syracuse, NY.

Sopchak, A. L. (1956). Projective study of Peter and his parents; revealing the necessary therapeutic limitations. *Journal of Child Psychiatry, 3,* 149–200.

Sopchak, A. L. (1958). Spearman correlations between MMPI scores of college students and their parents. *Journal of Consulting Psychology, 22,* 207–209.

Spivey, P. B., & Scherman, A. (1980). The effects of time lapse on personality characteristics and stress on divorced women. *Journal of Divorce, 4,* 49–59.

Strong, D. R., Greene, R. L., Hoppe, C., Johnston, T., & Olesen, N. (1999). Taxometric analysis of impression management and self-deception on the MMPI–2 in child-custody litigants. *Journal of Personality Assessment, 73,* 1–18.

Svanum, S., & McAdoo, W. G. (1991). Parental alcoholism: An examination of male and female alcoholics in treatment. *Journal of Studies on Alcohol, 52,* 127–132.

Swan, R. J. (1957). Using the MMPI in marriage counseling. *Journal of Counseling Psychology, 4,* 239–244.

Thomas, E., Rickel, A. U., Butler, C., & Montgomery, E. (1990). Adolescent pregnancy and parenting. *Journal of Primary Prevention, 10,* 195–206.

Townsend, J. K. (1969). Reports of parent behavior (RPBI) related to current behavior and MMPI scores in female psychiatric inpatients. *Dissertation Abstracts International, 29,* 2642.

Tuchman, S. (2003). Personality characteristics of parents who have been court-ordered to have supervised visitation with their children: An exploratory study. *Dissertation Abstracts International: Section B: The Sciences and Engineering, 64,* 1538.

Valliant, P. M., Jensen, B., & Raven-Brook, L. (1995). Brief cognitive behavioural therapy with male adolescent offenders in open custody or on probation: An evaluation of management of anger. *Psychological Reports, 76,* 1056–1058.

Velligan, D., Christensen, A., Goldstein, M. J., & Margolin, G. (1988). Parental communication deviance: Its relationship to parent, child, and family system variables. *Psychiatry Research, 26,* 313–325.

Vincent, K. R., Linsz, N. L., & Greene, M. I. (1966). The *L* scale on the MMPI as an index of falsification. *Journal of Clinical and Consulting Psychology, 12,* 214–215.

Vogel, W., & Lauterbach, C. (1963). Relationships between normal and disturbed sons' percepts of their parents' behavior and personality attributes of the parents and sons. *Journal of Clinical Psychology, 19,* 52–56.

Wangberg, D. K. (2000). Child custody evaluation practices: A survey of experienced clinical psychologists. *Dissertation Abstracts International: Section B: The Sciences and Engineering, 61*(2-B), 1100.

White R. J. (1997, June). *An examination of marital satisfaction and MMPI–2 profiles of veterans wives.* Paper presented at the 32nd Annual Symposium on Recent Developments in the Use of the MMPI–2/MMPI–A Workshop and Symposia, Minneapolis, MN.

Williams, C. L., Perry, C. L., Farbakhsh, K., & Veblen-Mortenson, S. (1999). Project Northland: Comprehensive alcohol use prevention for young adolescents, their parents, schools, peers and communities. *Journal of Studies on Alcohol—Supplement, 13,* 112–124.

Williams, J. T. (1951). *A study of the parents of cerebral palsied and non-cerebral palsied children using the Minnesota Multiphasic Personality Inventory.* Madison: University of Wisconsin.

Williams, J. T. (1952). A study of the parents of cerebral palsied and non-cerebral palsied children using the Minnesota Multiphasic Personality Inventory. *Speech Monographs, 19,* 199.

Wilson, D. L. (1995). College students' alcohol use, parental–familial alcohol use, and family of origin. *Dissertation Abstracts International, 56,* 2949.

Wilson, I. C., Carson, R., & Rabon, A. (1969). Parental bereavement in childhood: MMPI profiles in a depressed population. *North Carolina Journal of Mental Health, 3,* 58–59.

Wilson, T. E., White, T. L., & Heiber, R. G. (1985). Reparenting schizophrenic youth in a hospital setting. *Transactional Analysis Journal, 15,* 211–215.

Winder, P. H., Rosenthal, D., Rainer, J. D., Greenhill, L., & Sarling, B. (1977). Schizophrenics' adopting parents. *Archives of General Psychiatry, 34,* 777–784.

Wolff, W. M., & Morris, L. A. (1971). Intellectual and personality characteristics of parents of autistic children. *Journal of Abnormal Psychology, 77,* 155–161.

Wolking, W. (1966). MMPI profiles of the parents of behaviorally disturbed children and parents from the general population. *Journal of Clinical Psychology, 22,* 39–48.

Wolking, W. D., Dunteman, G. H., & Bailey, J. P. (1967). Multivariate analyses of parents' MMPIs based on the psychiatric diagnoses of their children. *Journal of Consulting Psychology, 31,* 521–524.

Wood, D. D. (1971). Parental identification in thought, feeling, and action in schizophrenic males. *Dissertation Abstracts International, 31,* 6272–6273.

Woodward, W. T. (1991). Psychopathic deviate subscales in the MMPI profiles of marital counselees: A comparison of those who remain married and those who divorce. *Dissertation Abstracts International, 51,* 6122.

Workman, M., & Beer, J. (1992). Aggression, alcohol dependency, and self-consciousness among high school students of divorced and nondivorced parents. *Psychological Reports, 71,* 279–286.

Wright, L. (1976). The "sick but slick" syndrome as a personality component of parents of battered children. *Journal of Clinical Psychology, 32,* 41–45.

Wrobel, N. H., & Lacher, D. (1992). Refining adolescent MMPI interpretations: Moderating effects of gender in prediction of descriptions from parents. *Psychological Assessment, 4,* 375–381.

Yanagida, E., & Chin, W. J. (1993). MMPI profiles of child abusers. *Journal of Clinical Psychology, 49,* 569–576.

Zokik, E., & Welsand, E. (1963). Changes in parental attitudes as a function of anxiety and authoritarianism. *Journal of Social Psychology, 60,* 293–300.

Assessment in Criminal/Prison Settings References

This appendix covers topics related to crime, delinquency, and imprisonment: pre-trial assessments; classification of felons; assessment of various criminal populations such as murderers, sex offenders, and delinquents; and evaluation of prison variables including prison adjustment, rehabilitation, and parole.

Aalsma, M. C. (2000). An empirical typology of adolescent delinquency. *Dissertation Abstracts International, 61,* 1107.

Abdel-Meguid, S. G. M. (1954). Delinquency related to personality, intelligence, school achievement, and environmental factors. *Dissertation Abstracts International Stanford University, 14,* 1204.

Abe, M. (1969). The Japanese MMPI and its delinquency scale. *Tohoku Psychologica Folia, 28,* 54–68.

Adams, T. C. (1976). Some MMPI differences between first and multiple admissions with a state prison population. *Journal of Clinical Psychology, 32,* 555–558.

Aldridge, N. C. (1999). Evaluating treatment for sex offenders: A pretest–posttest and follow-up study (treatment evaluation, recidivism). *Dissertation Abstracts International: Section B: The Sciences and Engineering. 60*(5-B), 2376.

Altus, W. D. (1953). Adjustment items which differentiate between psychiatric categories of military general prisoners. *Journal of General Psychology, 49,* 293–301.

Anderson, W. P., & Holcomb, W. (1983). Accused murderers: Five MMPI personality types. *Journal of Clinical Psychology, 39,* 761–768.

Anderson, W. P., Kunce, J. T., & Rich, B. (1979). Sex offenders: Three personality types. *Journal of Clinical Psychology, 35*(3), 671–676.

Arce, R., del Carmen Pampillon, M., & Farina, F. (2002). *Desarrollo y evaluación de un procedimiento empirico para detección de la simulación de enajenación mental en ei contexto legal* [Development and assessment of an empirical procedure for detecting simulated mental insanity in the legal context]. *Anuario de Psicologia, 33*(3), 385–408.

Archer, R. P., Bollnskey, P. K., Morton, T. L., & Farris, K. L. (2003). MMPI–A characteristics of male adolescents in juvenile justice and clinical treatment settings. *Assessment, 10*(4), 400–410.

Armentrout, J. A., & Hauer, A. L. (1978). MMPIs of rapists of adults, rapists of children, and non-rapist sex offenders. *Journal of Clinical Psychology, 34*(2), 330–332.

Ashbaugh, J. H. (1953). Personality patterns of juvenile delinquents in an area of small population. In S. R. Hathaway & E. D. Monachesi (Eds.), *Analyzing and predicting juvenile delinquency with the MMPI* (pp. 54–60). Minneapolis: University of Minnesota Press.

Austin, J. S. (1990). The detection of malingering in forensic inpatients: A look at the MMPI and MCMI. *Dissertation Abstracts International, 50*(7-A), 1981.

Bailey, C., Diehl, S., Dujardin, J. P., & Garrido, M. (2001, March). *MMPI–2 scales as indicators of rehabilitative needs of prison inmates: Exploring the importance of crime committed and substance abuse patterns.* Paper presented at the 36th Annual Symposium on Recent Developments in the Use of the MMPI–2/MMPI–A, Safety Harbor, FL.

Baldwin, K. C. (1997). Factors associated with denial in a sample of alleged sex offenders. *Dissertation Abstracts International: Section B: The Sciences and Engineering, 57*(8-B), 5315.

Baldwin, K., & Roys, D. T. (1998). Factors associated with denial in a sample of alleged adult sexual offenders. *Sexual Abuse: Journal of Research and Treatment, 10*(3), 211–226.

Baltes, P. B., Wender, K., & Steigerwald, F. (1968). Discriminatory analysis with the help of the Saarbrucken MMPI on the problem of male juvenile delinquency. *Zeitschrift für Experimentelle und Angewandte Psychologie, 15,* 404–418.

Barnard, G. W., Robbins, L., Tingle, D., & Shaw, T. (1987). Development of a computerized sexual assessment laboratory. *Bulletin of the American Academy of Psychiatry and the Law, 15*(4), 339–347.

Baron, A. T. (2003). Differences in psychopathology, temperament, and family/social history relative to the onset of sexual perpetration in youthful offenders. *Dissertation Abstracts International: Section B: The Sciences and Engineering, 63*(10-B), 4889.

Barrilleaux, G. S. (1997). Patterns of change in outpatient group treatment of adult male child sexual offenders. *Dissertation Abstracts International: Section B: The Sciences and Engineering, 57*(9-B), 5906.

Bassett, J. E., Schellman, G. C., Gayton, W. F., & Tavormina, J. (1977). Efficacy of the Mini–Multi validity scales with prisoners. *Journal of Clinical Psychology, 33,* 729–731.

Bauer, G. E., & Clark, J. A. (1976). Personality deviancy and prison incarceration. *Journal of Clinical Psychology, 32,* 279–283.

Baughman, J., & Pierce, D. (1972). MMPI correlates of prisoners' ideal-self. *Correctional Psychologist,* 194–199.

Beall, H. S., & Panton J. H. (1957). *Development of a prison adjustment scale (PAS) for the MMPI.* Unpublished work.

Becker, P. W. (1965). Some correlates of delinquency and validity of questionnaire assessment methods. *Psychological Reports, 16,* 271–277.

Bennett, L. A. (1970). Test taking "insight" of prison inmates and subsequent parole adjustment. *Correctional Psychologist, 4,* 27–34.

Ben-Porath, Y. S., Shondrick, D., & Stafford, K. (1994). MMPI–2 and race in a forensic diagnostic sample. *Criminal Justice and Behavior, 22,* 19–32.

Blackburn, R. (1968). Personality in relation to extreme aggression in psychiatric offenders. *British Journal of Psychiatry, 114,* 821–828.

Blum, S. H. (1985). The prediction of recorded delinquency using obvious, subtle, and neutral MMPI psychopathic deviate (*Pd*) items. *Dissertation Abstracts International, 46,* 294–295.

Boardman, A. F. (1996). A comparative investigation of insanity acquittees and unsuccessful insanity evaluatees. *Dissertation Abstracts International: Section B: The Sciences and Engineering, 56*(12-B), 7038.

Boehnert, C. E. (1987). Characteristics of those evaluated for insanity. *Journal of Psychiatry and Law, 15*(2), 229–246.

Boehnert, C. E. (1987). Typology of men unsuccessfully raising the insanity defense. *Journal of Psychiatry and Law, 15*(3), 417–424.

Bohn, M. J., Jr. (1978, July). *Classification of offenders in an institution for young adults.* Paper presented at the 19th International Congress of Applied Psychology, Munich, Germany.

Bohn, M. J., Jr. (1979). Management classification for young adult inmates. *Federal Probation, 43*(4), 53–59.

Booth, R. J. (1980). Classification of prison inmates with the MMPI: An extension and validation of the Megargee typology. *Dissertation Abstracts International, 41,* 1493.

Booth, R. J., & Howell, R. J. (1980). Classification of prison inmates with the MMPI: An extension and validation of the Megargee typology. *Criminal Justice and Behavior, 7,* 407–422.

Borum, R., & Grisso, T. (1995). Psychological test use in criminal forensic evaluations. *Professional Psychology: Research and Practice, 26,* 465–473.

Briggs, P. F., Johnson, R., & Wirt, R. D. (1962). Achievement among delinquency-prone adolescents. *Journal of Clinical Psychology, 18,* 305–309.

Briggs, P. F., Wirt, R. D., & Johnson, R. (1961). An application of prediction tables to the study of delinquency. *Journal of Consulting Psychology, 25,* 46–50.

Brodsky, S. L. (1967). *Collected papers in prison psychology.* Fort Leavenworth, KS: U.S. Disciplinary-Barracks.

Brodsky, S. L. (1968). Excessive dispensary users in the military prison. *Military Medicine, 133,* 368–371.

Brodsky, S. L., Mehaffey, T. D., & Rhoads, R. H. (1965). Biographical and psychodiagnostic dimensions of behavioral adjustment to the military prison. *Military Medicine, 130,* 480–484.

Brown, H. (1985). Cognitions associated with a delay of gratification task: A study with psychopaths and normal prisoners. *Criminal Justice and Behavior, 12,* 453–462.

Butcher, J. N. (2001). Assessment in forensic practice: An objective approach. In B. Van Dorsten (Ed.), *Forensic psychology: From classroom to courtroom* (pp. 65–82). New York: Kluwer Academic Press.

Caldwell, M. G. (1953). The youthful male offender in Alabama: A study in delinquency causation. *Sociology and Social Research, 37,* 236–243.

Campbell, T. W. (1992). The "highest level of psychological certainty": Betraying standards of practice in forensic psychology. *American Journal of Forensic Psychology, 10*(2), 35–48.

Cannici, J. P., Glick, S., & Garmon, S. (1989). Ego-strength changes associated with incarceration in males and females. *Journal of Offender Counseling Services and Rehabilitation, 14*(1), 31–35.

Capasso, R. J. (1995). Identifying delinquency proneness in adolescents using the MMPI–A. *Dissertation Abstracts International, 55,* 4601.

Capwell, D. F. (1945). Personality patterns of adolescent girls, II. Delinquents and non-delinquents. *Journal of Applied Psychology, 29,* 284–297.

Capwell, D. F. (1953). Study 1, personality patterns of adolescent girls: Delinquents and nondelinquents. In S. R. Hathaway & E. O. Monachesi (Eds.), *Analyzing and predicting juvenile delinquency with the MMPI* (pp. 29–37). Minneapolis: University of Minnesota Press.

Carbonell, J. L., Moorhead, K. M., & Megargee, E. I. (1984). Predicting prison adjustment with structured personality inventories. *Journal of Consulting and Clinical Psychology, 52,* 280–294.

Card, R. D., & Dibble, A. (1995). Predictive value of the Card/Farrall stimuli in discriminating between gynephilic and pedophilic sexual offenders. *Sexual Abuse: Journal of Research and Treatment, 7*(2), 129–141.

Carey, R. J. (1985). The prediction of adjustment to prison by means of an MMPI-based classification system. *Dissertation Abstracts International, 46,* 1676.

Carey, R. J., Garske, J. P., & Ginsberg, J. (1986). The prediction of adjustment to prison by means of an MMPI-based classification system. *Criminal Justice and Behavior, 13,* 347–365.

Carrillo, T. L. (1992). MMPI findings of previously molested versus non-molested sex offenders. *Dissertation Abstracts International, 53*(4-B), 2054.

Chu, S. (2001). An analysis of the MMPI results of 47 male criminals. *Chinese Journal of Clinical Psychology, 9*(3), 224–225.

Claghorn, J., Hays, J. R., Webb, L., & Lewis, N. (1991). Juror personality characteristics and the insanity defense. *Forensic Reports, 4*(1), 61–65.

Clark, J. H. (1952). The relationship between MMPI scores and psychiatric classification of Army general prisoners. *Journal of Clinical Psychology, 8,* 86–89.

Clark, M. W. (1997). Characteristics of juvenile sex offenders who admit versus those who deny their offenses. *Dissertation Abstracts International: Section B: The Sciences and Engineering, 57*(12-B), 7718.

Climent, C. E., Plutchik, R., Ervin, F. R., & Rollins, A. (1977). Parental loss, depression and violence: III. Epidemiological studies of female prisoners. *Acta Psychiatrica Scandinavica, 55,* 261–268.

Climent, C. E., Rollins, A., Ervin, F. R., & Plutchik, P. R. (1973). Epidemiological study of women prisoners: Medical and psychiatric variables related to violent behavior. *American Journal of Psychiatry, 130,* 985–990.

Cooke, G. (1969). The court study unit: Patient characteristics and differences between patients judged competent and incompetent. *Journal of Clinical Psychology, 25,* 140–143.

Cooper, C. L., Murphy, W. D., & Haynes, M. R. (1996). Characteristics of abused and nonabused adolescent sexual offenders. *Sexual Abuse: Journal of Research and Treatment, 8*(2), 105–119.

Corsini, R. J., & Bartleme, K. (1952). Attitudes of San Quentin prisoners. *Journal of Correctional Education, 4,* 43–46.

Craddick, R. A. (1955). *MMPI scores of psychopathic and non-psychopathic prisoners of a provincial goal.* Unpublished master's thesis, University of Alberta, Alberta, Canada.

Craddick, R. A. (1962). Selection of psychopathic from non-psychopathic prisoners within a Canadian prison. *Psychological Reports, 10,* 495–499.

Craddick, R. A. (1963). MMPI scatter of psychopathic and non-psychopathic prisoners. *Psychological Reports, 12,* 238.

Crolley, J., Roys, D., Thyer, B. A., & Bordnick, P. S. (1998). Evaluating outpatient behavior therapy of sex offenders: A pretest–posttest study. *Behavior Modification, 22*(4), 485–501.

Crolley, J., Roys, D., Thyer, B. A., & Bordnick, P. S. (1999). "Evaluating outpatient behavior therapy of sex offenders: A pretest–posttest study": Erratum. *Behavior Modification, 23*(1), 169.

Cubitt, G. H., & Gendreau, P. (1972). Assessing the diagnostic utility of MMPI and 16 *PF* indexes of homosexuality in a prison sample. *Journal of Consulting and Clinical Psychology, 39,* 342.

Curnoe, S. (2002). Personality and deviant sexual fantasies: An examination of the MMPIs. *Journal of Clinical Psychology, 58,* 803–815.

Dahlstrom, W. G., Panton, J. H., Bain, K. P., & Dahlstrom, L. E. (1986). Utility of the Megargee–Bohn MMPI typological assignments: Study with a sample of death row inmates. *Criminal Justice and Behavior, 13,* 5–17.

Davis, G. C., & Brehm, M. L. (1971). Juvenile prisoners: Motivational factors in drug use. *Proceedings of the Annual Convention of the American Psychological Association* (Vol. 6, pp. 333–334). Washington, DC: American Psychological Association.

DeFrancesco, D. P. (1993). Identifying differences among male sex offenders: Child molesters versus exhibitionists versus voyeurs. *Dissertation Abstracts International, 53*(9-A), 3146.

Denberg, M., Phillips, R., & Pserazzo, G. (1961). The relationship between MMPI and prison disciplinary reports. In *Proceedings of the 91st Annual Congress of the American Correctional Association* (pp. 233–236). Chicago: American Correctional Association.

DeSouza, J. M., & Doyal, G. T. (1998). Differences between violent female and male offenders: An explanatory study. *American Journal of Forensic Psychology, 16*(3), 67–87.

DiFrancesca, K., & Meloy, J. R. (1989). A comparative clinical investigation of the "How" and "Charlie" MMPI subtypes. *Journal of Personality Assessment, 53,* 396–403.

Driscoll, P. J. (1952). Factors related to the institutional adjustment of prison inmates. *Journal of Abnormal and Social Psychology, 47,* 593–596.

Duncan, D. F. (1989). MMPI scores of tattooed and untattooed prisoners. *Psychological Reports, 65,* 685–686.

Duthie, B., & McIvor, D. L. (1990). A new system for cluster-coding child molester MMPI profile types. *Criminal Justice and Behavior, 17*(2), 199–214.

Edinger, J. D. (1979). Cross-validation of the Megargee MMPI typology for prisoners. *Journal of Consulting and Clinical Psychology, 47,* 234–242.

Edinger, J. D. (1979). The utility of Wechsler Adult Intelligence Scale profile analysis with prisoners. *Journal of Clinical Psychology, 35,* 807–814.

Edwards, J. A. (1963). Rehabilitation potential in prison inmates as measured by the MMPI. *Journal of Criminal Law, Criminology and Police Science, 54,* 181–185.

Erickson, W. D, Luxenberg, M. G., Walbek, N. H., & Seely, R. K. (1987). Frequency of MMPI two-point code types among sex offenders. *Journal of Consulting and Clinical Psychology, 55,* 566–570.

Eronen, M., Tilhonen, J., & Hakola, P. (1996). Schizophrenia and homicidal behavior. *Schizophrenia Bulletin, 22*(1), 83–90.

Falek, A., Craddick, R. A., & Collum, J. (1970). An attempt to identify prisoners with an XYY chromosome complement by psychiatric and psychological means. *Journal of Nervous and Mental Disease, 1,* 165–170.

Fan, Q. (2000). A research on the personalities of 1,557 criminals and law-violators. *Psychological Science (China), 23,* 55–58.

Fisher, G. (1967). The performance of male prisoners on the Marlowe–Crowne Social Desirability Scale: II. Differences as a function of race and crime. *Journal of Clinical Psychology, 23,* 473–475.

Fisher, G. M., & Parsons, T. H. (1962). The performance of male prisoners on the Marlowe–Crowne social desirability scale. *Journal of Clinical Psychology, 18,* 140–141.

Flanagan, J. J., & Lewis, G. R. (1974). First prison admissions with juvenile histories and absolute first offenders: Frequencies and MMPI profiles. *Journal of Clinical Psychology, 30,* 358–360.

Floyd, M. (2000). MMPI–2 and PCL–R characteristics of female prison inmates. *Dissertation Abstracts International, 60,* 6360.

Follman, J. (1972). Delinquency prediction scales and personality inventories. *Child Study Journal, 2,* 99–103.

Forbey, J. D., & Ben-Porath, Y. S. (2002). Use of the MMPI–2 in the treatment of offenders. *International Journal of Offender Therapy and Comparative Criminology, 46*(3), 308–318.

Forgac, G. E., & Michaels, E. J. (1982). Personality characteristics of two types of male exhibitionists. *Journal of Abnormal Psychology, 91,* 287–293.

Forman, B. (1960). The effect of differential treatment on attitudes, personality traits, and behavior of adult parolees. *Dissertation Abstracts, 21,* 1652.

Fry, F. D. (1949). A study of the personality traits of college students, and of state prison inmates as measured by the Minnesota Multiphasic Personality Inventory. *Journal of Psychology, 28,* 439–449.

Fry, F. D. (1952). A normative study of the reactions manifested by college students and by state prison inmates in response to the Minnesota Multiphasic Personality Inventory, the Rosenzweig Picture–Frustration Study, and the Thematic Apperception Test. *Journal of Psychology, 34,* 27–30.

Fry, F. D. (1953). A normative study of the reactions manifested by college students, and by state prison inmates in response to the Minnesota Multiphasic Personality Inventory, the Rosenzweig Picture–Frustration Study, and the Thematic Apperception Test. *Secondary Publication, 15,* 548–552.

Gallagher, R. W., Ben-Porath, Y. S., & Briggs, S. (1997). Inmate views about the purpose of the MMPI–2 at the time of correctional intake. *Criminal Justice and Behavior, 24,* 360–369.

Gallenbeck, C. G. (1948). *The effects of prison confinement upon personality adjustment of inmates of Waupun State Prison.* Unpublished manuscript.

Ge, X., Donnellan, M. B., & Wenk, E. (2003). Differences in personality and patterns of recidivism between early starters and other serious male offenders. *Journal of the American Academy of Psychiatry and the Law, 31*(1), 68–77.

Gearing, M. L. (1979). The MMPI as a primary differentiator and predictor of behavior in prison: A methodological critique and review of the recent literature. *Psychological Bulletin, 86,* 929–963.

Gearing, M. L. (1981). The new MMPI typology for prisoners: The beginning of a new era in correctional research and (hopefully) practice. *Journal of Personality Assessment, 45,* 102–107.

Gearing, M. L. (1983). The relationship of Megargee and Bohn's MMPI personality subtypes and other MMPI dimensions to Kohlberg's moral stages in prisoners. *Dissertation Abstracts International, 43,* 2335.

Geer, T. M., Becker, J. V., Gray, S. R., & Krauss, D. (2001). Predictors of treatment completion in a correctional sex offender treatment program. *International Journal of Offender Therapy and Comparative Criminology, 45*(3), 302–313.

Gendreau, P., Irvine, M., & Knight, S. (1973). Evaluating response set styles on the MMPI with prisoners: Faking good adjustment and maladjustment. *Canadian Journal of Behavioural Science, 5,* 183–194.

Gibbens, T. (1958). The Porteus Maze Test and delinquency. *British Journal of Educational Psychology, 28,* 209–216.

Gibson-Madsen, K. A., & Karie, A. (2003). Detecting psychopathy using the MMPI–2: The Dangerousness Scale. *Dissertation Abstracts International: Section B: The Sciences and Engineering, 64*(5–B), 2003.

Gill, I. A. (1952). *An investigation of the psychological effects of the first three months of imprisonment on the personality of the first offender.* Unpublished doctoral dissertation, University of North Carolina, Chapel Hill.

Gillis, H. (1991). Project Choices: Adventure-based residential drug treatment for court-referred youth. *Journal of Addictions and Offender Counseling, 12,* 12–27.

Gironda, R. J. (1999). Comparative validity of MMPI–2 scores of African-Americans and Caucasians in a forensic diagnostic sample. *Dissertation Abstracts International: Section B: The Sciences and Engineering, 60*(6-B), 2942.

Glaser, B. A., Calhoun, G. B., & Petrocelli, J. V. (2002). Personality characteristics of male juvenile offenders by adjudicated offenses as indicated by the MMPI–A. *Criminal Justice and Behavior, 29*(2), 183–201.

Gough, H. G., & Peterson, D. R. (1952). The identification and measurement of predispositional factors in crime and delinquency. *Journal of Consulting Psychology, 16,* 207–212.

Gough, H. G., Wink, E. A., & Rozynko, V. V. (1965). Parole outcome as predicted from the CPI, the MMPI, and a base expectancy table. *Journal of Abnormal Psychology, 70,* 432–441.

Graham, K. R. (1993). Toward a better understanding and treatment of sex offenders. *International Journal of Offender Therapy and Comparative Criminology, 37*(1), 41–57.

Grassi, A. (1994). Tossicodipendenti detenuti: Analisi psicodinamica e descrittiva per l'individuazione di idonei programmi psicosocioriabilitativi [Drug-addicted prisoners: Psychodynamic and descriptive analysis favoring the individualization of suitable psychosociorehabilitative programs]. *Psichiatria e Psicoterapia Analitica, 13,* 99–113.

Green, A. N. (2000). Minnesota Multiphasic Personality Inventory—Adolescent excitatory scales and demographics as predictors of male juvenile delinquent placement. *Dissertation Abstracts International: Section B: The Sciences and Engineering, 61*(3-B), 1635.

Green, J. B. (2003). A comparison of personality characteristics between incarcerated male pedophiles and incarcerated male nonpedophiles as measured by the Minnesota Multiphasic Personality Inventory—2 (MMPI–2). *Dissertation Abstracts International: Section B: The Sciences and Engineering. 64*(4-B), 1933.

Gregory, I. (1965). Anterospective data following childhood loss of a parent: Delinquency and high school dropout. *Archives of General Psychiatry, 13,* 99–109.

Gregory, R. J. (1973). The actuarial description of delinquency: Seven MMPI code types. *Dissertation Abstracts International, 33,* 5017.

Gregory, R. J. (1974). Replicated actuarial correlates for three MMPI code types in juvenile delinquency. *Journal of Clinical Psychology, 30,* 390–394.

Griffiths, A. (1971). Prisoners of XYY Constitution: Psychological aspects. *British Journal of Psychiatry, 119,* 193–194.

Groff, M. G. (1987). Characteristics of incest offenders' wives. *Journal of Sex Research, 23*(1), 91–96.

Grossman, L. S., & Cavanaugh, J. L. (1990). Psychopathology and denial in alleged sex offenders. *Journal of Nervous and Mental Disease, 178,* 739–744.

Grossman, L. S., Haywood, T. W., & Wasyliw, O. E. (1992). The evaluation of truthfulness in alleged sex offenders' self-reports: 16*PF* and MMPI validity scales. *Journal of Personality Assessment, 59,* 264–275.

Grossman, L. S., & Wasyliw, O. E. (1988). A psychometric study of stereotypes: Assessment of malingering in a criminal forensic group. *Journal of Personality Assessment, 52,* 549–563.

Grossman, L. S., Wasyliw, O. E., & Benn, A. F. (2002). Can sex offenders who minimize on the MMPI conceal psychopathology on the Rorschach? *Journal of Personality Assessment, 78,* 484–501.

Grunberger, J. S. W. (1968). Clinical and psychological study of problem prisoners. *Wiener Zeitschrift für Nervenheilkunde, 26,* 168–184.

Gudjonsson, G. H., Petursson, H., Sigurdardottir, H., & Skulason, S. (1991). Overcontrolled hostility among prisoners and its relationship with denial and personality scores. *Personality and Individual Differences, 12,* 17–20.

Gumbiner, J., Arriaga, T., & Stevens, A. (1999). Comparison of MMPI–A, Marks and Briggs, and MMPI–2 norms for juvenile delinquents. *Psychological Reports, 84*(3, Pt. 1), 761–766.

Gurnani, D., & Dwyer, M. (1986). Serum testosterone levels in sex offenders. *Journal of Offender Counseling, Services and Rehabilitation, 11*(1), 39–45.

Guthrie, R. K. (1999). The prevalence of posttraumatic stress disorder among federal prison inmates. *Dissertation Abstracts International, 60,* 2943.

Guy, E., Platt, J. J., Zwerling, I., & Bullock, S. (1985). Mental health status of prisoners in an urban jail. *Criminal Justice and Behavior, 12,* 29–53.

Gynther, M. D., & McDonald, R. L. (1961). Personality characteristics of prisoners, psychiatric patients, and student nurses as depicted by the Leary system. *Journal of General Psychology, 64,* 387–395.

Hall, G. C. N. (1989). WAIS–R and MMPI profiles of men who have sexually assaulted children: Evidence of limited utility. *Journal of Personality Assessment, 53,* 404–412.

Hall, G. C., Graham, J., & Shepherd, J. (1991). Three methods of developing MMPI taxonomies of sexual offenders. *Journal of Personality Assessment, 56,* 2–16.

Hall, G. C. N., Maiuro, R. D., Vitaliano, P. P., & Proctor, W. C. (1986). The utility of the MMPI with men who have sexually assaulted children. *Journal of Consulting and Clinical Psychology, 54,* 493–496.

Hall, G. C., Shepherd, J. B., & Mudrak, P. (1992). MMPI taxonomies of child sexual and nonsexual offenders: A cross-validation and extension. *Journal of Personality Assessment, 58,* 127–137.

Halpern, S. K. (1990). Classification of sex offenders against children and minors with the MMPI. *Dissertation Abstracts International,* 50(8–B), 3696–3697.

Hammel, S. D. (2001). An investigation of the validity and clinical usefulness of the MMPI–A with female juvenile delinquents. *Dissertation Abstracts*

International: Section B: The Sciences and Engineering, 61(11-B), 6135.

Hannum, T. E., Borgen, F. H., & Anderson, R. M. (1978). Self-concept changes associated with incarceration in female prisoners. *Criminal Justice and Behavior, 5,* 271–279.

Hannum, T. E., Menne, J. W., Betz, E. L., & Rans, L. (1973). Differences in female prisoner characteristics: 1960–1970. *Corrective and Social Psychiatry and Journal of Applied Behavior Therapy, 19,* 39–41.

Hanson, R.W., Moss, C. S., Hosford, R. E., & Johnson, M. E. (1983). Predicting inmate penitentiary adjustment: An assessment of four classificatory methods. *Criminal Justice and Behavior, 10,* 293–309.

Harriman, B. L. (1956). Influence of group-centered therapy and mental health films on attitudes of prisoners. *Dissertation Abstracts International, 16,* 1494–1495.

Hathaway, S. R., Hastings, D. W., Capwell, D. F., & Bell, D. M. (1953). The relationship between MMPI profiles and later careers of juvenile delinquent girls. In S. R. Hathaway & E. Monachesi (Eds.), *Analyzing and predicting juvenile delinquency with the MMPI* (pp. 70–86). Minneapolis: University of Minnesota Press.

Hathaway, S. R., & Monachesi, E. D. (1951). The prediction of juvenile delinquency using the Minnesota Multiphasic Personality Inventory. *American Journal of Psychiatry, 108,* 469–473.

Hathaway, S. R., & Monachesi, E. D. (1953). *Analyzing and predicting juvenile delinquency with the MMPI.* Minneapolis: University of Minnesota Press.

Hathaway, S. R., & Monachesi, E. D. (1954). The occurrence of juvenile delinquency with patterns of maladjustment as exemplified in MMPI profiles. *American Psychologist, 9,* 391–392.

Hathaway, S. R., & Monachesi, E. D. (1963). *Adolescent personality and behavior.* Minneapolis: University of Minnesota Press.

Hathaway, S. R., Monachesi, E. D., & Young, L. A. (1960). Delinquency rates and personality. *Journal of Criminal Law and Criminology, 50,* 433–440.

Hays, F. M. (1999). A comparison of persons found not guilty by reason of insanity and mentally disordered offenders in outpatient treatment using Rorschach and MMPI–2 data. *Dissertation Abstracts International: Section B: The Sciences and Engineering, 60*(5-B), 2342.

Haywood, T. W., & Grossman, L. S. (1994). Denial of deviant sexual arousal and psychopathology in child molesters. *Behavior Therapy, 25*(2), 327–340.

Haywood, T. W., Grossman, L. S., Kravitz, H. M., & Wasyliw, O. E. (1994). Profiling psychological distortion in alleged child molesters. *Psychological Reports, 75*(2), 915–927.

Hazelrigg, P. J. (1996). Demographic, personality, and offense characteristics of men admitted to a maximum security psychiatric setting. *Dissertation Abstracts International: Section B: The Sciences and Engineering. 57*(2–B), 1441.

Heilbrun, A. B. (1971). Prediction of rehabilitation outcome in chronic court-case alcoholics. *Quarterly Journal of Studies on Alcohol, 32,* 328–333.

Heilbrun, K., & Heilbrun, A. (1995). Risk assessment with MMPI–2 in forensic evaluations. In Y. S. Ben-Porath, J. R. Graham, G. C. N. Hall, R. D. Hirschman, & M. S. Zaragoza (Eds.), *Forensic applications of MMPI–2* (pp. 160–178). Thousand Oaks, CA: Sage.

Herkov, M. J., Gynther, M. D., Thomas, S., & Myers, W. C. (1996). MMPI differences among adolescent inpatients, rapists, sodomists, and sexual abusers. *Journal of Personality Assessment, 66,* 81–90.

Hindelang, M. J. (1972). The relationship of self-reported delinquency to scales of the CPI and MMPI. *Journal of Criminal Law, Criminology and Police Science, 63,* 75–81.

Holcomb, W., Adams, N., & Ponder, H. (1985). The development and cross-validation of an MMPI typology of murderers. *Journal of Personality Assessment, 49,* 240–244.

Holcomb, W. R., Adams, W. P., Ponder, H. M., & Anderson W. (1984). Cognitive and behavioral predictors of MMPI scores in pretrial psychological evaluations of murderers. *Journal of Clinical Psychology, 40,* 592–597.

Holland, T. R. (1977). Multivariate analysis of personality correlates of alcohol and drug abuse in a prison population. *Journal of Abnormal Psychology, 86,* 644–650.

Holland, T. R., & Boik, R. J. (1978). Impression management in the ethical self-presentation of offenders undergoing presentence evaluation. *Criminal Justice and Behavior, 5*(3), 259–270.

Holland, T. R., & Holt, N. (1975). Personality patterns among short-term prisoners undergoing presentence evaluations. *Psychological Reports, 37,* 827–836.

Holland, T. R., & Holt, N. (1975). Prisoner intellectual and personality correlates of offense severity and recidivism probability. *Journal of Clinical Psychology, 31,* 667–672.

Horenstein, D., Solomon, S. J., & Houston, B. K. (1977). Preliminary report on a juvenile court testing program. *Corrective and Social Psychiatry and Journal of Behavior Technology, Methods and Therapy, 23,* 11–14.

House, T. H. (1974). Empathy in prison subjects at the extremes of the MMPI *Pd* and Welsch Anxiety scales viewing high or low levels of distress. *Dissertation Abstracts International, 34,* 4665.

House, T. H., & Milligan, W. (1973). Heart rate and galvanic skin responses to modeled distress in prison psychopaths. *Newsletter for Research in Mental Health and Behavioral Sciences, 15,* 36–40.

House, T. H., & Milligan, W. (1976). Autonomic responses to modeled distress in prison psychopaths. *Journal of Personality and Social Psychology, 34,* 556–560.

Hudson, A. H. (1996). Personality assessment of female sex offenders: A cluster analysis. *Dissertation Abstracts International: Section B: The Sciences and Engineering, 56*(9-B), 5212.

Hunter, J. A., Childers, S. E., & Esmaili, H. (1990). An examination of variables differentiating clinical sub-types of incestuous child molesters. *International Journal of Offender Therapy and Comparative Criminology, 34,* 95–104.

Hunter, L. M. (2000). Use of selected MMPI–A factors in the prediction of clinical outcomes in a community-based treatment program for juvenile sexual offenders. *Dissertation Abstracts International: Section B: The Sciences and Engineering, 60*(11-B), 5775.

Iverson, G. L., Franzen, M. D., & Hammond, J. A. (1995). Examination of inmates' ability to malinger on the MMPI–2. *Psychological Assessment, 7,* 118–121.

Jacobson, J., & Wirt, R. D. (1969). MMPI profiles associated with outcomes of group psychotherapy with prisoners. In J. N. Butcher (Ed.), *Recent developments in the use of the MMPI* (pp. 191–206). New York: McGraw-Hill.

Jemelka, R. P., Weigand, G. A., Walker, E. A., & Trupin, E. W. (1992). Computerized offender assessment: Validation study. *Psychological Assessment, 4,* 138–144.

Joesting, J., Jones, N., & Joesting, R. (1975). Male and female prison inmates' differences on MMPI scales and revised beta IQ. *Psychological Reports, 37,* 471–474.

Johnston, N., & Cooke, G. (1973). Relationship of MMPI alcoholism, prison escape, hostility control and recidivism scales to clinical judgments. *Journal of Clinical Psychology, 29,* 32–34.

Jones, T., Beidleman, W. B., & Fowler, R. D. (1981). Differentiating violent and nonviolent prison inmates by use of selected MMPI scales. *Journal of Clinical Psychology, 37,* 673–678.

Kalichman, S. C. (1990). Affective and personality characteristics of MMPI profile subgroups of incarcerated rapists. *Archives of Sexual Behavior, 19,* 443–459.

Kalichman, S. C. (1991). Psychopathology and personality characteristics of criminal sexual offenders as a function of victim age. *Archives of Sexual Behavior, 20*(2), 187–197.

Kalichman, S. C., Craig, M. E., Shealy, L., Taylor, J., Szymanowski, D., & McKee, G. (1989). An empirically derived typology of adult rapists based on the MMPI: A cross-validation study. *Journal of Psychology and Human Sexuality, 2,* 165–182.

Kalichman, S. C., Dwyer, S. M., Henderson, M. C., & Hoffman, L. (1992). Psychological and sexual functioning among outpatient sexual offenders against children: A Minnesota Multiphasic Personality Inventory (MMPI) cluster analytic study. *Journal of Psychopathology and Behavioral Assessment, 14*(3), 259–276.

Kalichman, S. C., & Henderson, M. C. (1991). MMPI profile subtypes of nonincarcerated child molesters. *Criminal Justice and Behavior, 18,* 379–396.

Kalichman, S. C., Shealy, L., & Craig, M. E. (1990). The use of the MMPI in predicting treatment participation among incarcerated adult rapists. *Journal of Psychology and Human Sexuality, 3*(2), 105–119.

Kalichman, S. C., Szymanowski, D., McKee, G., Taylor, J., & Craig, M. E. (1989). Cluster analytically derived MMPI profile subgroups of incarcerated adult rapists. *Journal of Clinical Psychology, 5,* 149–155.

Kanarr, L. (2003). The development of the Sexual Aggression Toward Partners Assessment Tool (SATPAT). *Dissertation Abstracts International: Section B: The Sciences and Engineering, 63*(8-B), 3920.

Kanun, C. (1956). Predicting delinquency from the MMPI using items instead of clinical scales. *Dissertation Abstracts International, 16,* 2547.

Kanun, C., & Monachesi, E. D. (1960). Delinquency and the validating scales of the Minnesota Multiphasic Personality Inventory. *Journal of Criminal Law, Criminology and Police Science, 50,* 525–534.

Karacan, I. (1974). Nocturnal penile tumescence and sleep of convicted rapists and other prisoners. *Archives of Sexual Behavior, 3,* 19–26.

Karle-Brueck, H. R. (2003). Denial in convicted sex offenders: A preliminary examination. *Dissertation Abstracts International: Section B: The Sciences and Engineering, 63*(12-B), 6097.

Kashiwamura, J. (1957). A study of the personality traits of prisoners as measured by the MMPI. *Journal of Correctional Medicine, 6,* 52–54.

Katz, L. (1967). The value of well-validated tests in courtroom testimony. *American Psychologist, 22,* 321.

Kennedy, T. D. (1986). Trends in inmate classification: A status report of two computerized psychometric approaches. *Criminal Justice and Behavior, 13,* 165–184.

Kieliszewski, J. T. (1999). A cluster analytic study of MMPI–2 profiles of convicted sex offenders of children. *Dissertation Abstracts International: Section B: The Sciences and Engineering, 60*(2-B), 833.

Kingsley, L. (1960). MMPI profiles of psychopaths and prisoners. *Journal of Clinical Psychology, 16,* 302–304.

Klonoff, H. (1976). The MMPI profile of prisoners of war. *Journal of Clinical Psychology, 32,* 623–627.

Knoff, R. H. (1984). The MMPI used as a "Lie detector": Prison data. *Tidsskrift for Norsk Psykologforening, 21,* 345–352.

Knox-Jones, P. A. (1995). Neuropsychological functioning among violent and nonviolent sex offenders. *Dissertation Abstracts International: Section B: The Sciences and Engineering, 56*(4-B), 2332.

Kodman, F., & Hopkins, R. W. (1970). Correlates of ego-strength in a sample of Kentucky prison inmates. *Correctional Psychologist, 4,* 20–26.

Kodman, F., & Hopkins, R. W. (1970). MMPI profile characteristics of Kentucky prison inmates. *Correctional Psychologist, 4,* 7–11.

Koeninger, R. (1954). A suggested system for classification of MMPI profiles of prison inmates. *Journal of Criminal Law, Criminology and Police Science, 44,* 628–630.

Korbanka, J. E. (1996). An MMPI–2 scale to identify history of sexual abuse. *Dissertation Abstracts*

International: Section B: The Sciences and Engineering, 56(11-B), 6396.

Koss, M. P., Leonard, K. E., Beezley, D. A., & Oros, C. J. (1985). Nonstranger sexual aggression: A discriminant analysis of the psychological characteristics of undetected offenders. *Sex Roles, 12,* 981–992.

Kucharski, L. T., Johnsen, D., & Procell, S. (2004). The utility of the MMPI–2 infrequency psychopathology *F(p)* and the revised infrequency psychopathology scales in the detection of malingering. *American Journal of Forensic Psychology, 22(1),* 33–40.

Kuroda, M. (1961). MMPI results of juveniles in reform and training schools: An examination in connection with profile patterns and delinquency scale scores. *Journal of Correctional Medicine, 10,* 144.

Langevin, R., & Bain, J. (1992). Diabetes in sex offenders: A pilot study. *Annals of Sex Research, 5(2),* 99–118.

Langevin, R., Lang, R., Reynolds, R., Wright, P., et al. (1988). Personality and sexual anomalies: An examination of the Millon Clinical Multiaxial Inventory. *Annals of Sex Research, 1(1),* 13–32.

Langevin, R., Wright, P., & Handy, L. (1989). Characteristics of sex offenders who were sexually victimized as children. *Annals of Sex Research, 2(3),* 227–253.

Langevin, R., Wright, P., & Handy, L. H. (1990). Use of the MMPI and its derived scales with sex offenders: I. Reliability and validity studies. *Annals of Sex Research, 3(3),* 245–291.

Langevin, R., Wright, P., & Handy, L. (1990). Use of the MMPI and its derived scales with sex offenders: II. Reliability and criterion validity. *Annals of Sex Research, 3(4),* 453–486.

Lanier, N. S. (1973). MMPI role taking by sociopathic and non-sociopathic prison inmates. *Dissertation Abstracts International, 33,* 5021–5022.

Lanyon, R. I. (1993). Validity of MMPI sex offender scales with admitters and nonadmitters *Psychological Assessment, 5,* 302–306.

Lanyon, R. I., & Lutz, R. W. (1984). MMPI discrimination of defensive and nondefensive felony sex offenders. *Journal of Consulting and Clinical Psychology, 52,* 841–843.

Lapham, S. C., Skipper, B. J., Hunt, W. C., & Chang, I. (2000). Do risk factors for re-arrest differ for female and male drunk-driving offenders? *Alcoholism: Clinical and Experimental Research, 24,* 1647–1655.

Lapham, S. C., Skipper, B. J., Owen, J. P., Kleyboecker, K., et al. (1995). Alcohol abuse screening instruments: Normative test data collected from a first DWI offender screening program. *Journal of Studies on Alcohol, 56(1),* 51–59.

Lauber, M., & Dahlstrom, W. G. (1953). MMPI findings in the rehabilitation of delinquent girls. In S. R. Hathaway & E. D. Monachesi (Eds.), *Analyzing and predicting juvenile delinquency with the MMPI* (pp. 39–47). Minneapolis: University of Minnesota Press.

Laudeman, K. A. (1978). Personality, drinking patterns and problem drinking among young adult offenders. *Journal of Drug Education, 7(3),* 259–269.

Lavelle, T., Hammersley, R., & Forsyth, A. (1993). Is the "addictive personality" merely delinquency? *Addiction Research, 1,* 27–37.

Lawson, K. A. (1997). Prediction of premature termination of adult male sexual offenders from outpatient treatment. *Dissertation Abstracts International: Section B: The Sciences and Engineering, 57(11-B),* 7229.

Lawton, M. (1965). Prisoners' faking on the MMPI. *Journal of Clinical Psychology, 21,* 269–271.

Lebo, D., Toal, R. A., & Brick, H. (1958). Manifest anxiety in prisoners before and after CO_2. *Journal of Consulting Psychology, 22,* 51–55.

Lennings, C. J. (1988). The effect of court appearances on personality: Therapy or torture: A case study. *International Journal of Offender Therapy and Comparative Criminology, 32,* 249–252.

Lessin, L. H. (1997). Predicting recidivism among sex offenders: A long-term survival analysis utilizing the Minnesota Multiphasic Personality Inventory and demographic variables. *Dissertation Abstracts International: Section B: The Sciences and Engineering, 57*(11-B), 7229.

Levin, S. M., & Stava, L. (1987). Personality characteristics of sex offenders: A review. *Archives of Sexual Behavior, 16*(1), 57–79.

Levy, S., & Freeman, R. (1954). Use of the MMPI in measuring adjustment of prisoners. *Journal of Social Therapy, 1*, 33–39.

Lilienfeld, S. O. (1996). The MMPI–2 Antisocial Practices content scale: Construct validity and comparison with the Psychopathic Deviate scale. *Psychological Assessment, 8*, 281–293.

Lim, E. O. (2003). Neuropsychological impairment and risk characteristics of offenders facing the death penalty. *Dissertation Abstracts International: Section B: The Sciences and Engineering, 64*(6-B), 2927.

Liu, Z., Chen, X., Qin, S., Xue, J., Hao, W., Lu, X., et al. (2002). Risk factors for female criminals. *Chinese Mental Health Journal, 16*(2), 106–108.

Losada-Paisey, G. (1998). Use of the MMPI–A to assess personality of juvenile male delinquents who are sex offenders and nonsex offenders. *Psychological Reports, 83*(1), 115–122.

Louscher, P. K., Hosford, R. E., & Moss, C. S. (1983). Predicting dangerous behavior in a penitentiary using the Megargee typology. *Criminal Justice and Behavior, 10*, 269–284.

Lovestrand, S. P. (1995). Comparability of the MMPI–2 in a prison population. *Dissertation Abstracts International, 56*, 3500.

Lyne, M. E. W. (1985). Childhood sexual victimization of men who later were convicted of rape or sexual child abuse. *Dissertation Abstracts International, 54*(2-B), 1104.

Mabli, J. (1985). Prerelease stress in prison inmates. *Journal of Offender Counseling, Services and Rehabilitation, 9*, 43–56.

Mack, J. L. (1968). An objective comparison of parole successes and failures in terms of their history

and personality adjustment. *Dissertation Abstracts, 28*, 3475B.

Maness, P., Silkowski, S., Velasquez, R. J., Savino, A. V., & Frank, J. (2001, March). *Ethnic comparisons on the MMPI–2 and male sex offenders.* Paper presented at the 36th Annual Symposium on Recent Developments in the Use of the MMPI–2/MMPI–A, Safety Harbor, FL.

Mann, J., Stenning, W., & Borman, C. (1992). The utility of the MMPI–2 with pedophiles. *Journal of Offender Rehabilitation, 18*(3–4), 59–74.

McCreary, C. P. (1975). Personality differences among child molesters. *Journal of Personality Assessment, 39*, 591–593.

McCreary, C. P. (1976). Trait and type differences among male and female assaultive and nonassaultive offenders. *Journal of Personality Assessment, 40*, 617–621.

McCreary, C. P., & Mensh, I. N. (1977). Personality differences associated with age in law offenders. *Journal of Gerontology, 32*, 164–167.

McDaniels, W., C. (1997, June). *The relation of sexual abuse history to the MMPI–2 profiles and criminal involvement of incarcerated women.* Paper presented at the 32nd Annual Symposium on Recent Developments in the Use of the MMPI–2/MMPI–A Workshop and Symposia, Minneapolis, MN.

McLaughlin, R. H. (1999). An examination of MMPI–2 content scale performances among a sample of criminal offenders (social discomfort, correctional norms, gender). *Dissertations International: Section B: The Sciences and Engineering, 59*(10-B), 5610.

McGovern, F. J., & Nevid, J. S. (1986). Evaluation apprehension on psychological inventories in a prison-based setting. *Journal of Consulting and Clinical Psychology, 54*, 576–578.

McGovern, K., & Peters, J. (1988). Guidelines for assessing sex offenders. In L. E. Walker (Ed.), *Handbook on sexual abuse of children: Assessment and treatment issues* (pp. 216–246). New York: Springer.

McGrath, R. E., & Ingersoll, J. (1999). Writing a good cookbook. I. A review of MMPI high-point studies. *Journal of Personality Assessment, 73,* 149–178.

McKee, G. R., Shea, S. J., Mogy, R. B., & Holden, C. E. (2001). MMPI–2 profiles of filicidal, mariticidal, and homicidal women. *Journal of Clinical Psychology, 57*(3), 367–374.

Megargee, E. I. (Ed.). (1977). A new classification system for criminal offenders. *Criminal Justice and Behavior* [Special issue], *4*(2).

Megargee, E. I. (1994). Using the Megargee MMPI-based classification system with MMPI–2s of male prison inmates. *Psychological Assessment, 6,* 337–344.

Megargee, E. I. (1997). Using the Megargee MMPI-based classification system with MMPI–2s of female prison inmates. *Psychological Assessment, 9,* 75–82.

Megargee, E. I. (2000). *User's guide: MMPI–2 criminal justice and correctional report for men.* Minneapolis, MN: National Computer Systems.

Megargee, E. I. (2002). Assessing the risk of aggression and violence. In J. N. Butcher (Ed.), *Clinical personality assessment: Practical approaches* (2nd. ed., pp. 435–451). New York: Oxford University Press.

Megargee, E. I. (2003). Psychological assessment in correctional settings. In J. R. Graham & J. A. Naglieri (Eds.), *Handbook of psychology. Vol. 10: Assessment psychology* (pp. 365–388). Hoboken, NJ: Wiley.

Megargee, E. I. (2004, May). *Development and validation of an MMPI–2 Infrequency Scale (FC) for use with criminal offenders.* Paper presented at the 39th annual symposium on recent developments of the MMPI–2/ MMPI–A, Minneapolis, MN.

Megargee, E. I. (2006). Use of the MMPI–2 in correctional settings. In J. N. Butcher (Ed.), *MMPI–2: A practitioner's guide* (pp. 327–360). Washington, DC: American Psychological Association.

Megargee, E. I. (in press). *Using MMPI–2 in criminal justice and correctional settings: An empirical approach.* Minneapolis: University of Minnesota Press.

Megargee, E. I., Bohn, M. J., Jr., Meyer, J., & Sink, F. (1979). *Classifying criminal offenders: A new system based on the MMPI.* Beverly Hills, CA: Sage.

Megargee, E. I., & Carbonell, J. L. (1985). Predicting prison adjustment with MMPI correctional scales. *Journal of Consulting and Clinical Psychology, 53,* 874–883.

Megargee, E. I., & Carbonell, J. L. (1995). Use of the MMPI–2 in correctional settings. In Y. S. Ben-Porath, J. R. Graham, G. C. N. Hirschman, & M. S. Zaragoza (Eds.), *Forensic applications of the MMPI–2* (pp. 127–159). Thousand Oaks, CA: Sage.

Megargee, E. I., Carbonell, J. L., Bohn, Jr., M. B., & Sliger, G. L. (2001) *Classifying criminal offenders with MMPI–2: The Megargee system.* Minneapolis: University of Minnesota Press.

Megargee, E. I., Mercer, S. J., & Carbonell, J. L. (1999). MMPI–2 with male and female state and federal prison inmates. *Psychological Assessment, 11,* 177–185.

Megargee, E. I., Rivera, P., & Fly J. T. (1991, March). *MMPI–2 and the Megargee offender classification system.* Paper presented at the 26th Annual Symposium on Recent Developments in the Use of the MMPI (MMPI–2), St. Petersburg, FL.

Melonas, I. A. (1998). A comparison of psychopathology in male adolescent child molesters and other male adolescent sex offenders. *Dissertation Abstracts International: Section B: The Sciences and Engineering, 58*(9-B), 5130.

Miller, G. R., Jr. (1999). The MTC: CM3 Axis I classification system for child molesters and its relationship to psychopathy, arousal, and the social introversion scale of the MMPI (Minnesota Multiphasic Personality Inventory, Massachusetts treatment center child molester typology). *Dissertation Abstracts International: Section B: The Sciences and Engineering, 60*(6-B), 2953.

Miller, H. A. (2004). Examining the use of the M–FAST with criminal defendants incompetent to stand trial. *International Journal of Offender Therapy and Comparative Criminology, 48*(3), 268–280.

Miller, T. W., Martin, W., & Spiro, K. (1989). Traumatic stress disorder: Diagnostic and clinical issues in former prisoners of war. *Comprehensive Psychiatry, 30,* 139–148.

Miner, M. H., & Dwyer, S. M. (1995). Analysis of dropouts from outpatient sex offender treatment. *Journal of Psychology and Human Sexuality, 7(3),* 77–93.

Miner, M. H., Marques, J. K., Day, D. M., & Nelson, C. (1990). Impact of relapse prevention in treating sex offenders: Preliminary findings. *Annals of Sex Research 3(2),* 165–185.

Minor, K. I., Karr, S. K., & Jain, S. K. (1987). An examination of the utility of the MMPI in predicting male prison inmates' abusive parenting attitudes. *Psychological Record, 37,* 429–436.

Monachesi, E. D., & Hathaway, S. R. (1953). *Adolescent personality and behavior.* Minneapolis: University of Minnesota Press.

Moore, R. (1966). *A revised MMPI scale for measuring psychopathy among prison inmates.* Marshall University, Master's thesis, Huntington, WV.

Morrice, J. (1957). The Minnesota Multiphasic Personality Inventory in recidivist prisoners. *Journal of Mental Science, 103,* 632–635.

Morton, T. L., Farris, K. L., & Brenowitz, L. H. (2002). MMPI–A scores and high points of male juvenile delinquents: Scales 4, 5, and 6 as markers of juvenile delinquency. *Psychological Assessment, 14,* 311–319.

Moskowitz, J. L. (1997). A comparison of the MMPI–2 profiles of not guilty by reason of insanity and civil inpatients. *Dissertation Abstracts International: Section B: The Sciences and Engineering, 58(1-B),* 423.

Moskowitz, J. L., Lewis, R. J., Ito, M. S., & Ehrmentraut, J. (1999). MMPI–2 profiles of NGRI and civil patients. *Journal of Clinical Psychology, 55(5),* 659–668.

Moss, C. S., Hosford, R. E., Anderson, W. R., & Petracca, M. (1977). Personality variables of Blacks participating in a prison riot. *Journal of Consulting and Clinical Psychology, 45,* 505–512.

Moss, C. S., Johnson, M. E., & Hosford, R. E. (1984). An assessment of the Megargee typology in lifelong criminal violence. *Criminal Justice and Behavior, 11,* 225–234.

Motiuk, L. L., Bonta, J., & Andrews, D. A. (1986). Classification in correctional halfway houses: The relative and incremental predictive criterion validities of the Megargee–MMPI and LSI systems. *Criminal Justice and Behavior, 13,* 33–46.

Motyka, G. A. (1998). MMPI–2 profile differences between first and multiple DUI offenders at a community-based correctional facility. *Dissertation Abstracts International: Section B: The Sciences and Engineering, 58(7-B),* 3956.

Mrad, D. F., Kabacoff, R. I., & Duckro, P. (1983). Validation of the Megargee typology in a halfway house setting. *Criminal Justice and Behavior, 10,* 252–262.

Neal, L. A., Hill, N., Hughes, J., & Middleton, A. (1995). Convergent validity of measures of PTSD in an elderly population of former prisoners of war. *International Journal of Geriatric Psychiatry, 10,* 617–622.

Nelson, D. M. (1980). Short-term stability of sex types in the MMPI-based adult offender classification system. *Dissertation Abstracts International, 41(3-B),* 1120–1121.

Nichols, W. L. (1980). The classification of law offenders with the MMPI: A methodological study. *Dissertation Abstracts International, 41,* 333.

Nieberding, J. E. (1976). MMPI personality type and the effect of imprisonment upon self concept. *Dissertation Abstracts International, 36,* 5274.

Nieberding, R. J., Moore, J. T., & Dematatis, A. P. (2002). Psychological assessment of forensic psychiatric outpatients. *International Journal of Offender Therapy and Comparative Criminology, 46(3),* 350–363.

O'Connor Boes, J. A. (1997). Individual differences and corruption: An investigation of the MMPI in a law enforcement setting. *Dissertation Abstracts International, 58,* 2166.

Ogloff, J. R. P. (1995). The legal basis of forensic application of the MMPI–2. In Y. S. Ben-Porath, J. R. Graham, G. C. N. Hall, R. D. Hirschman, & M. S. Zaragoza (Eds.), *Forensic applications of the MMPI–2* (pp. 18–47). Thousand Oaks, CA: Sage.

Ohanian, M. F. (1993). Identification of parole violation potential: Development of a contemporary measure using the MMPI–2. *Dissertation Abstracts International, 53,* 2996.

Oho, N., Shindo, H., & Kataoka, G. (1968). Some discussions on the measurement of delinquency with the MMPI. *Proceedings of the 32nd Annual Convention of the Japanese Psychological Association,* 411–413.

Olander, R. (2004). Defensive styles and other factors that differentiate between two types of child molesters: Use of the MCMI–II, MMPI–2, and the 16PF. *Dissertation Abstracts International: Section B: The Sciences and Engineering, 64*(7-B), 3537.

Orme-Johnson, D. W., & Moore, R. M. (2003). Section II: Original research on rehabilitation. First prison study using the Transcendental Meditation program: La Tuna Federal Penitentiary, 1971. *Journal of Offender Rehabilitation, 36,* 89–95.

Osberg, T. M., & Harrigan, P. (1999). Comparative validity of the MMPI–2 Wiener–Harmon subtle–obvious scales in male prison inmates. *Journal of Personality Assessment, 72,* 36–48.

Panton, J. H. (1958). MMPI profile characteristics of physically disabled prison inmates. *Psychological Reports, 4,* 529–530.

Panton, J. H. (1958). Predicting prison adjustment with the Minnesota Multiphasic Personality Inventory. *Journal of Clinical Psychology, 14,* 308–312.

Panton, J. H. (1959). *MMPI high-point codes on samples of male and female prison inmates.* Unpublished manuscript.

Panton, J. H. (1959). *Personality differences appearing between male and female prison inmates as measured by the MMPI.* Unpublished paper, North Car-

olina Department of Social Rehabilitation and Control, Raleigh.

Panton, J. H. (1959). The response of prison inmates to seven new MMPI scales. *Journal of Clinical Psychology, 15,* 196–197.

Panton, J. H. (1960). MMPI code configurations as related to measures of intelligence among a state prison population. *Journal of Social Psychology, 51,* 403–407.

Panton, J. H. (1961). Characteristics associated with alcoholism among a state prison population. *Tri-State Medical Journal, 11,* 6–8.

Panton, J. H. (1962). The identification of predispositional factors in self-mutilation within a state prison population. *Journal of Clinical Psychology, 18,* 63–67.

Panton, J. H. (1962). Use of the MMPI as an index to successful parole. *Journal of Criminal Law, Criminology and Police Science, 53,* 484–488.

Panton, J. H. (1970). *Manual for a Prison Classification Inventory (PCI) for the MMPI.* Raleigh, NC: Department of Social Rehabilitation and Control.

Panton, J. H. (1973). Personality characteristics of management problem prison inmates. *Journal of Community Psychology, 1,* 185–191.

Panton, J. H. (1974). Personality differences between male and female prison inmates measured by the MMPI. *Criminal Justice and Behavior, 1,* 332–339.

Panton, J. H. (1976). Personality characteristics of death-row prison inmates. *Journal of Clinical Psychology, 32,* 306–309.

Panton, J. H. (1976). Significant increase in MMPI *Mf* scores within a state prison population. *Journal of Clinical Psychology, 32,* 604–606.

Panton, J. H. (1977). Personality characteristics of drug pushers incarcerated within a state prison population. *Quarterly Journal of Corrections, 1,* 11–13.

Panton, J. H. (1978). Pre and post personality test responses of prison inmates who have had their death sentences commuted to life imprisonment.

Research Communications in Psychology, Psychiatry and Behavior, 3, 143–156.

Panton, J. H. (1979). Longitudinal post-validation of the MMPI Escape (*Ec*) and Prison Adjustment (*Ap*) scales. *Journal of Clinical Psychology, 35*, 101–103.

Panton, J. H. (1979). An MMPI item content scale to measure religious identification within a state prison population. *Journal of Clinical Psychology, 35*, 588–591.

Panton, J. H. (1979). MMPI profiles associated with outcomes of intensive psychotherapeutic counseling with youthful first offender prison inmates. *Research Communications in Psychology, Psychiatry and Behavior, 4*, 383–395.

Panton, J. H., & Behre, C. (1973). Characteristics associated with drug addiction within a state prison population. *Journal of Community Psychology, 1*, 411–416.

Panton, J. H., & Brisson, R. C. (1971). Characteristics associated with drug abuse within a state prison population. *Corrective Psychiatry and Journal of Social Therapy, 17*, 3–33.

Panton, J. H., & Brisson, R. C. (1973). *Characteristics associated with drug addiction within a state prison population.* Unpublished work.

Panton, J. H., & Brisson, R. C. (1973). *An experiment in attitude change among prison inmates.* Unpublished manuscript.

Parwatikar, S. D., Holcomb, W. R., & Menninger, K. A. (1985). The detection of malingered amnesia in accused murderers. *Bulletin of the American Academy of Psychiatry and the Law, 13*, 97–103.

Pavelka, F. L. (1986). Psychosocial characteristics of parolees in forensic social work. *Journal of Psychiatry and Law, 14*, 217–223.

Pawlak, A. E. (1996). Factors associated with sexual aggression among rapists and non-offenders. *Dissertation Abstracts International: Section B: The Sciences and Engineering, 56*(8–B), 4590.

Pena, L., & Megargee, E. (1994, May). *MMPI–A patterns among juvenile delinquents.* Paper presented at the 29th Annual Symposium on Recent Developments in the Use of the MMPI–2/MMPI–A Workshop and Symposia, Minneapolis, MN.

Pena, L., & Megargee, E. (1997, June). *Application of the Megargee typology for criminal offenders to adolescents with the MMPI–A.* Paper presented at the 32nd Annual Symposium on Recent Developments in the Use of the MMPI–2/MMPI–A, Minneapolis, MN.

Pena, L. M., Megargee, E. I., & Brody, E. (1996). MMPI–A patterns of male juvenile delinquents. *Psychological Assessment, 8*, 388–397.

Penn, N., Savino, A. V., Velasquez. R. J., Boscan, D., & Gomez, F. C., Jr. (1999, April). *MMPI–2 Performance of Mexican Prison Inmates: Clinical Correlates.* Paper presented at the 34th Annual Symposium on Recent Developments in the Use of the MMPI–2/MMPI–A, Huntington Beach, CA.

Pensinger, K. A. (1996). Breaking the incest taboo: The role of emotional alienation, cognitive distortions, and proximity of relationship in child sexual abuse. *Dissertation Abstracts International: Section B: The Sciences and Engineering, 57*(5-B), 3418.

Petroskey, L. J., Ben-Porath, Y. S., & Stafford, K. P. (2003, June). *Forensic correlates of the MMPI–2 PSY–5 scales.* Paper presented at the 38th MMPI–2 Conference on Recent Developments in the Use of the MMPI–2 and MMPI–A Workshop and Symposia, Minneapolis, MN.

Pirrello, V. E. (1999). An empirically derived classification system for adolescent sex offenders. *Dissertation Abstracts International: Section B: The Sciences and Engineering, 60*(3-B), 1311.

Plante, T. G., Manuel, G., & Bryant, C. (1996). Personality and cognitive functioning among hospitalized sexual offending Roman Catholic priests. *Pastoral Psychology, 45*(2), 129–139.

Quay, H. (1965). *Juvenile delinquency.* Princeton, NJ: Van Nostrand.

Posey, C. (1984). The fakability of subtle and obvious measures of aggression by male prisoners. *Journal of Personality Assessment, 48*, 137–144.

Rader, C. M. (1977). MMPI profile types of exposers, rapists, and assaulters in a court services population. *Journal of Consulting and Clinical Psychology, 45,* 61–69.

Rapaport, G. M., & Marshall, R. J. (1962). The prediction of rehabilitative potential of stockade prisoners using clinical psychological tests. *Journal of Clinical Psychology, 18,* 444–446.

Rasch, W. (1981). The effects of indeterminate detention: A study of men sentenced to life imprisonment. *International Journal of Law and Psychiatry, 4,* 417–431.

Rathus, S. A., Fox, J. A., & Ortins, J. (1980). The MacAndrew Scale as a measure of substance abuse and delinquency among adolescents. *Journal of Clinical Psychology, 36,* 579–583.

Reed, C. F., & Cuadra, C. A. (1957). The role-taking hypothesis in delinquency. *Journal of Consulting Psychology, 21,* 386–390.

Rice, M., Arnold, L., & Tate, D. (1983). Faking good and bad adjustment on the MMPI and over-controlled-hostility in maximum security psychiatric patients. *Canadian Journal of Behavioral Sciences, 15,* 43–51.

Rogers, R., Gillis, J. R., McMain, S., & Dickens, S. E. (1988). Fitness evaluations: A retrospective study of clinical, criminal, and sociodemographic characteristics. *Canadian Journal of Behavioural Science, 20*(2), 192–200.

Rogers, R., & McKee, G. R. (1995). Use of the MMPI–2 in the assessment of criminal responsibility. In Y. S. Ben-Porath, J. R. Graham, G. C. Hall, R. D. Hirschman, & M. S. Zavagoza (Eds.), *Forensic applications of the MMPI–2* (pp. 103–126). Thousand Oaks, CA: Sage.

Roman, D. D., & Gerbing, D. W. (1989). The mentally disordered criminal offender: A description based on demographic, clinical, and MMPI data. *Journal of Clinical Psychology 45,* 983–990.

Roman, D. D., Tuley, M. R., Villanueva, M. R., & Mitchell, W. E. (1990). Evaluating MMPI validity in a forensic psychiatric population. *Criminal Justice and Behavior, 17,* 186–198.

Rosen, E. M., & Mink, S. H. (1959). Desirability of personality traits as perceived by prisoners. *Rivista Sperimentale di Freniatria, 83,* 1251–1260.

Rosen, E., & Mink, S. H. (1961). Desirability of personality traits as perceived by prisoners. *Journal of Clinical Psychology, 17,* 147–151.

Rosstti, S., Anthony, P., Cimbolic, P., & Wright, T. L. (1996). Development and preliminary validation of the MMPI–2 scale for same-sex priest child molesters. *Sexual Addiction and Compulsivity, 3*(4), 341–356.

Roth, L., Rosenberg, N., & Levinson, R. (1971). Prison adjustment of alcoholic felons. *Quarterly Journal of Studies on Alcohol, 32,* 382–392.

Roys, D. T., & Timms, R. J. (1995). Personality profiles of adult males sexually molested by their maternal caregivers: Preliminary findings. *Journal of Child Sexual Abuse, 4*(4), 63–77.

Ruff, C. F., Templer, D. I., Ayers, J. L., & Barthlow, V. L. (1977). WAIS Digit Span differences between prisoners and psychiatric patients. *Perceptual and Motor Skills, 44,* 497–498.

Salcedo, R. F. (1984). Minnesota Multiphasic Personality Inventory (MMPI) response patterns among prisoners under varied instructional sets. *Dissertation Abstracts International, 45,* 133.

Sanchez Martin, M. (1991). Psychopathology and delinquency: A sample of a prison population at the Penitentiary Center of Salamanca. *Psiquis, 12,* 46–55.

Schaedler, T. (1974). Personality and attitude characteristics as a function of delinquency dimensions. *Dissertation Abstracts International, 34,* 3508B.

Schattner, T. J. (2003). Sex offenders and the use of the validity scales of the MMPI–2 to confirm treatment progress. *Dissertation Abstracts International: Section B: The Sciences and Engineering, 64*(5-B), 2404.

Schlank, A. M. (1993). The utility of the MMPI and the MSI for identifying a sex offender typology. *Dissertation Abstracts International, 54*(1-B), 508.

Schlank, A. M. (1995). The utility of the MMPI and the MSI for identifying a sexual offender typology. *Sexual Abuse: Journal of Research and Treatment,* 7(3), 185–194.

Schmalz, B. J., Fehr, R. C., & Dalby, J. T. (1989). Distinguishing forensic, psychiatric and inmate groups with the MMPI. *American Journal of Forensic Psychology, 7,* 37–47.

Schretlen, D., & Arkowitz, H. (1990). A psychological test battery to detect prison inmates who fake insanity or mental retardation. *Behavioral Sciences and the Law, 8,* 75–84.

Schulein, M. J. (1983). A cross-validation study of Megargee's MMPI Inmate Classification System at the Montana State Prison. *Dissertation Abstracts International, 44,* 1608.

Scott, N. A., Mount, M. K., & Duffy, P. S. (1977). MMPI and demographic correlates and predictions of female prison escape. *Criminal Justice and Behavior, 4,* 285–300.

Shands, H. C. (1958). *A report on an investigation of psychiatric problems in felons in the North Carolina prison system.* Unpublished manuscript.

Shea, S. J. (1993). Personality characteristics of self-mutilating male prisoners. *Journal of Clinical Psychology, 49,* 576–585.

Shea, S. J., McKee, G. R., Craig Shea, M. E., & Culley, D. C. (1996). MMPI–2 profiles of male pre-trial defendants. *Behavioral Sciences and the Law, 14,* 331–338.

Shealy, L., Kalichman, S. C., Henderson, M. C., Szymanowski, D., & McKee, G. (1991). MMPI profile subtypes of incarcerated sex offenders against children. *Violence and Victims, 6(3),* 201–212.

Shindo, H., & Kataoka, G. (1970). Some discussions on the measurement of delinquency with the MMPI: Report 5, In connection with findings of the factorial analysis of its 13 scales; Part 2. *Proceedings of the 34th Annual Convention of the Japanese Psychological Association, 498.*

Shindo, H., Ono, N., & Kataoka, G. (1969). Some discussions on the measurement of delinquency with the MMPI: Report 4, In connection with findings of the factorial analysis of its 13 scales. *Japanese Journal of Criminal Psychology, 7,* 14–20.

Shondrick, D. D., Ben-Porath, Y. S., & Stafford, K. (1992, May). *Forensic assessment with the MMPI–2: Characteristics of individuals undergoing court-ordered evaluations.* Paper presented at the 27th Annual Symposium on Recent Developments in the Use of the MMPI (MMPI–2), Minneapolis, MN.

Siegel, S. L. (2002). Typologies of sex offenders: A Minnesota Multiphasic Personality Inventory (MMPI) cluster analytic study. *Dissertation Abstracts International: Section B: The Sciences and Engineering, 62(9-B),* 4236.

Siemsen, R. A. (1999). Relationships of Rorschach and MMPI–2 variables to the Hare Psychopathy Checklist—Revised among mentally ill incarcerated felons. *Dissertations International: Section B: The Sciences and Engineering, 60(5-B),* 2367.

Simkins, L. (1993). Characteristics of sexually repressed child molesters. *Journal of Interpersonal Violence, 8(1),* 3–17.

Sittler, W. V., Webb, R. L., & Mandel, N. G. (1966). *A follow-up study of parole violation of individuals release from Minnesota correctional facilities from January 1, 1964, through December 31, 1964.* Unpublished manuscript.

Skolnick, N. J., & Zuckerman, M. (1979). Personality change in drug abusers: A comparison of therapeutic community and prison groups. *Journal of Consulting and Clinical Psychology, 47,* 768–770.

Sloore, H., Rossi, G., & Pham, T. (2004). MMPI–2 et diagnostic des troubles de la personnalité [MMPI–2 and the diagnosis of personality disorders]. In C. de Beaurepaire, M. Bénézech, & C. Kottler (Eds.), *Les dangerosités: de la criminologie à la psychopathologie, entre justice et psychiatrie* (pp. 211–221). Paris: John Libbey Eurotext.

Smith, L. B., Silber, D. E., & Karp, S. A. (1988). Validity of the Megargee–Bohn MMPI typology with women incarcerated in a state prison. *Psychological Reports, 62,* 107–113.

Smith, W. R., Monastersky, C., & Deisher, R. M. (1987). MMPI-based personality types among juvenile sexual offenders. *Journal of Clinical Psychology, 43*(4), 422–430.

Snortum, J. (1970). The relationship of self-concept and parent image to rule violations in a women's prison. *Journal of Clinical Psychology, 26,* 284–287.

Stanton, J. M. (1955). *The use of the MMPI to determine the group personality profile of state prison inmates and the relation of selected aspects of known anti-social behavior to profile components.* Unpublished doctoral dissertation, Fordham University, New York City.

Steigerwald, F., & Schmidt, L. (1974). On the diagnosis of juvenile delinquency with the Saarbrucken MMPI. *Psychologie und Praxis, 18,* 49–60.

Stein, K. B. (1967). Correlates of the ideational preference dimension among prison inmates. *Psychological Reports, 21,* 553–562.

Stein, K. B. (1968). Motoric and ideational dimensions: A study of personality styles among prison inmates. *Psychological Reports, 22,* 119–129.

Steininger, E. H. (1959). Changes in the MMPI profiles of first prison offenders during their first year of imprisonment. *Dissertation Abstracts International, 19,* 3394–3395.

Stoffer, S. S., Sapira, J. D., & Meketon, B. F. (1969). Behavior in ex-addict female prisoners participating in a research study. *Comprehensive Psychiatry, 10,* 224–232.

Stricklin, A. B., & Penk, M. L. (1980). Levels of imagery and personality dimensions in a female prison population. *Journal of Personality Assessment, 44,* 390–395.

Sutker, P. B. (1971). Personality differences and sociopathy in heroin addicts and nonaddict prisoners. *Journal of Abnormal Psychology, 78,* 247–251.

Sutker, P. B., Allain, A. N., & Geyer, S. (1978). Female criminal violence and differential MMPI characteristics. *Journal of Consulting and Clinical Psychology, 46,* 1141–1143.

Sutker, P. B., Moan, C. E., & Swanson, W. C. (1972). Porteus Maze Test qualitative performance in pure sociopaths, prison normals and antisocial psychotics. *Journal of Clinical Psychology, 28,* 349–353.

Sutker, P. B., & Moan, C. E. (1973). Prediction of socially maladaptive behavior within a state prison system. *Journal of Community Psychology, 1,* 74–78.

Sutker, P. B., Moan, C. E., & Allain, A. N. (1983). Assessment of cognitive control in psychopathic and normal prisoners. *Journal of Behavioral Assessment, 5,* 275–287.

Taylor, A. J. (1967). Prediction for parole: A pilot study with delinquent girls. *British Journal of Criminology, 7,* 418–424.

Templer, D. I., Kaiser, G., & Siscoe, K. (1993). Correlates of pathological gambling propensity in prison inmates. *Comprehensive Psychiatry, 34,* 347–351.

Thurston, D. R. (1955). *An investigation of the possibilities of parole prediction through the use of five personality inventories.* Unpublished doctoral dissertation, Michigan State University, Ann Arbor.

Tidefors-Andersson, I. (1995). Sexual abuse as a symptom of mental suffering, why? A qualitative pilot study of three incestuous fathers. *Nordisk Sexologi, 13*(3), 182–186.

Tohyama, B. (1971). An approach to the measurement of delinquency by the MMPI. *Psychological Test Data for Users, 1,* 25–27.

Tolan, J. C. (1981). The application of Megargee's MMPI prisoner typology within an incarcerated adolescent male population. *Dissertation Abstracts International, 42,* 2553.

Traub, G. S., & Bohn, M. J. (1985). Note on the reliability of the MMPI with Spanish-speaking inmates in the federal prison system. *Psychological Reports, 56,* 373–374.

Ullman, M. I. (1981). An MMPI study of the relationship between personality and criminal sexual behavior. *Dissertation Abstracts International, 41*(11-B), 4279.

Ulrich, J. F. (1997). A case study comparison of brief group treatment and brief individual treatment in the modification of denial among child sexual abusers. *Dissertation Abstracts International: Section B: The Sciences and Engineering, 57*(11-B), 7239.

Valliant, P. M., & Antonowicz, D. H. (1992). Rapists, incest offenders, and child molesters in treatment: Cognitive and social skills training. *International Journal of Offender Therapy and Comparative Criminology, 36*(3), 221–230.

Valliant, P. M., Asu, M. E., Cooper, D., & Mammola, D. (1984). Profile of dangerous and non-dangerous offenders referred for pre-trial psychiatric assessment. *Psychological Reports, 54*, 411–418.

Valliant, P. M., & Blasutti, B. (1992). Personality differences of sex offenders referred for treatment. *Psychological Reports, 71*(3, Pt 2), 1067–1074.

Valliant, P. M., Maksymchuck, L. L., & Antonowicz, D. (1995). Attitudes and personality traits of female adult victims of childhood abuse: A comparison of university students and incarcerated women. *Social Behavior and Personality, 23*(2), 205–215.

Van Cleve, E., Jemelka, R., & Trupin, E. (1991). Reliability of psychological test scores for offenders entering a state prison system. *Criminal Justice and Behavior, 18*, 159–165.

Van Dyke, P. (1954). *An investigation of self-mutilation at the Texas prison system in terms of the MMPI and other measures.* Unpublished doctoral dissertation, University of Texas, Austin.

Van Voorhis, P. (1994). *Psychological classification of the adult male prison inmate* (16th ed.). Albany: State University of New York Press.

Velasquez, R. J., Callahan, W. J., & Carrillo, R. (1989). MMPI profiles of Hispanic-American inpatient and outpatient sex offenders. *Psychological Reports, 65*(3, Pt. 1), 1055–1058.

Walters, G. D. (1986). Correlates of the Megargee criminal classification system: A military correctional setting. *Criminal Justice and Behavior, 13*, 19–32.

Walters, G. D. (1986). Screening for psychopathology in groups of Black and White prison inmates by means of the MMPI. *Journal of Personality Assessment, 50*, 257–264.

Walters, G. D. (1987). Child sex offenders and rapists in a military prison setting. *International Journal of Offender Therapy and Comparative Criminology, 31*, 261–269.

Walters, G. D., White, T. W., & Greene, R. L. (1988). Use of the MMPI to identify malingering and exaggeration of psychiatric symptomatology in male prison inmates. *Journal of Consulting and Clinical Psychology, 56*, 111–117.

Wang, X., Yang, D., Li, L., & Gao, B. (1997). Controlled study of aggressive behaviors and related factors in male schizophrenics and prisoners. *Chinese Mental Health Journal, 11*, 103–106.

Warman, R., & Hannum, T. (1965). MMPI pattern changes in female prisoners. *Journal of Research in Crime and Delinquency, 2*, 72–76.

Wasyliw, O. E., Benn, A. F., Grossman, L. S., & Haywood, T. W. (1998). Detection of minimization of psychopathology on the Rorschach in cleric and noncleric alleged sex offenders. *Assessment, 5*(4), 389–397.

Wasyliw, O. E., Grossman, L. S., & Haywood, T. W. (1994). Denial of hostility and psychopathology in the evaluation of child molestation. *Journal of Personality Assessment, 63*, 185–190.

Wasyliw, O. E., Grossman, L. S., Haywood, T. W., & Cavanaugh, J. L. (1988). The detection of malingering in criminal forensic groups: MMPI validity scales. *Journal of Personality Assessment, 52*, 321–333.

Watkins, E. R. (2000). MMPI profile configurations associated with convicted sex offenders from two West Virginia department of corrections facilities. *Dissertation Abstracts International: Section B: The Sciences and Engineering, 60*(11-B), 5798.

Watman, W. A. (1966). The relationship between acting out behavior and some psychological test indices in a prison population. *Journal of Clinical Psychology, 22,* 279–280.

Wattron, J. B. (1958). Validity of the March–Hilliard–Liechti MMPI Sexual Deviation Scale in a state prison population. *Journal of Consulting Psychology, 22,* 16.

Wattron, J. (1963). A prison maladjustment scale for the MMPI. *Journal of Clinical Psychology, 19,* 109–110.

Weiner, L. R. (1997). The presence of posttraumatic stress disorder in adult, male sex offenders as measured the Keane and Schlenger scales of the MMPI–2: The implication for addictions theory. *Dissertation Abstracts International: Section B: The Sciences and Engineering, 57*(8-B), 5349.

Weiss, J. M. (2000). Idiographic use of the MMPI–2 in the assessment of dangerousness among incarcerated felons. *International Journal of Offender Therapy and Comparative Criminology, 44*(1), 70–83.

Weissman, L., Moore, J. D., Thomas, G. B., & Whitman, E. N. (1972). Personality factors in prison volunteers related to response in clinical drug trials. *Journal of Clinical Pharmacology and New Drugs, 12,* 5–10.

Wheaton, D. K. (1973). A longitudinal study of prison recidivism with the Minnesota Multiphasic Personality Inventory and the Purpose in Life Test. *Dissertation Abstracts International, 33,* 7050–7051.

Whitacre, W. S. (1995, March). *MMPI–2 invalidity rates of incarcerated youthful sex offenders.* Paper presented at the 30th Annual Symposium on Recent Developments in the Use of the MMPI–2/MMPI–A, St. Petersburg, FL.

Whitaker, D., & Wodarski, J. S. (1988). Treatment of sexual offenders in a community mental health center: An evaluation. *Journal of Social Work and Human Sexuality, 7*(2), 49–68.

White, J. B. (1999). An efficacy study of the laws of living cognitive restructuring program for the rehabilitation of criminals, using an historical–descriptive meta-analysis method. *Dissertation Abstracts International, 59,* 3729.

White, R. B. (1979). Relationship of scores on the Escapism Scale of the MMPI to escape from minimum security federal custody. *Journal of Clinical Psychology, 35,* 467–470.

White, R. B. (1980). Prediction of adjustment to prison in a federal correctional population. *Journal of Clinical Psychology, 36,* 1031–1034.

White, R. B. (1981). Validity of the MMPI Prison Maladjustment scale in identifying disciplinary transfers among federally incarcerated male offenders. *Psychological Reports, 49,* 32–34.

Wirt, R. D., & Briggs, P. F. (1959). Personality and environmental factors in the development of delinquency. *Psychological Monographs, 73,* 47.

Wright, K. N. (1988). The relationship of risk, needs, and personality classification systems and prison adjustment. *Criminal Justice and Behavior, 15,* 454–471.

Wright, P., Nussbaum, D., Lynett, E., & Buis, T. (1997). Forensic MMPI–2 profiles: Normative limitations impose interpretive restrictions with both males and females. *American Journal of Forensic Psychology, 15*(4), 19–37.

Wynkoop, T. F. (1995). Development and validation of a classification system for child sexual abusers using the MMPI–2. *Dissertation Abstracts International: Section B: The Sciences and Engineering, 55*(8-B), 3605.

Yanagida, E. H., & Ching, J. W. (1993). MMPI profiles of child abusers. *Journal of Clinical Psychology, 49*(4), 569–576.

Zager, L. D. (1983). Response to Simmons and associates: Conclusions about the MMPI-based classification system's stability are premature. *Criminal Justice and Behavior, 10,* 310–315.

Zager, L. D. (1988). The MMPI–based criminal classification system: A review, current status, and future directions. *Criminal Justice and Behavior, 15,* 39–57.

Health Insurance Portability and Accountability Act Regulations: Frequently Asked Questions

BUYING AND SCORING PEARSON ASSESSMENTS TESTS

Q: Is Pearson Assessments a covered entity[1] under HIPAA?

A: No.

Q: Is Pearson Assessments a business associate[2] to customers who use Pearson Assessments' MICROTEST Q™ or Q Local™ software or scoring services? Should these customers enter into a *business associate agreement* with Pearson Assessments?

A: No. Business associates must receive, create or use individually identifiable health information[3] for or on behalf of a covered entity. Our customers may be covered entities, but they do not disclose individually identifiable health information to us. For that reason, Pearson Assessments is not a business associate to its customers.

- Purchasing test materials or administrations from Pearson Assessments: No individually identifiable health information is disclosed by the customer to Pearson Assessments in the course of purchasing our tests or MICROTEST Q or Q Local test administrations.
- Scoring tests using MICROTEST Q or Q Local software: Because the software resides entirely on our customer's computer system, there is no disclosure of individually identifiable health in-

formation to Pearson Assessments in the course of scoring tests using the software.

- Scoring tests using Pearson Assessments' scoring services: Pearson Assessments does not require individually identifiable health information in order to score answer sheets sent by mail or fax. Over the past year, we have removed name grids and spaces for other identifying information from most of our forms, leaving the forms identified only by a (non-social security number) ID number that is selected by the customer. We have no way of linking the ID number with an individual. Therefore, the information contained in the answer sheets is not individually identifiable health information when it arrives at Pearson Assessments for scoring.

Q: What if the customer has answer sheets that include name grids and other such identifiable information? Can these still be scored by Pearson Assessments?

A: Yes, with a little modification. The HIPAA regulations allow individually identifiable health information to be de-identified prior to disclosure by the covered entity.[4] Because we do not need the answer sheet to be individually identifiable in order to score the test and return it to their customer, we ask you to de-identify the answer sheet before

From Pearson Assessments "HIPAA Regulations (Frequently Asked Questions)" © 2005 Pearson Assessments. Reprinted with permission. Retrieved January 17, 2006, from http://www.pearsonassessments.com/catalog/hipaa.pdf.

[1] See 45 CFR 160.103.
[2] See 45 CFR 160.103.
[3] See 45 CFR 160.103.
[4] See 45 CFR 164.514 (a) and (b).

sending. In simple terms, that means that the customer will omit or use a marker to completely conceal the name and other individually identifiable information prior to sending the form. If you have questions about what information to omit or conceal, our client relations representatives will be happy to provide test-specific guidance.

Patient Access To and Right To Copy Test Information and Results Under HIPAA

As you know, most Pearson Assessments' test materials and output reports were never intended to be handed to the patient. They are sold for use only by qualified professionals. Testing material is protected by intellectual property law including copyright and trade secret law. The disclosure of test material could damage the test's integrity and usefulness in evaluation, diagnosis and treatment. Therefore, Pearson Assessments recommends that its customers do not provide access to or copies of test materials and/or reports unless disclosure is clearly required. Under the HIPAA statute,[5] *covered entities* are not required to provide a patient with access to and or the right to copy any test materials or reports to the extent that doing so would result in the disclosure of trade secrets.

Your organization, as a covered entity, may have generated HIPAA disclosure guidelines for your use. In creating those guidelines, your organization may or may not have given assessments any specific attention. The following information may be helpful to both you and your organization. Please read this entire section and share it with your HIPAA compliance officer and/or legal counsel.

Q: If a patient makes a HIPAA request for access to or copies of test materials and/or reports, what kind of disclosure is required?

A: Under HIPAA, covered entities are not required to provide a patient with access to and/or the right to copy any material or information that is not Protected Health Information or PHI.

Q: What is Protected Health Information or PHI?

A: Under HIPAA, protected health information or PHI[6] is individually identifiable health information that is used to make decisions about an individual and is maintained in the designated record set.

The following portions of our test materials are NOT PHI because they do not contain individually identifiable health information. Therefore, PATIENTS SHOULD BE DENIED ACCESS TO AND COPIES OF THE FOLLOWING under a HIPAA request:

1. Test booklets (when answers are entered on a separate form)
2. Test questions (by themselves)
3. Test manuals
4. Test user guides
5. Wall charts
6. Scoring templates
7. Scoring keys
8. Computer scoring programs such as MICROTEST Q or Q Local software.
9. Profile and Interpretive Reports are addressed in the next question. PLEASE READ ON.

Q: Are covered entities required to provide access to and copies of Profile and Interpretive reports?

A: No, there is an explicit exception in the HIPAA[7] statute that exempts trade secrets from disclosure. Because Pearson Assessments protects MICROTEST Q software and Q Local software and the computerized output reports generated using MICROTEST Q and Q Local as trade secrets, PATIENTS SHOULD BE ALSO DENIED ACCESS TO THE FOLLOWING (Note that this denial applies to requests under HIPAA or any other data disclosure law that exempts trade secrets from disclosure):

1. MICROTEST Q or Q Local Software containing patient files,

---

[5] Social Security Act § 1172(e) (codified at 42 U.S.C. § 1320d-1(e)).
[6] See 45 CFR 164.501.
[7] Social Security Act § 1172(e) (codified at 42 U.S.C. § 1320d-1(e)).

2. Profile or Interpretive Reports generated using MICROTEST Q OR Q Local profile reports software, and

3. Profile or Interpretive Reports obtained by mailing or faxing answer sheets to Pearson Assessments mail-in scoring service.

Q: What might the patient expect to be provided access to and copies of?

A: Unless there is an explicit exception in the HIPAA regulation, an individual has the right to inspect and obtain a copy of protected health information or PHI about the individual in a designated record set, for so long as the PHI is maintained in the designated record set.

If the request is not subject to denial (read further to learn about exceptions in the HIPAA regulations that permit denial of access), the patient may expect disclosure of:

1. Answer sheets stored by the covered entity that are identified by the patient's ID number, and on which the patient has marked the bubbles or filled in the blanks.
2. The Item Response page (only) generated by MICROTEST Q or Q Local software.

Q: May a covered entity provide a patient with summary information rather than access to or copies of test answer sheets and reports?

A: Yes. The HIPAA regulations allow a covered entity to provide an individual with summary information rather than underlying file documents but only if the patient agrees in advance to receive such a summary. Note, however, an individual who earlier agrees to receive summary information does not relinquish the right to later request access to the underlying documents. Access to and copies of MICROTEST Q or Q Local Software or Profile and Interpretive Reports should be denied under such a later request.

Q: Under what other circumstances may a covered entity deny access to or copies of Protected Health Information?

A: Denials can also be based on the application of professional judgment on the part of the covered entity. HIPAA regulations state that a covered entity may deny an individual access, provided that the individual is given a right to have such denials reviewed . . . in the following circumstances:

(i) A licensed health care professional has determined, in the exercise of professional judgment, that the access requested is reasonably likely to endanger the life or physical safety of the individual or another person;

(ii) The protected health information makes reference to another person (unless such other person is a health care provider) and a licensed health care professional has determined, in the exercise of professional judgment, that the access requested is reasonably likely to cause substantial harm to such other person; or

(iii) The request for access is made by the individual's personal representative and a licensed health care professional has determined, in the exercise of professional judgment, that the provision of access to such personal representative is reasonably likely to cause substantial harm to the individual or another person.

Denials by correctional facilities or those covered entities supporting correctional facilities, in response to requests by inmates are specifically addressed in the regulations. Covered entities providing services to inmates should be familiar with those provisions of the privacy regulations.

Access to Protected Health Information may be denied if the PHI was compiled "in reasonable anticipation of, or for use in, a civil, criminal, or administrative action or proceeding."[8] Pearson Assessments believes this provision of the privacy regulation should apply as follows: Covered entities may deny access to and the right to copy if PHI was compiled in reasonable anticipation of or for use in:

---

[8] 45 C.F.R. 164.524(a)(1)(ii).

FORENSIC

- Child custody disputes
- Commitment hearings (mental health institutions)
- Conservator/guardianship/competency hearings
- Competency to stand trial/commitment hearings
- Civil/criminal/pre-trial/pre-sentence criminal evaluations
    - Getting back driver's license after DUI
- Insanity defense
- Personal injury lawsuits/neurological evaluations
- Determine malingering, lying, acting
    - Workers Compensation
    - Work hardening programs
    - Social Security Disability evaluations
    - Personal injury evaluations
    - Insanity defense

CIVIL, CRIMINAL TRIALS

- To support or impeach expert testimony

CORRECTIONAL: To support classification, treatment, and management decisions at intake and throughout incarceration in criminal justice and correctional settings. (Housing placement) (security level), parole, pre-sentence investigation, probation)

- Readiness to be released
- Assess behaviors
- Security risks
- Rehabilitation potential
- Assess substance abuse, sexual predation, or mental instability (for placement in certain programs)

MARRIAGE AND FAMILY COUNSELING (in legal proceedings)

- Parental fitness
- Adoption evaluations

Q: Are there any other issues that customers should be aware of related to Pearson Assessments' tests and HIPAA regulations?

A: You should check with your HIPAA compliance officer for legal advice and information specific to your covered entity. As you know, all Pearson Assessments' tests and output reports are protected by copyright and other intellectual property rights. As the HIPAA regulations are clarified, the information in these pages is subject to change. The issue of whether copyrighted material may be disclosed under HIPAA remains an open legal question. Even though MICROTEST Q software, Q Local Software, and Profile and Interpretive reports are exempt from disclosure as trade secrets and test booklets, manuals, user guides, wall charts, scoring keys and templates are exempt from disclosure because they are not PHI, nevertheless, some patients may be entitled to inspect and/or copy portions of PHI such as their bubble answer sheet (without question text) and the Item Responses page (only) generated by MICROTEST Q or Q Local software.

The covered entity's HIPAA compliance officer or legal counsel should advise you regarding changes and modifications to the regulations, and the outcome of HIPAA-related litigation. If you have additional questions specifically related to HIPAA and Pearson Assessments, please call our client relations representatives at 1-800-627-7271.

FHIPAAFL 757-GEN 03/05 http://www.pearsonassessments.com | order by phone: 1-888-627-7271 | order by fax: 1-800-632-9011 CCL HIPAA REGULATIONS http://www.pearsonassessments.com | order by phone: 1-888-627-7271 | order by fax: 1-800-632-9011.

Health Insurance Portability and Accountability Act Position Statement

Many of our customers have inquired regarding Harcourt Assessment's position on whether test record forms must be disclosed to patients in order to comply with the Privacy Rule of the Health Insurance Portability and Accountability Act (HIPAA). The HIPAA Privacy Rule provides that individuals have a qualified right of access to individually identifiable health information maintained by health care providers covered by HIPAA. The widespread dissemination of record forms (which may disclose test questions and answers) would violate restrictions on providers' use of Harcourt Assessment's materials and would render test instruments invalid and therefore useless to the clinical community and to the public at large. In order to obtain clarification regarding this matter, Harcourt Assessment requested an opinion from the U.S. Department of Health and Human Services (HHS), which is responsible for HIPAA. We received a response from Richard Campanelli, the Director of the Office for Civil Rights at HHS, who stated in response:

> [A]ny requirement for disclosure of protected health information pursuant to the Privacy Rule is subject to Section 1172(e) of HIPAA, "Protection of Trade Secrets." As such, we confirm that it would not be a violation of the Privacy Rule for a covered entity to refrain from providing access to an individual's protected health information, to the extent that doing so would result in a disclosure of trade secrets.

Accordingly, as we have done for many years, we will continue to advise our customers that Harcourt Assessment's test instruments are trade secrets and their usefulness and value would be compromised if they were generally available to the public. We have stated this position in correspondence, court cases, news articles and on our website for many years. This position is also consistent with our longstanding practice of ensuring through our terms and conditions of use that all purchasers have the appropriate qualifications to administer and interpret the instruments being purchased and that such purchasers agree to maintain the confidentiality of the instruments.

Given the above-quoted support from HHS, Harcourt Assessment reiterates that customers may not disseminate copies of test record forms or protocols to persons who erroneously claim that they are entitled to copies under HIPAA. As the HHS has now confirmed, HIPAA does not require any person to disclose any trade secret materials, and all restrictions on the dissemination of test record forms and protocols remain in effect.

Multi-Health Systems Inc. Test Disclosure Policy

Adopted by leading Canadian test publishers and the Canadian Psychological Association ("CPA")

Client Access to Test Results in Canada

The position of Multi-Health Systems Inc. ("MHS") and Harcourt Assessment on the issue of test disclosure and the release of test results takes into consideration access rights to test information and results under the Canadian *Personal Information Protection and Electronic Documents Act* ("PIPEDA") and the United States' *Health Insurance Portability and Accountability Act* ("HIPAA"). For over 20 years, we have consistently applied and continue to maintain our non-disclosure policies regarding test items, response/answer sheets (which include test items), test manuals, user guides, wall charts, scoring templates, scoring keys, scoring programs and other test protocols ("Test Materials"), which is consistent with new privacy legislation in both Canada and the United States.

CPA, leading test developers, and the release of test results under PIPEDA and provincial privacy legislation

The Canadian Psychological Association ("CPA") (www.cpa.ca), MHS, and Harcourt Assessment maintain a policy of non-disclosure of Test Materials to clients who request such material under PIPEDA and provincial legislation. Psychologists and other qualified test purchasers are encouraged to follow this policy in order to protect the integrity/ validity of the assessment, protect the public, and the publisher's intellectual property rights.

Canadian legislation is not applicable to defined intra-provincial transactions of some organizations where that province has "substantially similar" legislation to PIPEDA. The Quebec *Act Respecting the Protection of Personal Information in the Private Sector*, the British Columbia and Alberta *Personal Information Protection Acts* and the Ontario *Personal Health Information Act* are expected to be declared "substantially similar" by the federal Cabinet. These Acts therefore govern disclosure requests in those provinces. In practical terms, an organization in compliance with these Acts will generally be in compliance with PIPEDA. In all other provinces and territories, the federal legislation PIPEDA applies. These pieces of legislation apply to all personal information, including personal health information about an identifiable individual collected, retained, used, or disclosed in the course of commercial activities. This could include responses to items, test results, test data, reports, name, age, and gender of each client who has been administered an assessment by you, the qualified purchaser of an assessment.

Under PIPEDA, Principle 4.9 states that upon request, an individual must be informed of the existence, use, and disclosure of his or her personal information and must be given access to that information if requested. **Section 9(3)(b) is an exemption provision stipulating that you are not required to give access to personal information** if to do so would reveal confidential commercial information. However, under certain circumstances, access is permissible if the confidential commercial information is severable from the record containing any other information for which access is requested. In all cases, the requested information shall be provided or made available in a form that is generally understandable to the client. Section 23 (b) in the BC Act and Section 24 (2) (b) in the Alberta Acts contain a similar "confidential commercial information" exemption as described above. The Quebec Act does not contain such an exemption; however, release of personal health information may be refused on the basis that release would bring serious harm to the client, third party, or public safety, and would reveal third party personal information. Unlike PIPEDA and provincial legislation, the new Ontario Personal Health Information Act, 2004 effective November 1, 2004, at Section 51(1)(c) provides that an individual's access rights do NOT apply to a record that contains "raw data from standardized psychological tests or assessments," unless reasonably severable. Access can also be refused on the basis that access may cause serious bodily harm.

Regarding the release of such material to individuals who claim access rights under PIPEDA and provincial legislation, we advise that Test Materials fall outside the definition of "personal information" since these materials are not "about" the individual and are thus not releasable to a client.

Even if Test Materials are considered personal information and thereby releasable, we advise that our Test Materials are proprietary, copyrighted, confidential commercial information, analogous to trade secrets, and we treat and protect them accordingly. Test Materials thus fall under the exception to release and access under PIPEDA and provincial legislation in order to ensure the ongoing safeguarding of such material. To provide clients with test items, scoring criteria, and other test protocols would be to reveal confidential commercial information on which the scores are based and would render the Test Materials useless. Studies confirm that if test items and test protocols were readily available, the integrity of the test and scor-

ing model could be compromised and would harm the public. There are a limited number of tests for particular purposes that cannot be easily replaced or substituted if made available upon request.

Other jurisdictions such as in the United States have indicated through the U.S. Department of Health and Human Services (HHS) that the similar "trade secret" exemption under HIPAA is applicable to Testing Material which makes the application of the confidential commercial information exemption claim neither *fanciful nor disingenuous in the Canadian context.*

The test publishing industry considers Test Materials to be confidential information and trade secrets and protects these accordingly. To secure and protect Test Materials, MHS and Harcourt Assessment have required, for the past 20 years, the completion of a Test User Agreement which prohibits purchasers from copying and releasing the tests to others who are not qualified to interpret the results or do not have the same ethical obligations to maintain test security, nor have we permitted licensees, distributors, or employees to disclose such material.

The CPA acknowledges that it is in the best interest of the public to protect the validity and integrity of Test Materials. As such, CPA, MHS, and Harcourt Assessment encourage you to apply the confidential commercial information exemption under PIPEDA to access requests to ensure the ongoing safeguarding of Test Materials. Release of such material would compromise the validity and utility of the tests with resulting significant negative impact on the health of Canadians, lead to the violation of purchase agreements, and infringe on the intellectual property rights of MHS and Harcourt Assessment. Ontario legislation appears to recognize the inherent difficulty in releasing raw data including test protocols from assessments and has specifically denied access right to this material unless severable from the record.

In accordance with PIPEDA and provincial legislation, MHS, Harcourt Assessment, and CPA's policy supports the release of test results provided that the test results can be severed from the confidential commercial information embedded in the Test Materials and released in an understandable form. This policy permits the release of test results with an explanation of the results in a summary format (such as a feedback summary) that does not reveal the protected test items and other test protocols. Under no circumstances are individuals requesting results or other information entitled to copies of Test Materials.

Upon written request for access and release of Test Materials from your clients under PIPEDA and provincial legislation, the following steps should be followed:

(1) Provide the client with a detailed description/ interpretation of the test results and offer to meet with the client.

(2) If the client wants a copy of the item booklet, or response sheet that also contain the items, and/or any materials that contain the scoring criteria, algorithm, model, or other test protocols, explain to them in writing that release of these materials is not possible as it will compromise the integrity of the tests and goes against the policy of the CPA and test developers.

The requested materials are considered confidential commercial information of the test developers, MHS and Harcourt Assessment, and are therefore exempt from disclosure under PIPEDA or provincial legislation. Release of such materials may breach the conditions of the Test User Agreements, invalidate the assessment, and/or lead to a violation of intellectual property rights.

(3) You may release the client's test results provided you are able to remove test items and scoring criteria, or other test protocols that may be attached to the results or within the document, which are considered confidential commercial information. The test results must be issued in an understandable form, such as a summary format. We suggest the provision of a detailed description/interpretation of the test results as stated in step 1, which does not release any confidential commercial information,

is sufficient for the purposes of PIPEDA and provincial legislation.

(4) Contact MHS or Harcourt Assessment for support if the client appeals your decision to deny access and release of Test Materials to the Privacy Commissioner of Canada, Alberta, BC, Quebec, and Ontario as the case may be.

For more information regarding CPA's policy regarding PIPEDA and provincial legislation go to their website www.cpa.ca. For information regarding release of Test Materials in the litigation context see [below].

Test Disclosure in the United States

In the US context, the HIPAA Privacy Rule provides that individuals have a qualified right of access to individually "identifiable health information" maintained in their "designated record set" by health care providers covered by HIPAA. MHS advises that Test Materials, such as test protocols, items, scoring criteria, and manuals by themselves are not "identifiable health information" and are thus not releasable. Since HIPAA does not state that the requested information should be made available in a form that is generally understandable to the client, MHS advises health care providers to retain Test Materials, such as item booklets, manuals, and scoring criteria separate from the client's designated record set. In these circumstances, upon written request, a client may gain access to only the test results.

Even if Test Materials are considered releasable, Section 1172 (e) states that health care providers are not required to disclose any information that is a trade secret or confidential commercial information. The U.S. Department of Health and Human Services (HHS) has confirmed by way of a letter dated August 6, 2003, that a client's access request is subject to the trade secret exemption:

[A]ny requirement for disclosure of protected health information pursuant to the Privacy Rule is subject to Section 1172 (e) of HIPAA, 'Protection of Trade Secrets.' As such, we confirm that it would not be a violation of the Privacy Rule for a covered entity to refrain from providing access to an individual's protected health information, to the extent that doing so would result in a disclosure of trade secrets.

HHS has confirmed that the trade secret exemption applies to proprietary Test Materials. MHS has adopted Harcourt Assessment's position statement on HIPAA which states: "HIPAA does not require any person to disclose trade secret material, and all restriction on dissemination of test record forms and protocols remain in effect." As already stated, MHS considers all of its Test Materials to be trade secrets and confidential commercial information, the release of which would violate the Test User Agreement, and compromise the validity, integrity, and value of the assessments. Health care providers may refrain from providing access to and copies of a client's identifiable health information, in so far as to do so would reveal valuable trade secrets and propriety information. It is our recommendation that you obtain consent from your clients and that you provide clients with summary information.

For additional information regarding MHS' policy on HIPAA, visit www.mhs.com/legal, email customerservice@mhs.com, or call 1-416-492-2627. For additional information regarding Harcourt Assessment's policy on HIPAA, visit www.psychcorp.com, email legalaffairs@harcourt.com, or contact Legal Affairs at 1-800-228-0752.

Release of Test Materials in the Litigation Context and Ethical Obligations

We recognize that, given the nature of our legal system, compelling reasons for disclosure of secured testing material may arise. To abide by the terms of purchase, we expect purchasers to do all they can to protect copyright material and to protect the items and scoring criteria as confidential, copyrighted, and trade secret material in response to written requests and/or subpoenas. An exception to releasing test data by a subpoena exists when the qualified purchaser obtains a court order extinguishing, also known as "quashing" or modifying, the subpoena. In this case, we require qualified purchasers to bring to the court's attention con-

cerns regarding test security and to take steps to resolve the conflict in a responsible manner. When faced with a subpoena or court order for the reproduction of Test Materials, you should secure a court order or protective agreement (to the extent possible) containing the following requirements:

(a) restricted access to materials and the testimony regarding materials to the most limited audience possible, preferably only to individuals who satisfy the test publisher's qualification policy;

(b) restricted copying of Test materials;

(c) assurance of the return or destruction of the materials at the conclusion of the proceeding (and confirmation of such return or destruction); and

(d) the sealing of and/or removing from the record to the extent any portion of such materials are disclosed in pleadings, testimony, or other documents in order to safeguard the integrity of the assessments. It is crucial that the Test Materials do not become part of the public record.

In the absence of a protective court order, we do not support the release of Test Materials to unqualified users who do not have an interest in maintaining the security of the test for the reasons stated above. You may wish to consult a lawyer to assist you with the above.

How to Contact Us Re: Test Disclosure

If you have any questions or concerns about the release of protected test materials, please contact MHS by email at privacyofficer@mhs.com or call 1-800-268-6011 (within Canada) or 1-800-456-3003 (within the U.S) or 1-416-492-2627 (outside of Canada & the U.S.); or contact Harcourt Assessments by email at CS_Canada@Harcourt.com or call 1-800-387-7278.

Personal Information of Our Customers

MHS is committed to safeguarding the privacy of our customers' personal information. We regularly review our qualification and purchase administration procedures and have established a comprehensive Privacy Policy that complies with PIPEDA and specifically defines how and why we collect, use, and disclose personal information.

To purchase our products and/or become a certified user of our assessments, customers must complete a Qualification Form (online, via email, or mail-in) to determine eligibility and, through the purchase process, we ask for your name, address, license number, credit card information, and other personal data required to process your request to purchase and maintain your customer account. We also collect information that allows us to enhance our products and services and provide you with more personalized services and a greater selection of products.

Personal Information of our Customers' Clients

In general, purchasing test materials and administrations, or becoming certified does not involve the transfer of personal information of our clients' customers.

No personal information is disclosed to MHS while using scoring software. Scoring software (e.g., SmarthLink™) are stand-alone platforms intended to run on a single desktop, but which can be integrated into a network of PCs.

In regards to our mail/fax scoring services, MHS encourages our customers to provide client ID numbers (not a Social Insurance Number (SIN) or a Social Security Number (SSN)) rather than a client's name on the response sheet so that MHS does not receive any identifiable personal information. By doing this, MHS has no way to link an ID number with a specific individual. MHS will accept, for scoring purposes, any response sheets that contain a client's name, age, responses, and other personal information. Answer sheets, once received, are kept in a locked, access-restricted cabinet. Those that are faxed, are accessible on our internal network only by client service representatives and others authorized to access such material.

As of April 5, 2004, to further protect the data transmitted to MHS, MHS' online scoring services has encrypted access passwords, which means that identifiable data will be made accessible only to our customers or their designated administrators ("Administrators"). Administrators are prompted to change their existing password the first time they log into the MHS Scoring Organizer. The client's information, including any personal information, will no longer be accessible by MHS unless an Administrator provides MHS with his or her protected password. However, MHS will be able to reset a password, at the request of an Administrator if necessary.

If MHS makes changes to our policy, we will post a prominent notice on our home page at www.mhs.com and may send you a notice by mail or email, if required. We would appreciate your help in keeping your contact information current and complete.

If you have any questions or concerns about the privacy of your personal information or that of your clients, please email customerservice@ mhs.com or call 1-800-268-6011 (within Canada) or 1-800-456-3003 (within the U.S) or 1-416-492-2627 (outside of Canada & the U.S.).

Last updated September 1, 2004.

MMPI–2 and MMPI–A Translations

MMPI–2

Arabic:
> Abdalla M. Soliman
> Department of Psychology
> Faculty of Education
> United Arab Emirates University
> AL-AIN, P.O. Box 17771
> United Arab Emirates
>> 97-13-5063310, (fax) 97-13-656457

Chile:
> Fernando J. Rissetti
> Departamentlo de Salud Estudiantil
> Pontificia Universidad
> Catolicia de Chile
> JV Lastarria 65
> Santiago, Chile SA5
>> (fax) 562-638-0638,
>>> (E-mail) frissett@lascar.puc.cl

Chinese:
> 1. Fanny Cheung
> Chinese University of Hong Kong
> Department of Psychology
> Shatin, N.T. Hong Kong
>> 852-2-6096498, (fax) 852-2-6035019,
>>> (E-mail) fmcheung@cuhk.edu.hk

> 2. Song Wei Zhen
> Institute of Psychology
> Chinese Academy of Sciences
> P.O. Box 1603, Postcode 100012
> Bejing, China

Croatian:
> Naklada Slap[1]

Czech:
> Testcentrum, a subsidiary of Hans Huber Verlag,
> Bratislava

Danish:
> In process.

Dutch/Flemish:
> 1. PEN Test Publishers
> P.O. Box 6537
> 6503 GA Nijmegen, The Netherlands
>> 31-24-3240884, (fax) 31-481-465867

> 2. Hedwig Sloore
> Free University of Brussels
> Department of Psychology
> Pleinlaan 2
> Brussels, Belgium
>> 32-2-629-2516, (fax) 32-2-6292489,
>>> (E-mail) hsloore@vnet3.uub.ac.be

Ethiopian:
> Tenbit Emiru
> Department of Psychology
> University of Minnesota
> Minneapolis, MN 55455
>> (E-mail) Emir0001@tc.umn.edu

---

[1] When complete contact information is not available, we have provided as much information as possible.

Farsi:
   1. Elahe Nezami
   Institute for Health Promotion and Disease
      Prevention Research
   School of Medicine
   3375 S. Hoover St.
   University Village, Suite E210
   MC-7798
   Los Angeles, CA 90089-7798
      213-821-1600

   2. Reza Zamani (University of Teheran)

French:
   Edition du Centre de Psychologie Appliqué
   25 rue de la Plaine
   75980 Paris, Cedex 20, France
      33-1-40-09-62-62, (fax) 33-1-40-09-62-80

French-Canadian:
   Canadian customers contact:
   Multi-Health Systems
   65 Overlea Blvd., Suite 210
   Toronto, Ontario M4H 1PI
      416-424-1700

German:
   Jurgen Hogrefe
   Verlag Hans Huber
   Langgass-Strasse 76
   CH-3000
   Bern 9
   Switzerland
      41-31-242533 (fax) 41-31-243380

Greek:
   Anna Kokkevi
   Department of Psychiatry
   Athens University Medical School
   Eginition Hospital
   72-74 Vassilissis Sopphias Ave.
   Athens, 11528 Greece
      33-1-721-7763, (fax) 30-1-724-3905

Hebrew:
   Moshe Almagor
   University of Haifa

Faculty of Social Sciences
Mount Carmel, Haifa 31905, Israel
   972-4-240-111, (fax) 972-4-246814
   or -240966

Hmong:
   Customer Service
   Pearson (National Computer Systems)
   5601 Green Valley Drive
   Bloomington, MN 55437-1099
      1-800-627-7271, (fax) 952-681-3259

Icelandic (Old Norse):
   Solvina Konrads, Erlendur Haraldsson, and
      Jakob Smari
   University of Iceland
   Hrisholti 7
   210 Garoabae, Iceland

Indonesian:
   Lena Halim
   PEN, Nijmegen
   Postbus 6537-6503 GA
   Nijmegen, The Netherlands
      (E-mail) magdalenah@fp.atmajaya.ac.id

Italian:
   1. Roberto Mattei
   Organizzazioni Speciali
   Via Scipione Ammirato 37-50136 Firenze, Italy
      55-660-997, (fax) 55-669-446

   2. Saolo Sirigatti
   Dip. Psicologia
   Universita di Firenze
   Via S. Niccolo, 93, Italy
      39-55-2491618, (fax) 39-55-2345326

   3. Paolo Pancheri
   CIC Edizioni Internazionali
   5a Cattedra di clinica Psichiatrica
   36, Viale Dell' Universita
   00185 Roma Italia
      39-6-902-49244 x501, (fax) 39-6-3210494

Japanese:
   Noriko Shiota
   Department of Psychology

Villanova University
Villanova, PA 19085
610-519-7772, (fax) 610-519-4269

Current researcher/norm developer
Takashi Hayama
Mental Health and Welfare Division
Minato-Chop NAKA-KU
Yokohama 231-0017-JAPAN
81-45-671-3935 (fax) 81-45-681-2533
(E-mail) xn3t-hym@asahi-net.or.jp

Korean:
1. Kyunghee Han
Central Michigan University
Department of Psychology
Mount Pleasant, MI 48859
989-774-6488

2. Maumsarang Co. Ltd.

3. JeeYoung Lim

Latvian:
Zinta Sarma

Spanish/Mexico:
1. Manual Moderno
Av Sonora 206
Col. Hipodromo, 06100 Mexico, D.F.
52-5-265-1100, (fax) 52-5-265-1162

2. Emilia Lucio G.M. and Isabel Reyes-Lagunes
Corregidora 30-1
Col. Miguel Hidalgo Tialpan
CP 14410
Mexico, DF
525-665-6325, (fax) 525-528-5253

Norwegian:
Bjorn Ellertsen
University of Bergen
Clinical Neuropsychology
Arstadveien 21
Bergen, Norway N-5009
47-55-29170, (fax) 47-55-589873

Romanian:
Michael Stevens

Russian:
1. Vladimar Martens
Institute of Biophysics
Zilapistnaya 46
Moscow, 182 Russia

2. Victor Koscheyev

Spanish/Argentina:
Maria Casullo
University of Buenos Aires
Faculty of Psychology
Tucuman 2162, 8th Floor A
1050 Buenos Aires, Argentina
541-953-1218, (fax) 541-49-4332,
(E-mail) casullo@insinv.psi.uba.ar

Spanish/Spain:
Alejando Avila-Espade
Universidad de Salamanca
Department of Psychology

Thai:
La-or Pongpanich
Psychiatric Department
Army General Hospital
Bangkok, Thailand
(fax) 66-02-245-5702 or 66-02-245-5641

Turkish:
Merla Culha
Koc University
Cayir Caddesi No. 5
Istinye, 80860
Istanbul, Turkey
212-229-3006 x 502
(fax) 212-229-3602-229-50

United States:
1. Customer Service
Pearson (National Computer Systems)
5601 Green Valley Drive
Bloomington, MN 55437-1099
1-800-627-7271, (fax) 952-681-3259

2. Alex Azan
Florida International University
Student Counseling Services
University Park-GC 211
Miami, FL 33199
305-348-2880, (fax) 305-348-3448

3. Rosa Garcia-Peltoniemi
Center for the Victims of Torture
717 East River Road
Minneapolis, MN 55455
612-626-1400, (fax) 612-626-2465

Vietnamese:
Pauline Tran
1258 Capistrano Lane
Vista, CA 92083
760-630-1680, (fax) 760-630-1680

MMPI–A

Chinese:
Fanny Cheung
Chinese University of Hong Kong
Department of Psychology
Shatin, N.T. Hong Kong
852-2-6096498, (fax) 852-2-6035019,
(E-mail) fmcheung @cuhk.edu.hk

French:
Edition du Centre de Psychologie Appliqué
25 rue de la Plaine
75980 Paris, Cedex 20, France
33-1-40-09-62-62, (fax) 33-1-40-09-62-80

Greek:
Anna Kokkevi
Department of Psychiatry
Athens University Medical School
Eginition Hospital
72-74 Vassilissis Sopphias Ave.
Athens, 11528 Greece
33-1-721-7763, (fax) 30-1-724-3905

Hebrew:
Moshe Almagor
University of Haifa
Faculty of Social Sciences

Mount Carmel, Haifa 31905, Israel
972-4-240-111, (fax) 972-4-246814 or
240966

Italian:
Roberto Mattei
Organizzazioni Speciali
Via Scipione Ammirato 37-50136 Firenze, Italy
55-660-997, (fax) 55-669-446

Korean:
Jeeyoung Lim
802-501 Hanjin APT
Jeongdun-Maul
193 Jeongja-Dong, Boondang-Gu
Sungnam-City, Kynuggi-Do
South Korea
822-729-9191, (fax) 822-729-9082,
(E-mail) mmpi2@samsung.co.kr

Norwegian:
Bjorn Ellertsen
University of Bergen
Clinical Neuropsychology
Arstadveien 21
Bergen, Norway N-5009
47-55-29170, (fax) 47-55-589873

Russian
Mera Atlis 510
Everett St.
El Cerrito, CA 94530
510-524-4426

Spanish/Mexico:
1. Manual Moderno
Av Sonora 206
Col. Hipodromo, 06100 Mexico, D.F.
52-5-265-1100, (fax) 52-5-265-1162

2. Emilia Lucio G.M. and Isabel Reyes-Lagunes
Corregidora 30-1
Col. Miguel Hidalgo Tialpan
CP 14410
Mexico, DF
525-665-6325, (fax) 525-528-5253

Thai:
  La-or Pongpanich
  Psychiatric Department
  Army General Hospital
  Bangkok, Thailand
    (fax) 66-02-245-5702 or 66-02-245-5641

United States:
  Pearson (National Computer Systems)
  5601 Green Valley Drive
  Bloomington, MN 55437-1099
    1-800-627-7271, (fax) 952-681-3259

Sample Agreement Between Expert Witness and Attorney

Chapter 5 discussed the different approaches that expert witnesses and attorneys use to reach agreement on fees. This appendix sets forth an example of a fee agreement. What is important is that the written agreement provide a clear understanding between attorney and expert witness about how fees are to be calculated and paid. The example given requires payment of all fees in advance. Advance payment prevents situations in which the expert witness has conducted an assessment, written a report, billed the attorney, but not received full payment when due.

Any sample agreement, of course, should be adapted to meet the needs of the individual expert witness, the specific circumstances of the assessment, and any applicable legislation, case law, and other standards or regulations in the relevant jurisdiction.

Before using any agreement, the expert witness should always and in all circumstances review the form with his or her own professional liability attorney (i.e., not the attorney who is hiring the individual as an expert witness) to ensure that it fully meets the applicable legal, ethical, and professional standards as well as the needs and approaches of the expert witness.

CONSULTANT AGREEMENT
[NAME OF EXPERT WITNESS]

Initial Case Review and Consultation

There is an initial, nonrefundable case-opening, review, and consultation fee of [an amount equal to 10 times the professional's hourly rate] to be paid in advance of opening work on the case.

If work in the [city or town in which expert witness practices] area (i.e., the area within 20 miles of [location of expert witness's office]) during this phase (i.e., before I am retained or disclosed as an expert witness) exceeds 10 hours, an advance of [an amount equal to 10 times the professional's hourly rate] is due immediately; each additional hour (beyond the initial 10) will be billed at the rate of [professional's hourly rate] per hour.

Each time the advance is depleted, a subsequent advance of [an amount equal to 10 times the clinician's hourly rate] is due immediately, against which each additional hour will be billed at the rate of [hourly rate] per hour. Unlike the initial case-opening, review, and consultation fee of [an amount equal to 10 times the expert witness's hourly rate], which is nonrefundable, the unused portion of any of these subsequent [an amount equal to 10 times the expert witness's hourly rate] advances (during this period prior to naming or endorsing me as an expert witness) will be returned should my services no longer be needed.

Disclosure as an Expert Witness

If, on the basis of the initial review and consultation, you decide to disclose me as an expert witness in the case, an additional nonrefundable payment of [an amount equal to 10 times the expert witness's hourly rate] must be received by me in advance of my being named as an expert witness.

If work in the [city or town] area (i.e., the area within 20 miles of [office]) during this phase exceeds 10 hours, an advance of [an amount equal to 10 times the professional's hourly rate] is due immediately; each additional hour (beyond the initial 10) will be billed at the rate of [hourly rate] per hour. Each time the advance is depleted, a subsequent advance (for work to be done within [city or town]) of [an amount equal to 10 times the expert witness's hourly rate] is due immediately, against which each additional hour will be billed at the rate of [hourly rate] per hour. Unlike the [an amount equal to 10 times the professional's hourly rate] fee for case opening and the [an amount equal to 10 times the professional's hourly rate] fee for endorsement as expert witness—both of which are nonrefundable—the unused portion of any of these subsequent [an amount equal to 10 times the professional's hourly rate] advances (during this period prior to naming or endorsing me as an expert witness) will be returned should my services no longer be needed.

It is understood that the opposing attorney(s) will pay my hourly fee for the deposition itself at the time that I am deposed. [As noted in chap. 5, this volume, the party or parties responsible for paying an expert witness for time spent in deposition varies from jurisdiction to jurisdiction.]

Work Conducted Outside the [City or Town] Area

For any travel out of [city or town] area, the charge is [eight times the hourly rate] per 24-hour period (or fraction thereof), plus expenses (transportation as discussed, food, lodging, and delivery of documents via such carriers such as Federal Express), to be received by me at least 1 week prior to the scheduled departure from the [city or town] area.

If I do not receive any of the payments called for hereunder exactly when due, I shall stop all work and vacate all appointments, in which event you agree to assume sole responsibility for any and all damages or expenses that may result to you or your client(s).

In the event of any litigation arising under the terms of this agreement, the prevailing party shall recover their reasonable attorneys' fees.

If you agree to these terms, please sign below and return a signed copy to me along with the case-opening fee.

_____   _____

Signature   Date

Sample Informed Consent Form for Conducting Forensic Assessments

As with agreements between expert witnesses and attorneys (see chap. 5 and Appendix L, this volume), there are many approaches to issues of informed consent when conducting forensic assessment. This appendix presents one possible example of a written informed consent form for assessments involving the MMPI–2. Such forms must be tailored to the specific nature, purpose, and circumstances of the assessment; the approach of the expert witness; the needs of the individual being assessed; and to all applicable legislation, case law, standards, and regulations.

Expert witnesses may find it useful to have several versions of these forms on a computer file. Experts can choose the most appropriate version and modify it before printing it out so that it fits a particular client and situation.

Before using any such agreement, the expert witness should always review the form with his or her own professional liability attorney (i.e., not the attorney who is hiring the individual as an expert witness) to ensure that it fully meets the applicable legal, ethical, and professional standards (e.g., regarding informed consent) as well as the needs and approaches of the expert witness.

Where appropriate, and where time permits, the expert witness may fax or mail copies of the form to both the attorney who has arranged the assessment and to the individual who is to be assessed. This provides each of them an opportunity to study the form and to consult with each other—and perhaps with other people—before the initial assessment session. At the initial assessment session, the expert witness can review the form with the indi-

vidual to ensure that he or she adequately understands and consents to the assessment process.

Providing the consent form to both the attorney and the individual to be assessed in advance of the first session can help prevent situations in which the attorney told the client only the following.

- "I want you to talk with Dr. _____ this Wednesday morning at 10:00 a.m."
- "Please call the Generic Institute and make an appointment. Just tell them who you are and that I referred you, and they'll know what to do."
- "This afternoon, the paralegal will drive you to another set of offices where they'll give you some tests."
- "Please have my secretary arrange for you to meet with the Generic Group sometime next week."

In the absence of adequate advance explanation, clients may show up at the expert witness's office having literally no idea why their attorney has asked them to make the trip.

It is important for the expert witness to take time to review the form on a point-by-point basis to ensure that the client adequately understands the process. The expert witness can use the form as part of the process of informed consent but must not assume that the mere presence of the form completes the process.

Providing information in written form can be vital in ensuring that clients have the information they need. But the form is no substitute for an adequate process of informed consent. At a minimum, the clinician must discuss the information with the client and arrive at a professional judgment that the client adequately understands the assessment and its implications.

Clinicians using consent forms must ensure that their clients have the requisite reading skills. Illiteracy is a major problem in the United States. Moreover, some clients may not be well versed in English, perhaps having only rudimentary skills in spoken English as a second or third language (Pope & Vasquez, 1998, p. 155).[1]

INFORMED CONSENT FOR FORENSIC ASSESSMENT

Your attorney has asked that I conduct a psychological assessment in connection with your court case. This form's purpose is to help you understand the assessment process.

The assessment will contain two parts. In the first part, I will give you a form (called the MMPI–2) containing a number of statements. You will be asked whether you believe that each statement applies to you. (We will discuss the instructions in detail when I give you the form.)

In the second part of the assessment, I will interview you. During the interview, I will ask you questions about yourself and ask you to talk about yourself. There may, of course, be areas that you are reluctant to talk about. If so, please be sure to tell me that the questions are making you uncomfortable or that you have reasons for not providing the information. We can then talk about your concerns.

It is important that you follow the directions to the MMPI–2 that are printed on the booklet cover. [Read the directions to the client.]

Although I will try to be thorough when I interview you, I may not ask about some areas, facts, or concerns that you believe are important. If so, please tell me so that we can discuss it.

I am a [psychologist, psychiatrist, or other professional title] licensed by the state of [name of state]. If you believe that I am behaving unethically or unprofessionally during the course of this assessment, I urge you to let me know at once so that we can discuss it. If you believe that I have not adequately addressed your complaints in this area, there are several agencies whom you may consult, and, if you believe it appropriate, you may file a formal complaint against me. One agency is the state governmental board that licenses me to practice: [name, address, and phone number of the licensing board]. Other agencies are the ethics committees of my state professional association, [name, address, and phone number], and national professional association, [name, address, and phone number]. However, you have assurance that I will conduct this assessment in an ethical and professional manner and will be open to discussing any complaints you have in this area.

Please check each item below to indicate that you have read it carefully and understand it.

- ❑ I understand that Dr. _____ has been hired by my attorney, [fill in attorney's name], to conduct a psychological assessment using the MMPI–2 and a clinical interview.
- ❑ I understand that Dr. _____ intends to administer a test called the Minnesota Multiphasic Personality Inventory-Revised (MMPI–2), which takes about 1 1/2 or 2 hours for me to fill out.
- ❑ I understand that Dr. _____ will score, interpret, and write a formal report about me on the basis of the results of the MMPI–2.
- ❑ I authorize Dr. _____ to send a copy of this formal report to my attorney and to discuss the report with him or her.

---

[1] For a more extended discussion, see Pope and Vasquez's (1998) chapter "Informed Consent and Informed Refusal" (pp. 126–142).

❑ I understand that Dr. _____ will not provide me with this written report but that I may, if I choose, schedule an additional appointment with Dr. _____ to discuss the results of this assessment.

❑ I authorize Dr. _____ to testify about me and this assessment in depositions and trial(s) related to my legal case.

❑ I understand that if I disclose certain types of special information to Dr. _____, he or she may be required or permitted to communicate this information to other people. As previously discussed with _____, examples of such special information include reports of child or elder abuse and threats to kill or violently attack a specific person.

If you have read, understood, and checked off each of the prior sections, please read carefully the following statement and, if you agree with it, please sign the statement.

Do not sign if you have any further questions or if there are any aspects that you do not understand or agree to; contact your attorney for guidance concerning how to proceed so that you fully understand the process and can decide whether you wish to continue.

Consent Agreement: I have read, agreed to, and checked off each of the previous sections. I have asked questions about any parts that I did not understand fully. I have also asked questions about any parts that I was concerned about. By signing below, I indicate that I understand and agree to the nature and purpose of this testing, how it will be reported, and to each of the points listed above.

_____   _____
Signature   Date

_____
Name (please print)

Expert Witness's Checklist for Forensic MMPI–2 Assessment

- Reached explicit agreement (preferably written) with the attorney on the purpose and scope of the testing.
- Reached explicit agreement (preferably written) with the attorney on deadlines.
- Reached explicit agreement (see Appendix L, this volume) with the attorney on fees.
- Reached explicit agreement (preferably written) with the attorney on the nature and form in which the assessment will be reported (i.e., written report, deposition, and trial testimony).
- Reached explicit agreement (preferably written) with the attorney on any relevant issues of privilege, confidentiality, and privacy.
- Reached explicit agreement (preferably written) with the attorney on who (i.e., the expert witness, the attorney, the client, or someone else) will be responsible for obtaining additional documents (e.g., reports of previous assessments, assessment reports prepared by other expert witnesses in this case).
- Informed the client about the assessment and obtained written informed consent (Appendix M, this volume).
- Determined whether there are any issues regarding vision, hearing, mobility, and so forth that need to be addressed in the assessment, report, or both.
- Determined whether there are any language issues (e.g., familiarity with English, reading difficulty) that need to be addressed in the assessment, report, or both.
- Determined whether there are any acute or chronic physical illnesses or disorders that need to be addressed in the assessment, report, or both.

- Determined whether there are any other factors that may affect the validity of the assessment or that may require special attention.
- Provided adequately monitored environment for assessment (e.g., client had quiet room—free from conversation with and distraction by other people—in which to fill out the inventory; client did not take the inventory home or elsewhere to fill out).
- Checked for any scoring inaccuracies.
- Determined whether the protocol is valid; if invalid, refrained from attempting to interpret an invalid protocol (beyond interpretation of the validity scales themselves).
- If using a computerized interpretive report, made sure that the interpretive statements are empirically based (rather than, e.g., a clinician's hunches, intuitions, and dicta set forth by a computer program).
- If using a computerized interpretive report, evaluated each hypothesis set forth to determine whether there is evidence that it is basically accurate, basically inaccurate, or nonapplicable (completely inaccurate).
- If any special scales (i.e., patterns of particular MMPI–2 items) are used, ensured that they have been appropriately normed and validated on the population of which the client is a member.
- In any oral or written report or discussion of the findings and their implications, explicitly noted any factors that may have influenced the validity of this assessment (see Appendix P, this volume, for a checklist for written report of forensic assessment).

Attorney's Checklist for Forensic MMPI–2 Assessment

- Evaluate the need for a forensic MMPI–2 assessment early in the case—long before any expert designations are due. Consider the purpose of the MMPI–2 assessment—whether for damages, liability, mitigation, affirmative defense—and decide if it would likely be helpful to an issue in the case.
- Collect all records relevant to the purpose of the assessment.
- Meet with the potential expert and explore his or her background, including resolved or unresolved complaints. Independently verify claims in his or her curriculum vitae about training, licensure, employment, and so forth.
- Discuss the nature of the assessment and decide whether he or she has adequate familiarity with and expertise in the MMPI–2.
- Determine whether the expert is able to tell a compelling story through the use of vivid and powerful language.
- Disclose the names of all parties to ensure that there are no conflicts.
- Provide to the expert a list of the deadlines in the case to ensure that the expert has the time and ability to comply with the deadlines. Send updates to the expert when those deadlines change.
- Evaluate the status of the law in jurisdiction to determine the extent to which the initial MMPI–2 evaluation can be done confidentially. (For example, in most jurisdictions, an expert may be hired to review previous MMPI–2 tests without requiring disclosure of the expert to the other side. On the other hand, where a party

such as a plaintiff actually meets with an expert, any MMPI–2 results would likely require disclosure.)

- Before having an evaluation performed that must be disclosed, attempt to determine whether the test will likely provide information that will help the fact finder to resolve an issue in the case.
- Reach an agreement with the expert on the purpose and scope of the evaluation. Explain to the expert relevant legal requirements (e.g., that local rules required tendering his or her entire file to the other party, including notes, drafts, and impressions).
- Reach an agreement, preferably in writing, concerning the expert's fees.
- Discuss with the client the general evaluation process.
- Discuss with the client the relevant issues of privilege, confidentiality, and privacy.
- Discuss with the expert any need for additional documents, independent investigation, consultations, and so forth.
- Decide, with the expert's input, the most appropriate procedure for obtaining additional information requested by the expert, whether through discovery or independent consultation by the expert. (Some ethical guidelines require an expert to do any independent inquiry that he or she decides is appropriate. For the attorney to gather some kinds of information for the expert may create unnecessary areas of cross-examination.)
- Discuss with the expert the results of the testing

and the specific issues that need to be addressed in a report.

- Reach an agreement with the expert on the nature and form of the assessment report—whether written or oral—and discuss any timeline changes.

- Review the assessment report and discuss with the expert any parts of the report that are confusing.

- Discuss the results with the client.

- Decide whether to endorse the expert for trial. If the expert is endorsed, follow local procedures and notify the expert, well in advance, of the trial date. If possible, the expert should be consulted before finalizing the trial date to avoid scheduling conflicts. Even if the expert is not endorsed, local rules in some jurisdictions require disclosure of the evaluation to other parties.

- Work with the opposing party in a cooperative spirit to ensure that any raw data is tendered to a qualified psychologist rather than to an attorney, when the expert witness requests that procedure.

- Once the expert is endorsed, discuss with the expert his or her role at trial, and coordinate any deposition with his or her calendar.

- Discuss with the expert any areas likely requir-

ing follow-up work, the timing of such follow-up, and local rules directing timing and content of supplemental disclosures to the court or to opposing parties. Explain relevant local rules (e.g., that the expert may not be able to testify to conclusions reached after his or her initial report unless they are disclosed in a timely fashion).

- Make certain that the expert understands *Daubert* and related issues. The court needs to be convinced that the MMPI results are reliable and that they are relevant to a controversy at issue.

- Prepare pretrial motions *in limine* to address specific MMPI issues. For example, some case law precludes cross-examining a party on individual responses to the MMPI. Other case law precludes introducing a computer-generated profile. Still other case law precludes using language such as "lie scale" as unduly inflammatory.

- Make prompt payment to the expert on every billing. Prompt and ongoing payment minimizes communication difficulties and potential areas of cross-examination suggesting that payment may be conditioned on the content of the testimony.

A Checklist for Reports of Forensic Assessment

There is no one-size-fits-all for a forensic assessment. The structure depends on whether the report addresses one narrow question or an array of complex issues. It depends on whether the assessment uses only one instrument or a battery of instruments. It depends on the background information, the assessment data, and other factors unique to the individual case.

The following checklist, drawing from the material presented in this book (especially chap. 5, this volume), can help practitioners to think through how to organize and present their findings, and to make sure, once the report is drafted, that all important issues are addressed clearly.

- Does the report clearly identify the person who was assessed?
- Does the report clearly identify the referral questions or the issues addressed by the assessment (e.g., competence to stand trial, custody hearing, personal injury suit)?
- Does the report clearly describe relevant background, demographic, or biographical information?
- Does the report identify other sources of information besides the assessment sessions? For example, did the assessment include review of law enforcement documents, court records, employment documents, medical records, records of previous assessments, school records, reports filed by attorneys or private detectives, audiotapes, videotapes, or other recordings?
- Did the assessment involve relevant special needs and circumstances, as discussed in

chapter 5? These might include (but are not limited to) vision, hearing, mobility and accessibility, reading and writing (and other language issues), physical illnesses and disorders, drugs and medications, and circumstances preceding the testing.

- Does the assessment report clearly identify each assessment instrument (e.g., Minnesota Multiphasic Personality Inventory—2) or method (e.g., interview)—at least once in an unabbreviated form—along with the date(s) on which each was used? If there is more than one form of a test, more than one kind of answer sheet or response form, more than one scoring system, and so forth, does the report clearly indicate which was used?
- Does the report clearly describe any unusual conditions of the assessment?
- Does the report clearly describe any departures from the administration, scoring, and interpretation of the instruments as described in the instrument's manual?
- Does the report clearly describe who administered each assessment procedure (e.g., the licensed psychologist writing and signing the report, an unlicensed psychology student or assistant, a secretary or office manager)?
- Does the report clearly indicate whether the assessment was always monitored? If there were any instances in which it was unmonitored, are these clearly described (e.g., Mr. X asked if he might take the MMPI–2 home with him and return it later in the day so that he might have an opportunity to discuss with his attorneys which

responses to various MMPI–2 items he should write on the form)?

- Does the report describe relevant aspects of the test taker's attitude and demeanor?
- Does the report clearly present the results from each assessment instrument or method?
- Does the report address validity issues explicitly and adequately?
- Does the report include any relevant base-rate information?
- Does the report present interpretations and professional opinions (including recommendations, if any) clearly so that (a) they address the referral questions or the issues that were the focus of the assessment, and (b) they flow clearly from the results of each assessment instrument or method?
- Does the report discuss any contradictions (seeming or actual) or ambiguities in the data?
- Does the report present the data and interpretations presented in a clear manner? Could someone without advanced training in psychology understand it? Is it jargon-free?
- Does the report present the data and interpretations in a fair and unbiased way?
- Does the report make clear how strong (or uncertain) the results, interpretations, and recommendations are? Does it make clear which points you are virtually certain about and which points you are not so sure of?
- Did you sign the report? Is the person who signed the report the person who conducted the assessment?
- Does the report include—in addition to the signature—the signer's full name typed or printed?
- Does the report include the signer's degree and job title or credential (e.g., Jane Doe, PhD, ABPP, Chief of Staff, Hypothetical Hospital, Licensed Psychologist)?

Ethical Principles of Psychologists and Code of Conduct

CONTENTS

Reprinted from *American Psychologist*, 57, 1060–1073. Copyright © 2002 by the American Psychological Association.

INTRODUCTION AND APPLICABILITY

The American Psychological Association's (APA's) Ethical Principles of Psychologists and Code of Conduct (hereinafter referred to as the Ethics Code) consists of an Introduction, a Preamble, five General Principles (A–E), and specific Ethical Standards. The Introduction discusses the intent, organization, procedural considerations, and scope of application of the Ethics Code. The Preamble and General Principles are aspirational goals to guide psychologists toward the highest ideals of psychology. Although the Preamble and General Principles are not themselves enforceable rules, they should be considered by psychologists in arriving at an ethical course of action. The Ethical Standards set forth enforceable rules for conduct as psychologists. Most of the Ethical Standards are written broadly, in order to apply to psychologists in varied roles, although the application of an Ethical Standard may vary depending on the context. The Ethical Standards are not exhaustive. The fact that a given conduct is not specifically addressed by an Ethical Standard does not mean that it is necessarily either ethical or unethical.

This Ethics Code applies only to psychologists' activities that are part of their scientific, educational, or professional roles as psychologists. Areas covered include but are not limited to the clinical, counseling, and school practice of psychology; research; teaching; supervision of trainees; public service; policy development; social intervention; development of assessment instruments; conducting assessments; educational counseling; organizational consulting; forensic activities; program design and evaluation; and administration. This Ethics Code applies to these activities across a variety of contexts, such as in person, postal, telephone, internet, and other electronic transmissions. These activities shall be distinguished from the purely private conduct of psychologists, which is not within the purview of the Ethics Code.

Membership in the APA commits members and student affiliates to comply with the standards of the APA Ethics Code and to the rules and procedures used to enforce them. Lack of awareness or misunderstanding of an Ethical Standard is not itself a defense to a charge of unethical conduct.

The procedures for filing, investigating, and resolving complaints of unethical conduct are described in the current Rules and Procedures of the APA Ethics Committee. APA may impose sanctions on its members for violations of the standards of the Ethics Code, including termination of APA membership, and may notify other bodies and individuals of its actions. Actions that violate the standards of the Ethics Code may also lead to the imposition of sanctions on psychologists or students whether or not they are APA members by bodies other than APA, including state psychological associations, other professional groups, psychology boards, other state or federal agencies, and payors for health services. In addition, APA may take action against a member after his or her conviction of a felony, expulsion or suspension from an affiliated state psychological association, or suspension or loss of licensure. When the sanction to be imposed by APA is less than expulsion, the 2001 Rules and Procedures do not guarantee an opportunity for an in-person hearing, but generally provide that complaints will be resolved only on the basis of a submitted record.

The Ethics Code is intended to provide guidance for psychologists and standards of professional conduct that can be applied by the APA and by other bodies that choose to adopt them. The Ethics Code is not intended to be a basis of civil liability. Whether a psychologist has violated the Ethics Code standards does not by itself determine whether the psychologist is legally liable in a court action, whether a contract is enforceable, or whether other legal consequences occur.

The modifiers used in some of the standards of this Ethics Code (e.g., reasonably, appropriate, potentially) are included in the standards when they would (1) allow professional judgment on the part of psychologists, (2) eliminate injustice or inequality that would occur without the modifier, (3) ensure applicability across the broad range of activities conducted by psychologists, or (4) guard against a set of rigid rules that might be quickly outdated. As used in this Ethics Code, the term reasonable means the prevailing professional judgment of psychologists engaged in similar activities in similar circumstances, given the knowledge the psychologist had or should have had at the time.

In the process of making decisions regarding their professional behavior, psychologists must consider this Ethics Code in addition to applicable laws and psychology board regulations. In applying the Ethics Code to their professional work, psychologists may consider other materials and guidelines that have been adopted or endorsed by scientific and professional psychological organizations and the dictates of their own conscience, as well as consult with others within the field. If this Ethics Code establishes a higher standard of conduct than is required by law, psychologists must meet the higher ethical standard. If psychologists' ethical responsibilities conflict with law, regulations, or other governing legal authority, psychologists make known their commitment to this Ethics Code and take steps to resolve the conflict in a responsible manner. If the conflict is unresolvable via such means, psychologists may adhere to the requirements of the law, regulations, or other governing authority in keeping with basic principles of human rights.

This version of the APA Ethics Code was adopted by the American Psychological Association's Council of Representatives during its meeting, August 21, 2002, and is effective beginning June 1, 2003. Inquiries concerning the substance or interpretation of the APA Ethics Code should be addressed to the Director, Office of Ethics, American Psychological Association, 750 First Street, NE, Washington, DC 20002-4242. The Ethics Code and information regarding the Code can be found on the APA Web site, http://www.apa.org/ethics.

The standards in this Ethics Code will be used to adjudicate complaints brought concerning alleged conduct occurring on or after the effective date. Complaints regarding conduct occurring prior to the effective date will be adjudicated on the basis of the version of the Ethics Code that was in effect at the time the conduct occurred.

The APA has previously published its Ethics Code as follows:

American Psychological Association. (1953). *Ethical standards of psychologists.* Washington, DC: Author.
American Psychological Association. (1959). Ethical standards of psychologists. *American Psychologist, 14,* 279–282.
American Psychological Association. (1963). Ethical standards of psychologists. *American Psychologist, 18,* 56–60.
American Psychological Association. (1968). Ethical standards of psychologists. *American Psychologist, 23,* 357–361.
American Psychological Association. (1977, March). Ethical standards of psychologists. *APA Monitor,* 22–23.
American Psychological Association. (1979). *Ethical standards of psychologists.* Washington, DC: Author.
American Psychological Association. (1981). Ethical principles of psychologists. *American Psychologist, 36,* 633–638.
American Psychological Association. (1990). Ethical principles of psychologists (Amended June 2, 1989). *American Psychologist, 45,* 390–395.
American Psychological Association. (1992). Ethical principles of psychologists and code of conduct. *American Psychologist, 47,* 1597–1611.

Request copies of the APA's Ethical Principles of Psychologists and Code of Conduct from the APA Order Department, 750 First Street, NE, Washington, DC 20002-4242, or phone (202) 336-5510.

PREAMBLE

Psychologists are committed to increasing scientific and professional knowledge of behavior and people's understanding of themselves and others and to the use of such knowledge to improve the condition of individuals, organizations, and society. Psychologists respect and protect civil and human rights and the central importance of freedom of inquiry and expression in research, teaching, and publication. They strive to help the public in developing informed judgments and choices concerning human behavior. In doing so, they perform many roles, such as researcher, educator, diagnostician, therapist, supervisor, consultant, administrator, social interventionist, and expert witness. This Ethics Code provides a common set of principles and standards upon which psychologists build their professional and scientific work.

This Ethics Code is intended to provide specific standards to cover most situations encountered by psychologists. It has as its goals the welfare and protection of the individuals and groups with whom psychologists work and the education of members, students, and the public regarding ethical standards of the discipline.

The development of a dynamic set of ethical standards for psychologists' work-related conduct requires a personal commitment and lifelong effort to act ethically; to encourage ethical behavior by students, supervisees, employees, and colleagues; and to consult with others concerning ethical problems.

GENERAL PRINCIPLES

This section consists of General Principles. General Principles, as opposed to Ethical Standards, are aspirational in nature. Their intent is to guide and inspire psychologists toward the very highest ethical ideals of the profession. General Principles, in contrast to Ethical Standards, do not represent obligations and should not form the basis for imposing sanctions. Relying upon General Principles for either of these reasons distorts both their meaning and purpose.

Principle A: Beneficence and Nonmaleficence

Psychologists strive to benefit those with whom they work and take care to do no harm. In their professional actions, psychologists seek to safeguard the welfare and rights of those with whom they interact professionally and other affected persons, and the welfare of animal subjects of research. When conflicts occur among psychologists' obligations or concerns, they attempt to resolve these conflicts in a responsible fashion that avoids or minimizes harm. Because psychologists' scientific and professional judgments and actions may affect the lives of others, they are alert to and guard against personal, financial, social, organizational, or political factors that might lead to misuse of their influence. Psychologists strive to be aware of the possible effect of their own physical and mental health on their ability to help those with whom they work.

Principle B: Fidelity and Responsibility

Psychologists establish relationships of trust with those with whom they work. They are aware of their professional and scientific responsibilities to society and to the specific communities in which they work. Psychologists uphold professional standards of conduct, clarify their professional roles and obligations, accept appropriate responsibility for their behavior, and seek to manage conflicts of interest that could lead to exploitation or harm. Psychologists consult with, refer to, or cooperate with other professionals and institutions to the extent needed to serve the best interests of those with whom they work. They are concerned about the ethical compliance of their colleagues' scientific and professional conduct. Psychologists strive to contribute a portion of their professional time for little or no compensation or personal advantage.

Principle C: Integrity

Psychologists seek to promote accuracy, honesty, and truthfulness in the science, teaching, and practice of psychology. In these activities psychologists do not steal, cheat, or engage in fraud, subterfuge, or intentional misrepresentation of fact. Psychologists strive to keep their promises and to avoid unwise or unclear commitments. In situations in which deception may be ethically justifiable to maximize benefits and minimize harm, psychologists have a serious obligation to consider the need for, the possible consequences of, and their responsibility to correct any resulting mistrust or other harmful effects that arise from the use of such techniques.

Principle D: Justice

Psychologists recognize that fairness and justice entitle all persons to access to and benefit from the contributions of psychology and to equal quality in the processes, procedures, and services being conducted by psychologists. Psychologists exercise reasonable judgment and take precautions to ensure that their potential biases, the boundaries of their competence, and the limitations of their expertise do not lead to or condone unjust practices.

Principle E: Respect for People's Rights and Dignity

Psychologists respect the dignity and worth of all people, and the rights of individuals to privacy, confidentiality, and self-determination. Psychologists are aware that special safeguards may be necessary to protect the rights and welfare of persons or communities whose vulnerabilities impair autonomous decision making. Psychologists are aware of and respect cultural, individual, and role differences, including those based on age, gender, gender identity, race, ethnicity, culture, national origin, religion, sexual orientation, disability, language, and socioeconomic status and consider these factors when working with members of such groups. Psychologists try to eliminate the effect on their work of biases based on those factors, and they do not knowingly participate in or condone activities of others based upon such prejudices.

ETHICAL STANDARDS

1. Resolving Ethical Issues

1.01 Misuse of Psychologists' Work

If psychologists learn of misuse or misrepresentation of their work, they take reasonable steps to correct or minimize the misuse or misrepresentation.

1.02 Conflicts Between Ethics and Law, Regulations, or Other Governing Legal Authority

If psychologists' ethical responsibilities conflict with law, regulations, or other governing legal authority, psychologists make known their commitment to the Ethics Code and take steps to resolve the conflict. If the conflict is unresolvable via such means, psychologists may adhere to the requirements of the law, regulations, or other governing legal authority.

1.03 Conflicts Between Ethics and Organizational Demands

If the demands of an organization with which psychologists are affiliated or for whom they are working conflict with this Ethics Code, psychologists clarify the nature of the conflict, make known their commitment to the Ethics Code, and to the extent feasible, resolve the conflict in a way that permits adherence to the Ethics Code.

1.04 Informal Resolution of Ethical Violations

When psychologists believe that there may have been an ethical violation by another psychologist, they attempt to resolve the issue by bringing it to the attention of that individual, if an informal resolution appears appropriate and the intervention does not violate any confidentiality rights that may be involved. (See also Standards 1.02, Conflicts Between Ethics and Law, Regulations, or Other Governing Legal Authority, and 1.03, Conflicts Between Ethics and Organizational Demands.)

1.05 Reporting Ethical Violations

If an apparent ethical violation has substantially harmed or is likely to substantially harm a person or organization and is not appropriate for informal resolution under Standard 1.04, Informal Resolution of Ethical Violations, or is not resolved properly in that fashion, psychologists take further action appropriate to the situation. Such action might include referral to state or national committees on professional ethics, to state licensing boards, or to the appropriate institutional authorities. This standard does not apply when an intervention would

violate confidentiality rights or when psychologists have been retained to review the work of another psychologist whose professional conduct is in question. (See also Standard 1.02, Conflicts Between Ethics and Law, Regulations, or Other Governing Legal Authority.)

1.06 Cooperating With Ethics Committees

Psychologists cooperate in ethics investigations, proceedings, and resulting requirements of the APA or any affiliated state psychological association to which they belong. In doing so, they address any confidentiality issues. Failure to cooperate is itself an ethics violation. However, making a request for deferment of adjudication of an ethics complaint pending the outcome of litigation does not alone constitute noncooperation.

1.07 Improper Complaints

Psychologists do not file or encourage the filing of ethics complaints that are made with reckless disregard for or willful ignorance of facts that would disprove the allegation.

1.08 Unfair Discrimination Against Complainants and Respondents

Psychologists do not deny persons employment, advancement, admissions to academic or other programs, tenure, or promotion, based solely upon their having made or their being the subject of an ethics complaint. This does not preclude taking action based upon the outcome of such proceedings or considering other appropriate information.

2. Competence

2.01 Boundaries of Competence

(a) Psychologists provide services, teach, and conduct research with populations and in areas only within the boundaries of their competence, based on their education, training, supervised experience, consultation, study, or professional experience.

(b) Where scientific or professional knowledge in the discipline of psychology establishes that an understanding of factors associated with age, gender, gender identity, race, ethnicity, culture, national origin, religion, sexual orientation, disability, language, or socioeconomic status is essential for effective implementation of their services or research, psychologists have or obtain the training, experience, consultation, or supervision necessary to ensure the competence of their services, or they make appropriate referrals, except as provided in Standard 2.02, Providing Services in Emergencies.

(c) Psychologists planning to provide services, teach, or conduct research involving populations, areas, techniques, or technologies new to them undertake relevant education, training, supervised experience, consultation, or study.

(d) When psychologists are asked to provide services to individuals for whom appropriate mental health services are not available and for which psychologists have not obtained the competence necessary, psychologists with closely related prior training or experience may provide such services in order to ensure that services are not denied if they make a reasonable effort to obtain the competence required by using relevant research, training, consultation, or study.

(e) In those emerging areas in which generally recognized standards for preparatory training do not yet exist, psychologists nevertheless take reasonable steps to ensure the competence of their work and to protect clients/patients, students, supervisees, research participants, organizational clients, and others from harm.

(f) When assuming forensic roles, psychologists are or become reasonably familiar with the judicial or administrative rules governing their roles.

2.02 Providing Services in Emergencies

In emergencies, when psychologists provide services to individuals for whom other mental health services are not available and for which psychologists have not obtained the necessary training, psychologists may provide such services in order to ensure that services are not denied. The services are discontinued as soon as the emergency has ended or appropriate services are available.

2.03 Maintaining Competence

Psychologists undertake ongoing efforts to develop and maintain their competence.

2.04 Bases for Scientific and Professional Judgments

Psychologists' work is based upon established scientific and professional knowledge of the discipline. (See also Standards 2.01e, Boundaries of Competence, and 10.01b, Informed Consent to Therapy.)

2.05 Delegation of Work to Others

Psychologists who delegate work to employees, supervisees, or research or teaching assistants or who use the services of others, such as interpreters, take reasonable steps to (1) avoid delegating such work to persons who have a multiple relationship with those being served that would likely lead to exploitation or loss of objectivity; (2) authorize only those responsibilities that such persons can be expected to perform competently on the basis of their education, training, or experience, either independently or with the level of supervision being provided; and (3) see that such persons perform these services competently. (See also Standards 2.02, Providing Services in Emergencies; 3.05, Multiple Relationships; 4.01, Maintaining Confidentiality; 9.01, Bases for Assessments; 9.02, Use of Assessments; 9.03, Informed Consent in Assessments; and 9.07, Assessment by Unqualified Persons.)

2.06 Personal Problems and Conflicts

(a) Psychologists refrain from initiating an activity when they know or should know that there is a substantial likelihood that their personal problems will prevent them from performing their work-related activities in a competent manner.

(b) When psychologists become aware of personal problems that may interfere with their performing work-related duties adequately, they take appropriate measures, such as obtaining professional consultation or assistance, and determine whether they should limit, suspend, or terminate their work-related duties. (See also Standard 10.10, Terminating Therapy.)

3. Human Relations

3.01 Unfair Discrimination

In their work-related activities, psychologists do not engage in unfair discrimination based on age, gender, gender identity, race, ethnicity, culture, national origin, religion, sexual orientation, disability, socioeconomic status, or any basis proscribed by law.

3.02 Sexual Harassment

Psychologists do not engage in sexual harassment. Sexual harassment is sexual solicitation, physical advances, or verbal or nonverbal conduct that is sexual in nature, that occurs in connection with the psychologist's activities or roles as a psychologist, and that either (1) is unwelcome, is offensive, or creates a hostile workplace or educational environment, and the psychologist knows or is told this or (2) is sufficiently severe or intense to be abusive to a reasonable person in the context. Sexual harassment can consist of a single intense or severe act or of multiple persistent or pervasive acts. (See also Standard 1.08, Unfair Discrimination Against Complainants and Respondents.)

3.03 Other Harassment

Psychologists do not knowingly engage in behavior that is harassing or demeaning to persons with whom they interact in their work based on factors such as those persons' age, gender, gender identity, race, ethnicity, culture, national origin, religion, sexual orientation, disability, language, or socioeconomic status.

3.04 Avoiding Harm

Psychologists take reasonable steps to avoid harming their clients/patients, students, supervisees, research participants, organizational clients, and others with whom they work, and to minimize harm where it is foreseeable and unavoidable.

3.05 Multiple Relationships

(a) A multiple relationship occurs when a psychologist is in a professional role with a person and (1) at the same time is in another role with the same person, (2) at the same time is in a relationship with a person closely associated with or related to the person with whom the psychologist has the professional relationship, or (3) promises to enter into another relationship in the future with the per-

son or a person closely associated with or related to the person.

A psychologist refrains from entering into a multiple relationship if the multiple relationship could reasonably be expected to impair the psychologist's objectivity, competence, or effectiveness in performing his or her functions as a psychologist, or otherwise risks exploitation or harm to the person with whom the professional relationship exists.

Multiple relationships that would not reasonably be expected to cause impairment or risk exploitation or harm are not unethical.

(b) If a psychologist finds that, due to unforeseen factors, a potentially harmful multiple relationship has arisen, the psychologist takes reasonable steps to resolve it with due regard for the best interests of the affected person and maximal compliance with the Ethics Code.

(c) When psychologists are required by law, institutional policy, or extraordinary circumstances to serve in more than one role in judicial or administrative proceedings, at the outset they clarify role expectations and the extent of confidentiality and thereafter as changes occur. (See also Standards 3.04, Avoiding Harm, and 3.07, Third-Party Requests for Services.)

3.06 Conflict of Interest

Psychologists refrain from taking on a professional role when personal, scientific, professional, legal, financial, or other interests or relationships could reasonably be expected to (1) impair their objectivity, competence, or effectiveness in performing their functions as psychologists or (2) expose the person or organization with whom the professional relationship exists to harm or exploitation.

3.07 Third-Party Requests for Services

When psychologists agree to provide services to a person or entity at the request of a third party, psychologists attempt to clarify at the outset of the service the nature of the relationship with all individuals or organizations involved. This clarification includes the role of the psychologist (e.g., therapist, consultant, diagnostician, or expert witness), an identification of who is the client, the probable uses of the services provided or the information obtained, and the fact that there may be limits to confidentiality. (See also Standards 3.05, Multiple Relationships, and 4.02, Discussing the Limits of Confidentiality.)

3.08 Exploitative Relationships

Psychologists do not exploit persons over whom they have supervisory, evaluative, or other authority such as clients/patients, students, supervisees, research participants, and employees. (See also Standards 3.05, Multiple Relationships; 6.04, Fees and Financial Arrangements; 6.05, Barter With Clients/Patients; 7.07, Sexual Relationships With Students and Supervisees; 10.05, Sexual Intimacies With Current Therapy Clients/Patients; 10.06, Sexual Intimacies With Relatives or Significant Others of Current Therapy Clients/Patients; 10.07, Therapy With Former Sexual Partners; and 10.08, Sexual Intimacies With Former Therapy Clients/Patients.)

3.09 Cooperation With Other Professionals

When indicated and professionally appropriate, psychologists cooperate with other professionals in order to serve their clients/patients effectively and appropriately. (See also Standard 4.05, Disclosures.)

3.10 Informed Consent

(a) When psychologists conduct research or provide assessment, therapy, counseling, or consulting services in person or via electronic transmission or other forms of communication, they obtain the informed consent of the individual or individuals using language that is reasonably understandable to that person or persons except when conducting such activities without consent is mandated by law or governmental regulation or as otherwise provided in this Ethics Code. (See also Standards 8.02, Informed Consent to Research; 9.03, Informed Consent in Assessments; and 10.01, Informed Consent to Therapy.)

(b) For persons who are legally incapable of giving informed consent, psychologists nevertheless (1) provide an appropriate explanation, (2) seek the individual's assent, (3) consider such persons' preferences and best interests, and (4) obtain appropriate permission from a legally authorized person, if such substitute consent is permitted or required by law. When consent by a legally authorized person is not permitted or required by law, psychologists take reasonable steps to protect the individual's rights and welfare.

(c) When psychological services are court ordered or otherwise mandated, psychologists inform the individual of the nature of the anticipated services, including whether the services are court ordered or mandated and any limits of confidentiality, before proceeding.

(d) Psychologists appropriately document written or oral consent, permission, and assent. (See also Standards 8.02, Informed Consent to Research; 9.03, Informed Consent in Assessments; and 10.01, Informed Consent to Therapy.)

3.11 Psychological Services Delivered To or Through Organizations

(a) Psychologists delivering services to or through organizations provide information beforehand to clients and when appropriate those directly affected by the services about (1) the nature and objectives of the services, (2) the intended recipients, (3) which of the individuals are clients, (4) the relationship the psychologist will have with each person and the organization, (5) the probable uses of services provided and information obtained, (6) who will have access to the information, and (7) limits of confidentiality. As soon as feasible, they provide information about the results and conclusions of such services to appropriate persons.

(b) If psychologists will be precluded by law or by organizational roles from providing such information to particular individuals or groups, they so inform those individuals or groups at the outset of the service.

3.12 Interruption of Psychological Services

Unless otherwise covered by contract, psychologists make reasonable efforts to plan for facilitating services in the event that psychological services are interrupted by factors such as the psychologist's illness, death, unavailability, relocation, or retirement or by the client's/patient's relocation or financial limitations. (See also Standard 6.02c, Maintenance, Dissemination, and Disposal of Confidential Records of Professional and Scientific Work.)

4. Privacy And Confidentiality

4.01 Maintaining Confidentiality

Psychologists have a primary obligation and take reasonable precautions to protect confidential information obtained through or stored in any medium, recognizing that the extent and limits of confidentiality may be regulated by law or established by institutional rules or professional or scientific relationship. (See also Standard 2.05, Delegation of Work to Others.)

4.02 Discussing the Limits of Confidentiality

(a) Psychologists discuss with persons (including, to the extent feasible, persons who are legally incapable of giving informed consent and their legal representatives) and organizations with whom they establish a scientific or professional relationship (1) the relevant limits of confidentiality and (2) the foreseeable uses of the information generated through their psychological activities. (See also Standard 3.10, Informed Consent.)

(b) Unless it is not feasible or is contraindicated, the discussion of confidentiality occurs at the outset of the relationship and thereafter as new circumstances may warrant.

(c) Psychologists who offer services, products, or information via electronic transmission inform clients/patients of the risks to privacy and limits of confidentiality.

4.03 Recording

Before recording the voices or images of individuals to whom they provide services, psychologists obtain permission from all such persons or their legal representatives. (See also Standards 8.03, Informed Consent for Recording Voices and Images in Research; 8.05, Dispensing With Informed Consent for Research; and 8.07, Deception in Research.)

4.04 Minimizing Intrusions on Privacy

(a) Psychologists include in written and oral reports and consultations, only information germane to the purpose for which the communication is made.

(b) Psychologists discuss confidential information obtained in their work only for appropriate scientific or professional purposes and only with persons clearly concerned with such matters.

4.05 Disclosures

(a) Psychologists may disclose confidential information with the appropriate consent of the organizational client, the individual client/patient, or another legally authorized person on behalf of the client/patient unless prohibited by law.

(b) Psychologists disclose confidential information without the consent of the individual only as mandated by law, or where permitted by law for a valid purpose such as to (1) provide needed professional services; (2) obtain appropriate professional consultations; (3) protect the client/patient, psychologist, or others from harm; or (4) obtain payment for services from a client/patient, in which instance disclosure is limited to the minimum that is necessary to achieve the purpose. (See also Standard 6.04e, Fees and Financial Arrangements.)

4.06 Consultations

When consulting with colleagues, (1) psychologists do not disclose confidential information that reasonably could lead to the identification of a client/patient, research participant, or other person or organization with whom they have a confidential relationship unless they have obtained the prior consent of the person or organization or the disclosure cannot be avoided, and (2) they disclose information only to the extent necessary to achieve the purposes of the consultation. (See also Standard 4.01, Maintaining Confidentiality.)

4.07 Use of Confidential Information for Didactic or Other Purposes

Psychologists do not disclose in their writings, lectures, or other public media, confidential, personally identifiable information concerning their clients/patients, students, research participants, organizational clients, or other recipients of their services that they obtained during the course of their work, unless (1) they take reasonable steps to disguise the person or organization, (2) the person or organization has consented in writing, or (3) there is legal authorization for doing so.

5. Advertising and Other Public Statements

5.01 Avoidance of False or Deceptive Statements

(a) Public statements include but are not limited to paid or unpaid advertising, product endorsements, grant applications, licensing applications, other credentialing applications, brochures, printed matter, directory listings, personal resumes or curricula vitae, or comments for use in media such as print or electronic transmission, statements in legal proceedings, lectures and public oral presentations, and published materials. Psychologists do not knowingly make public statements that are false, deceptive, or fraudulent concerning their research, practice, or other work activities or those of persons or organizations with which they are affiliated.

(b) Psychologists do not make false, deceptive, or fraudulent statements concerning (1) their training, experience, or competence; (2) their academic degrees; (3) their credentials; (4) their institutional or association affiliations; (5) their services; (6) the scientific or clinical basis for, or results or degree of success of, their services; (7) their fees; or (8) their publications or research findings.

(c) Psychologists claim degrees as credentials for their health services only if those degrees (1) were earned from a regionally accredited educational institution or (2) were the basis for psychology licensure by the state in which they practice.

5.02 Statements by Others

(a) Psychologists who engage others to create or place public statements that promote their professional practice, products, or activities retain professional responsibility for such statements.

(b) Psychologists do not compensate employees of press, radio, television, or other communication media in return for publicity in a news item. (See also Standard 1.01, Misuse of Psychologists' Work.)

(c) A paid advertisement relating to psychologists' activities must be identified or clearly recognizable as such.

5.03 Descriptions of Workshops and Non-Degree-Granting Educational Programs

To the degree to which they exercise control, psychologists responsible for announcements, catalogs, brochures, or advertisements describing workshops, seminars, or other non-degree-granting educational programs ensure that they accurately describe the audience for which the program is intended, the educational objectives, the presenters, and the fees involved.

5.04 Media Presentations

When psychologists provide public advice or comment via print, internet, or other electronic transmission, they take precautions to ensure that statements (1) are based on their professional knowledge, training, or experience in accord with appropriate psychological literature and practice; (2) are otherwise consistent with this Ethics Code; and (3) do not indicate that a professional relationship has been established with the recipient. (See also Standard 2.04, Bases for Scientific and Professional Judgments.)

5.05 Testimonials

Psychologists do not solicit testimonials from current therapy clients/patients or other persons who because of their particular circumstances are vulnerable to undue influence.

5.06 In-Person Solicitation

Psychologists do not engage, directly or through agents, in uninvited in-person solicitation of business from actual or potential therapy clients/patients or other persons who because of their particular circumstances are vulnerable to undue influence. However, this prohibition does not preclude (1) attempting to implement appropriate collateral contacts for the purpose of benefiting an already engaged therapy client/patient or (2) providing disaster or community outreach services.

6. Record Keeping and Fees

6.01 Documentation of Professional and Scientific Work and Maintenance of Records

Psychologists create, and to the extent the records are under their control, maintain, disseminate, store, retain, and dispose of records and data relating to their professional and scientific work in order to (1) facilitate provision of services later by them or by other professionals, (2) allow for replication of research design and analyses, (3) meet institutional requirements, (4) ensure accuracy of billing and payments, and (5) ensure compliance with law. (See also Standard 4.01, Maintaining Confidentiality.)

6.02 Maintenance, Dissemination, and Disposal of Confidential Records of Professional and Scientific Work

(a) Psychologists maintain confidentiality in creating, storing, accessing, transferring, and disposing of records under their control, whether these are written, automated, or in any other medium. (See also Standards 4.01, Maintaining Confidentiality, and 6.01, Documentation of Professional and Scientific Work and Maintenance of Records.)

(b) If confidential information concerning recipients of psychological services is entered into databases or systems of records available to persons whose access has not been consented to by the recipient, psychologists use coding or other techniques to avoid the inclusion of personal identifiers.

(c) Psychologists make plans in advance to facilitate the appropriate transfer and to protect the confidentiality of records and data in the event of psychologists' withdrawal from positions or practice. (See also Standards 3.12, Interruption of Psychological Services, and 10.09, Interruption of Therapy.)

6.03 Withholding Records for Nonpayment

Psychologists may not withhold records under their control that are requested and needed for a client's/patient's emergency treatment solely because payment has not been received.

6.04 Fees and Financial Arrangements

(a) As early as is feasible in a professional or scientific relationship, psychologists and recipients of psychological services reach an agreement specifying compensation and billing arrangements.

(b) Psychologists' fee practices are consistent with law.

(c) Psychologists do not misrepresent their fees.

(d) If limitations to services can be anticipated because of limitations in financing, this is discussed with the recipient of services as early as is feasible. (See also Standards 10.09, Interruption of Therapy, and 10.10, Terminating Therapy.)

(e) If the recipient of services does not pay for services as agreed, and if psychologists intend to use collection agencies or legal measures to collect the fees, psychologists first inform the person that such measures will be taken and provide that person an opportunity to make prompt payment. (See also Standards 4.05, Disclosures; 6.03, Withholding Records for Nonpayment; and 10.01, Informed Consent to Therapy.)

6.05 Barter With Clients/Patients

Barter is the acceptance of goods, services, or other nonmonetary remuneration from clients/patients in return for psychological services. Psychologists may barter only if (1) it is not clinically contraindicated, and (2) the resulting arrangement is not exploitative. (See also Standards 3.05, Multiple Relationships, and 6.04, Fees and Financial Arrangements.)

6.06 Accuracy in Reports to Payors and Funding Sources

In their reports to payors for services or sources of research funding, psychologists take reasonable steps to ensure the accurate reporting of the nature of the service provided or research conducted, the fees, charges, or payments, and where applicable, the identity of the provider, the findings, and the diagnosis. (See also Standards 4.01, Maintaining Confidentiality; 4.04, Minimizing Intrusions on Privacy; and 4.05, Disclosures.)

6.07 Referrals and Fees

When psychologists pay, receive payment from, or divide fees with another professional, other than in an employer-employee relationship, the payment to each is based on the services provided (clinical, consultative, administrative, or other) and is not based on the referral itself. (See also Standard 3.09, Cooperation With Other Professionals.)

7. Education and Training

7.01 Design of Education and Training Programs

Psychologists responsible for education and training programs take reasonable steps to ensure that the programs are designed to provide the appropriate knowledge and proper experiences, and to meet the requirements for licensure, certification, or other goals for which claims are made by the program. (See also Standard 5.03, Descriptions of Workshops and Non-Degree-Granting Educational Programs.)

7.02 Descriptions of Education and Training Programs

Psychologists responsible for education and training programs take reasonable steps to ensure that there is a current and accurate description of the program content (including participation in required course- or program-related counseling, psychotherapy, experiential groups, consulting projects, or community service), training goals and objectives, stipends and benefits, and requirements that must be met for satisfactory completion of the program. This information must be made readily available to all interested parties.

7.03 Accuracy in Teaching

(a) Psychologists take reasonable steps to ensure that course syllabi are accurate regarding the subject matter to be covered, bases for evaluating progress, and the nature of course experiences. This standard does not preclude an instructor from modifying course content or requirements when the instructor considers it pedagogically necessary or desirable, so long as students are made aware of these modifications in a manner that enables them to fulfill course requirements. (See also Standard 5.01, Avoidance of False or Deceptive Statements.)

(b) When engaged in teaching or training, psychologists present psychological information

accurately. (See also Standard 2.03, Maintaining Competence.)

7.04 Student Disclosure of Personal Information

Psychologists do not require students or supervisees to disclose personal information in course- or program-related activities, either orally or in writing, regarding sexual history, history of abuse and neglect, psychological treatment, and relationships with parents, peers, and spouses or significant others except if (1) the program or training facility has clearly identified this requirement in its admissions and program materials or (2) the information is necessary to evaluate or obtain assistance for students whose personal problems could reasonably be judged to be preventing them from performing their training- or professionally related activities in a competent manner or posing a threat to the students or others.

7.05 Mandatory Individual or Group Therapy

(a) When individual or group therapy is a program or course requirement, psychologists responsible for that program allow students in undergraduate and graduate programs the option of selecting such therapy from practitioners unaffiliated with the program. (See also Standard 7.02, Descriptions of Education and Training Programs.)

(b) Faculty who are or are likely to be responsible for evaluating students' academic performance do not themselves provide that therapy. (See also Standard 3.05, Multiple Relationships.)

7.06 Assessing Student and Supervisee Performance

(a) In academic and supervisory relationships, psychologists establish a timely and specific process for providing feedback to students and supervisees. Information regarding the process is provided to the student at the beginning of supervision.

(b) Psychologists evaluate students and supervisees on the basis of their actual performance on relevant and established program requirements.

7.07 Sexual Relationships With Students and Supervisees

Psychologists do not engage in sexual relationships with students or supervisees who are in their department, agency, or training center or over whom psychologists have or are likely to have evaluative authority. (See also Standard 3.05, Multiple Relationships.)

8. Research and Publication

8.01 Institutional Approval

When institutional approval is required, psychologists provide accurate information about their research proposals and obtain approval prior to conducting the research. They conduct the research in accordance with the approved research protocol.

8.02 Informed Consent to Research

(a) When obtaining informed consent as required in Standard 3.10, Informed Consent, psychologists inform participants about (1) the purpose of the research, expected duration, and procedures; (2) their right to decline to participate and to withdraw from the research once participation has begun; (3) the foreseeable consequences of declining or withdrawing; (4) reasonably foreseeable factors that may be expected to influence their willingness to participate such as potential risks, discomfort, or adverse effects; (5) any prospective research benefits; (6) limits of confidentiality; (7) incentives for participation; and (8) whom to contact for questions about the research and research participants' rights. They provide opportunity for the prospective participants to ask questions and receive answers. (See also Standards 8.03, Informed Consent for Recording Voices and Images in Research; 8.05, Dispensing With Informed Consent for Research; and 8.07, Deception in Research.)

(b) Psychologists conducting intervention research involving the use of experimental treatments clarify to participants at the outset of the research (1) the experimental nature of the treatment; (2) the services that will or will not be available to the control group(s) if appropriate; (3) the means by which assignment to treatment and control groups will be made; (4) available treatment alternatives if

an individual does not wish to participate in the research or wishes to withdraw once a study has begun; and (5) compensation for or monetary costs of participating including, if appropriate, whether reimbursement from the participant or a third-party payor will be sought. (See also Standard 8.02a, Informed Consent to Research.)

8.03 Informed Consent for Recording Voices and Images in Research

Psychologists obtain informed consent from research participants prior to recording their voices or images for data collection unless (1) the research consists solely of naturalistic observations in public places, and it is not anticipated that the recording will be used in a manner that could cause personal identification or harm, or (2) the research design includes deception, and consent for the use of the recording is obtained during debriefing. (See also Standard 8.07, Deception in Research.)

8.04 Client/Patient, Student, and Subordinate Research Participants

(a) When psychologists conduct research with clients/patients, students, or subordinates as participants, psychologists take steps to protect the prospective participants from adverse consequences of declining or withdrawing from participation.

(b) When research participation is a course requirement or an opportunity for extra credit, the prospective participant is given the choice of equitable alternative activities.

8.05 Dispensing With Informed Consent for Research

Psychologists may dispense with informed consent only (1) where research would not reasonably be assumed to create distress or harm and involves (a) the study of normal educational practices, curricula, or classroom management methods conducted in educational settings; (b) only anonymous questionnaires, naturalistic observations, or archival research for which disclosure of responses would not place participants at risk of criminal or civil liability or damage their financial standing, employability, or reputation, and confidentiality is protected; or (c) the study of factors related to job or organization effectiveness conducted in organizational settings for which there is no risk to participants' employability, and confidentiality is protected or (2) where otherwise permitted by law or federal or institutional regulations.

8.06 Offering Inducements for Research Participation

(a) Psychologists make reasonable efforts to avoid offering excessive or inappropriate financial or other inducements for research participation when such inducements are likely to coerce participation.

(b) When offering professional services as an inducement for research participation, psychologists clarify the nature of the services, as well as the risks, obligations, and limitations. (See also Standard 6.05, Barter With Clients/Patients.)

8.07 Deception in Research

(a) Psychologists do not conduct a study involving deception unless they have determined that the use of deceptive techniques is justified by the study's significant prospective scientific, educational, or applied value and that effective nondeceptive alternative procedures are not feasible.

(b) Psychologists do not deceive prospective participants about research that is reasonably expected to cause physical pain or severe emotional distress.

(c) Psychologists explain any deception that is an integral feature of the design and conduct of an experiment to participants as early as is feasible, preferably at the conclusion of their participation, but no later than at the conclusion of the data collection, and permit participants to withdraw their data. (See also Standard 8.08, Debriefing.)

8.08 Debriefing

(a) Psychologists provide a prompt opportunity for participants to obtain appropriate information about the nature, results, and conclusions of the research, and they take reasonable steps to correct any misconceptions that participants may have of which the psychologists are aware.

(b) If scientific or humane values justify delaying or withholding this information, psychologists

take reasonable measures to reduce the risk of harm.

(c) When psychologists become aware that research procedures have harmed a participant, they take reasonable steps to minimize the harm.

8.09 Humane Care and Use of Animals in Research

(a) Psychologists acquire, care for, use, and dispose of animals in compliance with current federal, state, and local laws and regulations, and with professional standards.

(b) Psychologists trained in research methods and experienced in the care of laboratory animals supervise all procedures involving animals and are responsible for ensuring appropriate consideration of their comfort, health, and humane treatment.

(c) Psychologists ensure that all individuals under their supervision who are using animals have received instruction in research methods and in the care, maintenance, and handling of the species being used, to the extent appropriate to their role. (See also Standard 2.05, Delegation of Work to Others.)

(d) Psychologists make reasonable efforts to minimize the discomfort, infection, illness, and pain of animal subjects.

(e) Psychologists use a procedure subjecting animals to pain, stress, or privation only when an alternative procedure is unavailable and the goal is justified by its prospective scientific, educational, or applied value.

(f) Psychologists perform surgical procedures under appropriate anesthesia and follow techniques to avoid infection and minimize pain during and after surgery.

(g) When it is appropriate that an animal's life be terminated, psychologists proceed rapidly, with an effort to minimize pain and in accordance with accepted procedures.

8.10 Reporting Research Results

(a) Psychologists do not fabricate data. (See also Standard 5.01a, Avoidance of False or Deceptive Statements.)

(b) If psychologists discover significant errors in their published data, they take reasonable steps to correct such errors in a correction, retraction, erratum, or other appropriate publication means.

8.11 Plagiarism

Psychologists do not present portions of another's work or data as their own, even if the other work or data source is cited occasionally.

8.12 Publication Credit

(a) Psychologists take responsibility and credit, including authorship credit, only for work they have actually performed or to which they have substantially contributed. (See also Standard 8.12b, Publication Credit.)

(b) Principal authorship and other publication credits accurately reflect the relative scientific or professional contributions of the individuals involved, regardless of their relative status. Mere possession of an institutional position, such as department chair, does not justify authorship credit. Minor contributions to the research or to the writing for publications are acknowledged appropriately, such as in footnotes or in an introductory statement.

(c) Except under exceptional circumstances, a student is listed as principal author on any multiple-authored article that is substantially based on the student's doctoral dissertation. Faculty advisors discuss publication credit with students as early as feasible and throughout the research and publication process as appropriate. (See also Standard 8.12b, Publication Credit.)

8.13 Duplicate Publication of Data

Psychologists do not publish, as original data, data that have been previously published. This does not preclude republishing data when they are accompanied by proper acknowledgment.

8.14 Sharing Research Data for Verification

(a) After research results are published, psychologists do not withhold the data on which their conclusions are based from other competent professionals who seek to verify the substantive claims through reanalysis and who intend to use such data only for that purpose, provided that the confiden-

tiality of the participants can be protected and unless legal rights concerning proprietary data preclude their release. This does not preclude psychologists from requiring that such individuals or groups be responsible for costs associated with the provision of such information.

(b) Psychologists who request data from other psychologists to verify the substantive claims through reanalysis may use shared data only for the declared purpose. Requesting psychologists obtain prior written agreement for all other uses of the data.

8.15 Reviewers

Psychologists who review material submitted for presentation, publication, grant, or research proposal review respect the confidentiality of and the proprietary rights in such information of those who submitted it.

9. Assessment

9.01 Bases for Assessments

(a) Psychologists base the opinions contained in their recommendations, reports, and diagnostic or evaluative statements, including forensic testimony, on information and techniques sufficient to substantiate their findings. (See also Standard 2.04, Bases for Scientific and Professional Judgments.)

(b) Except as noted in 9.01c, psychologists provide opinions of the psychological characteristics of individuals only after they have conducted an examination of the individuals adequate to support their statements or conclusions. When, despite reasonable efforts, such an examination is not practical, psychologists document the efforts they made and the result of those efforts, clarify the probable impact of their limited information on the reliability and validity of their opinions, and appropriately limit the nature and extent of their conclusions or recommendations. (See also Standards 2.01, Boundaries of Competence, and 9.06, Interpreting Assessment Results.)

(c) When psychologists conduct a record review or provide consultation or supervision and an individual examination is not warranted or necessary for the opinion, psychologists explain this and the sources of information on which they based their conclusions and recommendations.

9.02 Use of Assessments

(a) Psychologists administer, adapt, score, interpret, or use assessment techniques, interviews, tests, or instruments in a manner and for purposes that are appropriate in light of the research on or evidence of the usefulness and proper application of the techniques.

(b) Psychologists use assessment instruments whose validity and reliability have been established for use with members of the population tested. When such validity or reliability has not been established, psychologists describe the strengths and limitations of test results and interpretation.

(c) Psychologists use assessment methods that are appropriate to an individual's language preference and competence, unless the use of an alternative language is relevant to the assessment issues.

9.03 Informed Consent in Assessments

(a) Psychologists obtain informed consent for assessments, evaluations, or diagnostic services, as described in Standard 3.10, Informed Consent, except when (1) testing is mandated by law or governmental regulations; (2) informed consent is implied because testing is conducted as a routine educational, institutional, or organizational activity (e.g., when participants voluntarily agree to assessment when applying for a job); or (3) one purpose of the testing is to evaluate decisional capacity. Informed consent includes an explanation of the nature and purpose of the assessment, fees, involvement of third parties, and limits of confidentiality and sufficient opportunity for the client/patient to ask questions and receive answers.

(b) Psychologists inform persons with questionable capacity to consent or for whom testing is mandated by law or governmental regulations about the nature and purpose of the proposed assessment services, using language that is reasonably understandable to the person being assessed.

(c) Psychologists using the services of an interpreter obtain informed consent from the client/patient to use that interpreter, ensure that confidentiality of test results and test security are

maintained, and include in their recommendations, reports, and diagnostic or evaluative statements, including forensic testimony, discussion of any limitations on the data obtained. (See also Standards 2.05, Delegation of Work to Others; 4.01, Maintaining Confidentiality; 9.01, Bases for Assessments; 9.06, Interpreting Assessment Results; and 9.07, Assessment by Unqualified Persons.)

9.04 Release of Test Data

(a) The term test data refers to raw and scaled scores, client/patient responses to test questions or stimuli, and psychologists' notes and recordings concerning client/patient statements and behavior during an examination. Those portions of test materials that include client/patient responses are included in the definition of test data. Pursuant to a client/patient release, psychologists provide test data to the client/patient or other persons identified in the release. Psychologists may refrain from releasing test data to protect a client/patient or others from substantial harm or misuse or misrepresentation of the data or the test, recognizing that in many instances release of confidential information under these circumstances is regulated by law. (See also Standard 9.11, Maintaining Test Security.)

(b) In the absence of a client/patient release, psychologists provide test data only as required by law or court order.

9.05 Test Construction

Psychologists who develop tests and other assessment techniques use appropriate psychometric procedures and current scientific or professional knowledge for test design, standardization, validation, reduction or elimination of bias, and recommendations for use.

9.06 Interpreting Assessment Results

When interpreting assessment results, including automated interpretations, psychologists take into account the purpose of the assessment as well as the various test factors, test-taking abilities, and other characteristics of the person being assessed, such as situational, personal, linguistic, and cultural differences, that might affect psychologists' judgments or reduce the accuracy of their interpretations. They indicate any significant limitations of their interpretations. (See also Standards 2.01b and c, Boundaries of Competence, and 3.01, Unfair Discrimination.)

9.07 Assessment by Unqualified Persons
Psychologists do not promote the use of psychological assessment techniques by unqualified persons, except when such use is conducted for training purposes with appropriate supervision. (See also Standard 2.05, Delegation of Work to Others.)

9.08 Obsolete Tests and Outdated Test Results
(a) Psychologists do not base their assessment or intervention decisions or recommendations on data or test results that are outdated for the current purpose.

(b) Psychologists do not base such decisions or recommendations on tests and measures that are obsolete and not useful for the current purpose.

9.09 Test Scoring and Interpretation Services
(a) Psychologists who offer assessment or scoring services to other professionals accurately describe the purpose, norms, validity, reliability, and applications of the procedures and any special qualifications applicable to their use.

(b) Psychologists select scoring and interpretation services (including automated services) on the basis of evidence of the validity of the program and procedures as well as on other appropriate considerations. (See also Standard 2.01b and c, Boundaries of Competence.)

(c) Psychologists retain responsibility for the appropriate application, interpretation, and use of assessment instruments, whether they score and interpret such tests themselves or use automated or other services.

9.10 Explaining Assessment Results
Regardless of whether the scoring and interpretation are done by psychologists, by employees or assistants, or by automated or other outside services, psychologists take reasonable steps to ensure that explanations of results are given to the individual or designated representative unless the nature of the relationship precludes provision of an explanation of results (such as in some organizational consulting, preemployment or security screenings, and forensic evaluations), and this fact has been clearly explained to the person being assessed in advance.

9.11 Maintaining Test Security
The term test materials refers to manuals, instruments, protocols, and test questions or stimuli and does not include test data as defined in Standard 9.04, Release of Test Data. Psychologists make reasonable efforts to maintain the integrity and security of test materials and other assessment techniques consistent with law and contractual obligations, and in a manner that permits adherence to this Ethics Code.

10. Therapy

10.01 Informed Consent to Therapy
(a) When obtaining informed consent to therapy as required in Standard 3.10, Informed Consent, psychologists inform clients/patients as early as is feasible in the therapeutic relationship about the nature and anticipated course of therapy, fees, involvement of third parties, and limits of confidentiality and provide sufficient opportunity for the client/patient to ask questions and receive answers. (See also Standards 4.02, Discussing the Limits of Confidentiality, and 6.04, Fees and Financial Arrangements.)

(b) When obtaining informed consent for treatment for which generally recognized techniques and procedures have not been established, psychologists inform their clients/patients of the developing nature of the treatment, the potential risks involved, alternative treatments that may be available, and the voluntary nature of their participation. (See also Standards 2.01e, Boundaries of Competence, and 3.10, Informed Consent.)

(c) When the therapist is a trainee and the legal responsibility for the treatment provided resides with the supervisor, the client/patient, as part of the informed consent procedure, is informed that the therapist is in training and is being supervised and is given the name of the supervisor.

10.02 Therapy Involving Couples or Families

(a) When psychologists agree to provide services to several persons who have a relationship (such as spouses, significant others, or parents and children), they take reasonable steps to clarify at the outset (1) which of the individuals are clients/patients and (2) the relationship the psychologist will have with each person. This clarification includes the psychologist's role and the probable uses of the services provided or the information obtained. (See also Standard 4.02, Discussing the Limits of Confidentiality.)

(b) If it becomes apparent that psychologists may be called on to perform potentially conflicting roles (such as family therapist and then witness for one party in divorce proceedings), psychologists take reasonable steps to clarify and modify, or withdraw from, roles appropriately. (See also Standard 3.05c, Multiple Relationships.)

10.03 Group Therapy

When psychologists provide services to several persons in a group setting, they describe at the outset the roles and responsibilities of all parties and the limits of confidentiality.

10.04 Providing Therapy to Those Served by Others

In deciding whether to offer or provide services to those already receiving mental health services elsewhere, psychologists carefully consider the treatment issues and the potential client's/patient's welfare. Psychologists discuss these issues with the client/patient or another legally authorized person on behalf of the client/patient in order to minimize the risk of confusion and conflict, consult with the other service providers when appropriate, and proceed with caution and sensitivity to the therapeutic issues.

10.05 Sexual Intimacies With Current Therapy Clients/Patients

Psychologists do not engage in sexual intimacies with current therapy clients/patients.

10.06 Sexual Intimacies With Relatives or Significant Others of Current Therapy Clients/Patients

Psychologists do not engage in sexual intimacies with individuals they know to be close relatives, guardians, or significant others of current clients/patients. Psychologists do not terminate therapy to circumvent this standard.

10.07 Therapy With Former Sexual Partners

Psychologists do not accept as therapy clients/patients persons with whom they have engaged in sexual intimacies.

10.08 Sexual Intimacies With Former Therapy Clients/Patients

(a) Psychologists do not engage in sexual intimacies with former clients/patients for at least two years after cessation or termination of therapy.

(b) Psychologists do not engage in sexual intimacies with former clients/patients even after a two-year interval except in the most unusual circumstances. Psychologists who engage in such activity after the two years following cessation or termination of therapy and of having no sexual contact with the former client/patient bear the burden of demonstrating that there has been no exploitation, in light of all relevant factors, including (1) the amount of time that has passed since therapy terminated; (2) the nature, duration, and intensity of the therapy; (3) the circumstances of termination; (4) the client's/patient's personal history; (5) the client's/patient's current mental status; (6) the likelihood of adverse impact on the client/patient; and (7) any statements or actions made by the therapist during the course of therapy suggesting or inviting the possibility of a posttermination sexual or romantic relationship with the client/patient. (See also Standard 3.05, Multiple Relationships.)

10.09 Interruption of Therapy

When entering into employment or contractual relationships, psychologists make reasonable efforts to provide for orderly and appropriate resolution of responsibility for client/patient care in the event that the employment or contractual relationship ends, with paramount consideration given to the welfare of the client/patient. (See also Standard 3.12, Interruption of Psychological Services.)

10.10 Terminating Therapy

(a) Psychologists terminate therapy when it becomes reasonably clear that the client/patient no longer needs the service, is not likely to benefit, or is being harmed by continued service.

(b) Psychologists may terminate therapy when threatened or otherwise endangered by the client/patient or another person with whom the client/patient has a relationship.

(c) Except where precluded by the actions of clients/patients or third-party payors, prior to termination psychologists provide pretermination counseling and suggest alternative service providers as appropriate.

American Psychological Association Policy on Training for Psychologists Wishing to Change Their Specialty

Possession of a doctoral degree from an accredited institution does not, in and of itself, constitute adequate educational preparation to practice in all areas of psychology. A doctorate in experimental psychology, for example, does not provide adequate preparation for clinical practice. In assessing their own competence as it is relevant to an area of forensic practice, psychologists may find it helpful to consider the two policy statements of the American Psychological Association (APA) that follow.

The first policy statement was adopted by the APA's Council of Representatives at the January 23–25, 1976, meeting.[1]

Council adopts the following as official policy of the APA:

1. We strongly urge psychology departments currently engaged in doctoral training to offer training for individuals, already holding the doctoral degree in psychology, who wish to change their specialty. Such programs should be individualized, since background and career objectives vary greatly. It is desirable that financial assistance be made available to students in such programs.

2. Programs engaging in such training should declare so publicly and include a statement to that effect as a formal part of their program description and/or application for accreditation.

3. Psychologists seeking to change their specialty should take training in a program of the highest quality, and, where appropriate, exemplified by the doctoral training programs and internships accredited by the APA.

4. With respect to subject matter and professional skills, psychologists taking such training must meet all requirements of doctoral training in the new psychological specialty, being given due credit for relevant course work or requirements they have previously satisfied.

5. It must be stressed, however, that merely taking an internship or acquiring experience in a practicum setting is not, for example, considered adequate preparation for becoming a clinical, counseling, or school psychologist when prior training had not been in the relevant area.

6. Upon fulfillment of all formal requirements of such training program, the students should be awarded a certificate indicating the successful completion of preparation in the particular specialty, thus according them due recognition for their additional education and experience.

7. This policy statement shall be incorporated in the guidelines of the Committee on Accreditation so that appropriate sanctions can be brought to bear on university and internship training programs which violate paragraphs 4 and/or 5 of the above.

In reaffirming and amending its previous policy, the Council of Representatives approved the fol-

[1] From "Proceedings of the American Psychological Association, Incorporated, for the year 1975: Minutes of the Annual Meeting of the Council of Representatives, August 29 and September 2, 1975, Chicago, IL, and January 23–25, 1976, Washington, DC," by J. J. Conger, 1976, *American Psychologist, 31,* p. 424. Copyright 1976 by the American Psychological Association.

lowing statement of policy at its January 22–24, 1982, meeting.[2]

The American Psychological Association holds that respecialization education and training for psychologists possessing the doctoral degree should be conducted by those academic units in regionally accredited universities and professional schools currently offering doctoral training in the relevant specialty, and in conjunction with regularly organized internship agencies where appropriate. Respecialization for purposes of offering services in clinical, counseling, or school psychology should be linked to relevant APA approved programs.

[2] From "Proceedings of the American Psychological Association, Incorporated, for the year 1981. Minutes of the Annual Meeting of the Council of Representatives," by N. Abeles, 1982, *American Psychologist, 37,* p. 656. Copyright 1982 by the American Psychological Association.

Specialty Guidelines for Forensic Psychologists

Committee on Ethical Guidelines for Forensic Psychologists

The "Specialty Guidelines for Forensic Psychologists," while informed by the *Ethical Principles of Psychologists and Code of Conduct* (American Psychological Association [APA], 1992) and meant to be consistent with them, are designed to provide more specific guidance to forensic psychologists in monitoring their professional conduct when acting in assistance to courts, parties to legal proceedings, correctional and forensic mental health facilities, and legislative agencies. The primary goal of the *Guidelines* is to improve the quality of forensic psychological services offered to individual clients and the legal system and thereby to enhance forensic psychology as a discipline and profession. The *Specialty Guidelines for Forensic Psychologists* represent a joint statement of the American Psychology–Law Society and Division 41 of the American Psychological Association and are endorsed by the American Academy of Forensic Psychology. The *Guidelines* do not represent an official statement of the American Psychological Association.

The *Guidelines* provide an aspirational model of desirable professional practice by psychologists within any subdiscipline of psychology (e.g., clinical, developmental, social, or experimental), when they are engaged regularly as experts and represent themselves as such, in an activity primarily intended to provide professional psychological expertise to the judicial system. This would include, for example, clinical forensic examiners; psychologists employed by correctional or forensic mental health systems; researchers who offer direct testimony about the relevance of scientific data to a psycholegal issue; trial behavior consultants; psychologists engaged in preparation of amicus briefs; or psychologists, appearing as forensic experts, who consult with, or testify before, judicial, legislative, or administrative agencies acting in an adjudicative capacity. Individuals who provide only occasional service to the legal system and who do so without representing themselves as forensic experts may find these *Guidelines* helpful, particularly in consultation with colleagues who are forensic experts.

While the *Guidelines* are concerned with a model of desirable professional practice, to the extent that they may be construed as being applicable to the advertisement of services or the solicitation of clients, they are intended to prevent false or deceptive advertisement or solicitations and should be construed in a manner consistent with that intent.

I. PURPOSE AND SCOPE

A. Purpose

1. While the professional standards for the ethical practice of psychology, as a general discipline, are addressed in the American Psychological Association's *Ethical Principles of Psychologists*, these ethical principles do not relate, in sufficient detail, to current aspirations of desirable professional conduct for forensic psychologists. By design, none of

the *Guidelines* contradicts any of the *Ethical Principles of Psychologists*; rather, they amplify those *Principles* in the context of the practice of forensic psychology, as herein defined.

2. The *Guidelines* have been designed to be national in scope and are intended to conform with state and Federal law. In situations where the forensic psychologist believes that the requirements of law are in conflict with the *Guidelines*, attempts to resolve the conflict should be made in accordance with the procedures set forth in these *Guidelines* [IV(G)] and in the *Ethical Principles of Psychologists*.

B. Scope

1. The *Guidelines* specify the nature of the desirable professional practice by forensic psychologists, within any subdiscipline of psychology (e.g., clinical, developmental, social, experimental), when engaged regularly as forensic psychologists.

    a. "Psychologist" means any individual whose professional activities are defined by the American Psychological Association or by regulation of the title by state registration or licensure, as the practice of psychology.

    b. "Forensic psychology" means all forms of professional psychological conduct when acting, with definable foreknowledge, as a psychological expert on explicitly psycholegal issues, in direct assistance to courts, parties to legal proceedings, correctional and forensic mental health facilities, and administrative, judicial, and legislative agencies acting in an adjudicative capacity.

    c. "Forensic psychologist" means psychologists who regularly engage in the practice of forensic psychology as defined in I(B)(1)(b).

2. The *Guidelines* do not apply to a psychologist who is asked to provide professional psychological services when the psychologist was not informed at the time of delivery of the services that they were to be used as forensic psychological services as defined above. The *Guidelines* may be helpful, however, in preparing the psychologist for the experience of communicating psychological data in a forensic context.

3. Psychologists who are not forensic psychologists as defined in I(B)(1)(c), but who occasionally provide limited forensic psychological services, may find the *Guidelines* useful in the preparation and presentation of their professional services.

C. Related Standards

1. Forensic psychologists also conduct their professional activities in accord with the *Ethical Principles of Psychologists* and the various other statements of the American Psychological Association that may apply to particular subdisciplines or areas of practice that are relevant to their professional activities.

2. The standards of practice and ethical guidelines of other relevant "expert professional organizations" contain useful guidance and should be consulted even though the present *Guidelines* take precedence for forensic psychologists.

II. RESPONSIBILITY

A. Forensic psychologists have an obligation to provide services in a manner consistent with the highest standards of their profession. They are responsible for their own conduct and the conduct of those individuals under their direct supervision.

B. Forensic psychologists make a reasonable effort to ensure that their services and the products of their services are used in a forthright and responsible manner.

III. COMPETENCE

A. Forensic psychologists provide services only in areas of psychology in which they have specialized knowledge, skill, experience, and education.

B. Forensic psychologists have an obligation to present to the court, regarding the specific matters to which they will testify, the boundaries of their competence, the factual bases (knowledge, skill, experience, training, and education) for their qualification as an expert on the specific matters at issue.

C. Forensic psychologists are responsible for a fundamental and reasonable level of knowledge and understanding of the legal and professional standards that govern their participation as experts in legal proceedings.

D. Forensic psychologists have an obligation to understand the civil rights of parties in legal proceedings in which they participate, and manage their professional conduct in a manner that does not diminish or threaten those rights.

E. Forensic psychologists recognize that their own personal values, moral beliefs, or personal and professional relationships with parties to a legal proceeding may interfere with their ability to practice competently. Under such circumstances, forensic psychologists are obligated to decline participation or to limit their assistance in a manner consistent with professional obligations.

IV. RELATIONSHIPS

A. During initial consultation with the legal representative of the party seeking services, forensic psychologists have an obligation to inform the party of factors that might reasonably affect the decision to contract with the forensic psychologist. These factors include, but are not limited to,

1. the fee structure for anticipated professional services;

2. prior and current personal or professional activities, obligations, and relationships that might produce a conflict of interest;

3. their areas of competence and the limits of their competence; and

4. the known scientific bases and limitations of the methods and procedures that they employ and their qualifications to employ such methods and procedures.

B. Forensic psychologists do not provide professional services to parties to a legal proceeding on the basis of "contingent fees," when those services involve the offering of expert testimony to a court or administrative body, or when they call upon the psychologist to make affirmations or representations intended to be relied upon by third parties.

C. Forensic psychologists who derive a substantial portion of their income from fee-for-service arrangements should offer some portion of their professional services on a *pro bono* or reduced fee basis where the public interest or the welfare of clients may be inhibited by insufficient financial resources.

D. Forensic psychologists recognize potential conflicts of interest in dual relationships with parties to a legal proceeding, and they seek to minimize their effects.

1. Forensic psychologists avoid providing professional services to parties in a legal proceeding with whom they have personal or professional relationships that are inconsistent with the anticipated relationship.

2. When it is necessary to provide both evaluation and treatment services to a party in a legal proceeding (as may be the case in small forensic hospital settings or small communities), the forensic psychologist takes reasonable steps to minimize the potential negative effects of these circumstances on the rights of the party, confidentiality, and the process of treatment and evaluation.

E. Forensic psychologists have an obligation to ensure that prospective clients are informed of their legal rights with respect to the anticipated forensic service, of the purposes of any evaluation, of the nature of the procedures to be employed, of the intended uses of any product of their services, and of the party who has employed the forensic psychologist.

1. Unless court ordered, forensic psychologists obtain the informed consent of the client or party, or their legal representative, before proceeding with such evaluations and procedures. If the client appears unwilling to proceed after receiving a thorough notification of the purposes, methods, and intended uses of the forensic evaluation, the evaluation should be postponed and the psychologist should take steps to place the client in contact with his/her attorney for the purpose of legal advice on the issues of participation.

2. In situations where the client or party may not have the capacity to provide informed consent to services or the evaluation is pursuant to court order, the forensic psychologist provides reasonable notice to the client's legal representative of the nature of the anticipated forensic service before proceeding. If the client's legal representative objects to the evaluation, the forensic psychologist notifies the court issuing the order and responds as directed.

3. After a psychologist has advised the subject of a clinical forensic evaluation of the intended use of the evaluation and its work product, the psychologist may not use the evaluation work product for other purposes without explicit waiver to do so by the client or the client's legal representative.

F. When forensic psychologists engage in research or scholarly activities that are compensated financially by a client or party to a legal proceeding, or when the psychologist provides those services on a *pro bono* basis, the psychologist clarifies any anticipated further use of such research or scholarly product, and obtains whatever consent or agreement is required by law or professional standards.

G. When conflicts arise between the forensic psychologist's professional standards and the requirements of legal standards, a particular court, or a directive by an officer of the court or legal authorities, the forensic psychologist has an obligation to make those legal authorities aware of the source of the conflict and to take reasonable steps to resolve it. Such steps may include, but are not limited to, obtaining the consultation of fellow forensic professionals, obtaining the advice of independent counsel, and conferring directly with the legal representatives involved.

V. CONFIDENTIALITY AND PRIVILEGE

A. Forensic psychologists have an obligation to be aware of the legal standards that may affect or limit the confidentiality or privilege that may attach to their services or their products, and they conduct their professional activities in a manner that respects those known rights and privileges.

1. Forensic psychologists establish and maintain a system of record keeping and professional communication that safeguards a client's privilege.

2. Forensic psychologists maintain active control over records and information. They only release information pursuant to statutory requirements, court order, or the consent of the client.

B. Forensic psychologists inform their clients of the limitations to the confidentiality of their services and their products (See also Guideline IV[E]) by providing them with an understandable statement of their rights, privileges, and the limitations of confidentiality.

C. In situations where the right of the client or party to confidentiality is limited, the forensic psychologist makes every effort to maintain confidentiality with regard to any information that does not bear directly upon the legal purpose of the evaluation.

D. Forensic psychologists provide clients or their authorized legal representatives with access to the information in their records and a meaningful explanation of that information, consistent with existing federal and state statutes, the *Ethical Principles of Psychologists*, the *Standards for Educational and Psychological Testing*, and institutional rules and regulations.

VI. METHODS AND PROCEDURES

A. Because of their special status as persons qualified as experts to the court, forensic psychologists have an obligation to maintain current knowledge of scientific, professional and legal developments within their area of claimed competence. They are obligated also to use that knowledge, consistent with accepted clinical and scientific standards, in selecting data collection methods and procedures for an evaluation, treatment, consultation or scholarly/empirical investigations.

B. Forensic psychologists have an obligation to document and be prepared to make available, subject to court order or the rules of evidence, all data that form the basis for their evidence or services. The standard to be applied to such documentation will be subject to reasonable judicial scrutiny; this standard is higher than the normative standard for general clinical practice. When forensic psychologists conduct an examination or engage in the treatment of a party to a legal proceeding, with foreknowledge that their professional services will be used in an adjudicative forum, they incur a special responsibility to provide the best documentation possible under the circumstances.

1. Documentation of the data upon which one's evidence is based is subject to the normal rules of discovery, disclosure, confidentiality, and privilege that operate in the jurisdiction in which the data were obtained. Forensic psychologists have an obligation to be aware of those rules and to regulate their conduct in accordance with them.

2. The duties and obligations of forensic psychologists with respect to documentation of data that form the basis for their evidence apply from the moment they know or have a reasonable basis for knowing that their data and evidence derived from it are likely to enter into legally relevant decisions.

C. In providing forensic psychological services, forensic psychologists take special care to avoid undue influence upon their methods, procedures, and products, such as might emanate from the party to a legal proceeding by financial compensation or other gains. As an expert conducting an evaluation, treatment, consultation, or scholarly/empirical investigation, the forensic psychologist maintains professional integrity by examining the issue at hand from all reasonable perspectives, actively seeking information that will differentially test plausible rival hypotheses.

D. Forensic psychologists do not provide professional forensic services to a defendant or to any party in, or in contemplation of, a legal proceeding prior to that individual's representation by counsel, except for persons judicially determined, where appropriate, to be handling their representation *pro se*. When the forensic services are pursuant to court order and the client is not represented by counsel, the forensic psychologist makes reasonable efforts to inform the court prior to providing the services.

1. A forensic psychologist may provide emergency mental health services to a pretrial defendant prior to court order or the appointment of counsel where there are reasonable grounds to believe that such emergency services are needed for the protection and improvement of the defendant's mental health and where failure to provide such mental health services would constitute a substantial risk of imminent harm to the defendant or to others. In providing such services the forensic psychologist neverthe-

less seeks to inform the defendant's counsel in a manner consistent with the requirements of the emergency situation.

2. Forensic psychologists who provide such emergency mental health services should attempt to avoid providing further professional forensic services to that defendant unless that relationship is reasonably unavoidable [see IV(D)(2)].

E. When forensic psychologists seek data from third parties, prior records, or other sources, they do so only with the prior approval of the relevant legal party or as a consequence of an order of a court to conduct the forensic evaluation.

F. Forensic psychologists are aware that hearsay exceptions and other rules governing expert testimony place a special ethical burden upon them. When hearsay or otherwise inadmissible evidence forms the basis of their opinion, evidence, or professional product, they seek to minimize sole reliance upon such evidence. Where circumstances reasonably permit, forensic psychologists seek to obtain independent and personal verification of data relied upon as part of their professional services to the court or to a party to a legal proceeding.

1. While many forms of data used by forensic psychologists are hearsay, forensic psychologists attempt to corroborate critical data that form the basis for their professional product. When using hearsay data that have not been corroborated, but are nevertheless utilized, forensic psychologists have an affirmative responsibility to acknowledge the uncorroborated status of those data and the reasons for relying upon such data.

2. With respect to evidence of any type, forensic psychologists avoid offering information from their investigations or evaluations that does not bear directly upon the legal purpose of their professional services and that is not critical as support for their

product, evidence, or testimony, except where such disclosure is required by law.

3. When a forensic psychologist relies upon data or information gathered by others, the origins of those data are clarified in any professional product. In addition, the forensic psychologist bears a special responsibility to ensure that such data, if relied upon, were gathered in a manner standard for the profession.

G. Unless otherwise stipulated by the parties, forensic psychologists are aware that no statements made by a defendant, in the court of any (forensic) examination, no testimony by the expert based upon such statements, nor any other fruits of the statements can be admitted into evidence against the defendant in any criminal proceeding, except on an issue respecting mental condition on which the defendant has introduced testimony. Forensic psychologists have an affirmative duty to ensure that their written products and oral testimony conform to this Federal Rule of Procedure (12.2[c]), or its state equivalent.

1. Because forensic psychologists are often not in a position to know what evidence, documentation, or element of written product may be or may lend to a "fruit of the statement," they exercise extreme caution in preparing reports or offering testimony prior to the defendant's assertion of a mental state claim or the defendant's introduction of testimony regarding a mental condition. Consistent with the reporting requirements of state or federal law, forensic psychologists avoid including statements from the defendant relating to the time period of the alleged offense.

2. Once a defendant has proceeded to the trial state, and all pretrial mental health issues such as competency have been resolved, forensic psychologists may include in their reports or testimony any statements made by the defendant that are directly relevant to

supporting their expert evidence, providing that the defendant has "introduced" mental state evidence or testimony within the meaning of Federal Rule of Procedure 12.2(c), or its state equivalent.

H. Forensic psychologists avoid giving written or oral evidence about the psychological characteristics of particular individuals when they have not had an opportunity to conduct an examination of the individual adequate to the scope of the statements, opinions, or conclusions to be issued. Forensic psychologists make every reasonable effort to conduct such examinations. When it is not possible or feasible to do so, they make clear the impact of such limitations on the reliability and validity of their professional products, evidence, or testimony.

VII. PUBLIC AND PROFESSIONAL COMMUNICATIONS

A. Forensic psychologists make reasonable efforts to ensure that the products of their services, as well as their own public statements and professional testimony, are communicated in ways that will promote understanding and avoid deception, given the particular characteristics, roles, and abilities of various recipients of the communications.

1. Forensic psychologists take reasonable steps to correct misuse or misrepresentation of their professional products, evidence, and testimony.

B. Forensic psychologists provide information about professional work to clients in a manner consistent with professional and legal standards for the disclosure of test results, interpretations of data, and the factual bases for conclusions. A full explanation of the results of tests and the bases for conclusions should be given in language that the client can understand.

1. When disclosing information about a client to third parties who are not qualified to interpret tests results and data, the forensic

psychologist complies with Principle 16 of the *Standards for Educational and Psychological Testing.* When required to disclose results to a nonpsychologist, every attempt is made to ensure that test security is maintained and access to information is restricted to individuals with a legitimate and professional interest in the data. Other qualified mental health professionals who make a request for information pursuant to a lawful order are, by definition, "individuals with a legitimate and professional interest."

2. In providing records and raw data, the forensic psychologist takes reasonable steps to ensure that the receiving party is informed that raw scores must be interpreted by a qualified professional in order to provide reliable and valid information.

C. Forensic psychologists realize that their public role as "expert to the court" or as "expert representing the profession" confers upon them a special responsibility for fairness and accuracy in their public statements. When evaluating or commenting upon the professional work product or qualifications of another expert or party to a legal proceeding, forensic psychologists represent their professional disagreements with reference to a fair and accurate evaluation of the data, theories, standards, and opinions of other expert or party.

D. Ordinarily, forensic psychologists avoid making detailed public (out-of-court) statements about particular legal proceedings in which they have been involved. When there is a strong justification to do so, such public statements are designed to assure accurate representation of their role or their evidence, not to advocate the positions of parties in the legal proceeding. Forensic psychologists address particular legal proceedings in publications or communications only to the extent that the information relied upon is part of a public record or consent for that use has been properly obtained from the party holding any privilege.

E. When testifying, forensic psychologists have an obligation to all parties to a legal proceeding to present their findings, conclusions, evidence, or other professional products in a fair manner. This principle does not preclude forceful representation of the data and reasoning upon which a conclusion or professional product is based. It does, however, preclude an attempt, whether active or passive, to engage in partisan distortion or misrepresentation. Forensic psychologists do not, by either commission or omission, participate in a misrepresentation of their evidence, nor do they participate in partisan attempts to avoid, deny, or subvert the presentation of evidence contrary to their own position.

F. Forensic psychologists, by virtue of their competence and rules of discovery, actively disclose all sources of information obtained in the court of their professional services; they actively disclose which information from which source was used in formulating a particular written product or oral testimony.

G. Forensic psychologists are aware that their essential role as expert to the court is to assist the trier of fact to understand the evidence or to determine a fact in issue. In offering expert evidence, they are aware that their own professional observations, inferences, and conclusions must be distinguished from legal facts, opinions, and conclusions. Forensic psychologists are prepared to explain the relationship between their expert testimony and the legal issues and facts of an instant case.

Statement of Principles Relating to the Responsibilities of Attorneys and Psychologists in Their Interprofessional Relations

An Interdisciplinary Agreement Between the New Mexico Bar Association and the New Mexico Psychological Association

These principles should govern the interprofessional relations of psychologists and attorneys.

I. THE PATIENT–CLIENT

The welfare of the patient–client is the paramount and joint goal of these principles.

II. THE PSYCHOLOGISTS AND THE LAW

1. Psychologists shall refrain from giving legal advice.

2. Psychologists shall refrain from interfering with established lawyer–client relationships.

III. ATTORNEYS AND PSYCHOLOGICAL CARE

1. Attorneys shall refrain from giving psychodiagnostic opinions.

2. Attorneys shall refrain from interfering with established psychologist–patient relationships.

IV. AN ATTORNEY'S RESPONSIBILITIES

An attorney's responsibility is always first to his [or her] client. However, in his [or her] relationships with psychologists, an attorney has the following responsibilities:

1. Testimony: An attorney should keep the psychologist informed as to the status of the litigation and in particular inform him [or her] sufficiently in advance of:

a. deposition and trial settings;

b. vacated deposition and trial settings; and

c. pretrial settlements.

2. Fees: The services of a psychologist in a legal matter involve the consumption of the psychologist's time and the utilization of his [or her] facilities and his [or her] expertise. As a result, the attorney shall make proper arrangements with all involved psychologists beforehand for payment for the psychologist's services either directly by his [or her] client or by the attorney himself [or herself] through advancement of costs. An attorney is not expected to advance costs for psychologist services involving treatment.

An attorney who requests information from a psychologist solely to advance his [or her] knowledge of psychology is responsible personally for prompt payment of those services.

3. Background: An attorney should attempt to familiarize himself [or herself] with the psychological literature in order that he [or she] may have some initial understanding of the problem and so that he [or she] might be able to specify the information requested from the psychologist and understand the psychologist's explanation and report.

4. Confidentiality: An attorney must know the applicable law relating to confidentiality in the psychologist–patient relationship, such as the psychotherapist–patient privilege, Rule 504,

New Mexico Rules of Evidence and the disclosure of information provision of the New Mexico Mental Health and Developmental Disabilities Code, N. M. Stat. Ann. Section 43-1-19 (1978). The attorney shall refrain from asking a psychologist to disclose confidential information other than as provided by law.

5. Client Preparation: An attorney should inform his [or her] client as to the nature and purposes of any psychological evaluation and should identify the potential uses of information to be gathered during the evaluation.

V. A PSYCHOLOGIST'S RESPONSIBILITIES

A psychologist's primary responsibility is always the well-being of his [or her] patient. The psychologist must maintain the confidentiality of patient communications as provided by New Mexico law. The psychologist acting as psychotherapist must claim the psychotherapist–patient privilege on behalf of his [or her] patient, recognizing that this privilege may be waived or excepted under New Mexico law. In any event, the psychologist must obtain a valid authorization from his [or her] patient or the patient's guardian before confidential information may be disclosed. A psychologist involved in the legal process has the following responsibilities.

1. Records: Given a valid authorization, the psychologist should promptly transfer information from his [or her] records to the requesting attorney. Psychologists have no proprietary interest in test or interview responses, whether written, taped, or otherwise recorded.

2. Reports: Given a valid authorization, reports covering a summation of psychological facts and opinions and their significance shall be furnished upon request by the treating psychologist or the psychologist specifically engaged to do such work. The attorney should specify the items he [or she] wishes covered in that report.

3. Psychological Testing Materials: Secured instruments, such as Rorschach or TAT [Thematic Apperception Test] cards, testing manuals, or other copyrighted materials, should be for-

warded only to certified psychologists retained by the requesting attorney.

4. Psychological Evaluations: Before evaluating a person, the psychologist must inform the person of the nature and purposes of the psychological evaluation and must identify the potential uses of the information to be gathered during the evaluation.

5. Conferences: Given a valid authorization, attorneys may confer with psychologists either to:

a. gain psychological information on a topic of the attorney's interest, or

b. discuss psychological aspects of the case of a particular client with the treating psychologist or with one engaged to render such opinions. This may include a discussion of testimony that may be elicited at trial.

6. Testimony: Psychologists may be requested to testify either in court or by deposition. Cooperation between both attorneys and psychologists should allow for setting of court or deposition testimony for mutual convenience; while a subpoena may be necessary, it is not a substitute for direct communication between the attorney and psychologist for purpose of setting a time for testimony.

A psychologist should familiarize himself [or herself] with the basic requirements of court procedure.

A psychologist should limit his [or her] testimony to his [or her] opinion and its basis. He [or she] should leave the representation of his [or her] patient and advancement of the patient's interest to the patient's attorney.

7. Fees: Psychologists may use the expenditure of their time, office facilities, and funds as a basis for arriving at a reasonable fee for services rendered pursuant to these principles. If an attorney fails to give timely notification of a change in the scheduled time for the psychologist's services, which makes the psychologist unavailable for other remunerative work, the psychologist may charge for the time set aside. A reasonable fee for the psychologist's time spent in prepara-

tion for testimony by deposition or in the court-room is the same rate charged for usual psychological services. A reasonable fee for deposition or courtroom testimony is no more than double the usual rate for psychological services.

VI. GRIEVANCE PROCEDURE

Any grievance regarding the Principles set forth above shall be referred to a grievance panel for hearing. The New Mexico Bar Association and the New Mexico Psychological Association will each provide six committee members and one cochairman to serve on grievance panels which will be composed of two lawyers, two psychologists, and one cochairman. The cochairman for a grievance panel will choose two panel members from each profession.

Grievance panels are intended to resolve disputes arising out of the Principles set forth above; they are not intended as a substitute for the bodies governing the ethical conduct of the respective professions. Breaches of the ethical code of either profession or violations of law are to be referred to the appropriate body for consideration.

Twelve Deadly Traps of Forensic Assessment

1. Using psychological tests without having well-grounded expertise and up-to-date training in assessment, the relevant assessment instruments and methods, the relevant population, and the relevant issues (e.g., developmental disabilities, schizophrenia, sexual abuse, malingering).

2. Accepting new psychological tests, measures, or other assessment methods and instruments uncritically from a test publisher or other source without ensuring that they have been sufficiently researched and validated for *forensic* uses involving the *population* and *issues at hand*.

3. Administering tests without adequately addressing relevant issues of informed consent.

4. Using any modified form of a psychological test or method of administering a psychological test that has not been adequately and objectively validated for the relevant forensic uses.

5. Using obsolete forms of a test as though they met an acceptable current standard.

6. Failing to assess and document factors that might reasonably affect the assessment's validity (e.g., medications taken by client, client's difficulties seeing or hearing, client's limited ability to speak or read English, disruptions occurring during the testing).

7. Administering a test without close and continuous monitoring (e.g., sending tests home with the client).

8. Interpreting or otherwise making inferences about the clinical scales on an invalid MMPI profile.

9. Shaping a psychological test interpretation to help win a case, or allowing other factors to bias an assessment report.

10. Failing to distinguish clearly and explicitly among unsubstantiated hypotheses, probabilistic statements based on actuarial data, and reasonable or absolute certainties.

11. Using nonstandard interpretations of scales, patterns, or profiles (e.g., idiosyncratic interpretations) that have not been adequately validated for the relevant forensic populations and purposes in well-designed empirical research published in peer-reviewed journals.

12. Failing to acknowledge explicitly, honestly, and adequately any inconsistent or anomalous findings (i.e., those that "don't fit"), uncertainties, possibility of error, and the limitations of the assessment instruments and methods.

Strategy for Forensic Use of Computer-Based Reports

BEFORE TESTING

- Determine if the client was briefed by an attorney about taking the test or if he or she is predisposed to respond in a particular way (e.g., dissimulating).
- Obtain any earlier MMPI, MMPI–2, or MMPI–A results so that they can inform the current assessment.
- Address relevant informed consent issues, including informed consent for release of information. Obtain signature on any relevant consent forms.

TEST ADMINISTRATION PROCEDURES

- If you are testing the client, it is important to provide a comfortable, private place to administer the test in a standard manner and monitored setting. Clients should not take the MMPI–2 in an unmonitored setting, and they should not be allowed to take the test at home or out of the testing room.
- If another person administered the test, find out if standard procedures were followed and evaluate the circumstances under which the test was given (for example, was the test given for a workers' compensation claim, employment placement, possible admission to a hospital, a court case, etc.).

- It is critical to ensure that the appropriate form of the instrument is used. The MMPI–2 should be used for adults who are 18 or older. The MMPI–A should be used for individuals between the ages of 14 and 18.
- If the client's reading level is below sixth grade, consider using a standardized audiocassette version of the inventory.
- If the client cannot read English at an adequate level, check to see if a standardized translation is available (see Appendix K, this volume).
- Administer *all* of the items in the inventory.
- Be sure that the computer scoring program used is licensed and has been checked for accuracy.
- After the test is administered, examine the answer sheet carefully to determine if the client changed any answers. If so, be sure the original response was completely erased. Make sure all responses are properly marked (not too light or too dark, etc.). Check for any double-marked items. Ask the client to correct any errors on the answer sheet.
- Make sure that the MMPI–2 report is actually for *this* client. This step is necessary because the answer sheet does not contain the client's name, only an identification number.
- Follow procedures to handle and store the answer sheet, scored protocol, and interpretive material safely, securely, and in compliance with all applicable legal and ethical requirements.

EVALUATING THE VALIDITY OF TEST RESULTS

Eight conditions will cause a forensics report to be invalid. They are listed below. In an invalid report, the scores are reported but not plotted and a message is printed indicating that the report is invalid. The narrative is suppressed with the exception of the validity statement. Scores approximating the conservative cut-offs listed below should also be viewed with caution. (Note: If the forensic setting is omitted, the narrative will be suppressed, but unless there are other conditions invalidating the report, the scores can still be interpreted.)

- Cannot Say > 30 and at least 1 of the 8 clinical, 15 content, or 3 substance abuse scales have a response percentage of less than 90%;
- At least 95% of the items are marked true;
- At least 95% of the items are marked false;
- $F–K$ (raw) score ≥ 16;
- $TRIN \geq 90\ T$;
- $VRIN \geq 90\ T$;
- $F \geq 100\ T$; and
- $Fp \geq 100\ T$.

Although the following conditions may not invalidate a report, they should be evaluated. They may indicate that the test results are of questionable validity and should be interpreted with caution.

- Omitted items. Ensure that the individual endorsed a sufficient number of items on scales that will be used in testimony. If he or she omitted items, determine if the omissions focus on a particular theme or have an adverse impact on particular scales. Check the response percentage for each scale to determine if item omissions adversely affect any scales.
- Noncontent-oriented responding. Look for
  Cannot Say ≥ 10
  $VRIN > 80$
  $TRIN > 80$
  Preponderance of *true* or *false* responses
- Defensive self-reporting. Some forensic clients present an overly defensive pattern.
  Overly positive self-presentation leading to an attenuated record can occur if any of the following conditions are present:

Cannot Say = 5–30
L = 61–64 (inclusive)
K = 61–64 (inclusive)
$S > 65$
The following conditions, which indicate defensive responding, make MMPI–2 results highly questionable at best:
$L \geq 65$
$K > 70$
$S > 70$

- Although high F, $F(p)$, and FB scores often indicate invalid or questionable test results because the client probably exaggerated his or her problems and claimed to have excessive symptoms, the clinician may be able to gain information from the degree to which these scales are elevated.
  Exaggerated
  F (infrequency) = 90–99 (inclusive) or
  FB = 90–99 (inclusive) or
  Fp = 81–89 (inclusive)
  Highly exaggerated
  F = 100–109 (inclusive) or
  FB = 100–109 (inclusive) or
  Fp = 90–99 (inclusive)
  Likely malingering
  $F \geq 110$ and $VRIN < 79$ or
  $FB \geq 110$ and $VRIN < 79$ or
  $Fp \geq 100$ and $VRIN < 79$

CLINICAL SCALE INTERPRETATION

- For clinical scales elevated in the interpretive range ($T \geq 65$), determine if single-scale elevations or code-type configurations are the primary prototype for determining the scale/profile empirical correlates.
- If a clinical scale is elevated, determine if the Harris–Lingoes subscales or other relevant content measures support the correlates.
- Determine how well defined the profile is: Profiles with 10-point differences (or more) from one scale to the next have *very high* profile definition and can be interpreted with confidence that the scores will remain prominent on retest.

Profiles with 5- to 9-point differences from one scale to the next have *high* profile definition and can be interpreted with some confidence that the scores will remain prominent on retest.

Profiles with less than a 5-point difference from one scale to the next have *low* profile definition. Other scales in the code could be prominent on retest.

- Determine if there are any expected salient variables that seem to be missing from the profile features and if the scale elevations are consistent with other prominent scale elevations.

OBJECTIVE SYMPTOM DESCRIPTION

The heart of MMPI–2 interpretation is the actuarial description of personality. The Minnesota Report summarizes the known correlates for the code type obtained. The Symptomatic Patterns, Interpersonal Relations, and Mental Health Considerations sections of the report provide objection descriptions.

- Keep in mind that traditional empirical correlates apply to cases in which the individual responded in a manner that is not defensive or exaggerated.
- When evaluating clinical scale patterns, keep the frequency of the prototype in perspective by referring to the appropriate base rates provided in the report.
- Supplement the empirical personality descriptions with content-based interpretations where appropriate. Content-based hypotheses are credible as long as validity indicators are within acceptable boundaries.
- Incorporate supplementary MMPI–2 descriptions and predictions from such measures as the addiction scales or the Marital Distress Scale as appropriate to the individual's self-report and case disposition requirements.

TAILORING THE FORENSIC EVALUATION TO THE SETTING

The forensic practitioner's experience with clients in a given court setting can be brought to bear on the final case interpretation. The forensic considerations section (Child Custody, Personal Injury, Personal Injury [Neurological], Pretrial Criminal, General Corrections, Competency/Commitment) of the report is a step in that direction. Implications for a particular profile are drawn from characteristics of cases in a particular setting.

Observe the following cautions when using computer-based reports in forensic evaluation and when preparing for testimony:

- Ensure appropriate "chain-of-custody" for answer sheets and processed materials.
- Pay particular attention to the computer-based validity interpretations because clients in forensic evaluations are often motivated to distort their answers.
- Make sure that there is an appropriate match between the prototypal report and the client's other background or test information.
- Check your report to ensure that it incorporates all relevant information.
- Discuss any possible discrepancies between the test findings and other information regarding the client.

GENERAL CONSIDERATIONS AND CAUTIONS

- Avoid using subjective or unproven measures such as the Wiener–Harmon subtle scales in forensic evaluations.
- Do not incorporate item-level data in forensic reports.

Description of MMPI, MMPI–2, and MMPI–A Scales

SECTION 1: MMPI AND MMPI–2 SCALES

Validity Scales

Cannot Say Score (?). This score is not a psychometric scale but rather the number of items the individual omitted; it is used as an index of cooperativeness. If the test taker has omitted more than 30 items, the response record is probably insufficient for interpretation. This is particularly the case if the item deletions occur in the first 370 items. If the item deletions are at the end of the booklet (beyond Item 370), the validity and clinical scales can be interpreted, but the supplemental and MMPI–2 content scales should not be interpreted.

Lie Scale (L). In the MMPI–2, as in the original MMPI, the L scale is a measure of the individual's willingness to self-disclose personal information and to endorse negative self-views. Individuals who score high on this scale (T > 60) are presenting an overly favorable picture of themselves. If the L score is greater than 65, the individual is claiming virtue not found among people in general.

Defensiveness Scale (K). The K scale was developed as a measure of test defensiveness and as a correction for the tendency of some people to deny problems. Five MMPI scales are corrected by adding a portion of K to the total score: Hysteria, Psychopathic Deviate, Psychasthenia, Schizophrenia, and Mania. The K scale appeared to operate for

MMPI–2 normative test takers much as it did for the original MMPI research participants. As a consequence, the K weights originally derived by Meehl were maintained in the MMPI–2. Slight changes in the norms for K in the MMPI–2 make the scale somewhat less elevated for higher socioeconomic status individuals than in the past. The slightly higher K score for the MMPI–2 normative sample does not raise the T scores for corrected scales (Butcher, 1990a). Low socioeconomic status clients appear slightly lower on the K scale than do individuals from the normative sample. Some adjustment in the interpretation of profiles from test takers from very low socioeconomic or educational levels may be needed.

In the MMPI–2, practitioners can evaluate both K-corrected and non–K-corrected profiles if they desire, because non–K-corrected profiles are now available.

Infrequency Scale F and Infrequency-Back Scale F(B). The F scale was developed for the original MMPI as a measure of symptom exaggeration or the tendency to claim an excessive number of psychological problems. (See more extensive discussion in chap. 7, this volume.) Originally, the F scale contained 64 items. The F scale in the MMPI–2 contains 60 items. If the F score is approximately 30 raw score points, it is suggestive of a random response set.

References consulted to compile this appendix are as follows: Butcher (1992c); Butcher, Graham, Williams, et al. (1990); Butcher and Williams (1992a, 1992b); and C. L. Williams et al. (1992).

An additional invalidity measure, the F(B) scale was developed for the revised version of the MMPI to detect possible deviant responding to items located toward the end of the item pool. Some test takers may modify their approach to the items part way through the test and answer in a random or unselective manner. Because the items on the *F* scale occur earlier in the test, before Item 370, the *F* scale might not detect deviant response patterns occurring later in the booklet.

The 40-item F(B) scale was developed following the same method used for the original *F* scale, by including items that had low endorsement percentages in the normal population.

Consistency Scales: Variable Response Inconsistency Scale (*VRIN*) and True Response Inconsistency Scale (*TRIN*).

Two validity scales have been introduced in the MMPI–2 and MMPI–A to assist the practitioner in evaluating the validity of the profile. These scales are based on the analysis of the individual's response to the items in a consistent or inconsistent manner.

The first scale, *TRIN* is made up of pairs of items in which a combination of two *true* or two *false* responses is semantically inconsistent. For example, "I am awake most of the day" and "Most of the day I am asleep" cannot be answered in the same direction if the test taker is responding consistently to the content. The *TRIN* scale can aid in interpreting scores on the *L* and *K* scales, because the former is made up of items that are keyed *false* and the latter is made up of items all but one of which is keyed *false*. Thus, an individual who inconsistently responds *false* to MMPI–2 items will have elevated scores on Scales *L* and *K* that do not reflect intentional misrepresentation or defensiveness. An individual whose *TRIN* score indicates inconsistent *true* responding will have deflated scores on Scales *L* and *K* that do not reflect a particularly honest response pattern or lack of ego resources.

The *VRIN* scale may be used to help interpret a high score on *F*. *VRIN* is made up of pairs of (*true–false; false–true; true–true; false–false*) patterns. The scale is scored by summing the number of inconsistent responses. A high *F* score in conjunction with a low to moderate

VRIN score rules out the possibility that the *F* score reflects random responding.

Clinical Scales

As explained in chapter 2, the clinical scales are virtually identical in the MMPI and MMPI–2 in terms of item composition and psychometric properties. Their distributions and recommended cutoff points differ slightly because the *T*-score distributions are based on different samples and use a slightly different *T*-score generation procedure. Empirical correlates for the clinical scales are essentially the same in all three versions. It is important to emphasize again that not all correlates will fit all test takers who score in a particular range.

Scale 1: Hypochondriasis (*Hs*). *High Scorers.* Excessive bodily concern; somatic symptoms that tend to be vague and undefined; epigastric complaints; fatigue, pain, and weakness; lacks manifest anxiety; selfish, self-centered, and narcissistic; pessimistic, defeatist, and cynical outlook on life; dissatisfied and unhappy; makes others miserable; whines and complains; demanding and critical of others; expresses hostility indirectly; rarely acts out; dull, unenthusiastic, and unambitious; ineffective in oral expression; has longstanding health concerns; functions at a reduced level of efficiency without major incapacity; not very responsive to therapy and tends to terminate therapy when therapist is seen as not giving enough attention and support; seeks medical solutions to problems. (See the test manual for more details [Butcher et al., 2001].)

Scale 2: Depression (*D*). *High Scorers.* Depressed, unhappy, and dysphoric; pessimistic; self-deprecating; guilty; sluggish; somatic complaints; weakness, fatigue, and loss of energy; agitated, tense, high strung, and irritable; prone to worry; lacks self-confidence; feels useless and unable to function; feels like a failure at school or on the job; introverted, shy, retiring, timid, and seclusive; aloof; maintains psychological distance; avoids interpersonal involvement; cautious and conventional; has difficulty making decisions; nonaggressive; overcontrolled; denies impulses; makes concessions to avoid conflict; motivated for therapy.

Scale 3: Hysteria (*Hy*). *High Scorers.* Reacts to stress and avoids responsibility through development of physical symptoms; has headaches, chest pains, weakness, tachycardia, and anxiety attacks; symptoms appear and disappear suddenly; lacks insight about causes of symptoms; lacks insight about own motives and feelings; lacks anxiety, tension, and depression; rarely reports delusions, hallucinations, or suspiciousness; psychologically immature, childish, and infantile; self-centered, narcissistic, and egocentric; expects attention and affection from others; uses indirect and devious means to get attention and affection; does not express hostility and resentment openly; socially involved; friendly, talkative, and enthusiastic; superficial and immature in interpersonal relationships; shows interest in others for selfish reasons; occasionally acts out in sexual or aggressive manner with little apparent insight; initially enthusiastic about treatment; responds well to direct advice or suggestion; slow to gain insight into causes of own behavior; resistant to psychological interpretations.

Scale 4: Psychopathic Deviate (*Pd*). *High Scorers.* Antisocial behavior; rebellious toward authority figures; stormy family relationships; blames parents for problems; history of underachievement in school; poor work history; marital problems; impulsive; strives for immediate gratification of impulses; does not plan well; acts without considering consequences of actions; impatient; limited frustration tolerance; poor judgment; takes risks; does not profit from experience; immature, childish, narcissistic, self-centered, and selfish; ostentatious and exhibitionistic; insensitive; interested in others in terms of how they can be used; likeable and usually creates a good first impression; forms shallow and superficial relationships and is unable to form warm attachments; extroverted and outgoing; talkative, active, energetic, and spontaneous; intelligent; asserts self-confidence; has a wide range of interests; lacks definite goals; hostile, aggressive, sarcastic, and cynical; resentful and rebellious; acts out; antagonistic; aggressive outbursts, assaultive behavior; little guilt over negative behavior; may feign guilt and remorse when in trouble; is free from disabling anxiety, depression, and psychotic symptoms; likely to have personality disorder diagnosis (antisocial or passive–aggressive); prone to worry; is dissatisfied; shows absence of deep emotional response; feels bored and empty; poor prognosis for change in therapy; blames others for problems; intellectualizes; may agree to treatment to avoid jail or some other unpleasant experience but is likely to terminate before change is effected.

Scale 5: Masculinity–Femininity (*Mf*). *Men: Very High Scorers (T > 80).* Shows conflicts about sexual identity; insecure in masculine role; effeminate; aesthetic and artistic interests; intelligent and capable; values cognitive pursuits; ambitious, competitive, and persevering; clever, clear thinking, organized, and logical; shows good judgment and common sense; curious; creative, imaginative, and individualistic in approach to problems; sociable; sensitive to others; tolerant; capable of expressing warm feelings toward others; passive, dependent, and submissive; peace loving; makes concessions to avoid confrontations; good self-control; rarely acts out.

Men: High Scorers (T = 70–79). May be viewed as sensitive; insightful; tolerant; effeminate; showing broad cultural interests; submissive and passive. (In clinical settings, the patient might show sex-role confusion or heterosexual adjustment problems.)

Men: Low Scorers (T < 35). "Macho" self-image, presents self as extremely masculine; overemphasizes strength and physical prowess; aggressive, thrill seeking, adventurous, and reckless; coarse, crude, and vulgar; harbors doubts about own masculinity; has limited intellectual ability; narrow range of interests; inflexible and unoriginal approach to problems; prefers action to thought; is practical and nontheoretical; easy-going, leisurely, and relaxed; cheerful, jolly, and humorous; contented; willing to settle down; unaware of social stimulus value; lacks insight into own motives; unsophisticated.

Women: High Scorers (T > 70). Rejects traditional feminine roles and activities; traditional masculine interests in work, sports, and hobbies; active, vigorous, and assertive; competitive, aggressive, and dominating; coarse, rough, and tough; outgoing, uninhibited, and self-confident; easy-going, relaxed, and balanced; logical and calculated; un-emotional and unfriendly.

Women: Low Scorers (T < 35). Describes self in terms of stereotypical female role; doubts about own femininity; passive, submissive, and yielding; defers to males in decision making; self-pitying; complaining and fault finding; constricted; sensitive; modest; and idealistic.

Scale 6: Paranoia (Pa). *Extremely High Scorers (T > 75).*

Blatantly psychotic behavior; disturbed thinking; delusions of persecution and/or grandeur; ideas of reference; feels mistreated and picked on; angry and resentful; harbors grudges; uses projection as defense; most frequently diagnosed as schizophrenia or paranoid state.

Moderate Scorers (T = 65–74 for men; T = 71–74 for women). Paranoid predisposition; sensitive; overly responsive to reactions of others; feels he or she is getting a raw deal from life; rationalizes and blames others; suspicious and guarded; hostile, resentful, and argumentative; moralistic and rigid; overemphasizes rationality; poor prognosis for therapy; does not like to talk about emotional problems; difficulty in establishing rapport with therapist.

Extremely Low Scorers (T < 35). Should be interpreted with caution. In a clinical setting, low Scale 6 scores, in the context of a defensive response set, may suggest frankly psychotic disorder; delusions, suspiciousness, ideas of reference; symptoms less obvious than for high scorers; evasive, defensive, and guarded; shy, secretive, and withdrawn.

Scale 7: Psychasthenia (Pt). *High Scorers.*

Anxious, tense, and agitated; high discomfort; worried and apprehensive; high strung and jumpy; difficulties in concentrating; introspective and ruminative; obsessive and compulsive; feels insecure and inferior; lacks self-confidence; self-doubting, self-critical, self-conscious, and self-derogatory; rigid and moralistic; maintains high standards for self and others; overly perfectionistic and conscientious; guilty and depressed; neat, orderly, organized, and meticulous; persistent; reliable; lacks ingenuity and originality in problem solving; dull and formal; vacillates; is indecisive; distorts importance of problems and overreacts; shy; does not interact

well socially; hard to get to know; worries about popularity and acceptance; sensitive; physical complaints; shows some insight into problems; intellectualizes and rationalizes; resistant to interpretations in therapy; expresses hostility toward therapist; remains in therapy longer than most patients; makes slow but steady progress in therapy.

Scale 8: Schizophrenia (Sc). *Very High Scorers (T = 80–90).*

Blatantly psychotic behavior; confused, disorganized, and disoriented; unusual thoughts or attitudes; delusions; hallucinations; poor judgment.

High Scorers (T = 65–79). Schizoid lifestyle; does not feel a part of social environment; feels isolated, alienated, and misunderstood; feels unaccepted by peers; withdrawn, seclusive, secretive, and inaccessible; avoids dealing with people and new situations; shy, aloof, and uninvolved; experiences generalized anxiety; resentful, hostile, and aggressive; unable to express feelings; reacts to stress by withdrawing into fantasy and daydreaming; difficulty separating reality and fantasy; self-doubts; feels inferior, incompetent, and dissatisfied; sexual preoccupation and sex-role confusion; nonconforming, unusual, unconventional, and eccentric; vague, longstanding physical complaints; stubborn, moody, and opinionated; immature and impulsive; high-strung; imaginative; abstract and vague goals; lacks basic information for problem solving; poor prognosis for therapy; reluctant to relate in meaningful way to therapist; stays in therapy longer than most patients; may eventually come to trust therapist.

Scale 9: Mania (Ma). *High Scorers (T > 75).*

Overactivity; accelerated speech; may have hallucinations or delusions of grandeur; energetic and talkative; prefers action to thought; wide range of interests; does not use energy wisely; does not see projects through to completion; creative, enterprising, and ingenious; little interest in routine or detail; easily bored and restless; low frustration tolerance; difficulty inhibiting expression of impulses; episodes of irritability, hostility, and aggressive outbursts; unrealistic and unqualified optimism; grandiose aspirations; exaggerates self-worth and self-importance; unable to see own limitations; outgoing, sociable, and gregarious; likes to be around other people; creates good first impression; friendly, pleasant, and enthusiastic; poised and self-confident; superficial relationships; manipulative, deceptive, and unreliable; feelings of dissatisfaction; agitated; may have periodic episodes of depression; difficulties at school or work; resistant to interpretations in therapy; attends therapy irregularly; may terminate therapy prematurely; repeats problems in stereotyped manner; not likely to become dependent on therapists; becomes hostile and aggressive toward therapist.

Moderate Scorers (T > 65, ≤ 74). Overactivity; exaggerated sense of self-worth; energetic and talkative; prefers action to thought; wide range of interests; does not use energy wisely; does not see projects through to completion; enterprising and ingenious; lacks interest in routine matters; becomes bored and restless easily; low frustration tolerance; impulsive; has episodes of irritability, hostility, and aggressive outbursts; unrealistic and overly optimistic at times; shows some grandiose aspirations; unable to see own limitations; outgoing, sociable, and gregarious; likes to be around other people; creates good first impression; friendly, pleasant, and enthusiastic; poised and self-confident; superficial relationships; manipulative, deceptive, and unreliable; feelings of dissatisfaction; agitated; views therapy as unnecessary; resistant to interpretations in therapy; attends therapy irregularly; may terminate therapy prematurely; repeats problems in stereotyped manner; not likely to become dependent on therapist; becomes hostile and aggressive toward therapist.

Low Scorers (T < 35). Low energy level; low activity level; lethargic, listless, apathetic, and phlegmatic; difficult to motivate; reports chronic fatigue and physical exhaustion; depressed, anxious, and tense; reliable, responsible, and dependable; approaches problems in conventional, practical, and reasonable way; lacks self-confidence; sincere, quiet, modest, withdrawn, and seclusive; unpopular; overcontrolled; unlikely to express feelings openly.

Scale 0: Social Introversion–Extraversion (*Si*).

High Scorers (T > 65). Socially introverted; is more comfortable alone or with a few close friends; reserved, shy, and retiring; uncomfortable around members of opposite sex; hard to get to know; sensitive to what others think; troubled by lack of involvement with other people; overcontrolled; not likely to display feelings openly; submissive and compliant; overly accepting of authority; serious; slow personal tempo; reliable and dependable; cautious, conventional, and unoriginal in approach to problems; rigid and inflexible in attitudes and opinions; difficulty making even minor decisions; enjoys work; gains pleasure from productive personal achievement; tends to worry; is irritable and anxious; moody; experiences guilt feelings; has episodes of depression or low mood.

Low Scorers (T < 45). Sociable and extroverted; outgoing, gregarious, friendly, and talkative; strong need to be around other people; mixes well; intelligent, expressive, and verbally fluent; active, energetic, and vigorous; interested in status, power, and recognition; seeks out competitive situations; has problem with impulse control; acts without considering the consequences of actions; immature and self-indulgent; superficial and insincere relationships; manipulative and opportunistic; arouses resentment and hostility in others.

MMPI–2 Supplemental Scales

Addiction Acknowledgement Scale (*AAS*). This scale assesses the extent to which the individual has endorsed content relevant to alcohol or drug use and abuse.

Addiction Potential Scale (*APS*). This scale assesses the tendency for the individual to have lifestyle characteristics associated with the development of alcohol and drug abuse problems. High scorers endorse items reflecting hedonistic, irresponsible, and impulsive behavior.

MacAndrew Scale—Revised (*MAC–R*). High scorers have been found to be prone to developing problems of addiction such as alcohol or drug abuse, pathological gambling, or other addictive problems.

Anxiety (*A*). Individuals scoring high on this scale are viewed as anxious, tense, obsessional, and generally maladjusted.

Repression (R). Individuals scoring high on this scale tend to be overcontrolled. They deny problems and tend to gloss over personal frailties. They are seen as constricted and inhibited.

Ego Strength (Es). This scale assesses the ability of the individual to tolerate stress and to benefit from treatment.

Dominance (Do). This scale measures the extent to which the individual is dominant in social and interpersonal contexts.

Responsibility (Re). This scale addresses the extent to which the individual holds attitudes of social responsibility.

Hostility (Ho). This scale assesses the personality style of chronic hostile behavior.

Post-traumatic Stress Disorder Scale—Keane (Pk). This scale assesses the symptoms of the syndrome of posttraumatic stress disorder.

Marital Distress Scale (MDS). This scale assesses marital relationship problems.

MMPI–2 Content Scales

Anxiety Scale (ANX). High scorers on *ANX* report general symptoms of anxiety, including tension, somatic problems (i.e., heart pounding and shortness of breath), sleep difficulties, worries, and poor concentration. They fear losing their minds, find life a strain, and have difficulties making decisions. They appear to be readily aware of these symptoms and problems, and they are willing to admit them.

Fears Scale (FRS). A high score on *FRS* indicates an individual with many specific fears. These specific fears can include blood; high places; money; animals such as snakes, mice, or spiders; leaving home; fire; storms and natural disasters; water; the dark; being indoors; and dirt.

Obsessiveness Scale (OBS). High scorers on *OBS* have tremendous difficulties making decisions and are likely to ruminate excessively about issues and problems, causing others to become impatient. Having to make changes distresses them, and they may report some compulsive behaviors, such as counting or saving unimportant things. They are excessive worriers who frequently become overwhelmed by their own thoughts.

Depression Scale (DEP). High scores on this scale characterize individuals with significant depressive thoughts. They report feeling blue, uncertain about their future, and uninterested in their lives. They are likely to brood, be unhappy, cry easily, and feel hopeless and empty. They may report thoughts of suicide or wishes that they were dead. They may believe that they are condemned or have committed unpardonable sins. Other people may not be viewed as a source of support.

Health Concerns Scale (HEA). Individuals with high scores on *HEA* report many physical symptoms across several body systems. Included are gastrointestinal symptoms (e.g., constipation, nausea and vomiting, or stomach trouble), neurological problems (e.g., convulsions, dizzy and fainting spells, or paralysis), sensory problems (e.g., poor hearing or eyesight), cardiovascular symptoms (e.g., heart or chest pains), skin problems, pain (e.g., headaches or neck pains), and respiratory troubles (e.g., coughs, hay fever, or asthma). These individuals worry about their health and feel sicker than the average person.

Bizarre Mentation Scale (BIZ). Psychotic thought processes characterize individuals high on *BIZ*. They may report auditory, visual, or olfactory hallucinations and may recognize that their thoughts are strange and peculiar. Paranoid ideation (e.g., the belief that they are being plotted against or that someone is trying to poison them) may be reported as well. These individuals may feel that they have a special mission or powers.

Anger Scale (ANG). High scores on *ANG* suggest anger control problems. These individuals report being irritable, grouchy, impatient, hot-headed, annoyed, and stubborn. They sometimes feel like swearing or smashing things. They may lose self-control and report having been physically abusive toward people and objects.

Cynicism Scale (CYN). Misanthropic beliefs characterize high scorers on *CYN*. They expect hidden, negative motives behind the acts of others, for example, believing that most people are honest simply because of fear of being caught. Other people are to be distrusted because people use each other and are only friendly for selfish reasons. They likely hold negative attitudes about those close to them, including fellow workers, family, and friends.

Antisocial Practices Scale (*ASP*). In addition to holding similar misanthropic attitudes as high scorers on *CYN,* high scorers on *ASP* report problem behaviors during their school years and other antisocial practices, such as being in trouble with the law, stealing, or shoplifting. They report sometimes enjoying the antics of criminals and believe that it is all right to get around the law, as long as it is not broken.

Type A Scale (*TPA*). High scorers on *TPA* are hard-driving, fast-moving, and work-oriented individuals who frequently become impatient, irritable, and annoyed. They do not like to wait or to be interrupted. There is never enough time in a day for them to complete their tasks. They are direct and may be overbearing in their relationship with others.

Low Self-Esteem Scale (*LSE*). High scores on *LSE* characterize individuals with low opinions of themselves. They do not believe that they are liked by others or that they are important. They hold many negative attitudes about themselves, including beliefs that they are unattractive, awkward and clumsy, useless, and a burden to others. They certainly lack self-confidence and find it hard to accept compliments from others. They may be overwhelmed by all the faults they see in themselves.

Social Discomfort Scale (*SOD*). High scorers on *SOD* are uneasy around others, preferring to be by themselves. When in social situations, they are likely to sit alone rather than joining in the group. They see themselves as shy and dislike parties and other group events.

Family Problems Scale (*FAM*). Considerable family discord is reported by high scorers on *FAM.* Their families are described as lacking in love, quarrelsome, and unpleasant. They even may report hating members of their families. Their childhood may be portrayed as abusive, and their marriages may be seen as unhappy and lacking in affection.

Work Interference Scale (*WRK*). A high score on *WRK* is indicative of behaviors or attitudes likely to contribute to poor work performance. Some of the problems relate to low self-confidence, concentration difficulties, obsessiveness, tension and pressure, and decision-making problems. Others suggest lack of family support for career choice, personal questioning of career choice, and negative attitudes toward coworkers.

Negative Treatment Indicators Scale (*TRT*). High scores on *TRT* characterize individuals with negative attitudes toward doctors and mental health treatment. High scorers do not believe that anyone can understand or help them. They have issues or problems that they are not comfortable discussing with anyone. They may not want to change anything in their lives, nor do they feel that change is possible. They prefer giving up rather than facing a crisis or difficulty.

SECTION 2: MMPI–A SCALES

Validity Scales

Cannot Say (*?*). This score equals the total number of unanswered items. A defensive protocol is suggested if the raw score is greater than 30.

Lie (*L*). As in the MMPI–2, this scale is a measure of a rather unsophisticated, overly "virtuous" test-taking attitude. Elevated scores ($T > 65$) suggest that the individual is presenting him- or herself in an overly positive light and attempting to create an unrealistically favorable view of his or her adjustment.

Infrequency (*F*). Adolescent response to personality items has traditionally been shown to be somewhat exaggerated or extreme. Adolescents tend to score high on the original MMPI *F* scale. One reason for this is that many of the original MMPI *F* items were inappropriate as infrequency indicators for adolescents—they were endorsed differently than in adult samples. As a consequence, for the MMPI–A, new infrequency items were obtained by examining endorsement frequencies of the normative sample. Items that were endorsed by fewer than 20% of the sample were identified as *F* items. The *F* scale in the MMPI–A contains 66 items. As a consequence, the number of *F* items suggestive of a random response set is 33. The items on this scale are answered in the nonkeyed direction by most people. High scores ($T > 80$) suggest some extreme responding that may be due to reading difficulties, confusion, inconsistent responding, exaggeration, or possibly serious psychopathology.

F_1 and F_2. These subscales were developed by dividing the 66-item *F* scale into two equal halves. Extreme elevations on F_2, in the absence of extreme elevations on F_1, suggest that the first half of the MMPI–A (i.e., the basic scales) can be interpreted but that scales in the second half of the booklet (i.e., content scales and supplementary scales) are invalid.

Defensiveness (*K*). As in the original MMPI, this scale measures an individual's willingness to disclose personal information and to discuss his or her problems. High scores ($T > 65$) reflect possible reluctance to disclose personal information, provided *TRIN* is not elevated above 74. The *K* score is not used to correct for defensiveness in adolescent profiles as it is for adults.

True Response Inconsistency (*TRIN*). The *TRIN* scale is made up of pairs of items to which a combination of *true* or *false* responses is semantically inconsistent. Extreme scores ($T \leq 75$) on either end of the range reflect a tendency to answer inconsistently false (i.e., nea saying, at the low end of the range) or to answer inconsistently true (i.e., yea saying, at the upper end of the distribution). Raw scores are converted to linear *T* scores that are based on the adolescent normative sample.

Variable Response Inconsistency (*VRIN*). The *VRIN* scale is made up of pairs of items for which one or two of four possible configurations (*true–false, false–true, true–true,* and *false–false*) represents semantically inconsistent responses. The scale is scored by summing the number of inconsistent

responses. Extreme *VRIN* scores ($T \leq 75$) indicate the presence of an invalid response style.

Basic Scales

Scale 1: Hypochondriasis (*Hs*). High scorers present numerous vague physical problems and may be unhappy, self-centered, whiny, complaining, and attention-demanding. They are dissatisfied with life and cynical toward others.

Scale 2: Depression (*D*). High scores reflect depressed mood, low self-esteem, and feelings of inadequacy. Elevations may reflect great discomfort and need for change or symptomatic relief. High scorers are pessimistic, unhappy, indecisive, withdrawn, and feel useless.

Scale 3: Hysteria (*Hy*). High scorers may rely on defenses such as denial and repression to deal with stress. They tend to be dependent and naive. They show little insight into problems. High levels of stress may be accompanied by physical symptoms.

Scale 4: Psychopathic Deviate (*Pd*). Elevations measure acting-out behaviors and rebelliousness; disrupted family relations; lying; impulsiveness; and school or legal difficulties. Alcohol or drug problems may be present.

Scale 5: Masculinity–Femininity (*Mf*). High-scoring boys are described as having an unusual pattern of feminine interests. Because the direction of scoring is reversed, high-scoring girls are seen as having stereotypically masculine or more "macho" interests.

Scale 6: Paranoia (*Pa*). Elevations on this scale are often associated with being suspicious, aloof, shrewd, guarded, worrying, and overly sensitive. High scorers may be hostile and argumentative. Problems in school are common.

Scale 7: Psychasthenia (*Pt*). High scorers may be tense, anxious, preoccupied, obsessional, and rigid. They tend to have low self-confidence.

Scale 8: Schizophrenia (*Sc*). High scorers may have an unconventional or schizoid lifestyle. They can be withdrawn, shy, and moody, and feel inadequate, tense, and confused. They may have unusual or strange thoughts, poor judgment, and erratic moods. School problems and low personal achievement are probable.

Scale 9: Mania (*Ma*). High scorers may be impulsive and overly energetic. Acting-out behavior and school problems occur among high-scoring adolescents.

Scale 0: Social Introversion–Extraversion (*Si*). High scorers are introverted, shy, withdrawn, socially reversed, submissive, overcontrolled, lethargic, conventional, tense, inflexible, and guilt prone. Low scorers are extroverted, outgoing, gregarious, expressive, and talkative.

Supplementary Scales

Anxiety (*A*). High scores suggest anxious, tense, obsessional, and generally maladjusted individuals.

Repression (*R*). High scorers tend to be overcontrolled. They deny problems and gloss over personal frailties.

MacAndrew Scale—Revised (*MAC–R*). High scorers are prone to developing problems with addiction and tend to be risk takers and exhibitionistic.

Alcohol and Drug Problem Acknowledgment (*ACK*). High scores indicate the individual has endorsed content relevant to alcohol or drug use and related problems.

Alcohol and Drug Problem Proneness (*PRO*). High scores suggest the tendency to develop alcohol or drug use problems, including association with a negative peer group.

Immaturity (*IMM*). The *IMM* scale was developed in accordance with Loevinger's distinction between the preconformist and conformist stages of maturation.

Content Scales

Anxiety (*a–anx*). Adolescents who score high on *a–anx* report many symptoms of anxiety, including tension, frequent worrying, and difficulties sleeping (e.g., nightmares, disturbed sleep, and difficulty falling asleep). They report difficulties concentrating, confusion, and an inability to stay on task. They appear aware of their problems and how they differ from others.

Obsessiveness (*a–obs*). Adolescent high scorers on *a–obs* report worrying beyond reason, often over trivial matters. They may have ruminative thoughts about "bad words" or may count unimportant items. They have times when they are unable to sleep because of their worries. They report great difficulty making decisions and frequently dread having to make changes in their lives. They report that others sometimes lose patience with them.

Depression (*a–dep*). Adolescents who score high on *a–dep* report many symptoms of depression. Frequent crying spells and fatigue are problems. They are dissatisfied with their lives, and they feel that others are happier. They have many self-deprecative thoughts, including beliefs that they have not lived the right kind of life, feelings of uselessness, and beliefs that they are condemned and their sins unpardonable. Their future seems hopeless and their lives seem uninteresting and not worthwhile. Suicidal ideation is possible. They report loneliness even when with other people. Their future seems too uncertain for them to make serious plans, and they have periods when they are unable to "get going." A sense of hopelessness is characteristic.

Health (*a–hea*). Adolescents with high scores on *a–hea* report numerous physical problems that interfere with their enjoyment of afterschool activities and that contribute to significant school absence. They may report that their physical health is worse than that of their friends. Their physical complaints cross several body systems. Included are gastrointestinal problems (e.g., constipation, nausea and vomiting, or stomach trouble), neurological problems (e.g., numbness, convulsions, fainting and dizzy spells, or paralysis), sensory problems (e.g., hearing difficulty or poor eyesight), cardiovascular symptoms (e.g., heart or chest pain), skin problems, pain (e.g., headaches or neck pain), and respiratory problems.

Alienation (*a–aln*). High scorers on *a–aln*, one of the adolescent-specific content scales, report considerable emotional distance from others. They believe that they are getting a raw deal from life and that no one cares about or understands them. They do not believe that they are liked by others nor do they get along with others. They feel that they have no one, including parents or close friends, who understands them. They feel that others are out to get them and are unkind to them. They have difficulty self-disclosing and report feeling awkward when having to talk in groups of people. They do not appreciate hearing others give their opinions.

Bizarre Mentation (*a–biz*). Adolescents scoring high on *a–biz* report strange thoughts and experiences, including possible auditory, visual, and olfactory hallucinations. They characterize their experiences as strange and unusual, and they believe that there is something wrong with their minds. Paranoid ideation (e.g., the belief that they are being plotted against or that someone is trying to poison them) may also be reported. They may believe that others are trying to steal their thoughts and ideas or control their minds, perhaps through hypnosis. They may believe that evil spirits or ghosts possess or influence them.

Anger (*a–ang*). Adolescents with high scores on *a–ang* report considerable anger control problems. They often feel like swearing, smashing things, or starting a fistfight, and they frequently get into trouble for breaking or destroying things. They report having considerable problems with irritability and impatience with others. They have been told that they throw temper tantrums to get their own way. They indicate that they are hot headed and often have to yell to make a point. Occasionally they get into fights, especially when drinking.

Cynicism (*a–cyn*). Misanthropic attitudes are held by adolescents scoring high on *a–cyn*. They believe that others are out to get them and will use unfair means to gain an advantage. They look for hidden motives whenever someone does something nice for them. They believe that it is safer to trust nobody because people make friends to use them.

Conduct Problems (*a–con*). Adolescents scoring high on *a–con* report a number of different behavioral problems, including stealing, shoplifting, lying, breaking or destroying things, being disrespectful, swearing, and being oppositional. Members of their peer group are often in trouble and frequently talk them into doing things they know they should not do. At times they try to make other people afraid of them, just for the fun of it.

Low Self-Esteem (*a–lse*). Adolescents with high *a–lse* scores have negative opinions of themselves, including being unattractive, lacking self-confidence, feeling useless, having little ability, having several faults, and not being able to do anything well. They are likely to yield to others' pressure, changing their minds or giving up in arguments. They tend to let other people take charge when problems have to be solved and do not feel that they are capable of planning their own future.

Low Aspirations (*a–las*). High scorers on *a–las*, an adolescent-specific content scale, are disinterested in being successful. They do not like to study or to read about things, dislike science, dislike lectures on serious topics, and prefer work that allows them to be careless. They do not expect to be successful. They report difficulty starting things, and they quickly give up when things go wrong. They let other people solve problems, and they avoid facing difficulties. Others also tell them that they are lazy.

Social Discomfort (*a–sod*). Adolescents with high scores on *a–sod* find it difficult to be around others. They report being shy, and they much prefer to be alone. They dislike having people around them and frequently avoid others. They do not like parties, crowds, dances, or other social gatherings. They · have difficulty making friends and do not like to meet strangers.

Family Problems (*a–fam*). Adolescents with high *a–fam* scores report considerable problems with their parents and other family members. Family discord, jealousy, fault finding, anger, beatings, serious disagreements, lack of love and understanding, and limited communication characterize these families. These adolescents do not believe they can count on their families in times of trouble.

School Problems (*a–sch*). Numerous difficulties in school characterize adolescents scoring high on *a–sch*, another of the adolescent-specific content scales. Poor grades, suspension, truancy, negative attitudes toward teachers, and dislike of school are characteristic of high scorers. The only pleasant aspect of school for such youth is their friends. They do not participate in school activities or sports. They believe that school is a waste of time. Some of these individuals may report being afraid to go to school. Others indicate that they are told that they are lazy, and they are frequently bored and sleepy at school.

Negative Treatment Indicators (*a–trt*). High scorers on *a–trt* indicate negative attitudes toward doctors and mental health professionals. They do not believe that others are capable of understanding them or that others care what happens to them. They are unwilling to take charge and face their problems or difficulties. They report several faults and bad habits that they feel are insurmountable. They do not feel they can plan their own future. They will not assume responsibility for negative things in their lives. They also report great unwillingness to discuss their problems with others and indicate that there are some issues that they would never be able to share with anyone. They report being nervous when others ask them personal questions, and they have many secrets they feel are best kept to themselves.

Psychometric Properties of the MMPI, MMPI–2, and MMPI–A Compared

Original MMPI[1]	MMPI–2	MMPI–A
Contains 566 items.	Contains 567 items.	Contains 478 items.
Contains 16 repeated items.	Contains no repeated items.	Contains no repeated items.
Contains a number of objectionable content areas: sexual preference, religion, and bowel and bladder functioning. Some items contain outmoded language.	Objectionable and outmoded items have been deleted. About 14% of items were reworded in more modern language.	Objectionable items have been eliminated, and items were reworded from the adolescent's perspective.
Contains numerous nonworking, nonscored items	Eliminated nonworking items. Substituted new items dealing with suicide, drug and alcohol abuse, Type A behavior, interpersonal relations, and treatment compliance.	Nonworking items have been eliminated, and specific adolescent items have been included.
Contains four validity scales: ?, L, F, and K.	Contains nine validity scales: ?, L, F, K, F(B), F(p), VRIN, S, and TRIN.	Contains eight validity scales: ?, L, F, F_1, F_2, K, VRIN, and TRIN.
Contains the 10 standard scales: Hs, D, Hy, Pd, Mf, Pa, Pt, Sc, Ma, and Si.	Contains the 10 nearly identical standard scales in the original MMPI: Hs, D, Hy, Pd, Mf, Pa, Pt, Sc, Ma, and Si. The difference is that a few items with objectionable content were eliminated from F, Hs, D, Mf, and Si.	Contains the traditional standard scales as in the MMPI–2. The number of items on the Mf and Si scales was reduced slightly to shorten the inventory.
K correction added to Hs, Pd, Pt, Sc, and Ma.	K correction added to Hs, Pd, Pt, Sc, and Ma.	K correction is not used in the MMPI–A.
Age range of normative sample: 16–65 years.	Age range of normative sample: 18–84 years.	Age range of normative sample: 14–18 years.

Reprinted from "Comparison of the Original MMPI, MMPI–2, and MMPI–A," by J. N. Butcher (1992b). Workshop presented at MMPI/MMPI–2/ MMPI–A Workshops and Symposia, University of Minnesota, Minneapolis. Reprinted with permission of the author.
[1] As of September 1999, the original MMPI was withdrawn from use by the publisher.

Original MMPI	MMPI–2	MMPI–A
Assesses alcohol and drug problems; contains the 49-item *MAC* Scale.	Assesses alcohol and drug problems; contains the 49-item *MAC–R* Scale. Four objectionable items have been deleted; however, four new items, which empirically separated alcoholic patients from other psychiatric patients, were substituted.	Assesses alcohol and drug problems; contains *MAC–R* Scale to assess addiction potential.
	Two new substance abuse indicators have been developed. *PRO* (Alcohol and Drug Problem Proneness Scale) and *ACK* (Alcohol and Drug Problem Acknowledgment Scale).	Two new substance abuse indicators have been developed: *APS* (Addiction Potential Scale) and *AAS* (Addiction Acknowledgment Scale).
When the 13 validity and standard scale scores are factor analyzed, typically, four factors emerge: *A, R, Mf,* and *Si.*	When the MMPI–2 validity and standard scores are factor analyzed the same four factors emerge in similar magnitude: *A, R, Mf,* and *Si.*	When MMPI–A validity and standard scales are factor analyzed the same four factors emerge and are similar: *A, R, Mf,* and *Si.*
The Harris–Lingoes subscales are available for providing content-based hypotheses for clinical scale interpretation.	The Harris–Lingoes subscales are available in the MMPI–2.	The Harris–Lingoes subscales are available in the MMPI–A.
The Serkownek subscales for *Si* are available for developing content-based hypotheses.	New subscales for *Si* are available for generating content-based hypotheses.	The *Si* subscales from the MMPI–2 are contained in the MMPI–A.
The Koss–Butcher empirically based "critical items" are available for the MMPI.	The Koss–Butcher "critical items" are virtually intact in the MMPI–2. Moreover, two item sets (depressed–suicide and alcohol–crises) have been expanded by about four items each on the basis of new empirical item analyses.	No empirically derived "critical item" lists have been developed for the MMPI–A.
The Wiggins content scales provide a psychometrically sound measurement of the content of an individual's responses.	A new set of 15 content scales has been developed to assess the major content dimensions in the MMPI–2. These rationally and statistically constructed scales provide highly reliable and valid indicants of the major content themes in the MMPI–2.	A new set of 15 adolescent problem-oriented content scales has been developed according to a rational and statistical strategy.
The original MMPI norms were based on 724 visitors to the university hospitals and some special groups such as CCC [Civilian Conservation Corp] Workers.	The MMPI–2 normative sample was randomly solicited from several states: California, Minnesota, North Carolina, Ohio, Pennsylvania, Virginia, and Washington. A total of 1,138 men and 1,462 women were included.	The MMPI–A normative sample was obtained from private and public schools in California, Minnesota, New York, North Carolina, Ohio, Pennsylvania, Virginia, and Washington state. A total of 805 boys and 815 girls were included.

Original MMPI	MMPI–2	MMPI–A

Original MMPI

Mean educational level of the original sample was 8th grade, similar to the 1940 census data.

Item omissions were allowed and actually encouraged in the original MMPI data collection, producing high Cannot Say scores. This resulted in a lower mean profile for the normative group compared with more contemporary samples when omitted items are discouraged.

The original *T* scores for the MMPI were linear *T* scores. No effort was made to have equivalent *T* scores across scales.

Percentile ranks across scales vary for a given *T*-score elevation.

No test–retest data were collected from the original normative sample.

MMPI–2

Mean educational level was 13 years, similar to the 1980 census data.

Response to all items in the MMPI–2 was encouraged. Mean profiles are less affected by item omission.

The MMPI–2 *T* scores for the 8 clinical scales and the 15 content scales are uniform *T* scores that are based on a single composite scale score distribution. A given level of *T* is *equivalent* in terms of percentile rank across the clinical scales.

The percentile rank for a given *T* score is uniform across the original 8 clinical scales and 15 content scales.

T score	Percentile
50	55
55	73
60	85
65	92
70	96
75	98
80	99

One-week test–retest data are available for a subsample of the MMPI–2 normative sample (*n* = 82 men and 111 women):

	Men	Women
L	.77	.81
F	.78	.69
K	.84	.81
1	.85	.85
2	.75	.77
3	.72	.76
4	.81	.79
5	.82	.73
6	.67	.58
7	.89	.88
8	.87	.80
9	.83	.68
0	.92	.91

MMPI–A

Educational level of normative sample was 8th, 9th, 10th, 11th, and 12th grade.

Item omissions were discouraged in the MMPI–A normative data collection.

The MMPI–A *T* scores for the 8 clinical scales and the 15 content scales are uniform and comparable with MMPI–2 *T* scores.

The percentile rank for a given *T* score is uniform across the 8 original clinical scales and 15 content scales.

T score	Percentile
50	55
55	73
60	85
65	92
70	96
75	98
80	99

One-week test–retest data are given for boys and girls in the normative sample (*n* = 45 boys and 109 girls):

	Boys and Girls
L	.61
F	.55
K	.75
1	.79
2	.78
3	.70
4	.80
5	.82
6	.65
7	.83
8	.83
9	.70
0	.84

Original MMPI	MMPI–2	MMPI–A
Only age and gender were obtained from individuals from the original normative sample.	Extensive biographical and life-event information was obtained from the MMPI–2 normative sample.	Extensive biographical and life-event information was obtained from the MMPI–A normative sample.
The original normative sample was essentially rural, White men and women in Minnesota.	The MMPI–2 normative sample is more diverse in terms of socioeconomic level, ethnic group membership, and residence.	The MMPI–A normative sample is diverse in terms of ethnicity and residence.

Men		Boys	
White	82.0%	White	76.5%
Black	11.1%	Black	12.4%
American Indian	3.3%	American Indian	2.6%
Hispanic	3.1%	Hispanic	2.2%
Asian	0.5%	Asian	2.9%

Women		Girls	
White	81.0%	White	75.9%
Black	12.9%	Black	12.3%
American Indian	2.7%	American Indian	3.2%
Hispanic	2.6%	Hispanic	2.0%
Asian	0.9%	Asian	2.8%

Original MMPI	MMPI–2	MMPI–A
Manual scoring keys are available for the MMPI.	Manual scoring keys are available for the MMPI–2.	Manual scoring keys are available for the MMPI–A.
Tape-recorded and computer-administered format versions are available for the MMPI.	Tape-recorded and computer-administered format versions are available for the MMPI–2.	Tape-recorded and computer-administered format versions are available for the MMPI–A.
An MMPI scoring and interpretation system for the MMPI is available from National Computer Systems (NCS).	A computer scoring and interpretation program (Minnesota Report) for the MMPI–2 is available from NCS.	A computer interpretation program (Minnesota Report) for the MMPI–A is available from NCS.

Procedure for Converting MMPI Scores to New Norms

Plotting original MMPI raw scores on MMPI–2 norms provides a contemporary comparison of a client's MMPI scores. The original raw scores and the item response records (answer sheet) are needed to complete this four-step process.

Step 1: Begin by looking at the MMPI answer sheet to find out how the person responded to the following:

Infrequency [F] Scale
- 14.   (T)
- 53.   (T)
- 206.   (T)
- 258.   (F)

Hypochondriasis [Hs] Scale
- 63.   (F)

Depression [D] Scale
- 58.   (F)
- 95.   (F)
- 98.   (F)

Masculinity–Femininity [Mf] Scale
For men:
- 69.   (T)
- 70.   (T)
- 249.   (F)
- 295.   (T)

For women:
- 69.   (F)
- 70.   (T)
- 249.   (F)
- 295.   (T)

Social Introversion–Extraversion [Si] Scale
- 462.   (F)

Step 2: Note the direction (*true* or *false*) on which the individual responded to each of the 13 items.

Step 3: Modify the person's raw score for the scales on which these 13 items appear. Subtract any of these raw score modifications from the original raw score to develop a revised raw score. For example, if the person endorsed three items that appear on the F scale in the direction noted, then reduce the F raw score by 3 points.

Step 4: Plot the revised raw score using an MMPI–2 profile form.

Note: Only the original validity scales (Lie scale [L], Infrequency scale [F], and Defensiveness scale [K]) and 10 standard or clinical scales can be processed in this manner. The MMPI–2 content scales and most of the special scales cannot be scored from the original MMPI.

Suggestions for Presenting the MMPI–2 and MMPI–A in Court

- Describe the extensive validation and research base—presented in peer-reviewed scientific and professional journals—that supports this objective, paper and pencil personality scale.
- Describe the wide use and acceptance of the instrument, and cite studies to support your descriptions.
- Describe how to administer the test in a standardized way, and discuss the meaning, importance, and implications of a "standardized test administered under standardized conditions."
- Explain *briefly* the rationale underlying development of the original MMPI as an objective way to classify psychological problems.
- Explain empirical scale construction and describe how the clinical scales were developed through external validation.
- Describe and illustrate how the MMPI measures have been validated, and explain the correlate base for the clinical scales.
- Emphasize that your assessment has only used MMPI–2 or MMPI–A measures that have been validated for the forensic application.

- Illustrate how the MMPI is typically used in personality description and clinical assessment. Focus particularly on the use of established correlates in the assessment.
- Explain how the original MMPI was revised to address critical problems of items and norms that were out of date and that produced findings that were no longer valid (e.g., the problem of overpathologizing).
- Describe and illustrate how the clinical scales of the revised versions (i.e., MMPI–2 and MMPI–A) use the same items and have the same psychometric properties as the original version of the scales.
- Describe and illustrate how the validity scales work to assess a particular profile's credibility and validity. Illustrate any relevant test-taking strategy that might apply for the particular case being tried.
- Explain how the findings of the profile at hand help us to understand the test taker in light of the issues relevant to this legal case.

Note. Chapters 2, 3, 4, and 7 present the background for these suggestions.

Glossary

In this Glossary we have provided a quick guide to some of the technical terms and abbreviations relevant to forensic evaluations and expert testimony. It is by no means comprehensive and does not purport to provide detailed, technical definitions accompanied by qualifications and proper context. The attorney reading a report of psychological and neuropsychological assessment, studying published psychological research relevant to a trial, or listening to deposition or trial testimony by an expert witness may need a convenient and easily used source to look up technical terms. A clinician who specializes in the Minnesota Multiphasic Personality Inventory (MMPI) and who has not previously testified in court may wish, during preparation, to review terms relevant to some of the other major testing instruments and may find it useful to become familiar with some of the terms used in judicial proceedings (such as forms of objection). Many books have been published over the years devoted exclusively to listing and defining psychological or legal terms; in making the difficult decisions regarding which terms to include in this relatively brief list, we have inevitably used our own experience concerning which terms are most likely to arise in cases involving a version of the MMPI and to be unknown to attorneys or witnesses.

A final note: There is a lack of consistency in the literature of neuropsychology in regard to the use of terms that differ according to whether the prefix is *a-* or *dys-* (e.g., agraphia, dysgraphia). In the list that follows, we have used the *a-* prefix to denote a complete lack or absence of the function and the *dys-* prefix to denote a partial (not complete) impairment of function.

ABREACTION　A term usually used within a psychoanalytic or psychodynamic framework in which the individual lets out or expresses strong emotions that had been held in or repressed.

ACALCULIA　Acalculia is the lack of ability to recognize and use numbers because of organic impairment (see DYSCALCULIA).

ACTING OUT　This is a term usually used within a psychoanalytic or psychodynamic framework to denote a defense in which the individual expresses painful or "unacceptable" emotions through behavior as a way to keep the emotions unconscious (or out of awareness).

ACTUARIAL APPROACH　The actuarial approach is the application of probability statistics to human behavior, as in insurance mortality tables.

ACUTE POSTTRAUMATIC STRESS DISORDER　This is a disorder in which symptoms develop within 6 months of an extremely stressful or traumatic experience.

ADAPTIVE TESTING　Adaptive testing is an approach to test administration using the rapid computational capability of a computer. A different set of items is administered for each person, depending on the person's previous responses. Rather than administering all items for each person, the items are specifically chosen for each individual.

ADMINISTRATIVE LAW JUDGE (ALJ) An ALJ is an impartial hearing officer who presides at formal adversary hearings involving a variety of contests, including disputes over workers' compensation, disability requests, and complaints to regulatory boards, such as state psychology licensing boards.

ADMISSIBLE EVIDENCE Admissible evidence comprises information that can be communicated or displayed to the trier of fact (e.g., judge or jury); certain information (e.g., hearsay or privileged communications) may be inadmissible under the applicable laws of evidence.

AFFECT Affect is feelings or emotion.

AFFIDAVIT An affidavit is a statement given under oath.

AGGRAVATED ASSAULT This is an attack on another person in which, according to criteria enacted under state statute, serious bodily injury is inflicted or a deadly weapon is used.

AGNOSIA Agnosia is a state or condition in which the individual lacks knowledge in the relevant area (as in the adjective *agnostic*).

AGRAPHIA This is the lack of ability to write the letters of the alphabet due to organic impairment (see DYSGRAPHIA).

ALIENATION This is loss or lack of a relationship with others.

ALPHA ERROR See TYPE I ERROR.

AMERICAN ASSOCIATION FOR CORRECTIONAL AND FORENSIC PSYCHOLOGY (AACFP) The American Association for Correctional and Forensic Psychology is an organization of behavioral scientists and practitioners focusing on causes, assessment, and interventions related to criminal behavior

AMERICAN BOARD OF FORENSIC PSYCHIATRY This board provides advanced certification as an expert witness to psychiatrists who have previously been certified by the American Board of Psychiatry and Neurology.

AMERICAN BOARD OF PROFESSIONAL PSYCHOLOGY (ABPP) This organization, incorporated originally in 1947 as the American Board of Examiners in Professional Psychology, grants diplomas to psychologists in various areas of practice: clinical child and adolescent psychology, clinical health psychology, clinical psychology, clinical neuropsychology, cognitive and behaviorial psychology, counseling psychology, forensic psychology, group psychology, industrial/organizational psychology, organizational and business consulting psychology, psychoanalysis, rehabilitative psychology, and school psychology. "The Board encourages the pursuit of excellence via its program of certification at an advanced professional level. The ABPP diploma signifies, to the public and to the profession, the highest recognition of competence as judged by one's professional peers" (American Board of Professional Psychology, 1984, p. 1).

AMERICAN PSYCHIATRIC ASSOCIATION The American Psychiatric Association is the largest voluntary association of psychiatrists in the United States. Founded in 1844, the association publishes a variety of journals (e.g., *American Journal of Psychiatry*, which is the official or archival journal, and *Psychiatric Services*) and books.

AMERICAN PSYCHOLOGICAL ASSOCIATION (APA) Holding its first meeting in 1892, the APA incorporated in 1925 (see Fernberger, 1932). The largest association of psychologists in the United States, with 114,000 members and affiliates, the APA publishes numerous scientific and professional journals (the first in 1925), including *American Psychologist*, the official or archival journal, *Behavioral Neuroscience, Journal of Abnormal Psychology, Journal of Consulting and Clinical Psychology, Journal of Personality and Social Psychology, Professional Psychology: Research and Practice*, and *Psychological Assessment*, as well as books.

AMICUS CURIAE   Literally a "friend of the court," this term generally refers to someone who is not a party to a case who offers a brief bearing on the case. For example, both the APA and the American Psychiatric Association have provided briefs in cases in which an individual's ability to accurately predict whether a convicted murderer was likely to kill again was at issue.

ANALYSAND   Analysand is a term for a patient in psychoanalysis.

ANG   *ANG* is an abbreviation for the Anger content scale on the MMPI–2 (see chap. 2 and Appendix W, this volume).

ANHEDONIA   Anhedonia is the impairment of the ability to experience pleasure or to engage in pleasurable activities.

ANTISOCIAL PERSONALITY   This is a personality disorder involving a marked lack of ethical or moral development.

ANX   *ANX* is the abbreviation for the Anxiety content scale on the MMPI–2 (see chap. 2 and Appendix W, this volume).

APHASIA   Aphasia is the lack of an ability to recognize or produce words (i.e., to process language; see DYSPHASIA).

APHONIA   Aphonia is the lack of ability to make vocal sounds due to organic impairment (i.e., loss of voice; see DYSPHONIA).

APPELLANT   An appellant is an individual who appeals a decision of the court.

ARITHMETIC SUBTEST   This is a verbal subtest of the Wechsler Adult Intelligence Scale—III (WAIS–III).

ASKED AND ANSWERED   This is a form of objection during a trial in which the attorney who is not currently questioning a witness asserts that the attorney who is questioning a witness is posing a question that has already been adequately answered by the witness.

ASP   *ASP* is the abbreviation for the Antisocial Practices content scale on the MMPI–2 (see chap. 2 and Appendix W, this volume).

ASSOCIATION FOR PSYCHOLOGICAL SCIENCE   The Association for Psychological Science was founded in 1988 as an independent, multipurpose organization to advance the discipline of psychology, to preserve the scientific base of psychology, to promote public understanding of psychological science and its application, to enhance the quality of graduate education, and to encourage the 'giving away' of psychology in the public interest" (APS, 1990, p. 311; see also Holden, 1988). The APS publishes such journals as *Psychological Science* and *Current Directions in Psychological Science.*

ATAXIA   Ataxia is the lack of ability to coordinate voluntary movements.

ATTEST   Attest is a legal term denoting that an individual swears or otherwise affirms that certain information is true and accurate (e.g., an expert witness attests that an MMPI–2 has been incorrectly scored).

AUTOMATED ASSESSMENT   This is a psychological test interpretation by computer or some other mechanical procedures.

AVERSION THERAPY   Aversion therapy is a term usually used within a behavioral or cognitive–behavioral framework to denote treatment in which an unwanted, punishing, or aversive stimulus is used to eliminate unwanted behaviors.

BATTERY   Battery is an unlawful touching, beating, or physical violence done to another without consent.

BEHAVIOR MODIFICATION   Behavior modification is an intervention to change behavior on the basis of altering contingencies of reinforcement according to the principles of operant conditioning.

BEHAVIOR THERAPY   This is an intervention on the basis of the laws of learning (e.g., classical or operant conditioning).

BEHAVIORAL ASSESSMENT   Behavioral assessment is a technique to determine the functional relationships between an individual's behavior and environmental stimuli.

BEHAVIORISM   Behaviorism is a framework in which the study of people (or animals) focuses primarily or exclusively on observable behavior.

BENDER-GESTALT (or BENDER VISUAL MOTOR GESTALT TEST)   This is a test for neuropsychological impairment in which the individual is asked to copy nine geometric forms (see Bender, 1938; Lacks, 1984).

BENTON VISUAL RETENTION TEST   This is a test for neuropsychological impairment focusing on visual memory; it takes about 5 or 10 minutes to administer and is appropriate for individuals ages 8 and older.

BETA ERROR   See TYPE II ERROR.

BETWEEN-SUBJECTS RESEARCH   Between-subjects research is a study in which different but comparable groups of people (generally in which participants have been randomly assigned to the different groups) receive different interventions (e.g., behavior modification, dynamic therapy, and medication) or levels of interventions. Results are obtained by comparing (and contrasting) the possible effects of the values, forms, or levels of the variable as manifested in the differences between subjects or groups of subjects (see WITHIN-SUBJECTS RESEARCH).

BEYOND THE SCOPE   This is a form of objection during a trial in which the attorney who is not currently questioning a witness asserts that the attorney who is questioning a witness is posing a legally impermissible cross-examination question because it goes beyond the scope of the material covered during direct examination.

BIMODAL DISTRIBUTION   Bimodal distribution is a statistical term indicating a distribution in which there are two values (or scores) that are tied in terms of being most frequent; thus the distribution has two modes (i.e., is bimodal; see MODE; see also chap. 9, this volume).

BIZ   *BIZ* is an abbreviation for the Bizarre Mentation content scale on the MMPI–2 (see chap. 2 and Appendix W, this volume).

BLOCK DESIGN SUBTEST   This is a performance subtest of the WAIS–III.

BONA FIDE   Bona fide indicates that an action has been made in good faith, without fraud or deceit.

BOOKLET CATEGORY TEST   This is an altered form (making the test easier to administer) of the Category Test, one of the tests included in the Halstead–Reitan Neuropsychological Test Battery.

BRIEF   A brief is a document prepared by counsel as a statement of the case, defining issues, presenting arguments, and citing authorities on the matter.

CANNOT SAY   Cannot Say (?) is an MMPI validity scale (see chaps. 2 and 7, this volume) of the total number of unanswered items.

CATEGORY TEST   A category test is one of the tests included in the Halstead–Reitan Neuropsychological Test Battery.

CATHEXIS   Cathexis is the investment of psychological energy into a specific person, thing, or activity.

CENTRAL NERVOUS SYSTEM   This is the portion of the nervous system that includes the brain and spinal cord.

CENTRAL TENDENCY   Central tendency is a statistical term indicating the average; measures of central tendency include the mean, the median, and the mode (see MEAN, MEDIAN, and MODE; see also chap. 9, this volume).

CHARACTER DISORDER   See PERSONALITY DISORDER.

CIVIL COMMITMENT   Civil commitment is a legal process in which an individual can be confined (e.g., in a mental hospital) against his or her will because of a mental, emotional, or behavioral disorder that meets certain criteria (e.g., the individual is assessed as constituting an immediate threat to him- or herself or others or is assessed as gravely disabled).

CLANG ASSOCIATIONS   This is language characterized by a sequence of words and phrases determined not so much by logical expression as by the similarity of word sounds and associations (e.g., "Two plus two. Too much. Let out the clutch. Clutch my heart. I'm heart of hearing. See my earring? Ringing in my ears. Clinging to my tears.").

CLIENT-CENTERED THERAPY   Predominantly originated and developed by psychologist Carl Rogers, this intervention is nondirective, tends to involve statements by the therapist that reflect (e.g., summarize or restate) what the client has just expressed, and focuses on trust, accurate empathy, and acceptance.

COGNITION   Cognition is thinking or the processes involved in thinking; the intellectual processes by which a person takes in and processes information (e.g., intellectual learning, judging, planning, and reasoning).

COGNITIVE–BEHAVIOR MODIFICATION
This is behavior modification (an intervention to change behavior on the basis of altering contingencies of reinforcement according to the principles of operant conditioning) that also focuses on cognitive processes as mediating factors.

COGNITIVE THERAPY   Cognitive therapy is an intervention that focuses on altering negative, self-defeating, and distorted thought processes.

COMPETENCY   In a legal setting, competency is the ability to make a reasoned decision. There is no one standard that defines competency. Rather, the standard fluctuates depending on the decision at issue. A "competent" criminal defendant must have sufficient capacity to assist an attorney in a defense. "Competency" required for informed consent to medical care requires the ability to consider alternatives and weigh benefits and risks. A "competent" witness must understand the oath to tell the truth and must be able to communicate.

COMPREHENSION SUBTEST   This is a verbal subtest of the WAIS–III.

CONCRETE THINKING   Concrete thinking is the impaired ability to engage in abstract thought.

CONFABULATION   Confabulation is inventing information to hide the fact that the individual cannot remember (e.g., an individual suffering from the early stages of Alzheimer's disease, asked what she had for breakfast but unable to remember, might make up what seems to her to be a plausible answer).

CONTINUANCE   Continuance is a postponement of an action or a session, hearing, trial, or other legal proceeding to a subsequent time.

CONTRAST ERROR   This is a term of assessment or research denoting a tendency to erroneously inflate perceived differences (e.g., in assessing individuals or characteristics) because of (comparison to or contrast with) previous ratings.

CONTROL GROUP   A control group is a comparison group used in research that attempts to assess the effect(s) of one or more independent variables (e.g., to assess the efficacy of client-centered therapy for depression, depressed individuals might be randomly assigned to two groups, one of which receives client-centered therapy, the other, as the control group, receives educational instruction about depression).

CORRELATION COEFFICIENT   This is a statistic indicating the degree to which two variables are related (i.e., to which they covary, or vary together). The coefficient falls somewhere on the continuum ranging from -1 (perfectly negatively correlated) to 0 (no relationship whatsoever) to 1 (perfectly positively correlated; see chap. 9, this volume).

COUNTERTRANSFERENCE   This term has been defined in a variety of (sometimes inconsistent) ways, but generally refers to the therapist experiencing (sometimes on an unconscious level) feelings that are stirred up or elicited by the patient.

CYN CYN is the abbreviation for the Cynicism content scale on the MMPI–2 (see chap. 2 and Appendix W, this volume).

D D is the abbreviation for the Depression clinical scale (i.e., Scale 2) on the MMPI (see chap. 2 and Appendix W, this volume).

DAUBERT ANALYSIS This refers to a case law standard articulated by the United States Supreme Court in 1993 in *Daubert v. Merrell Dow Pharmaceuticals, Inc.* (509 U.S. 579 (1993)) that governs the admissibility of expert testimony (see chap. 4, this volume).

DECOMPENSATION This is a deterioration of an individual's personality, condition, or functioning.

DEFENSE MECHANISM The term *defense mechanism* is usually used within a psychoanalytic or psychodynamic framework to denote a strategy that a person uses to ward off awareness of unpleasant, frightening, or anxiety-inducing thoughts or experiences; the strategy is carried out on an unconscious level (i.e., the individual is not aware of it).

DELUSION A delusion is a rigid belief not consistent with reality and maintained in spite of strong evidence to the contrary.

DEMENTIA Dementia refers to a substantial loss of mental or cognitive abilities.

DEMUR To demur is to allege in a legal proceeding that the facts as charged, even if true, do not form an adequate legal basis for the case to go forth.

DEP DEP is the abbreviation for the Depression content scale on the MMPI–2 (see chap. 2 and Appendix W, this volume).

DEPENDENT VARIABLE A dependent variable is a research term indicating the measure that, according to the hypothesis, will reflect changes in the independent variable (i.e., changes in the dependent variable are dependent on the presence or absence or changes in the independent variable).

DEPERSONALIZATION Depersonalization is a state in which the individual feels that his or her self or body is somehow unreal, unfamiliar, different, or strange.

DEPOSITION Deposition is a legal term indicating the process in which an attorney may take the testimony—under oath—of a witness before the trial (see chaps. 6 and 9, this volume).

DEREALIZATION This is a state in which the individual feels that his or her surroundings are somehow unreal, unfamiliar, different, or strange.

DESCRIPTIVE STATISTICS These are statistics that apply only to cases that have actually been counted or otherwise measured (e.g., the number of words in this book and the average number of letters in the words in this book); in descriptive statistics, no attempt is made to draw inferences about a wider population than has actually been counted or measured (e.g., in the example above, no attempt would be made to use the number and length of words in this book to generalize about other books; see INFERENTIAL STATISTICS).

DESENSITIZATION This is a term usually used within the behavioral or cognitive–behavioral framework to refer to a process in which repeated exposure to a stimulus may tend to reduce the occurrence of a response (or the response's intensity) to the stimulus (e.g., in cognitive–behavioral therapy, an individual who has been traumatized by an event may be guided to experience much milder versions of the event in his or her imagination until the effects of the trauma are diminished).

DIAGNOSTIC AND STATISTICAL MANUAL OF MENTAL DISORDERS (DSM) One of the classification systems by which mental, emotional, or behavior disorders have been defined, described, and labeled, the American Psychiatric Association publishes this volume. The first edition, influenced by Adolf Meyer's view of personality, appeared in 1952. After the second edition (1968), the manual adopted a new multiaxial system of diagnosis (American Psychiatric Association, 1980, 1987, 1994): Axis I presents clinical disorders or syndromes (as well as treatment issues that do not constitute mental disorders and some supplementary codes); Axis II presents personality and developmental disorders; Axis III presents physical disorders; Axis IV indicates the level of psychosocial stress; and Axis V indicates the best level of functioning the individual has experienced during the past year. The *DSM* includes a cautionary statement that there is no implication that categories meet legal criteria for various diseases, disorders, or disabilities. The cautionary statement further admonishes that the "clinical and scientific considerations" of this classification system "may not be wholly relevant to legal judgments" (American Psychiatric Association, 1987, p. xxix).

DICHOTOMOUS VARIABLE   This is a statistical term denoting a scale that is divided into two mutually exclusive categories (e.g., a nominal scale that divides individuals into boys and girls; an age scale that divides all survey participants into those who are under 45 and all those who are 45 or older).

DIGIT SPAN   A digit span is a verbal subtest of the WAIS–III as well as of the mental status examination and other assessment approaches.

DIGIT SYMBOL SUBTEST   This is a performance subtest of the WAIS–III.

DISCOVERY   Discovery is a legal term indicating the process that occurs before the trial begins in which attorneys are able to obtain documents, information, and testimony from opposition parties, expert witnesses, and others.

DOUBLE JEOPARDY   This is a prohibition against a second prosecution or punishment for the same offense, as defined through common law, state constitutions, and the Fifth Amendment to the United States Constitution.

DYSCALCULIA   Dyscalculia is the impaired ability to recognize and use numbers because of organic impairment (see ACALCULIA).

DYSGRAPHIA   Dysgraphia is the impaired ability to write the letters of the alphabet because of organic impairment (see AGRAPHIA).

DYSKINESIA   Dyskinesia is the impaired ability to produce voluntary movements (as in the side-effect tardive dyskinesia sometimes produced by antipsychotic medications).

DYSLEXIA   Dyslexia is the impaired ability to read because of organic impairment.

DYSPHASIA   Dyphasia is the impaired ability to recognize or produce words (i.e., to process language; see APHASIA).

DYSPHONIA   Dysponia is the impaired ability to make vocal sounds because of organic impairment (i.e., loss of voice; see APHONIA).

DYSPRAXIA   Dyspraxia is the impaired ability to conduct voluntary, coordinated, intentional movements, actions, or expressions.

ECHOLALIA   This is a condition in which the individual constantly (and perhaps exclusively) mimics or repeats what others are saying.

ECHOPRAXIA   This is a condition in which the individual mimics or repeats the behaviors of those around him or her.

EGO PSYCHOLOGY   Ego psychology is a branch, development, or revision of psychoanalytic theory focusing on the processes of the ego rather than the id; the relative emphasis is on the person's attempts to cope with reality rather than to express unconscious wishes and themes.

EXISTENTIAL PSYCHOLOGY OR THERAPY   This is a framework for psychology or therapy in which the focus is the individual's immediate human experience rather than observable behaviors, cognitive processes, or unconscious motives.

EXPERT WITNESS   This is a testifying person who may render an opinion on the basis of specialized knowledge or skill if proper foundation is laid under FED. R. EVID. 702 and FED. R. EVID. 703 (see PERCIPIENT OR LAY WITNESS).

F SCALE   The *F* scale is the abbreviation for the Infrequency Scale, which is a validity scale on the MMPI (see chapters chaps. 2 and 7, this volume) created to measure exaggeration of symptoms.

FACTOR ANALYSIS   Factor analysis is a statistical technique used in research to reduce a large array of measurements or data into more concise or fundamental dimensions.

FALSE NEGATIVE   A false negative is an error in assessment in which a test falsely indicates that the individual does not have a particular condition (that the test was designed to identify) when in fact the person does have the condition (see FALSE POSITIVE, SENSITIVITY, and SPECIFICITY).

FALSE POSITIVE   A false positive is an error in assessment in which a test falsely indicates that the individual has a particular condition (that the test was designed to identify) when in fact the person does not have the condition (see FALSE NEGATIVE, SENSITIVITY, and SPECIFICITY).

FAM   *FAM* is the abbreviation for the Family Problems content scale on the MMPI–2 (see chap. 2 and Appendix W, this volume).

F(B)   The Infrequency-Back scale is a measure of exaggerated responding similar to the *F* scale, whose items appear toward the end of the test booklet.

FEDERAL RULES OF EVIDENCE (Fed. R. Evid.)   These are uniform rules of evidence used in all federal courts. The rules define how and when evidence is presented to the trier of fact. Most states have adopted the Federal Rules of Evidence in total or in part.

FELONY   A felony is a serious crime for which a person can be sentenced to long-term penitentiary incarceration or death.

FINGER OSCILLATION TEST   This is one of the tests included in the Halstead–Reitan Neuropsychological Test Battery. This is also known as the finger-tapping test.

FRS   *FRS* is the abbreviation for the Fears content scale on the MMPI–2 (see chap. 2 and Appendix W, this volume).

FUNCTIONAL DISORDER   This is a form of psychopathological distress or dysfunction for which a physiological cause is neither known nor presumed.

FUNCTIONAL PSYCHOSES   Functional psychoses are severe mental disorders that are attributed primarily to psychological causes such as stress.

GESTALT THERAPY   Gestalt therapy is a form of therapy focusing on integrating behavior, thinking, and feeling.

GRIP STRENGTH   Grip strength is one of the tests included in the Halstead–Reitan Neuropsychological Test Battery.

HABEAS CORPUS   Habeas corpus is the name given to a variety of writs designed to bring a party before a court or judge. Whenever the words are used alone, the primary function of the writ is to release the party from unlawful imprisonment.

HALSTEAD IMPAIRMENT INDEX   This is a number from 0.0 (none of the scores suggesting brain damage) to 1.0 (all seven scores suggesting brain damage) representing the proportion of seven (originally 10) Halstead–Reitan Neuropsychology tests on which the individual scored in the range characteristic of neuropsychologically damaged individuals.

HAPTIC   The term *haptic* relates to touch.

HEA   *HEA* is the abbreviation for the Health Concerns content scale on the MMPI–2 (see chap. 2 and Appendix W, this volume).

HEALTH INSURANCE PORTABILITY AND ACCOUNTABILITY ACT (HIPAA)   HIPPA (1996) is broad-ranging federal regulation of health insurance, professional confidentiality, and patient privacy.

HEARSAY   Hearsay is a form of objection during a trial in which the attorney who is not currently questioning a witness asserts that the attorney who is questioning a witness is eliciting (or that the witness is providing) testimony that is inadmissible because it is based on information that was overheard.

HEARSAY RULE   The hearsay rule excludes statements made out of court when offered to prove the truth of the matter asserted.

Hs   *Hs* is the abbreviation for the Hypochondriasis clinical scale (i.e., Scale 1) on the MMPI (see chap. 2 and Appendix W, this volume) measuring somatic concerns.

Hy   *Hy* is the abbreviation for the Hysteria clinical scale (i.e., Scale 3) on the MMPI (see chap. 2 and Appendix W, this volume).

IMPLOSIVE THERAPY   This is an intervention within the behavioral or cognitive–behavioral framework in which an "implosion" (sometimes termed "flooding") of anxiety or fear is evoked in an effort to desensitize an individual to a specific stimulus.

INCIDENCE   Incidence is a statistical term that refers to the number of *new* cases of a particular event or phenomenon within a specified period of time (see PREVALENCE).

INDEPENDENT VARIABLE   An independent variable is a research factor that, according to a hypothesis, will cause a change in at least one other (dependent) variable in the study; the independent variable is often presented at different levels whereas other factors are held constant.

INFERENTIAL STATISTICS   Inferential statistics are techniques allowing inferences to be made about a larger population on the basis of counts and measurements of a (presumably representative) sample or subset of that population (see DESCRIPTIVE STATISTICS).

INFORMATION   In this context, Information is a verbal subtest of the WAIS–III.

INSANITY, LEGAL   In federal criminal cases, legal insanity is a defense through which the de-

fendant is not responsible for otherwise criminal conduct if, at the time of the commission of the acts charged, the defendant, as a result of a severe mental disease or defect, was unable to appreciate the nature or the wrongfulness of his or her acts. State standards for legal insanity vary.

INTERROGATORIES   Interrogatories is a set of questions set forth in writing by the attorneys in a case to which someone involved in the case (e.g., one of the litigants) must respond in writing as part of the pretrial discovery process.

IQ   IQ is the abbreviation for Intelligence Quotient; in general, this is the relation of mental age to chronological age, or the person's likely intellectual ranking in the population.

IRRELEVANT   In this context, irrelevant refers to a form of objection during a trial in which the attorney who is not currently questioning a witness asserts that the attorney who is questioning a witness is posing a question that is irrelevant to the case.

ITEM RESPONSE THEORY (IRT)   IRT, sometimes referred to as latent trait theory, is an approach to test construction that is different from classical development strategies. Item-level analyses are used to explore the functioning of items in predicting the presence of a criterion variable—for example, to estimate the strength of an underlying trait or characteristic. IRT is used to develop and guide assessments that are adapted to each client. Not all items are administered to each client; only those items that are needed, contingent on the individual's response to earlier items, are administered.

K **CORRECTION**   This score refers to a proportion of the *K* scale that has been empirically determined as a correction for test defensiveness. The percentage of the *K* score is added to five clinical scales of the MMPI (*Hs*, *Pd*, *Pt*, *Sc*, and *Ma*) as a means of making the scale more sensitive to psychopathology.

K **SCALE**   *K* scale is an abbreviation for Defensiveness on the MMPI validity scale (see chaps. 2 and 7, this volume).

KELLY–FRYE TEST This refers to a case law standard that expert testimony, to be admissible, must be generally accepted by the relevant scientific or professional community (see chap. 3, this volume). In most states the *Kelly–Frye* test has been replaced with a *Daubert* analysis.

KURTOSIS This is a statistical term describing the degree to which scores or measurements are clustered closely around or are spread far from the mean.

L SCALE *L* is an abbreviation for the Lie scale, an MMPI validity scale (see chaps. 2 and 7, this volume) created to measure the tendency to claim excessive virtue.

LAMBDA Lambda is a statistical term indicating the degree to which two dichotomous variables are related or associated; it is also a variable used in the Rorschach Comprehensive System (Exner, 1991).

LAW OF EFFECT This is a term generally used within the behavioral or cognitive–behavioral framework to denote the phenomenon by which behaviors that are followed by pleasing consequences (positive reinforcers) tend to be repeated whereas behaviors that are followed by aversive consequences are less likely to be repeated.

LEADING Leading is a form of objection during a trial in which the attorney who is not currently questioning a witness asserts that the attorney who is questioning a witness is posing a question that is legally improper because it indicates to a witness how to respond (e.g., "When you saw the defendant that night did you think to yourself, 'This must be the man who killed the shopkeeper?'").

LEARNED HELPLESSNESS Learned helplessness is a phenomenon in which the individual erroneously "learns" (perhaps from one or more traumatic situations in which his or her behavior produced no significant result) that his or her behaviors have little or no relationship to consequences.

LESION A lesion is damage, a wound, or pathology occurring in tissue.

LINEAR T SCORES This is a statistical term (see *T* SCORES) in which the mean of the distribution is 50 and the standard deviation is 10; this is the type of scaling used by the original MMPI (see chaps. 2 and 9, this volume).

LITIGANT A litigant is any party to a lawsuit, including the plaintiff, defendant, petitioner, respondent, cross-complainant, and cross-defendant, but does not refer to an attorney, witness, or judge.

LSE *LSE* is the abbreviation for the Low Self-Esteem content scale on the MMPI–2 (see chap. 2 and Appendix W, this volume).

LURIA-NEBRASKA This is a neuropsychological assessment battery.

Ma *Ma* is the abbreviation for the Mania clinical scale (i.e., Scale 9) on the MMPI (see chap. 2 and Appendix W, this volume).

MALINGERING Malingering is an intentional behavior that can range from exaggerating the symptoms or impact of actual illness to completely falsifying symptoms to achieve some external goal.

MATERIAL EVIDENCE This is the quality of evidence that tends to influence the trier of fact because of its logical connection with the issue. Referred to as "relevant evidence" in FED. R. EVID. 401, it includes "evidence having any tendency to make the existence of any fact that is of consequence to the determination of the action more probable or less probable than it would be without the evidence."

MEAN A mean is an arithmetic average in which the scores (or other numbers) are added and then the resulting sum is divided by the number of scores.

MEDIAN This is a statistical term indicating that score or measurement that divides all the scores or measurements into two equal groups: those falling below the median and those falling above the median (see chap. 9, this volume).

MEGARGEE FELONY CLASSIFICATION RULES   This is an MMPI-based classification system designed to group felons' MMPI profiles into similar personality clusters (see chap. 2, this volume).

MENTAL STATUS EXAMINATION   A mental status examination is a generic term (i.e., numerous articles, texts, and guidebooks present different outlines for conducting the examination) that describes a structured observation and interview technique in which the examiner evaluates a comprehensive set of characteristics (e.g., appearance, orientation, attention, concentration, memory, and insight) related to the individual's current mental status.

Mf   *Mf* is an abbreviation for the Masculinity–Femininity clinical scale (i.e., Scale 5) on the basic MMPI profile (see chap. 2 and Appendix W, this volume).

MILLON CLINICAL MULTIAXIAL INVENTORY (MCMI, MCMI–II, and MCMI–III)   This is a rationally derived scale that assesses individuals according to Millon's (e.g., 1969, 1981, 1987, 1994) conceptualization of clinical and personality disorders. As the title of the scale indicates, it focuses on clinical (rather than nonclinical) assessment.

MISDEMEANOR   A misdemeanor is an offense that is not a felony and is punishable by a fine or short period of incarceration generally in a facility other than a penitentiary.

MODE   A mode is a statistical term indicating the most frequently occurring score or measurement in a distribution (see chap. 9, this volume).

MOTION IN LIMINE   This is a written request made to the presiding judge before or after the beginning of a jury trial for a protective order against prejudicial statements.

NATIONAL ASSOCIATION OF SOCIAL WORKERS (NASW)   The NASW is a voluntary professional association that emerged in 1955 when seven previously established social work associations merged.

NO FOUNDATION   This is a form of objection during a trial in which the attorney who is not currently questioning a witness asserts that the attorney who is questioning a witness is posing a question that is legally impermissible because no foundation has been provided for this area of testimony.

NONDIRECTIVE THERAPY   See CLIENT-CENTERED THERAPY.

NORM-REFERENCED TESTS   Norm-reference tests are those that compare test takers with each other. Grading on a curve is an example of norm-referenced tests.

NOT GUILTY BY REASON OF INSANITY DEFENSE (NGRI)   In federal jurisdictions, an NGRI is a criminal defense asserting that, at the time of commission of acts constituting the offense, the defendant, as a result of a severe mental disease or defect, was unable to appreciate the nature and quality or the wrongfulness of his or her acts. In federal jurisdictions, the defendant has the burden of proving the defense of insanity by clear and convincing evidence. The burden of proof and the nature of the disease or defect required to prove the insanity defense varies in state jurisdictions. For additional information, please see Cheatham and Litwack (2003); Giorgi-Guarnieri et al. (2002); Litwack (2003); Matthews (2004); Melville and Naimark (2002); Nwokike (2005); Van Susteren (2002); and Zolovska and Bursztajn (2005).

NULL HYPOTHESIS   In experimental research, the null hypothesis is that independent or experimental variable exerts no effect so that there will be no statistically significant difference in outcome between the experimental group(s) and the control group(s).

OBJECT ASSEMBLY SUBTEST   This is a performance subtest of the WAIS–III.

OBJECT RELATIONS THEORY   Object relations theory is a psychoanalytic view that the development of the ego (self) and social relationships is based on or strongly influenced by the infant's attachment to the significant people (generally the parents).

OBS OBS is the abbreviation for the Obsessiveness content scale on the MMPI–2 (see chap. 2 and Appendix W, this volume).

OPERANT CONDITIONING Operant conditioning is the influence on behavior by the positive or negative reinforcements that follow the behavior (see BEHAVIOR MODIFICATION).

Pa Pa is the abbreviation for the Paranoia clinical scale (i.e., Scale 6) on the MMPI (see chap. 2 and Appendix W, this volume).

PARAPRAXIS Parapraxis is an incident in which a person says or does something that is different from what he or she intends to say or do, resulting in an error of which the person may be unaware. An example is a "Freudian slip."

PATHOGNOMONIC SYMPTOM OR SIGN This is a sufficient indicant for assigning a particular diagnosis or classification (e.g., complete lack of brain activity is a pathognomic sign of death).

Pd Pd is an abbreviation for the Psychopathic Deviate clinical scale (i.e., Scale 4) on the MMPI (see chap. 2 and Appendix W, this volume).

PERCENTILE RANK This tells what proportion of the group falls below a particular point.

PERCENTILE SCORE The rank from the bottom of a scale is expressed in percentage form.

PERCIPIENT OR LAY WITNESS This is a testifying person who does not possess any expertise in the matters about which he or she testifies (used in contrast to expert witness). A percipient witness is often called a witness of fact.

PERJURY Perjury is the intentional providing of false sworn testimony (sometimes with additional qualifiers such as pertaining to a material fact important to the case).

PERSONALITY DISORDER This is a group of maladaptive behavioral syndromes originating in the developmental years (usually considered learning-based disorders) and not characterized by neurotic or psychotic symptoms.

PICTURE ARRANGEMENT SUBTEST This is a performance subtest of the WAIS–III.

PICTURE COMPLETION SUBTEST This is a performance subtest of the WAIS–III.

PRACTICE EFFECTS This is a phenomenon in which the validity of a test may be affected because an individual has previously taken the test (e.g., the test is now familiar).

PREDICTIVE ACCURACY Predictive accuracy is the level of success, expressed as a probability, that a test demonstrates in predicting performance, behavior, symptoms, or other specific criteria that it was created to predict.

PREDICTIVE BIAS Predictive bias is the tendency of an assessment instrument to systematically underpredict or overpredict performance, behavior, symptoms, or other specific criteria based on demographics or other variables that are not relevant to the specific criteria.

PREDICTIVE VALIDITY Predictive validity indicates the degree to which test results are accurate in forecasting some outcome.

PREPONDERANCE OF EVIDENCE This is a standard of proof in which the evidence presented to the court appears more convincing than the evidence provided by the opposition. The evidence, as a whole, shows that the fact sought to be proved is more probable than not.

PREVALENCE This is a statistical term that refers to the total number of cases of a particular event or phenomenon within a specified time (see also INCIDENCE).

PROFILE A profile is a method of displaying test scores to provide a visual comparison of relative performance on similar scales.

PROJECTIVE TEST A projective test is an assessment instrument in which the test materials (e.g., Rorschach cards, Thematic Apperception Test pictures) contain some stimulus ambiguity;

the individual's responses are hypothesized to reveal personality attributes.

PSYCHOLOGICAL TEST   A psychological test is a procedure or task developed to assess psychological characteristics, abilities, or conditions, such as personality factors, memory, concentration, attitudes, beliefs, behavioral tendencies, or symptoms. Cronbach (1960) wrote, "A test is a systematic procedure for comparing the behavior of two or more persons" (p. 21).

PSYCHOPATHOLOGY FIVE (PSY–5) SCALES   This is a set of five MMPI–2 scales developed to assess the five major personality dimensions (often referred to as the "Big Five") using MMPI items that address psychopathology (Harkness & Butcher, 2002; Harkness, McNulty, & Ben-Porath, 1995; Harkness, McNulty, Strack, & Lorr, 1994; McNulty et al., 2002).

PSYCHOPHYSIOLOGIC (PSYCHOSOMATIC) DISORDERS   These are physical disorders in which psychological factors are considered to play a major causative role.

Pt   *Pt* is the abbreviation for the Psychasthenia clinical scale (i.e., Scale 7) on the MMPI, created to measure anxiety (see chap. 2 and Appendix W, this volume).

RANDOM SAMPLE   A random sample is a subgroup selected from a larger group (termed the *population*) in such a way that each member of the larger group has an equal probability of being chosen.

RATIONAL–EMOTIVE THERAPY   Predominantly originated and developed by psychologist Albert Ellis, this therapy attempts to identify and correct errors in thinking and misconnections between thinking and feeling.

RATIONAL SCALE DEVELOPMENT   This refers to developing scales on the basis of the content of the items by simply grouping items according to their explicit meaning.

REASONABLE DOUBT   A reasonable doubt is one that would cause a reasonably prudent person to hesitate to act in matters of importance.

RECIDIVISM   Recidivism is a return to a previous form of undesirable behavior after a course of intervention.

REITAN–INDIANA APHASIA SCREENING TEST   This is one of the tests included in the Halstead–Reitan Neuropsychological Test Battery.

REITAN–KLOVE LATERAL DOMINANCE EXAMINATION   This is one of the tests included in the Halstead–Reitan Neuropsychological Test Battery.

REITAN–KLOVE SENSORY-PERCEPTION EXAMINATION   This is one of the tests included in the Halstead–Reitan Neuropsychological Test Battery.

REITAN–KLOVE TACTILE FORM RECOGNITION TEST   This is one of the tests included in the Halstead–Reitan Neuropsychological Test Battery.

RELIABILITY   Reliability is the degree to which a test or other form of measurement is consistent in producing the same result every time it is used to assess or measure a particular person who has not changed significantly between testings (see chap. 9, this volume).

REPLICATION   Replication in this context is research that attempts to repeat previous research (either identically or with specific changes) to see if the original results are reliable.

RES IPSA LOQUITUR   Literally from the Latin, this means, "The thing speaks for itself." In legal proceedings, the *res ipsa loquitur* principle of evidence or inference indicates that, under certain circumstances, the mere existence of an event may establish culpability.

RESPONSE RATE   This is a statistical term indicating the percentage of those invited to participate in a study who actually participated in the study (e.g., if surveys were mailed out to 200 randomly selected individuals and 150 individuals completed and returned the survey form, the response rate would be 75%).

RESTRUCTURED CLINICAL (*RC*) SCALES
The *RC* scales are a new set of experimental scales that were developed, using correlational statistical procedures, to assess the main constructs measured by the MMPI clinical scales. The redevelopment procedures attempted to develop newer measures of the underlying constructs by removing the influence of a dimension called demoralization that was considered to influence the traditional measures. (See chap. 2, this volume.)

RETROSPECTIVE ACCURACY   In contrast to "predictive accuracy,"—which is the likelihood that those who score positive (or manifest some other score or pattern of scores) on a hypothetical predictor variable will fall into a specific group—"retrospective accuracy" is the likelihood that those in a specific group will score positive (or manifest some other score or specific pattern of scores) on the predictor variable.

ROGERIAN THERAPY   See CLIENT-CENTERED THERAPY.

RORSCHACH   Rorschach is a projective technique in which the individual is shown 10 symmetrical "inkblots" in specific sequence and is asked to describe each blot and the specific attributes of the card that, according to the individual, make up or determine what the individual sees in the card.

Sc   *Sc* is the abbreviation for the Schizophrenia clinical scale (i.e., Scale 8) on the MMPI (see chap. 2 and Appendix W, this volume).

SCALE   A scale is a systematic framework for assigning names or measurements; for definitions of *nominal, ordinal, interval,* and *ratio scales,* see chapter 9.

SEASHORE RHYTHM   This is one of the tests originally developed as part of the Seashore Tests of Musical Talent and now included in the Halstead–Reitan Neuropsychological Test Battery.

SELF-REPORT QUESTIONNAIRE   This is a questionnaire or inventory designed to obtain self-descriptions from an individual.

SENSITIVITY   If a psychological test has been validated to identify a certain condition, the sensitivity refers to the proportion of tested individuals who test positive who actually have the condition (see SPECIFICITY, FALSE POSITIVE, and FALSE NEGATIVE).

SENTENCE COMPLETION TEST   This is a projective test appearing in many forms; the basic procedure involves presenting an individual with a word or phrase that begins a sentence and asking the individual to complete the sentence immediately.

SEQUELAE   Sequelae comprise distress, dysfunction, symptoms, and other consequences that linger in the aftermath of a trauma, disease, or disorder.

SERIAL SEVENS   The individual is asked to count by sevens either forward (e.g., 7, 14, 21) or backward (100, 93, 86).

Si   *Si* is the abbreviation for the Social Introversion–Extraversion clinical scale (i.e., Scale 0) on the MMPI (see chap. 2 and Appendix W, this volume).

SIGNIFICANT DIFFERENCE   In inferential statistics, this is a difference that is unlikely to be due to chance (see TYPE I and TYPE II ERRORS).

SIMILARITIES SUBTEST   This is a verbal subtest of the WAIS–R.

SKEWNESS   This is a statistical term indicating the degree to which measurements fall in a symmetrical (i.e., not skewed) or asymmetrical (i.e., skewed) pattern around the mean.

SOCIAL APPROVAL OR SOCIAL DESIRABILITY BIAS   This is the potential tendency for an individual participating in research or assessment to provide answers that would be perceived as socially approved or socially desirable.

SOCIOTHERAPY Sociotherapy is an intervention focusing on an individual's social or interpersonal relationships and functioning.

SOD *SOD* is the abbreviation for the Social Discomfort content scale on the MMPI–2 (see chap. 2 and Appendix W, this volume).

SOMATIC This term relates to the body (e.g., headaches and abdominal pain would be characterized as somatic complaints).

SPECIFICITY If a psychological test has been validated to identify a certain condition, the specificity refers to the proportion of tested individuals who test negative who actually do not have the condition (see SENSITIVITY, FALSE POSITIVE, and FALSE NEGATIVE).

SPEECH SOUNDS PERCEPTION TEST This is one of the tests included in the Halstead–Reitan Neuropsychological Test Battery.

STANDARD DEVIATION This is a statistical measure of the spread or dispersion of scores (or other measures) around the mean, or the square root of the variance (see chap. 9, this volume).

STANDARD SCORE A standard score is one that is calculated in terms of standard deviations from the statistical mean of scores.

STANDARDIZED TEST A standardized test is an assessment instrument that is administered, scored, and interpreted using uniform procedures and that has been developed using a specific population as a reference group to provide test norms to which an individual's score(s) can be compared.

STANFORD–BINET This is a standardized test of the intellectual abilities of children.

SUBPOENA DUCES TECUM Literally translated from the Latin, this means, "Under penalty, bring forth [this material] with you." It is a legal document requiring the individual to produce certain materials (see chap. 6, this volume).

SUBSCALES Subscales are groups of items for a particular scale or construct that focus on a subfacet of the scale in question. For example, the Depression scale has been rationally divided into five subsets of homogeneous contents.

SUBTLE/OBVIOUS SCALES This is a set of subscales developed for some MMPI scales considered by the developer, Daniel Wiener, to measure the constructs underlying the scale with core items that are not obviously related to the scale. The subtle scales are items that are not seemingly related to the major content of the scale construct, for example, depression. The "subtle" items were thought to have special meaning because they were thought to be valid indicators but not recognizable as such by the test taker. However, the subtle items have proven to be largely chance items and not actually related to external criteria as the obvious items are.

SYNDROME This is a group or pattern of symptoms, sequelae, or characteristics of a disorder.

T **SCORES** These are scores falling along a distribution in which the mean is 50 and the standard deviation is 10 (see chaps. 2 and 9, this volume).

TACTILE Tactile relates to touch.

TACTUAL PERFORMANCE TEST This is one of the tests included in the Halstead–Reitan Neuropsychological Test Battery.

TELEPROCESSING This is a computer-based data processing procedure by which psychological tests are processed, scored, and interpreted through telephone link-up with a central processing center.

TEST A test is defined as a "systematic procedure for observing behavior and describing it on a numerical scale, or in terms of categories" (Cronbach, 1990, p. 706).

TEST–RETEST RELIABILITY This is a measure, often expressed as a coefficient, of the degree to which the same group of people will produce the same or similar scores on two separate administrations of the same test.

TEST USER QUALIFICATIONS   These are guidelines established by a professional organization (e.g., the APA) specifying the level of training and experience required for different tests.

THEMATIC APPERCEPTION TEST   This is a projective technique developed by psychologist Henry Murray (see Murray, 1943) in which an individual is shown a sequence of pictures and is asked to make up a story that goes with each picture.

TINNITUS   Tinnitus is a condition in which the individual hears noise (e.g., static, roaring, ringing) in the absence of an external stimulus for the noise.

TORT   A tort is a legal term denoting a wrong for which the injured party may sue in civil court for damages to "be made whole."   .

TPA   *TPA* is the abbreviation for the Type A content scale on the MMPI–2 (see chap. 2 and Appendix W, this volume).

TR (or T–R)   TR is an abbreviation for test–retest variation, a form of test reliability usually expressed as a correlation; changes in test scores for an individual test taker may reflect the imperfect reliability of the test (generally chance or error variance), an actual change in the individual's condition, or the possibility that the individual is intentionally or unconsciously distorting responses but is not doing so in a consistent manner.

TRAIL MAKING TEST   One such test is included in the Halstead–Reitan Neuropsychological Test Battery.

TRANSACTIONAL ANALYSIS   This is a form of therapy focusing on three aspects of the self: parent, child, and adult.

TRANSFERENCE   Transference is a phenomenon in which a patient transfers to or projects onto the therapist feelings from an earlier relationship (e.g., the child's relationship to a parent); the process is initially unconscious.

TRIN   *TRIN* is the abbreviation for the True Response Inconsistency scale, one of the validity scales of the MMPI–2 (see chap. 7 and Appendix W, this volume).

TRT   *TRT* is the abbreviation for the Negative Treatment Indicators content scale on the MMPI–2 (see chap. 2 and Appendix W, this volume).

TWO POINT CODE   This is an MMPI–2 variable that comprises the highest two scores on the clinical scale profile; for example, if the highest two scale scores are on the Depression (Scale 2) and Psychasthenia scale (Scale 7), then the 2-point code would be a 2-7/7-2.

TYPE I ERROR   This is a research term indicating that a decision (in interpreting results) was made that there was an actual (i.e., not due to chance) difference or finding when in reality there was no such actual difference or finding; this is also known as an alpha error.

TYPE II ERROR   This is a research term indicating that a decision (in interpreting results) was made that there was no actual (i.e., not due to chance) difference or finding when in reality there *was* such actual difference or finding; this is also known as a beta error.

UNIFORM *T* SCORES   This is a statistical term (see *T* SCORES) for the type of scaling used by the MMPI–2 and MMPI–A resulting in comparable percentile values for a given *T* score across various clinical or content scales (see chaps. 2 and 9, this volume).

VALIDITY   Validity is the degree to which a test or other form of measurement actually assesses or measures what it is designed to assess or measure (see chaps. 7 and 9, this volume).

VARIABLE   A variable is a characteristic, attribute, or measurement that has at least two levels or categories. "Work" may be a variable that can be divided into "paid" and "unpaid" (i.e., two levels), although it is also possible to define work as a variable with many more levels or categories (e.g., work as "hard," "medium," or "light" as experienced or defined by the individual doing the work).

VARIANCE   Variance is a statistical measure of the spread or dispersion of scores (or other measures) around the mean; the square of the standard deviation (see chap. 9, this volume).

VERBAL TEST   This is a test in which the person's ability to understand and use words and concepts is important in making the required responses.

VOCABULARY SUBTEST   This is a verbal subtest of the WAIS–R and other tests.

VOIR DIRE   *Voir dire* is a process by which attorneys and judges question potential jurors to determine whether the individuals are appropriate (e.g., lack bias) to serve as jurors in a specific trial.

VRIN   VRIN is the abbreviation for the Variable Response Inconsistency scale, one of the validity scales of the MMPI-2 (see chap. 7 and Appendix W, this volume).

WECHSLER ADULT INTELLIGENCE SCALE—III (WAIS–III)   The WAIS–III comprises verbal/numerical (Verbal) and perceptual/motor (Performance) subtests.

WECHSLER–BELLEVUE SCALE   This is a test (comprising 11 subtests) divided into two main parts (Verbal and Performance) developed in the 1930s as a general intelligence test and later revised into the WAIS.

WECHSLER MEMORY SCALE   The original (WMS) and revised (WMS–R) versions contain subtests assessing such aspects of memory as forward and backward digit span, logical memory, visual reproduction, and associate learning.

WELL-DEFINED (PROFILE)   With respect to an MMPI variable this refers to differences in scores that make up the code type and those not included in the code. A well-defined profile is an MMPI profile that has a scale elevation or two-point code elevation that is more than 5 *T* score points above the next score in the profile.

WESTERN APHASIA BATTERY   This is a set of subtests that yield an AQ (aphasia quotient) and a CQ (cortical quotient), a more general measure of cognitive functioning.

WISCONSIN CARD SORTING TEST   This is an untimed test focusing on perseverative and abstract thinking used to help identify neuropsychological impairment.

WITHIN-SUBJECTS RESEARCH   Within-subjects research is a study in which each participant receives (generally in sequence) the different interventions or different levels of the intervention. The (possible) effects of the different values, forms, or levels of the variable are compared and contrasted in terms of (or within) each subject (see BETWEEN-SUBJECTS RESEARCH).

WORK PRODUCT   This is a legal term denoting the materials that the attorney (and in some instances consultants and others who work for the attorney) prepares leading up to trial that, depending on circumstances and applicable law, are not subject to pretrial discovery by opposing counsel.

WRK   WRK is the abbreviation for the Work Interference content scale on the MMPI-2 (see chap. 2 and Appendix W, this volume).

Z SCORES   These are standardized scores falling along a distribution in which the mean is 0 and the standard deviation is 1.

References

Note. The following references are for works cited in chapters 1 through 10. However, Appendixes C, D, E, F, and G contain lists of published works relevant to the MMPI, MMPI–2, and MMPI–A in specific forensic areas. Unless the works in Appendixes C through G were also cited in the chapters, they do not appear in the reference list that follows.

Abeles, N. (1982). Proceedings of the American Psychological Association, Incorporated, for the year 1981. Minutes of the annual meeting of the Council of Representatives. *American Psychologist, 37,* 632–666.

Ackerman, M. J., & Ackerman, M. C. (1997). Custody evaluation practices: A survey of experienced professionals (revisited). *Professional Psychology: Research and Practice, 28,* 137–145.

Adams, K. B., & Putnam, S. (1992, May). *Use of the MMPI–2 in neuropsychological evaluations.* Paper presented at a workshop conducted at the 27th Annual Symposium on Recent Developments in the Use of the MMPI (MMPI–2), Minneapolis, MN.

Adams, T. C. (1976). Some MMPI differences between first and multiple admissions with a state prison population. *Journal of Clinical Psychology, 32,* 555–558.

Adelman, R. M., & Howard A. (1984). Expert testimony on malingering: The admissibility of clinical procedures for the detection of deception. *Behavioral Sciences and the Law, 2,* 5–19.

Albrecht, N. N., Talbert, F. S., Albrecht, J. W., Boudewyns, P. A., Hyer, L. A., Touze, J., et al. (1994). A comparison of MMPI and MMPI–2 in PTSD assessment. *Journal of Clinical Psychology, 50,* 578–585.

Aldridge, N. C. (1999, December). Evaluating treatment for sex offenders: A pretest–posttest and follow-up study (treatment evaluation, recidivism). *Dissertation Abstracts International: Section B: The Sciences and Engineering, 60*(5-B), 2376.

Alexy, W. D., & Webb, P. M. (1999). Utility of the MMPI–2 in work-hardening rehabilitation. *Rehabilitation Psychology, 44,* 266–273.

Alfano, D. P., Paniak, C. E., & Finlayson, M. A. (1993). The MMPI and closed head injury: A neurocorrective approach. *Neuropsychiatry, Neuropsychology, and Behavioral Neurology, 6,* 111–116.

Alperin, J. J., Archer, R. P., & Coates, G. D. (1996). Development and effects of an MMPI–A K-correction procedure. *Journal of Personality Assessment, 67,* 155–168.

American Academy of Clinical Neuropsychology. (2001). Policy statement on the presence of third party observers in neuropsychological assessment. *Clinical Neuropsychologist, 15*(4), 433–439.

American Bar Association. (1989). *American Bar Association criminal justice mental health standards.* Washington, DC: Author.

American Board of Professional Psychology. (1984). *Policies and procedures for the creation of diplomates in professional psychology.* Columbia, MO: Author.

American Psychiatric Association. (1952). *Diagnostic and statistical manual of mental disorders.* Washington, DC: Author.

American Psychiatric Association. (1968). *Diagnostic and statistical manual of mental disorders* (2nd ed.). Washington, DC: Author.

American Psychiatric Association. (1980). *Diagnostic and statistical manual of mental disorders.* Washington, DC: Author.

American Psychiatric Association. (1987). *Diagnostic and statistical manual of mental disorders* (3rd ed., rev.). Washington, DC: Author.

American Psychiatric Association. (1994). *Diagnostic and statistical manual of mental disorders* (4th ed.). Washington, DC: Author.

American Psychological Association. (1981). Specialty guidelines for the delivery of services by clinical (counseling, industrial/organizational, and school) psychologists. *American Psychologist, 36,* 639–681.

American Psychological Association. (1983). *Publication manual of the American Psychological Association.* Washington, DC: Author.

American Psychological Association. (1985). *Standards for educational and psychological testing.* Washington, DC: Author.

American Psychological Association. (1986a). *Accreditation handbook.* Washington, DC: Author.

American Psychological Association. (1986b). *Guidelines for computer-based tests and interpretations.* Washington, DC: Author.

American Psychological Association. (1987a). *Casebook on ethical principles of psychologists.* Washington, DC: Author.

American Psychological Association. (1987b). *General guidelines for providers of psychological services.* Washington, DC: Author.

American Psychological Association. (1987c). Model Act for State Licensure of Psychologists. *American Psychologist, 42,* 696–703.

American Psychological Association. (1992). Ethical principles of psychologists and code of conduct. *American Psychologist, 47,* 1597–1611.

American Psychological Association. (1993). *Guidelines for ethical conduct in the care and use of animals.* Washington, DC: Author.

American Psychological Association. (2002). Ethical principles of psychologists and code of conduct. *American Psychologist, 57,* 1060–1073.

American Psychological Association. (2005). *HIPAA security rule online compliance workbook.* Retrieved October 13, 2005, from http://www.apapractice. org/apo/hipaa.html

American Psychological Association, American Educational Research Association, and National Council on Measurement in Education. (1999). *Standards for educational and psychological testing.* Washington, DC: Author.

American Psychological Society. (1990). American Psychological Society. *Psychological Science, 1,* 311.

Anastasi, A., & Urbine, S. (1997). *Psychological testing.* New York: Prentice Hall.

Anderson, W., & Holcomb, W. (1983). Accused murderers: Five MMPI personality types. *Journal of Clinical Psychology, 39,* 761–768.

Anderson, W. P., Kunce, J. T., & Rich, B. (1979). Sex offenders: Three personality types. *Journal of Clinical Psychology, 35*(3), 671–676.

Anthony, N. (1971). Comparison of clients' standard, exaggerated, and matching MMPI profiles. *Journal of Consulting and Clinical Psychology, 38,* 100–103.

Arbisi, P. A. (2006). Use of the MMPI–2 in personal injury and disability evaluations. In J. N. Butcher (Ed.), *MMPI–2: A practioner's guide* (pp. 407–441). Washington, DC: American Psychological Association.

Arbisi, P., & Ben-Porath, Y. S. (1995). An MMPI–2 infrequency scale for use with psychopathological populations: The Infrequency–Psychopathology Scale F(p). *Psychological Assessment, 7,* 424–431.

Arbisi, P., & Ben-Porath, Y. S. (1997). Characteristics of the MMPI–2 F(p) scale as a function of diagnosis in an inpatient sample of veterans. *Psychological Assessment, 9,* 102–105.

Arbisi, P. A., Ben-Porath, Y. S., & McNulty, J. L. (2003). Empirical correlates of common MMPI–2 two-point codes in male psychiatric inpatients. *Assessment, 10*(3), 237–247.

Arbisi, P. A., & Butcher, J. N. (2004a). Failure of the FBS to predict malingering of somatic symptoms: Response to critiques by Greve and Bianchini and Lees Haley and Fox. *Archives of Clinical Neuropsychology, 19*(3), 341–345.

Arbisi, P. A., & Butcher, J. N. (2004b). Psychometric perspectives on detection of malingering of pain: The use of the MMPI–2. *Clinical Journal of Pain, 20,* 383–398.

Arbisi, P., & Butcher, J. N. (2004c). Relationship between personality and health symptoms: Use of the MMPI–2 in medical assessments. *International Journal of Health and Clinical Psychology, 4,* 571–595.

Arbisi, P. A., Murdoch, M., Fortier, L., & McNulty, J. (2004). MMPI–2 validity and award of service connection for PTSD during the VA compensation and pension evaluation. *Psychological Services, 1*(1), 56–67.

Arbisi, P. A., & Seime, R. J. (2006). Use of the MMPI–2 in medical settings. In J. N. Butcher (Ed.), *MMPI–2: A practioner's guide* (pp. 273–299). Washington, DC: American Psychological Association.

Arce, R., del Carmen Pampillon, M., & Farina, F. (2002). *Desarrollo y evaluacion de un procedimiento empirico para deteccion de la simulacion de enajenacion mental en el contexto legal* [Development and assessment of an empirical procedure for detecting simulated mental insanity in the legal context]. *Anuario de Psicologia, 33*(3), 385–408.

Archer, R. P. (1989). Use of the MMPI with adolescents in forensic settings. *Forensic Reports, 2,* 65–87.

Archer, R. P. (1997a). Future directions for the MMPI–A: Research and clinical issues. *Journal of Personality Assessment, 68,* 95–109.

Archer, R. (1997b). *MMPI–A: Assessing adolescent psychopathology.* Hillsdale, NJ: Erlbaum.

Archer, R. P. (2005). *MMPI–A: Assessing adolescent psychopathology.* Mahway, NJ: Erlbaum.

Archer, R. P., Fontaine, J., & McCrae, R. R. (1998). Effects of two MMPI–2 validity scales on basic relations to external criteria. *Journal of Personality Assessment, 70,* 87–102.

Archer, R. P., Griffin, R., & Aiduk, R. (1995). Clinical correlates for ten common code types. *Journal of Personality Assessment, 65,* 391–408.

Archer, R. P., Handel, R. W., Lynch, K. D., & Elkins, D. E. (2002). MMPI–A validity scale uses and limitations in detecting varying levels of random responding. *Journal of Personality Assessment, 78,* 417–431.

Arkes, H. R., Saville, P. D., Wortmann, R. L., & Harkness, A. R. (1981). Hindsight bias among physicians weighing the likelihood of diagnoses. *Journal of Applied Psychology, 66,* 252–254.

Armentrout, J. A., & Hauer, A. L. (1978). MMPIs of rapists of adults, rapists of children, and non-rapist sex offenders. *Journal of Clinical Psychology, 34*(2), 330–332.

Arnold, P. D. (1970). *Recurring MMPI two-point codes of marriage counselors and "normal" couples with implications for interpreting marital interaction behavior.* Unpublished doctoral dissertation, University of Minnesota, Minneapolis.

Asch, S. E. (1956). Studies of independence and conformity: I. A minority of one against a unanimous majority. *Psychological Monographs, 70*(9, Whole No. 416).

Atlis, M. M., Hahn, J., & Butcher, J. N. (2006). Computer-based assessment with the MMPI–2. In J. N. Butcher (Ed.), *MMPI–2: A practioner's guide* (pp. 445–476). Washington, DC: American Psychological Association.

Axelrod, B., Barth, J., Faust, D., Fisher, J., Heilbronner, R., Larrabee, G., et al. (2000). Presence of third party observers during neuropsychological testing: Official statement of the National Academy of Neuropsychology. *Archives of Clinical Neuropsychology, 15*(5), 379–380.

Baer, R. A., & Miller, J. (2002). Underreporting of psychopathology on the MMPI–2: A meta-analytic review. *Psychological Assessment, 14,* 16–26.

Baer, R., & Sekirnjak, G. (1997). Detection of underreporting on the MMPI–2 in a clinical population: Effects of information about validity scales. *Journal of Personality Assessment, 69,* 555–567.

Baer, R. A., Wetter, M. W., & Berry, D. T. R. (1992). Detection of underreporting of psychopathology on the MMPI: A meta analysis. *Clinical Psychology Review, 12,* 509–525.

Baer, R., Wetter, M., & Berry, D. T. R. (1995). Effects of information about validity scales on underreporting of symptoms on the MMPI–2: An analog investigation. *Assessment, 2,* 189–199.

Baer, R. A., Wetter, M. W., Nichols, D., Greene, R., & Berry, D. T. (1995). Sensitivity of MMPI–2 validity scales to underreporting of symptoms. *Psychological Assessment, 7,* 419–423.

Bagby, R. M., & Marshall, M. B. (2004). Assessing underreporting response bias on the *MMPI–2. Assessment, 11,* 115–126.

Bagby, R. M., Marshall, M. B., Basso, M. R., Nicholson, R. A., Bacchiochi, J., & Miller, L. S. (2005). Distinguishing bipolar depression, major depression, and schizophrenia with the MMPI–2 clinical and content scales. *Journal of Personality Assessment, 84,* 89–95.

Bagby, R. M., Marshall, M. B., Bury, A. B., & Bacchiochi, J. R. (2006). Assessing underreporting and overreporting response style on the MMPI–2. In J. N. Butcher (Ed.), *MMPI–2: A practitioner's guide* (pp. 39–69). Washington, DC: American Psychological Association.

Bagby, R. M., Nicholson, R. A., Bacchiochi, J. R., Ryder, A. G., & Bury, A. S. (2002). The predictive capacity of the MMPI–2 and PAI validity scales and indexes to detect coached and uncoached feigning. *Journal of Personality Assessment, 78,* 69–86.

Bagby, R. M., Nicholson, R. A., Rogers, R., Buis, T., Seeman, M. V., & Rector, N. A. (1997). Effectiveness of the MMPI–2 validity indicators in the detection of defensive responding in clinical and nonclinical samples. *Psychological Assessment, 9,* 406–413.

Bagby, R. M., Rogers, R., Buis, T., & Kalemba, V. (1994). Malingered and defensive response styles on the MMPI–2: An examination of validity scales. *Assessment, 1,* 31–38.

Bagby, R. M., Rogers, R., Buis, T., Nicholson, R. A., Cameron, S. L., Rector, N. A., et al. (1997). Detecting feigned depression and schizophrenia on the MMPI–2. *Journal of Personality Assessment, 68,* 650–664.

Bakan, P. (1978). Two streams of consciousness: A typological approach. In K. S. Pope & J. L. Singer (Eds.), *The stream of consciousness: Scientific investigations into the flow of human experience* (pp. 159–184). New York: Plenum Press.

Baldwin, K., & Roys, D. T. (1998). Factors associated with denial in a sample of alleged adult sexual offenders. *Sexual Abuse: Journal of Research and Treatment, 10*(3), 211–226.

Bank, S. C., & Poythress, N. G. (1982). The elements of persuasion in expert testimony. *Journal of Psychiatry and Law, 10,* 173–204.

Barnard, C. P., & Jenson, G. (1984). Child custody evaluations: A rational process for an emotion-laden event. *American Journal of Family Therapy, 12*(2), 61–67.

Barrett, R. K. (1973). *Relationship of emotional disorder to marital maladjustment and disruption*. Unpublished doctoral dissertation, Kent State University, Kent, OH.

Barry, J. R., Anderson, H. E., & Thomas, O. R. (1967). MMPI characteristics of alcoholic males who are well and poorly adjusted to marriage. *Journal of Clinical Psychology, 23,* 355–360.

Barthlow, D. L., Graham, J. R., Ben-Porath, Y. S, & McNulty, J. L. (1999). Incremental validity of the MMPI–2 content scales in an outpatient mental health setting. *Psychological Assessment, 11,* 39–47.

Barthlow, D. L., Graham, J. R., Ben-Porath, Y. S., & McNulty, J. L. (2004). Construct validity of the MMPI–2 college maladjustment (*Mt*) scale. *Assessment, 11*(3), 251–262.

Barthlow, D. L., Graham, J., Ben-Porath, Y. S., Tellegen, A. M., & McNulty, J. L. (2002). The appropriateness of the MMPI–2 *K* correction. *Assessment, 9,* 219–229.

Barton, W. A. (1990). *Recovering for psychological injuries*. Washington, DC: Association of Trial Lawyers of America.

Bathurst, K., Gottfried, A. W., & Gottfried, A. E. (1997). Normative data for the MMPI–2 in child litigation. *Psychological Assessment, 9,* 205–211.

Bazelon, D. L. (1974). Psychiatrists and the adversary process. *Scientific American, 230,* 8–23.

Bell, B. E., & Loftus, E. F. (1985). Vivid persuasion in the courtroom. *Journal of Personality Assessment, 49,* 659–664.

Belli, M. M., & Carlova, J. (1986). *Belli for your malpractice defense*. Oradell, NJ: Medical Economics Books.

Bender, L. (1938). A visual motor gestalt test and its clinical use. *Research Monographs of the American Orthopsychiatric Association, 3,* x–176.

Beniak, T., Heck, D., & Erdahl, P. E. (1992, May). *Intractable epilepsy: MMPI and MMPI–2 profiles*. Paper presented at the 27th Annual Symposium on Recent Developments in the Use of the MMPI (MMPI–2), Minneapolis, MN.

Ben-Porath, Y. S. (2003). Introducing the MMPI–2 Restructured Clinical (*RC*) Scales. *SPA Exchange, 15,* 16–17, 23.

Ben-Porath, Y. S., & Butcher, J. N. (1989a). The comparability of MMPI and MMPI–2 scales and profiles. *Psychological Assessment, 1,* 345–347.

Ben-Porath, Y. S., & Butcher, J. N. (1989b). Psychometric stability of rewritten MMPI items. *Journal of Personality Assessment, 53,* 645–653.

Ben-Porath, Y. S., Butcher, J. N., & Graham, J. R. (1991). Contribution of the MMPI–2 scales to the differential diagnosis of schizophrenia and major depression. *Psychological Assessment, 3,* 634–640.

Ben-Porath, Y. S., & Forbey, J. D. (2003). *Non-gendered norms for the MMPI–2*. Minneapolis: University of Minnesota Press.

Ben-Porath, Y. S., & Forbey, J. D. (2004, May). *Detrimental effects of the K correction on clinical scale validity*. Paper presented at the 39th Annual Symposium on Recent Developments on the MMPI–2/MMPI–A, Minneapolis, MN.

Ben-Porath, Y. S., McCully, E., & Almagor, M. (1993). Incremental validity of the MMPI–2 content scales in the assessment of personality and psychopathology by self-report. *Journal of Personality Assessment, 61,* 557–575.

Ben-Porath, Y. S., Shondrick, D. D., & Stafford, K. P. (1995). MMPI–2 and race in a forensic diagnostic sample. *Criminal Justice and Behavior, 22,* 19–32.

Ben-Porath, Y. S., Slutske, W. S., & Butcher, J. N. (1989). A real-data simulation of computerized administration of the MMPI. *Psychological Assessment, 1,* 18–22.

Ben-Porath, Y. S., & Tellegen, A. (1992). Continuity and changes in MMPI–2 validity indicators: Points of clarification. *MMPI–2 News and Profiles 3*(2), 6–8.

Berry, D. T. R. (1995). Detecting distortion in forensic evaluations with the MMPI–2. In Y. S. Ben-Porath, J. R. Graham, G. C. N. Hall, R. D. Hirschman, & M. S. Zargoza (Eds.), *Forensic applications of the MMPI–2* (pp. 82–102). Thousand Oaks, CA: Sage.

Berry, D. T. R., Adams, J. J., Smith, G. T., Greene, R., Sekirnjak, G. C., Wieland, G., et al. (1997). MMPI–2 clinical scales and two-point codes: Impact of varying levels of omitted items. *Psychological Assessment, 9,* 158–160.

Berry, D. T., Baer, R. A., & Harris, M. J. (1991). Detection of malingering on the MMPI: A meta-analysis. *Clinical Psychology Review, 11,* 585–591.

Berry, D., & Butcher, J. N. (1997). Detection of feigning of head injury symptoms on the MMPI–2. In C. Reynolds (Ed.), *Detection of malingering in head injury litigation* (pp. 209–238). New York: Plenum Press.

Berry, D. T., Wetter, M. W., Baer, R. A., Larsen, L., Clark, C., & Monroe, K. (1992). MMPI–2 random responding indices: Validation using a self-report methodology. *Psychological Assessment, 4,* 340–345.

Berry, D. T., Wetter, M. W., Baer, R. A., Widiger, T. A., Sumpter, J. C., Reynolds, S. K., et al. (1991). Detection of random responding on the MMPI–2: Utility of *F,* back *F,* and *VRIN* scales. *Psychological Assessment, 3,* 418–423.

Berry, D. T. R., Wetter, M. W., Baer, R. A., Youngjohn, J., Gass, C. S., Lamb, D. G., et al. (1995). Overreporting of closed-head injury symptoms on the MMPI-2. *Psychological Assessment, 7,* 517–523.

Binder, L. M., & Rohling, M. L. (1996). Money matters: A meta-analytic review of the effects of financial incentives on recovery after closed head injury. *American Journal of Psychiatry, 153,* 7–10.

Black, J. B., & Bower, G. H. (1979). Episodes as chunks in narrative memory. *Journal of Verbal Learning and Verbal Behavior, 18,* 309–318.

Blackburn, R. (1968). Personality in relation to extreme aggression in psychiatric offenders. *British Journal of Psychiatry, 114,* 821–828.

Blake, D. D., Penk, W. E., Mori, D. L., Kleespies, P. M., Walsh, S. S., & Keane, T. M. (1992). Validity and clinical scale comparisons between the MMPI and MMPI-2 with psychiatric patients. *Psychological Reports, 70,* 323–332.

Blanchard, D. D., McGrath, R. E., Pogge, D. L., & Khadivi, A. (2003). A comparison of the PAI and MMPI-2 as predictors of faking bad in college students. *Journal of Personality Assessment, 80,* 197–205.

Blau, T. H. (1984a). Psychological tests in the courtroom. *Professional Psychology, 15,* 176–186.

Blau, T. H. (1984b). *The psychologist as expert witness.* New York: Wiley-Interscience.

Block, J. (1965). *The challenge of response sets: Unconfounding meaning, acquiescence, and social desirability in the MMPI.* New York: Appleton-Century-Crofts.

Bloom, B. L. (1992). Computer-assisted psychological intervention: A review and commentary. *Clinical Psychology Review, 12,* 169–197.

Bloomquist, M. L., & Harris, W. G. (1984). Measuring family functioning with the MMPI: A reliability and concurrent validity study of three MMPI family scales. *Journal of Clinical Psychology, 40,* 1209–1214.

Boardman, A. F. (1996, June). A comparative investigation of insanity acquittees and unsuccessful insanity evaluatees. *Dissertation Abstracts International: Section B: The Sciences and Engineering, 56*(12-B), 7038.

Bobb, P. (1992, March). *Ultimate advocacy course: Art of persuasion.* Paper presented at the Association of Trial Lawyers of America Workshop, Washington, DC.

Boccaccini, M. T., & Brodsky, S. (1999). Diagnostic test usage by forensic psychologists in emotional injury cases. *Professional Psychology: Research and Practice, 30,* 253–259.

Boehnert, C. E. (1987a). Characteristics of those evaluated for insanity. *Journal of Psychiatry and Law, 15,* 229–246.

Boehnert, C. E. (1987b). Typology of men unsuccessfully raising the insanity defense. *Journal of Psychiatry and Law, 15*(3), 417–424.

Boer, D. P., Tough, S., & Haaven, J. (2004). Assessment of risk manageability of intellectually disabled sex offenders. *Journal of Applied Research in Intellectual Disabilities, 17,* 275–283.

Bohn, M. J. (1979). Management classification for young adult inmates. *Federal Probation, 43,* 53–59.

Boies, D. (2004). *Courting justice.* New York: Miramax Books.

Booth, R. J., & Howell, R. J. (1980). Classification of prison inmates with the MMPI: An extension and validation of the Megargee typology. *Criminal Justice and Behavior, 7,* 407–422.

Borum, R., & Grisso, T. (1995). Psychological test use in criminal forensic evaluations. *Professional Psychology: Research and Practice, 26,* 465–473.

Bosquet, M., & Egeland, B. (2000). Predicting parent behaviors from antisocial practices content scale scores of the MMPI-2 administered during pregnancy. *Journal of Personality Assessment, 74,* 146–162.

Bower, G. H., & Clark, M. C. (1969). Narrative stories as mediators for serial learning. *Psychonomic Science, 14,* 181–182.

Bower, G. H., & Morrow, D. G. (1990). Mental models in narrative comprehension. *Science, 247,* 44–48.

Bowler, R. M., Rauch, S. S., Becker, C. H., Hawes, A., & Cone, J. D. (1989). Three patterns of MMPI profiles following neurotoxin exposure. *American Journal of Forensic Psychology, 7,* 15–31.

Boyle, G. J. (1996). Psychometric limitations of the Personality Assessment Inventory: A reply to Morey's. *Journal of Psychopathology and Behavioral Assessment, 18*(2), 197–204.

Brauer, B. A. (1992). The signer effect on MMPI performance of deaf respondents. *Journal of Personality Assessment, 58,* 380–388.

Brauer, B. A., Braden, J. P., Pollard, R. Q., & Hardy-Braz, S. T. (1998). Hearing impairments and test interpretation. In J. H. Sandoval, C. L. Frisby, K. F. Geisinger, J. Ramos-Grenier, & J. Dowd-Scheuneman (Eds.), *Test interpretation and diversity: Achieving equity in assessment* (pp. 297–315). Washington, DC: American Psychological Association.

Brems, C., & Lloyd, P. (1995). Validation of the MMPI-2 Low Self-Esteem content scale. *Journal of Personality Assessment, 65,* 550–556.

Briere, J., & Zaidi, L. Y. (1989). Sexual abuse histories and sequelae in female psychiatric emergency room patients. *American Journal of Psychiatry, 146,* 1602–1606.

Brodsky, S. L. (1989). Advocacy in the guise of scientific objectivity: An examination of Faust and Ziskin. *Computers in Human Behavior, 5,* 261–264.

Brodsky S. L. (1991). *Testifying in court: Guidelines and maxims for the expert witness.* Washington, DC: American Psychological Association.

Brooten, K. E., & Chapman, S. (1987). *Malpractice: A guide to avoidance and treatment.* New York: Grune & Stratton.

Brophy, A. L. (1995). Educational level, occupation, and the MMPI–2 F-K index. *Psychological Reports, 77*(1), 175–178.

Brozek, J., Franklin, J. C., Guetzkow, H., & Keys, A. (1947). Recovery after 12 weeks of controlled nutritional rehabilitation following experimental semistarvation in man. Part I. Experimental design and physical changes. *American Psychologist, 2,* 329–330.

Brozek, J. H., & Schiele B. (1948). Clinical significance of the Minnesota Multiphasic F scale evaluated in experimental neurosis. *American Journal of Psychiatry, 105,* 259–266.

Bruck, M. (1998). The trials and tribulations of a novice expert witness. In S. J. Ceci & H. Hembrooke (Eds.), *Expert witnesses in child abuse cases: What can and should be said in court* (pp. 85–104). Washington, DC: American Psychological Association.

Brunetti, D. G., Schlottman, R. S., Scott, A. B., & Hollrah, J. L. (1998). Instructed faking and MMPI–2 response latencies: The potential for assessing response validity. *Journal of Clinical Psychology, 34,* 143–153.

Buechley, R., & Ball, H. (1952). A new test of "validity" for the group MMPI. *Journal of Consulting Psychology, 16,* 299–301.

Burgess, J. A. (1984). Principles and techniques of cross-examination. In B. G. Warschaw (Ed.), *The trial masters: A handbook of strategies and techniques that win cases* (pp. 249–255). Englewood Cliffs, NJ: Prentice Hall.

Burish, T. G., & Houston, B. K. (1976). Construct validity of the Lie Scale as a measure of defensiveness. *Journal of Clinical Psychology, 32,* 310–314.

Bury, A. S., & Bagby, R. M. (2002). The detection of feigned uncoached and coached posttraumatic stress disorder with the MMPI–2 in a sample of workplace accident victims. *Psychological Assessment, 14,* 472–484.

Butcher, J. N. (1972). *Objective personality assessment: Changing perspectives.* New York: Academic Press.

Butcher, J. N. (1985a). Assessing psychological characteristics of personal injury or worker's compensation litigants. *Clinical Psychologist, 38,* 84–87.

Butcher, J. N. (1985b). Current developments in MMPI use: An international perspective. In J. N. Butcher & C. D. Spielberger (Eds.), *Advances in personality assessment* (Vol. 4, pp. 83–94). Hillsdale, NJ: Erlbaum.

Butcher, J. N. (1987). *Computerized psychological assessment.* New York: Basic Books.

Butcher, J. N. (1990a). Education level and MMPI–2 measured psychopathology: A case of negligible influence. *MMPI–2 News and Profiles 1*(2) 2–3.

Butcher, J. N. (1990b). *Use of the MMPI–2 in treatment planning.* New York: Oxford University Press.

Butcher, J. N. (1992a, March). *Clinical applications of the MMPI–2.* Paper presented at a workshop at the MMPI/MMPI–2/MMPI–A Workshops & Symposia, University of Minnesota, Minneapolis.

Butcher, J. N. (1992b). *Comparison of the original MMPI, MMPI–2, and MMPI–A.* Paper presented at a workshop at the MMPI/MMPI–2/MMPI–A Workshops & Symposia, University of Minnesota, Minneapolis.

Butcher, J. N. (1992c). [Psychological assessment of airline pilot applicants: Validity and clinical scores]. Unpublished raw data, University of Minnesota, Minneapolis.

Butcher, J. N. (1994). Psychological assessment of airline pilot applicants with the MMPI–2. *Journal of Personality Assessment, 62,* 31–44.

Butcher, J. N. (1995). Personality patterns of personal injury litigants: The role of computer-based MMPI–2 evaluations. In Y. S. Ben-Porath, J. R. Graham, G. C. N. Hall, R. D. Hirschman, & M. S. Zaragoza (Eds.), *Forensic applications of the MMPI–2* (pp. 179–201). Thousand Oaks, CA: Sage.

Butcher, J. N. (1996). *International adaptations of the MMPI–2: Research and clinical applications.* Minneapolis: University of Minnesota Press.

Butcher, J. N. (1997). Frequency of MMPI–2 scores in forensic evaluations. *MMPI–2 News and Profiles, 8*(1), 2–4.

Butcher, J. N. (1998a, March). *Analysis of MMPI–2 S scale subscales to refine interpretation of "good impression."* Paper presented at the 34th Annual Conference on Recent Developments in the Use of the MMPI/MMPI–2, Clearwater, FL.

Butcher, J. N. (1998b). *User's guide to the Minnesota Report: Forensic settings.* Minneapolis, MN: National Computer Systems.

Butcher, J. N. (1999). *A beginner's guide to the MMPI–2.* Washington, DC: American Psychological Association.

Butcher, J. N. (2000a). *Basic sources on the MMPI–2.* Minneapolis, MN: University of Minnesota Press.

Butcher, J. N. (2000b). Revising psychological tests: Lessons learned from the revision of the MMPI. *Psychological Assessment, 12*(3), 263–271.

Butcher, J. N. (2004). Personality assessment without borders: Adaptation of the MMPI–2 across cultures. *Journal of Personality Assessment, 83*(2), 90–104.

Butcher, J. N. (2005). *A beginner's guide to the MMPI–2* (2nd ed.). Washington, DC: American Psychological Association.

Butcher, J. N. (2006). *MMPI–2: A practitioner's guide*. Washington, DC: American Psychological Association.

Butcher, J. N., Aldwin, C., Levenson, M., Ben-Porath, Y. S., Spiro, A., & Bossé, R. (1991). Personality and aging: A study of the MMPI–2 among elderly men. *Psychology of Aging, 6*, 361–370.

Butcher, J. N., Arbisi, P. A., Atlis, M. M., & McNulty, J. L. (2003). The construct validity of the Lees–Haley Fake Bad Scale (FBS): Does this scale measure malingering and feigned emotional distress? *Archives of Clinical Neuropsychology, 18*, 473–485.

Butcher, J. N., Atlis, M. M., & Fang, L. (2000). Effect of altered instructions on the MMPI–2 profiles of college students who are not motivated to distort their responses. *Journal of Personality Assessment, 75*, 492–501.

Butcher, J. N., Atlis, M., & Hahn, J. (2003). Assessment with the MMPI–2: Research base and future developments. In D. Segal (Ed.), *Comprehensive handbook of psychological assessment* (pp. 30–38). New York: Wiley.

Butcher, J. N., Berah, E., Ellertsen, B., Miach, P., Lim, J., Nezami, E., et al. (1998). Objective personality assessment: Computer-based MMPI–2 interpretation in international clinical settings. In C. Belar (Ed.), *Comprehensive clinical psychology: Sociocultural and individual differences* (pp. 277–312). New York: Elsevier.

Butcher, J. N., Cabiya, J. J., Lucio, E., Pena, L., Scott, R., & Ruben, D. (1998). *Hispanic version of the MMPI–A (manual supplement)*. Minneapolis: University of Minnesota Press.

Butcher, J. N., Cheung, F. M., & Lim, J. (2003). Use of the MMPI–2 with Asian populations. *Psychological Assessment, 15*, 248–256.

Butcher, J. N., Dahlstrom, W. G., Graham, J. R., Tellegen, A., & Kaemmer, B. (1989). *Minnesota Multiphasic Personality Inventory–2 (MMPI–2): Manual for administration and scoring*. Minneapolis: University of Minnesota Press.

Butcher, J. N., Derksen, J., Sloore, H., & Sirigatti, S. (2003). Objective personality assessment of people in diverse cultures: European adaptations of the MMPI–2. *Behavior Research and Therapy, 41*, 819–840.

Butcher, J. N., Egli, E. A., Shiota, N. K., & Ben-Porath, Y. S. (1988). *Psychological interventions with refugees*. Rockville, MD: National Institute of Mental Health.

Butcher, J. N., Ellertsen, B., Ubostad, B., Bubb, E, Lucio, E., Lim, J., et al. (2000). *International case studies on the MMPI–A: An objective approach*. Minneapolis: University of Minnesota Press.

Butcher, J. N., Graham, J. R., & Ben-Porath, Y. S. (1995). Methodological problems and issues in MMPI/MMPI–2/MMPI–A research. *Psychological Assessment, 7*, 320–329.

Butcher, J. N., Graham, J. R., Ben-Porath, Y. S., Tellegen, Y. S., Dahlstrom, W. G., & Kaemmer, B. (2001). *Minnesota Multiphasic Personality Inventory–2: Manual for administration and scoring* (Rev. ed.). Minneapolis: University of Minnesota Press.

Butcher, J. N., Graham, J. R., Dahlstrom, W. G., & Bowman, E. (1990). The MMPI–2 with college students. *Journal of Personality Assessment, 54*, 1–15.

Butcher, J. N., Graham, J. R., Williams, C. L., & Ben-Porath, Y. S. (1990). *Development and use of the MMPI–2 content scales*. Minneapolis: University of Minnesota Press.

Butcher, J. N., Hamilton, C. K., Rouse, S. V., & Cumella, E. J. (in press). The Deconstruction of the *Hy* scale of MMPI–2: Failure of RC3 in measuring somatic symptom expression. *Journal of Personality Assessment*.

Butcher, J. N., & Han, K. (1995). Development of an MMPI–2 scale to assess the presentation of self in a superlative manner: The *S* scale. In J. N. Butcher & C. D. Spielberger (Eds.), *Advances in personality assessment* (Vol. 10, pp. 25–50). Hillsdale, NJ: Erlbaum.

Butcher, J. N., & Harlow, T. (1987). Psychological assessment in personal injury cases. In A. Hess & I. Weiner (Eds.), *Handbook of forensic psychology* (pp. 128–154). New York: Wiley.

Butcher, J. N., & Hostetler, K. (1990). Abbreviating MMPI item administration: What can be learned from the MMPI for the MMPI–2? *Psychological Assessment, 2*, 12–21.

Butcher, J. N., Jeffrey, T., Cayton, T. G., Colligan, S., DeVore, J., & Minnegawa, R. (1990). A study of active duty military personnel with the MMPI–2. *Military Psychology, 2*, 47–61.

Butcher, J. N., Keller, L. S., & Bacon, S. F. (1985). Current developments and future directions in computerized personality assessment. *Journal of Consulting and Clinical Psychology, 53*, 803–815.

Butcher, J. N., Kendall, P. C., & Holmback, G. (1999). *Handbook of research methods in clinical psychology* (2nd ed.). New York: Wiley.

Butcher, J. N., & Miller, K. B. (1998). Personality assessment in personal injury litigation. In A. Hess & I. Weiner (Eds.), *Handbook of forensic psychology* (pp. 104–126). New York: Wiley.

Butcher, J. N., & Miller, K. B. (2006). Personality assessment in personal injury litigation. In A. Hess & I. B. Weiner (Eds.), *Handbook of forensic psychology* (3rd ed., pp. 140–166). New York: Wiley.

Butcher, J. N., Mineka, S., & Hooley, J. (2004). *Abnormal psychology and modern life* (12th ed.). Boston: Addison Wesley Longman.

Butcher, J. N., Morfitt, R., Rouse, S. V., & Holden, R. R. (1997). Reducing MMPI–2 defensiveness: The effect of specialized instructions on retest validity in a job applicant sample. *Journal of Personality Assessment, 68,* 385–401.

Butcher, J. N., Nezami, E., & Exner, J. (1998). Psychological assessment of people in diverse cultures. In S. Kazarian & D. R. Evans (Eds.), *Cross cultural clinical psychology* (pp. 61–105). New York: Oxford University Press.

Butcher, J. N., & Owen, P. (1978). Survey of personality inventories: Recent research developments and contemporary issues. In B. Wolman (Ed.), *Handbook of clinical diagnosis* (pp. 475–546). New York: Plenum Press.

Butcher, J. N., & Pancheri, P. (1976). *Handbook of cross-national MMPI research.* Minneapolis: University of Minnesota Press.

Butcher, J. N., Perry, J., & Atlis, M. (2000). Validity of computer-based interpretations: Current status. *Psychological Assessment, 12,* 6–18.

Butcher, J. N., Perry, J., & Hahn, J. (2004). Computers in clinical assessment: Historical developments, present status, and future challenges. *Journal of Clinical Psychology, 60,* 331–346.

Butcher, J. N., & Pope, K. S. (1990). MMPI–2: A practical guide to psychometric, clinical, and ethical issues. *Independent Practitioner, 10*(1), 33–40.

Butcher, J. N., & Pope, K. S. (1992). Forensic psychology: Psychological evaluation in family custody cases—Role of the MMPI–2 and MMPI–A. *Family Law News, 15,* 25–28.

Butcher, J. N., Rouse, S. V., & Perry, J. N. (2000). Empirical description of psychopathology in therapy clients: Correlates of MMPI–2 scales. In J. N. Butcher (Ed.), *Basic sources on the MMPI–2* (pp. 487–500). Minneapolis: University of Minnesota Press.

Butcher, J. N., & Tellegen, A. (1966). Objections to MMPI items. *Journal of Consulting Psychology, 30,* 527–534.

Butcher, J. N., & Tellegen, A. (1978). Common methodological problems in MMPI research. *Journal of Consulting and Clinical Psychology, 46,* 620–628.

Butcher, J. N., Tsai, J., Coelho, S., & Nezami, E. (2006). Cross cultural applications of the MMPI–2. In J. N. Butcher (Ed.), *MMPI–2: A practioner's guide* (pp. 505–537). Washington, DC: American Psychological Association.

Butcher, J. N., & Williams, C. L. (1992a). *Essentials of MMPI–2 and MMPI–A interpretation.* Minneapolis: University of Minnesota Press.

Butcher, J. N., & Williams, C. L. (1992b). *User's guide to the Minnesota Report: Adolescent clinical system.* Minneapolis, MN: National Computer Systems.

Butcher, J. N., & Williams, C. L. (2000). *MMPI–2/MMPI–A: Essentials of interpretation* (2nd ed.). Minneapolis: University of Minnesota Press.

Butcher, J. N., Williams, C. L., Graham, J. R., Archer, R., Tellegen, A., Ben-Porath, Y. S., et al. (1992). *MMPI–A manual for administration, scoring, and interpretation.* Minneapolis: University of Minnesota Press.

Cairns, D., Mooney, V., & Crane, P. (1984). Spinal pain rehabilitation: Inpatient and outpatient treatment results and development of predictors for outcome. *Spine, 9,* 91–95.

Camara, W. J., Nathan, J. S., & Puente, A. E. (2000). Psychological test usage: Implications in professional psychology. *Professional Psychology: Research and Practice, 31,* 141–154.

Capwell, D. F. (1945). Personality patterns of adolescent girls, II. Delinquents and non-delinquents. *Journal of Applied Psychology, 29,* 284–297.

Carlson, D. A. J. (2001). Computerized vs. written administration of the MMPI–A in clinical and non-clinical settings. *Dissertation Abstracts International: Section B: The Sciences and Engineering, 62*(2-B), 1130.

Carragee, E. J. (2001). Psychological screening in the surgical treatment of lumbar disc herniation. *Clinical Journal of Pain, 17,* 215–219.

Cartwright, R. E. (1984). Winning psychological principles in summation. In B. G. Warshaw (Ed.), *The trial masters: A handbook of strategies and tactics that win cases* (pp. 338–349). Englewood Cliffs, NJ: Prentice Hall.

Cashel, M. L., Ovaert, L., & Holliman, N. G. (2000). Evaluating PTSD in incarcerated male juveniles with the MMPI–A: An exploratory analysis. *Journal of Clinical Psychology, 56,* 1535–1549.

Caudill, B., & Pope, K. S. (1995). *Law and mental health professionals: California.* Washington, DC: American Psychological Association.

Chandler, M. J., Greenspan, S., & Barenboim, C. (1973). Judgments of intentionality of response to videotapes and verbally presented moral dilemmas: The medium is the message. *Child Development, 44,* 315–320.

Chanowitz, B., & Langer, E. J. (1981). Premature cognitive commitment. *Journal of Personality and Social Psychology, 41,* 1051–1063.

Charles, S. C., & Kennedy, E. (1985). *Defendant.* New York: Free Press.

Charlton, M., Fowler, T., & Ivandick, M. J. (2006). *Law and mental health professionals: Colorado.* Washington, DC: American Psychological Association.

Charter, R. A., & Lopez, M. N. (2003). MMPI–2: Confidence intervals for random responding to the *F, F* back and *VRIN* Scales. *Journal of Clinical Psychology, 59,* 985–991.

Cheatham, C. S., & Litwack, T. R. (2003). Professionals' attitudes regarding whether a New York defendant who delusionally refuses a viable, counsel-recommended insanity defense should be found competent or incompetent to stand trial. *Journal of Psychiatry and Law, 31*(4), 433–460.

Cheung, F. M., & Song, W. Z. (1989). A review on the clinical applications of the Chinese MMPI. *Psychological Assessment, 1,* 230–237.

Cheung, F. M., Song, W. Z., & Butcher, J. N. (1991). An infrequency scale for the Chinese MMPI. *Psychological Assessment, 3,* 648–653.

Cheung, F. M., Zhao, J., & Wu, C. (1992). Chinese MMPI profiles among neurotic patients. *Psychological Assessment, 4,* 214–218.

Chisholm, S. M., Crowther, J. H., & Ben-Porath, Y. S. (1997). Selected MMPI–2 scales' ability to predict premature termination and outcome from psychotherapy. *Journal of Personality Assessment, 69,* 127–144.

Chojenackie, J. T., & Walsh, W. B. (1992). The consistency of scores and configural patterns between the MMPI and MMPI–2. *Journal of Personality Assessment, 59,* 276–289.

Choudhry, N., Fletcher, R., & Soumerai, S. (2005). Systematic review: The relationship between clinical experience and quality of health care. *Annals of Internal Medicine, 142,* 260–273.

Cigrang, J. A., & Staal, M. A. (2001). Readministration of the MMPI–2 following defensive invalidation in a military job applicant sample. *Journal of Personality Assessment, 76,* 472–481.

Claghorn, J., Hays, J. R., Webb, L., & Lewis, N. (1991, January–March). Juror personality characteristics and the insanity defense. *Forensic Reports, 4*(1), 61–65.

Clark, L. A. (1985). A consolidated version of the MMPI in Japan. In J. N. Butcher & C. D. Spielberger (Eds.), *Advances in personality assessment* (Vol. 4, pp. 95–130). Hillsdale, NJ: Erlbaum.

Clark, M. E. (1994). Interpretive limitations of the MMPI–2 Anger and Cynicism content scales. *Journal of Personality Assessment, 63,* 89–96.

Clark, M. E. (1996). MMPI–2 negative treatment indicators content and content component scales: Clinical correlates and outcome prediction for men with chronic pain. *Psychological Assessment, 8,* 32–47.

Clark, M. E., Gironda, R. J., & Young, R. W. (2003). Detection of back random responding: Effectiveness of MMPI–2 and Personality Assessment Inventory validity indices. *Psychological Assessment, 15,* 223–234.

Clark, M. W. (1997, June). Characteristics of juvenile sex offenders who admit versus those who deny their offenses. *Dissertation Abstracts International: Section B: The Sciences and Engineering, 57*(12-B), 7718.

Clawar, S. S. (1984). How to determine whether a family report is scientific. *Conciliation Courts Review, 22,* 71–76.

Clements, R., & Heintz, J. M. (2002). Diagnostic accuracy and factor structure of the *AAS* and *APS* scales of the MMPI–2. *Journal of Personality Assessment, 79,* 564–582.

Clopton, J. R., & Neuringer, C. (1977). MMPI cannot say scores: Normative data and degree of profile distortion. *Journal of Personality Assessment, 41,* 511–513.

Clopton, J. R., Shanks, D. A., & Preng, K. W. (1987). Classification accuracy of the MacAndrew scale with and without *K* corrections. *International Journal of Addictions, 22,* 1049–1051.

Cofer, C. N., Chance, J., & Judson, A. J. (1949). A study of malingering on the MMPI. *Journal of Psychology, 27,* 491–499.

Colby, F. (1989). Usefulness of the *K* correction in MMPI profiles of patients and nonpatients. *Psychological Assessment, 1,* 142–145.

Coles, R. (1973a, February 22). Shrinking history (Part 1). *New York Times Review of Books,* pp. 15–21.

Coles, R. (1973b, March 8). Shrinking history (Part 2). *New York Times Review of Books,* pp. 25–29.

Colligan, R. C., & Offord, K. P. (1991). Adolescents, the MMPI, and the issue of *K* correction: A contemporary normative study. *Journal of Clinical Psychology, 47*(5), 607–631.

Colligan, R. C., Osborne, D., Swenson, W. M., & Offord, K. P. (1983). *The MMPI: A contemporary normative study.* New York: Praeger.

Colotla, V. A., Bowman, M. L., & Shercliffe, R. J. (2001). Test–retest stability of injured workers' MMPI–2 profiles. *Psychological Assessment, 13,* 572–576.

Committee on Ethical Guidelines for Forensic Psychologists. (1991). Specialty guidelines for forensic psychologists. *Law and Human Behavior, 15,* 655–665.

Committee on Legal Issues for the American Psychological Association. (1996). Strategy for private practitioners coping with subpoenas or compelled testimony for client records or test data. *Professional Psychology: Research and Practice, 27,* 245–251.

Committee on Professional Standards of the American Psychological Association. (1984). Casebook for providers of psychological services. *American Psychologist, 39,* 663–668.

Conger, A. J., & Conger, J. C. (1996). Did too, did not!: Controversies in the construct validation of the PAI. *Journal of Psychopathology and Behavioral Assessment, 18,* 205–212.

Conger, J. J. (1976). Proceedings of the American Psychological Association, Incorporated, for the year 1975: Minutes of the annual meeting of the Council of Representatives, August 29 and September 2, 1975, Chicago, IL, and January 23–25, 1976, Washington, DC. *American Psychologist, 31,* 406–434.

Conger, J. J. (1977). Proceedings of the American Psychological Association, Incorporated, for the year 1976: Minutes of the annual meeting of the Council of Representatives, September 2 and 5, 1976, Washington, DC, and January 28–30, 1977, Washington, DC. *American Psychologist, 32,* 408–438.

Conkey, V. A. (2000). Determining the sensitivity of the MMPI–A to random responding and malingering in adolescents (Minnesota Multiphasic Personality Index, validity scales). *Dissertation Abstracts International: Section B: The Sciences and Engineering, 60*(7-B), 3608.

Conley, J. M., O'Barr, W. M., & Lind, E. A. (1978). The power of language: Presentational style in the courtroom. *Duke Law Journal, 6,* 1375–1399.

Connell, M., & Koocher, G. P. (2003). HIPAA and forensic practice. *American Psychology Law News, 23*(2), 16–19.

Constans, J. I., Lenhoff, K., & McCarthy, M. (1997). Depression subtyping in PTSD patients. *Annals of Clinical Psychiatry, 9*(4), 235–240.

Constantinou, M., Ashendorf, L., & McCaffrey, R. J. (2002). When the third party observer of a neuropsychological evaluation is an audio-recorder. *Clinical Neuropsychologist, 16*(3), 407–412.

Contini de Gonzalez, E. N., Figueroa, M. I., Cohen Imach, S., & Coronel de Pace, P. (2001). *El MMPI–A en la identificationn de rasgos psicopatologicos. Un estuido con adolescents de Tucumán* [The use of the MMPI–A in the identification of psychopathological traits in adolescents of Tucuman]. *Revista Iberoamericana de Diagnostico y Evaluacion Psicologica, 12*(2), 85–96.

Cookerly, J. R. (1974). The reduction of psychopathology as measured by the MMPI clinical scales in three forms of marriage counseling. *Journal of Marriage and Family, 36,* 332–340.

Costanzo, M., & Costanzo, S. (1992). Jury decision making in the capital penalty phase: Legal assumptions, empirical findings, and a research agenda. *Law and Human Behavior, 16,* 185–202.

Couric, E. (1988). *The trial lawyers.* New York: St. Martin's Press.

Coyle, W. C., & Heap, R. F. (1965). Interpreting the MMPI *L* scale. *Psychological Reports, 17,* 722.

Craddick, R. A. (1962). Selection of psychopathic from non-psychopathic prisoners within a Canadian prison. *Psychological Reports, 10,* 495–499.

Cripe, L., Maxwell, J. K., & Hill, E. (1995). Multivariate discrimination analysis of neurologic, pain, and psychiatric patients with the MMPI. *Journal of Clinical Psychology, 51,* 258–268.

Cronbach, L. J. (1960). *Essentials of psychological testing* (2nd ed.). New York: Harper & Row.

Cronbach, L. J. (1990). *Essentials of psychological testing* (5th ed.). New York: HarperCollins.

Dahir, V. B., Richardson, J. T., Ginsburg, G. P., Gatowski, S. I., Dobbin, S. A., & Merlino, M. L. (2005). Judicial application of *Daubert* to psychological syndrome and profile evidence: A research note. *Psychology, Public Policy, and Law, 11,* 62–82.

Dahlstrom, W. G. (1980). Altered versions of the MMPI. In W. G. Dahlstrom & L. E. Dahlstrom (Eds.), *Basic readings on the MMPI* (pp. 386–393). Minneapolis: University of Minnesota Press.

Dahlstrom, W. G. (1992). Comparability of two-point high-point code patterns from original MMPI norms to MMPI–2 norms for the restandardization sample. *Journal of Personality Assessment, 59,* 153–164.

Dahlstrom, W. G., & Archer, R. P. (2000). A shortened version of the MMPI–2. *Assessment, 7,* 131–141.

Dahlstrom, W. G., Archer, R. P., Hopkins, D. G., Jackson, E., & Dahlstrom, L. E. (1994). *Assessing the readability of the Minnesota Multiphasic Personality Inventory instruments—MMPI, MMPI–2, and MMPI–A.* Minneapolis: University of Minnesota Press.

Dahlstrom, W. G., & Dahlstrom, L. E. (1980). *Basic readings on the MMPI: A new selection on personality measurement.* Minneapolis: University of Minnesota Press.

Dahlstrom, W. G., Panton, J. H., Bain, K. P., & Dahlstrom, L. E. (1986). Utility of the Megargee–Bohn MMPI typological assignments: Study with a sample of death row inmates. *Criminal Justice and Behavior, 13,* 5–17.

Dahlstrom, W. G., Welsh, G. S., & Dahlstrom, L. E. (1972). *An MMPI handbook* (Vol. I). Minneapolis: University of Minnesota Press.

Dahlstrom, W. G., Welsh, G. S., & Dahlstrom L. E. (1975). *An MMPI handbook. Vol. 2: Research applications*. Minneapolis: University of Minnesota Press.

Dalby, J. T. (1988). Detecting faking in the pretrial psychological assessment. *American Journal of Forensic Psychology, 6,* 49–55.

Dawes, R. M. (1988a). *Rational choice in an uncertain world*. San Diego, CA: Harcourt Brace Jovanovich.

Dawes, R. M. (1988b). You can't systematize human judgment: Dyslexia. In J. Dowie & A. Alstein (Eds.), *Professional judgment: A reader in clinical decision making* (pp. 150–162). Cambridge, England: Cambridge University Press.

Dearth, C. S., Berry, D. T., Vickery, C. D., Vagnini, V. L., Baser, R. E., Orey, S. A., et al. (2005). Detection of feigned head injury symptoms on the MMPI–2 in head injured patients and community controls. *Archives of Clinical Neuropsychology, 20,* 37–48.

Deed, M. L. (1991). Court-ordered child custody evaluations: Helping or victimizing vulnerable families. *Psychotherapy, 28,* 76–84.

Deinard, A. S., Butcher, J. N., Thao, U. D., Moua Vang, S. H., & Hang, K. (1996). Development of a Hmong translation of the MMPI–2. In J. N. Butcher (Ed.), *International adaptations of the MMPI–2* (pp. 194–205). Minneapolis: University of Minnesota Press.

Demarco, A. D. (2002). MMPI–2 content scale interpretation in cases of chronic low back pain: Do adjustment differences among sufferers lead to different content scores? *Dissertation Abstracts International: Section B: The Sciences and Engineering, 62*(11-B), 5368.

Department of Health and Human Services. (2004). *The Health Insurance Portability and Accountability Act of 1996 (HIPAA)*. Retrieved October 13, 2005, from http://www.cms.hhs.gov/hipaa

Dershowitz, A. M. (1982). *The best defense*. New York: Random House.

Detrick, P., Chibnall, J. T., & Rosso, M. (2001). Minnesota Multiphasic Personality Inventory—MMPI–2 in police officer selection normative data and relation to the Inwald Personality Inventory. *Professional Psychology: Research and Practice, 32,* 484–490.

Dickman, S., & Sechrest, L. (1985). Research on memory and clinical practice. In G. Stricker & R. H. Keisner (Eds.), *From research to clinical practice: Implications of social and developmental research for psychotherapy* (pp. 15–44). New York: Plenum Press.

Didion, J. (1979). *The white album*. New York: Simon & Schuster.

Drasgow, J., & Dreher, R. (1965). Predicting client readiness for training and placement in vocational rehabilitation. *Rehabilitation Counseling Bulletin, 8,* 94–98.

Dush, D. M., Simons, L. E., Platt, M., & Nation, P. C. (1994). Psychological profiles distinquishing litigating and nonlitigating pain patients: Subtle, and not so subtle. *Journal of Personality Assessment, 62,* 299–313.

Duthie, B., & McIvor, D. (1990). A new system for cluster-coding child molester MMPI profile types. *Criminal Justice and Behavior, 17,* 199–214.

Dzioba, R. B., & Doxey, N. C. (1984). A prospective investigation into the orthopaedic and psychologic predictors of outcome of first lumbar surgery following industrial injury. *Spine, 9,* 614–623.

Eberly, R. E., Harkness, A. R., & Engdahl, B. E. (1991). An adaptational view of trauma response as illustrated by the prisoner of war experience. *Journal of Traumatic Stress, 4,* 363–380.

Edinger, J. D. (1979). Cross-validation of the Megargee MMPI typology for prisoners. *Journal of Consulting and Clinical Psychology, 47,* 234–242.

Edinger, J. D., Reuterfors, D., & Logue, P. E. (1982). Cross-validation of the Megargee MMPI typology: A study of specialized inmate populations. *Criminal Justice and Behavior, 9,* 184–203.

Edwards, A. (1957). *The social desirability variable in personality assessment and research*. New York: Dryden Press.

Egeland, B., Erickson, M., Butcher, J. N., & Ben-Porath, Y. S. (1991). MMPI–2 profiles of women at risk for child abuse. *Journal of Personality Assessment, 57,* 254–263.

Elhai, J. D. (2000). The detection of genuine and malingered posttraumatic stress disorder: An examination of fake bad indices on the MMPI–2. *Dissertation Abstracts International: Section B: The Sciences and Engineering, 61*(5-B), 2755.

Elhai, J. D., Baugher, S. N., Quevillon, R. P., Sauvageot, J., & Frueh, B. C. (2004). Psychiatric symptoms and health service utilization in rural and urban combat veterans with posttraumatic stress disorder. *Journal of Nervous and Mental Disease, 192,* 701–704.

Elhai, J. D., Flitter, J. M. K., Gold, S. N., & Sellers, A. H. (2001). Identifying subtypes of women survivors of childhood sexual abuse: An MMPI–2 cluster analysis. *Journal of Traumatic Stress, 14*(1), 157–175.

Elhai, J. D., Forbes, D., Creamer, M., McHugh, T. F., & Frueh, B. C. (2003). Clinical symptomatology of posttraumatic stress disorder-diagnosed Australian and United States Vietnam combat veterans: An MMPI–2 comparison. *Journal of Nervous and Mental Disease, 191,* 458–464.

Elhai, J. D., & Frueh, B. C. (2001). Subtypes of clinical presentations in malingerers of posttraumatic stress disorder: An MMPI–2 cluster analysis. *Assessment, 8*(1), 75–84.

Elhai, J. D., Frueh, B. C., Davis, J. L., Jacobs, G. A., & Hammer, M. B. (2003). Clinical presentations in combat veterans diagnosed with posttraumatic stress disorder. *Journal of Clinical Psychology, 59*(3), 385–397.

Elhai, J. D., Frueh, B. C., Gold, P. B., Hamner, M. B., & Gold, S. N. (2003). Posttraumatic stress, depression and dissociation as predictors of MMPI–2 Scale 8 scores in combat veterans with PTSD. *Journal of Trauma and Dissociation, 4*(1), 51–64.

Elhai, J. D., Gold, P. B., Frueh, B. C., & Gold, S. N. (2000). Cross-validation of the MMPI–2 in detecting malingered posttraumatic stress disorder. *Journal of Personality Assessment, 75,* 449–463.

Elhai, J. D., Gold, P. B., Frueh, B. C., & Gold, S. N. (2001). Cross-validation of the MMPI–2 in detecting malingered posttraumatic stress disorder: Errata. *Journal of Personality Assessment, 77,* 189.

Elhai, J. D., Gold, S. N., Mateus, L. F., & Astaphan, T. A. (2001). Scale 8 elevations on the MMPI–2 among women survivors of childhood sexual abuse: Evaluating posttraumatic stress, depression, and dissociation as predictors. *Journal of Family Violence, 16*(1), 47–57.

Elhai, J. D., Gold, S. N., Sellers, A. H., & Dorfman, W. I. (2001). The detection of malingered posttraumatic stress disorder with MMPI–2 Fake Bad indices. *Assessment, 8*(2), 221–236.

Elhai, J. D., Naifeh, J. A., Zucker, I. S., Gold, S. N., Deitsch, S. E., & Frueh, B. C. (2004). Discriminating malingered from genuine civilian posttraumatic stress disorder: A validation of three MMPI–2 infrequency scales (*F, Fp,* and *Fptsd*): Erratum. *Assessment, 11*(3), 271.

Elhai, J. D., Naifeh, J. A., Zucker, I. S., Gold, S. N., Deitsch, S. E., Frueh, B. C., et al. (2004). Discriminating malingered from genuine civilian posttraumatic stress disorder: A validation of three MMPI–2 infrequency scales (*F, Fp,* and *Fptsd*). *Assessment, 11*(2), 139–144.

Elhai, J. D., Ruggiero, K. J., Frueh, B. C., Beckham, J. C., & Gold, P. B. (2002). The Infrequency-Posttraumatic Stress Disorder Scale (*Fptsd*) for the MMPI–2: Development and initial validation with veterans presenting with combat-related PTSD. *Journal of Personality Assessment, 79,* 531–549.

Elwork, A. (1992). Psycholegal treatment and intervention: The next challenge. *Law and Human Behavior, 16,* 175–183.

Elwork, A., & Sales, B. D. (1985). Jury instructions. In S. Kassin & L. Wrightsman (Eds.), *The psychology of evidence and trial procedure* (pp. 280–297). Beverly Hills, CA: Sage.

Elwork, A., Sales, B. D., & Alfini, J. J. (1977). Juridic decisions: In ignorance of the law or in light of it? *Law and Human Behavior, 1,* 163–189.

Elwork, A., Sales, B. D., & Alfini, J. J. (1982). *Making jury instructions understandable.* Charlottesville, VA: Michie.

Emery, O. B., & Csikszentmihalyi, M. (1981). The specialization effects of cultural role models in ontogenetic development. *Child Psychiatry and Human Development, 12,* 3–18.

Endler, N. S., Parker, J. D., & Butcher, J. N. (1993). A factor analytic study of coping styles and the MMPI–2 content scales. *Journal of Clinical Psychology, 49,* 523–527.

Englert, D. R., Weed, N. C., & Watson, G. S. (2000). Convergent, discriminant, and internal properties of the Minnesota Multiphasic Personality Inventory (2nd ed.) Low Self-Esteem Content Scale. *Measurement and Evaluation in Counseling and Development, 33*(1), 42–49.

Epstein, L., & Feiner, A. H. (1979). *Countertransference.* New York: Aronson.

Erard, R. E. (2004). Release of test data under the 2002 ethics code and the HIPAA privacy rule: A raw deal or just a half-baked idea? *Journal of Personality Assessment, 82,* 23–30.

Erdberg, S. P. (1970). MMPI differences associated with sex, race, and residence in a southern sample (Doctoral dissertation, University of Alabama, 1969). *Dissertation Abstracts International, 30,* 5236B.

Erdberg, S. P. (1988, August). *How clinicians can achieve competence in testing procedures.* Paper presented at the 96th Annual Convention of the American Psychological Association, Atlanta, GA.

Erickson, B., Lind, E. A., Johnson, B. C., & O'Barr, W. M. (1978). Speech style and impression formation in a court setting: The effects of "powerful" and "powerless" speech. *Journal of Experimental Social Psychology, 14,* 266–279.

Erickson, W., Luxenberg, M., Walbeck, N., & Seely, R. (1987). The frequency of MMPI two-point code types among sex offenders. *Journal of Consulting and Clinical Psychology, 55,* 566–570.

Ethics codes & practice guidelines for assessment, therapy, counseling, & forensic practice. (2005). Retrieved October 13, 2005, from http://kspope.com/ethcode/index.php

Evans, J. (1989). *Bias in human reasoning: Causes and consequences.* Hillsdale, NJ: Erlbaum.

Evans, R. W. (1994). The effects of litigation on treatment outcome with personal injury patients. *American Journal of Forensic Psychology, 12*(4), 19–34.

Exner, J. E. (1991). *The Rorschach: A comprehensive system* (Vol. 2). New York: Wiley.

Exner, J., McDowell, E., Pabst, J., Stackman, W., & Kirk, L. (1963). On the detection of willful falsification in the MMPI. *Journal of Consulting Psychology, 27*, 91–94.

Eyde, L., Kowal, D., & Fishburne, F. J. (1991). In T. B. Gutkin & S. L. Wise (Eds.), *The computer & the decision-making process* (pp. 75–123). Hillsdale, NJ: Erlbaum.

Fairbank, J. A., Keane, T. M., & Malloy, P. F. (1983). Some preliminary data on the psychological characteristics of Vietnam veterans with posttraumatic stress disorders. *Journal of Consulting and Clinical Psychology, 51*, 912–919.

Fairbank, J. A., McCaffrey, R., & Keane, T. M. (1985). Psychometric detection of fabricated symptoms of post-traumatic stress disorder. *American Journal of Psychiatry, 142*, 501–503.

Faschingbauer, T. R. (1974). A 166-item short form for the group MMPI: The FAM. *Journal of Consulting and Clinical Psychology, 42*, 645–655.

Faschingbauer, T. R. (1979). The future of the MMPI. In C. S. Newmark (Ed.), *MMPI: Clinical and research trends* (pp. 201–215). New York: Praeger.

Fernberger, S. W. (1932). The American Psychological Association: A historical summary, 1892–1930. *Psychological Bulletin, 29*, 1–89.

Fersch, E. A. (1980). Ethical issues for psychologists in court settings. In J. Monahan (Ed.), *Who is the client? The ethics psychological intervention in the criminal justice system* (pp. 43–62). Washington, DC: American Psychological Association.

Fink, A., & Butcher, J. N. (1972). Reducing objections to personality inventories with special instructions. *Educational and Psychological Measurements, 27*, 631–639.

Finn, S., & Butcher, J. N. (1990). Clinical objective personality assessment. In M. Hersen, A. E. Kazdin, & A. S. Bellack (Eds.), *The clinical psychology handbook* (pp. 362–373). New York: Pergamon.

Finn, S., & Tonsager, M. (1992). Therapeutic effects of providing MMPI–2 test feedback to college students awaiting therapy. *Psychological Assessment, 4*, 278–287.

Fischer, C. T. (1985). *Individualized psychological assessment*. Belmont, CA: Brooks/Cole.

Fischer, C. T. (2004). Individualized assessment moderates the impact of HIPAA privacy rules. *Journal of Personality Assessment, 82*, 35–38.

Fischoff, B. (1982). For those condemned to study the past: Heuristics and biases in hindsight. In D. Kahneman, P. Slovic, & A. Tversky (Eds.), *Judgment under uncertainty: Heuristics and biases* (pp. 335–351). Cambridge, England: Cambridge University Press.

Fjordbak, T. (1985). Clinical correlates of high *L* scale elevations among forensic patients. *Journal of Personality Assessment, 49*, 252–255.

Flamer, S., & Buch, W. (1992, May). *Differential diagnosis of post-traumatic stress disorder in injured workers: Evaluating the MMPI–2*. Paper presented at the 27th Annual Symposium on Recent Developments in the Use of the MMPI (MMPI–2), Minneapolis, MN.

Flitter, J., Elhai, J., & Gold, S. (2003). MMPI–2 *F* scale elevations in adult victims of child sexual abuse. *Journal of Traumatic Stress, 16*, 269–274.

Flynn, R., & Salomone, P. R. (1977). Performance of the MMPI in predicting rehabilitation outcome: A discriminant analysis, double cross-validation assessment. *Rehabilitation Literature, 38*, 12–15.

Follette, W. C., Naugle, A. E., & Follette, V. M. (1997). MMPI–2 profiles of adult women with child sexual abuse histories: Cluster-analytic findings. *Journal of Consulting and Clinical Psychology, 65*, 858–866.

Fontaine, J. L., Archer, R. P., Elkins, D. E., & Johansen, J. (2001). The effects of MMPI–A *T*-score elevation on classification accuracy for normal and clinical adolescent samples. *Journal of Personality Assessment, 76*, 264–281.

Forbes, D., Creamer, M., & McHugh, T. (1999). MMPI–2 data for Australian Vietnam veterans with combat-related PTSD. *Journal of Traumatic Stress, 12*(2), 371–378.

Forbey, J. D. (2002). Incremental validity of the MMPI–A content scales and interpretive utility of the content component scales of the MMPI–A in a residential treatment facility. *Dissertation Abstracts International: Section B: The Sciences and Engineering, 63*(1-B), 522.

Forbey, J. D., & Ben-Porath, Y. S. (2001). Minnesota Multiphasic Personality Inventory—Adolescent (MMPI–A). In W. L. Dorfman & M. Hersen (Eds.), *Understanding psychological assessment. Perspectives on individual differences* (pp. 313–334). Norwell, MA: Kluwer.

Forbey, J. D., Ben-Porath, Y. S., & Davis, D. L. (2000). A comparison of sexually abused and non-sexually abused adolescents in a clinical treatment facility using the MMPI–A. *Child Abuse and Neglect, 24*, 557–568.

Forbey, J. D., Handel, R. W., & Ben-Porath, Y. S. (2000). A real-data simulation of computerized adaptive administration of the MMPI–A. *Computers in Human Behavior, 16*(1), 83–96.

Forfar, C. S. (1993). Keane's MMPI–PTSD scale: A false positive analysis. *Dissertation Abstracts International, 54*(3-B), 1664.

Forgac, G. E., & Michaels, E. J. (1982). Personality characteristics of two types of male exhibitionists. *Journal of Abnormal Psychology, 91*, 287–293.

Fowler, R. D. (1969). Automated interpretation of personality test data. In J. N. Butcher (Ed.), *MMPI research developments and clinical applications* (pp. 105–125). New York: McGraw-Hill.

Fowler, R. D. (1987). Developing a computer-based test interpretation system. In J. N. Butcher (Ed.), *Computerized psychological assessment* (pp. 50–63). New York: Basic Books.

Fowler, R. D., & Butcher, J. N. (1986). Critique of Matarazzo's views on computerized testing: All sigma and no meaning. *American Psychologist, 41*, 94–96.

Franklin, C. L., Repasky, S. A., Thompson, K. E., Shelton, S. A., & Uddo, M. (2002). Differentiating overreporting and extreme distress: MMPI–2 use with compensation-seeking veterans with PTSD. *Journal of Personality Assessment, 79*, 274–285.

Franklin, C. L., Repasky, S., Thompson, K. E., Shelton, S. A., & Uddo, M. (2003). Assessment of response style in combat veterans seeking compensation for posttraumatic stress disorder. *Journal of Traumatic Stress, 16*(3), 251–255.

Freeman, L., & Roy, J. (1976). *Betrayal.* New York: Stein & Day.

Freides, D. (1993). Proposed standard of professional practice: Neuropsychological reports display all quantitative data. *Clinical Neuropsychologist, 7*, 234–235.

Fromm, E., & Pope, K. S. (1990). Countertransference in hypnotherapy and hypnoanalysis. *Independent Practitioner, 10*(3), 48–50.

Frueh, B. C., Smith, D. W., & Barker, S. E. (1996). Compensation seeking status and psychometric assessment of combat veterans seeking treatment for PTSD. *Journal of Traumatic Stress, 9*(3), 427–439.

Fry, F. D. (1949). A study of the personality traits of college students and of state prison inmates as measured by the MMPI. *Journal of Psychology, 28*, 439–449.

Gallagher, R. W. (1997). *Detection of malingering at the time of intake in a correctional setting with the MMPI–2 validity scales.* Unpublished doctoral dissertation, Kent State University, Kent, OH.

Gallen, R. T., & Berry, D. T. R. (1996). Detection of random responding in MMPI–2 protocols. *Assessment, 1*, 61–68.

Gallucci, N. (1984). Prediction of dissimulation on the MMPI in a clinical field setting. *Journal of Consulting and Clinical Psychology, 52*, 917–918.

Gandolfo, R. (1995). MMPI–2 profiles of worker's compensation claimants who present with complaints of harassment. *Journal of Clinical Psychology, 51*, 711–715.

Garb, H. N. (1984). The incremental validity of information used in personality assessment. *Clinical Psychology Review, 4*, 641–655.

Garb, H. N. (1988). Comment on "The study of clinical judgment: An ecological approach." *Clinical Psychology Review, 8*, 441–444.

Garb, H. N. (1992). The debate over the use of computer based test reports. *Clinical Psychologist, 45*, 95–100.

Garrido, M., & Velasquez, R. (2006). Interpretation of Latino/Latina MMPI–2 profiles: Review and application of empirical findings and cultural–linguistic considerations. In J. N. Butcher (Ed.), *MMPI–2: A practitioners guide* (pp. 477–504). Washington, DC: American Psychological Association.

Garson, R. J. (1965, July 26). The better half [Letter to the Editor]. *Newsweek*, p. 2.

Gass, C. S. (1991). MMPI–2 interpretation and closed head injury: A correction factor. *Psychological Assessment, 3*, 27–31.

Gass, C. S. (1992). MMPI–2 interpretation of patients with cerebrovascular disease: A correction factor. *Archives of Neuropsychology, 7*, 17–27.

Gass, C. S. (2000). Personality evaluation in neuropsychological assessment. In R. D. Vanderploeg (Ed.), *Clinician's guide to neuropsychological assessment* (2nd ed., pp. 155–194). Hillsdale, NJ: Erlbaum.

Gass, C. S. (2006). Use of the MMPI–2 in neuropsychological evaluations. In J. N. Butcher (Ed.), *MMPI–2: A practitioners guide* (pp. 301–326). Washington, DC: American Psychological Association.

Gass, C., & Brown, M. C. (1992). Neuropsychological test feedback to patients with brain dysfunction. *Psychological Assessment, 4*, 272–277.

Gass, C. S., & Gonazalez, C. (2003). MMPI–2 short form proposal: CAUTION. *Archives of Clinical Neuropsychology, 18*, 521–527.

Gass, C. S., & Luis, C. A. (2001). MMPI–2 scale *F(p)* and symptom feigning: Scale refinement. *Assessment, 8*, 425–429.

Gass, C. S., Luis, C. A., Rayls, K., & Mittenberg, W. B. (1999). Psychological status and its influences in acute traumatic brain injury: An MMPI–2 study [Abstract]. *Archives of Clinical Neuropsychology, 14*, 30.

Gaston, L., Brunet, A., Koszycki, D., & Bradwejn, J. (1996). MMPI profiles of acute and chronic PTSD in a civilian sample. *Journal of Traumatic Stress, 9*, 817–832.

Gatchel, R. J., & Gardea, M. A. (1999). Psychosocial issues: Their importance in predicting disability, response to treatment, and search for compensation. *Neurologic Clinics, 17*, 149–166.

Geisinger, K. F. (1992). The metamorphosis of test validation. *Educational Psychologist, 27*, 197–222.

Gendreau, P. M., Irvine, M., & Knight, S. (1973). Evaluating response set styles on the MMPI with prisoners faking good adjustment and maladjustment. *Canadian Journal of Abnormal Psychology, 82,* 139–140.

General guidelines for providers of psychological services. (1987). *American Psychologist, 42,* 712–723.

Gilberstadt, H. (1969). Construction and application of MMPI codebooks. In J. N. Butcher (Ed.), *MMPI research developments and clinical applications* (pp. 55–70). New York: McGraw-Hill.

Gilbert, D. H., & Lester, J. T. (1970). *The relationship of certain personality and demographic variables to success in vocational rehabilitation.* Los Angeles: Los Angeles Orthopedic Hospital.

Giorgi-Guarnieri, D., Janofsky, J., Keram, E., Lawsky, S., Merideth, P., Mossman, D., et al. (2002). AAPL practice guideline for forensic psychiatric evaluation of defendants raising the insanity defense. *Journal of the American Academy of Psychiatry and the Law, 30*(2), S3–S40.

Glaser, B. A., Calhoun, G. B., & Petrocelli, J. V. (2002). Personality characteristics of male juvenile offenders by adjudicated offenses as indicated by the MMPI–A. *Criminal Justice and Behavior, 29*(2), 183–201.

Gold, P. B., & Frueh, C. B. (1999). Compensation-seeking and extreme exaggeration of psychopathology among combat veterans evaluated for posttraumatic stress disorder. *Journal of Nervous and Mental Disease, 187,* 680–684.

Gough, H. G. (1947). Simulated patterns on the MMPI. *Journal of Abnormal and Social Psychology, 42,* 215–225.

Gough, H. G. (1950). The *F* minus *K* dissimulation index for the MMPI. *Journal of Consulting Psychology, 14,* 408–413.

Graham, J. R. (1963). *The meaning of cannot say scores on the MMPI.* Unpublished master's thesis, University of North Carolina, Chapel Hill.

Graham, J. R. (1977). *The MMPI: A practical guide.* New York: Oxford University Press.

Graham, J. R. (1988, August). *Establishing validity of the revised form of the MMPI.* Paper presented at the 96th Annual Convention of the American Psychological Association, Atlanta, GA.

Graham, J. R. (2000). *MMPI–2: Assessing personality and psychopathology* (3rd ed.). New York: Oxford University Press.

Graham, J. R. (2006). *MMPI–2: Assessing personality and psychopathology* (4th ed.). New York: Oxford University Press.

Graham, J. R., Ben-Porath, Y. S., & McNulty, J. (1999). *MMPI–2 correlates for outpatient mental health settings.* Minneapolis: University of Minnesota Press.

Graham, J. R., Timbrook, R., Ben-Porath, Y. S., & Butcher, J. N. (1991). Code-type congruence between MMPI and MMPI–2: Separating fact from artifact. *Journal of Personality Assessment, 57,* 205–215.

Graham, J. R., Watts, D., & Timbrook, R. (1991). Detecting fake–good and fake–bad MMPI–2 profiles. *Journal of Personality Assessment, 57,* 264–277.

Greenberg, S. A., & Shuman, D. W. (1997). Irreconcilable conflict between therapeutic and forensic roles. *Professional Psychology: Research and Practice, 28,* 50–75.

Greenblatt, R. L., & Davis, W. E. (1999). Differential diagnosis of PTSD, schizophrenia, and depression with the MMPI–2. *Journal of Clinical Psychology, 55,* 217–223.

Greene, B. (1997). *Ethnic and cultural diversity among lesbians and gay men.* Thousand Oaks, CA: Sage.

Greene, R. L. (1979). Response consistency on the MMPI: The *T–R* index. *Journal of Personality Assessment, 43,* 69–71.

Greene, R. L. (1980). *The MMPI: An interpretive manual.* New York: Grune & Stratton.

Greene, R. L. (1991). *The MMPI–2/MMPI: An interpretive manual.* Needham Heights, MA: Allyn & Bacon.

Greene, R. L. (2000). *The MMPI–2: An interpretive manual* (2nd ed.). Needham Heights, MA: Allyn & Bacon.

Greene, R. L., Gwin, R., & Staal, M. (1997). Current status of MMPI–2 research: A methodologic overview. *Journal of Personality Assessment, 68,* 20–36.

Greene, R. L., Robin, R. W., Albaugh, B., Caldwell, A., & Goldman, D. (2003). Use of the MMPI–2 in American Indians II. Empirical correlates. *Psychological Assessment, 15,* 360–369.

Greenfield, P. (1983–1984). Cognitive impact of the media. *Imagination, Cognition, and Personality: Consciousness in Theory, Research, and Clinical Practice, 3,* 3–16.

Greiffenstein, M. F., Baker, W. J., Axelrod, B., Peck, E. A., & Gervais, R. (2004). The Fake Bad Scale and MMPI–2 *F*-family in detection of implausible psychological trauma claims. *Clinical Neuropsychologist, 18*(4), 573–590.

Greiffenstein, M. F., Baker, W. J., Gola, T., Donders, J., & Miller, L. (2002). The Fake Bad Scale in a typical and severe closed head injury litigants. *Journal of Clinical Psychology, 58,* 1591–1600.

Greve, K. W., & Bianchini, K. J. (2004). Response to Butcher et al., The construct validity of the Lees–Haley Fake–Bad Scale. *Archives of Clinical Neuropsychology, 19*(3), 337–339.

Grossman, L. S., & Cavanaugh, J. L. (1989). Do sex offenders minimize psychiatric symptoms? *Journal of Forensic Sciences, 34,* 881–886.

Grossman, L. S., Haywood, T. W., Ostrov, E., Wasyliw, O., & Cavanaugh, J. L. (1990). Sensitivity of MMPI validity indicators to motivational factors in psychological evaluations of police officers. *Journal of Personality Assessment, 55,* 549–561.

Grossman, L. S., & Wasyliw, O. E. (1988). A psychometric study of stereotypes: Assessment of malingering in a criminal forensic group. *Journal of Personality Assessment, 52,* 549–563.

Grow, R., McVaugh, W., & Eno, T. (1980). Faking and the MMPI. *Journal of Clinical Psychology, 36,* 910–917.

Grutman, R., & Thomas, B. (1990). *Lawyers and thieves.* New York: Simon & Schuster.

Gucker, D., & McNulty, J. (2004, May). *The MMPI-2, defensiveness, and an analytic strategy.* Paper presented at the 39th Annual Symposium on Recent Developments in the Use of the MMPI-2, Minneapolis, MN.

Gynther, M. D., Altman, H., & Warbin, R. (1973). Interpretation of uninterpretable MMPI profiles. *Journal of Clinical Psychology, 40,* 78–83.

Gynther, M. D., Fowler, R. D., & Erdberg, S. P (1971). False positives galore: The application of standard MMPI criteria to a rural, isolated, Negro sample. *Journal of Clinical Psychology, 27,* 234–237.

Habush, R. L. (1984). Maximizing damages through trial techniques. *Trial, 20,* 68–72.

Hafner, A. J., Butcher, J. N., Hall, M., & Quast, W. (1969). Parent pathology and childhood disorders: A review of MMPI findings. In J. N. Butcher (Ed.), *MMPI: Research developments and clinical applications* (pp. 181–190). New York: McGraw-Hill.

Hall, G. C. N., Bansal, A., & Lopez, I. R. (1999). Ethnicity and psychopathology: A meta-analytic review of 31 years of comparative MMPI/MMPI-2 research. *Psychological Assessment, 11,* 186–197.

Hall, G. C., Graham, J., & Shepherd, J. (1991). Three methods of developing MMPI taxonomies of sexual offenders. *Journal of Personality Assessment, 56,* 2–16.

Hall, G. C., Maiuro, R., Vitaliano, P., & Proctor, W. (1986). The utility of the MMPI with men who have sexually assaulted children. *Journal of Consulting and Clinical Psychology, 54,* 111–112.

Hall, G. C., Shepherd, J. B., & Mudrak, P. (1992). MMPI taxonomies of child sexual and nonsexual offenders: A cross-validation and extension. *Journal of Personality Assessment, 58,* 127–137.

Hammel, S. D. (2001). An investigation of the validity and clinical usefulness of the MMPI-A with female juvenile delinquents. *Dissertation Abstracts International: Section B: The Sciences and Engineering, 61*(11-B), 6135.

Handel, R. W., Ben-Porath, Y. S., & Watt, M. (1999). Computerized adaptive assessment with the MMPI-2 in a clinical setting. *Psychological Assessment, 11,* 369–380.

Hanson, R. W., Moss, C. S., Hosford, R. E., & Johnson, M. E. (1983). Predicting inmate penitentiary adjustment: An assessment of four classificatory methods. *Criminal Justice and Behavior, 10,* 293–309.

Harkness, A. R., & Butcher, J. N. (2002). Theory and measurement of personality traits. In *Clinical personality assessment: Practical approaches* (2nd ed., pp. 24–39). London: Oxford University Press.

Harkness, A. R., McNulty, J. L., & Ben-Porath, Y. S. (1995). The Personality Psychopathology Five (PSY-5): Constructs and MMPI-2 scales. *Psychological Assessment, 7,* 104–114.

Harkness, A. R., McNulty, J. L., Strack, S., & Lorr, M. (1994). The Personality Psychopathology Five (PSY-5): Issues from the pages of a diagnostic manual instead of a dictionary. In *Differentiating normal and abnormal personality* (pp. 291–315). New York: Springer.

Harris, A. J. R., & Tough, S. (2004). Should actuarial risk assessments be used with sex offenders who are intellectually disabled? *Journal of Applied Research in Intellectual Disabilities, 17,* 235–241.

Hartshorne, H., & May, M. A. (1928). *Studies in deceit.* New York: Macmillan.

Harvey, V. S. (1997). Improving readability of psychological reports. *Professional Psychology: Research and Practice, 28,* 271–274.

Hastie, R. (1986). Notes on the psychologist as expert witness. *Law and Human Behavior, 10,* 79–82.

Hathaway, S. R. (1965). Personality inventories. In B. Wolman (Ed.), *Handbook of clinical psychology* (pp. 451–476). New York: McGraw-Hill.

Hathaway, S. R., & McKinley, J. C. (1940). A multiphasic personality schedule (Minnesota): I. Construction of the schedule. *Journal of Psychology, 10,* 249–254.

Hathaway, S. R., & McKinley, J. C. (1943). *Manual for administering and scoring the MMPI.* Minneapolis: University of Minnesota Press.

Hathaway, S. R., & Monachesi, E. D. (1963). *Adolescent personality and behavior.* Minneapolis: University of Minnesota Press.

Hawk, G., & Cornell, D. (1989). MMPI profiles of malingerers diagnosed in pretrial forensic evaluations. *Journal of Clinical Psychology, 45,* 673–678.

Hays, F. M. (1999). A comparison of persons found not guilty by reason of insanity and mentally disordered offenders in outpatient treatment using Rorschach and MMPI-2 data. *Dissertations International: Section B: The Sciences and Engineering, 60*(5-B), 2342.

Heaton, R. K., Chelune, G. J., & Lehman, R. A. W. (1978). Using neuropsychological and personality tests to assess the likelihood of patient employment. *Journal of Nervous and Mental Disease, 166,* 408–416.

Heaton, R. K., Smith, H. H., Lehman, R. A. W., & Vogt, A. T. (1978). Prospects for faking believable deficits on neuropsychological testing. *Journal of Consulting and Clinical Psychology, 46,* 892–900.

Heilbrun, A. B. (1963). Revision of the MMPI *K* correction procedure for improved detection of maladjustment in a normal college population. *Journal of Consulting Psychology, 27*(2), 161–165.

Heilbrun, K. (1992). The role of psychological testing in forensic assessment. *Law and Human Behavior, 16,* 257–272.

Heilbrun, K., Bennett, W. S., White, A. J., & Kelly, J. (1990). An MMPI-based empirical model of malingering and deception. *Behavioral Sciences and the Law, 8,* 45–53.

Heimann, P. (1950). On countertransference. *International Journal of Psychoanalysis, 31,* 81–84.

Helmes, E., & Reddon, J. R. (1993). A perspective on developments in assessing psychopathology: A critical review of the MMPI and MMPI–2. *Psychological Bulletin, 113,* 453–471.

Henry, L. M. (1999). Comparison of MMPI and MMPI–A response patterns of African American adolescents. *Dissertations International: Section B: The Sciences and Engineering, 60*(6-B), 2945.

Herkov, M. J., Archer, R., & Gordon, R. A. (1991). MMPI response sets among adolescents: An evaluation of the limitations of the Subtle–Obvious subscales. *Psychological Assessment, 3,* 424–426.

Herman, J. L. (1992). *Trauma and recovery.* New York: Basic Books.

Herman, J. L., Perry, J. C., & van der Kolk, B. A. (1989). Childhood trauma in borderline personality disorder. *American Journal of Psychiatry, 146,* 490–495.

Hess, H. (1992). Affective response in group therapy process and outcome. *Psychotherapie Psychosomatik Medizinische Psychologie, 42,* 120–126.

Hiley-Young, B., Blake, D. D., Abueg, F., & Rozynko, V. (1995). War zone violence in Vietnam: An examination of premilitary, military, and postmilitary factors in PTSD in-patients. *Journal of Traumatic Stress, 8*(1), 125–141.

Hjemboe, S., Almagor, M., & Butcher, J. N. (1992). Empirical assessment of marital distress: The Marital Distress Scale (MDS) for the MMPI–2. In C. D. Spielberger & J. N. Butcher (Eds.), *Advances in personality assessment* (Vol. 9, pp. 141–152). Hillsdale, NJ: Erlbaum.

Hjemboe, S., & Butcher, J. N. (1991). Couples in marital distress: A study of demographic and personality factors as measured by the MMPI–2. *Journal of Personality Assessment, 57,* 216–237.

Hoffman, B. (1986). How to write a psychiatric report for litigation following a personal injury. *American Journal of Psychiatry, 143,* 164–169.

Hoffman, B., & Spiegel, H. (1989). Legal principles in the psychiatric assessment of personal injury litigants. *American Journal of Psychiatry, 146,* 304–310.

Holcolmb, W., Adams, N., & Ponder, H. (1985). The development and cross-validation of an MMPI typology of murderers. *Journal of Personality Assessment, 49,* 240–244.

Holcomb, W. R., Adams, W. P., Ponder, H. M., & Anderson, W. (1984). Cognitive and behavioral predictors of MMPI scores in pretrial psychological evaluations of murderers. *Journal of Clinical Psychology, 40,* 592–597.

Holden, C. (1988). Research psychologists break with APA. *Science, 241,* 1036.

Holifield, J., Nelson, W., & Hart, K. (2002). MMPI profiles of sexually abused and nonabused outpatient adolescents. *Journal of Adolescent Research, 17,* 188–195.

Hsu, L. M. (1986). Implications of differences in elevations of *K*-corrected and non–*K*-corrected MMPI *T* scores. *Journal of Consulting and Clinical Psychology, 54,* 552–557.

Hudson, A. H. (1996). Personality assessment of female sex offenders: A cluster analysis. *Dissertation Abstracts International: Section B: The Sciences and Engineering, 56*(9-B), 5212.

Hunt, H. F. (1948). The effect of deliberate deception on MMPI performance. *Journal of Consulting Psychology, 12,* 396–402.

Hunt, H. F., Carp, W. A., Cass, A., Winder, L., & Kantor, R. E. (1947). A study of the differential diagnostic efficiency of the MMPI. *Journal of Consulting Psychology, 12,* 331–336.

Hunt, H. F., Cass, W. A., Carp, A., & Winder, C. L. (1947). A study of the effect of the *K* correction on the differential diagnostic efficiency of the Minnesota Multiphasic Personality Inventory. *American Psychologist, 2,* 273.

Hunter, J. A., Childers, S. E., & Esmaili, H. (1990). An examination of variables differentiating clinical subtypes of incestuous child molesters. *International Journal of Offender Therapy and Comparative Criminology, 34,* 95–104.

Hunter, L. M. (2000). Use of selected MMPI–A factors in the prediction of clinical outcomes in a community-based treatment program for juvenile sexual offenders. *Dissertation Abstracts International: Section B: The Sciences & Engineering, 60*(11-B), 5775.

Hutton, H. E., Miner, M. H., Blades, J. R., & Langfeldt, V. C. (1992). Ethnic differences on the MMPI Overcontrolled–Hostility Scale. *Journal of Personality Assessment, 58,* 260–268.

Hyer, L., Leach, P., Boudewyns, P. A., & Davis, H. (1991). Hidden PTSD in substance abuse inpatients among Vietnam veterans. *Journal of Substance Abuse Treatment, 8,* 213–219.

Imwinkelried, E. J. (1982). *The methods of attacking scientific evidence.* Charlottesville, VA: Michie.

Imwinkelrind, E. J. (1994). The next step after *Daubert:* Developing a similarly epistemological approach to ensuring the reliability of nonscientific expert testimony. *Cardoza Law Review, 15,* 2271–2294.

Iverson, G. L., & Barton, E. (1999). Interscorer reliability of the MMPI–2: Should *TRIN* and *VRIN* be computer scored? *Journal of Clinical Psychology, 55*(1), 65–69.

Iverson, G. L., Franzen, M. D., & Hammond, J. A. (1995). Examination of inmates' ability to malinger on the MMPI–2. *Psychological Assessment, 7,* 118–121.

Iverson, G. L., Henrichs, T. F., Barton, E. A., & Allen, S. (2002). Specificity of the MMPI–2 Fake Bad Scale as a marker for personal injury malingering *Psychological Reports, 90*(1), 131–136.

Jackson, D. (1971). The dynamics of structured personality tests: 1971. *Psychological Review, 78,* 229–248.

Jackson, D. N. (1989). *Basic Personality Inventory manual.* Goshen, NY: Sigma Assessment Systems.

Jackson, D. N., Fraboni, M., & Helmes, E. (1997). MMPI–2 content scales: How much content do they measure? *Assessment, 4,* 111–117.

Jackson, D., & Messick, S. (1962). Response styles and the assessment of psychopathology In S. Messick & J. Ross (Eds.), *Measurement of personality and cognition* (pp. 129–155). New York: Wiley.

Janis, I. L. (1972). *Victims of groupthink.* Boston: Houghton Mifflin.

Janis, I. L. (1982). *Stress, attitudes, and decisions.* New York: Praeger.

Janis, I. L., & Mann, L. (1979). *Decision making: A psychological analysis of conflict, choice, & commitment.* New York: Free Press.

Jaranson, J., Butcher, J. N., Halcón, L., Johnson, D. R., Robertson, C., Savik, K., et al. (2004). Somali and Oromo refugee: Correlates of torture and trauma. *American Journal of Public Health, 94,* 591–597.

Jaranson, J. M., & Popkin, M. K. (1998). *Caring for victims of torture.* Washington, DC: American Psychiatric Association.

Jemelka, R. P., Weigand, G. A., Walker, E. A., & Trupin, E. W. (1992). Computerized offender assessment: Validation study. *Psychological Assessment, 4,* 138–144.

Jenkins, J. A. (1989). *The litigators.* New York: Doubleday.

Jensen, A. R. (1972). *Genetics and education.* New York: Harper & Row.

Ji, S., Gao, C., Li, M., Ji, Y., Guo, C., & Fang, M. (1999). Effect of *K* correction on the profile of the MMPI. *Chinese Journal of Clinical Psychology, 7*(1), 12–15.

Johnson, D. L., Simmons, J. G., & Gordon, B. C. (1983). Temporal consistency of the Meyer–Megargee inmate typology. *Criminal Justice and Behavior, 10,* 263–268.

Jordan, B. K., Schlenger, W. E., Hough, R. L., Kukla, R. A., Fairbank, J. A., Marmar, C. R., et al. (1991). Lifetime and current prevalence of specific psychiatric disorders among Vietnam veterans and controls. *Archives of General Psychiatry, 48,* 207–215.

Julien, A. (1984). The opening statement. In B. G. Warshaw (Ed.), *The trial masters: A handbook of strategies and tactics that win cases* (pp. 139–147). Englewood Cliffs, NJ: Prentice Hall.

Kalichman, S. C. (1990). Affective and personality characteristics of MMPI profile subgroups of incarcerated rapists. *Archives of Sexual Behavior, 19,* 443–459.

Kalichman, S. C. (1991). Psychopathology and personality characteristics of criminal sex offenders as a function of victim age. *Archives of Sexual Behavior, 20,* 187–197.

Kalichman, S. C., Craig, M. E., Shealy, L., Taylor, J., Szymanowski, D., & McKee, G. (1989). An empirically derived typology of adult rapists based on the MMPI: A cross-validation study. *Journal of Psychology and Human Sexuality, 2,* 165–182.

Kalichman, S. C., & Henderson, M. C. (1991). MMPI profile subtypes of nonincarcerated child molesters. *Criminal Justice and Behavior, 18,* 379–396.

Kalichman, S. C., Shealy, L., & Craig, M. E. (1990). The use of the MMPI in predicting treatment participation among incarcerated adult rapists. *Journal of Psychology and Human Sexuality, 3,* 105–119.

Kalichman, S. C., Szymanowski, D., McKee, G., Taylor, J., & Craig, M. E. (1989). Cluster analytically derived MMPI profile subgroups of incarcerated adult rapists. *Journal of Clinical Psychology, 45,* 149–155.

Kamphuis, J. H., & Finn, S. E. (2002). Implementing base rates into daily clinical decision making. In J. N. Butcher (Ed.), *Clinical personality assessment* (2nd ed., pp. 257–268). New York: Oxford University Press.

Karle-Brueck, H. R. (2003). Denial in convicted sex offenders: A preliminary examination. *Dissertation Abstracts International: Section B: The Sciences and Engineering, 63*(12-B), 6097.

Kassin, S. M., Williams, L. N., & Saunders, C. L. (1990). Dirty tricks of cross-examination: The influence of conjectural evidence on the jury. *Law and Human Behavior, 14,* 373–384.

Keane, T. M., Malloy, P. E., & Fairbank, J. A. (1984). Empirical development of an MMPI subscale for the assessment of combat-related posttraumatic stress disorder. *Journal of Consulting and Clinical Psychology, 52,* 888–891.

Keane, T. M., Weathers, F. W., & Kaloupek, D. G. (1992). Psychological assessment of post-traumatic stress disorder. *PTSD Research Quarterly, 3,* 1–3.

Keane, T. M., Wolfe, J., & Taylor, K. L. (1987). Posttraumatic stress disorder: Evidence for diagnostic validity and methods of psychological assessment. *Journal of Clinical Psychology, 43,* 32–43.

Keefe, K., Sue, S., Enomoto, K., Durvasula, R. S., & Chao, R. (1996). Asian American and White college students' performance on the MMPI–2. In J. N. Butcher (Ed.), *International adaptations of the MMPI–2* (pp. 206–220). Minneapolis: University of Minnesota Press.

Kelin, W. G., & Bloom, L. J. (1986). Child custody evaluation practices: A survey of experienced professionals. *Professional Psychology: Research and Practice, 17,* 338–346.

Keller, L. S., & Butcher, J. N. (1991). *Assessment of chronic pain patients with the MMPI–2.* Minneapolis: University of Minnesota Press.

Keller, R. A., Wigdor, B. T., & Lundell, F. W. (1973). Adjustment of welfare recipients and applicants: Investigation of some relevant factors. *Canadian Psychiatric Association Journal, 18,* 511–517.

Kelven, H., & Zeisel, H. (1966). *The American jury.* Boston: Little, Brown.

Kendall, P. C., Edinger, J., & Eberly, C. (1978). Taylor's MMPI correction for spinal cord injury: Empirical endorsement. *Journal of Consulting and Clinical Psychology, 46,* 370–371.

Kenderdine, S. K., Phillips, E. J., & Scurfield, R. M. (1992). Comparison of the MMPI–PTSD subscale with PTSD and substance abuse patient populations. *Journal of Clinical Psychology, 48,* 136–139.

Kennedy, R. D. (1983). *California expert witness guide.* Berkeley: California Continuing Education of the Bar.

Kennedy, R. D., & Martin, J. C. (1987). *California expert witness guide: Supplement.* Berkeley: California Continuing Education of the Bar.

Kennedy, T. D. (1986). Trends in inmate classification: A status report of two computerized psychometric approaches. *Criminal Justice and Behavior, 13,* 165–184.

Keys, A. (1946). Human starvation and its consequences. *Journal of the American Dietetic Association, 22,* 582–587.

Keys, A., Brozek, J., Henschel, A., Mickelson, O., & Taylor, H. L. (1950). *The biology of human starvation.* Minneapolis: University of Minnesota Press.

Khan, F. I., Welch, T., & Zilmer, E. (1993). MMPI–2 profiles of battered women in transition. *Journal of Personality Assessment, 60,* 100–111.

Kieliszewski, J. T. (1999). A cluster analytic study of MMPI–2 profiles of convicted sex offenders of children. *Dissertation Abstracts International: Section B: The Sciences and Engineering, 60*(2-B), 0833.

Kincannon, J. C. (1968). Prediction of the standard MMPI scale scores from 71 items: The Mini-Mult. *Journal of Consulting and Clinical Psychology, 32,* 319–325.

Klawans, H. L. (1991). *Trials of an expert witness: Tales of clinical neurology and the law.* Boston: Little, Brown.

Knisely, J. S., Barker, S. B., Ingersoll, K. S., & Dawson, K. S. (2000). Psychopathology in substance abusing women reporting childhood sexual abuse. *Journal of Addictive Diseases, 19*(1), 31–44.

Knox-Jones, P. A. (1995). Neuropsychological functioning among violent and nonviolent sex offenders. *Dissertation Abstracts International: Section B: The Sciences and Engineering, 56*(4-B), 2332.

Kopper, B. A., Osman, A., & Barrios, F. X. (2001). Assessment of suicidal ideation in young men and women: The incremental validity of the MMPI–2 content scales. *Death Studies, 25,* 593–607.

Korestzky, M. B., & Peck, A. H. (1990). Validation and cross-validation of the PTSD subscale of the MMPI with civilian trauma victims. *Journal of Clinical Psychology, 46*(3), 296–299.

Korgeski, G. P., & Leon, G. R. (1983). Correlates of self-reported and objectively determined exposure to Agent Orange. *American Journal of Psychiatry, 140,* 1443–1449.

Koss, M. P., Leonard, K. E., Beezley, D. A., & Oros, C. J. (1985). Nonstranger sexual aggression: A discriminant analysis of the psychological characteristics of undetected offenders. *Sex Roles, 12,* 981–992.

Krakauer, S. Y., Archer, R. P., & Gordon, R. (1993). The development of the Items-Easy (IE) Items-Difficult (d) subscales of the MMPI–A. *Journal of Personality Assessment, 80,* 561–571.

Krishnamurthy, R., & Archer, R. P. (1999). A comparison of two interpretive approaches for the MMPI–A structural summary. *Journal of Personality Assessment, 73,* 245–259.

Kubiszyn, T. (1984, August). *The MMPI, litigation, and back pain treatment: A curvilinear relationship.* Paper presented at the 92nd Annual Convention of the American Psychological Association, Toronto, Ontario, Canada.

Kuehnle, K. (1998). Ethics and the forensic expert. *Ethics and Behavior, 8*, 1–18.

Kuperman, S. K., & Golden, C. J. (1979). Predicting pain treatment results by personality variables in organic and functional patients. *Journal of Clinical Psychology, 35*, 832–837.

Kurman, R. G., Hursey, K. G., & Mathew, N. T. (1992). Assessment of chronic refractory headache: The role of the MMPI–2. *Headache, 32*, 432–435.

Lachar, D. (1974). The prediction of early USAF freshman cadet adaptation with the MMPI. *Journal of Counseling Psychology, 21*, 404–408.

Lachar, D., & Sharp, J. R. (1979). Use of parent's MMPIs in the research and evaluation of children: A review of the literature and some new data. In J. N. Butcher (Ed.), *New directions in MMPI research* (pp. 203–240). Minneapolis: University of Minnesota Press.

Lacks, P. (1984). *Bender gestalt screening for brain dysfunction.* New York: Wiley.

Lahey, B. B., Russo, M. F., Walker, J. L., & Piacentini, J. C. (1989). Personality characteristics of mothers of children with disruptive behavior disorders. *Journal of Consulting and Clinical Psychology, 57*, 512–515.

Lakoff, R. T. (1990). *Talking power: The politics of language.* New York: Basic Books.

Lally, S. L. (2003). What tests are acceptable for use in forensic evaluations? A survey of experts. *Professional Psychology: Research and Practice, 34*, 491–498.

LaMarca, G. A. (1984). How to prepare and present effective opening statements. In B. G. Warshaw (Ed.), *The trial masters: A handbook of strategies and tactics that win cases* (pp. 148–157). Englewood Cliffs, NJ: Prentice Hall.

Lamb, D., Berry, D. T. R., Wetter, M., & Baer, R. (1994). Effects of two types of information on malingering of closed head injury on the MMPI–2: An analog investigation. *Psychological Assessment, 6*, 8–13.

Land, H. M. (1968). Child abuse: Differential diagnosis, differential treatment. *Child Welfare, 65*, 33–44.

Landberg, G. (1982). Proposed model for the intervention of the mental health specialist in the resolution of difficult child custody disputes. *Journal of Preventive Psychiatry, 1*, 309–318.

Langer, E. J. (1989). *Mindfulness.* Reading, MA: Addison-Wesley.

Langer, E. J., & Piper, A. I. (1987). The prevention of mindlessness. *Journal of Personality and Social Psychology, 53*, 280–287.

Langevin, R., & Bain, J. (1992). Diabetes in sex offenders: A pilot study. *Annals of Sex Research, 5*(2), 99–118.

Langevin, R., Wright, P., & Handy, L. (1989). Characteristics of sex offenders who were sexually victimized as children. *Annals of Sex Research, 2*(3), 227–253.

Langevin, R., Wright, P., & Handy, L. H. (1990a). Use of the MMPI and its derived scales with sex offenders: I. Reliability and validity studies. *Annals of Sex Research, 3*(3), 245–291.

Langevin, R., Wright, P., & Handy, L. (1990b). Use of the MMPI and its derived scales with sex offenders: II. Reliability and criterion validity. *Annals of Sex Research, 3*(4), 453–486.

Lanyon, R. I. (1993). Validity of MMPI sex offender scales with admitters and nonadmitters. *Psychological Assessment, 5*, 302–306.

Lanyon, R. I. (1997). Detecting deception: Current models and directions. *Clinical Psychology Science and Practice, 4*, 377–387.

Lanyon, R. I., & Almer, E. R. (2002). Characteristics of compensable disability patients who choose to litigate. *Journal of American Academy of Psychiatry and Law, 30*(3), 400–404.

Lanyon, R. I., & Lutz, R. W. (1984). MMPI discrimination of defensive and nondefensive felony sex offenders. *Journal of Consulting and Clinical Psychology, 52*, 841–843.

Larrabee, G. J. (2003). Exaggerated MMPI–2 symptom report in personal injury litigants with malingered neurocognitive deficit. *Archives of Clinical Neuropsychology, 18*(6), 673–686.

Lee, D., Reynolds, C., & Willson, V. (2003). Standardized test administration: Why bother? *Journal of Forensic Neuropsychology, 3*, 55–81.

Lee, H. B., Cheung, F. M., Man, H., & Hsu, S. Y. (1992). Psychological characteristics of Chinese low back pain patients: An exploratory study. *Psychology and Health, 6*, 119–128.

Lees-Haley, P. R. (1989). Malingering post-traumatic stress disorder on the MMPI. *Forensic Reports, 2*, 89–91.

Lees-Haley, P. R. (1992). Psychodiagnostic test usage by forensic psychologists. *American Journal of Forensic Psychology, 10*, 25–30.

Lees-Haley, P. R. (1997a). Attorneys influence expert evidence in forensic psychological and neuropsychological examinations. *Assessment, 4*, 321–324.

Lees-Haley, P. R. (1997b). MMPI–2 base rates for 492 personal injury plaintiffs: Implications and challenges for forensic assessment. *Journal of Clinical Psychology, 53*, 745–756.

Lees-Haley, P. R., English, L. T., & Glenn, W. J. (1991). A fake bad scale on the MMPI–2 for personal injury claimants. *Psychological Reports, 68*, 203–210.

Lees-Haley, P. R., & Fox, D. D. (2004). Commentary on Butcher, Arbisi, Atlis, and McNulty (2003) on the

Fake Bad Scale. *Archives of Clinical Neuropsychology, 19*(3), 333–336.

Lees-Haley, P. R., Smith, H. H., Williams, C. W., & Dunn, J. T. (1996). Forensic neuropsychological test usage: An empirical survey. *Archives of Clinical Neuropsychology, 11,* 45–51.

Leon, G., Gillum, B., Gillum, R., & Gouze, M. (1979). Personality stability and change over a 30-year-period—Middle age to old age. *Journal of Consulting and Clinical Psychology, 47,* 517–524.

Lessin, L. H. (1997). Predicting recidivism among sex offenders: A long-term survival analysis utilizing the Minnesota Multiphasic Personality Inventory and demographic variables. *Dissertation Abstracts International: Section B: The Sciences and Engineering, 57*(11-B), 7229.

Levenson, H., Hirschfeld, M. L., & Hirschfeld, A. H. (1985). *Duration of chronic pain and the MMPI: Profiles of industrially-injured workers.* Paper presented at the 20th Symposium on Recent Developments in the Use of the MMPI, Honolulu, HI.

Levin, F. G. (1984). Strategy for opening statement: A case study. In B. G. Warshaw (Ed.), *The trial masters: A handbook of strategies and tactics that win cases* (pp. 158–195). Englewood Cliffs, NJ: Prentice Hall.

Levin, S. M., & Stava, L. (1987). Personality characteristics of sex offenders: A review. *Archives of Sexual Behavior, 16*(1), 57–79.

Lewis, A. (1991). *Make no law: The Sullivan case and the First Amendment.* New York: Random House.

Lezak, M. D. (1983). *Neuropsychological assessment.* New York: Oxford University Press.

Lilienfeld, S. O. (1996). The MMPI–2 Antisocial Practices content scale: Construct validity and comparison with the Psychopathic Deviate Scale. *Psychological Assessment, 8,* 281–293.

Lim, J., & Butcher, J. N. (1996). Detection of faking on the MMPI–2: Differentiation between faking-bad, denial, and claiming extreme virtue. *Journal of Personality Assessment, 67,* 1–26.

Litwack, T. (2003). The competency of criminal defendants to refuse, for delusional reasons, a viable insanity defense recommended by counsel. *Behavioral Sciences and the Law, 21*(2), 135–156.

Litz, B. T., Penk, W., Walsh, S., Hyer, L., Blake, D. D., Marz, B., et al. (1991). Similarities and differences between Minnesota Multiphasic Personality Inventory (MMPI) and MMPI–2 applications to the assessment of post-traumatic stress disorder. *Journal of Personality Assessment, 57,* 238–254.

Liu, J.-x., Jiang, C.-q., & Zhang, X.-d. (2002). Effect of *K* correction on the profile of MMPI in different mentally disordered patients. *Chinese Journal of Clinical Psychology, 10*(2), 140–142.

Loftus, E. F. (1986). Experimental psychologist as advocate or impartial educator. *Law and Human Behavior, 10,* 63–78.

Loftus, E. F. (1999). Lost in the mall: Misrepresentations and misunderstandings. *Ethics and Behavior, 9,* 51–60.

Loftus, E., & Ketcham, K. (1991). *Witness for the defense.* New York: St. Martin's Press.

Long, B., Rouse, S. V., Nelson, R. O., & Butcher, J. N. (2004). The MMPI–2 in sexual harassment and discrimination cases. *Journal of Clinical Psychology, 60,* 643–658.

Losada-Paisey, G. (1998). Use of the MMPI–A to assess personality of juvenile male delinquents who are sex offenders and nonsex offenders. *Psychological Reports, 83*(1), 115–122.

Louscher, P. K., Hosford, R. E., & Moss, C. S. (1983). Predicting dangerous behavior in a penitentiary using the Megargee typology. *Criminal Justice and Behavior, 10,* 269–284.

Lubin, B., Larsen, R. M., & Matarazzo, J. (1984). Patterns of psychological test usage in the United States: 1935–1982. *American Psychologist, 39,* 451–454.

Lucio, E., Palacios, H., Duran, C., & Butcher, J. N. (1999). MMPI–2 with Mexican psychiatric inpatients: Basic and content scales. *Journal of Clinical Psychology, 55,* 1541–1552.

Luginbuhl, J. (1992). Comprehension of judges' instructions in the penalty phase of a capital trial: Focus on mitigating circumstances. *Law and Human Behavior, 16,* 203–218.

Lund, S. N. (1975). *Personality and personal history factors of child abusing parents.* Unpublished doctoral dissertation, University of Minnesota, Minneapolis.

Lundy, R., Geselowitz, L., & Shertzer, C. (1985). Role-played and hypnotically induced simulation of psychopathology on the MMPI: A partial replication. *International Journal of Clinical and Experimental Hypnosis, 33,* 302–309.

Lyons, J. A., & Keane, T. M. (1992). Keane PTSD scale: MMPI and MMPI–2 update. *Journal of Traumatic Stress, 5,* 111–117.

Lyons, J. A., & Wheeler-Cox, T. (1999). MMPI, MMPI–2 and PTSD: Overview of scores, scales and profiles. *Journal of Traumatic Stress, 12*(1),175–183.

MacDonald, J. D. (1968). *No deadly drug.* New York: Doubleday.

MacDonald, J. M. (1976). *Psychiatry and the criminal: A guide to psychiatric examinations for the criminal courts.* Springfield, IL: Charles C. Thomas.

Maness, P., Silkowski, S., Velasquez, R. J., Savino, A. V., & Frank, J. (2001, March). *Ethnic comparisons on the MMPI–2 and male sex offenders.* Paper presented at the 36th Annual Symposium on Recent

Developments in the Use of the MMPI–2/MMPI–A, Safety Harbor, FL.

Manos, N. (1985). Adaptation of the MMPI in Greece: Translation, standardization, and cross-cultural comparison. In J. N. Butcher & C. D. Spielberger (Eds.), *Advances in personality assessment* (Vol. 4, pp. 159–208). Hillsdale, NJ: Erlbaum.

Manos, N., & Butcher, J. N. (1982). *MMPI: User's manual for the MMPI (Greek)*. Thessaloniki, Greece: University Studio.

Mantell, E. H. (1994). A modest proposal to dress the emperor: Psychiatric and psychological opinion in the courts. *Widener Journal of Public Law, 4*, 53, 57.

Marcus, E. H. (1983). Causation in psychiatry: Realities and speculations. *Medical Trial Technical Quarterly, 29*, 424–433.

Marcus, E. H. (1987). Defending mental injury claims: Cross-examining the plaintiff's expert witness. *Medical Trial Technique Quarterly, 33*, 430–439.

Martin, H. C. (1981–1982). The story underground. *Imagination, Cognition, and Personality: Consciousness in Theory, Research, and Clinical Practice, 1*, 171–184.

Martin, J. C. (1985). *California expert witness guide: Supplement*. Berkeley: California Continuing Education of the Bar.

Martins, M., Donders, J., & Millis, S. R. (2001). Evaluation of invalid response sets after traumatic head injury. *Journal of Forensic Neuropsychology, 2*(1), 1–18.

Matarazzo, J. D. (1955). MMPI validity scores as a function of increasing levels of anxiety. *Journal of Consulting Psychology, 19*, 213–217.

Matarazzo, J. (1986). Computerized clinical psychological test interpretations: Unvalidated plus all mean and no sigma. *American Psychologist, 41*, 14–24.

Matthews, S. (2004). Failed agency and the insanity defense. *International Journal of Law and Psychiatry, 27*, 413–424.

Matz, P. A., Altepeter, T. S., & Perlman, B. (1992). MMPI–2 reliability with college students. *Journal of Clinical Psychology, 48*, 330–334.

McAdoo, G., & Connolly, F. J. (1975). MMPIs of parents in dysfunctional families. *Journal of Consulting and Clinical Psychology, 43*, 270.

McCaffrey, R., & Bellamy-Campbell, R. (1989). Psychometric detection of fabricated symptoms of combat-related PTSD: A systematic replication. *Journal of Clinical Psychology, 45*, 76–79.

McCall, R. J. (1958). Face validity in the scale of the MMPI. *Journal of Clinical Psychology, 14*, 77–80.

McCloskey, M., Egeth, H., & McKenna, J. (1986). The experimental psychologist in court: The ethics of expert testimony. *Law and Human Behavior, 10*, 1–13.

McCormick, R. A., Taber, J. I., & Kruedelbach, N. (1989). The relationship between attributional type and post-traumatic stress disorder in addicted patients. *Journal of Traumatic Stress, 2*, 477–487.

McCrae, R. R., Costa, P. T., Dahlstrom, W. G., Barefoot, J. C., Siegler, I. C., & Williams, R. B. (1989). A caution on the use of the MMPI *K*-correction in research on psychosomatic medicine. *Psychosomatic Medicine, 51*(1), 58–65.

McDermott, J. F., Tseng, W., Char, W. F., & Fukunaga, C. S. (1978). Child custody decision making: The search for improvement. *American Academy of Child Psychiatry, 17*, 104–116.

Mcentee, B. K. (1999). MMPI–A Personality Psychopathology Five. *Dissertations International: Section B: The Sciences and Engineering, 60*(2-B), 0837.

McGrath, R. E., Pogge, D. L., Stein, L. A. R., Graham, J. R., Zaccario, M., & Piacentini, T. (2000). Development of an Infrequency–Psychopathology scale for the MMPI–A: The *Fp*–A scale. *Journal of Personality Assessment, 74*, 282–295.

McGrath, R. E., Pogge, D. L., & Stokes, J. M. (2002). Incremental validity of selected MMPI–A content scales in an inpatient setting. *Psychological Assessment, 14*, 401–409.

McGrath, R. E., Sweeney, M., O'Malley, W. B., & Carlton, T. K. (1998). Identifying psychological contributions to chronic pain complaints with the MMPI–2: The role of the *K* scale. *Journal of Personality Assessment, 70*, 448–459.

McGrath, R. E., Terranova, R., Pogge, D. L., & Kravic, C. (2003). Development of a short form for the MMPI–2 based on scale elevation congruence. *Assessment, 10*, 13–28.

McLaughlin, R. H. (1999). An examination of MMPI–2 content scale performances among a sample of criminal offenders (social discomfort, correctional norms, gender). *Dissertations International: Section B: The Sciences and Engineering, 59*(10-B), 5610.

McNulty, J., Graham, J. R., Ben-Porath, Y. S., & Stein, L. A. R. (1997). Comparative validity of MMPI–2 scores of African-American and Caucasian mental health clients. *Psychological Assessment, 9*, 464–470.

McNulty, J. L., Harkness, A. R., & de Raad, B. (2002). The MMPI–2 personality psychopathology–Five (PSY–5) scales and the five factor model. In *Big five assessment* (pp. 436–452). Ashland, OH: Hogrefe & Huber.

McSweeny, A. J., Becker, B. C., Naugle, R. I., Snow, W. G., Binder, L. M., & Thompson, L. L. (1998). Ethical issues related to the presence of third party observers in clinical neuropsychological evaluations. *Clinical Neuropsychologist, 12*(4), 552–559.

Meaney, J. (1995). From *Frye* to *Daubert*: Is a pattern unfolding? *Juristics, 35*, 191–201.

Meehl, P. E., & Hathaway, S. R. (1946). The factor as a suppressor variable in the MMPI. *Journal of Applied Psychology, 30*, 525–564.

Megargee, E. I. (1979). *How to do publishable research with the MMPI: Clinical notes of the MMPI*. Minneapolis, MN: National Computer Systems.

Megargee, E. I. (1984). A new classification system for criminal offenders: VI. Differences among the types on the Adjective Checklist. *Criminal Justice and Behavior, 11*, 349–376.

Megargee, E. I. (1992). *Impact of the revised MMPI (MMPI–2) on the Megargee MMPI–based offender classification system*. Washington, DC: National Institute of Justice.

Megargee, E. I. (1994). Using the Megargee MMPI-based classification system with the MMPI–2 of male prison inmates. *Psychological Assessment, 6*, 337–344.

Megargee, E. I. (1995). Use of the MMPI–2 in correctional settings. In Y. S. Ben-Porath, J. R. Graham, G. C. N. Hall, R. D. Hirschman, & M. S. Zaragoza (Eds.), *Forensic applications of the MMPI–2* (pp. 127–159). Thousand Oaks, CA: Sage.

Megargee, E. I. (1997). Using the Megargee MMPI–based classification system with the MMPI–2s of female prison inmates. *Psychological Assessment, 9*, 75–82.

Megargee, E. I. (2004, May). *Development and validation of an MMPI–2 Infrequency Scale (FC) for use with criminal offenders*. Paper presented at the 39th annual symposium on recent developments of the MMPI–2/ MMPI–A, Minneapolis, MN.

Megargee, E. I. (2006). Using the MMPI–2 in correctional settings. In J. N. Butcher (Ed.), *MMPI–2: A practitioner's guide* (pp. 327–360). Washington, DC: American Psychological Association.

Megargee, E. I., & Bohn, M. J. (1977). A new classification system for criminal offenders: IV. Empirically determined characteristics of the ten types. *Criminal Justice and Behavior, 4*, 149–210.

Megargee, E. I., & Bohn, M. J. (1979). *Classifying criminal offenders: A new system based on the MMPI*. Newbury Park, CA: Sage.

Megargee, E. I., & Carbonell, J. L. (1995). Use of the MMPI–2 in correctional settings. In Y. S. Ben-Porath, J. R. Graham, G. C. N. Hirschman, & M. S. Zaragoza (Eds.), *Forensic applications of the MMPI–2* (pp. 127 –159). Thousand Oaks, CA: Sage.

Megargee, E. I., Carbonell, J. L., Bohn, M. B., & Sliger, G. L. (2001). *Classifying criminal offenders with the MMPI–2*. Minneapolis: University of Minnesota Press.

Meier, P. (1986). Damned liars and expert witnesses. *Journal of the American Statistical Association, 81*, 269–276.

Melonas, I. A. (1998). A comparison of psychopathology in male adolescent child molesters and other male adolescent sex offenders. *Dissertation Abstracts International: Section B: The Sciences and Engineering, 58*(9-B), 5130.

Melville, J. D., & Naimark, D. (2002). Punishing the insane: The verdict of guilty but mentally ill. *Journal of the American Academy of Psychiatry and the Law, 30*(4), 553–555.

Menninger, K. A. (1945). *The human mind*. New York: Knopf.

Meringoff, L. K. (1980). A story, a story. *Journal of Educational Psychology, 72*, 240–249.

Micucci, J. A. (2002). Accuracy of MMPI–A scales *ACK, MAC–R*, and *PRO* in detecting comorbid substance abuse among psychiatric inpatients. *Assessment, 9*(2), 111–122.

Miller, H. R., Goldberg, J. O., & Streiner, D. L. (1995). What's in a name? The MMPI–2 PTSD scales. *Journal of Clinical Psychology, 51*, 626–631.

Miller, M. O., & Sales, B. D. (1986). *Law and mental health professionals: Arizona*. Washington, DC: American Psychological Association.

Miller, R. D. (1990). Prearrangement forensic evaluation: The odyssey moves east of the Pecos. *Bulletin of the American Academy of Psychiatry and Law, 18*, 311–321.

Millon, T. (1969). *Modern psychopathology: A biosocial approach to maladaptive learning and functioning*. Philadelphia: W. B. Saunders.

Millon, T. (1981). *Disorders of personality: DSM–III: Axis II*. New York: Wiley.

Millon, T. (1987). *Manual for the Millon Clinical Multiaxial Inventory—II*. Minneapolis, MN: National Computer Systems.

Millon, T. F. (1994). *MCMI–III: Manual*. Minneapolis, MN: National Computer Systems.

Millon, T. (1997). *The MCMI–III*. Minneapolis, MN: Pearson Assessments.

Miner, M. H., & Dwyer, S. M. (1995). Analysis of dropouts from outpatient sex offender treatment. *Journal of Psychology and Human Sexuality, 7*(3), 77–93.

Miner, M. H., Marques, J. K., Day, D. M., & Nelson, C. (1990). Impact of relapse prevention in treating sex offenders: Preliminary findings. *Annals of Sex Research, 3*(2), 165–185.

Monahan, J. (1980). *Who is the client? The ethics of psychological intervention in the criminal justice system*. Washington, DC: American Psychological Association.

Moore, J. M., Thompson-Pope, S. K., & Whited, R. M. (1996). MMPI–A profiles of adolescent boys with a history of firesetting. *Journal of Personality Assessment, 67,* 116–126.

Moreland, K. (1987). Computerized psychological assessment: What's available? In J. N. Butcher (Ed.), *Computerized psychological assessment* (pp. 26–49). New York: Basic Books.

Morey, L. C. (1991). *The Personality Assessment Inventory.* Lutz, FL: Psychological Assessment Resources.

Morey, L. C. (1996). *An interpretive guide to the Personality Assessment Inventory (PAI).* Lutz, FL: Psychological Assessment Resources.

Morey, L. C. (2003). *Essentials of PAI assessment.* Wiley.

Morrell, J. S., & Rubin, J. L. (2001). The Minnesota Multiphasic Personality Inventory—2, posttraumatic stress disorder, and women domestic violence survivors. *Professional psychology: Research and Practice, 32,* 151–156.

Morrow, D. G., Greenspan, S. L., & Bower, G. H. (1987). Accessibility and situation models in narrative comprehension. *Journal of Memory and Comprehension, 26,* 165–187.

Morton, T. L., & Farris, K. L. (2002). MMPI–A structural summary characteristics of male juvenile delinquents. *Assessment, 9,* 327–333.

Morton, T. L., Farris, K. L., & Brenowitz, L. H. (2002). MMPI–A scores and high points of male juvenile delinquents: Scales 4, 5, and 6 as markers of juvenile delinquency. *Psychological Assessment, 14,* 311–319.

Moskowitz, J. L., Lewis, R. J., Ito, M. S., & Ehrmentraut, J. (1999). MMPI–2 profiles of NGRI and civil patients. *Journal of Clinical Psychology, 55,* 659–668.

Moss, C. S., Johnson, M. E., & Hosford, R. E. (1984). An assessment of the Megargee typology in lifelong criminal violence. *Criminal Justice and Behavior, 11,* 225–234.

Motiuk, L. L., Bonta, J., & Andrews, D. A. (1986). Classification in correctional halfway houses: The relative and incremental predictive criterion validities of the Megargee–MMPI and LSI systems. *Criminal Justice and Behavior, 13,* 33–46.

Moyer, D. M., Burkhardt, B., & Gordon, R. M. (2002). Faking PTSD from a motor vehicle accident on the MMPI–2. *American Journal of Forensic Psychology, 20*(2), 81–89.

Mrad, D. F., Kabacoff, R. I., & Duckro, P. (1983). Validation of the Megargee typology in a halfway house setting. *Criminal Justice and Behavior, 10,* 252–262.

Munley, P. H., Bains, D. S., Bloem, W. D., & Busby, R. M. (1995). Post-traumatic stress disorder and the MMPI–2. *Journal of Traumatic Stress, 8*(1), 171–178.

Munley, P. H., Germain, J. M., Tovar-Murray, D. & Borgman, A. L. (2004). MMPI–2 profile code types

and measurement error. *Journal of Personality Assessment, 82,* 179–188.

Murray, H. A. (1943). *Thematic Apperception Test: Manual.* Cambridge, MA: Harvard University.

Murstein, B. I., & Glaudin, V. (1968). The use of the MMPI in the determination of marital adjustment. *Journal of Marriage and Family, 30,* 651–655.

Neighbours, J. S. (1991). The use of the MMPI and a cross-validation of the Keane PTSD subscale in the differential diagnosis of posttraumatic stress disorder in workers' compensation patients. *Dissertation Abstracts International, 51*(12-B, Pt 1), 6147.

Nelson, L. (1987). Measuring depression in a clinical population using the MMPI. *Journal of Consulting and Clinical Psychology, 55,* 788–790.

Nelson, L. (1995). Use of the MMPI and MMPI–2 in forensic neurological evaluations. In Y. S. Ben-Porath, J. R. Graham, G. C. N. Hall, R. D. Hirschman, & M. S. Zaragoza (Eds.), *Forensic applications of the MMPI–2* (pp. 202–221). Thousand Oaks, CA: Sage.

Nelson, L., & Cicchetti, D. (1991). Validity of the MMPI Depression Scale for outpatients. *Psychological Assessment, 3,* 55–59.

Nelson, L. D., Pham, D., & Uchiyama, C. (1996). Subtlety of the MMPI–2 Depression Scale: A subject laid to rest. *Psychological Assessment, 8,* 331–333.

Newnan, O. S., Heaton, R. S., & Lehman, R. A. W. (1978). Neuropsychological and MMPI correlates of patient's future employment characteristics. *Perceptual and Motor Skills, 46,* 635–642.

Newsome, C. R., Archer, R. P., Trumbetta, S., & Gottesman, I. I. (2003). Changes in adolescent response patterns on the MMPI/MMPI–A across four decades. *Journal of Personality Assessment, 81,* 74–84.

Nichols, D. S. (in press). The trials of separating bath water from baby: A review and critique of the MMPI–2 Restructured Clinical Scales. *Journal of Personality Assessment.*

Nichols, B. L., & Czirr, R. (1986). Post-traumatic stress disorder: Hidden syndrome in elders. *Clinical Gerontologist, 5,* 417–433.

Nicholson, R. A., Mouton, G. J., Bagby, R. M., Buis, T., Peterson, S. A., & Buigas, R. A. (1997). Utility of MMPI–2 indicators of response distortion: Receiver operating characteristic analysis. *Psychological Assessment, 9,* 471–479.

Nizer, L. (1961). *My life in court.* Garden City, NY: Doubleday.

Noel, B., & Watterson, K. (1992). *You must be dreaming.* New York: Poseidon.

Nwokike, J. (2005). Federal insanity acquittees. *Journal of the American Academy of Psychiatry and the Law, 33*(1), 126–128.

O'Dell, J. W. (1972). P. T. Barnum explores the computer. *Journal of Consulting and Clinical Psychology, 38,* 270–273.

Office of Civil Rights. (2005). *Medical privacy—National standards to protect the privacy of personal health information.* Retrieved October 13, 2005, from http://www.hhs.gov/ocr/hipaa

Ogloff, J. R. P. (1995). The legal basis of forensic applications of the MMPI–2. In Y. S. Ben-Porath, J. R. Graham, G. C. N. Hall, R. D. Hirschman, & M. S. Zargoza (Eds.), *Forensic applications of the MMPI–2* (pp. 18–47). Thousand Oaks, CA: Sage.

Oleske, D. M., Andersson, G. B. J., Lavender, S. A., & Hahn, J. J. (2000). Association between recovery outcomes for work-related low back disorders and personal, family, and work factors. *Spine, 25,* 1259–1265.

Olio, K. A., & Cornell, W. F. (1998). The facade of scientific documentation: A case study of Richard Ofshe's analysis of the Paul Ingram case. *Psychology, Public Policy, and Law, 4,* 1182–1197.

Ollendick, D. G. (1984). Scores on three MMPI alcohol scales of parents who receive child custody. *Psychological Reports, 55,* 337–338.

Ollendick, D. G., & Otto, B. J. (1983). MMPI characteristics of parents referred for child-custody studies. *Journal of Psychology, 117,* 227–232.

Ollendick, D. G., Otto, B. J., & Heider, S. M. (1983). Marital MMPI characteristics: A test of Arnold's signs. *Journal of Clinical Psychology, 39,* 240–245.

Osberg, T. M. (1999). Comparative validity of the MMPI–2 Wiener–Harmon subtle–obvious scales in male prison inmates. *Journal of Personality Assessment, 72,* 36–48.

Osberg, T. M., & Poland, D. L. (2001). Validity of the MMPI–2 basic and Harris–Lingoes subscales in a forensic sample. *Journal of Clinical Psychology, 57,* 1369–1380.

Osberg, T. M., & Poland, D. L. (2002). Comparative accuracy of the MMPI–2 and the MMPI–A in the diagnosis of psychopathology in 18-year-olds. *Psychological Assessment, 14,* 164–169.

Osborne, D. (1971). An MMPI index of disturbed marital interaction. *Psychological Reports, 29,* 851–854.

Otto, R. (2002). Use of the MMPI in forensic settings. *Journal of Forensic Psychology Practice, 2,* 73–91.

Otto, R., & Butcher, J. N. (1995). Computer-assisted psychological assessment in child custody evaluations. *Family Law Quarterly, 29,* 79–96.

Otto, R., & Collins, R. P. (1995). Use of the MMPI–2/MMPI–A in child custody evaluations. In Y. S. Ben-Porath, J. R. Graham, G. C. N. Hall, R. D. Hirschman, & M. S. Zaragoza (Eds.), *Forensic applications of the MMPI–2* (pp. 222–252). Thousand Oaks, CA: Sage.

Overall, J. E., & Gomez-Mont, F. (1974). The MMPI–168 for psychiatric screening. *Educational and Psychological Measurement, 34,* 315–319.

Ownby, R. L. (1987). *Psychological reports: A guide to report writing in professional psychology.* Brandon, VT: Clinical Psychology.

Palav, A., Ortega, A., & McCaffrey, R. J. (2001). Incremental validity of the MMPI–2 content scales: A preliminary study with brain-injured patients. *Journal of Head Trauma Rehabilitation, 16*(3), 275–283.

Pancoast, D. L., & Archer, R. (1989). Original adult MMPI norms in normal samples: A review with implications for future developments. *Journal of Personality Assessment, 53,* 376–395.

Panton, J. H. (1970). *Manual for a Prison Classification Inventory (PCI) for the MMPI.* Raleigh, NC: Department of Social Rehabilitation and Control.

Panton, J. H. (1973). Personality characteristics of management problem prison inmates. *Journal of Community Psychology, 1,* 185–191.

Paolo, A., Ryan, J., & Smith, A. J. (1991). Reading difficulty of MMPI–2 subscales. *Journal of Clinical Psychology, 47,* 529–532.

Parker, J. C., Doerfler, L. A., Tatten, H. A., & Hewett, J. E. (1983). Psychological factors that influence self-reported pain. *Journal of Clinical Psychology, 39,* 22–25.

Parkison, S., & Fishburne, F. (1984). MMPI normative data for a male active duty Army population. In *Proceedings of Psychology in the Department of Defense, ninth symposium* (USAFA-TR-84-2). Colorado Springs, CO: USAF Academy, Department of Behavioral Sciences.

Parwatikar, S. D., Holcomb, W. R., & Menninger, K. A. (1985). The detection of malingered amnesia in accused murderers. *Bulletin of the American Academy of Psychiatry and the Law, 13,* 97–103.

Patrick, J. (1988). Personality characteristics of work-ready workers' compensation clients. *Journal of Clinical Psychology, 44,* 1009–1012.

Patterson, J. T. (1987). *The dread disease: Cancer and modern American culture.* Cambridge, MA: Harvard University Press.

Paulhus, D. L. (1986). Self deception and impression management in test responses. In A. Angleitner & J. Wiggins (Eds.), *Personality assessment via questionnaires* (pp. 143–165). Berlin, Germany: Springer-Verlag.

Paulson, M. J., Afifi, A., Chaleff, A., Thomason, M., & Lui, V. (1975). An MMPI scale for identifying at-risk abusive parents. *Journal of Clinical Child Psychology, 4,* 22–24.

Paulson, M. J., Afifi, A., Thomason, M., & Chaleff, A. (1974). The MMPI: A descriptive measure of psychopathology in abusive parents. *Journal of Clinical Psychology, 30,* 387–390.

Paulson, M. J., Schwemer, G. T., & Bendel, R. B. (1976). Clinical applications of the *Pd, Ma,* and *OH,* and experimental MMPI scales to further understanding of abusive parents. *Journal of Clinical Psychology, 32,* 558–564.

Pearson, C., & Pope, K. (1981–1982). Consciousness in the feminist novel. *Imagination, Cognition, and Personality: Consciousness in Theory, Research, and Clinical Practice, 1,* 185–192.

Pena, C., Cabiya, J. J., & Echevarria, N. (1998, March). *Changes in the MMPI–2 mean T scores of prisoners convicted of violent crimes who were enrolled in a treatment program based on the social learning model.* Paper presented at the 34th Annual Conference on Recent Developments in the Use of the MMPI–2, Clearwater, FL.

Pena, L. M. (2001). The association of MMPI–A scales with measures of adjustment among institutionalized male juvenile delinquents. *Dissertation Abstracts International: Section B: The Sciences and Engineering, 62*(5-B), 2527.

Pena, L. M., Megargee, E. I., & Brody, E. (1996). MMPI–A patterns of male juvenile delinquents. *Psychological Assessment, 8,* 388–397.

Penk, W. E., Drebing, C., & Schutt, R. (2002). PTSD in the workplace. In J. C. Thomas & M. Hersen (Eds.), *Handbook of mental health in the workplace* (pp. 215–249). Thousand Oaks, CA: Sage.

Penk, W. E., Rierdan, J., Losardo, M., & Robinowitz, R. (2006). The MMPI–2 and assessment of post-traumatic stress disorder (PTSD). In J. N. Butcher (Ed.), *MMPI–2: A practitioners guide* (pp. 121–141). Washington, DC: American Psychological Association.

Penk, W. E., Robinowitz, R., Dorsett, D., Black, J., Dolan, M. P., & Bell, W. (1989). Co-morbidity: Lessons learned about post-traumatic stress disorder (PTSD) from developing PTSD scales for the MMPI. *Journal of Clinical Psychology, 45,* 709–717.

Pennington, N., & Hastie, R. (1981). Juror decision-making models: The generalization gap. *Psychological Bulletin, 89,* 246–287.

Pennington, N., & Hastie, R. (1988). Explanation-based decision making: Effects of memory structure on judgment. *Journal of Experimental Psychology: Learning, Memory, and Cognition, 14,* 521–533.

Pennington, N., & Hastie, R. (1991). A cognitive theory of juror decision making: The story model. *Cardozo Law Review, 13,* 5001–5039.

Pennington, N., & Hastie, R. (1992). Explaining the evidence: Tests of the story model for juror decision making. *Journal of Personality and Social Psychology, 62,* 189–206.

Perrin, S., Van Hasselt, V. B., & Hersen, M. (1997). Validation of the Keane MMPI–PTSD scale against *DSM–III–R* criteria in a sample of battered women. *Violence and Victims, 12*(1), 99–104.

Perspectives. (1990, April 23). *Newsweek,* p. 17.

Peters, F. (1984). Cross-examination of the adverse medical expert: Keep the jury laughing. In B. G. Warshaw (Ed.), *The trial masters: A handbook of strategies and tactics that win cases* (pp. 287–304). New York: Prentice Hall.

Physicians for Human Rights. (1991). *Medical testimony on victims of torture: A physician's guide to political asylum cases.* Boston: Author.

Piotrowski, C. (1998). Assessment of pain: A survey of practicing clinicians. *Perceptual and Motor Skills, 86,* 181–192.

Pirrello, V. E. (1999). An empirically derived classification system for adolescent sex offenders. *Dissertation Abstracts International: Section B: The Sciences and Engineering, 60*(3-B), 1311.

Plante, T. G., Manuel, G., & Bryant, C. (1996). Personality and cognitive functioning among hospitalized sexual offending Roman Catholic priests. *Pastoral Psychology, 45*(2), 129–139.

Pogge, D. L., Stokes, J. M., McGrath, R. E., Bilginer, L., & DeLuca, V. A. (2002). MMPI–A Structural Summary variables: Prevalence and correlates in an adolescent inpatient psychiatric sample. *Assessment, 9*(4), 334–342.

Pollack, D. R., & Grainey, T. F. (1984). A comparison of MMPI profiles for state and private disability insurance applicants. *Journal of Personality Assessment, 48,* 121–125.

Pollard, R. Q. (2002). Ethical conduct in research involving deaf people. In V. A. Gutman (Ed.), *Ethics in mental health and deafness* (pp. 162–178). Washington, DC: Gallaudet University Press.

Pope, K. S. (1990). Ethical and malpractice issues in hospital practice. *American Psychologist, 45,* 1066–1070.

Pope, K. S. (1992). Responsibilities in providing psychological test feedback to clients. *Psychological Assessment, 4,* 268–271.

Pope, K. S. (1994). *Sexual involvement with therapists: Patient assessment, subsequent therapy, forensics.* Washington, DC: American Psychological Association.

Pope, K. S. (1995). What psychologists better know about recovered memories, research, lawsuits, and the pivotal experiment. *Clinical Psychology: Science and Practice, 2,* 304–315.

Pope, K. S. (1996). Memory, abuse, and science: Questioning claims about the false memory syndrome epidemic. *American Psychologist, 51,* 957–974.

Pope, K. S. (1997). Science as careful questioning: Are claims of a false memory syndrome epidemic based on empirical evidence? *American Psychologist, 52,* 997–1006.

Pope, K. S. (1998). Pseudoscience, cross-examination, and scientific evidence in the recovered memory controversy. *Psychology, Public Policy, and the Law, 4,* 1160–1181.

Pope, K. S. (2003). Developing and practicing ethics. In J. M. Prinstein & M. D. Patterson (Eds.), *The portable mentor: Expert guide to a successful career in psychology* (pp. 33–43). New York: Kluwer Academic/Plenum Press.

Pope, K. S. (2005a). *Malingering research update.* Retrieved October 17, 2005, from http://kspope.com/assess/malinger.php

Pope, K. S. (2005b). *Torture.* Retrieved October 11, 2005, from http://kspope.com/torvic/torture.php

Pope, K. S. (2006). *The therapist as a person.* Retrieved January 12, 2006, from http://kspope.com

Pope, K. S., & Bajt, T. R. (1988). When laws and values conflict: A dilemma for psychologists. *American Psychologist, 43,* 828.

Pope, K. S., & Bouhoutsos, J. C. (1986). *Sexual intimacy between therapists and patients.* New York: Praeger/Greenwood.

Pope, K. S., & Brown, L. S. (1996). *Recovered memories of abuse: Assessment, therapy, forensics.* Washington, DC: American Psychological Association.

Pope, K. S., & Feldman-Summers, S. (1992). National survey of psychologists' sexual and physical abuse history and their evaluation of training and competence in these areas. *Professional Psychology: Research and Practice, 23,* 353–361.

Pope, K. S., & Garcia-Peltoniemi, R. E. (1991). Responding to victims of torture: Clinical issues, professional responsibilities, and useful resources. *Professional Psychology: Research and Practice, 22,* 269–276.

Pope, K. S., Sonne, J. L., & Greene, B. (2006). *What therapists don't talk about and why: Understanding taboos that hurt us and our clients.* Washington, DC: American Psychological Association.

Pope, K. S., Sonne, J. L., & Holroyd, J. (1993). *Sexual feelings in psychotherapy: Explorations for therapists and therapists-in-training.* Washington, DC: American Psychological Association.

Pope, K. S., & Tabachnick, B. G. (1993). Therapists' anger, hate, fear, and sexual feelings: National survey of therapists' responses, client characteristics, critical events, formal complaints, and training. *Pro-fessional Psychology: Research and Practice, 24,* 142–152.

Pope, K. S., & Tabachnick, B. G. (1994). Therapists as patients: A national study of psychologists' experiences, problems, and beliefs. *Professional Psychology: Research and Practice, 25,* 247–258.

Pope, K. S., Tabachnick, B. G., & Keith-Spiegel, P. (1987). Ethics of practice: The beliefs and behaviors of psychologists as therapists. *American Psychologist, 42,* 993–1006.

Pope, K. S., Tabachnick, B. G., & Keith-Spiegel, P. (1988). Good and poor practices in psychotherapy: A national survey of beliefs of psychologists. *Professional Psychology: Research and Practice, 19,* 547–552.

Pope, K. S., & Vasquez, M. J. T. (1998). *Ethics in psychotherapy and counseling: A practical guide* (2nd ed.). San Francisco: Jossey-Bass.

Pope, K. S., & Vasquez, M. J. T. (2005). *How to survive and thrive as a therapist: Information, ideas, and resources for psychologists in practice.* Washington, DC: American Psychological Association.

Pope, K. S., & Vasquez, M. J. T. (in press). *Ethics in psychotherapy and counseling: A practical guide for psychologists* (3rd ed.). San Francisco: Jossey-Bass.

Pope, K. S., & Vetter, V. A. (1991). Prior therapist–patient sexual involvement among patients seen by psychologists. *Psychotherapy, 28,* 429–438.

Pope, K. S., & Vetter, V. A. (1992). Ethical dilemmas encountered by members of the American Psychological Association: A national survey. *American Psychologist, 47,* 397–411.

Postuma, A. B., & Harper, J. F. (1998). Comparison of MMPI–2 responses of child custody and personal injury litigants. *Professional Psychology: Research and Practice, 29,* 437–443.

Powell, M., Illovsky, M., O'Leary, W. C., & Gazda, G. M. (1988). Life-skills training with hospitalized psychiatric patients. *International Journal of Group Psychotherapy, 38,* 109–117.

Powis, D. M. (1999). Actuarial use of the MMPI–A: Generation of clinical correlate data for frequently occurring codetypes in an adolescent inpatient sample. *Dissertations International: Section B: The Sciences and Engineering, 59*(11-B), 6107.

Putzke, J. D., Williams, M. A., Daniel, F. J., & Boll, T. J. (1999). The utility of *K*-correction to adjust for a defensive response set on the MMPI. *Assessment, 6*(1), 61–70.

Rader, C. M. (1977). MMPI profile types of exposers, rapists, and assaulters in a court service population. *Journal of Consulting and Clinical Psychology, 45,* 61–69.

Rathus, S. A., & Siegel, L. J. (1980). Crime and personality revisited. *Criminology, 18,* 245–251.

Rayls, K. R., Mittenberg, W., Burns, W. J., & Theroux, S. (2000). Prospective study of the MMPI–2 correction factor after mild head injury. *Clinical Neuropsychologist, 14,* 546–550.

Reed, M. K., Walker, B., Williams, G., McCloud, S., & Jones, S. (1996). MMPI–2 patterns in African-American females. *Journal of Clinical Psychology, 52,* 437–441.

Reitan, R. M., & Wolfson, D. (1985). *The Halstead–Reitan Neuropsychological Test Battery: Theory and clinical interpretation.* Tucson, AZ: Neuropsychology Press.

Reitan, R. M., & Wolfson, D. (1997). Emotional disturbances and their interaction with neuropsychological deficits. *Neuropsychology Review, 7,* 3–19.

Repko, G. R., & Cooper, R. (1983). A study of the average worker's compensation case. *Journal of Clinical Psychology, 39,* 287–295.

Resource finder for torture victims, asylum-seekers, and refugees. (2005). Retrieved October 11, 2005, from http://kspope.com/torvic/php

Responding to victims of torture: Clinical issues, professional responsibilities, and useful resources. (2005). Retrieved October 11, 2005, from http://kspope.com/torvic/torture1.php

Rice, M., Arnold, L., & Tate, D. (1983). Faking good and bad adjustment on the MMPI and over-controlled-hostility in maximum security psychiatric patients. *Canadian Journal of Behavioral Sciences, 15,* 43–51.

Rissetti, F., & Maltes, S. (1985). Use of the MMPI in Chile. In J. N. Butcher & C. D. Spielberger (Eds.), *Advances in personality assessment* (Vol. 4, pp. 209–257). Hillsdale, NJ: Erlbaum.

Roberts, A. H. (1984). The operant approach to the management of pain and excess disability. In A. D. Holzman & D. C. Turk (Eds.), *Pain management: A handbook of psychological treatment approaches* (pp. 10–30). New York: Pergamon Press.

Roberts, A. H., & Reinhardt, L. (1980). The behavioral management of chronic pain: Long-term follow-up with comparison groups. *Pain, 8,* 151–162.

Rogers, R. (1983). Malingering or random? A research note on obvious vs. subtle subscales of the MMPI. *Journal of Clinical Psychology, 39,* 257–258.

Rogers, R. (1984). Towards an empirical model of malingering and deception. *Behavioral Sciences and the Law, 2,* 93–111.

Rogers, R. (2003). Forensic use and abuse of psychological tests: Multiscale inventories. *Journal of Psychiatric Practice, 9,* 316–320.

Rogers, R., Bagby, R. M., & Chakraborty, D. (1993). Feigning schizophrenic disorders on the MMPI–2: Detection of coached simulators. *Journal of Personality Assessment, 60,* 215–226.

Rogers, R., & Cruise, K. R. (1998). Assessment of malingering with simulation designs: Threats to external validity. *Law and Human Behavior, 23,* 273–285.

Rogers, R., Dolmetsch, R., & Cavanaugh, J. L. (1983). Identification of random responders on MMPI protocols. *Journal of Personality Assessment, 47,* 364–368.

Rogers, R., Gillis, J. R., McMain, S., & Dickens, S. E. (1988). Fitness evaluations: A retrospective study of clinical, criminal, and sociodemographic characteristics. *Canadian Journal of Behavioral Science, 20,* 192–200.

Rogers, R., Harris, M., & Thatcher, A. A. (1983). Identification of random responders on the MMPI: An actuarial approach. *Psychological Reports, 53,* 1171–1174.

Rogers, R., & McKee, G. R. (1995). Use of the MMPI–2 in the assessment of criminal responsibility. In Y. S. Ben-Porath, J. R. Graham, G. C. N. Hall, R. D. Hirschman, & M. S. Zargoza (Eds.), *Forensic applications of the MMPI–2* (pp. 103–126). Thousand Oaks, CA: Sage.

Rogers, R., Salekin, R. T., & Sewell, K. W. (1999). Validation of the Millon Clinical Multiaxial Inventory for Axis II disorders: Does it meet the *Daubert* standard? *Law and Human Behavior, 23,* 425–443.

Rogers, R., Salekin, R. T., Sewell, K. W., Goldstein, A., & Leonard, K. (1998). A comparison of forensic and nonforensic malingerers: A prototypical analysis of explanatory models. *Law and Human Behavior, 22,* 353–367.

Rogers, R., Sewell, K. W., Cruise, K. R., Wang, E. W., & Ustad, K. L. (1998). The PAI and feigning: A cautionary note on its use in forensic-correctional settings. *Assessment, 5,* 399–405.

Rogers, R., Sewell, K. W., Martin, M. A., & Vitacco, M. J. (2003). Detection of feigned mental disorders: A meta-analysis of the MMPI–2 and malingering. *Assessment, 10,* 160–177.

Rogers, R., Sewell, K., & Saleken, R. (1994). A meta-analysis of malingering on the MMPI–2. *Assessment, 1,* 227–237.

Rohling, M. L., Binder, L. M., & Langhinrichsen-Rohling, J. (1995). Money matters: A meta-analytic review of the association between financial compensation and the experience and treatment of chronic pain. *Health Psychology, 14,* 537–547.

Roman, D. D., & Gerbing, D. W. (1989). The mentally disordered criminal offender: A description based on demographic, clinical, and MMPI data. *Journal of Clinical Psychology, 45,* 983–990.

Roman, D. D., Tuley, M. R., Villanueva, M. R., & Mitchell, W. E. (1990). Evaluating MMPI validity in a forensic psychiatric population. *Criminal Justice and Behavior, 17,* 186–198.

Roper, B. L., Ben-Porath, Y. S., & Butcher, J. N. (1991). Comparability of computerized adaptive and conventional testing with the MMPI–2. *Journal of Personality Assessment, 57,* 278–290.

Rosenbaum, R. (1991). *Travels with Dr. Death.* New York: Penguin Books.

Ross, S. R., Millis, S. R., Krukowski, R. A., Putnam, S. H., & Adams, K. M. (2004). Detecting incomplete effort on the MMPI–2: An examination of the Fake–Bad Scale in mild head injury. *Journal of Clinical and Experimental Neuropsychology, 26*(1), 115–124.

Rothke, S. E., Friedman, A. F., Dahlstrom, W. G., & Greene, R. L. (1994). MMPI–2 normative data for the *F-K* index: Implications for clinical, neuropsychological, and forensic practice. *Assessment, 1*(1), 1–15.

Rubenzer, S. (1991). Computerized testing and clinical judgment: Cause for concern. *Clinical Psychologist, 44,* 63–66.

Ruch, F. L., & Ruch, W. M. (1967). The *K* factor as a (validity) suppressor variable in predicting success in selling. *Journal of Applied Psychology, 51,* 201–204.

Ruiz, M. A., Drake, E. B., Glass, A., Marcotte, D., & van Gorp, W. G. (2002). Trying to beat the system: Misuse of the Internet to assist in avoiding the detection of psychological symptom dissimulation. *Professional Psychology: Research and Practice, 33,* 294–299.

Sadoff, R. L. (1975). *Forensic psychiatry: A practical guide for lawyers and psychiatrists.* Springfield, IL: Charles C. Thomas.

Saks, M. J. (1977). *Jury verdicts: The role of group size and social decision rule.* Lexington, MA: Lexington Books.

Sales, B. D., & VandenBos, G. R. (1994). The value of psychology to the law and law to psychology. In B. D. Sales & G. R. VandenBos (Eds.), *Psychology in litigation and legislation* (pp. 1–10). Washington, DC: American Psychological Association.

Salomone, P. R. (1972). Client motivation and rehabilitation counseling outcome. *Rehabilitation Counseling Bulletin, 16,* 11–20.

Salter, A. C. (1988). *Treating child sex offenders and victims: A practical guide.* Thousand Oaks, CA: Sage.

Salter, A. C. (2003). *Predators: Pedophiles, rapists, and other sex offenders.* New York: Basic Books.

Savasir, I., & Erol, N. (1990). The Turkish MMPI: Translation, standardization, and validation. In J. N. Butcher & C. D. Spielberger (Eds.), *Advances in personality assessment* (Vol. 8, pp. 49–62). Hillsdale, NJ: Erlbaum.

Schafer, R. (1992). *Retelling a life.* New York: Basic Books.

Schank, R. C. (1980). Language and memory. *Cognitive Science, 4,* 243–284.

Schank, R. C. (1990). *Tell me a story: A new look at real and artificial memory.* New York: Scribner.

Schank, R. C., & Abelson, R. P. (1977). *Scripts, plans, goals, and understanding.* Hillsdale, NJ: Erlbaum.

Schank, R. C., Collins, G. C., & Hunter, L. E. (1986). Transcending inductive category formation in learning. *Behavioral and Brain Sciences, 9,* 639–651.

Schattner, T. J. (2003). Sex offenders and the use of the validity scales of the MMPI–2 to confirm treatment progress. *Dissertation Abstracts International: Section B: The Sciences and Engineering, 64*(5-B), 2404.

Scheibe, S., Bagby, R. M., Miller, L. S., & Dorian, B. J. (2001). Assessing posttraumatic disorder with the MMPI–2 in a sample of workplace accident victims. *Psychological Assessment, 13,* 369–374.

Schiele, B. C., & Brozek, J. (1948). "Experimental neurosis" resulting from semistarvation in man. *Psychosomatic Medicine, 10,* 31–50.

Schill, T., & Wang, T. (1990). Correlates of the MMPI–2 Anger Content Scale. *Psychological Reports, 67,* 800–804.

Schinka, J. A., & LaLone, L. (1997). MMPI–2 norms: Comparisons with a census-matched subsample. *Psychological Assessment, 9,* 307–311.

Schlank, A. M. (1995). The utility of the MMPI and the MSI for identifying a sexual offender typology. *Sexual Abuse: Journal of Research and Treatment 7*(3), 185–194.

Schlenger, W. E., & Kukla, R. A. (1987, August). *Performance of the Keane–Fairbank MMPI Scale and other self-report measures in identifying posttraumatic stress disorder.* Paper presented at the 95th Annual Convention of the American Psychological Association, New York.

Schlenger, W. E., Kukla, R. A., Fairbank, J. A., Hough, R. L., Jordan, B. K., Marmar, C. R., et al. (1989). *The prevalence of post-traumatic stress disorder in the Vietnam generation: Findings from the National Vietnam Veterans Readjustment Study [Report] Research.* Triangle Park, NC: Research Triangle Institute.

Schmalz, B. J., Fehr, R. C., & Dalby, J. T. (1989). Distinguishing forensic, psychiatric and inmate groups with the MMPI. *American Journal of Forensic Psychology, 7,* 37–47.

Schmidt, H. O. (1948). Notes on the MMPI: The factor. *Journal of Consulting Psychology, 12,* 337–342.

Schneider, S. (1979). Disability payments for psychiatric patients: Is patient assessment affected? *Journal of Clinical Psychology, 35,* 259–264.

Schretlen, D. (1988). The use of psychological tests to identify malingered symptoms of mental disorder. *Clinical Psychology Review, 8,* 451–476.

Schretlen, D. (1990). A limitation of using Wiener and Harmon Obvious and Subtle Scales to detect faking on the MMPI. *Journal of Clinical Psychology, 46,* 1090–1095.

Schretlen, D., & Arkowitz, H. (1990). A psychological test battery to detect prison inmates who fake insanity or mental retardation. *Behavioral Sciences and the Law, 8,* 75–84.

Schretlen, D., Wilkins, S. S., Van Gorp, W. G., & Bobholz, J. H. (1992). Cross-validation of a psychological test battery to detect faked insanity. *Psychological Assessment, 4,* 77–83.

Scott, R., & Stone, D. (1986a). Measures of psychological disturbance in adolescent and adult victims of father–daughter incest. *Journal of Clinical Psychology, 42,* 251–269.

Scott, R., & Stone, D. (1986b). MMPI profile constellations in incest families. *Journal of Consulting and Clinical Psychology, 54,* 364–368.

Scotti, J. R., Sturges, L. V., & Lyons, J. A. (1996). The Keane PTSD scale extracted from the MMPI: Sensitivity and specificity with Vietnam veterans. *Journal of Traumatic Stress, 9,* 643–650.

Sellbom, M., & Ben-Porath, Y. S. (in press). Mapping the MMPI–2 Restructured Clinical (RC) Scales onto normal personality traits: Evidence of construct validity. *Journal of Personality Assessment.*

Sellbom, M., Ben-Porath, Y. S., Lilienfeld, S. O., Patrick, C. J., & Graham, J. R. (in press). Assessing psychopathic personality traits with the MMPI–2. *Journal of Personality Assessment.*

Serrano, R. A. (1992, March 27). Expert says baton swings missed King; testimony purged. *Los Angeles Times,* pp. B3–B4.

Shafer, R. (1954). *Psychoanalytic interpretation in Rorschach testing: Theory and application.* New York: Grune & Stratton.

Shaffer, J. W. (1981). Using the MMPI to evaluate mental impairment in disability determination. In J. N. Butcher, G. Dahlstrom, M. Gynther, & W. Schofield (Eds.), *Clinical notes on the MMPI* (pp. 1–12). Nutley, NJ: Hoffman-La Roche Laboratories/ National Computer Systems.

Shaffer, J. W., Nussbaum, K., & Little, J. M. (1972). MMPI profiles of disability insurance claimants. *American Journal of Psychiatry, 129,* 63–67.

Shapiro, D. L. (1984). *Psychological evaluation and expert testimony.* New York: Van Nostrand Reinhold.

Shapiro, D. L. (1991). *Forensic psychological assessment: An integrative approach.* Boston: Allyn & Bacon.

Shealy, L., Kalichman, S. C., Henderson, M. C., & Szymanowski, D. (1991). MMPI profile subtypes of incarcerated sex offenders against children. *Violence and Victims, 6*(3), 201–212

Shepard, M. (1971). *The love treatment: Sexual intimacies between patients and psychotherapists.* New York: Wyden.

Shondrick, D. D., Ben-Porath, Y. S., & Stafford, K. (1992, May). *Forensic assessment with the MMPI–2: Characteristics of individuals undergoing court-ordered evaluations.* Paper presented at the 27th Annual Symposium on Recent Developments in the Use of the MMPI (MMPI–2), Minneapolis, MN.

Shores, A., & Carstairs, J. R. (1998). Accuracy of the MMPI–2 computerized Minnesota Report in identifying fake–good and fake–bad response sets. *Clinical Neuropsychologist, 12,* 101–106.

Siegel, S. L. (2002). Typologies of sex offenders: A Minnesota Multiphasic Personality Inventory (MMPI) cluster analytic study. *Dissertation Abstracts International: Section B: The Sciences and Engineering, 62*(9-B), 4236.

Silver, R., & Sines, L. K. (1962). Diagnostic efficiency of the MMPI with and without correction. *Journal of Clinical Psychology, 18,* 312–314.

Simkins, L. (1993). Characteristics of sexually repressed child molesters. *Journal of Interpersonal Violence, 8*(1), 3–17.

Simmons, J. G., Johnson, D. L., Gouvier, W. D., & Muzyczka, M. J. (1981). The Myer–Megargee inmate typology: Dynamic or unstable? *Criminal Justice and Behavior, 8,* 49–54.

Simms, L. J., Casillas, A., Clark, L. A., Watson, D., & Doebbeling, B. N. (in press). Psychometric evaluation of the restructured clinical scales of the MMPI–2. *Psychological Assessment, 17,* 345–358.

Sines, L. K., Baucom, D. H., & Gruba, G. H. (1979). A validity scale sign calling for caution in the interpretation of MMPIs among psychiatric inpatients. *Journal of Personality Assessment, 43,* 604–607.

Singer, J., & Pope, K. S. (1978). *The power of human imagination: New methods of psychotherapy.* New York: Plenum Press.

Singer, J. L., Sincoff, J. B., & Kolligian, J. (1989). Counter-transference and cognition: Studying the psychotherapist's distortions as consequences of normal information processing. *Psychotherapy, 26,* 344–355.

Sirigatti, S., Giannini, M., Laura-Grotto, R., & Giangrasso, B. (2002). *Classificare i detenuti con il MMPI–2: il sistema di Megargee. Primi dati su un campione italiano* [Classifying prison inmates with the MMPI–2: The Megargee system. First data from an Italian sample]. *Bollettino di Psicologia Applicata, 238,* 17–23.

Sivec, H. J., Hilsenroth, M. J., & Lynn, S. J. (1995). Impact of simulating borderline personality disorder on the MMPI–2: A costs–benefits model employing base rates. *Journal of Personality Assessment, 64,* 295–311.

Sivec, H. J., Lynn, S. J., & Garske, J. P. (1994). The effect of somatoform disorder and paranoid psychotic role-related dissimulations as a response set on the MMPI–2. *Assessment, 1,* 69–81.

Slick, D. J., Hopp, G., Strauss, E., & Spellacy, F. J. (1996). Victoria Symptom Validity Test: Efficiency for detecting feigned memory impairment and relationship to neuropsychological tests and MMPI–2 validity scales. *Journal of Clinical and Experimental Neuropsychology, 18,* 911–922.

Sloan, P., Arsenault, L., & Hilsenroth, M. J. (1998). A longitudinal evaluation of the Mississippi Scale for Combat-Related PTSD in detecting war-related stress symptomatology. *Journal of Clinical Psychology, 54,* 1085–1090.

Sloan, P., Arsenault, L., McCormick, W. A., Dunn, S., & Scalf, L. (1992). Initial contact interviews with Marine reservists in Operation Desert Storm. In U.S. Department of Veteran's Affairs (Ed.), *Persian Gulf returnees: First year findings* (pp. 10–18). Westhaven, CT: Northeast Program Evaluation Center.

Smith, J. D., & Nelson, K. R. (1989). *The sterilization of Carrie Buck.* Far Hills, NJ: New Horizon Press.

Smith, S. R, Hilsenroth, M. J., Castlebury, F. D., & Durham, T. W. (1999). The clinical utility of the MMPI–2 Antisocial Practices Content Scale. *Journal of Personality Disorders, 13,* 385–393.

Smith, V. L. (1991). Prototypes in the courtroom: Lay representations of legal concepts. *Journal of Personality and Social Psychology, 61,* 857–872.

Sneyers, M., Sloore, H., Rossi, G., & Derksen, J. (2005). *Using the Megargee system among Belgian prisoners: Cross-cultural prevalence of the MMPI–2 based types.* Manuscript submitted for publication.

Snibbe, J. R., Peterson, P. J., & Sosner, B. (1980). Study of psychological characteristics of a worker's compensation sample using the MMPI and the Millon Clinical Multiaxial Inventory. *Psychological Reports, 47,* 959–966.

Snyder, D., & Regts, J. M. (1990). Personality correlates of marital satisfaction: A comparison of psychiatric, maritally distressed, and nonclinic samples. *Journal of Sex and Marital Therapy, 16,* 34–43.

Sonne, L., & Pope, K. S. (1991). Treating victims of therapist–patient sexual involvement. *Psychotherapy, 28,* 174–187.

Spence, G. (1983). *Of murder and madness.* Garden City, NY: Doubleday.

Spence, G., & Polk, A. (1982). *Gunning for justice.* Garden City, NY: Doubleday.

Spiro, A., III, Butcher, J. N., Levenson, M. R., Aldwin, C., & Bossé, R. (2000). Change and stability in personality: A five-year study of the MMPI–2 in older men. In J. N. Butcher (Ed.), *Basic sources on the MMPI–2*

(pp. 443–462). Minneapolis: University of Minnesota Press.

Spring, F. L., & Foote, W. L. (1986). Statement of principles relating to the responsibilities of attorneys and psychologists in their interprofessional relations: An interdisciplinary agreement between the New Mexico Bar Association and the New Mexico Psychological Association. Adopted August 30, 1986, by the Board of Bar Commissioners of the State Bar of New Mexico and New Mexico Psychological Association.

Stein, L. A. R., & Graham, J. R. (2005). Ability of substance abusers to escape detection on the Minnesota Multiphasic Personality Inventory–Adolescent (MMPI–A) in a juvenile correctional facility. *Assessment, 12*(1), 28–39.

Steinberg, E. R. (1982–1983). The stream-of-consciousness technique in the novel. *Imagination, Cognition, and Personality: Consciousness in Theory, Research, and Clinical Practice, 2,* 241–250.

Sternbach, R. A., Wolf, S. R., Murphy, R. W., & Akeson, W. H. (1973). Traits of pain patients: The low back "loser." *Psychosomatics, 14,* 226–229.

Storm, J., & Graham, J. R. (1998, March). *The effects of validity scale coaching on the ability to malinger psychopathology.* Paper presented at the 33rd Annual Symposium on Recent Developments in the Use of the MMPI–2, Clearwater, FL.

Storm, J., & Graham, J. R. (2000). Detection of coached general malingering on the MMPI–2. *Psychological Assessment, 12,* 158–165.

Strassberg, D. S., Clutton, S., & Korboot, P. (1991). A descriptive and validity study of the Minnesota Multiphasic Personality Inventory—2 (MMPI–2) in an elderly Australian sample. *Journal of Psychopathology and Behavioral Assessment, 13,* 301–312.

Strassberg, D. S., & Russell, S. W. (2000). MMPI–2 content scales validity within a sample of chronic pain patients. *Journal of Psychopathology and Behavioral Assessment, 22,* 47–61.

Strong, D. R., Greene, R. L., & Schinka, J. A. (2000). A taxometric analysis of MMPI–2 infrequency scales [F and $F(p)$] in clinical settings. *Psychological Assessment, 12,* 166–173.

Sutker, P. B., Allain, A. N., & Geyer, S. (1978). Female criminal violence and differential MMPI characteristics. *Journal of Consulting and Clinical Psychology, 46,* 1141–1143.

Sutker, P. B., Bugg, F., & Allain, A. N. (1991). Psychometric prediction of PTSD among POW survivors. *Psychological Assessment, 3,* 105–110.

Swan, R. J. (1957). Using the MMPI in marriage counseling. *Journal of Counseling Psychology, 4,* 239–244.

Sweetland, A. (1948). Hypnotic neurosis: Hypochondriasis and depression. *Journal of General Psychology, 39,* 91–105.

Tallent, N. (1992). *The practice of psychological assessment*. Englewood Cliffs, NJ: Prentice Hall.

Tallent, N. (1993). *Psychological report writing*. Englewood Cliffs, NJ: Prentice Hall.

Tellegen, A., & Ben-Porath, Y. S. (1992). The new uniform scores for the MMPI–2: Rationale, derivation, and appraisal. *Psychological Assessment, 4,* 145–155.

Tellegen, A., & Ben-Porath, Y. S. (1993). Code type comparability of the MMPI and MMPI–2: Analysis of recent findings and criticisms. *Journal of Personality Assessment, 61,* 489–500.

Tellegen, A., Ben-Porath, Y. S., McNulty, J. L., Arbisi, P. A., Graham, J. R., & Kaemmer, B. (2003). *MMPI–2 Restructured Clinical (RC) Scales: Development, validation, and interpretation.* Minneapolis: University of Minnesota Press.

Tellegen, A., Butcher, J. N., & Hoeglund, T. (1993). Are unisex norms for the MMPI–2 needed? Would they work? *MMPI–2 News and Profiles, 4,* 4–5.

The Therapist as a person. (2005). Retrieved October 13, 2005, from http://kspope.com/therapist/index/php

Thomsen, J. L., Helwig-Larsen, K., & Rasmussen, O. V. (1984). Amnesty International and the forensic sciences. *American Journal of Forensic Medicine, 5,* 305–311.

Tierney, J. (1982). Doctor, is this man dangerous? Psychiatrists' predictions of criminal behavior are more often wrong than right. *Science, 82,* 28–31.

Timbrook, R., & Graham, J. R. (1994). Ethnic differences on the MMPI? *Psychological Assessment, 6,* 212–217.

Timbrook, R., Graham, J. R., Keiller, S., & Watts, D. (1991, March). *Failure of the Weiner–Harmon subscales to discriminate between valid and invalid profiles.* Paper presented at the 26th Annual Symposium on Recent Developments in the Use of the MMPI (MMPI–2), St. Petersburg, FL.

Tinius, T., & Ben-Porath, Y. S. (1993, March). *A comparative study of Native Americans and Caucasian Americans undergoing substance abuse treatment.* Paper given at the 28th Annual Conference on Recent Developments in the Use of the MMPI/MMPI–2, St. Petersburg, FL.

Tran, B. N. (1996). Vietnamese translation and adaptation of the MMPI–2. In J. N. Butcher (Ed.), *International adaptation of the MMPI–2* (pp. 175–193). Minnesota: University of Minnesota Press.

Tsushima, W. T., & Tsushima, V. G. (2001). Comparison of the fake bad scale and other MMPI–2 validity scales with personal injury litigants. *Assessment, 8,* 205–211.

Tulsky, D., Saklofske, D. H., Chelune, G. J., Heaton, R. K., Ivnik, R. J., Bornstein, R., et al. (Eds.). (2003). *Clinical interpretation of the WAIS–III and WMS–III.* San Diego, CA: Academic Press.

Valliant, P. M., & Blasutti, B. (1992). Personality differences of sex offenders referred for treatment. *Psychological Reports, 71,* 1067–1074.

Van Cleve, E., Jemelka, R., & Trupin, E. (1991). Reliability of psychological test scores for offenders entering a state prison system. *Criminal Justice and Behavior, 18,* 159–165.

Van Susteren, L. (2002). The insanity defense, continued. *Journal of the American Academy of Psychiatry and the Law, 30*(4), 474–475.

Velasquez, R. J., Callahan, W. J., & Carrillo, R. (1989). MMPI profiles of Hispanic-American inpatient and outpatient sex offenders. *Psychological Reports, 65,* 1055–1058.

Velasquez, R., Gonzales, M., Butcher, J. N., Castillo-Canez, I., Apodaca, J. X., & Chavira, D. (1997). Use of the MMPI–2 with Chicanos: Strategies for counselors. *Journal of Multicultural Counseling and Development, 25,* 107–120.

Veneziano, C., Veneziano, L., LeGrand, S., & Richards, L. (2004). Neuropsychological executive functions of adolescent sex offenders and nonsex offenders. *Perceptual and Motor Skills, 98,* 661–674.

Victor, T. L., & Abeles, N. (2004). Coaching clients to take psychological and neuropsychological tests: A clash of ethical obligations. *Professional Psychology: Research and Practice, 35,* 373–379.

Villanueva, M. R., Roman, D. D., & Tuley, M. R. (1988). Determining forensic rehabilitation potential with the MMPI: Practical implications for residential treatment populations. *American Journal of Forensic Psychology, 6,* 27–35.

Vincent, K. R., Linsz, N. L., & Greene, M. I. (1966). The scale of the MMPI as an index of falsification. *Journal of Consulting and Clinical Psychology, 22,* 214–215.

Wagenaar, W. A. (1988). The proper seat: A Bayesian discussion of the position of expert witness. *Law and Human Behavior, 12,* 499–510.

Waller, N. G., & Reise, S. P. (1989). Computerized adaptive personality assessment: An illustration with the Absorption scale. *Journal of Personality and Social Psychology, 57,* 1051–1058.

Walter, M. J. (1982). Using the opponent's expert to prove your case. *Litigation, 8,* 10–12, 59–60.

Walters, G. D. (1986). Correlates of the Megargee criminal classification system: A military correctional setting. *Criminal Justice and Behavior, 13,* 19–32.

Walters, G. D. (1987). Child sex offenders and rapists in a military prison setting. *International Journal of Offender Therapy and Comparative Criminology, 31,* 261–269.

Walters, G. D., White, T., & Greene, R. (1988). Use of the MMPI to identify malingering and exaggeration of psychiatric symptomatology in male prison inmates. *Journal of Consulting and Clinical Psychology, 56,* 111–117.

Ward, L. C. (1997). Confirmatory factor analyses of the Anxiety and Depression Content Scales of the MMPI–2. *Journal of Personality Assessment, 68,* 678–691.

Warren, L. W., & Weiss, D. J. (1969). Relationship between disability type and measured personality characteristics. In *Proceedings of the 77th Annual Convention of the American Psychological Association* (Pt. 2, pp. 773–774). Washington, DC: American Psychological Association.

Warshaw, B. G. (1984). *The trial masters: A handbook of strategies and techniques that win cases.* New York: Prentice Hall.

Wasyliw, O. E., Grossman, L. S., & Haywood, T. W. (1994). Denial of hostility and psychopathology in the evaluation of child molestation. *Journal of Personality Assessment, 63,* 185–190.

Wasyliw, O. E., Grossman, L. S., Haywood, T. W., & Cavanaugh, J. L. (1988). The detection of malingering in criminal forensic groups: MMPI validity scales. *Journal of Personality Assessment, 52,* 321–333.

Watkins, C. E., Campbell, V. L., Nieberding, R., & Hallmark, R. (1995). Contemporary practice of psychological assessment by clinical psychologists. *Professional Psychology: Research and Practice, 26,* 54–60.

Weed, N. C. (1993). An evaluation of the efficacy of MMPI–2 indicators of validity. *Dissertation Abstracts International, 53,* 3800.

Weed, N., Ben-Porath, Y. S., & Butcher, J. N. (1990). Failure of the Wiener–Harmon Minnesota Multiphasic Personality Inventory (MMPI) subtle scales as predictors of psychopathology and as validity indicators. *Psychological Assessment, 2,* 281–285.

Weed, N. C., Butcher, J. N., Ben-Porath, Y. S., & McKenna, T. (1992). New measures for assessing alcohol and drug abuse with the MMPI–2: The APS and AAS. *Journal of Personality Assessment, 58,* 389–404.

Weed, N., & Han, K. (1992, May). *Is K correct?* Paper presented at the 27th Annual Symposium on Recent Developments in the Use of the MMPI, Minneapolis, MN.

Weiner, I. B. (1987). Writing forensic reports. In I. B. Weiner & A. Hess (Eds.), *Handbook of forensic psychology* (pp. 511–528). New York: Wiley.

Weiner, I. B. (1989). On competence and ethicality in psychodiagnostic assessment. *Journal of Personality Assessment, 53,* 827–831.

Weiner, I. B. (1995). How to anticipate ethical and legal challenges in personality assessments. In J. N. Butcher (Ed.), *Clinical personality assessment* (pp. 95–103). New York: Oxford University Press.

Weiner, I. B. (2006). Writing forensic reports. In I. B. Weiner & A. Hess (Eds.), *The handbook of forensic psychology* (pp. 631–652). New York: Wiley.

Weiner, L. R. (1997). The presence of posttraumatic stress disorder in adult, male sex offenders as measured by the Keane and Schlenger scales of the MMPI–2: The implication for addictions theory. *Dissertation Abstracts International: Section B: The Sciences and Engineering, 57*(8-B), 5349.

Weis, R., Crockett, T. E., & Vieth, S. (2004). Using MMPI–A profiles to predict success in a military-style residential treatment program for adolescents with academic and conduct problems. *Psychology in the Schools, 41,* 563–574.

Weiss, D. J. (1985). Adaptive testing by computer. *Journal of Consulting and Clinical Psychology, 53,* 774–789.

Weissman, H. N. (1984). Psychological assessment and psycholegal formulations in psychiatric traumatology. *Psychiatric Annals, 14,* 517–529.

Wellman, F. L. (1936). *The art of cross-examination.* New York: Macmillan. (Original work published 1903)

Westermeyer, J., Williams, C., & Nguyen, N. (1992). *Refugee mental health and adjustment.* Washington, DC: U.S. Government Printing Office.

Wetter, M. W., Baer, R. A., Berry, D. T. R., & Reynolds, S. K. (1994). The effect of symptom information on faking the MMPI–2. *Assessment, 1,* 199–207.

Wetter, M. W., Baer, R. A., Berry, D. T. R., Smith, G. T., & Larsen, L. H. (1992). Sensitivity of MMPI–2 validity scales to random responding and malingering. *Psychological Assessment, 4,* 369–374.

Wetter, M. W., & Corrigan, S. K. (1995). Providing information to clients about psychological tests: A survey of attorneys' and law students' attitudes. *Professional Psychology, 26,* 465–474.

Wetter, M. W., & Deitsch, S. E. (1996). Faking specific disorders and temporal response consistency on the MMPI–2. *Psychological Assessment, 8,* 39–47.

Wetzler, S., & Marlowe, D. (1990). "Faking bad" on the MMPI, MMPI–2, and Millon–II. *Psychological Reports, 67,* 1117–1118.

Whitacre, W. S. (1995, March). *MMPI–2 invalidity rates of incarcerated youthful sex offenders.* Paper presented at the 30th Annual Symposium on Recent Developments in the Use of the MMPI–2/MMPI–A Workshop and Symposia, St. Petersburg, FL.

Wiener, D. N. (1948a). Personality characteristics of selected disability groups. In G. S. Welsh & W. G. Dahlstrom (Eds.), *Basic readings on the MMPI in psychology and medicine* (pp. 435–451). Minneapolis: University of Minnesota Press.

Wiener, D. N. (1948b). Subtle and obvious keys for the Minnesota Multiphasic Personality Inventory. *Journal of Consulting Psychology, 12,* 164–170.

Wiggins, J. S. (1966). Substantive dimensions of self-report in the MMPI item pool. *Psychological Monographs: General and Applied, 80,* 42.

Wilcock, K. D. (1964). Neurotic differences between individualized and socialized criminals. *Journal of Consulting Psychology, 28,* 141–145.

Wilcox, P., & Dawson, J. (1977). Role-played and hypnotically induced simulation of psychopathology on the MMPI. *Journal of Clinical Psychology, 33,* 743–745.

Williams, C. L., & Butcher, J. N. (1989). An MMPI study of adolescents: I. Empirical validity of the standard scales. *Psychological Assessment, 1,* 251–259.

Williams, C. L., Butcher, J. N., Ben-Porath, Y. S., & Graham, J. R. (1992). *MMPI–A content scales: Assessing psychopathology in adolescents.* Minneapolis: University of Minnesota Press.

Williams, M. A., & Boll, T. J. (2000). Report writing in clinical neuropsychology. In G. Groth-Marnat (Ed.), *Neuropsychological assessment in clinical practice* (pp. 575–602). New York: Wiley.

Williams, R. D. (1988). Corporate policies for creation and retention of documents. In K. Ross & B. Wrubel (Eds.), *Product liability of manufacturers 1988: Prevention and defense* (pp. 529–596). New York: Practicing Law Institute.

Williams, M. A., Putzke, J. D., LaMarche, J. A., Bourge, R. C., Kirklin, J. K., McGiffin, D. C., et al. (2000). Psychological defensiveness among heart transplant candidates. *Journal of Clinical Psychology in Medical Settings, 7*(3), 167–174.

Wilson, J. P., & Walker, A. J. (1990). Toward an MMPI trauma profile. *Journal of Traumatic Stress, 3,* 151–168.

Wiltse, L. L., & Rocchio, P. H. (1975). Preoperative psychological tests as predictors of success of chemonucleolysis and treatment of low back pain syndrome. *Journal of Bone and Joint Surgery, 57,* 478–483.

Wise, E. A. (1996). Diagnosing posttraumatic stress disorder with the MMPI clinical scales: A review of the literature. *Journal of Psychopathology and Behavioral Assessment, 18,* 71–82.

Witt, P. H. (2003). Writing and defending your expert report: The step-by-step guide with models. *Journal of Psychiatry and Law, 31*(3), 355–360.

Wooten, A. J. (1984). Effectiveness of the *K* correction in the detection of psychopathology and its impact on profile height and configuration among young adult men. *Journal of Consulting and Clinical Psychology, 52,* 468–473.

Wright, L. (1970). Psychologic aspects of the battered child syndrome. *Southern Medical Bulletin, 58,* 14–18.

Wright, L. (1976). The sick but slick syndrome as a personality component of parents of battered children. *Journal of Clinical Psychology, 32,* 41–45.

Wrobel, T. A., Calovini, P. K., & Martin, T. O. (1991). Application of the Megargee MMPI typology to a population of defendants referred for psychiatric evaluation *Criminal Justice and Behavior, 18,* 397–405.

Wrobel, T. A., & Lachar, D. (1982). Validity of the Wiener subtle and obvious empirically derived psychological test items under faking conditions. *Journal of Consulting and Clinical Psychology, 50,* 469–470.

Xiong, C. (2005, March 23). Purported expert on sex offenders is charged with perjury. *Minneapolis Star-Tribune,* p. 7B.

Younger, I. (1986a). *Credibility and cross-examination.* Hopkins, MN: Professional Education Group.

Younger, I. (1986b). *Expert witnesses.* Hopkins, MN: Professional Education Group.

Younger, I. (1986c). *Thomas Murphey's cross-examination of Dr. Carl A. Binger.* Hopkins, MN: Professional Education Group.

Youngjohn, J. R., Davis, D., & Wolf, I. (1997). Head injury and the MMPI–2: Paradoxical severity effects and the influence of litigation. *Psychological Assessment, 9,* 177–184.

Zachary, R. A., & Pope, K. S. (1984). Legal and ethical issues in the clinical use of computerized testing. In M. D. Schwartz (Ed.), *Using computers in clinical practice* (pp. 151–164). New York: Haworth.

Zager, L. D. (1983). Response to Simmons and associates: Conclusions about the MMPI–based classification system's stability are premature. *Criminal Justice and Behavior, 10,* 310–315.

Zager, L. D. (1988). The MMPI-based criminal classification system: A review, current status, and future directions. *Criminal Justice and Behavior, 15,* 39–57.

Ziskin, J. (1969). *Coping with psychiatric and psychological testimony.* Marina Del Rey, CA: Law & Psychology Press.

Ziskin J. (1981a). *Coping with psychiatric and psychological testimony* (2nd ed.). Marina Del Rey, CA: Law and Psychology Press.

Ziskin, J. (1981b). Use of the MMPI in forensic settings. In J. N. Butcher, W. G. Dahlstrom, M. D. Gynther, & W. Schofield (Eds.), *Clinical notes on the MMPI* (pp. 1–12). Nutley, NJ: Hoffman-La Roche Laboratories/National Computer Systems.

Zolovska, B., & Bursztajn, H. J. (2005). "Are you there alone?" The unspeakable crime of Andrea Yates. *American Journal of Psychiatry, 162,* 821–822.

Zwart, J. A., Ellertsen, B., & Bovim, G. (1996). Psychosocial factors and MMPI–2 patterns in migraine, cluster headache, tension-type headache, and cervicogenic headache. *New Trends in Experimental and Clinical Psychiatry, 12,* 167–164.

Table of Cases

Index

About the Authors

Ken Pope, PhD, ABPP, received graduate degrees from Harvard and Yale and has been in independent practice as a licensed psychologist since the mid-1980s. A diplomate in clinical psychology, he has authored or coauthored more than 100 articles and chapters in peer-reviewed scientific and professional journals and books. He is a charter fellow of the Association for Scientific Psychology and was elected a fellow of American Psychological Association (APA) Divisions 1, 2, 12, 29, 35, 41, 42, 44, and 51. He has testified as an expert witness in various states on assessment, interventions, and standards of care.

Based on his research in the 1970s on therapist–patient sex, he cofounded the UCLA Post-Therapy Support Program, the first center offering services, conducting research, and providing university-based training for graduate students and therapists seeking to work with people who had been sexually exploited by therapists. Ken taught courses in psychological and neuropsychological assessment, abnormal psychology, and professional standards of care at the University of California, Los Angeles, where he served as a psychotherapy supervisor. He chaired the Ethics Committees of the APA and the American Board of Professional Psychology.

In the early 1980s, Ken was the director of clinical programs for a consortium of community mental health centers and hospitals. He worked with the community, the hospitals, and the centers to find ways to meet community needs in accordance with its own cultures and ecology. By the end of his work in those areas, their programs included home-bound services (in which therapists and others went to the homes of people whose chronic or terminal illnesses or disabilities prevented them from traveling), legal services for people who were poor or homeless, Manos de Esperanza serving people whose primary language is Spanish, a 24-hour crisis service, peer-support services, and group homes so that people who were mentally disabled could live independently.

His publications include 10 articles in the *American Psychologist* and 11 books (including *Ethics in Psychotherapy and Counseling, 2nd Edition,* with Melba Vasquez; *Sexual Involvement With Patients: Patient Assessment, Subsequent Therapy, Forensics; The Stream of Consciousness: Scientific Investigations Into the Flow of Human Experience,* with Jerome Singer; *Law and Mental Health Professionals: California,* with Brandt Caudill; *What Therapists Don't Talk About and Why: Understanding Taboos That Hurt Us and Our Clients,* with Janet Sonne and Beverly Greene; and *Surviving and Thriving as a Therapist: Information, Ideas, and Resources for Psychologists,* with Melba Vasquez).

One of his main interests is the family of special-needs dogs and cats who live in his home and whose photos and stories can be seen at http://kenpope.com. He also maintains three other Web sites: *Articles, Research, & Resources in Psychology* at http://kspope.com; *Accessibility & Disability Information & Resources in Psychology Training & Practice* at http://kpope.com; and *Resources for Companion Animals, Assistance Animals, & Special-Needs Animals* at http://catanddoghelp.com.

He provides a free psychology news service for approximately 1,000 psychologists, attorneys, and psychiatrists. (Anyone is welcome to join the list.) Each day he E-mails three to six messages, including excerpts from new and in-press articles in scientific and professional journals and from psychology-related articles in that morning's newspapers, job announcements, requests for information and resources from list members, and so forth.

Ken received the Belle Mayer Bromberg Award for Literature; the Frances Mosseker Award for Fiction; the APA Division 42 Presidential Citation "In Recognition of His Voluntary Contributions, His Generosity of Time, the Sharing of His Caring Spirit [and] His Personal Resources"; the APA Division 44 Citation of Appreciation; the APA Division 12 Award for Distinguished Professional Contributions to Clinical Psychology; and the APA Award for Distinguished Contributions to Public Service, which includes the following citation:

> For rigorous empirical research, landmark articles and books, courageous leadership, fostering the careers of others, and making services available to those with no means to pay. His works include 9 books and 100 other publications on topics ranging from treating victims of torture to psychometrics to memory to ethics. His pioneering research has increased our understanding of therapist–patient sex, especially in the areas of effects on patients, tendencies to deny or discount risks, factors enabling known perpetrators to continue or resume not only practicing but also abusing patients, and approaches to prevention. As the title—*What Therapists Don't Talk About and Why*—of his acceptance talk for the Division 12 Award for Distinguished Professional Contributions to Clinical Psychology suggests, Pope's research frequently addresses concerns that are relatively neglected because they tend to cause anxiety, such as therapists' feelings of anger, hate, fear, or sexual attraction toward patients, or therapists' own histories of sexual and physical abuse. He frequently declines compensation for his work to advance psychology in the public interest. This is evident in his recent book, *Sexual Involvement With Therapists: Patient Assessment, Subsequent Therapy, Forensics*, published by the American Psychological Association. Pope waived all royalties for the volume in order that it might be sold at reduced price and be more readily available and useful. His integrity, good will, humor, and tireless work in the public interest represent the finest ideals of our profession. (*American Psychologist*, 1995, pp. 241–243)

James N. Butcher, PhD, is professor emeritus in the department of psychology at the University of Minnesota. He graduated from Guilford College in North Carolina with a BA in psychology in 1960, received an MA in experimental psychology from the University of North Carolina at Chapel Hill in 1962, and received a PhD in clinical psychology at the University of North Carolina at Chapel Hill in 1964. He was awarded honorary doctorates for his international personality assessment research (Doctor Honoris Causa) from the Free

University of Brussels, Belgium, in 1990 and from the University of Florence, Italy (Laurea ad Honorem in psychology) in 2005. He received the Bruno Klopfer Award from the Society for Personality Assessment in 2004 for longstanding contributions to personality assessment.

He has maintained an active research program in the areas of personality assessment, abnormal psychology, cross-cultural personality factors, and computer-based personality assessment. He is a past member of the University of Minnesota Press's Minnesota Multiphasic Personality Inventory (MMPI) Consultative Committee. Since 1982, the committee has been actively engaged in a large-scale project to revise and restandardize the MMPI. He is the former editor of *Psychological Assessment*, and he currently serves as consulting editor for numerous other journals in psychology and psychiatry. He has served on the Board of Trustees of the Society for Personality Assessment and the executive committees of Divisions 1 (General Psychology) and 5 (Division of Measurement and Evaluation) of the American Psychological Association (APA). He is an active fellow of the APA.

In 1965, Butcher, a new faculty member of the University of Minnesota and just out of graduate school at the University of North Carolina, founded the Symposium on Recent Developments in the Use of the MMPI to provide a forum for researchers to discuss current and proposed research on the MMPI. Over the years of its existence, the annual symposium has served as a vehicle for many important new developments in the MMPI and generated numerous research investigations that have opened new research directions for the instrument. A year after the MMPI symposium began, the need for practical training in the use of the test became apparent because many psychologists were not receiving assessment training in their graduate programs. The MMPI symposium was expanded to include practical workshops on the clinical application of the MMPI. Since its inception, the MMPI Workshop Series has provided professional training on the MMPI and MMPI–2 to thousands of psychologists in the United States.

Throughout his career in psychology, Butcher has been involved in studying the use of the MMPI in intercultural contexts. In 1970, he founded the International Conference on Personality Assessment, which has been held ever since every 2 years. The conference provides the opportunity for scholars from a range of countries to discuss their research and to exchange views on issues and techniques in personality assessment with professionals from other countries. Programs devoted to facilitating international research on personality assessment have been conducted in several countries—Australia, Belgium, Chile, China, Denmark, Egypt, Greece, Holland, Hong Kong, Iran, Israel, Italy, Japan, Korea, Mexico, Norway, and South Africa.

Butcher has conducted extensive research on the MMPI for more than 44 years in a broad range of contexts and published 50 books and more than 175 articles in the areas of personality assessment, abnormal psychology, and psychotherapy. His publications include basic research works in abnormal psychology, personality assessment, and the MMPI, including research methodology and computer applications of psychological tests. He was a central figure in the revision of the MMPI and the development of the MMPI–2 and MMPI–A. Butcher's contribution to the MMPI revision began in 1969, when he organized a national symposium to address the question of whether the MMPI needed to be revised and, if so, how. During the 1970s, he published articles and held additional meetings to keep alive the possibility of an MMPI revision. Finally, in 1982, the test publisher initiated a revision with a team composed of Butcher, Grant Dahlstrom, Jack R. Graham, and Auke Tellegen (who participated in the later stages of the project). The MMPI revision effort spanned 10 years and included scores of empirical studies with a broad range of normal and clinical populations. This revision effort culminated in the publication of the MMPI–2 in 1989 and the MMPI–A in 1992. His published books include *MMPI–2: A Beginner's Guide* (2nd ed., APA, 2005); *International Adaptations of the MMPI–2* (1996); *Use of the MMPI–2 in Treatment Planning* (1990); *A Practitioner's Guide to Computerized Psychological Assessment* (1987); *Essentials of MMPI–2 and MMPI–A Interpretation* (2nd ed., with Carolyn L. Williams, 2003); *Abnormal Psychology and Modern Life* (12th ed., with Sue Mineka and Jill Hooley, 2004); *Clinical Personality Assessment* (2nd ed., 2002); and *Handbook of Research Methods in Clinical Psychology* (2nd ed., with Philip C. Kendall and Grayson Holmback, 1999).

He has been actively involved in developing and organizing disaster response programs for dealing with human problems following airline disasters. Butcher organized a model crisis intervention disaster response for the Minneapolis–St. Paul Airport and organized and supervised psychological services following two major airline disasters, Northwest Flight 255 and Aloha Airlines's Maui accident.

Butcher's forensic testimony, the source of much material included in this book, has been extensive and covers many types of legal cases. As might be expected, his testimony almost always centers on the interpretation of MMPI–2 scores. Issues concerning technical aspects of the test or the likely meaning of a particular MMPI configuration are common themes in his court testimony. His forensic experience includes personal injury, criminal, family custody, and medical malpractice.

The *Journal of Personality Assessment* invited Butcher to describe his professional development and adventures, and this account appeared as "Discontinuities, Side Steps, and Finding a Proper Place: An Autobiographical Account" in 2003 (Vol. *80*(3), pp. 223–236).

Recently Butcher has taken up watercolors as a hobby, and an example of his work is on the cover of this book, as well as on the cover of the October 2005 *American Psychologist*, and at http://kspope.com/sexiss/JimButcherWatercolor.php.

Joyce Seelen, **JD**, received her BA in journalism from the University of Minnesota and her JD from the University of Denver School of Law. She practiced in Denver as a Colorado state public defender, beginning in 1980, where she defended indigent people charged with crimes. In 1982, she successfully defended a poor person charged with first-degree murder, after which she began a private practice that emphasizes representation of the victims of abuse by people in positions of trust. An active litigator, she has tried several civil cases to jury verdicts in excess of $1 million each. In two of her cases, *Moses v. the Diocese* (863 P.2d 310 (Colo. 1993)) and *The Bear Valley Church of Christ v. DeBose* (928 P.2d 1315 (Colo. 1996)), the Colorado supreme court became the leading court in the country in extending civil protection to people harmed by the negligence of religious institutions. In 1995, her peers in the Colorado Trial Lawyers Association created a special award of merit for her "in recognition of her zealous advocacy of victims while advancing public understanding of the civil justice system." In another of her cases, *Bohrer v. Church Mutual* (965 P.2d 1258 (Colo. 1998)), for the first time in the state's history, the Colorado supreme court in 1998 ordered an insurance company to pay for damages caused by negligent counseling, despite the fact that the individual being counseled had been sexually abused by the insured minister and the policy had excluded coverage for sexual abuse. Seelen generally restricts her practice to the representation of personal injury plaintiffs who are often denied access to the civil justice system because of the prejudices within that system concerning "emotional damages." In addition, she prosecutes a mix of large and small cases because of her belief that plaintiffs in smaller cases are often denied effective access to the civil justice system.

In 2003, Seelen moved to the Big Island of Hawaii and began combining an active long-distance law practice in Denver with a new real estate career in Hawaii. What began as an effort by Seelen to "slow down" has generated a series of opportunities. In 2004, she successfully represented a child in Denver in ground-breaking civil litigation against Children's Hospital, currently on appeal (*Liggett v. Nelligan and The Children's Hospital Association*, Case No. 04Ca2262, Colorado Court of Appeals). In the same year, the Kobe Bryant criminal prosecution team called on Seelen and her special expertise to assist them in picking a jury in the difficult Eagle, Colorado, case, *People v. Bryant* (03CR204, Eagle County, Colorado), which was dismissed at the end of the first week.